Dance Cultures Around the World

Lynn E. Frederiksen, MFA

Clark University

Shih-Ming Li Chang, MFA

Wittenberg University

EDITORS

HUMAN KINETICS

Library of Congress Cataloging-in-Publication Data

Names: Frederiksen, Lynn E., editor. | Chang, Shih-Ming Li, editor.
Title: Dance cultures around the world / Lynn E. Frederiksen, Shih-Ming Li
  Chang, editors.
Description: Champaign, IL : Human Kinetics, 2024. | Includes
  bibliographical references and index.
Identifiers: LCCN 2022052081 (print) | LCCN 2022052082 (ebook) | ISBN
  9781492572329 (paperback) | ISBN 9781492594574 (epub) | ISBN
  9781492594581 (pdf)
Subjects: LCSH: Dance--Cross-cultural studies. | Dance--Social aspects.
Classification: LCC GV1588.6 .D366 2024 (print) | LCC GV1588.6 (ebook) |
  DDC 306.4/84--dc23/eng/20230109
LC record available at https://lccn.loc.gov/2022052081
LC ebook record available at https://lccn.loc.gov/2022052082

ISBN: 978-1-4925-7232-9 (print)

Acquisitions Editor: Bethany J. Bentley
Developmental Editor: Melissa J. Zavala
Copyeditor: E before I Editing
Proofreader: Erin Cler
Indexer: Andrea J. Hepner
Permissions Manager: Laurel Mitchell
Senior Graphic Designer: Nancy Rasmus
Cover Designer: Keri Evans
Cover Design Specialist: Susan Rothermel Allen
Photographs (interior): Courtesy of the chapter authors, unless otherwise noted
Photo Asset Manager: Laura Fitch
Photo Production Manager: Jason Allen
Senior Art Manager: Kelly Hendren
Art Style Development: Joanne Brummet
Illustrations: © Human Kinetics, unless otherwise noted
Printer: Walsworth

Printed in the United States of America   10 9 8 7 6 5 4 3 2 1

The paper in this book was manufactured using responsible forestry methods.

Human Kinetics
1607 N. Market Street
Champaign, IL 61820
USA

United States and International
Website: **US.HumanKinetics.com**
Email: info@hkusa.com
Phone: 1-800-747-4457

Canada
Website: **Canada.HumanKinetics.com**
Email: info@hkcanada.com

E7434 (paperback)

Contents

PART II   Central and South America

PART III   Caribbean

PART IV Africa

PART V   Europe and Russia

PART VI Middle East

PART IX   Oceania

Preface

Dance is a prism that can reveal cultural dynamics over time and space. This textbook considers several guiding questions: What is dance? Who dances? Why do they dance? And how can the answers to these questions enrich your experience of your own culture, as well as those of others? On a broad level, the first two questions seem fairly easy to answer. In her foundational book *To Dance Is Human*, dance ethnologist Judith Lynne Hanna defines dance as "human behavior composed, from the dancer's perspective, of purposeful, intentionally rhythmical, and culturally patterned sequences of nonverbal body movements other than ordinary motor activities, the motion having inherent and aesthetic value" (1979, 57). This definition seeks to encompass the characteristics of dance found the world over, and in so doing answers the next question as to who dances: Every culture has some form of dance. However, *why* people dance—and further, how they define and create dance—are the difficult questions at the core of this text. Once you understand why dance exists and examine the factors that explain particular dance forms, you can engage more fully with many cultures of dance, including your own.

All culture emerges from the human body. Therefore, any exploration of dance must start with the bipedal human body and how it deals with its surroundings, as well as how these methods of engagement are passed on to subsequent generations. The latter requires that dance be inherently attractive and emotionally fulfilling to ensure its long-term survival. Rhythm often lies at the heart of this dynamic.

The rhythms of walking and running undergird all human motion, and related concepts of balance and upward orientation become milestones of human growth and progress. Parents applaud a child's first wobbling steps because standing and moving on two feet is still the key to human survival. A human body in efficient, rhythmic motion can move through and engage with the environment more easily. Consequently, this process shapes how the mind remembers and communicates everyday experiences, as well as

concepts such as cosmology (origin stories, such as how humans came to be), moral and aesthetic values, community history, and more. Balance on two legs ultimately determines how your human brain experiences the world and also how you express these experiences. Through the art of dance, you engage directly with balance in motion as a physical and conceptual reality.

Along with other arts, dance helps people to deal with intangible and uncontrollable aspects of life by giving them form through metaphor. While you may think of metaphor mostly as a figure of speech, such as "life is a bowl of cherries," it is actually a basic mode of human thought that developed with the importance of balance—a side effect of having two legs. People use metaphors to learn about unknown things by comparing them—balancing them—with familiar things (Johnson 1987).

Metaphors stir emotions that are similar to those experienced in real-life situations. This function of metaphor is at the core of all education, because emotional engagement heightens learning. The arts evolved as a vital part of human existence by activating the emotion–learning link within the safe setting of a community. Thus, dance—through its metaphors and its physical grounding in our human bodies—is a prism through which the many facets of culture can be revealed and appreciated.

Purpose of This Book

All dances use familiar elements—costumes, props, group and solo arrangements, gesture, pose, locomotion, and a host of other factors—to create effective metaphors within a given culture. Outsiders, however, might view these metaphors through their own cultural lenses and misinterpret their relevance. Videos and the Internet allow people to see many different dances from around the globe, but mostly through their own—largely unconscious—cultural assumptions and preferences. Often, dance is considered a "universal language" that needs no translation. This viewpoint is supported by the way that education and arts institutions—focused on the society within which they operate—often consider dance to be primarily physical, relatively simple, and universally accessible. But just as you would not expect to understand a foreign language simply because it is human speech, you cannot expect to understand foreign dance without some "translation." The multiple layers of meaning and history in foreign dances are often left unrevealed, and therefore the opportunity for true cross-cultural understanding is missed.

The first step of translation is to understand the general patterns of how dance develops within a culture, because dance does not happen in a vacuum. Like any other human behavior, it arises to meet the needs of a community and will continue as long as it still meets those needs—whether they are for entertainment, religious observation, economic exchange, education, aesthetic validation, political resistance, or some other purpose. However, while all cultures have the same potential range of reasons for creating dance, the specific details vary greatly. This book illuminates the details by having cultural insiders describe the specific contexts and forces that shape their dances and how these patterns might shift over time to alter both the qualities of the dance and its place in society. These dynamics are complex, and what you see of a dance today might not represent the full background. You need the insider's viewpoint. Learning how migration, slavery, colonialism, or other forces could give rise to specific dance "languages" helps you understand the overall patterns at play in every culture. And, just as with learning a foreign language, encountering other dance "languages" through cultural insiders helps you recognize the patterns at play in your own culture. With this realization, you are less likely to make unconscious or erroneous assumptions about the dances explored in the text. You will also be better prepared to engage with dance cultures beyond the scope of this textbook.

All arts are the product of their cultures, regardless of whether the cultural values and history are acknowledged, and familiar elements within your own culture support unconscious assumptions simply because they are ubiquitous—trees obscuring the forest. To offset this tendency, the contributors for each chapter have been asked to think carefully about cultural principles they might take for granted because of their familiarity and to examine how these principles operate through the dance. In this manner, they also help you understand the parameters of your own assumptions and how these might emerge in the exploration of dance around the world.

How This Book Is Organized

The geopolitical boundaries of the nine regions addressed in this book provide a consistent and logical structure for exploring a wide range of dance cultures. However, the regions are by no means covered comprehensively, given the limitations of space and the availability of contributors. A brief introduction to each region highlights some of the key dynamics shaping the dance cultures, and the subsequent chapters give a limited sampling of what you might expect to see in dance. Of course, most regions have such a wide variety of dance cultures that this small sample cannot be taken to represent the specific histories, techniques, and purposes of all the dances. Nonetheless, the dance-culture dynamics in each region reveal general patterns that operate throughout the world, adjusted for historical, political, and geographical differences. We hope that your understanding of these patterns will open the door to experiencing dance cultures far beyond the 25 chapters in this book.

Each chapter begins with learning objectives specific to the culture at hand, a list of key terms to recognize, and a short vignette describing a signature dance or dance-related feature of the culture, followed by a brief introduction to its history and geography. Sidebars throughout the chapter highlight significant events, people, or qualities of the dance culture, while icons indicate web-based supplementary materials, including videos, images, articles, and more. Additionally, cultural highlights or short stories from the lives of individual dancers, choreographers, historians, or educators within the culture give you a more personal view. Most chapters also include a Crosscurrents section to illuminate cross-cultural dynamics—regional or global, historical or contemporary—that affect the culture's dance. At the end of the chapter are discussion questions, glossary terms, and suggested references and resources.

Instructor Resources

Several instructor resources are available within the online instructor pack in HK*Propel* to help you use this text in your class.

- The instructor guide includes a sample syllabus and chapter-specific files that contain chapter summaries and suggested answers for the discussion questions.
- The presentation package contains PowerPoint slides of the key points of each chapter. Instructors can use these slides as is or edit them to create unique presentations.
- The test package provides over 700 questions in multiple-choice, true or false, and fill-in-the-blank formats. The files may be downloaded for integration with a learning management system or printed as paper-based tests. Instructors may also create their own customized quizzes or tests from the test bank questions to assign to students directly through HK*Propel*. Multiple-choice, true-or-false, multiple-response, and matching questions are automatically graded, and student scores can be easily reviewed by instructors in the platform.
- Ready-made chapter quizzes allow instructors to assess student comprehension of the most important concepts in each chapter. Each quiz contains 10 questions, drawn from the larger test bank. Each quiz may be downloaded or assigned to students within HK*Propel*. The chapter quizzes are automatically graded with scores available for review in the platform.

Instructor ancillaries are free to adopting instructors, including an ebook version of the text that allows instructors to add highlights, annotations, and bookmarks. Please contact your sales manager for details about how to access instructor resources in HK*Propel*.

Student Resources

Throughout the chapters, you'll notice icons at the ends of major sections to indicate additional material is available in HK*Propel*. This robust online resource supplements your textbook with the following elements:

- Links to videos, articles, and websites: You are invited to use these links to explore cultures of dance around the world and learn more about the concepts discussed in the chapters, including viewing videos of many dances discussed. These links have been curated to provide more information than can be covered in the book.
- Full lists of glossary terms and definitions and references and resources: The book chapters contain lists of selected glossary terms and resources. The complete lists appear in HK*Propel*.
- Application activities: Each chapter in HK*Propel* includes an application activity related to the topic of each chapter. These practical and easy-to-understand activities are designed to enhance your learning experience.
- Quizzes: Your instructor may assign you short quizzes to complete within HK*Propel* to demonstrate your mastery of each chapter's content.

As you start your journey through cultures of dance, remember that what you see today might not be the same tomorrow. The settings in which dance cultures operate can change in response to altered political, environmental, technological, and other conditions—even public health, as the COVID-19 pandemic has illustrated. (Often these changes have synergistic effects, such as how the pandemic spurred technology for remote "gatherings.") Additionally, the terminology we use when exploring dance cultures around the world must shift as our understanding of cultural assumptions deepens. The term "world dance" is now recognized as being culturally biased, constraining our ability to engage meaningfully with dances from cultures outside our immediate experience (Blumenfield 2021).

New dances and new reasons for dance will always emerge as crosscurrents of people and technology carry influences around the globe. Nonetheless, the methodology for exploring dance cultures that this text provides will help you find your way even as circumstances change. This book is designed both as an overview of dance cultures and as a guide to the *ways* that dance develops and evolves. The examples are given in each chapter primarily to highlight factors at play in the evolution of dance—politics, economics, geography, religion, technology, and more—and how their interactions might be revealed through the dance. The methodology is flexible enough to account for new categories and qualifications, and the book will help you learn how to look for these. In addition, the materials in the web-based supplement can be updated continually to bring new examples within reach of the concepts that the book outlines. With these two resources, you will have both a reliable guide and a well-crafted gateway to dance cultures in our world. Bon voyage!

References and Resources

Blumenfield, Alice. 2021. "Can We Please Stop Using the Term 'World Dance'?" *Dance Magazine.* https://www.dancemagazine.com/world-dance/ Accessed January 2, 2023.

Hanna, Judith Lynne. 1979. *To Dance Is Human.* Chicago, London: The University of Chicago Press.

Johnson, Mark. 1987. *The Body in the Mind.* Chicago, London: The University of Chicago Press.

Acknowledgments

First and foremost, we give riotous applause to our wonderful authors who contributed chapters for the 25 cultures in this book. Their commitment to the project never wavered, despite unprecedented challenges wrought by the COVID-19 pandemic, localized natural disasters, technological meltdowns, and a writing process that stretched over several years and around the world. We are truly humbled and inspired by their perseverance, expertise, and generosity in sharing their dance cultures. We are also grateful to those who, though they did not become contributors after answering the call for authors, nonetheless expressed enthusiasm and shared many ideas for the project.

Several organizations generously publicized our call for authors:

- Dance Studies Association
- International Dance Council CID UNESCO
- International Council for Traditional Music
- National Dance Education Organization
- Society for Ethnomusicology
- World Dance Alliance

We are also grateful to Wittenberg University and Clark University for their support and assistance in this project. At Human Kinetics, kudos go to acquisitions editor, Bethany Bentley, for convincing us to create a textbook (rather than an annotated online database of dance videos) and guiding our collaborations with multiple authors around the world; to developmental editor, Melissa Zavala, for shepherding the project through its complex production process; and to the entire staff whose careful attention to details kept us steady in the frenzy of publication.

From the early days, our heartfelt thanks go to Dr. Linda Caldwell (1950-2018) who convinced us that the project was a worthy pursuit—her spirit continues in this work.

Our sincere gratitude also goes to a nearly endless list of people who have helped us along the way. To name but a few: Ranjanaa Devi, Yvonne Daniel, Mary Jo Freshley, and Eric Galm, who gave us welcome insights on cross-cultural collaborations and helped us search for contributors; Heather McCartney at the Joyce Theater who invited us to the 2020 American Dance Platform Symposium in NYC, resulting in much positive encouragement for the project from like-minded dance scholars; staff and faculty at Clark University and Wittenberg University; and countless others who shared their expertise and reinforced our belief that this textbook was a long-awaited resource for students and teachers in the world of dance.

And to our families, our deep, abiding gratitude for your patience, love, and support as we tussled with this project over several years and numerous video chats from multiple places around the world at all hours of the day and night. Quite simply, we could not have done it without you.

PART I

North America

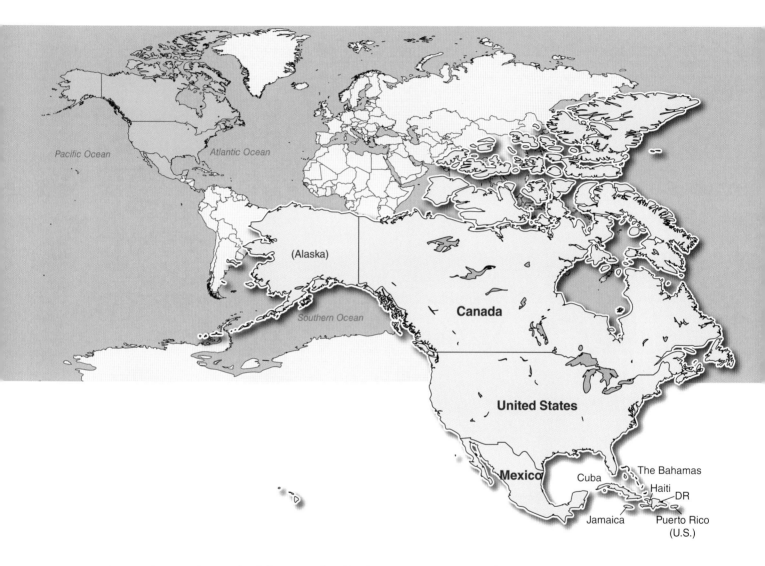

In North America, colonialism resulted in the unique creation of entirely new countries populated by immigrants—both voluntary and involuntary. Indigenous peoples, especially in Canada and the United States, were marginalized in their own lands. While many voluntary immigrants came from European countries, involuntary immigrants were largely represented by enslaved Africans and to a lesser extent indentured servants and exiles from various European and Asian countries affected by European colonial ambitions. For immigrants, dance can be a way to maintain connections to their homeland. Although Indigenous Americans were not exiled from North America, their land was taken away from them, and their dance became a way of maintaining their identity and sense of "home." The key colonial powers in North America were Spain, France, and Britain, though others played significant roles throughout the

"New World." The chapters in part I address Native American dance, social dance in the United States, and dances of Mexico to illuminate patterns of interaction and influence that continue to shape the dance cultures of North America.

 HK*Propel* includes web links to additional resources for this section.

Native American and First Nations Dance

Robin Prichard

Learning Objectives

After reading this chapter you will be able to do the following:

- Articulate how one can respectfully study Native American dance.
- Understand the importance of powwow dance to Native American identity, history, and cultural continuity.
- Summarize various influences on current-day powwow dances.
- Describe the importance of powwow elements such as circles, drums, and regalia.
- Compare and contrast various powwow dances, including social, contest, exhibition, and special dances.
- Identify how age, gender, and veteran status affect powwow dancers.

Key Terms

evolutionary fallacy—The discredited idea that cultures evolve on a single unitary time line from primitive to advanced. It falsely equates the complexity of a society's technology with the complexity of its art. It creates a hierarchy wherein so-called primitive cultures are worth less than "civilized."

intertribal powwow—A gathering where Native Americans from many tribes celebrate their cultures through music and dance.

"kill the Indian to save the man"—The policy of the U.S. government after 1890 to eliminate all Indian culture and force Native Americans to assimilate. This was enacted through draconian restrictions and the forced removal of children from Native American homes. The policy was designed to enact cultural genocide.

pan-Indian identity—A shared sense of common identity among Native Americans that unites the indigenous of North America. Pan-Indian identity does not erase tribal identity, which remains primary, but is a layer on top of it.

regalia—The clothing worn by Native Americans during dances. Regalia is specific to the type of dance being performed and is never called a *costume*.

Powwow Dance

Cars, campers, and tents ring the fairgrounds. Fry bread stands, jewelry booths, and T-shirt tables form an inner ring, catering to the hundreds of dancers and spectators who have arrived for the **powwow** weekend. The innermost ring, consisting of flattened and packed earth, holds a heightened sense of possibility: This is where dancers will exhibit, share, and compete. A group of musicians sits in a circle at one end of the dance ring, poised to drum and sing; judges sit at intervals around the ring, and audience members surround the circle with blankets and lawn chairs. Dancers of all ages in intricate **regalia** line up outside the arena. Some are here to dance socially; some are here to compete and win prize money; all will pass on Native traditions and form new ones. As the head drummer begins to steadily beat, the head military veteran, carrying an eagle feather staff, enters first, followed by male and female veterans bearing flags of the nation and the branches of the armed forces. The **Grand Entry** opening the powwow has begun.

An **intertribal powwow** is an event centered around dance and music in which Native Americans from different tribes come together to celebrate their cultures. They can be the length of an afternoon or several days in duration. Most powwows are outdoor events, and many are held in fairgrounds where participants camp for several days. Some participants are dedicated dancers, driving from powwow to powwow from spring to fall following the "**powwow circuit/ highway**" and hoping to win prize money; some are there to support family members and dance in social dances; some are there to sell jewelry and fry bread; and some are "powwow potatoes" (like couch potatoes), attending for food, entertainment, and dating possibilities.

Intertribal powwows in the United States and Canada number in the hundreds each summer. Chances are, if you live in the United States, a powwow is held within a half-day drive from your home. Powwow music and dances are the most widespread forms of Native American musical and movement expression, yet they are the least studied. A dance in one region can be radically different than another 500 miles away, despite the same song, dance, and order structures, reflecting great diversity of Native American tribes and traditions.

Powwows demonstrate both the continuity and evolution of North America's oldest dance traditions. Older practices coexist alongside new innovations in song and dance, but they do not always coexist easily. Traditionalists demand strict adherence to the past, while others insist on transformations to more accurately reflect 21st century Native American life.

For Native Americans, powwows have many meanings. One significance is social—powwows

Terminology: What to Call Native Americans?

There are many terms for Native Americans, not all of which are appropriate for all situations.

- *Native American:* Most commonly used in the United States; when in doubt, this is a safe term to use.
- *First Nations:* Generally synonymous with Native American, this term is most common in Canada and refers to any original nation of North America.
- *Indian:* An older term, still used by many Native Americans and in names of organizations and titles. This term is considered offensive in Canada and by some in the United States.
- *Indigenous:* Refers to the original inhabitants of the land; not a settler or colonial culture. This includes original inhabitants of North America, Africa, and Australia, among others.
- *Aboriginal:* Generally synonymous with *indigenous*; however, when capitalized, it refers to the indigenous peoples of Australia.
- There are other terms, such as the former name of the Washington NFL football team, that are racial slurs, considered extremely offensive, and should never be used.

are opportunities to continue old friendships and begin new ones. Performing and maintaining tribal identity have a critical role at a powwow: As members of various indigenous nations mix and share traditions, individual tribal identity is maintained and strengthened. Participants also celebrate the commonalities of indigeneity across tribes, and this shared identity is called **pan-Indian identity**. Powwows are credited as having a fundamental role in creating and sustaining pan-Indian identity, but this shared identity does not diminish or erase one's tribal affiliation, which remains primary. Native Americans also identify as American or Canadian. Most powwow participants consider affiliation in that order of importance—first the tribe, then Native American, then country. Significantly, powwows are a way of remembering and performing for ancestors. An unseen outer circle of ancestor spirits is present for powwow dancers, and performers speak of dancing for their ancestors. Therefore, powwow dances are both spiritual and secular, social and ritualistic, traditional and contemporary.

Studying Native American Cultures

In order to respectfully study Native American cultures, three premises must be understood. The first is that the designation *Native American* encompasses a wide multiplicity and diversity of cultures. Currently, there are over 500 federally recognized tribes in the United States and over 600 First Nations in Canada, with 220 different languages spoken; each holds its own distinct culture and tradition. At the time of Christopher Columbus' landing in 1492, the New World was more populated and sophisticated than it is commonly thought to be. In Charles Mann's book *1491* (2005), Mann estimates the New World population as between 50 to 100 million—a higher population than Europe—mostly living in complex, highly organized tribes. North America had far greater diversity in language and culture than Europe, as well. For example, the differences in languages between the **Diné (Navajo)** and the **Hopi**, who geographically are next-door neighbors in current day Arizona and New Mexico, are far greater than the differences between the English and the Dutch languages. Therefore, whenever one talks about Native dances, one

must situate them within a particular tribe as well as a particular historical time. The dances discussed in this chapter are dances shared at intertribal powwows and thus serve only as an example of intertribal Native American dances in the 20th and 21st centuries.

The second premise is to understand authenticity as a concept that applies to contemporary and popular Native American dance. All cultures are living, changing entities that constantly evolve: An authentic Native American dance in the 21st century is different from a dance a hundred years ago. Native American cultures are the most frequently studied by anthropologists, and have become among the most fetishized and commercialized. Americans and Europeans can get caught up looking for the "authentic" Native American dance, which usually means looking for a dance from before contact with Europeans. The viewpoint that sees Native dance as authentic only when practiced in isolation from contemporary culture is damaging to Native American artists. Creativity and innovation are essential to the ongoing development of artistic forms; to deny this to indigenous artists denies them the basic tenets of both culture and artistry. Contemporary forms of Native American dance are just as "authentic" as older forms.

Third, the **evolutionary fallacy** must be addressed when studying Native cultures. The *evolutionary fallacy* is the discredited idea that cultures move in a single line from most primitive to most civilized. This false notion was popular in the early part of the 20th century, and it assumed that indigenous dance was less developed and less valuable than Western concert dance, which was seen as the pinnacle of dance evolution. It also contributed to the bizarre idea that indigenous dance was somehow a precursor to ballet and modern dance. Dispelling the evolutionary fallacy means understanding that dance forms evolve and develop along their own continuum. Dance that happens later, historically, is neither less nor more valuable than earlier dance. It also means understanding that all dance that happens in the 21st century is contemporary dance. Dispelling the evolutionary fallacy breaks down the hierarchical thinking that considers some dance forms as more evolved, sophisticated, or valuable than others.

Last, it is important to remember that Native Americans are contemporary people—they are not symbols, mascots, or reminders of the past. Their cultures exist within and beside American mainstream culture and are subjected to the same pressures and influences, as well as challenges that are distinct for contemporary indigenous peoples.

Indian Sports Mascots

While the debates rage on, there is a great deal of agreement among Native Americans that sports mascots are offensive. Native Americans also consider it offensive when people without cultural ties claim indigenous status (a great-grandma Cherokee princess is not sufficient), which particularly surfaces when some people claim that they are not offended by Indian mascots. For comparison, place another ethnic group in the mascot's place and see if you still find it inoffensive. Akin to blackface, Native Americans consider mascots to be **brownface**, and, regardless of the intention, they are *not* honored. Where non-Native imagery prevails, Native voices are silenced.

 See resource 1.1 in HK*Propel* for web links.

History of Intertribal Powwows

The root of every dance and song performed in a powwow lies in a Native American tribal tradition of a particular First Nation. Occasionally, such as in the **hoop dance** and the **fancy dances** (as described below), specific origins can be identified and are agreed upon. Often, however, a dance's origins are contested, and oral histories conflict. While it is impossible to trace origins of all dances, it is easier to discern the effects of American colonialism, which had a large influence on powwow dances, particularly from 1890 onward. One can therefore recognize powwows as a constantly evolving practice, shaped from Native American roots, influenced by Euro-Western cultures, then reappropriated for the continuing expression of Native Americans.

Native Americans have faced continuing hardships in maintaining cultural and artistic traditions. In particular, the U.S. federal policy in the 19th century was first to eradicate the Indian population through genocide and war and then to relocate them when that proved impossible. When killing was no longer popular or politically feasible, the policy transformed into one of eradicating Native traditions and forcing Native Americans to conform to Christian beliefs and white American ways of life. The U.S. policy was to "**kill the Indian to save the man**." This meant wiping out all Native cultures, traditions, and practices in order to make Native Americans indistinguishable from white Americans and to assimilate them into the lower echelons of society.

By 1890, the U.S. government considered the "Indian problem" contained when the last of the **Lakota** were confined to South Dakota reservations. Native Americans were wards of the U.S. federal government, were excluded from U.S. citizenship, and had few rights. The **Bureau of Indian Affairs**, a federal agency under the Department of War, exerted extreme control over Indian life, and it banned most forms of Indian dance. Dances were "dangerous" because they continued Native customs, interfered with assimilation, and were not Christian. Government officials also worried that large-scale gatherings could incite Native Americans to war, and that they could disguise warlike preparations. Moreover, tribe members would often have to travel for days to attend dances, and this was inconducive to the federal project of turning nomadic cultures into sedentary farmers. Furthermore, many dances included "**giveaways**," in which tribal members would gift large portions of their wealth to others. Native American beliefs hold that the stature of an individual is increased by what one gives away, rather than what one accumulates. This was unacceptable to mainstream American culture and infuriated those that tried to enforce individual ownership of the land onto Native Americans, instead of their collective or tribal ownership. Government officials and missionaries felt that giveaways further distanced Native Americans from Christian and Western beliefs and that Indians would need to develop a stronger sense of greed before they would become "civilized." For these reasons, dances had to occur in secret and in remote locations, away from the prying eyes of the Indian Affairs commissioners.

Simultaneously, Europeans and non-Native Americans were fascinated with Indian culture, and pageant-style shows were created to fulfill this curiosity. The most well-known of these shows, ***Buffalo Bill's Wild West*** show, employed hundreds of Native Americans at a time to perform in arenas to audiences of 30,000 or more. Native American performers, mostly male, toured America and Europe, showing off horse-riding skills and Native dances. These pageants told a narrative of the disappearing Indian: Theatrical scenes played out famous battles and always ended with Buffalo Bill as the hero and Indians as the losers. Thus, Native Americans played out their own demise daily in Wild West shows. Ironically, since dancing was banned on reservations, the only place Native Americans could legally dance was in Wild West shows. Yet, they had to play a version of "Indian" that was acceptable to white audiences—namely, enacting their own disappearance.

Wild West shows are acknowledged as a strong influence on current powwow practices. Parts of the powwow, such as the Grand Entry, can be directly linked to these large-scale pageants, and many styles of dance were directly influenced by the theatrical demands of the shows. **Rodeos**, with their competitive events and rankings, were

another influence that became folded into contest powwows.

Intertribal powwows as we know them today were first held in Oklahoma after World War I. Powwows began as a way of welcoming Native soldiers home from war. Native Americans have had the highest participation rate in the U.S. military of any ethnic group throughout the 20th and 21st centuries; warrior culture and celebration of veterans are strongly entrenched in Native American values. Pan-Indian identity was created and strengthened when Native American soldiers served side by side in regiments with soldiers from many different tribes and nations.

Tribal members who interacted with each other during wartime began to identify with a common experience of being indigenous in America, sharing elements of history as well as challenges with mainstream America. Powwows became large-scale homecoming celebrations, and their popularity accelerated after World War II. The homecoming celebrations also pre-

Historical photo of Native Americans featured in *Buffalo Bill's Wild West* show.

Buyenlarge/Getty Images

cipitated more women's involvement in dancing within the powwow circle. Dancing in the interior of the arena was associated with veteran status, and since women served in the U.S. armed forces in large numbers, they began to be included in powwow dances in more central ways. Today, the celebration of military veterans is still a fundamental part of the powwow. Native American veterans always lead the Grand Entry and carry flags, and all veterans, Native or non-Native, performing or spectating, are acknowledged and celebrated.

Thus, powwow dances are an amalgamation of Native American traditions, acted upon by American colonialism, reenacted by 20th century Native peoples, and incorporated as new traditions and shared among First Nations in a pan-Indian practice.

 See resource 1.2 in HK*Propel* for web links.

Powwow Elements

Intertribal powwows are events between different tribes, meaning they are open to all First Nations as well as casual attendees and observers. Native Americans continue many traditions within a given tribe through **intratribal powwows** and rituals; however, outsiders would not be invited or welcome to these. Intertribal powwows can be traditional or contest. Traditional and contest powwows hold the same dances, but traditional powwows focus on unity and tribal identity and do not judge dances nor hand out prize money. The contest elements of powwows are a more recent invention: The idea of competitive dancing and prizes in Native American dancing did not exist prior to the 20th century.

Contest powwows have grown to be the most popular in recent decades and generally have higher attendance. Winners of contest dances earn money, and a following of dancers has developed, with dancers traveling "the powwow circuit" moving from powwow to powwow during summer months. Prize money is modest—from a few hundred dollars to a few thousand—but it can be enough to fund the travel for a few months. Although there is a competitive element to contest dances, unity and appreciation of all dancers remains the underlying concern. Spectators may have favorite tribes and dancers, but they do not cheer for a specific dancer, and booing would be extremely rude. The act of watching a competitive powwow dance is one of reverence and appreciation.

Types of powwows can be further divided into Northern powwows, whose songs and dances originate in the Northern Great Plains and Great Lakes regions, and Southern powwows, whose origins are traced to Oklahoma. Northern and Southern powwows historically have different dances, styles, and spatial arrangements; however, because dancers from both types mix, regional powwow differences have become less distinct, and large powwows usually represent both Northern and Southern styles in dance and drum.

In these styles, the circle is the main organizing spatial principle as a symbol of unity, the connectedness of all things on Mother Earth, and the cycles of nature and life. It symbolizes the link between ancestors, the living, and future generations. Powwow grounds are a nexus between the spiritual and physical worlds, inhabited by both seen and unseen entities, the known and the unknowable.

Concern for the Earth and Notions of Ownership

The Native American worldview embraces stewardship and shared responsibility for the earth, as opposed to notions of dominance and individual ownership.

We are part of something much grander in scale, and we should take care of this place where we live, because one day the earth may decide to shake us off and be done with the abuse. (Cody Boettner [Muskogee Creek], World Hoop Dance Champion)

Powwow grounds are blessed by elders, who create a consecrated space by clearing the grounds of negative influences. Dancers purify themselves with the smoke from **smudging** (burning) sage or sweetgrass before entering the arena. Consecrated spaces are important because they are considered neutral grounds where personal conflicts are set aside. Powwows are designed to create unity, and elements that may interfere with harmony are left outside. Alcohol and drugs are strictly prohibited at powwows, and anyone breaking this rule will be asked to leave. Powwows honor the human body as a site of interconnectedness and harmony. Powwow dancers are expected to show respect for oneself as a way of respecting both life and Mother Earth; for many dancers, this means living an alcohol- and drug-free life.

Music

Drums are a fundamental element of powwows, and musicians are given the highest respect. The sound of the drum represents a heartbeat, and, as a heartbeat sustains life, the drumbeat sustains the dance. Dancers should follow the drum at all times; ending with both feet on the ground on the last drum beat of a song is compulsory, and dancers who do not are disqualified from competitions. Drummers are almost always men, but women have been making strides into drumming roles in recent years. Nevertheless, female drummers are still considered controversial among many powwow participants. More commonly, women sit behind the male drummers and singers and come in later in songs as support vocals.

Gender

A hierarchy of status exists in powwows in which importance is delineated by age, military veteran status, and gender. The Grand Entry illustrates this by the order in which dancers enter. First men enter, then women; juniors enter with boys first, followed by girls; then children, with boys leading and girls following. Some people would argue that this does not suggest importance and that the categories are "separate but equal"; however, it is impossible to deny that participants are divided into these fundamental categories and that the order never varies. This connotes status and importance. Furthermore, certain genders are expected to perform only in certain dances. As cultures and societies change, so do gender roles and gender participation: Several powwows exist that are gender-free and queer or **two-spirit** friendly, in which any person can perform any role. These **LGBTQ**/two-spirit powwows are designed to question the gender hierarchies

and expectations of conventional powwows and create a welcoming space for people regardless of gender or sexuality.

Gender, Sexuality, and Two-Spirit

Two-spirit is a modern pan-Indian term that denotes a third gender or gender variant that does not conform to male or female. Many Native Americans agree that traditional indigenous societies had acceptance of people of nonconforming gender; the strict male-female binary is considered a colonial influence. *Two-spirit* is not interchangeable with *LGBTQ*, and it is used only to refer to Native Americans.

Clothing

Regalia plays an essential role in powwow dances. The clothing worn has symbolic significance that may denote tribe, family, or kin. Each dance has a preexisting template for what can be worn, determined by custom and tribal origin of the dance. Colors, patterns, and fabrics are often personal choice. Regalia is intricate, colorful, and complex, and it is often handed down through families. A typical powwow dancer wears regalia items that are handmade, bought, inherited, and gifted. Regalia is never called a *costume*—a term that powwow dancers find offensive. As one dancer explains, "I am not pretending to be someone else. This is who I am" (Conlin 2016).

 See resource 1.3 in HK*Propel* for web links.

Powwow Dances

Powwows contain more than a dozen different types of dances. These include men's and women's traditional dances; competitive dances such as men's and women's fancy dance; social dances like the **round dance**; and exhibition dances, such as the hoop dance. Below are descriptions of sample dances one would experience at a powwow.

Round Dance (or Friendship Dance)

It is understood that there are no nonparticipants in powwow grounds; those spectating are participants as much as those dancing. The round dance brings performing participants and spectating participants together in the dance ring. Dancers go into the audience and invite people to join them in the arena. It is considered rude to refuse, and announcers will say that anyone who refuses must pay the dancer. Participants join hands around the outer ring of the dance arena. The head dancers lead the group around in a circle sunwise (clockwise), using a side-to-side step. The head dancers break off and lead the group into spirals, often making several circles within the larger circle. The participants' main task is to follow the drumbeat and the spatial pattern, and they can add their own variations and style as long as they achieve this. The round dance is also called the friendship dance, and its function is to connect people through movement and music. In powwows, round dances often happen in between rounds or while judges' scores are tabulated, and they can happen numerous times during a powwow.

Round dances have become well recognized internationally on social media and are an established part of the **Idle No More** grassroots indigenous movement. Begun in 2012, Idle No More began as a protest against the Canadian government's plan to weaken environmental protections to allow for oil pipelines to be built across First Nations' lands. **Flash mob** round dances held in Canadian and U.S. shopping malls became a signature event in Idle No More's protests against resource exploitation on First Nations' territory, and they continue to be held in various locations as peaceful events that bring awareness to the plights of First Nations. Examples of round dance flash mobs held in varying locations and times and with groups both large and small are plentiful on the Internet.

Men's and Women's Fancy Dance

Dances called *fancy dance style*, as contrasted with the straight style that is more traditional, are contemporary dances that are fast, athletic, and showy. The dances are characterized by quick footwork timed to the drum, to which dancers add jumps, splits, cartwheels, and other athletic moves. Men's fancy dance regalia is intricate from top to toe; bustles on the shoulders move and dancers hold spinners that must be kept in constant motion. Dancers must keep track of the movement of their regalia as they follow the drums, improvising while adding their individual signature to their dance. Other than the requirement to keep time to the drum and end on the last beat, men's fancy dance is free-form and improvisatory.

Compared to other powwow dances, the origins of the men's and women's fancy dance are not contested. The name *fancy dance* came about when Buffalo Bill asked Native American performers to take their traditional dances from warrior society and "fancy it up" for American and European audiences. Here we see traditional Native American dances changing to be more palatable for Western spectators. However, most powwow people agree that the men's fancy dance that is seen today began in Oklahoma after World War I. Since then, Native Americans have performed the fancy dance as an expression of Native American culture, predominantly for their families, their tribes, and the wider network of Native Americans. Men's fancy dance has become the iconic representation of powwows; it is the most well-known and most spectacular, and it holds the highest prize money.

Women's fancy dance grew out of men's fancy dance. In some traditional dances, women are bound by the restriction to keep one foot on the ground at all times; this symbolizes the idea that women are closer to the earth. According to powwow tradition, in the early 1940s a group of teenage girls rebelled at not being able to perform the fancy dance. They dressed up in men's outfits and danced at a South Dakota powwow. This action and other similar contestations of powwow conventions led to women developing their own fancy dance tradition.

Women's fancy dance is also called the **shawl dance** or **butterfly dance**. The dance represents a caterpillar emerging from a cocoon and transforming into a butterfly, much like a young girl transforms into a woman. The regalia is more sedate than the men's, consisting of a basic dress, a yoke, leggings, and moccasins. The showpiece of the regalia is the shawl, which adorns the dancer's shoulders and represents a cocoon or wings. Oral sources place the dance's birthplace as the Lakota reservations in South Dakota. The dance is more structured than the men's fancy dance, and because of its athleticism and quickness, it is also considered a dance for young adults.

Hoop Dance

The hoop dance is an exhibition dance, or **blanket dance**, at most powwows. This designation means that a competition is not held; dancers perform it to share with participants. A blanket is placed in the arena and spectators are encouraged to donate by placing money on the blanket. Although at regular powwows the hoop dance is not a competition dance, the Heard Museum in Phoenix, Arizona, holds the largest event for hoop dancers, the **Annual World Champion Hoop Dance Contest**.

The hoop dance is one of the most spectacular, virtuosic, and well known of the powwow dances. Dancers display quick, precise footwork and hoop handling skills that take decades to perfect. The hoop dance requires stamina, cardiorespiratory endurance, flexibility, speed, and agility and is therefore considered a dance ideal for young adults in their 20s and 30s. Nonetheless, dancers of any age and gender can perform hoop dances.

The hoop dance serves as an excellent example of a Native American dance that has transformed many times to reach its current 21st century form. Its roots are in the **Pueblo** people's ceremonies of what is now the southwestern United States. In the early 20th century, **Tony White Cloud** of the Jemez Pueblo took the traditional hoop dance, transformed it into an exhibition dance, and popularized it by performing it in the 1942 movie *The Valley of the Sun*. He toured with actor/singer/rodeo performer Gene Autry ("the Singing Cowboy") through the United States and Europe during World War II, promoting war bonds to fund the war effort. He subsequently performed in more Hollywood movies. As such, White Cloud is considered the father of the modern hoop dance. Throughout the 20th century, Native Americans of various tribes adopted the hoop dance as their own, transforming it from a Pueblo ceremony to a pan-Indian dance that expresses Native identity. It has become an authentic dance form for many indigenous Americans, particularly practiced among the First Nations of the western United States and Canada.

The hoop is a symbol of unity, the life cycle, Mother Earth, and the connectedness of all beings within her. A hoop has no beginning and no end, representing the never-ending cycle of life. It is a

A Native American man performs the hoop dance.

Tim Mosenfelder/Corbis via Getty Images

dance of healing and a prayer for the earth. The dancers mix athleticism and artistry to tell stories of the earth, sun, and moon, and everything that lives in between, from the biggest living creatures to the smallest.

Hoop dancers use between 4 and 40 hoops to create shapes that represent eagles, butterflies, trees, Mother Earth, deities, and humans. Hoop dancers continue to create new symbols; in a contemporary hoop dance, a spectator might see a bronco-riding cowboy, a bull, or a car represented in the hoop shapes. Similarly, dancers incorporate new steps into their routines; it would not be unusual to see the **moonwalk** or **break dancing** moves in a hoop dance.

Dancers must pass through every hoop they use, they must catch hoops when thrown or spun, and designs should not fall apart. Dancers must be in time with the drum and stop with the end of the music, and bells or deer hooves are required. Dancers choose the number of hoops they use; those using only a few hoops must bring more

Cultural Highlight

FIRST FEMALE HOOP DANCE CHAMPION

Ginger Sykes Torres is used to breaking new ground. Torres is a member of the Navajo Nation, of the Tó Dích'íi'nii Clan born for Bilagáana, and in 1997, she was the first female to win a world title in the Heard Museum's Annual World Championship Hoop Dance Contest. "When I started dancing the hoop dance, there were only two or three other female hoop dancers and I sometimes felt like I didn't belong. But my parents were very supportive. Now, there are many more women hoop dancing and I am happy that young women feel more accepted. It is empowering and inspiring to see many young girls now learning to hoop dance."

For Torres, there can be a tension between the traditional and the contemporary elements in the hoop dance. "A good hoop dance is one that has all the traditional elements of precision, rhythm, and speed, but also shows the unique style and strengths of the dancer—which might include limited elements of modern dance or athletic display. A good dancer should show technique and style with traditional Native dance steps, not just the hoops, and should have short, seamless transitions between formations. The movement must be continuous. And there should always be some engagement with the audience—there should be some showmanship without being too flashy."

Torres is a Stanford University graduate with a degree in the earth systems program and works as an environmental consultant, advocating for renewable energy and climate change action. She sees the hoop dance as an extension of her work in environmental sustainability. "The hoop dance honors the earth. It reminds us to take care of the planet for future generations." Torres creates formations of animals and plants with her hoops that she feels are important. Another dancer might make the same hoop formations and mean something different with them. Each dance reflects the dancer's tribal origin and personality.

Torres now teaches the hoop dance to Native American children of all genders. "It is essential for girls and women to be involved, and it's vital that the girls know they can win when they compete in the same competitions as boys." Torres dances to maintain connections to her culture, and she has performed internationally. "It's crucial to share our culture in ways that honor our past but also reflect who we are today. It shows that Native American cultures are resilient, and it helps people to understand that we are modern day people."

 See resource 1.4 in HK*Propel* for web links.

creativity to their routine than dancers using as many as 40. There is a balance between speed and creativity: Hoop dancers who use fewer hoops dance to extremely fast songs, while dancers with 20 or more hoops dance to a slower drumbeat.

Special Dances

Powwows include special dances that are held at an individual's or family's request. Honor songs and dances mark a person's special achievement, such as a graduation or return from military service, or as a memorial for a deceased relative. Giveaways often accompany the honor songs, where family members give expensive goods, such as cloth, shawls, and regalia, to the arena director, head judges, head dancers, and special friends. Lesser gifts can include bags of groceries, dish towels, or DVD players, and dancers from other dance categories are called up to select gifts. Leftovers are given away during an open call to the children in the audience. Giveaways are planned for months and are often preceded by a period of hardship by the family as they save for giveaways. Outsiders are often shocked by the cost and amount of goods distributed during giveaways. For Native Americans, prestige comes from acts of generosity, and status is represented by the amount one gives away. Audience members are expected to stand during honor songs and dances.

 **See resource 1.5 in HK*Propel* for web links.**

Crosscurrents

Powwows continue to change as mainstream culture and Native American culture change. Gender restrictions continue to be challenged, and women are demanding to perform drum and singing roles. Powwows now exist that are specifically gender-free and LGBTQ friendly, where no role is determined by gender or sexuality. As participants travel greater distances for powwows, Northern and Southern styles are becoming less distinct and are incorporating more elements from each other to include all dancers. Powwow dances are becoming more recognizable, and dancers are performing in other types of dance productions, such as the circus arts of **Cirque du Soleil**, *The Nutcracker* ballet, and peaceful flash mob protests.

Electronic and social media have affected the ways the powwow dances are learned, shared, and enacted. Videos of powwows are regularly shared on YouTube. It is now possible to learn basic powwow steps from website tutorials originally begun by individuals and now supported by tribal and outside funding. During the 2020/2021 coronavirus pandemic, powwows moved online, and a new practice of socially distanced powwows began. The Facebook site **Social Distance Powwow** reveals the crucial functions that powwows perform for Native American communities, with posts of real-time dance competitions, vendors selling crafts, personal anniversaries of sobriety, celebrations of first powwows and other life events, and calls for prayers and support during hardships. Powwows continue to transform as they create and reflect the needs of Native Americans in the 21st century.

 See resource 1.6 in HK*Propel* for web links.

Summary

In order to respectfully study Native American dance, one must acknowledge the diversity of Native American cultures, understand Native Americans as contemporary people whose current dances have as much merit as historical ones, and eschew the evolutionary fallacy. Intertribal powwows are events widespread throughout North America where Native Americans come together to celebrate their culture through music and dance. Powwow songs and dances are the most common form of Native American music and dance today, and they have roots in traditional tribal societies, although some origins are better known than others. American colonialism has affected powwow dances and structures, and Native Americans have adapted dances as their needs evolved. Powwow dances include social dances, such as the round dance; competitive styles, such as the men's and women's fancy dance; exhibition styles, such as the hoop dance; and special dances that include memorials, honor songs and dances, and giveaways. Through powwows, Native Americans affirm their tribal identity, Native identity, and national identity; participate in ancient tribal traditions; and create new rituals and aesthetics for the 21st century.

Discussion Questions

1. What images and portrayals of Native Americans have you encountered, and where did you encounter them? Did this chapter challenge those portrayals? Did it reinforce them?

2. In the future, what can you do to ensure that you receive accurate portrayals of and information about Native Americans?

3. What is pan-Indian identity, and how have powwows contributed to its formation?

4. Summarize the many influences on powwow dances.

5. Describe the significance of circles to Native American cultures. In what ways do powwows manifest this symbolism?

6. Compare and contrast the different movement styles and elements of different powwow dances. What values are expressed in each?

 Visit HK*Propel* for access to this chapter's Application Activity.

Selected Glossary

brownface—When Europeans or Euro-Americans dress up as and adopt the cultural markers of Native Americans. Similar to blackface with African Americans.

Buffalo Bill's Wild West—Large pageant-style arena shows in which the battles between the U.S. Cavalry and Native Americans were featured. Native American cultures were highlighted, including horseback riding and dance. Most active between 1890 and 1920.

butterfly dance/shawl dance—A specific powwow dance done by women. Also known as the women's fancy dance, it contains fast footwork and traveling, and it is often a competition dance. The shawl is used to indicate a journey of the butterfly.

evolutionary fallacy— The discredited idea that cultures evolve on a single unitary time line from primitive to advanced. It falsely equates the complexity of a society's technology with the complexity of its art. It creates a hierarchy wherein so-called primitive cultures are worth less than "civilized."

fancy dances—A category of powwow dances that are showy, athletic, and fast paced. Fancy dances are more contemporary than traditional powwow dances and are often performed competitively. Both women and men have their own types of fancy dances.

Grand Entry—The formal opening of a powwow; in the Grand Entry all participants enter the dance arena, parading in their regalia for the other performers and spectators. A highlight of a powwow.

hoop dance—A specific style of contemporary Native American dance, a hoop dance is an exhibition dance performed in powwows. Dancers use 4 to 40 hoops to create symbols of nature and the contemporary world. All genders can perform the hoop dance.

Idle No More—A social movement that began in Canada, created initially by four indigenous women. It protests environmental degradation of reservation land and asserts indigenous sovereignty. It has used round dances in shopping malls to great effect.

intertribal powwow—A gathering where Native Americans from many tribes celebrate their cultures through music and dance.

"kill the Indian to save the man"—The policy of the U.S. government after 1890 to eliminate all Indian culture and force Native Americans to assimilate. This was enacted through draconian restrictions and the forced removal of children from Native American homes. The policy was designed to enact cultural genocide.

pan-Indian identity—A shared sense of common identity among Native Americans that unites the indigenous of North America. Pan-Indian identity does not erase tribal identity, which remains primary, but is a layer on top of it.

regalia—The clothing worn by Native Americans during dances. Regalia is specific to the type of dance being performed and is never called a "costume."

two-spirit—*Two-spirit* is a modern, pan-Indian term that denotes a third gender or gender variant that does not conform to male or female. The term is not interchangeable with ***LGBTQ***, and it is used only to refer to Native Americans.

Selected References and Resources

Browner, T. 2002. *Heartbeat of the People*. Chicago: University of Illinois.

Conlin, Paula. 2016. "From Powwow to Stomp Dance." In *The Oxford Handbook of Dance and Ethnicity*, edited by Anthony Shay and Barbara Sellers-Young, 613-635. Oxford: Oxford University Press.

Grau, Andree. 1998. "Myths of Origin." In *The Routledge Dance Studies Reader*, edited by Alexandra Carter, 197-202. London and New York: Routledge.

Mann, Charles. 2005. *1491: New Revelations of the Americas Before Columbus*. New York: Knopf.

Prichard, Robin. 2016. "Honoring the Past, Changing the Future: Bringing Native American Voices Into Dance Theory Courses." *Journal of Dance Education* 16 (2): 39-47. https://doi.org/10.1080/15290824.2015.1055003.

2

Social Dance in the United States

Expression and Socialization

Nora Ambrosio

Learning Objectives

After reading this chapter you will be able to do the following:

- Recognize dance in the United States as a cultural phenomenon that has its roots in the cultures of many different countries, and therefore has developed under a range of political, geographical, religious, and other influences.

- See social dance as an illustration of how the relative youth of the United States as a nation and the unique features of its development are woven into the dance of this culture.

- Understand the relevance of social dance as a means of expression and socialization, and how these functions play out in the United States.

- Evaluate the different social dance subcultures described in this chapter.

Key Terms

ball culture—Also known as *drag ball culture*, an **LGBTQ+** subculture that originated in the 1920s in New York City.

cultural appropriation—The adoption of elements from another culture without proper attribution.

expression—In social dance, both individuals and groups express themselves, making thoughts or feelings known through bodily movements, often in confirmation of personal or group identity.

hip-hop—A late 20th century dance style and art movement whose musical roots grew from New York City's African American, Latino, and Caribbean cultures.

social dance—Dance that provides for socialization and a means for expression, often displaying a particular movement style or form of a specific group or subculture.

socialization—Interactions with others while navigating the norms of a culture or society.

subculture—A cultural group that has its own identity, purposes, and priorities within a larger, dominant culture.

Social Dance and the Drag Ball Culture in Harlem, New York

During the height of the **Harlem Renaissance**, poet and social activist Langston Hughes recounted his experience witnessing a 1920s **drag ball**: "Strangest and gaudiest of all Harlem spectacles in the '20s . . . the queerly assorted throng on the dance floor, males in flowing gowns and feathered headdresses and females in tuxedos and box-back suits" (Haider 2018). Underground **ball culture** became synonymous with queer Black culture beginning in the 1960s. By the 1970s, the balls had become a safe haven for all gay people of color to use **drag**, style, fashion, and dance as a means for **expression** and **socialization**. The 1991 documentary ***Paris Is Burning*** brought ball culture to the mainstream, highlighting several "houses" that operated as families, giving gay youth actual homes and communities. "[T]he drag houses instituted their own family structure, headed by mothers, and sometimes fathers, who oversaw their 'children,' some of whom faced rejection from their biological families or their working-class African American and Latino communities. While the houses were initially formed to prepare and promote their competitors in upcoming balls, they provided space for much broader, adaptable family roles" (Herzog and Rollins 2012). The drag ball **subculture** had a major effect and impact on much in popular culture, such as pop singer Madonna's hit song "Vogue" (1990), which featured **voguing**, a dance made popular in the balls. ***RuPaul's*** *Drag Race*, a popular television show, mirrors ball culture, as did the show *Pose*, a drama series that focused on ball culture of the 1980s and beyond. The balls continue into today, as do the different family houses, providing a powerful outlet for expression and an avenue for socialization for both the participants and viewers.

Drag ball culture is a prime example of dance as a means of expression and socialization for people in marginalized subcultures. The first drag ball reportedly took place in Harlem, New York, in 1869, but it became part of underground nightlife in New York during the Harlem Renaissance—a flowering of African American arts in Harlem between 1918 and 1937. Spurred by the **Great Migration** of African Americans fleeing the repressive aftermath of the Civil War, the Harlem Renaissance can be seen as a microcosm and nexus of the complex cross-cultural history and dynamics underlying **social dance** in the United States. Although U.S. dance includes concert forms such as modern, ballet, jazz, and tap (the focus of dance education in many K-12, higher education, and studio settings) this chapter focuses on social dance and will show that the cultural forces shaping this form are much more immediately apparent than they are through the individualized artistic vision and formalized settings of concert dance.

The drag ball phenomenon highlights several unique elements of social dance in the United States, a relatively young country whose dance forms reflect the many cultures woven into its history. These cultures were mostly foreign to American soil before the arrival of European colonizers in the 1500s. (Although indigenous American dances are maintained to varying degrees within their nations and communities throughout the continent, they have less visibility in mainstream U.S. culture.) The key threads of influence in U.S. dance are European, African, and Latin American/Caribbean—the latter being themselves a mixture of African, European, and indigenous cultures. The forces of colonialism, immigration, and slavery have shaped the economic, religious, and societal framework of the U.S. from its earliest days to the present. Among these forces, the enslavement and transport of African people to the New World have had perhaps the most enduring ramifications for the culture of dance in the United States.

Brief History

A complex array of Native American cultures inhabited North America for over 16,000 years before European colonists arrived in the early 1500s. The colonists decimated indigenous populations through introduction of European diseases, direct warfare, and governmental programs of cultural eradication. Along the way, European nations—primarily Britain, France, and Spain—fought for supremacy over the vast resources of the continent. Britain ultimately secured the strongest foothold in North America, while immigrants from a range of cultures,

Willie Ninja (left) voguing in a nightclub.

Catherine McGann/Getty Images

social positions, and religious affinities arrived on American shores. Concurrently, colonial powers expanded the enslavement of Africans, establishing the colony's economic and political foundations firmly in slavery. In the 1700s, colonists chafing under British rule sparked the American Revolution, forming the United States of America during the years of warfare that followed the 1776 Declaration of Independence. Over time, the nation expanded through appropriation of Native American land and skirmishes with other colonial powers and neighbors such as Mexico. By the mid-1800s, contours of the present-day continental United States were established, and European immigration swelled the country's population. Throughout this expansion, slavery continued as a major economic engine for the nation until the ratification of the Emancipation Proclamation after the Civil War (1861-1865). However, true emancipation and civil rights for African Americans would be thwarted for many years by the rise of white supremacists and institutionalized discrimination, leading to the Great

Migration from southern states to northern industrial cities in the early 20th century. Immigrants from Asia, Europe, the rest of the Americas, and the Caribbean added to the complex cultural and economic dynamics throughout the 19th and 20th centuries, as did a Great Depression (1929-1933), World Wars I and II (1914-1918 and 1939-1945), the **Civil Rights Movement** (1940s-1960s), and astonishing technological advancements. In the 21st century the nation continues to grapple with the cultural ramifications of its multifaceted population and history (see table 2.1).

As the United States developed, the balance of cultural influences shifted from external to internal forces, the latter heightened by technological changes that enhanced the sharing of social and artistic impulses. A look at one 20th century dance phenomenon sparked, in part, by a popular movie illustrates this process.

 See resource 2.1 in HK*Propel* for web links.

Table 2.1 20th-21st Century Social Dance Events in the United States Through the Decades

Decade	Events
1920s	The height of the Harlem Renaissance (c. 1918-1937). Social dances such as the Charleston and the black bottom became popular, as did the drag balls that continue today.
1930s	A pattern emerges. Social dances such as the Lindy hop began in Black communities and were then borrowed, adapted, and adopted by white communities. This becomes a pattern with many social dances, with movements often emanating from the African diaspora and Latin America.
1940s	Ballroom dancing came to the forefront. Dances from Europe and Latin America, such as the waltz, foxtrot, and rumba, became popular in the United States.
1950s	This decade saw the advent of rock and roll music, and this music influenced the social dances of the time, including the jitterbug (a take on the Lindy hop), the jive, and the rock and roll.
1960s	Dances such as the twist, monkey, and mashed potato emerged. Connections to the African diaspora are still apparent.
Late 1960s	Dance styles emerged that reflected turbulent times. Freestyle dancing, with or without a partner, became the popular form of social dance.
1970s	Disco music brought about such dances as the hustle, the bump, and the bus stop. Partner dancing once again became popular.
1980s	Breaking, developed in the 1970s, became popular in the mainstream. Hip-hop culture gave rise to rap music. Slam dancing and mosh dancing were also seen in certain punk rock and heavy metal circles. Music television (MTV, VH-1, BET) popularized the music video. Many social dance styles appeared in the videos of the music industry's most popular performers.
1990s	Rap music, hip-hop, and breaking remained popular. Rave dancing, which began in the 1980s as an underground dance craze, became the popular dance form leading into the 21st century. In 1995, David LaChapelle created the documentary *Rize,* which featured clowning and krumping, dance forms created in the African American community of South Central Los Angeles.
2000s	Concert dance and social dance forms continued to be fused and created an exciting and unique aesthetic for many dance companies, including Rennie Harris Puremovement (founded in 1992), which focuses on hip-hop. Social dance is brought to the mainstream by reality television shows such as *Dancing with the Stars, So You Think You Can Dance,* and *America's Best Dance Crew.* The medical profession reports on the significant health benefits, particularly for older adults, of participating in ballroom dance. Congresswoman Eleanor Holmes Norton introduces a National Dance Day resolution to promote dance and dance education. Celebrated on the last Saturday in July, this unofficial holiday was further introduced to the public by *So You Think You Can Dance* cocreator and Dizzy Feet Foundation copresident Nigel Lythgoe.
2011	National Dance Week Foundation was established as a nonprofit institution. Originally formed in 1981 to bring greater awareness and recognition to dance, the organization has inspired thousands of events during its 10-day annual celebration, which occurs every April.
2011-2017	*Dancing with the Stars* and *So You Think You Can Dance* are still popular television shows. Well-known social dance styles and genres are featured, but less familiar dance styles, such as the New Orleans bounce, are also introduced to the mainstream via these popular television shows.
2018-today	Popular music continues to be a catalyst for new fad dances, including the Harlem shake, juju on that beat, whip/nae nae, the dab, shmoney dance, wobble, and walk it out. Television programs such as *Dancing with the Stars* and *So You Think You Can Dance* are still popular, while new shows such as *World of Dance* and the Netflix original series *We Speak Dance* bring more viewing options to the public.

John Travolta in *Saturday Night Fever*.

Social Dance

When looking at dance in the United States from a cultural perspective, it is apparent that very few dance forms and styles were born entirely of this country. Most U.S. dances—social forms, staged forms, and hybrids thereof—utilize the movements and dances of the peoples who migrated, whether voluntarily or through force, to the United States. Social dances in particular, have a history of being passed from culture to culture, with participants borrowing movements and styles and adapting them to fit, or to go against, cultural norms. For this reason, social dance serves as an excellent example of the dynamics shaping U.S. dance over the past several centuries and into the present.

Social Dance in the United States—A Definition

Social dance provides for socialization, often displaying a particular movement style or form of a specific group or subculture. Unlike concert dance, social dances are mainly meant for participation, although there are professional dance choreographers that use social dance movements in their choreography. Several U.S. examples of social dance include line dancing, disco, ballroom, rock and roll, and hip-hop.

Cultural Highlight

WHATEVER HAPPENED TO DISCO?

In the late 1970s, **disco** music and dancing reigned supreme in the United States. Although a major part of the nightlife in New York City and other urban centers, disco came into the mainstream mainly due to the 1977 movie *Saturday Night Fever*, which starred John Travolta. The movie set a trend for social dancing, including **partner dances** such as the hustle and the bump, and the bus stop **line dance**. It also set the tone for fashion and glamour, and looking fabulous was required for all who wanted to fit in on the nightclub scene (Ambrosio 2018). In New York City, there were discotheques, or discos, such as Studio 54 and the Copacabana, that catered to an elite clientele.

There were also nightclubs that drew a more eclectic crowd, and some that catered to a mostly gay male population. Private parties were held at certain establishments (sometimes referred to as **loft parties**). Despite astronomical cover charges for admittance, lines of people waiting to get in often circled city blocks. Regardless of the club attended, ecstatic dancing with the flavor of African dance and jazz dance was seen everywhere, spurred on by music that had an identifiable disco beat. The music had almost an orchestral sound that relied heavily on string and horn instruments, synthesizers, drum machines, "chicken-scratch" guitars, and reverberated vocals. The sound was big and often played over audio systems at deafening, but also stimulating, volumes.

So, whatever happened to disco? Changes in the economy and the political landscape in the late 1970s and early 1980s may have led to the decline of disco in the United States. The conservatism ushered in by the **Reagan Era** called attention to what was seen as the self-indulgent nature of the disco scene. There was also a vocal "disco sucks" movement that was touted by some **DJs**, radio personalities, and rock musicians. Basically, they were a "coalition of predominantly straight white men who felt dispossessed by disco and vented their anger in frequently homophobic and . . . racist publicity stunts" (Malnig 2009). Rock musicians such as David Bowie, Rod Stewart, and the band Queen were ridiculed for adopting a disco sound in some of their music. By the early 1980s, many of the popular discos had closed their doors or reinvented themselves to cater to a different crowd. The disco sub-culture may have disappeared; however, the disco dance style and music influence has not. Remnants of disco dance styles can still be seen on today's dance floors, and disco dancing has been re-popularized by television dance shows such as *Dancing with the Stars* and *So You Think You Can Dance*.

 See resource 2.2 in HK*Propel* for web links.

In the United States, historic social dances, as well as many of the latest fad dances, reflect movement and style adapting and adopting from many different cultures, including European, African, Latin American, and Caribbean. Much has been written about **cultural appropriation** of dance, and particularly of social dance. Although not the emphasis of this chapter, acknowledging appropriation is crucial: Any study of social dance will uncover the embodiment of different cultures' movements and styles because "embodied practices can never be fully extracted from issues of cultural representation" (Bock and Borland 2011). Technology has further complicated the dynamics of cultural appropriation, as dances can be commodified through video and distributed worldwide. Without the need to be physically present when engaging another culture's dance, appropriation—intentional or not—becomes very easy. The best antidote is raising awareness of such pitfalls by understanding the cultural dynamics and history of the dances in question.

Although social dance in the United States does not have the centuries-long history found in many other cultures, there are in fact social dances that hold cultural significance for both the participants and viewers that were (and are) born from the cultures in which they exist. Many groups of people comprise dance subcultures in the population of the United States, where the dance itself creates a living, breathing culture, providing important outlets for the specific groups, as seen in the example of ball culture. Social dances, through the acts of participating and viewing, provide both individuals and groups with essential outlets of expression and socialization. Social dance is a cultural phenomenon that allows for self- and group expression, as well as an activity that affects socialization and community building in the United States.

 See resource 2.3 in HK*Propel* **for web links.**

Social Dance as Expression

Social dance in the United States is constantly being transformed, from era to era and culture to culture. The basic human affinity for the joy and release of dancing plays out in a wide range of social situations. Both dancers and viewers are active participants in these events.

When dancing is done in social situations, such as weddings, parties, proms, galas, cultural celebrations, or nightclubs, it is not arbitrary, but a major part of what people expect of these contemporary rituals. Similarly, group or partner social dances in the United States, such as **line dancing**, **folk dance**, **square dance**, and **ballroom dance**, are popular activities that many people prioritize in their social lives. Although social dances can be taught and learned, as in the case of ballroom and folk dances, many social dances are done in the moment, requiring the participants to improvise, connecting to the music and the people around them. Therefore, in the United States, the specific music choices and subcultures help shape the form of social dance at any given event. It is interesting to note that although some social dance forms may share a common heritage, different subcultures might only participate in the specific social dance form with which they align. For example, although some ballroom dances and line dances have roots in dances found in Europe, a ballroom dancer may never experience doing line dances, and vice versa.

Social Dance as Expression

"An exploration of what bodies can do together when left to their own devices, dancing cuts across the devotions of the professional and public passions. It occurs in tiny rooms and public arenas, streets, stages, kitchens, studios. Assembling all that dance has to offer provides a report on what sensibilities connect and disperse people through a physical culture. Taken together, dance supplies a record of where we have been and where we'd like to go, of how we move together and apart, of how we create the environments we inhabit and what we aspire to make of them" (Martin 2010, 56).

Though some social dance activities require prior knowledge of steps and patterns, such as folk and square dances, many others require the participants to do nothing more than cut loose. "Dance also makes legible the social kinesthetic, the shared physical sensibility and context we join as we rumble and tumble together" (Martin 2010, 59). Social dance creates environments of inclusion, which are particularly potent when looking at social dance and the need for expression of marginalized populations (see Ball Culture in the opening vignette).

Social Dance and Sexual Expression

Whether people identify as part of the **LGBTQ+**, cisgender, or straight community, dance and sexuality, and dance as sexual expression have also been part of social dance. What may be deemed an appropriate use of the body in social dance tends to be generational, as well as influenced by political, religious, and geographic characteristics (e.g., urban versus rural). Take, for example, the singer **Elvis Presley**'s third appearance on the ***Ed Sullivan Show*** in 1957, which ended up being his final appearance on that show. After Presley's gyrating hip movements shocked a portion of the audience during the first two shows (filmed by confused camera operators who panned in and out between full body shots and close ups), it was determined that for the third performance only the top half of his body would be shown. By today's standards, his hip movements were quite tame, but back in the conservative 1950s they scandalized a good portion of the (mostly older and white) population. A closer look at Presley's dance style shows adapting and adopting what had been seen in Black social dance for years and in indigenous African and Latin American dance before that. This lineage of movement adapting and adopting—from the African diaspora, Latin America, and the Caribbean, to Black American culture, to white American culture and beyond—appears in social dances through the decades (as seen in the discussion on hip-hop). As in years past, many African American singers and rap artists have started dance crazes to go along with their music that have quickly made their way through all races and cultures, such as the **wobble**, the **walk it out**, the **cupid shuffle**, and the **whip/nae nae**, to name a few.

Today, sexual expression is an inherent part of many forms of social dance in the United States. And an aura of sex, sexiness, and sensuality in social dance is sometimes perceived by viewers of social dance, whether the dancers are purposefully giving off a sexual vibe or not. The inability of some viewers to separate the dancer from the dance, or their misinterpretation of "leaving it all on the dance floor" as something other than what it is—ecstatic dancing—may say more about the viewer than the dancer. However, dancing for sexual expression, whether for titillation or because "that is just what I feel like doing," is also an accepted part of some social dance scenes, particularly the club scenes. Nevertheless, it is not just nightclubs where people display their sexuality, but in mainstream dance cultures and the media, as well. For example, both amateur and professional ballroom dance competitions sometimes feature women and men in revealing costumes and dance moves that are less than conservative. Although suggestive dance moves may ruffle a few feathers, there are just as many viewers who cheer on their favorite ballroom dance couples, regardless of, or maybe in response to, what they are doing on the dance floor.

Social Dance for Social Change

Social dance for social change also provides powerful means for expression, and social dance in this context was clearly seen in the **Black Lives Matter** protests of 2020. Throughout the United States (as well as the rest of the world), dance was seen at these protests as a way to not only express rage and sadness, but to show the power of using the dancing body to tell the story of the Black Lives Matter movement. The artistic expression of the dancers was on full display, and social dances such as voguing and **krumping** were used to depict how the dancers were feeling about oppression, inequality, and police brutality. Although some of these dance moments were planned, many were spontaneous and brought people from all walks of life together. At moments, the dancing was used to blow off steam, particularly line dances such as the cupid shuffle, which had hundreds of people joining in, including members of law enforcement. These dancing events served to diffuse tension between the protestors and the police, as well as highlight the passion and commitment of the protestors.

Black Lives Matter Movement of 2020

The Black Lives Matter movement was founded in 2013 in response to the acquittal of Trayvon Martin's killer. The mission of BLM is to "eradicate white supremacy and build local power to intervene in violence inflicted on Black communities by the state and vigilantes" (BLM website 2020). Protests formed around the country (and worldwide) to bring light to the injustices experienced by people of color, particularly as perpetrated by law enforcement. The killing of George Floyd by police in 2020 galvanized protestors from many age groups, races, and religions under the BLM banner.

Whether discussing social dance as a fun, enjoyable physical activity, as a means to highlight the need for social change, as a form of freedom of expression, or as an important part of marginalized cultures, the opportunity for people to express themselves through movement has had meaning and relevance throughout U.S. history.

 See resource 2.4 in HK*Propel* for web links.

Social Dance for Socialization

Socialization among humans is as important as the need for food, water, and shelter. Social dance can satisfy the need for connection with others and to feel part of a community. "Dance here provides an immediacy of the social. It takes up the question of what we can make together. It sends our imaginations back to the intimate rooms where all those dreadful decisions were made based upon failed intelligence and asks what smartness can be for" (Martin 2010, 59). When looking at dance as a means for socialization, participating as a doer or observer can satisfy the need for inclusion.

Dance for Socialization

"There is perhaps nothing more universal than the drive to move our bodies in sync with music. Studies show that dancing at parties and in groups encourages social bonding, whether it is a traditional stomp, a tango, or even the hokeypokey. Many researchers have argued that people experience a blurring of the self into their groups thanks to the synchronization that occurs while dancing" (Goldman 2016, para. 1).

The physical exertion dancing requires, like other forms of exercise, can also make people feel good. However, in the United States, the social aspect that dancing provides is key, whether the dancing occurs at a wedding celebration or other social events. While in the past these events were shared only with family members and close friends, the Internet has allowed the entire world into these once private occasions. The social impact of many dances that were developed in the United States can now be felt in different countries, where the form, function, and even context for the dances can be adopted and adapted to new cultural uses. In the United States the infamous engagement and wedding videos, along with "**promposals**" that feature dance sequences as part of the "ask," are as popular as any drama or comedy series on television. Watching these events on video provides a different type of socialization—although we may not know the people in the videos, we can enjoy their occasions and happiness and feel a positive and social response as viewers. Another example of the viewer–participant relationship can be seen in the **flash mob**, a phenomenon of U.S. origins that now occurs worldwide. The science underlying this viewer–participant relationship speaks to the key elements of socialization, expression, and communication through dance—where dancers and viewers alike experience feelings of community and empathy—as well as to how technology has emerged as a functional part of U.S. social dance.

Flash Mobs and Mirror Neurons

Flash mob dances are unannounced, seemingly spontaneous events in public venues, where participants start dancing together to a previously set choreography. They are organized via social media, text messages, or other communication technology, and the form of the dance can be rehearsed choreography, well-known popular dances, or any combination thereof. Flash mobs can be viewed both live and on the Internet, and those posted to social media have racked up thousands, even millions of views. The flash mobs that occur as a surprise to the unsuspecting, for example in a train station where loud music begins playing and seemingly random people next to you suddenly start dancing, are welcomed as a lovely treat by the onlookers. The delight lies in how the viewers truly become part of the event through its unexpectedness and the dynamics of human empathy.

When looking at the viewer as participant, neuroscientists point to the study of brain cells called **mirror neurons** that react both when a particular action is performed and when it is only observed. These scientists agree that the basis for empathy may stem from this system of mirror neurons. Thus, the emotional connection that naturally arises for humans through shared movement experience—even as a viewer—plays a significant role in both the form and function of social dances and is especially visible in the flash mob.

Not all flash mobs, however, are for purposes of feel-good moments. Some are done as a call to activism, such as when dozens of women danced and chanted outside a courthouse during the trial of film producer Harvey Weinstein, who was found guilty of sexual assault, among other

Flash mob performed at an outdoor event.

Charles Eshelman/Getty Images

charges. The LGBTQ dance group **WERK for Peace** stopped traffic on several roads in Washington, DC, as part of a protest to call attention to climate change. The company, whose members include queer and trans dancers, used all forms of dance to promote peace, and intend to "bring the dance floor to the streets to protest egregious social injustice" (werkforpeace.org 2020). Here, the flash mob provides for socialization of like-minded people, who use the power of dance to call attention to what they believe are important issues.

"The fact that dance is not reducible to any other form of human activity reveals its significance and justifies its existence. Therefore, dance has always been an important symbolic instrument in ritual contexts, in art events, in social communication, and political action" (Giurchescu 2001, 110).

 See resource 2.5 in HK*Propel* for web links.

Crosscurrents

Social dances that emerged from the unique history of the United States have taken root in cultures around the world, aided by technology and the resultant exponential growth of cross-cultural interactions. Cultural elements that previously took decades to spread beyond their origins now travel almost instantaneously via the Internet. The worldwide presence of **hip-hop** is a classic example of this phenomenon.

Hip-Hop Culture

The dance subculture of hip-hop and **breaking**, established by inner-city youths in the late 1960s and early 1970s in the Bronx, is an excellent example of a culture that developed out of the need for expression and socialization. Three prominent **DJs**—**DJ Kool Herc**, **Afrika Bambaataa**, and **Grandmaster Flash**—brought (primarily African

American) groups of people together in recreation rooms and block parties and mixed music in ways that inspired people to dance. Hip-hop is said to have first been influenced by the music that was coming out of Jamaica, particularly for Herc, who was raised there (Chang 2005).

All of these DJs created and enhanced the "break" in certain pieces of music, which allowed for longer periods of shifts in the music or for a section to be played and repeated where percussion instruments and syncopated rhythms—key elements of African diaspora music—were featured prominently. The breaks in the music are what got people excited and out on the dance floor, and the importance of this music's cultural lineage to the development of hip-hop cannot be overstated.

Although research backs up the claim of the power of music, the pioneering DJs of hip-hop were firmly rooted in African diasporic culture and understood "**being in the groove**" on intellectual, visceral, and cultural levels. They began to utilize their turntables and records to extend particularly dynamic breaks in order to give the dancers more time to "cut loose." This "cutting loose" developed into the iconic styles now associated with hip-hop: precise, gestural, percussive, highly athletic—even acrobatic, and inherently competitive.

In the early days in the Bronx, when Herc, Bambaataa, and Flash were creating the phenomenon called hip-hop, gang warfare was the rule of the day. The escalated violence and killing eventually led gang leaders to sign a peace treaty, which "had been momentous. Change was sweeping through the Bronx. Youthful energies turned from nihilistic implosion to creative explosion" (Chang 2005, 64). As outlined in the seminal book *Can't Stop Won't Stop*, the violence did not fully subside, but by 1975 Bambaataa, with his motto of peace, love, and unity, had developed the community organization called **Zulu Nation**, and out of that group came the Zulu King dancers (Chang 2005). Through the dance, the tensions of gang warfare were translated into highly charged choreographic competitions. Eventually the popularity of hip-hop, and ultimately rap music, spread beyond the Bronx to all areas of New York, and then beyond the New York borders. By the mid-1970s, Puerto Rican groups began adapting the **b-boy** style of dance and infusing new movements into breaking routines. These routines, now beginning to be performed by several races and ethnicities, showed movement similarities to the Angolan and Brazilian forms of capoeira, the Cuban rumba, and Chinese gung-fu (Chang 2005).

From its inception to today, hip-hop and breaking dance styles, including b-boying, and **b-girling**, **rocking**, **house**, krumping, **popping**, **locking**, and the **electric boogaloo** (the latter three coming out of California), have become more than just a social dance form, but a culture in and of itself, with its own style of fashion, language, graffiti art, **DJing**, **MCing**, and other cultural characteristics. When created, hip-hop and breaking provided a voice for inner-city youths. Nowadays, hip-hop and breaking are not only done by every race and gender in the United States, but also worldwide, even in some Middle Eastern countries where this dance style, by necessity, is done covertly. The power of and access to the Internet has allowed hip-hop to be borrowed, adapted, and adopted worldwide.

Hip-Hop in Concert Dance

Today, there are even professional dance companies that use the movement language of hip-hop and breaking in concert dance presentations, such as **Rennie Harris Puremovement**. Harris is considered a pioneer of street dance theater who characterizes hip-hop as a "contemporary indigenous form, one that expresses universal themes that extend beyond racial, religious, and economic boundaries, and one that (because of its pan-racial and transnational popularity) can help bridge these divisions" (Rennie Harris RHAW 2020).

Other dance companies, such as **Ephrat Asherie Dance** are "rooted in street and social dance and dedicated to revealing the inherent complexities of these forms. . . . EAD explores the expansive narrative qualities of various street and club styles, including breaking, hip-hop, house, and vogue, as a means to tell stories, develop innovative imagery, and find new modes of expression" (Ephrat Asherie Dance 2020). Both Harris and Asherie have brought hip-hop culture and dance into the mainstream, while at the same time keeping a connection to the historic nature and cultural accuracy of the form.

There are many practitioners, such as Harris and Asherie, who are committed to presenting hip-hop in ways that pay homage to the founders and the culture (particularly in terms of authenticity). However, what some deem as the commercialization of hip-hop has led to controversy. The originators of hip-hop believe that

Teena Marie, street dancer and performer with Ephrat Asherie Dance.

Photo: Joey Kennedy.

this dance form should be learned in the hip-hop communities: on the streets, in the clubs, and at the battles (competitions) where participants really get to show their abilities. Today we see versions and interpretations of hip-hop that are featured prominently on televisions shows. There are dance studios with students of all ages, and even college dance programs, where hip-hop is taught. Although there are teachers, artists, and academics that present hip-hop and breaking in their true and authentic form, there are just as many people promoting a watered-down version that does not display the accurate nature of the culture. Here is where adapting and adopting gets problematic. Whereas many practitioners of hip-hop and breaking approach the dancing from a cultural perspective and keep to the founders' original aesthetic and cultural principles, there are those who approach teaching and learning these forms as a technique to master, without seeking to incorporate or understand the cultural nuances of the form's origins and functions.

As in every culture, there are shifts in popularity, aesthetics, and significance (even the early days of hip-hop saw these occurrences), but the phenomenon of people from every race, class, and culture participating in hip-hop and breaking does not seem to be waning. An Internet search of hip-hop dance will yield millions of results from all over the world. Whether approaching hip-hop from a cultural or recreational point of view, there is no denying hip-hop's wide-reaching appeal, its powerful and enthralling connection to music, and the means for individual and group expression and socialization that it offers.

 See resource 2.6 in HK*Propel* for web links.

Summary

Social dance in the United States is a cultural phenomenon that has been known to elicit everything from wild acceptance to political controversy. Examining social dance in terms of expression and socialization reveals the unique interplay between mainstream and marginalized cultures that evolved over the complex centuries of U.S. history, and that perspective helps us to understand the rich potential of social dance for individuals and communities. From expressions of solidarity, statements of identity, and social protest to the power of empathic understanding and sheer physical joy of human movement, all participants—whether viewers or dancers—can experience powerful, lasting responses. Thus, social dance provides a unique window into cultural identity and resonance in the United States and allows for deeper participation in the humanity of dance.

Discussion Questions

1. What are some of the historical patterns that affected the development of dance in the United States? How does social dance exemplify the unique elements of dance culture and history in the United States?

2. What are some of the ways that social dance in the United States can serve as a means of expression and socialization? Discuss this topic in relation to different age groups, genders, socioeconomic status, geography, and other relevant issues.

3. What is drag ball dance culture, and how does it reflect key elements in the history and function of social dance in the United States?

4. Has your concept of United States dance culture changed after this reading, and if so, how and why?

 Visit HK*Propel* for access to this chapter's Application Activity.

Selected Glossary

ball culture/drag ball culture—An LGBTQ+ subculture that originated in the 1920s in New York City.

"being in the groove"—Hearing a specific type of music, such as funk, soul, electronic, or hip-hop, that drives people to move; connecting to the propulsive rhythmic "feel" of the music.

breaking/break dancing—An energetic form of dance, created and popularized by African Americans and U.S. Latinos, that includes athletic movements such as back and head spin, along with fast and intricate footwork. While "breaking" is the preferred term among practitioners, the general public and media often call it "break dancing."

cultural appropriation—The adoption of movements, dances, styles, and elements of one culture by members of another culture, which can be contentious when majority cultures appropriate from minority cultures without proper attribution.

DJs or DJing—An abbreviation for *disc jockey*; the person (or people) responsible for playing music at live events as well as on the radio and streaming services.

drag ball culture/ball culture—An LGBTQ+ subculture that originated in the 1920s in New York City.

expression (individual and group)—In social dance, both individuals and groups express themselves, making thoughts or feelings known through bodily movements, often in confirmation of personal or group identity.

flash mob—A preplanned dance that is performed before an unsuspecting audience, usually in a public space.

hip-hop—A dance style and art movement that is a subculture with specific characteristics, such as style of dress and fashion, language, graffiti art, hierarchy, and other cultural features such as **DJing** and **MCing**. Its musical roots grew from New York City's African American, Latino, and Caribbean cultures.

promposal—One of the many Internet sensations centering on dance, which features a surprise request for a prom date. These events usually display contemporary forms of jazz dance or hip-hop, with some featuring fully choreographed "productions."

social dance—Dance that provides for socialization and a means for expression, often displaying a particular movement style or form of a specific group or subculture. Unlike concert dance, social dances are mainly meant for participation, although there are professional dance choreographers that use social dance movements in their choreography.

socialization—In the broader sense, socialization includes being with people, meeting people, and feeling a connection with others, through dance and other means, and may include altering behaviors to the norms of a culture or society.

subculture—A cultural group within a larger culture that has its own identity, purposes, and priorities. Subcultures are often seen to be in opposition to the larger or dominant culture.

voguing—A dance style made famous in the drag balls and then brought to the mainstream by Madonna's music video "Vogue." The dancing is highly stylized and imitates the poses and characteristics that are performed by fashion models on a catwalk.

Selected References and Resources

Ambrosio, Nora. 2018. *Learning About Dance: Dance as an Art Form and Entertainment*. 8th ed. Dubuque, IA: Kendall Hunt Publishing.

Bock, Sheila, and Katherine Borland. 2011. "Exotic Identities: Dance, Difference, and Self-Fashioning." *Journal of Folklore Research*, (48), 1-36. https://doi.org/10.1353/jfr.2011.0000.

Chang, Jeff. 2005. *Can't Stop Won't Stop*. New York: St. Martin's Press.

Ephrat Asherie Dance.2020. www.ephratasheriedance.com/mission-statement.

Foster, Susan Leigh. 2016. "Why Is There Always Energy for Dancing?" *Dance Research Journal*, (48)3, 12-26. https://doi.org/10.1017/S0149767716000383.

Giurchescu, Anca. 2001. "The Power of Dance and Its Social and Political Uses." *Yearbook for Traditional Music*, (33), 109-121. JSTOR. www.jstor.org/stable/1519635.

Goldman, Jason G. 2016. "Why Dancing Leads to Bonding." *Scientific American Mind*, May 1, 2016. https://www.scientificamerican.com/article/why-dancing-leads-to-bonding/.

Green, Jesse. 1993. "Paris Has Burned." *New York Times*, April 18, 1993. www.nytimes.com/1993/04/18/style/paris-has-burned.html?auth=login-email&login=email.

Haider, Arwa. 2018. "How Drag Balls Went Mainstream." BBC, 20 August, 2018. www.bbc.com/culture/story/20180810-drag-balls-the-glamorous-performances-that-mean-resistance.

Herzog, Amy, and Joe Rollins. 2012. "Editors' Note: House Style." *Women's Studies Quarterly*, (41) 1/2, 9-13. JSTOR. www.jstor.org/stable/23611767.

LaMothe, Kimerer. 2013. "Did Humans Evolve to Dance? Movement and Mirror Neurons." Psychology Today blog, July 31, 2013. www.psychologytoday.com/us/blog/what-body-knows/201307/did-humans-evolve-dance-4-movement-and-mirror-neurons.

Malnig, Julie, ed. 2009. *Ballroom, Boogie, Shimmy Sham, Shake*. Champaign, IL: University of Illinois Press.

Martin, Randy. 2010. "Dancing Through the Crisis." *Affinities: A Journal of Radical Theory, Culture, and Action* (4)2, Fall 2010, 55-60.

Matthews T.E., M.A.G. Witek, O.A. Heggli, V.B. Penhune, and P. Vuust. 2019. "The Sensation of Groove Is Affected by the Interaction of Rhythmic and Harmonic Complexity" *PLoS ONE* 14(1): e0204539. https://doi.org/10.1371/journal.pone.0204539.

McGarry, L., and F. Russo. 2011. "Mirroring in Dance/Movement Therapy: Potential Mechanisms Behind Empathy Enhancement." *The Arts in Psychotherapy* 38(3), 178-184.

Rennie Harris RHAW. www.rennieharrisrhaw.org/rennie.php.

WERK for Peace. https://werkforpeace.org/.

3

Danza Folklórico and Mexican American Culture

¡Un Gran Fandango!

Colleen Porter Hearn

Learning Objectives

After reading this chapter, you will be able to do the following:

- Define folklórico and identify critical factors in its development and relationship to Mexican cultural history.
- Study religious, political, and geographical dynamics affecting dance culture, including composition, footwork, costuming, and meaning as ritual or entertainment.
- Take general knowledge from specifics of folklórico and compare to its shared heritage with the United States and other cultures.
- Understand how aesthetics, leyendas (legends), and traditions change through time and generations.

Key Terms

fandango—A dance style in triple meter, also named for a festival, with origins in Mexico, Spain, Portugal, and northern Africa.

indígenas—indigenous people of Mexico.

leyenda—Spanish for *legend*.

Náhuatl—A group of languages spoken by the ancient Aztecs and today by indígenas, mainly in central Mexico.

Nueva España—The viceroyalty of New Spain that controlled Mexico and other territories within the Spanish Empire.

zapateado/taconeo—Rhythmic stamping of the feet.

A Romantic Fandango of Old Mexico Reaching Into California

Envision a spacious courtyard cloistered within a Mexican estate's adobe walls. **El Rancho de Santa Margarita y Flores**, built by a prominent Mexican family in the 1840s, was its own kind of oasis within the desert, harbored in what is now Southern California. Now imagine an iconic 19th century social event—the **Fandango**! The hosts opened their doors to ranchers, clergy, and other powerful families throughout the area. During the day, **vaqueros** (skilled cowboys) demonstrated their horse management prowess to guests picnicking. In the evening's balls, flickering candles silhouetted a chamber orchestra and master of ceremonies, **el tecolero**, who called out directions for the dances. Ladies lifted their shortened full skirts, just skimming their ankles, to demonstrate their **zapateado** (footwork) with flair. And men, wearing wide-brimmed riding hats, boots, and vaquero-inspired clothing, executed their own footwork. Both might accentuate the rhythms with **castañuelas**. As with the complex rhythms and interconnections of the dance, the Fandango was a time of courtship and friendship with political intrigue amid the shadows.

Fandango may loosely be translated as "elaborate ornament," and the celebration's name stems from the fandango dance style. Some historians believe both originated in Spain, with its nuances of the energetic *jota* and elegant **flamenco** dances. Others attest the *indígenas* (**indigenous** people) first performed the dance in community and ritualistic gatherings in what is now Mexico, and then intrigued Spanish colonials restyled it to fit their cultural norm. The event provided social maneuvering on all levels, from romantic trysts to political liaisons. This suggests why the name may also have derived from the Portuguese *fado*, meaning "fate." Many Portuguese, neighbors to the Spanish on the Iberian Peninsula, also emigrated to the colonies and brought their own fandango traditions.

Reflective of Spanish tradition, the Fandango often followed a Roman Catholic holy week of penance and sacrifice. Under the mission system begun in the 16th century in **Nueva España** (New Spain), the friars realized music and dance were international languages to be shared with the indígenas. Under the Spanish Empire, Nueva España amassed great territory within North and South America, the Caribbean islands, and Oceania. Because many areas were then isolated, a Fandango event was most welcome. Interrelating worship with celebration, the Fandango "served as a replica of life in and out of the mission. Regardless of your social class or your ethnicity or your occupation or your gender, you're welcome to dance the Fandango" (Russell 2020).

The Fandango reveals a romantic image of Old Mexico prior to the Mexican–American War (1846-1848). That conflict determined which country would control California with other regions in what is now the western United States. Nevertheless, Mexican influence on the United States continues. When one passes through the iron gate of El Rancho de Santa Margarita y Flores, the vistas whisper of ancient times, of First Nations, Spanish conquests, Catholic missions, and Mexican versus U.S. occupations. Then, crossing into Mexico, we discover contrasting and shared landscapes within a rich multicultural society. Because Mexican dance study is massive, for this chapter we limit our scope to specific dances that illuminate historical and regional dynamics—a journey into Mexican folklórico.

Mexico's history plays against a backdrop of indigenous, enslaved, conquering, and immigrant cultures. From 1200 BCE to 1521 CE the land witnessed powerful indigenous empires. In 1519, the Spanish Conquest began. By 1521 Spanish rule was fully establish, significantly shaping the nation's identity for the next 300 years. As in other colonies, enslaved Africans were brought to labor on the plantations and ranches. After Mexico's War of Independence (1810-1821) the newly formed nation persisted through perturbations, intermittent warfare with the United States, occupation by France, and internal strife. With the end of the final revolution in 1920, the current Mexican government began its own journey through trials and accomplishments.

Throughout these historical complexities, dance and music interrelationships have played an important role. The aesthetics of the indígenas would later mesh with Spanish, African, and other cultural styles through storytelling, dance, music, and more. Dances related to polytheism might be transposed into Christian analogy yet maintain many original rituals while respond-

Dancers performing at a Fandango festival in Mexico.

Tania Victoria/Secretaría de Cultura de la Ciudad de México via Flickr.com

ing to a given era's societal views and resources. For example, how the dancers then and now interpreted their dances would be influenced by costuming representative of the times, which could be more restrictive or bold. Bare feet might be replaced by Cuban-heeled shoes; skirts might become fuller with sweeping effect. The ancient use of masks carries into the present. Thus, the prominence of an emerging Mexican culture, which included indigenous customs and rites, the ranchero lifestyle, Catholic influences, and immigrant and enslaved Africans' contributions, would be echoed in its arts. With the passage of time, some truths would transform into *leyenda*, depicted in folklórico, reaching across millennia to interweave Mexico's past, present, and future.

 See resource 3.1 in HK*Propel* for web links.

Ever-Evolving Dances of Ancient Culture

Mexico's ancient civilizations span over 13,000 years. Of the 63 indigenous cultures now recognized by Mexico's government, four empires once dominated. The **Olmecs** settled up and down the Atlantic coast, the **Mayans** settled in the area from the Pacific to the Yucatán Peninsula, the **Toltecs** went into Central Mexico, and the **Aztecs** migrated from above the **Rio Grande** to conquer lands coast-to-coast. As nobles and priests ruled over merchants, farmers, hunters, and slaves, their arts mirrored sophisticated languages and sciences.

The nations shared polytheistic beliefs based on nature and absorbed into rituals, many of which exist today, as discovered in the following dances. The dance–music connection has been and continues to be crucial to the indígenas. "The elemental and universal qualities of this music give it significance and virility [as] 'the living voice'" (Smithsonian Folkways 2020).

Los Quetzales—Dance of the Quetzales

This dance is among Mexico's oldest and honors the **quetzales**, birds revered for their vibrant plumage. Their name derives from the **Náhuatl** word meaning "precious." Mayans and Aztecs proclaimed the species **dioses del aire**—gods of the air—because the birds live on mountains wrapped in clouds that create an image of land floating in air. The Aztec god **Quetzalcoatl**—named for his birdlike and serpentine (*coatl*) characteristics—patronized the arts and, like the bird, protected his kin.

Male dancers' crimson uniforms represent god and creature, crowned with glorious rays of

ribbons woven into a reed frame. Accompanying instruments—flute, maracas, drums—resonate throughout. To prepare, the men pray and fast, then perform their dance in precise and intricate patterns, bowing toward the sun. Steps travel diagonally, in unison with the sun's rotation that may be measured through a wooden astrological instrument.

Los Voladores de Palatal—Palatal Flyers Dance

UNESCO proclaimed this dance part of Mexico's **intangible cultural heritage**. *Palatal* describes how dancers press their tongues against the palate to sing birdlike trills. Whether originally a fertility rite or an offering to the sun and moon, the dance is an athletic feat. Also called *palo volador* (flying pole), the exercise centers on a 120-foot pole, originally made of the ancient **ceiba** tree, an important symbolic element in the culture. In the modern version, five men scale

Los Quetzales dance.
Photo: The Mexican Folkloric Dance Company of Chicago.

the pole, and all but one suddenly drops with a rope securing each dancer's ankle—literally as a lifeline. The fifth man is the timekeeper who guides the dancers' rotation in correspondence to the ancient calendar—"13 rotations [around the *ceiba* pole] × 4 [dancers] = 52, the number of years in a Mesoamerican century" (Arghiris 2013). The pole vibrates as the four men, heads downward, whirl in unison for 13 rotations, landing feet first in perfect timing. The remaining competitor triumphantly stands at the apex, playing a drum and flute. The *palatal* sounds as observers cheer and the final man descends with his team's guidance. Be forewarned: Many regions outlaw this dangerous performance.

 See resource 3.2 in HK*Propel* for web links.

Spanish Conquest and Colonialism

Shipwrecked sailors were the first Spanish peoples on Mexico's shores, but by 1517 the colonial era commenced. **Moctezuma Xocoyotzin II** (1502-1520) was just one Aztec ruler whom the conquistador **Hernán Cortés** (1485-1547) destroyed. However, the Aztec capital **Tenochtitlan** did not fall until 1521, when its last king, **Cuauhtémoc** (c.1495-c.1521), was assassinated. Some indígenas aligned with the Spanish to defeat their Aztec foe, while the Mayans and the Chichimeca fought the Spanish for decades. Ultimately, the Spanish Empire would control Nueva España for over 300 years.

Political hierarchy based on race and birthplace established rule. Spaniards born in Spain held power; those born in the New World with Spanish ancestry were mainly merchants and landowners with limited political control. Roman Catholic priests and monks were to convert the populace. Those of both Spanish and indigenous blood had fewer rights, while the original inhabitants were generally servants or laborers, but a great many were enslaved. Although African slaves had no rights, a master could grant manumission, and mixed-race descendants hoped to break from the system's prejudice.

As with El Rancho de Santa Margarita, the Spanish established the ranch culture in Nueva España, which inadvertently formulated a sense of independence. Distancing from Spain and adapting to subcultures and landscapes brought distinctive forms of religious fervor and arts. Despite political oppression, dancing became a vehicle to assimilate cultures, as well as for protest.

Vaqueros

When the Spanish brought cattle and horses to the Americas in the 16th century, the cattle-rearing culture was established in Nueva España. The *vaquero*, horse-mounted cattle herder, was the precursor to the American cowboy. Although first forbidden from this profession by the Spanish, the indígenas, with their beliefs in anthropomorphism (human characteristics in animals and natural forces) became important contributors to this life. We must also recognize the *vaqueras* (cattle-driving women), and Afro-Mexican participation. All these highly skilled men and women were known for "horse whispering," natural horse management skills, demonstrated during a Fandango.

La Conquista and Chinelos

La Conquista (dance of the conquest) and the *chinelos* (masked dances of carnival) have similar themes: conflict between Spanish rulers and indigenous nations, but with different objectives. The first is a tragedy; the second, a satire. Again, the origins of such performances remain controversial because the ancient indigenous cultures mounted similar entertainment, and we will see how the Catholic clergy manipulated similar themes to connect indigenous practices to Christianity.

La Conquista portrays the execution of Aztec rulers Montezuma or Cuauhtémoc under the sword of Cortés. It is believed Franciscan monks adapted this from the Spanish *danza de moros y cristianos*, which reenacts Spanish Christian victory over the Moors. This theme, the monks believed, would help convince the indígenas of the Spanish holy right to rule. Although Spanish colonists may have endorsed the epic, an undertone for a defeated people hovered over the scene. Today it is a reminder for those of indigenous descent: *"No debemos olvidar; triunfaremos"*—*We must not forget; we will triumph* (Torres 2020).

The word *chinelos* originates from the Náhuatl "disguised." During Carnival, masked dancers join in parades, mocking Spanish royals, priests, or officials. Milky-white masks, elaborate robes, and bulky headdresses satirize ugly royals, priests, tax collectors, and overseers. The tradition has continued into modern Mexico, whether parodying evil landowners or overseers, political rivals, French rulers, or even American invaders. Professionals or amateurs perform in rural and urban venues, on stage and in the streets. Both dances continue to exemplify the complexities of Mexican history.

Carnival

Carnival, introduced to Mexico by the Roman Catholic Spaniards, lasts seven days before Ash Wednesday, which signifies the beginning of Christianity's Lent, 40 days of fasting and repentance before Easter. Lent recalls the 40 days in which Jesus, according to the New Testament, went into the desert, rejecting the devil's temptations. During Carnival, costuming hides identities to ward off sin.

Los Diablos—Devil Mask Dance

The ferocious devil masks of *Los Diablos* cast back to ancient indigenous empires, when it was believed masks held supernatural powers. Such masked dances were appropriated and adapted by Franciscan monks and Spanish rulers who wove them into Christian passion plays to persuade converts and reinforce royal domination. In *Los Diablos*, for example, the Christian image of the devil often appears brandishing a whip. Nonetheless, the dance still maintains an element of the oppressed mocking the oppressors. As a dancer in Fresno, California, explains, when one performs this dance: "You can be someone else. . . . It's like getting rid of your ego. It's like the rhythm of the heart. It's like the devil is on fire" (Guzmán 2019).

Tales of Three Slaves: *La Malinche, La China Poblana*, and *Los Negritos*

The histories and *leyendas* behind the following dances reveal complexities within the characters'

roles, enslavement, and the dynamics between clashing cultures. Thus, while the tales themselves may seem unfamiliar at first to outside viewers, they are important to Mexican culture while echoing universal themes.

Los Matachines Dance-drama

The roles of **La Malinche** and the mother from ***Los Negritos*** are sometimes interchanged in dance-dramas called ***matachines***, performed by Hispanic and indigenous peoples in Mexico and the southwestern United States. Ironically, the characters may be interpreted as either evil spirits or symbols of purity (Shea 2008).

La Malinche

La Malinche (c. 1500-c. 1529), a young Aztec princess whose family sold her into slavery, was gifted to the Spanish conquistador Hernán Cortés and ultimately found herself at his mercy. But she was a brilliant interpreter of many languages, and through her the Spaniards were able to suppress or make alliances with nations in the New World. Given freedom for her participation and for having a son by Cortés, she was seen as mother of or traitor to the *indígenas*, as goddess or witch in dances of the **Yaqui** and **Pueblo** peoples, even far above the Rio Grande. When mocked in a satirical dance, a man might imitate her; when revered, women and young girls portray her in dazzling costumes and intricate steps. In the epic ***La Danza de la Pluma***, reenacting the Spanish conquest, the honored La Malinche is played by a young dancer in native adornments who transforms into the Christianized **Doña** Marina, played by another dancer in Spanish colonial dress. Both crowned in royal feathers, they march together in a massive procession, then mirror each other in a highly energetic set.

La China Poblana—Asian Servant Girl of Puebla

La China Poblana concerns a princess whom pirates smuggled far from her native India to the city of Puebla in Nueva España, where she was sold as a ***chinita*** (servant). Respected for her visions and kindness to the poor, she was granted her freedom, lived her life, and ultimately was buried in the sacristy of the Jesuit temple (Temple

La Malinche

Photo: S. Sheppard, view from Casita Colibri blog.

de la Compañía de Jesús). Her tale would evolve as the dance *La China Poblana*, evoking both a lovely romance and patriotism. Today, several dances honor her in women's solos or couples' dances.

Los Negritos—Dance of the Black People

Los Negritos may seem of African origin, since by the 1520s the Spanish had shipped enslaved Africans to colonies. However, many dance scholars believe it originated as a **Totonac** parable. In one version, a slave and her son escape a plantation to find refuge among the indígenas, though the mother is devastated when her son is poisoned by a snake. Catholic monks and priests found this mother–son theme could blend into their Christian lessons through ***pastorelas***—reenactments of Christian nativity tales that also resembled indigenous plays portraying gods—thereby facilitating the conversion of the indígenas to Christianity.

Enslaved heroines of *La Malinche* and *La China Poblana* would receive their freedom in their lifetime, but the real slaves of African descent reflected in *Los Negritos* had to wait for Mexican independence from Spain before they, too, could be free.

 See resource 3.3 in HK*Propel* for web links.

Mexican Nation

Estados Unidos Mexicanos, 1821

Turmoil in Spain following the abdication of two Spanish kings, Charles IV (1748-1819) and Ferdinand VII (1784-1833), spurred revolt. In the city of Dolores, the Mexican priest Miguel Hidalgo y Costilla proclaimed *"Grito de Dolores"* (Cry/Shout of Dolores City) on September 16, 1810, to rally Mexicans to overthrow their Spanish rulers, and the date is now Mexico's Independence Day. The war ended in 1821, with the Treaty of Córdoba, when Spain conceded defeat, but the young Mexican republic would suffer through dictators, social upheavals, and constitutions written, destroyed, and rewritten, while claiming heroes, a public educational system, and a robust arts heritage.

Dance personified a heightening patriotism. The national flag's symbols—an eagle grasping a snake while perched upon a prickly pear cactus planted on a rock surrounded by water—signified the spiritual sign where the Aztecs were to build their capital, Tenochtitlan, now *Ciudad de México* (Mexico City). Its colors display red for the people's blood, white for purity, and green for hope. Female dancers, especially, would adapt this design to embellish their China Poblana skirts, while twisting ribbons of the same colors into their braids.

Mexico and the United States After Independence—1830s to 1848

In the 1800s, tensions flared between the newly independent neighbors. Mexican-controlled Texas became a battleground that generated the

Republic of Texas (1836), which then joined the United States (1845). Emboldened, the United States sparked the Mexican–American War (1846-1848), which forced Mexico to release its northern territories that would become the states of California, New Mexico, Arizona, Utah, Nevada, Kansas, and Colorado. (Spain had already ceded Louisiana, Mississippi, and Florida.) The resulting **Treaty of Guadalupe Hidalgo**, theoretically, presupposed Mexican landowners could keep their property and customs.

Mexico and the United States also argued over slavery. Spain's colonies had African slaves, but when Mexico's mixed-race President **Vicente Guerrero** (1782-1831) abolished the practice in 1829, he refused to return runaways to the United States. The freed slaves were endangered when the United States took over the aforementioned Mexican territories. From as far away as North Carolina, an estimated 10,000 slaves escaped to Mexico on the Southern Underground Railroad (Little 2020). Their new life was difficult, but now "African presence pervades Mexican culture. In story and legend, music and dance, proverb and song, the legacy of Africa touches the life of every Mexican" (Montiel 2020). And today, "Dance is one of the principal ways modern Afro-Mexicans are reclaiming their roots, as reported by [members of the] AJ+ Oaxacan Obatala dance troupe" (Cocking 2019). Thus, the heroine's yearning for freedom in *Los Negritos* was realized.

 See resource 3.4 in HK*Propel* for web links.

French Occupation of Mexico

1864 to 1867

While U.S. interference in Mexico's affairs was curtailed during Reconstruction following the American Civil War (1861-1865), French forces occupied Mexico (1864-1867) in order to retrieve a national debt. Appointed as emperor of Mexico, Maximilian I (1832-1867) invited highly skilled immigrants from across Europe and Asia to settle and make investments in Mexico. He also patronized the arts, especially marching bands that played popular European music. His reign would influence what would be called **Norteño** music and dance.

El Baile de las Cintas

In the Yucatán Peninsula, ***el baile de las cintas*** combines French traditional dance with "Spanish folklore with pentatonic sounds of Mayan music" and Afro-Caribbean elements (Ovalle 2017). With the women's loose, embroidered three-layered dress and the men's ***guayabera*** shirt and pants, both wore heeled shoes or boots for zapateado. Charming *cintas* is not a dance of protest and may seem simply a European maypole dance, but there is more to its story. Like *Palo Volador*, *las cintas* also traditionally manipulates a pole made of ceiba wood, but in contrast, earthbound dancers weave between each other until their ribbons wind tightly around it. Dancing under the ceiba tree symbolizes ***árbol de la vida*** (Tree of Life—the Mayan *Yaxche*, or silk-cotton tree). Roots dig into the underworld; the solid terrestrial trunk's branches reach to the heavens. For the Maya, "The world is a quincunx, consisting of four directional quadrants and a central space corresponding to the fifth direction" (Maestri 2019). Ribbon colors parallel this quincunx: red (east), white (north), black (west), yellow (south), and green (center). This truly Mexican dance is performed during Fandangos and may also have been done, albeit in a "Californio" style, at El Rancho de Santa Margarita y Flores.

 See resource 3.5 in HK*Propel* for web links.

The Mexican Revolution

La Revolución Mexicana 1910-1920

Folklórico grew as cultural expression throughout tumultuous times in reaction to political dissension at home and in neighboring countries. From 1910 until the early 1920s, *La Revolución Mexicana* raged, with Mexico's social classes trapped in a horrific civil war. In 1916, when Mexican revolutionaries cut a swath through the U.S. state of New Mexico, the United States sent troops to protect its borders.

Las Adelitas—Women Warriors of the Revolution

Amid this conflict, *las adelitas* romanticized Mexican women soldiers (*soldaderas*) in a *corrido* (historical ballad):

Popular entre la tropa era Adelita	Popular among the troop was Adelita
La mujer que el sargento idolatraba	The woman that the sergeant idolized
Que ademas de ser valiente era bonita	And besides being brave, she was pretty
Que hasta el mismo coronel la respetaba.	So that even the colonel respected her.

Unlike most ballads, however, the music has a pounding, militaristic beat as women dance in revolutionary dress, bearing rifles and ammunition, marching in strict precision. The soldaderas suffered greatly in their quest for equal rights, but they were inspired by tales of La Malinche, legendarily vindicated for riding a stallion through the heavens, shooting thunderbolts against their assailants (Saldaña 1996, 303).

Jarabe Tapatío

Jarabe tapatío, or the **Mexican hat dance**, finds its roots in freedom. *Jarabe* is translated as "syrup" or "herb mixture," describing the blending of zapateado with music. *Tapatío* is a colloquial term for the residents in Guadalajara city. Colonial bureaucrats saw this mixed couples' dance as such a threat amid its popularity and the closeness between dance partners (taboo in Spanish society) that, in 1790, they banned it. Inevitably, the people defiantly performed it in public. This patriotism was highlighted at the end of the Mexican Revolution when Secretary of Education José Vasconcelos proclaimed the jarabe tapatío Mexico's national dance and ordered it taught in public schools. Ladies often wear the China Poblana dress for this dance, but in the Jalisco state, a stunning multicolored ruf-

fled blouse and skirt reminiscent of the *ecuestre femenino* (female equestrian) dress is worn. This region also claims **mariachi** bands, and the male dancers wear a dramatic version of the **charro** (horse riders) uniform, with sombrero, bolero jacket, pants, and boots.

Charro Uniform and Mariachi Music

Charro is a cowboy from Mexico's central region known for riding athleticism and as a revolutionary. The traditional uniform was adopted as a costume by mariachi musicians. (Gómez 2018). Mariachi music is now an international sensation. Students join mariachi bands in American schools, and young San Antonio, Texas, native Sebastien de la Cruz wore his mariachi outfit when singing the national anthem at the NBA playoffs in 2013.

Ballet Folklorico Sol Huasteco dancing in the state of Chihuahua.

Courtesy of Ballet Folklorico Sol Huasteco, Las Vegas, Nevada.

Cultural Highlight

A PERSONAL TRIBUTE TO A MEXICAN MUSICAL ICON

In an interview, Alma Abrego, a language interpreter and dancer, described her respect for her father, Eugenio Abrego (1922-1988), master accordion player and first voice with the renowned Los Alegres de Terán. His band, with friend and member Tomás Ortiz, was instrumental in expanding the popularity of Norteño music. Artists of all genres, young and old, filled the Abrego home and celebrated their beloved Mexican music and dance. Alma described the gifts her father presented to her:

"My siblings and I knew our father was famous, not because anyone told us, but because of the artistic energy he radiated without trying, whether on stage, in film, and especially our home. [When the group was] traveling on tour in both Mexico and the United States, the audiences naturally danced to the Norteño sound. They enthusiastically applauded my father—which made us, as children, feel pride and love.

"As with most great artists, my father always kept his humbleness and priorities. He never turned down a job, whether it be the plainest or the most prestigious setting. My mother always made sure not to overburden him with unnecessary matters; she would say, 'Tu padre es un artista y necesita tener su mente clara para su arte'—(Your father is an artist, and he needs to have his mind clear for his art).

"Live music was always present in our family gatherings, be it northern regional music (Música Norteña), the genre my father was a master of, mariachi, salsa, cha-cha, mambo, or rock music. Thus, dance was always present. Everyone danced, even children. One of the beautiful gifts my father left me was the polka composition he named 'Alma Leti,' and when my daughter was born, he composed one for her too, naming it after her, 'Stephanie Angelique.'"

El Son de la Negra—Music of the Dark Lady

Dancer and choreographer **Kareli Montoya** stresses that *el son de la negra* —often called the second national dance of Mexico—is required for any serious folklórico dancer (personal communication, 2020). In her online tutorials, she describes one challenging step, the **tornillo**, in which the heel motion "resembles turning a screw into the floor." The musical arrangement for instruments evokes the revolution, with images of a train carrying a loved one home, away from war. Trumpets and heels start slowly, then go on to a faster tempo like a train revving up. One phrase, *"ojos de papel volando"* (eyes of fluttering paper), recalls flags decorating cars. Lyrics speak of a dark-haired or dark-skinned beauty, *la negra*, who had accepted a shawl as a token for a marriage proposal:

¿Cuando sme traes a mi negra?	When will you bring my dark lady?
Que la quiero vera qui	I want to see her here
Con su rebozo de seda	With her silk shawl
Que la traje de Tepic.	That I brought for her from Tepic.

As you can see from the songs of the revolution, Mexican music and dance are entwined throughout the nation's history. On the notes of its music, folklórico travels across many boundaries.

 See resource 3.6 in HK*Propel* for web links.

Crosscurrents

Today, folklórico prevails throughout Mexico and the United States. A look at individual dance styles with their musical underpinnings illuminates their complex cross-cultural legacies. A discussion of folklórico as integrative learning reveals how Mexican music and dance have become a familiar presence in many U.S. schools, especially in the Southwest.

Norteño and El Calabaceado— Northern Music and the Pumpkin Dance

Researcher Agustín Gurza recognizes Alma's father Eugenio Abrego (1922-1988) and his partner Tomás Ortiz (1924-2007) as "the fathers of modern Norteño music, the accordion-based country style that traversed borders as fluidly as its immigrant fans" (Guzra 2015). Norteño was influenced by the French in the 19th century under Maximilian I, who encouraged immigrants from as far as Europe and Asia to settle in the country. When his reign collapsed, supporters and artists he patronized fled to northern Mexico and the southwestern United States. By the 20th century and into today, Mexican artists would record, film, and play Norteño music with mass-market appeal in U.S. cities.

While Norteño choreography and sounds share roots with European cultures—the rancho (Portuguese), waltz (Austrian/Bavarian), jig (Irish), jota (Spanish), mazurka (Polish), and redova and polka (Czech)—how dancers and musicians perform is genuinely Mexican. Couples demonstrate fast zapateado or sway in romantic frames. In the Mexican state of Baja California, bordering California and Arizona in the United States, the rancho culture inspires the *calabaceado* (also called *huarachazo*, *taconeado*, and *huapango norteño*). *Calabaceado* loosely means picking and switching partners, like choosing a pumpkin (or squash) in the garden. This genre goes back at least to the 1940s, but probably earlier.

El Calabaceado—Pumpkin Dance

"Calabaceado originated about 150 years ago in the celebrations of pioneer families in Baja California. The dance is rooted in the lifestyle of cowboys and rural communities. . . . This vigorous dance requires great skill, stamina, and excellent physical condition. These attributes give rise to an explosive, energetic dance of resistance, grace, and competition, concluding when fatigue ends the dancers' furious movements to loud applause" (Curry 2022, para 2 and 3).

Son Jarocho (Jarocho Music) and La Bamba

The port city of **Veracruz** plays a crucial role in Mexican history. Centuries-old home to indígenas, it was claimed by the Spanish for its access to the Caribbean islands and other routes. Pirates, the French, and the United States repeatedly attacked the city. As noted in our Fandango discussion, Veracruz's music, *son jarocho*, combines flamenco, indigenous, and Afro-Caribbean sounds, often accompanied by a 39-string harp, "the very soul of '*Jarocho music*' [which] does carry not only the melody but also the harmony, the speed and the ambiance of the '*Son*'" (Ovalle 2017).

The city's *la bamba* music and couples' dance are known worldwide. On stage, ladies wear exquisite white gowns with lace overlay, full skirts, embroidered aprons, and flowers adorning their hair. Men wear the guayabera shirt, with pockets "big enough to hold more than one guava fruit" and straw hats (Ovalle/Yucatan, Campeche, and Quintana Roo, 2017). Dancers promenade, exhibiting zapateado with spins in set patterns. In one version, partners travel around a ribbon on the floor, and with their feet, tie it into a love knot.

 See resource 3.7 in HK*Propel* for web links.

Folklórico as Integrative Learning

Returning to her Cultural Highlight about growing up surrounded by Mexican music and dance, **Alma Abrego** said,

> While attending a Mexican party celebration in Europe, a German friend asked me, "How do you move so naturally dancing? I have taken many Latin dance classes, and I still cannot move like you!" I replied, "We grow up in Mexico dancing these kinds of dances, mainly in our family reunions." I always had more than one male dancer asking me to dance with him during the partnering class. Once, the instructor, renowned dancer/choreographer Daniel Nagrin, asked my partner and me to demonstrate. In the end, he applauded. "Perfect! The way partnering should be—a perfect union!" I attribute this partnering gift to those family reunions.

In Mexico and the United States, children may be taught simple versions of jarabe tapatío, and advocates like Abrego, through their personal journeys, understand how learning folklórico can be a positive experience for children.

Día de Muertos and All Saints Day

Folklórico reimagines its multiple cultures during **Día de Muertos** (Day of the Dead), a Mexican holiday taught in the public schools. In central and southern regions, it once honored **Mictēcacihuātl**, Aztec goddess of the underworld, who protected the dead. To assimilate into Catholic liturgy, the dates became October 31 to November 2, to coincide with All Saints Day, and is now celebrated throughout Mexico and the United States to remember ancestors. Dances include skull-like masks or makeup, while the monarch butterfly, a holiday symbol, flies amid Aztec marigolds to transport departed souls. "It's like a mystery" (Zaragoza 2020).

In the southwestern United States, where Mexican culture resonates, and through the influence of Mexican and Mexican American artists in other states, folklórico has become a vivid presence in schools and on stage:

- Advocate Gema Sandoval credits teacher **Sal Castro** (1933-2013) for bringing folkórico into California schools. Every public and four-year institution in the Los Angeles area now offers a folkórico class (Sandoval 2012).

- Mexican-born **José Luis Ovalle** cofounded *La Compañía de Danza Folklórica Mexicana de Chicago* **(MFDC)**, which has received countless awards and represented Mexico in the USA World Cup opening ceremony.

- With her De La Rosa Dance Company, Houston, Texas, educator **Elisa de la Rosa** weaves contemporary/modern dance and folkórico into Mexican and Mexican American themes.

- Rancho High School in Las Vegas, Nevada, offers a comprehensive folkórico program emphasizing students' artistic and psychomotor potentials. Under educator **Jacquelyn Guzman**'s guidance, they study the genre's importance to Mexican heritage while advancing their teamwork and individual skills.

- Uniting families, Kareli Montoya's Thee Academy in Los Angeles, California, offers a "Mommy, Daddy & Me" folkórico class and several technique levels. These young dancers dream of becoming members of the school's Ballet Folklórico de Los Angeles touring company and its mariachi ensembles.

 See resource 3.8 in HK*Propel* for web links.

Summary

Amalia Hernández (1917-2000), who founded *Ballet Folklórico de México* in Mexico City, was a groundbreaker in advancing Mexican culture to the world. She beautifully described folkórico essence as follows:

> The power of the native dance . . . is what makes the folklore so rich. Not just steps, it has a meaning. The sound of the bells, the masks, the dances in the churchyard, the social festivities—it's a beautiful environment, a beautiful feeling. . . . And the religious dances (have) tremendous devotion . . . they are dancing in heaven. (Smith 1991)

On stage or impromptu, at neighborhood gatherings or after mass, reenacting a legend or just for recreation, folkórico celebrates the Mexican identity, reaching across boundaries. And now, once a year, people gather against the backdrop of the wall at the California and Tijuana border, just 70 miles from El Rancho de Santa Margarita y Flores, for the *Fandango Fronterizo*. Attendees dance, play music, and welcome friends and strangers. Fandango magic from both sides exemplifies "what it has done for centuries—brought people together to knit a closer sense of togetherness. The sounds of guitars, voices, and dancing feet [last] late into the night" (Sheehy 2017).

In summary, Mexico's folkórico intertwines its indigenous cultures with those of European, Caribbean, Asian, and African peoples as an ever-evolving source of national identity and attests to the vitality and unique relationship with its neighbor the United States. Folkórico exemplifies a rich past living in the present, traveling into the future with heart and soul.

¡Siempre Folklórico!

Discussion Questions

1. What are the definition and origins of the Fandango? How is the annual Fandango Fronterizo relevant today at the border between Mexico and California?

2. Who are the three legendary enslaved peoples who continue to inspire Mexican dances today? Describe their stories and their respective dances.

3. How is Mexican dance assimilation of many cultures?

4. What animal exhibits such beauty and power that it inspired the ancient Indigenous empires before Spanish colonization and is enshrined in a dance performed today?

 Visit HK*Propel* for access to this chapter's Application Activity.

Selected Glossary

fandango—A dance style in triple meter, also named for a festival, with origins in Mexico, Spain, Portugal, and northern Africa.

indígenas—Indigenous people of Mexico.

jarabe tapatío—Often called the Mexican hat dance, originates in Guadalajara.

La China Poblana—Dance that tells the story of a servant girl from Asia who is granted freedom in Puebla during the colonial period. She was known for her unique Indian-inspired costume.

leyenda—Spanish for legend.

mariachi—Music and dance with trumpets, stringed instruments, and powerful voices, and was considered symbolic of Mexican music for almost 100 years. Its forerunners were Mestizo (mixed-race, Spanish/Indigenous) folk ensembles. The Mexican state of Jalisco is considered the mariachi heartland, though modern mariachi evolved mainly in the nation's capital, Mexico City, after traditional groups migrated to the city in the 1920s.

Náhuatl—A group of languages spoken by the ancient Aztecs and today by indígenas, mainly in central Mexico.

Nueva España—The viceroyalty of New Spain that controlled Mexico and other territories within the Spanish Empire.

zapateado/taconeo—Rhythmic stamping of the feet.

Selected References and Resources

Arghiris, Richard. "Danza de los Voladores." November 3, 2013. Accessed August 15, 2020. www.youtube.com/watch?v=ZS_cbYty4iE

Cocking, Lauren. "The Untold History of Afro-Mexicans, Mexico's Forgotten Ethnic Group." The CultureTrip, October 8, 2019. Accessed July 24, 2020. https://theculturetrip.com/north-america/mexico/articles/the-untold-history-of-afro-mexicos-mexicos-forgotten-ethnic-group/

Curry, Maria E. "Traditional Mexican Dance to be Designated." Save Our Heritage Organisation, 2022. http://sohosandiego.org/enews/0722mariacalabaceado.htm Accessed Oct. 31, 2022.

Guzmán, Raymundo. 2019. "If Cities Could Dance [Season 2 Episode 5]: 'Mexican Folk Dance in Fresno, CA.'" PBS. April 23, 2019. Accessed July 25, 2020. www.pbs.org/video/mexican-folk-dance-in-fresno-ca-lygqkp/

Maestri, Nicoletta. "Ceiba Pentandra: The Sacred Tree of the Maya, Connecting the Upper, Middle, and Lower Maya Realms." ThoughtCo, March 29, 2019. Accessed July 24, 2020. www.thoughtco.com/ceiba-pentandra-sacred-tree-maya-171615

Ovalle, José Luis. 2017. *Yucatán, Campeche and Quintana Roo*. Accessed July 24, 2020. www.mexfoldanco.org/mexican-dance/yucatan.html

Russell, Craig. *Mission Music: The Passion and Fervor of Fandango*. Public Media Group of Southern California: KCET. Accessed July 24, 2020. www.kcet.org/shows/socal-connected/mission-music-the-passion-and-fervor-of-fandango

Saldaña, Nancy H. "La Malinche: Her Representation in Dances of Mexico and the United States" *Ethnomusicology*, Vol. 10, No. 3. Society for Ethnomusicology: University of Illinois Press, September 1966, pp. 298-309.

Sandoval, Gema. "A History of Mexican Folklórico in Southern California, World Arts Culture & Context, May 16, 2012 Accessed July 24, 2020. www.dance-historyproject.org/index-of-artists/gema-sandoval/

Sheehy, Daniel. "Fandango Without Borders." Washington, DC: Smithsonian Center for Folklife and Cultural Heritage Newsletter. October 10, 2017. Accessed August 12, 2020. https://folklife.si.edu/talkstory/fandango-without-borders

Smith, James F. "Amalia Hernandez: Creator of Mexico's Ballet Folklórico," *Los Angeles Times*, September 20, 1991. www.latimes.com/archives/la-xpm-2000-nov-05-me-47382-story.html

Torres, Larry. "Understanding *Los Matachines*." New Mexico Department of Cultural Arts. 2020. www.nmarts.org/matachines/essays.php?p=torres

Zaragoza, Silvia. "Day of the Dead—Monarch Butterfly Migration to Michoacán, México," October 28, 2019. Accessed July 24, 2020. www.youtube.com/watch?v=s0t6mws2vgY

PART II

Central and South America

The impact of European colonial powers (primarily Spanish and Portuguese) on indigenous people of this region shared some characteristics with those in North America. However, unlike the more nomadic peoples in the north, Incas, Mayans, Aztecs, and other indigenous peoples had thriving cities with thousands of inhabitants when the Europeans arrived. Additionally, European colonials in this region were focused more on resource extraction and exploitation than on settlements. The combination of a powerful indigenous presence and fewer European settlements helped maintain the indigenous threads in the dances of the region. The chapters in part II explore dance cultures of Guatemala and Brazil. There are many other countries in both central and South America with unique dance cultures of their own; however, dances in Guatemala and Brazil highlight different forces brought to bear on their cultures by Spanish and Portuguese powers, respectively. These forces—including failed enslavement of indigenous peoples followed by a massive intensification of the African slave trade—operated to a greater or lesser degree throughout the continent. In the chapters that follow you will see how a multiplicity of dances within each country can reflect and express the intertwining of Indigenous, African, and European cultures that now characterize the region.

 HK*Propel* includes web links to additional resources for this section.

4

Dance in Guatemala

Sources for a Collective Identity in Motion

Beatriz Herrera Corado

Learning Objectives

After reading this chapter, you will be able to do the following:

- Develop a critical approach toward the sources for researching dance in the past.
- Identify ancestry as an analytical tool that describes social bonding, identity expressions, and the context in which a performance happens.
- Understand dance practice as a corporeal heritage that enables a sense of continuity in contexts of colonialism and violent repression.
- Approach critically the state institutionalized theatrical dance practices and its representations of the traditional dance from specific contexts.

Key Terms

ladino—A person of a mixed cultural ancestry who denies the indigenous kinship.

Maya—The native population of south Mexico and Central America.

mestizo—A descendant from Spanish and indigenous lineages who recognizes both origins.

marimba—Guatemala's national instrument.

syncretism—The process of acculturation when a cultural group adapts the elements of another. It is common that syncretism happens in contexts of oppression, as a group uses cultural elements from another group in order to survive.

son—A traditional rhythm of Guatemalan music.

Sotz'il Music and Dance Company

We arrived at the terrace of the National Theatre in Guatemala City, where chairs awaited us around a rectangular set. A carpet of pine leaves lay before us, delimiting the performance space from the audience. It was covered with sacred elements: candles, flowers, and incense. The performers from **Sotz'il** Music and Dance Company were dressed as Ancient Maya **Kaqchikel** warriors and were about to perform their most recent choreography, "Ajq'omal: A Commitment with Life." As cultural bearers from the Maya Kaqchikel ethnic group, the members of the group research the past to connect with their ancestors and myths of origin, creating new dances that resonate across the ages. In Ajq'omal, they represented warriors who sought power for their own sake, without the proper permission from the gods and spiritual beings (known as *nawales*). The deer (*kej*), representing the ultimate authority, held a scepter (*kawil*) as a sign of his power. Sotz'il members dance to reclaim their own Maya Kaqchikel identity and heritage—a heritage denied and kept secret for centuries after the Spanish Conquest (personal communication with Sotz'il company members Luis Cúmez and César Guarcax, 2019).

 See resource 4.1 in HK*Propel* for web links.

Guatemala's territory was occupied by the **Mayan** civilization from 2000 BCE until 1519 CE (table 4.1). The ancient Maya people encompassed communities speaking several languages and did not have a political unity; nevertheless, they shared cultural traits, such as religious artistic expressions. From 1519 onward, the conquest by the Spanish empire and the colonial regime established European worldview and traditions. Guatemala, an independent country since 1821, has been governed by dictatorial regimes. In 1871, the country received a second wave of European migrants who installed themselves as landowners of agricultural farms of coffee and sugar. The successive authoritarian governments were interested in modernizing the country according to European standards and architecture; nevertheless, freedom of expression was limited. In 1945, the Revolution, organized by the urban middle class of Guatemala City, established a socialist democratic regime that ended tragically in 1954 when the U.S.-engineered coup stopped a land reform that affected the business of the United Fruit Company. The coup led to a civil war that lasted 36 years. Despite the new constitution of 1985 that established democracy again, the war only ended when the peace accords were signed in 1996. Guatemala is still under the effects of the civil war, with high violence rates and a poorly managed cultural policy that complicates artistic labor.

A dancer from Sotz'il Music and Dance company performing as a warrior in "Ajq'omal: A Commitment with Life" (2019).

Creating Identity

Who are we? How do we manifest a sense of belonging to a collectivity and a shared identity? We may be the ones who speak the same lan-

Table 4.1   Chronological Periods of Pre-Columbian Mayan and Mesoamerican (Central American) Cultures

Period	Dates
Preclassic	2000 BCE-200 CE [development of hierarchical society]
Classic	200 CE-900 [Mayan cities flourish]
Postclassic	900 CE-1519 [decline of Mayan civilization, completed by Spanish Conquest]

Data from Arredondo and Barrientos (2012) p. XXVII.

guage, who live in the same nation-state, who know the same dance style, or who claim to descended from the same ancestor. In the example of Sotz'il, the language they speak is Maya Kaqchikel; they live in the same country—Guatemala—and in the same village of El Tablón. They know and create their own dance and choreographies and acknowledge their Maya Kaqchikel ancestors. Through this chapter, we will examine how these four dimensions of identity—language, geography, dance style, and shared ancestry—are deeply present in many of the dance practices of Guatemala, especially regarding the connection and recognition of the ancestors and their lineage.

As a nation-state, Guatemala reflects the intermingling of three cultures that took place after the Spanish Conquest: Mayan and native American cultures, European, and African. (Note that *American* in this chapter refers to belonging to the Americas as a continent, not as belonging to the United States.) So far, dance research in Guatemala has been categorized by each of the three roots and the **syncretism** that took place from the Spanish Conquest onward.

This chapter does not inventory all the dances that are currently performed in Guatemala but instead gives key historical and cultural interpretations to help you understand the dance in its local context. In this light, the Spanish Conquest of 1519 is a critical, devastating juncture with many consequences—especially regarding ethnicity and racism. As a result, dance became an essential vessel of symbols and traditions, gathering communities to commemorate past events, ancestors, and rituals. The critical role that dance plays in developing and supporting communities has never ceased, despite violence, repression, and severe economic and political inequality.

Nowadays, Guatemala is a multicultural country where at least 25 languages are spoken, including Spanish (Ministerio de Educación de Guatemala 2003). Within so much diversity,

language is conceived as the referent of ethnic identity. So, because there are 25 languages, there are 25 ethnic groups. Of the 25 languages, 22 are from Mayan origin, all of them spread in different territories. An exception is the **Garífuna** language, from the Garífuna community, an ethnic group that developed from African and Caribbean roots. Much like language reveals how diverse the country is, other practices, such as dance, can create shared bodily experience, thus establishing different ways of understanding identity.

 See resource 4.2 in HKPropel for web links.

Dance as a Calendrical Event

Ancient Maya Record of Dance

The Ancient Maya peoples developed a complex society featuring architectural work, writing, and mathematical systems, along with calendars to organize time and space. Ancient Mayan religion is regarded as **pantheistic** because it includes a plurality of entities encompassing the divine realm, ancestors, animals, and sacred places (Cohodas 2015). On buildings, **stelae** (upright stone slabs), and ceramics, the Maya depicted the royalty as dancing. Studies of ancient city ruins suggest that many of the plazas and open spaces were used as dance floors (Grube 1992, 216), where the occasion for dance could be an astronomical event, the ascension of a ruler, or the beginning or end of a cycle in the Maya calendar. Researchers mainly know about dance as an activity of the elite (Looper 2009). However, it might have been practiced by entire populations, as happens in 21st century Mayan communities.

Mayan Calendars

The most important calendars were (and still are) the ritual calendar of 260 days and the solar calendar of 365 days (Van Akkeren 2011, 401; Arredondo and Barrientos 2012, 19-22). The calendars were not only a count of days but showed how time itself had a special meaning in everyday life (Tedlock 2002, 1-3). Mayan cosmology regarded time and space as a way to understand and order the universe, human existence, and destiny. Hence, the calendar is directly linked to religious ceremonies and so to dance practices.

We know about Ancient Mayan culture from three sources of information: first, the **Maya Chronicles** and scripts of ancient dance-dramas, some of which were rewritten by European colonizers; second, the texts and iconography preserved in stelae, buildings, and ceramics; and third, the oral tradition and bodily knowledge of cultural bearers. Researchers have proposed that during the Classic period, Mayans celebrated a Great *Pokob* Dance to commemorate the end of a calendar cycle and the start of a new one (van Akkeren 2000, 279; 2011, 408). One version of the Pokob dance—even if not preserved in a "pure" state—is the dance-drama **Rabinal Achí**. It has survived until present days as a dance with **parlamentos** (written script). Though we can only guess at the specific steps of the ancient dances, their meanings and contexts still resonate today in the contemporary forms explored further in this chapter.

 See resource 4.3 in HK*Propel* for web links.

Continuity of Mayan Practices

The continuity of some Mayan practices and the referred sources of knowledge allow us to imagine how the ancient dances might have been. Evidence does show that the elite used dance in political events (following the sacred dates of the calendar) and that elements such as costumes and

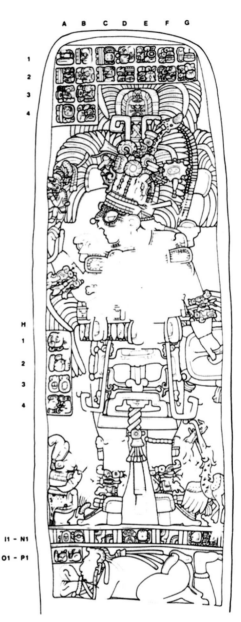

Evidence of dance in the Classic period: A dancer with a "kawil"'scepter used in accession ceremonies.

Used by permission of Stephen Houston, Brown University, Providence.

props had a meaning related to status and royalty.

Other important elements of the dance and artistic representations of ancient Maya are the masks, which are still worn for dance and festivities. Dancers wear a mask and a headdress, holding a scepter and a shield. Such was how a dancer from the elite might have appeared as he performed in an ancient plaza. The masks might personify a deity—an animal or an ancestor—

either of whom would imply a connection with the entities of the spirit world: "[T]he impersonation of supernaturals by Maya elites was no mere theatrical representation or disguise, but a ritual process by which numinous [ethereal] beings were thought to assume corporeal form. . . . The headdress effectively becomes a medium for the transformation of the performer's voice and eyesight into emanations from the spirit world" (Looper 2009, 50). Masks used today in traditional Mayan dances are still considered to be sacred, despite the drastic historical repression. Pre-Columbian traditions were hidden under what seem to be Christian practices, as we will see in the next sections.

How were traditions kept alive during the Spanish Conquest? A possible answer lies in the importance of cosmology as the abstract notion of cultural heritage, which has a verbal, as well as a bodily, manifestation. It is impossible to separate dance from the deep beliefs that the different ethnic groups build and share. It is a fact that practices were kept secret, as later some priests "rediscovered" the ancient dances, such as the Rabinal Achí (Van Akkeren 2011). Other dances were completely transformed during the colonial era, such as the dance of the deer (***danza del venado***), an animal considered both as a deity and an ancestor. Furthermore, religious and calendrical notions were (and still are) important for dance performances, either because dances build resistance to repression or reinforce pride of heritage and connections with the ancestors. Nowadays, calendars of sacred days still unite people in special events. Even if the calendar has changed to the Gregorian system, patron saint days are important for many communities, regardless of the ethnic group. Contemporary Mayan artists are reconstructing their own legacy by identifying the spiritual forces known as ***nawales***, in order to create their performances, as is the case of Sotz'il.

In the chronology of Guatemalan history, the postclassical Maya period was interrupted by the Spanish Conquest. As mentioned before, examples of ancient Maya dance traditions still survive today, but now we will see the implications of the Spanish Conquest and colonial era.

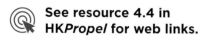 **See resource 4.4 in HK*Propel* for web links.**

Colonial Period

Christianity and Spanish Traditions

In many countries, October 12 is "celebrated" as Columbus Day, which is also known as the *Día de la Hispanidad* (day of the Spanish heritage): the day that Christopher Columbus arrived in America. In Guatemala, as many other American countries, no other event has had such deep consequences as the European conquest. The invasion of America was the moment when humanity came to realize how the globe was shaped, not only geographically but also culturally, because two groups of people that had never known that each other existed happened to meet (Todorov 2012, 15).

In the Guatemalan context, the Mayan cosmology and lifestyle were a shock to the Spanish conquerors, including the rituals, musical instruments, elaborate masks, and dance ceremonies that, in some cases, did involve human sacrifices. Because the Spanish sought not only a territorial expansion but also a spiritual dominance to save the souls of the so-called "primitive tribes," oppression of indigenous religion severely affected dance practices. From the field of semiotics (the study of signs and symbols) Todorov (2012) has explicated an extensive analysis of the first one hundred years that followed after the arrival of Columbus to America, focusing on the process of mutual understanding. He contests the racist belief that indigenous communities were ignorant and did not know how to react against the conquerors, and he highlights specific historical figures who sought strategies of understanding.

In a fictional manner, anthropologist Ruud van Akkeren (2011) wrote a novel that narrates the first encounter of Spanish priests with a Mayan dance ritual, namely the Rabinal Achí. This dance adapted to the colonial regime, and its practice continues until the present day. For example, the Spanish-style costume known as ***morerías*** is used, as are Spanish masks (light skin and blue or green eyes), and European-inspired musical instruments such as a trumpet and the *chirimía* (an imitation of the oboe). The dance is preceded by a ritual that nowadays combines both a Christian and a Mayan rite—a syncretism of deep beliefs known as La Costumbre (Cohodas 2015).

Day of the Patron Saint

The day of the patron saint is a yearly holiday that celebrates a Christian saint who protects a town. The holiday came to replace—and be adapted to—the sacred dates from the ancient Mayan calendar. All towns in Guatemala participate, celebrating a range of saints. In the case of the town of Rabinal, the Rabinal Achí is performed on January 25th, the day of Saint Paul, but unlike other patron saint day dances, it belongs only to that town. For this reason, the Rabinal Achí is acknowledged as a dance that survived the colonial regime.

During the conquest and the following colonial period—from 1519 to 1821—the three roots of ancestry become intertwined, because the Spanish conquerors brought African slaves with them. Because verbal language was insufficient for full communication, dance played an important role when Spanish priests tried to convert and educate the Mayans according to European standards. In Spain around the 15th century, a traditional dance called ***el baile de moros y cristianos*** (*dance of the Moors and Christians*) reenacted the conquest and conversion of Arabs who had occupied Spain during the late Middle Ages (Arrivillaga 2016, 58). The dance-drama extolling the victory of the Christians over the Moors was taught by the priests to the Mayans and developed locally as ***el baile de la conquista*** (*dance of the conquest*). Both dances are usually performed in an open space, with special costumes (morerías) that resemble how the 14th century Spanish represented Arabs. However, little is known, from the outside point of view, about the indigenous Mayan elements and layers of meaning that were adapted to the dance through costumes and choreographic use of the space. For example, the four cardinal points that have specific meanings in Mayan cosmology are used in the choreographic design of el baile de la conquista (Krystal 2011). The dance has a script,

In the town of Cubulco's patron saint celebration, two dancers stand dressed as Spanish conquerors wearing the *morería* suit.

Photo: Richard Chang Jonfe.

A dancer from the town of Sumpango is ready to perform the bull dance. There were no bulls before the Spanish Conquest, so this dance is also an adaptation by Mayan communities to the expectations of the conquerors.

Photo: Richard Chang Jonfe.

in which the Mayans intertwined the prayers for their own deities with the Christian names. It is not a surprise that, currently, both dance of the Moors and Christians and the dance of the conquest are still represented, conveying a sense of identity and community on the day of the patron saint of some Mayan townships (Arrivillaga 2016, 69; Krystal 2011, 28).

Religion

For the Spanish conquerors, religion was an absolute ideal, in which everything that was not Christian, or which contradicted Christian principles, was considered to be a sin and was therefore heresy. The Spanish gaze saw the Mayan dances as pagan rituals that could be worshipping the devil. The consequence to this intolerant point of view, for both Mayans and Afro-descendants, was that all ceremonies, dances, and behaviors that were different from the Christian way of life were banned and kept in secret. Nevertheless, some dances that actually hid the Mayan symbols within Spanish rituals were allowed, such as el baile de la conquista.

Christian Concepts of the Body in Dance

Christian religion itself is expressed in terms that divide the soul from the body. According to Christian beliefs, the soul can be saved after death, but the body will be "corrupted." From this point of view, the body is seen as sinful; therefore dance, if it is not executed in a proper manner, is seen as sinful as well.

Syncretism

The colonial era was a critical time in which the Spanish regime repressed and controlled the cultural expressions of two other groups of people that were previously unknown to them: native Americans, including Mayans and Caribbeans, and African populations. While Spanish-descendant people—embracing the music related to Christian rites—would fully adhere to Western conventions in art rather than the traditions of indigenous Guatemalans, the Mayans and Afro-descendant people employed syncretism. Mayans adapted themselves to the Christian calendar and traditions but hid symbols and messages from their own cosmology and beliefs in the Christian ceremonies. Similarly, Afro-Caribbean Garífunas adapted elements from a variety of origins to perform their religious celebrations, dances, and music.

 See resource 4.5 in HK*Propel* for web links.

The Garífuna

Afro-Caribbean roots

African ancestry came primarily from enslaved people who were brought to Guatemala from different African countries starting as early as 1519. The close connection between music and dance in Africa arrived, and the influence of Afro-descendants in Guatemala is seen in the African origins of Guatemala's national musical instrument, the **marimba**—a type of xylophone (Arrivillaga 2013, 138).

The slave trade during the colonial period engendered a dispute among the Spanish, English, and French colonizers. From this political context emerged the minority ethnic group that occupies Guatemala's Atlantic coast, the Garífuna, a community with African and native Caribbean roots. The case of this community reveals how dance is deeply linked with other artistic expressions, such as music, cosmology, and ritual practices, both sacred and secular.

The Garífuna (or Garinagu) culture originated in the Caribbean when a group of escaped African slaves found refuge on St. Vincent Island in 1635 (Arrivillaga 2010, 20-23). Over the next 150 years, the African newcomers and the indigenous inhabitants shaped a new language and culture with mixed traditions from both origins. But in 1797 the British defeated the Garífuna and some two thousand survivors of the subsequent violence were dispersed to the mainland, settling in Honduras, Guatemala, Belize, and elsewhere. It is remarkable how their culture has survived over centuries despite the geographic diaspora—a testament to the strength of Garífuna traditions.

Among the calendrical dances from the Garífuna tradition, **wanáragua** (or *yankunú*) allows improvisation in a sacred context. Wanáragua—celebrated for Christmas, New Year, and Epiphany Day (January 6th)—can be described as a "popular masked processional rite" (Greene 2005, 198). Unlike the Mayan public ritual dance, wanáragua lacks a script but consists of a procession that stops at specific places where the dance is performed, and there is an organized structure in which dancers take turns to challenge the drummers. In this case, the musicians have to follow the improvised sequence of the dancers. Outstanding features of this dance are the costumes: Dancers wear a mask that denotes a white person and a costume that resembles both British military regalia and costumes from traditional European dances, such as the **Morris dance**. The use of these costumes reveals how the wanáragua is a ritual that ridicules the British colonizers and also empowers and venerates Garífuna cultural identity.

Garífuna cosmology centers on ancestors and kinship (Cayetano 2013, 111-112), using music and dance for both sacred and secular activities. In the sacred domain, dance and music are used to connect people with dead ancestors, through, for example, the trance rituals *bügü* and *chugú*. The drum rhythm that guides the dance is called **hüngühüledi**, which refers to the beats of the heart (Arrivillaga 2010, 42). Families with extended kin who live in other countries still gather together to commemorate their ancestors through these same dances and ensure continuity of their tradition.

The Marimba

The marimba is an idiophone, a kind of xylophone, with a specially configured keyboard and made of particular types of wood. It is now the most popular music instrument that accompanies parties and celebrations all around Guatemala, and its origins date back to the colonial era, from the African migration.

 See resource 4.6 in HK*Propel* for web links.

Influences From Western Theatrical Dance

Despite extensive social segregation, ethnic groups inevitably mixed over the centuries. The terms **mestizo** and **ladino** arose to designate a mixed identity. However, while *mestizo* literally means mixed-race, in the Guatemalan context, the term *ladino* came to be synonymous with non-indigenous, non-Mayan, and non-Afro descendant. Ladinos essentially constructed a white identity, claiming to have "authentic" Spanish or European ancestry, denying the possibility of an ancestor from a different ethnic group. Following European values and beliefs, the ladinos controlled the government and managed the independence of the country from Spain in 1821. In this context, the ladinos would not conceive of traditional Mayan dance-dramas as art; for them, art should follow European conventions or, more accurately, what they imagined such conventions to be. It is not a surprise that in the late 1800s the first theaters were built in the cities where ladinos lived. As the Christian church determined the legitimacy of Spanish-descendant power from the colonial era onward, the church and clergy controlled and supervised all public discourse and artistic expressions. Music, for example, was mostly done in religious contexts. Even after independence in 1821, most governments were repressive dictatorships that squelched any cultural expression questioning or challenging their regime. (Móbil 2002, 453-457).

According to historians, theatrical dance started in Guatemala from 1948 onward, following the foundation of the *Ballet Nacional de Guatemala* (National Ballet of Guatemala) (Mertins 2009, 17-20). The circumstances of local and global dynamics explain how a foreign dance—European ballet—came to be the national representation of the country. The revolutionary left-wing government invited a Russian company that was defecting from the Soviet Union while touring in Latin America—as well as two Belgian artists who were running away from the aftermath of World War II—to move to Guatemala and teach ballet. This influence motivated the intellectual elite of bourgeois ladinos in 1950s' Guatemala City to consider supporting a national company of ballet dance as proper representation of delightful artistic taste. Citizens of Guatemala City started to negotiate with the government to fund the ballet company, a support that fluctuated greatly due to political instability and a civil war that engulfed the country from the 1960s onward.

Classical ballet was then, in the 1950s, the latest novelty for the ladino elite, the imitation of a European art form. Concerning repertoire, Guatemalan dancers who started training in ballet also represented Mayan traditional dances on the stage. An example is the premiere of the National Ballet in 1948, where a local newspaper reports three Mayan traditional dances re-created on the stage, even though the names of the dances are not mentioned (Mertins 2009, 20). Since this first experience, ladino ballet and modern dancers began to construct their own staged choreographies of the traditional dances that took place in the Mayan towns and brought them to the capital city in a theatrical version. Even if some of these traditional dances were already designed to be executed for an audience in a presentational mode, what drastically changed is the setting in a Western theater instead of an open space where the whole community could gather to witness dance. Other areas of misunderstandings are the sacred date of the tradition, the embodied knowledge from the Mayan culture bearers that was ignored, and the rituals involved, because Western theatrical dance is supposed to be secular. The Mayan dances were effectively mined as a resource and transformed into a commodity for elite consumption.

Commodification of traditional dance is ongoing even to this day, such as with the second national company: ***Ballet Moderno y Folklórico*** (Modern and Folk Ballet). Around the 1960s, after the establishment of the left-wing government, the Folk Ballet of Mexico visited Guatemala City. Guatemalans were amazed by the color and cheerfulness of Mexican traditional dance, which they had never seen before. A dance advocate of that time, who later became the director of the company, said that "unfortunately, the [Guatemalan] government did not know that we had not any researchers, we had not channeled the folk practices, we did not have musicians dedicated to the genre, we had nothing to create such a thing" (Mertins 2009, 57). So, because Guatemalan emergent dancers and choreographers from the capital city were not confident enough to build a company based only on folk dance—a lack of confidence that might be related to the perceived lesser artistic value of traditional practices plus the violence of the civil war that made research in indigenous villages impossible to do—they decided to found a company dedicated to both practices: American modern dance, as well as traditional dances.

At this point, identity defined in terms of ancestry becomes a decisive issue when looking at dance as art in a secular or theatrical context. The question "what is art?" in Guatemala is still related to ancestry and to the ethnic group that dares to ask the question—usually the intellectual elite of ladinos. It does not mean that indigenous art does not exist; it means that the state's discourse, policies, and educational plans regarding art would happen and be regulated by intellectual ladinos. The next section addresses the main features that distinguish the genres of dance in Guatemala, touching on the roots of ancestry seen so far.

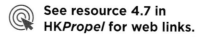 **See resource 4.7 in HK*Propel* for web links.**

Crosscurrents

The three main genres of dance can be identified according to their final cause or function:

- Mayan public ritual dance, which seeks to link a specific community with its ancestors, deities, and myths of origin

- Western theatrical dance, which might represent ethnic-others onstage, and, in the case of classical ballet and modern dance, enacts a quest for beauty

- Social dance, which is executed in secular spaces and times, encourages the spontaneous participation of people, whether or not they consider themselves dancers, and can also take place in events related to the life cycle of individuals.

Traditional Dance-Drama: Continuity of Pre-Columbian Dance Forms and Syncretism

Mayan dance-dramas, or "Mayan public ritual dances" (Cohodas 2015), are script-based performances that celebrate a patron saint or other religious event in a community. These dances might have pre-Columbian origins, such as Rabinal Achí, dance of the deer, dance of the snake, dance of the monkeys, and *el palo volador* or *la danza del volador* (the flying pole or the dance of the flyers). Other dances might have been articulated during the process of colonization such as el baile de la conquista and el baile de moros y cristianos.

Dance-dramas usually present humans, animals, and divine characters wearing identifying

From the colonial period onward, people celebrate the patron saint day by gathering to witness dance.
Photo: Richard Chang Jonfe.

masks. However, some of the masks are abstract, and not all of them directly represent a specific character (Krystal 2011). For instance, the *palo volador* or *la danza del volador* centers on a large standing pole from which two or four dancers dressed as monkeys suspend themselves, using ropes, and turn around the axis, like flying. Because this dance is performed in several places and in other Mesoamerican countries, there are hints of the exchange of ideas between the pre-Hispanic communities. Still, more research is needed to fully understand the contemporary meaning of the monkey characters.

Overall, Mayan public ritual dance is a genre devoted to Mayan communities' sense of identity and continuity. There is some income that circulates among musicians and costume and mask makers, but economics is not the main motivation for cultural bearers to keep the practice ongoing. The devotion of patron saints as a syncretic cult that stands for Mayan and Christian deities seems to be the strongest force that drives the enactment of the dances. As the experiences of anthropologists witnessing these dances convey, more research is necessary to fully identify the choreographic patterns and distinctive steps that take place. Some of these steps have been modified for the stage, as in theatrical dance.

The traditional Mayan dance in the 21st century, according to reports from Krystal (2011, 59), Arrivillaga (2016, 61), and Looper (2009, 191-200), can be summarized as follows:

- The performance takes place on a special date, in an open space, where the audience can see the dance. There are Christian and

Women carrying candles to the church as part of the rituals of the patron saint day. Women are usually excluded from performing dance but do participate in processions and rituals.

Photo: Richard Chang Jonfe.

Mayan rituals before and after the dance. Sometimes the dances are part of a bigger celebration in the town known as the *feria*.

- The full dance is a very long performance that can take up to 12 hours. It is composed of several music pieces for the characters to dance.

- The choreography is set around a narrative: Dance-dramas tell a story through dialogues and movement. However, scripts have been lost over time, so there are choreographies that do not include the spoken texts (García 2009, 32).

- They are performed by nonprofessional dancers. Nevertheless, it is an honor to be a dancer and to invest time and money for the ritual process and the costumes.

- The dances require special costumes and masks that are made at specific workshops called morerías. The masks are considered to be sacred and refer to pre-Columbian deities.

- The dances are organized by the "owner" of the dance, who usually possesses the script of the dialogues and knows the steps of the dance.

- Usually, the dances have a fixed choreography that has been rehearsed previously. Nevertheless, Looper (2009) reports some dances that do involve improvisation.

- Live musicians participate in the performance, with a specific set of melodies that correspond to the choreographies. Each dance has its own musical themes.

Theatrical Dance

Theatrical dance comes from the influence of European notions of dance as art that inspired ladino dancers in the 20th century, but it is widespread among all ethnic groups throughout the country. In contrast to traditional dance, the performances have no religious context or function. Nevertheless, theatrical dance today does not escape a calendar and special dates, such as **International Dance Day**, on April 29th, which is celebrated in Guatemala with a special performance organized by the government in the national theater.

The distinctiveness of theatrical dance in Guatemala is based on its system of transmission by foreigners or by ladinos connected with a foreign ancestry. Because the dance script, technique, and know-how have not been transmitted from generation to generation, but instead have come from foreign artists, theatrical dance still depends on the international scene or on artists who travel abroad and teach. Another alternative to strengthen the transmission is institutional support from the state, which is supposed to fund the National School of Dance, where only ballet and modern dance are taught. Nevertheless, repercussions from Guatemala's civil war and its aftermath have been a threat not only to strong artistic institutions, but also to all cultural expressions, regardless of the genre. In such a context, developing a tradition of know-how for stage dance is still a challenge in Guatemala.

A subgenre of theatrical dance is **secular folkloric dance**. This genre includes the folkloric repertoire staged by the Ballet Moderno y Folklórico, but also several communities throughout Guatemala that have organized dance troops that perform indigenous-like scenes and rituals. These dances might represent tokens of weddings or sowing and harvesting scenes taken from their original contexts, or full Mayan rituals, as in the case of the multiday *paabanc*. Masks are not necessarily used in these performances, and they are different from dance-dramas in that they can be performed by mestizos that represent an ethnic "other" without a ritual context. So, because the ancestral link is not fully addressed, these dances are usually the ones that dance troops perform internationally as "Guatemalan folk dance."

Social Dance

Social dance is distinguished by its participatory nature and spontaneity. In Guatemala towns, the wider celebrations of patron day saints include social dancing to a *marimba orquesta*. In secular and informal spaces and dates, social dancing happens during celebratory and commemorative events, with the marimba rhythm known as *son* played in all contexts. In mestizo cities, the music has also permeated the ballroom dances from the parties—where marimba is played, as well. Hence, it is not strange to find a marimba repertoire that usually includes foxtrot, Spanish two-step, *cumbia*, boleros, corridos, and blues. From the chapter author's personal experience at mestizo parties, the way people dance to all these different rhythms of music does not vary so much, and all of them are danced in couples.

From the Garífuna culture, the **punta** dance is the one mostly practiced at parties and social gatherings. It is considered to be a courtship dance (Greene 2002, 194; Arrivillaga 2010, 43). Punta is characterized by vigorous hip movements contrasted with an almost motionless upper torso. In the Garífuna towns, punta dancers face the drums in order to dance together with the musicians—an Afro-descendant practice. It is the most widespread Garífuna cultural expression throughout Guatemala and the world. In many parties at Guatemala City and other places, it is common to dance punta among other Afro-Caribbean rhythms such as **salsa**, **reggaetón**, **merengue**, and **bachata**.

 See resource 4.8 in HK*Propel* for web links.

Summary

As this chapter has shown, dance is a major force that conveys an embodied manifestation of Guatemala's history and ethnic identity. Among the three ethnic threads that appear in Guatemalan dance—Mayan, European, and Afro-Caribbean—historical events ultimately shaped the way each element exists today, as well as the cultural identities of those who practice the different dance forms. With the ancient calendrical dances woven into European Christian rituals and celebrations, the Afro-Caribbean heritage in Garífuna dances, and the weavings of Mayan sensibilities in folk dance performances and the contemporary choreographies of Sotz'il dance company, we see how dance helps answer these three basic questions: Who are our ancestors? What is our myth of origin? Why and for whom do we dance? These questions interlace the abstract cosmology with the everyday cultural practices that re-create traditional beliefs. Dance, as a practice of the body, is therefore deeply linked to a transcendental dimension that—even beyond personal identity—supports a notion of a collective entity. The colonial era and dictatorships subjected Guatemala to the politics of segregation and elimination of indigenous practices. Nevertheless, despite this repression, the focus on dance allows researchers from different fields to understand the sense of continuity and collectivity. Dance remains the power that brings people together both for the sacred dates and for the casual parties that release stress and unite the community.

 See resource 4.9 in HK*Propel* for web links.

Discussion Questions

1. Through which sources of knowledge have researchers found information about ancient Maya dance?

2. How did the Spanish Conquest and colonization affect the dance practice of ancient Mayan communities?

3. Why does dance function as a kin bonding practice in the case of Garífuna people?

4. What elements are different between Mayan public ritual dance and folkloric dance?

5. What was the political and global context that made possible the introduction of classical ballet in Guatemala?

 Visit HK*Propel* for access to this chapter's Application Activity.

Selected Glossary

cumbia—Legends say that "cumbia" is a Bantu-origin word. It is the most popular widespread music and dance rhythm throughout Spanish-speaking America. It is usually played by marimba and marimba orquestas at parties in many towns and communities.

Garífuna or **Garinagu**—The people from African and Caribbean origin who resisted the European colonial regimes in the island of St. Vincent and currently live in the Atlantic coast of Central America. The term also refers to their language.

ladino—A person of a mixed cultural ancestry who denies the indigenous kinship, speaks Spanish, and seeks or displays European cultural expressions.

marimba—An idiophone, similar to a xylophone, from African origin that was adapted to a Western keyboard and built with special woods from different countries. It is recognized as Guatemala's national instrument.

Maya/Mayan—The native population of the south of Mexico and Central America, an overarching ethnic group that includes different languages and diverse cultural heritage.

merengue and **bachata**—Dominican music and dances based on a 4/4 rhythmical structure. They differ in stepping structures and the syncopation in the percussion. They are both danced in Guatemala's mestizo parties.

mestizo—A descendant from Spanish and indigenous lineages who recognizes both origins.

punta—A Garífuna dance and music rhythm usually danced at parties. It has spread beyond Guatemala and Central America, and it's popularly known in the song "sopa de caracol."

reggaetón—A Puerto Rican music and dance rhythm, influenced by Jamaican dancehall music genre, that features a "dembow" percussion pattern, danced in Guatemala's mestizo parties.

salsa—An Afro-Caribbean music and dance rhythm formally defined in New York in the 1960s. It is usually danced in couples, with specific roles of leader and follower in Guatemala's mestizo parties.

son—A traditional rhythm of Guatemalan music.

syncretism—Hybridization; when a cultural group adapts the elements of another. It is common for syncretism to happen in contexts of oppression; groups combine cultural elements as ways of survival.

Selected References and Resources

Arredondo, Ernesto, and Tomás Barrientos. 2012. *2012: Calendarios Mayas y Orígenes del Fin del Mundo*. Guatemala City: FUNDESA/Pacunam, p. 129.

Arrivillaga, Alfonso. 2008. Cómo cantan los Cuchumatanes: Un recuento musical a partir de la mira etnográfica. *Senderos: Revista de Etnomusicología* 1, pp. 11-35.

Arrivillaga, Alfonso. 2013. La marimba en el salón de baile de los garínagu. *Senderos: Revista de Etnomusicología* 3, pp. 137-146.

Bremme, Ida, Estuardo González and Carlos García. 2003. Guatemala: Principales Danzas y Bailes. In *Nuestra música y danzas tradicionales*, edited by Giselle Chang. San José, Costa Rica: Coordinación Educativa y Cultural Centroamericana, pp. 245-273.

Casaús, Marta. 2005. *Las redes intelectuales centroamericanas: un siglo de imaginarios nacionales (1820-1920)*. Guatemala City: F&G Editores. 325 pp.

García, Carlos. 2008. Las danzas unificadas de San Pedro Necta, Huehuetenango. *Senderos: Revista de Etnomusicología* 1, 93-106.

Grube, Nikolai. 1992. Classic Maya Dance. *Ancient Mesoamerica* 3, 201-218.

Luján, Jorge. 2008. *Inicios del Dominio Español en Indias*. Guatemala City: Editorial Universitaria.

Mertins, Lizette. 2012. *La Danza Teatral en Guatemala (1978-2010)*. Guatemala City: Universidad de San Carlos de Guatemala.

Ministerio de Educación de Guatemala. 2003. *Mapa Etnolingüístico de Guatemala*. www.mineduc.gob.gt/digebi/mapaLinguistico.html.

Móbil, José. 2002. *Historia del arte guatemalteco*. Guatemala City: Editorial Serviprensa. S. A.

Todorov, Tzvetan. 2012. *La conquista de América: el problema del otro*. Buenos Aires, Argentina. Siglo Veintiuno editores.

van Akkeren, Ruud. 2011. *La danza del tambor: los últimos días del calendario maya*. Guatemala City. Piedra Santa Editorial.

5

Dance in Brazil

Amélia Conrado

Collaboration and Translation by Kelly Sabini

Learning Objectives

After reading this chapter you will be able to do the following:

- Understand the importance of dance within the dynamics of Brazilian culture, taking white-European colonization as a fact that signified enormous changes to this scenario.
- Recognize the period in which European colonization began as the imposition of a cultural model—through relationships riddled with conflict, genocides, and enslavements—that resulted in acculturation and reflects the complexity and diversity of the context in which Brazilian dances are formed.
- Understand the African presence, including its dances and cultural traditions, as an important factor in the reconfiguration of dance in Brazil.
- Encounter some of the dance forms that reveal characteristics of the country's five regions, recognizing the symbolic value of popular cultures as an expression of national culture.

Key Terms

capoeira—An Afro-Brazilian martial art that represents the Africans' struggle for freedom, stemming from a form of self-defense created during the 16th century by enslaved Africans in Brazil.

Casa Grande—A name that designates the farms with large houses belonging to the planters in the period of European colonization and enslavement of Africans in Brazil.

samba—A rhythm, music, and dance genre of Angolan origin that has recast itself in Brazil as a national symbol.

Sateré-Mawé—An indigenous ethnic group of the Amazon region.

tucandeira—A species of ants used in sacred indigenous rituals.

Samba de Roda—A Poetic View

Descendants of Africans maintain and have reinvented rich traditions in their daily lives. Let's be carried to the warm, often light-hearted, sometimes sensual ambiance of *samba de roda* ("samba in a circle"). Samba de roda is dancing, singing, indistinct instrumentation, and pulsating rhythms vibrating playfully through participants' bodies.

It comes to life in the private backyards of small, simple houses, and in public at the corner bar or under a tree in the town square. It erupts in the night on hills and in slums and on the brightly lit stages of the avenue's theaters. These are the places where samba ignites.

Its greatest wealth is that it originates from the people who transfer their feelings into poetic verses and songs, such as "I came here to hang around, I came here to dilly-dally, dilly-dally, dilly-dally, dilly-dally."

Each person who approaches this circle begins to clap their hands and follows along with the music's vibrant and pulsing rhythm.

The women, wearing their long, full, white or multicolored skirts, dance gracefully with a sway in their hips and shuffle in their feet, in pairs, into the center of the circle. Their heads are wrapped with beautiful scarves, their arms with showy bracelets, and their necks are looped with many strings of beads. The men are dressed in long pants, colorful shirts, and hats.

And that is how samba de roda happens—oftentimes unexpectedly, through the meeting of friends and family members who celebrate the joy of living. All that is needed is for one person to pick up a tambourine and another to sing a song and clap for whoever is present.

In this way of dancing, singing, drumming, and celebrating the coming together of people, there is no place for discrimination based on age, gender, race, religion, or ethnicity—everyone is included. Everyone participates!

The "Brazil" that most students of dance are familiar with today is the Brazil of **capoeira**—with its unusual instrumentation and acrobatic moves and fast footwork (which will be discussed more fully later in this chapter) and the Brazil of Rio's **Carnival**—with its larger-than-life floats, nudity, promiscuity, and days on end of wild dancing to pulsating rhythms of tambourines and drums. These highly commercialized, Eurocentric views of Brazilian culture are popular selling points that inevitably both color and limit one's understanding of dance in Brazil. Available records about the "history of dance" in Brazil reflect a discontinuous and minimally inclusive view of the multifaceted expressions of dance, their techniques, and the diversity of dance existing in Brazilian society. This is because, within the literature, the record of Western white culture that established itself in Brazil through European colonization prevails. A Eurocentric perspective spread throughout Brazilian culture, permeating dance companies and training schools, and continued into modernity with the avant-garde artistic movements and others that endorse this perspective in contemporary times. In this sense, the diverse dance expressions that arise in Brazil (re)write their own history, seeking to overcome these hallmarks of political and ideological domination of the territory.

Guided by these considerations, we focus on dance that presents itself as both a collective form, such as the rituals of traditional peoples, as well as in the so-called staged dances—that is, those forms that stem from formal dance teaching schools and whose purpose is the production of performances, staged presentations, and the development of and adherence to a certain model of thought in dance.

Geography and History

Brazil is a country of continental proportions. It has a geographic area of 3.3 million square miles, divided into five major regions (north, northeast, midwest, southeast, and south), that form a federation composed of 26 states, 5,560 municipalities, and a federal district—where sits the capital of the country, **Brasilia**. A significant portion of the world's largest rainforest, the **Amazon**, lies within Brazil. The population in 2020 was more than 214 million inhabitants, making it the sixth most populous country in the world.

Dance history books typically discuss dance in Brazil from a fragmented and ideologically white-European frame of reference. Here we are taking a counter-colonial approach. An extensive chronology of Brazilian dance history begins with the precolonial period, in which the societies and cultures of the original peoples occupied this large territory that was later called "Brazil." It continues through the centuries of European colonization, repression of indigenous cultures, enslavement of African peoples, and the complex crosscurrents of history that bring Brazil to its present day.

 See resource 5.1 in HK*Propel* for web links.

Dance and Ritual in Pre-Brazil

To discuss dance in Brazil, we must examine the period preceding colonization (1500-1822), when the territory, not yet colonized by the Europeans, was inhabited by thousands of ethnically distinct indigenous peoples. At the time of genocide caused by the European invasion, many of these peoples resisted by fleeing deep into the interior of the country. As a result of this resistance, there are currently around 800,000 indigenous people in Brazil—represented by 305 different ethnicities and 274 indigenous languages in the country, according to the 2010 census. Indigenous peoples of various ethnic groups throughout all of Brazil's territory have fought for more than 500 years for the right to their original lands that were invaded during European colonization. Presently, they continue to fight for legal recognition of their land rights, for the demarcation of indigenous lands, for protection of life policies due to the crimes they suffer at the hands of squatters and explorers who seek to criminally exploit the natural resources existing in protected indigenous locations, and for the protection of indigenous life.

> A calamity—rain for some, drought for others—will fall on us and we will not be able to do anything to protect ourselves from it, except to sing and dance to calm the fury of the creator gods and wait for the child to be born who will unite our peoples against the phantom-brothers. (Munduruku 2018, 6)

In bringing forth the prophecy mentioned in the fictional work *O Karaíba: A History of Pre-Brazil*, the indigenous philosopher Daniel Munduruku (2018) explains to us that, before the arrival of European colonizers, there was an organized system of life among the original peoples of this land, who enjoyed the abundance of all that nature had to offer. The various symbols, rituals, and expressions of the descendants of these cultures come to us today in the form of oral transmission, which requires imagination, interpretation, and in-depth study to provide a historical understanding of these indigenous and ancestral societies. The traditional lifestyles of indigenous societies are deeply entwined with nature. This harmonization of "the natural being" is seen in their philosophies and prophecies, the sounds of their languages, and the ways of life that express a worldview—in this sense, the signs, teachings, rituals, and dream-state visions transmitted by the tribal wise men, called *pajés*. So although this is a work of fiction extolling former ways of life, there are truths contained within it. Such ancestral knowledge and wisdom exalt the dance, song, musical instruments, objects, and prayers as rituals. These rituals, which are very sensorial, are manifested in the indigenous cultural celebrations.

Currently, there are many and diverse problems with regard to Brazil's government and its institutions for the protection of indigenous peoples, such as **FUNAI** (National Foundation of the Indian/Fundação Nacional do Índio). These institutions should comply with the laws that govern the preservation of these indigenous communities that live deep in the forests and wooded areas, and on long stretches of riverbanks, having little to no contact with people from urban areas. They are also intended to protect and preserve indigenous peoples that, for reasons of survival, currently find themselves in urban centers.

In reality, however, indigenous societies in Brazil endure constant struggle for the demarcation of their lands that have been criminally seized by national and foreign groups exploiting soil, water, minerals, and everything they own. In addition to threatening their fundamental rights to exist, the imperialist and capitalist models also impact indigenous ways of life, traditions, and cultures. For many years, indigenous societies have been attacked by landowners who are looking to extract ores such as iron, copper, aluminum, and gold, to mine gemstone deposits such as diamonds, amethysts, and emeralds,

Cultural Highlight

TUCANDEIRA (STINGING ANT) RITUAL—ANCIENT RITES FOR 21ST CENTURY BATTLES

The power and relevance of ancient rituals continues in 21st century Brazil. For example, the *Waumat*, a centuries-old rite of passage for young men of the **Sateré-Mawé** people, has recently been focused on preparing the men to lead in the fight against loggers, land-grabbers, and multinational corporations that seek to ravage the Amazon for private commercial gain. In the ritual, the men dance as they subject themselves to the venomous stings of the *tucandeira* ants, thereby proving their strength as leaders. For these traditional cultures, the rituals and dance are integrated with the dynamics of life, in which the body is a principal means of expression and communication. In an interview, indigenous practitioners of the Waumat spoke of its deep and continuous relevance: "I was born Sateré, I grew up Sateré so wherever I go, I am Sateré. I could even wear a tie, jacket, shoes, sneakers, social dress, but I will always be Sateré Mawé. Going through this ritual gives me this strength to show our right to our land, to fight, to show that we are not forgetting our culture, because our right, our identity, is our culture. Tucandeira is really the vaccine and medicine of the Sateré Mawé." (Transcript of dialogue spoken by the indigenous members Benito Miquilis, Érick Pereira da Batista, Franceia Açaí, and Tuxaua Dico. InfoAmazonia 2019)

 See resource 5.2 in HK*Propel* for web links.

to illegally log Brazil's ancient trees for timber exportation, or to clear-cut large swaths of land for cattle ranching, among other interests. These events—still taking place in the 21st century—harken back to the 16th century arrival of European colonizers to the then-new territory called "Brazil" and the accompanying massacres and genocides of indigenous peoples. In five centuries, these problems have not been resolved. To the contrary, indigenous populations continue to fight for their basic human right to exist and for possession of their original lands.

The **Jesuit** missions of previous centuries imposed upon the indigenous people conversion to Christianity, with its values vastly different from the life principles and worldviews of these indigenous societies. It is believed that, as a survival mechanism, these original peoples reinvented their rituals to incorporate Christian doctrines, disguising them so as to continue their own beliefs, rituals, and cultural practices. We can assume that ritualistic practices—including dance—responded similarly to the pressures of colonialism. There are some dances and cultural manifestations in different locations throughout contemporary Brazil that bring important elements from the re-signified indigenous memo-

ries. An example of these is the representation of remembrance and identity of the **Guaranis**, an important indigenous ethnic group in Brazil and elsewhere in South America, whose name means "warrior." These embodied memories, or cultural manifestations of identity, are explained in different ways by the elders. The Guaranis' remembrance is a procession with dances, songs, and flutes, usually paraded through the streets on January seventh, a date that memorializes the "owners of the land" who fought for the independence of the island of Itaparica, a region in the state of **Bahia**. In the states of Pernambuco and Paraíba, there are the manifestations of the *caboclinhos* dances, which are identified by the name of indigenous tribes who perform them, such as *caboclinhos Carijós* and *caboclinhos Sete Flexas*. As a form of cultural affirmation and memory, they found within Carnival (sometimes spelled *Carnaval*) a space to express themselves with their dances, stories, songs, and costumes. Throughout Brazil, traditional rituals are preserved by indigenous communities, which have managed to navigate the current socio-political-historical and cultural dynamics while maintaining their ethnic and cultural presence.

European Dances in Brazil

From Colonization to the Present

The arrival of the Portuguese royal family to the country in 1808 brought with it European dances. The staged performance of operas and ballets for the court were the first signs of permanence of this style of dance in Brazilian culture. In the state of Bahia, located in the Northeast region, the first opera house was established for the arrival of these companies. Later, in 1816, the **Royal Theater of São João** was built in the state of **Rio de Janeiro** (Vicenzia 1997, 13).

Italian and French ballet dancers—present in Brazil since the 19th century—performed seasonally at these various opera houses. However, it was only in 1927 that the first **School of Dance of the Municipal Theater of Rio de Janeiro** was established in Brazil. An invitation was issued to the Russian ballerina **Maria Olenewa** (1896-1965)—then dancing in the company directed by **Anna Pavlova** (1881-1931)—to develop the corps de ballet and ballet performances in the city. The first presentation took place in 1939 (Achcar 1980, 209).

In addition to the ballet tradition, initially appearing as court dances, other European and Asian cultural practices were disseminated in the Brazilian territory, mainly in the south and southeast of the country, where the political situation of Brazil of the day made possible the immigration of Italian, German, and Japanese peoples. Furthermore, from approximately 1888, when slavery was abolished, to the early 1900s, this migration of Europeans and Asians to Brazil highlighted a completely different type of immigrant colony—that of Afro-Brazilians. Unlike other immigrants to Brazil, African immigrants suffered for almost 400 years as enslaved laborers, forced to render service to the colony.

The Africans who served in the royal court, and on the plantations, ranches, and the so-called **Casa Grandes**, learned European dances and strategically refashioned them to disguise their ritual practices and customs that were prohibited by their "masters" and the laws of the time. The most common example of these strategies was how they "converted" to Christian Catholicism, whose feasts of Catholic saints were opportunities for enslaved Africans to wage rebellions and coordinate escapes to *quilombos*—distant lands of difficult access, where they organized themselves and lived as free communities. Thus, these peoples made use of religious celebrations to (re) invent their dances, songs, beliefs, and forms of power as a process of cultural resistance.

To return to the more obvious remnants of classical European dance in Brazil, we find the continuance of classical ballet today vis-à-vis its different training schools, such as French, English, and Russian, as well as dance trends emerging in the Americas, particularly Cuban ballet. While Russian and English methodologies predominated (as exemplified by the existence of the **Bolshoi Theater School** in Joinville, Brazil, the only branch of the famous Bolshoi Ballet outside Russia) the Cuban classical ballet is distinctive due to its technique developed specifically for the Latin American body. Similar developmental efforts took place in the emergence of Brazilian modern dance.

 See resource 5.3 in HK*Propel* for web links.

Founding of Modern Dance in Brazil

Around the 1940s, with the arrival of foreign dancers and choreographers and the return of Brazilians who had lived abroad, the modern school of dance emerged with influences from Europe and the United States. Over time, the relationship between the two countries has been one of domination and dependence: The United States' economic power and dominance and Brazil's economic instability and dependence. The implications of this politico-economic relationship play out similarly in the world of dance, that is, the exportation of North American cultures to Brazil with the dissemination of modern dance techniques, American music, industrialized products, and values of consumption imposed by capitalism. All this had a strong impact on the internalized values and mentality of the Brazilian people and their current perception that "what is outside is better." The discredit and discrimination of dances from Afro-Brazilian, indigenous, and other ethnic references based on the preservation of cultural traditions suffered from this ideology of "modernity."

In the state of São Paulo the Experimental Dance School of the Municipal Theater was inaugurated in 1940 with Czechoslovakian choreographer **Vaslav Veltchek** (1896-1968) as its director. He married Brazilian ballerina **Marília Franco** (1920-2006) interpreter of his work *The Dance of Bacchanal*, which critics considered a masterpiece of the modern style.

In the city of Porto Alegre, the master dancer **Lya Bastian Meyer** (1911-2005) brought the **Mary Wigman** (1886-1973) method of German modern dance and its ideas to the south of the country. In 1956, in the northern city of Salvador, Bahia, the first school of dance at the Federal University of Bahia, was founded, the first of its kind in higher education in the country. Polish dancer and choreographer Yanka Rudzka (1916-2008), also a follower of Wigman's expressionism, was its founder and director. German director Rolf Guelewisk, another follower of the German expressionist school, succeeded her (Vicenzia 1997, 16). Such legacies gave this institution modern and avant-garde dance as its basis of creative thought.

In the years 1971 to 1980, the arrival of African American dance master **Clyde Morgan** as director of the Contemporary Dance Group of the Federal University of Bahia School of Dance marks the beginning of a modern dance methodology based on **José Limón's** (1908-1972) technique and principles of African dances and cultures. In this way, he inspired and trained a generation of dancers who continue his approach. Some Brazilian masters of this methodology include **Raimundo Bispo dos Santos** ("Mestre King"), **Carlos Pereira dos Santos** (Negrizu), **Eusébio Lobo da Silva**, **José Carlos Arandiba** (Zebrinha), **Nadir Nóbrega Oliveira**, and **Edva Maria Barreto**, among others.

In addition to the North American and German techniques that circulated in Brazil, other styles draw their content from African Brazilian dances and the so-called popular dances reproduced by dance companies and independent troupes that also signal a time of searching for the newness in dance.

 **See resource 5.4 in HK*Propel* for web links.**

Regional Dances and Popular Cultural Events

Regional characteristics reflect the geography and the cultural history of each area, and the complexities of Brazil's history are immediately apparent in the nature of—and perspectives on—the dances in each region. Several historical influences resonate most significantly, such as the concentration of African cultural descendants in the coastal northeast region, where the majority of enslaved Africans were brought to Brazil. The indigenous presence in different regions, notably the northern and midwest regions, has similar implications for their dances, while the patterns of colonial occupation and later European immigration in the south and southeast regions constitute a third thread of influence on the nature of regional dances.

The way dances are perceived—and therefore accepted or repressed, documented or ignored—is also shaped through the intersection of history and culture. The term *popular dance* emerged from critical approaches that (re)define *folkloric* dances. This notion and origin come from European culture and make a distinction between that of the "people" and that of the "elite." The perspective of this definition values the knowledge and ideas of the "elite" over those of the "people." In Brazil this distinction was widespread. It was only in the second half of the 20th century that new research and conceptual reframing called these assumptions into question, and the issue remains under debate.

The existence of a dance and the manifestation of popular culture in one region does not preclude its existence in another, although some dances might be more prominent in a given location. Like capoeira and samba, which are expressions of popular culture found in all Brazilian states, many dances exist in multiple regions, but with different characteristics.

Throughout the vast Brazilian territory, there is a wealth of dances and popular manifestations that convey the original cultures, as well as those that came with the peoples of other nations and cultures, and which result in a plurality and cultural diversity. For this reason, popular dances cannot be understood in a Cartesian way that separates mind ("elite") and body ("popular"). Instead, they are characterized by an intertwining of aesthetic dialogues between dance, song, music, costumes, theatricality, and characters that interact in the staging and express the uniqueness of their distinct location(s), climate(s), people(s), way(s) of life, heritage(s), and identity(-ies) within the country. In other words, they are reflections of Brazil by region. The tremendous cultural wealth found in Brazil makes it difficult to list all of its traditions.

Folkloric Dance Troupes

Since the 1940s, the emergence of folkloric troupes and dance companies stands out on the national scene, with field research in popular dances. These companies include **Grupo Viva Bahia** (in the state of Bahia, 1962), **Balé Popular do Recife** (in Pernambuco, 1977), and **Balé Folclórico da Bahia** (in Bahia, 1988). It was also around the 1940s that **Mercedes Baptista's** Balé Folclórico appeared. Baptista was the first Black dancer to join the corps de ballet at the *Teatro Municipal* of Rio de Janeiro. She left Brazil to study in New York (USA) at the invitation of **Katherine Dunham** and, upon returning to Brazil, founded her own folkloric dance company.

Northern Region

Because the northern region is located in the Amazon, the largest area of preserved forest in the world and a region that experiences high temperatures and humidity, these characteristics of geography and climate are reflected in the people's way of life. In the seven states that make up the Amazon region, there is both a low population density and a predominance of indigenous ethnic groups. Dance is a present and integral part of indigenous rituals and cannot be understood separately. Due to the migrations of these and other peoples who settled there for various motives, there are cultural crossovers between indigenous peoples, Afro-descendants, European descendants, and Asians, among others. Dances such as the *toré*, *carimbó*, *siriri*, **boi-bumbá**,

lundu, *marabaixa*, *batuque*, and a variety of other dances make up this amalgamation.

Northeast Region

The dances of the northeast region also reflect a geography, climate, and way of life. The northeast borders the northern region and brings characteristics from there, for example, the caboclinho dance of indigenous memorialization that was recognized in 2016 as intangible cultural heritage of Brazil. Most states in the northeast region have a semiarid, hot, and dry climate. Dances such as *xaxado*, *forró*, *quadrilhas juninas*, and **bumba-meu-boi** reflect the cattle culture of these places. There is tremendous diversity of dances, such as **tambor de crioula** (in the state of Maranhão), bumba-meu-boi (Maranhão, Pernambuco), *frevo* (Pernambuco), and samba de roda (Bahia), among others, that reflect significant elements of the region's African heritage. The northeast coast's topography, with its vast maritime area, is also revealed in characteristics of its respective dances.

Midwest Region

The dances from the midwest region bring characteristics from marshes, savannas, and mountains, and also influences of the cattle culture. Indigenous peoples are significant. The *Kuarup* ritual in honor of the dead takes place in the Xingu National Park and annually gathers ethnic groups such as Mehinako, Kuikuro, Waura, Aweti, Matipu, Kalapalo, Nahukuá, and Yawalapiti. Dances such as *catira* or *cateretê*, *sarandi*, and others reflect the intersections between subjects and cultures of the great migratory flows through this region over time.

Southeast Region

The southeast region is Brazil's financial, cultural, and tourist hub, comprising four abutting states—São Paulo, Minas Gerais, Rio de Janeiro, and Espírito Santo. São Paulo, the capital of the state of São Paulo, is Brazil's financial center; Minas Gerais is the industrial and mining center; and the coastal states of Rio de Janeiro and Espírito Santo boast vibrant cultural and tourism industries. Popularly known as the "Marvelous

City," the city of Rio de Janeiro boasts the iconic Christ the Redeemer statue and Sugarloaf Mountain that juts into the bay. In this southeastern region, we find the dances *moçambique* (São Paulo), *congadas* (Minas Gerais), and *jongo* (Rio de Janeiro and São Paulo), among others.

South Region

The south region of Brazil comprises three coastal states—Paraná, Santa Catarina, and Rio Grande do Sul, where Brazil borders Uruguay. From the early 1800s to the late 1900s, millions of Europeans immigrated to Brazil's southern region. Italians and Germans were among the largest representative populations, and areas today retain a strong Italian and German culture. Agriculture, livestock, textiles, manufacturing, and chemical industries dominate the southern region of Brazil. Considered by some to be "the breadbasket" of Brazil, a pro-secession movement that has long existed in this region prompted, as recently as 2017, a referendum-style vote for their independence from Brazil. In the western corner of Paraná, bordering Argentina and Paraguay, are the majestic Foz de Iguaçu, with hundreds of cascading waterfalls that stretch for over a mile and a half. In the south region, the dances of *chimarrita* (Rio Grande do Sul), *pau-de-tapes* (Rio Grande do Sul), *caninha verde* and *fandango* (Paraná and Rio Grande do Sul), *pezinho dance* (Rio Grande do Sul) of the "gaúcho" or southern American "cowboy" culture of the pampas are found.

 See resource 5.5 in HK*Propel* for web links.

African Dance in Brazil

From Colonization to the Present

With the invasion of Brazil by Europeans in the year 1500, the colonization of Brazil commenced. Initially disputed by Spaniards, Dutch, and Portuguese—the latter remaining in command of the vast territory—the construction project that was colonial Brazil is defined by the kidnapping and trafficking of millions of Africans of different ethnicities. The enslaved people were forced to work on the sugarcane and coffee plantations, in

the gold mines, in the opening and construction of roads and cities, in the Casa Grandes (plantation estates), and in all types of physical labor. Yet even in enslavement, these peoples made use of their greatest assets—their bodies, their knowledge, and their wisdom—and continued to perform their rituals of combat, sports, dances, songs, and religious devotion whenever possible.

Capoeira is a well-known example of Afro-Brazilian dance that emerged from the complex dynamics of enslavement as an Afro-Brazilian self-defense art form. Recreated by African peoples at least four centuries ago, capoeira was a response to their enslavement and their struggle for freedom. It is through bodily wisdom that the technique was developed, whereby the greatest archive of memory and secrets—the body—became a powerful weapon of defense and attack. The capoeira moves come from African games and rituals, and in Brazil, their creators observed the movements of animals, the waves of the sea, the movements of work tools, the passage to areas of difficult access. All of these lent their names to the gestures that make up capoeira's vast repertoire: monkey, camel, stingray's tail, leg, bolt, half-moon-of-compass, dodge, cutting grass, head butt, and countless others.

From the 1960s until today, capoeira has been widespread across five continents where schools, academies, social projects, and shows were founded. In Brazil, the practice of capoeira depends on historical circumstances and can reinvent itself and incorporate modern values. Three divisions of Brazilian capoeira are most prominent.

- **Capoeira angola** represents the maintenance of African values in performance and preservation under the guidance of old capoeira masters.
- **Capoeira regional** is a more modern form whose philosophy and practice incorporate elements of institutional structures such as the school model and some academic elements of university education that enable greater social inclusion.
- **Capoeira contemporânea**, a dissident from the Angola and Regional divisions, is more commercialized, embracing the values of the consumer, market, and competitive society.

Finally, from its philosophical, technical, aesthetic, and historical principles, capoeira draws

Capoeira in Brazil.

Phil Clarke Hill/In Pictures via Getty Images Images

important knowledge and skills which imply that the body is the only weapon used to confront its opponent, and the capoeira *roda* (circle) is the ritualized space for the application of this knowledge.

National Identity Through Dance and Traditional and Popular Cultural Expressions in the 1930s

In the late 1930s, the Brazilian political environment was ruled by the *Estado Novo* (the "new state"), an authoritarian regime, the perspective of which was the modernization and affirmation of a national identity through symbols that emphasized an idea of social representativeness, such as the practice of samba, soccer, and capoeira, among other cultural expressions. During this time, Brazil's president was the military dictator **Getúlio Vargas**, who added to his populist political strategy a nationalism that had "the face of

the people." This period is also marked by the decriminalization of Black religious cults, such as **Candomblés**, and of capoeira, as well as loosened restrictions on Carnival. There was also a certain openness to the arts and traditional cultures.

African cultural experience in Brazil endured many struggles, reconstruction, and strategies to secure a permanence that represented a long process of cultural resistance. In the country's dance history and literature, work by many groups goes unreported: Black resistance groups in Afro-Brazilian religions such as the Candomblés, **Umbandas**, **Caboclos terreiros**; artistic and cultural institutions and associations, such as the **samba schools** (escolas de samba), **Afoxés**, **Blocos Afro**, and others; and dancers, choreographers, groups, and Afro dance companies. Only after the 1990s did the first critical writings emerge, coming from academic research carried out by the protagonists of Black militancy.

In the 21st century, the contribution of dances and cultural manifestations in this area results in a process that offers aesthetic and political

67

dialogues in a critical, conscious, and humanizing way.

 See resource 5.6 in HK*Propel* for web links.

Crosscurrents

Dance from the contemporary and avant-garde perspective is, at its essence, a break from conventional models. It is based on a revolutionary, ephemeral desire for freedom from techniques that highlight physical rigor and discipline. Technological advances, new means of communication, and globalization are some of the factors that corroborate this more introspective, individualistic, and minimalist tendency. Obviously, there are contradictions, since the desire for separation from traditional values does not prevent the possibility of new meanings for traditional dance in contemporary times. For example, recall how the tucandeira (stinging ants) ritual dance is now employed to fight corporate and government incursions on indigenous lands that are fueled by global economic trends and foreign rapaciousness. At the other end of the spectrum are Brazil's Carnival and capoeira culture, exports and representations of Brazil to the world.

The complex dynamics of Brazilian dance history have long intertwined with those of other countries, including the United States. Such interactions resonate through contemporary dance, engaging the dominance/dependence model (discussed earlier with respect to the United States), and illuminating unique opportunities for expanding the cultural reach and impact of Brazilian dance. Anthropologist and dancer Katherine Dunham's presence in Brazil is a key example of influences flowing from the United States in the mid-20th century; it highlights how complex issues such as racism played out in cultural exchanges. Indeed, the crosscurrents of contemporary dance seem to have provided a way for many otherwise repressed aspects of Brazilian dance culture to become visible and legitimized, under the aegis of individual artistic vision.

With modernity and the ease of travel among people from different countries, many people choose to live, educate themselves, and create in places around the globe far from where they originated. Dance knowledge follows this flux. Bodies cross borders and experience different techniques. People—and their ideas—immerse themselves in the existential dilemmas of the world and express themselves through artistic discourse.

Katherine Dunham teaching Brazilian dances to fellow actress.

Bettmann/Getty Images

Katherine Dunham and Racism in Brazil

When American anthropologist, choreographer, and activist Katherine Dunham took her dance company to São Paulo, Brazil, to perform in 1950, the Esplanada Hotel refused to house her upon learning she was Black. She threatened a lawsuit, and the streets of São Paulo filled with protestors to support her cause. Brazil's legislature quickly banned racial discrimination. To this day, all São Paulo elevators contain notices stating the prohibition against discrimination. Dunham's influence is present, even if her name is not officially attached (Das, 2018).

See resource 5.7 in HK*Propel* for web links.

Summary

From pre-Columbian times to the 21st century, Brazilian dance informs our understanding of the nation's history and culture. The complexities of ethnic identities; the repression of indigenous peoples and of Africans and their descendants, along with European domination; the emergence of a "national identity" discourse; and contemporary trends of globalization all play out through the dances that continue to represent Brazil to itself and the world. The aesthetic, subtle, and varied dance forms shift and position themselves in the world, reinforcing their importance as wisdom and memories that speak for themselves and for many bygone generations.

Discussion Questions

1. In understanding the characteristics of the historical, cultural, educational, and social trajectories of the dances in Brazil, what values can be highlighted in terms of their contribution to society?

2. Considering the large financial investments for shows such as *Carnival* in Brazil and, in contrast, the social inequalities that exist in the country, in what way can dance contribute to changing this reality?

3. When watching one of the suggested dance videos about the various trends present in Brazil, what are some characteristics that are similar to and different from your country's dance expressions?

 Visit HK*Propel* for access to this chapter's Application Activity.

Selected Glossary

bumba-meu-boi—A dance-drama with social criticism and audience participation. With characters both human and animal, performers of this Brazilian folkloric form enact various levels of social commentary through a story centered on the death and resurrection of an ox. Bumba-meu-boi is the second biggest folklore festival in Brazil, after Carnival.

caboclinhos/caboclinhas—Men and women performers embodying popular Brazilian manifestation of indigenous reminiscences present in some regions of the country, mainly in the Northeast.

Candomblé—An African-Brazilian religion in which the orixás, deities linked to nature, are worshipped in Brazil, with a diversity of national roots in Angola, Jeje, Keto, Nago, and Caboclo. In the hierarchy of positions and **Candomblé** doctrine, there are the "families-of-saints," as a way of reconnecting Africans across the African diaspora.

capoeira—Created during the 16th century as a form of self-defense by enslaved Africans in Brazil, capoeira is an Afro-Brazilian martial art representing the struggle for freedom. As a technical, aesthetic, and cultural language, it blends dance, athleticism, acrobatics, theatrics, song, and instrumentation, and is performed by pairs inside a circle of capoeira performers. The berimbau is the single-string percussive instrument played during the capoeira fight.

Carnival/Carnaval—Originating as a Roman Catholic festival in Europe, Carnival came to Brazil through Portuguese colonialism and has grown to be the largest such event in the world. The word "Carnival" comes from the Latin term "carnelevare" (meaning "to remove meat"). The festival of parades and street parties with elaborate costumes and masks precedes the Lenten season of austerity and restraint that culminates in Easter. Samba is the signature music and dance of Brazilian Carnival.

Casa Grandes—Farms with large houses of the planters in the period of European colonization and enslavement of Africans in Brazil.

Mercedes Baptista—An important master in Afro dance in Brazil, she was the first Black dancer to join the Municipal Ballet Theater of Rio de Janeiro. She later founded the Mercedes Baptista Folk Ballet in 1953 in the city of Rio de Janeiro.

samba—A rhythm, music, and dance genre of Angolan origin that recasts itself in Brazil; capitalizing on the significant tradition of Brazilian dance and music, samba is a national symbol and the single most important popular dance manifestation in Brazil. There are many variations and styles of samba (dance) throughout Brazil, such as samba de roda, samba do pé, samba pagode, and samba de gafieira.

Sateré-Mawé—An indigenous ethnic group of the Amazon region.

tucandeira—Species of ants used in sacred indigenous rituals.

Selected References and Resources

Achcar, Dalal. 1980. *Ballet, Art, Technique, Interpretation*. Rio de Janeiro: Brazilian Company of Graphic Arts.

Araújo, Lauana Vilaronga Cunha de. 2008. "Poetic Strategies in Times of Dictatorship: The Experience of the Experimental Dance Group of Salvador-Ba." 282f. Dissertation (Master in Performing Arts) Postgraduate Program in Performing Arts, School of Theater, Federal University of Bahia, Salvador, 2008.

Boccanera Junior, Silio. 2008. *Theater in Bahia: From Colony to Republic 1800-1925*. 2nd.ed. Salvador: Eduneb/Edufba.

Biriba, Raissa Conrado. 2019. "Salvador Dance Performances: An Analysis of the Contemporary Scene of Choreographic Works in Salvador." / BA. Dissertation (Master, Multidisciplinary Graduate Program in Culture and Society)—Federal University of Bahia, Institute of Humanities, Arts and Sciences Prof Milton Santos—IHAC, Salvador, 2019.

Brazilian Institute of Geography and Statistics. "Projection of Brazil and the Brazilian States by Population." www.ibge.gov.br/apps/populacao/projecao/index.html (7 mar 21).

Conrado, A.V.S. "Afro-Brazilian Dance as Black Activism." 2018. In *Dancing Bahia: Essays on Afro-Brazilian Dance, Education, Memory, and Race*, edited by L.M. Suarez, A. Conrado, and Y. Daniel. Chicago, USA / Bristol, UK: Intellect, pp. 17-38.

Das, Joanna Dee. "Katherine Dunham: The Artist as Activist." https://humanities.wustl.edu/features/Joanna-Dee-Das-Katherine-Dunham-Artist-Activist (2-9-18) Human Ties Features

Luz, Marco Aurélio de Oliveira. 2017. Agadá: Dynamics of African-Brazilian Civilization. 4a.ed. Salvador: Edufba.

Monteiro, Marianna F. Martins. 2011. *Popular Dance: Show and Devotion*. São Paulo: Third Name.

Munduruku, Daniel, and Mauritius Negro (Illustrator). 2018. *O Karaíba: A History of Pre-Brazil*. São Paulo: Editora.

Robatto, Lia and Mascarenhas, Lúcia. 2002. *Steps of the Dance—Bahia*. Casa de Jorge Amado Foundation. Melhoramentos, Salvador-Bahia.

Rodrigues, Nina. 1988. *Africans in Brazil*. 7.ed. São Paulo:Ed.Nacional [Brasília]. Ed.Universidade de Brasília.

Suárez, Lucia M. 2013. "Inclusion in Motion: Cultural Agency Through Dance in Bahia, Brazil." *Transforming Anthropology*, vol. 21, no. 2, pp.153-168. American Anthropological Association.

Vicenzia, Ida. 1997. *Dance in Brazil*. National Art Foundation—Funarte. Rio de Janeiro, RJ.

PART III

Caribbean

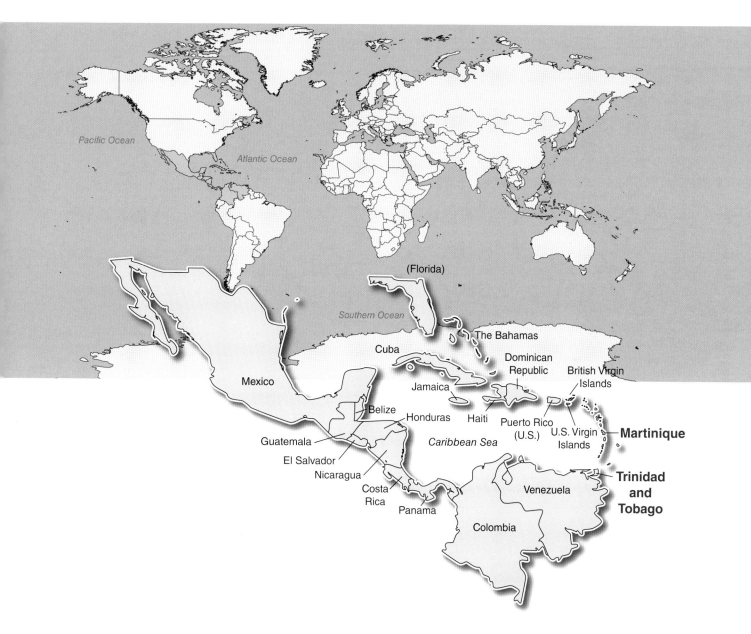

Dance cultures of the Caribbean reflect the aftermath of European colonialism, an intermingling of peoples from around the globe, and the challenges of independence for small nations in a vulnerable physical and economic environment. The Triangular Trade route between the Americas, West Africa, and Europe was a lucrative practice for colonial powers that traded enslaved Africans for the sugar, cotton, and other materials that their forced labor produced in the islands. Britain, Spain, France, Holland, and Denmark were the primary colonizers in the region, building sugar-producing empires as they expanded slavery and decimated indigenous populations on the islands. In response, marginalized and enslaved peoples used their dances as accommodation, imitation, and resistance to express their cultural identity and aid their survival under harsh conditions. While Spanish colonialism characterizes several islands in the Greater Antilles, such as Cuba, Hispaniola, and Puerto Rico, in this part we encounter Martinique and Trinidad-Tobago, both in the Lesser Antilles. Dance cultures in these islands illuminate patterns primarily of French and British colonization as they likewise reflect the uniquely Caribbean dance culture of the entire region.

 HK*Propel* includes web links to additional resources for this section.

6

Bèlè Drum-Dance Culture in Martinique

Camee Maddox-Wingfield

Learning Objectives

After reading this chapter you will be able to do the following:

- Identify the primary historical processes and cultural geographic factors that shaped the development of bèlè in the Caribbean region, and specifically in Martinique.
- Summarize the different performance contexts where bèlè has been practiced in the past and present-day Martinique.
- Analyze the sociopolitical realities of Martinique that are reflected in bèlè's decline and subsequent revival.
- Recognize and describe the different sociocultural functions of bèlè performance in contemporary Martinique.

Key Terms

Code Noir—Set of rules established in 1685 by King Louis XIV in French colonies to enforce the conversion and baptism of enslaved Africans.

danm bèlè—Female dance partner.

kavalyé—Male dance partner.

marronage—The enactment of resistance to oppression, particularly colonial or racist oppression, both small-scale (*petit marronage*) and large-scale (*grand marronage*).

tanbou bèlè—A goat-skinned conical drum that rests horizontally on its side and is straddled by the drummer.

A Bèlè Event

It is a mild summer evening just after nightfall and the sound of drums and call-and-response singing echo through the hills of a mountainside community. The moonlit open-air **swaré bèlè** event gathers bèlè practitioners from all over the island to honor the rich complex of ancestral drum-dance traditions through a spontaneous, unscripted rotation of performers.

On the ground-level dance floor are eight dancers in female/male pairs, four percussionists, a lead singer, and a chorus of background singers, surrounded by an audience of onlookers and fellow bèlè performers. As dancers take their turns on the dance floor, a captivating game ensues between the **danm bèlè** (female bèlè dancer) and her **kavalyé** (male dance partner). Through their danced interactions, it becomes clear that the danm bèlè has a special command over the encounter. She is beautifully adorned in a long, brightly colored dress, and the required **carré madras** "handkerchief"—a square piece of checkered fabric folded into a triangle—is tied around her waist.

Face-to-face with her kavalyé, she uses a range of facial expressions, strategic maneuvers, and playful devices. Her coquettish dance behaviors are reinforced by the reactions of her kavalyé and the observing public. One moment she gazes at her kavalyé, encouraging him to pursue with her inviting smile; then she abruptly switches it up with a conceited glare, daring him to come closer. She flutters her long, wide skirt as a prop for flirtatious play, while executing isolated hip rotations and side-to-side waist ticks, all while striking the ground with her bare feet perfectly in sync with the drummer's rhythmic breaks. Spectators wait in suspense to see the outcome of this flirtatious game.

The kavalyé makes his first advance, but she eludes him with a smooth dodging maneuver to enjoy a brief moment of play with the drummer. As their dance encounter comes to an end, she pulls her kavalyé in for a close embrace, grabs him by his waist and offers a light pelvic thrust. As she retreats from her kavalyé, who is overcome with satisfaction, she dances back to her place in the outer circle, clearing the dance space for the next pair of dancers in the sequence. The audience goes wild with applause and laughter.

 See resource 6.1 in HK*Propel* for web links.

In contemporary Martinique, *bèlè* is not simply the name of a traditional dance; the term *bèlè* is used to describe *an mannyè viv*, a way of life that is organized around participation in the island's rich complex of Afro-Creole drum-dance practices. The dynamics that shape Martinique's dance culture are complex and can be best understood through an exploration of Martinican bèlè, from the past to present day. Despite the tradition's near erasure from Martinican public life, especially in the years following World War II when the island fully integrated with the French state through a process known as **departmentalization**, bèlè and its associated practices like *ladja*/*danmyé* and *kalennda* flourish today within a community of devoted cultural activists working to preserve Martinique's Afro-Caribbean cultural heritage.

Because bèlè is a folk tradition partially adapted from European court dances by enslaved Africans, and several versions of bèlè can be found across different island communities, the story of bèlè's origins during the slavery era is fraught with conjecture about accommodation, imitation, and resistance. Some perspectives suggest that enslaved Africans and free people of color sought to replicate the styles and mannerisms of the white planter class when they danced the **quadrilles** (European court dance using a square configuration) of the local bourgeoisie with the goal of distancing themselves from African traditions and assimilating elitist European norms. Other perspectives suggest that mimicry and parody were at play when enslaved Africans danced the quadrille. With these different perspectives in mind, the legacy of bèlè in Martinique can be interpreted as a story of creative duplicity, resilience, and camouflaged protest under the dreadful conditions of slavery.

Martinique is an overseas department of France located in the Lesser **Antilles**—a group of islands comprising the eastern Caribbean archipelago. Originally inhabited by Arawak and Carib indigenous peoples, the island was settled in the 17th century by the **Compagnie des îles d'Amérique** (Company of American Islands), facing an intense period of colonization by France and participation in the transatlantic slave trade until the 1848 abolition. In 1946, the island fully integrated with the French state as a ***département d'outre mèr*** (DOM, overseas department).

Today, the population is estimated to be about 375,000, with a majority (85%) of African-descended Martinicans (Black and ***métis*** [mixed]). There is also a small population of Indo-Martinicans, the community formed by East Indian indentured labor migrants following the end of slavery. A small minority (5%) of the population, white ***békés***, are the descendants of colonial slave owners—planters who have maintained their concentration of wealth and status in the island's racialized social class hierarchy. Additionally, there is a small percentage of white island residents from metropolitan France, along with small Syrian, Lebanese, and Chinese ethnic communities. Like other Caribbean island societies, Martinique is characterized by diglossic (dual language) speech communities, with French designated as the official language and Martinican Creole (***Kréyòl***) spoken in a variety of contexts.

Martinique, a volcanic island that stretches about 425 square miles, has a mountainous northern region with dense lush vegetation, rainforests, and black volcanic sand beaches. In the south of the island, there is a landscape of hills and open pastures, mangroves, and popular tourist beach towns. The northern **communes** (municipalities) of Sainte-Marie and Basse-Pointe, and the southern commune of Les Anses-d'Arlet, are the most prominently known hometowns of different regional bèlè variants performed on the island today.

Defining Bèlè as a Regional Folk Tradition

Bèlè is a Caribbean dance term that generically refers to a group of folk traditions that were influenced by the **contredanse** (European country dances) and the quadrille and most visibly integrated African aesthetics, movement styles, and musical accompaniment (Cyrille 2009; Daniel 2009, 2010, 2011; Wason 2010). Bèlè traditions include elements of European court dances but communicate different attitudes and values

rooted in Afro-Caribbean cultural sensibilities. Different dances with the name bèlè exist in various Caribbean locales, and although these adaptations share overlapping historical processes and stylistic qualities that traversed the region with interisland circulation and travel during the colonial era, each island's bèlè tradition is performed differently. Variations of bèlè share the same basic logic, involving dance partners who playfully interact with one another in the center of a circle through intricate foot patterns, dynamic arm movements, turns, and bent-knee flat-footed body orientation. The playful and, at times, competitive interactive style between dance partners is reminiscent of the **Congo minuet**. Through expressions of salutation, dancers also interact with the drummers who provide polyrhythmic drum patterns based on the dancers' movements.

In bèlè traditions, the ***tanbou*** goat-skinned conical drum is played alongside call-and-response singing with a lead singer and a chorus of background singers. In Martinican bèlè, there is also the added ***tibwa*** percussive element—two wooden sticks that are beaten on the side of the drum with a steady tempo. The performing ensemble of dancers, drummers, and singers is normally encircled by a crowd of participating spectators who clap their hands, sway their bodies, and join in by singing the song's refrain. When functioning together in harmony, all of these elements provide the spirited energy that is required for a successful bèlè event.

Bèlè is understood to have its creole origins in the French colonies of Grenada, Saint-Domingue (present-day Haiti), Martinique, and Guadeloupe, and to have later traveled to other Caribbean island territories that were once occupied by French settlers, including Saint Lucia, Dominica, Carriacou, and Trinidad (Franco 1999; Johnson 2012). Some studies of bèlè argue that the dances are adaptations of African mating, fertility, and harvest dances that integrated Western European dance elements of 18th century quadrille and contredanse performance (Honychurch 1988, 63). In societies where both quadrille and bèlè exist, it is clear that the two dances have absorbed elements of one another (Wason 2010, 227). Unlike the more African-influenced bèlè that is accompanied by goat-skinned drums and other percussive instruments, traditional quadrille performance is accompanied by melodic instruments, and is danced with an erect body orientation, moderate foot and arm movements, and simple turns and curtsies between partners—characteristics that signified elegance and grace according to the Eurocentric aesthetic standards that established a prevailing dance hierarchy. If we think of Caribbean quadrilles as a dance spectrum, with some variations being more African influenced, and others more European, Martinique's bèlè repertoire has dance elements that are more recognizably inherited from West and Central African cultures.

 See resource 6.2 in HK*Propel* for web links.

Question of Origins

African or European, Resistance or Accommodation?

There are different interpretations regarding the etymology of bèlè, which include explanations based on the French term **belair** (meaning *pretty tunes*) and the Congolese dance terms **boela** and **mbele**. Not surprisingly, some dance and music forms in Martinique can be traced to specific peoples in regions of West and Central Africa that played prominently in the French slave trade. For example, some characteristics of bèlè correspond to the boela and mbele, dances that a British

missionary observed among the **Bakongo** peoples of southern Congo during the late 19th century. Similarly, the drum techniques used in bèlè share commonalities with those of the **Baaka** people in Congo. But identifying those elements that appear to have origins in West-Central African dance and music culture is only part of the challenge of tracing origins. The quadrille styles imported from Europe during the colonial era also left an imprint on the spatial configurations used in the bèlè group dances observed today in Martinique.

Dances of Assimilation, Imitation, and Resistance

European court dances that used both square and line group formations arrived in the Antilles from France through colonial settlement (Cyrille 2009). In many of these colonial contexts, the objective was to eradicate African dance behaviors and replace them with more "restrained European attitudes" (192). These dances were also for the enjoyment of the French planter class and aristocrats who craved Parisian entertainment and leisure. It was popularly believed by colonial observers that free people of color and enslaved Africans imitated the quadrille as

Dance partners engage in the playful exchange that characterizes the square *quadrille* configuration of bèlè linò.

Photo courtesy of Benny René-Charles

a way of distancing themselves from the African expressive practices that were prohibited by law and repressed by slave codes like the **Code Noir**. In the pursuit of upward mobility, it would have made sense for free people of color to imitate court dances in order to align themselves with their elite counterparts. For enslaved people, however, it is likely that parody, mimicry, and resistance played a role in their performance of these quadrille-based dances.

Disfiguring the colonists' most esteemed and cherished traditions brought some degree of agency in an institution that generally denied Black humanity. The dancing body of the enslaved Black person—with its animation and its "celebration of excess" (Gikandi 2011, 280)—was the antithesis of European cultural sensibilities of proper etiquette and reserved behavior. Another perspective argues that Black people appropriated elements of European court dance as a strategy to disguise their ritual worship practices that were outlawed under slavery (Cyrille 2002, 224). If they could execute sacred rituals under the guise of the quadrille, their practices would not be easily targeted and punished by the authorities. To outside observers, it would simply appear as though the slaves were amusing themselves for entertainment.

Community Performance Rituals: Bamboulas

Scholars often point to the **bamboulas** that were common during the slavery era to explain how bèlè developed into the variations observed in Martinique today. Bamboulas were "community performance rituals" held on weekends and holidays when the enslaved were permitted to socialize, and they were commonly organized by **mutual aid societies** whose traditions promoted solidarity and reciprocity for the Black community (Desch-Obi 2008, 127). These bamboulas provided the blueprint for the rural organization of the Martinican swaré bèlè tradition (Gerstin 1996, 117). By the early 19th century, Blacks in the rural plantation settings of Martinique had adopted the spatial choreography of European quadrille and merged it with the African-based musical expression of drumming and call-and-response singing that was traditionally used in bamboula gatherings.

Mutual Aid Societies

During slavery, mutual aid associations, known in the French colonies as *sociétés*, were in place to raise money and purchase freedom for the enslaved, pay for burial arrangements, practice worship and religious activities in a concealed environment, and organize entertainment events.

Bèlè as Communal Work Activity

Even though many African-derived music and dance practices were prohibited, particularly when they served religious purposes, they were certainly permitted, and even encouraged, when they served labor purposes because they helped to enhance slaves' productivity and generate revenue for planters. Beyond imitation, accommodation, and camouflaged resistance, enslaved Africans also practiced bèlè as a communal work activity (Gerstin 1996; Wason 2010). Work-related group expressions that form the foundation of bèlè include **belairs d'ateliers** and **belairs des coups de mains** (or **koudmèn** in Kréyòl) (Rosemain 1986). Belairs d'ateliers were improvised songs and dances that accompanied plantation work and helped to keep field laborers in sync while executing tasks, like tilling soil, clearing fields, cutting cane, and grating manioc (1986, 51). Belairs des coups de mains were song and dance gatherings that accompanied smaller group work in gardens, on provision grounds, or in any other mutual aid activity outside of the forced labor complex of plantation work that served the planters for economic gain.

According to elders of the bèlè tradition, bèlè is **une danse de la terre**—a dance of the land and earth. It was practiced by enslaved agricultural laborers who toiled to the sound of the bèlè drum and danced as a source of release after a hard day's work. Many of the dance movements in today's bèlè repertoire of gestures represent motions carried out in agricultural labor. The **tonbé-lévé** movement, for example, whereby the dancer leans forward and backward while stamping their feet and swinging their arms forward and backward alternately, reenacts the movement of cutting sugarcane (one hand is holding the stalk of cane while the other arm swings the machete in a steady, rhythmic pattern). **Grajé** is the name of another movement, whereby the repetitive pattern of the dancer's feet rubbing the ground evokes the image of grating manioc.

 See resource 6.3 in HK*Propel* for web links.

Bèlè Performance Contexts in Contemporary Martinique

The public performance of bèlè in contemporary Martinique is sustained by the swaré bèlè system—nocturnal, participatory events whereby "initiated" (experienced) dancers, drummers, and singers come together to play bèlè until the early hours of the morning. These events typically begin around seven o'clock in the evening, and, depending on the number of performers, can end anywhere from one to three o'clock in the morning. Swaré bèlè performance gatherings are ceremonially organized to uphold the values of mutual aid, collectivity, and solidarity that are instilled in bèlè schools. These events also provide a space to pay homage to the ancestors and Martinique's cultural heroes, as well as to protest the legacies of racism, colonialism, and capitalism.

Bèlè Linò

The typical swaré bèlè gathering follows a distinct sequence of performances, beginning with a few matches of ladja (also called danmyé), a martial art tradition between two combatants in the center of a circle. These matches help to warm up the energy of the space and get the audience excited about the night's events. The remainder of the event functions through an improvised, unscripted rotation of performers playing and dancing sets from the **bèlè linò** repertoire. Bèlè linò (also known as **bèlè samaritain**) are a set of six bèlè dance/music styles from the commune Sainte-Marie (municipality on the northern coast of Martinique) and surrounding communities. These dances use the quadrille configuration of pairing four **danm** (female dancers) with four **kavalyé** (male dancers). Opening with a circular

procession called the **wondi-dewondi**, the dancers move counterclockwise, then clockwise before returning to their original positions and dancing with their partners in squares (**carré**). After each of the two carré squares have completed their sequence, each pair dances a **monté o tanbou** sequence, whereby the two dancers come together in the center of the circle for a playful exchange, then dance toward the drummers to give them a salutation.

Among the many bèlè variations in Martinique, several bèlè linò styles are most commonly taught in bèlè schools and frequently performed in public bèlè gatherings such as swaré bèlè: Bèlè (a dance with explosive energy); *gran bèlè* (solemn circle dance); and *bélya* (a call to assemble that also expresses hope).

After several hours of bèlè linò rotations in an event, the performance concludes with a segment of **lalin klè**, which is a set of "full moon" group dances: Partners bump each other to the chant "zip, zap, zabap" (**mabèlo**); ballroom style movements flow in double line formation (*kannigwé*) and single and double-line variants (*bénézwel*); women use **bidjin bal** side-to-side motion derived from the popular **biguine** social dance).

Other bèlè and kalennda variations are practiced in Martinique today but appear less frequently in swaré bèlè gatherings. Occasionally, swaré events are dedicated exclusively to one of these practices (such as the annual swaré kalennda held by the cultural association **AM4**).

 See resource 6.4 in HK*Propel* for web links.

Bèlè's Pre-Revival Eclipse in Martinique

For **Antilleans** (Caribbean islanders) living in France's overseas departments, French national belonging is ideologically premised on a model of cultural assimilation (Daniel 2001; Browne 2004; Agard-Jones 2009; Bonilla 2015). In the years following Martinique's 1946 departmentalization, island residents faced tremendous pressure to follow French values and norms, alongside local struggles to define and assert Martinican cultural specificity (Price 1998; Beriss 2004). During the post-WWII era, Afro-Creole traditions, such as those associated with bèlè, danmyé, and kalennda

Cultural Highlight

ÉMILE "TI-ÉMILE" CASÉRUS

The renowned bèlè singer **Émile "Ti-Émile" Casérus** and other members of the Casérus family were recruited from their countryside homes in Sainte-Marie to perform bèlè on the city stages of Fort-de-France and on cruise ships filled with tourists. Ti-Émile founded and led the professional performance troupes *Les Foulards Jaunes* (later named *Lévé Yo Ka*) and *La Fleur Créole*. Bèlè was preserved during this time thanks to the early audio recordings of Ti-Émile and other prominent bèlè families from Sainte-Marie, as well as the cultural programming initiatives of Aimé Césaire during his tenure as mayor of Fort-de-France. Despite these efforts to valorize the bèlè heritage of Martinique, the overwhelming majority of Martinicans held the perception that these traditions were backward, outdated symbols of Martinique's troubled past.

 See resource 6.5 in HK*Propel* for web links.

were discouraged, while French media, art, education, and consumption practices were firmly planted in Martinique's institutions—what Martinican intellectuals referred to as "cultural genocide," or "genocide by substitution" (Burton 1995, 5; Glissant 1981, 173). Families with children during this period of intense assimilation raised them to identify as French and prohibited them from practicing drum traditions. They associated bèlè with negative stereotypes, such as **bagay vyé nèg**—a pejorative Kréyòl expression for old, unsophisticated aspects of Black culture—or **bagay ki ja pasé**—something of the past, or antiquated.

The bèlè tradition survived this post-war eclipse on the peripheries of Martinican public life through the performances of folkloric troupes whose theatrical renditions of bèlè were geared toward the tourist market. The **Groupe Folklorique Martiniquais**, established the same year as Martinique's departmentalization in 1946, was known for performing folk traditions such as the *biguine*, **mazurka**, and **valse** (waltz) in staged productions.

Professional folkloric troupes gave rural tradition bearers and performers the opportunity to establish urban reputations for themselves and for their drum-dance practices. Many of those performers were from celebrated bèlè families of the northern Atlantic commune Sainte-Marie, the home of bèlè linò that was relatively accessible from the capital city Fort-de-France.

 See resource 6.6 in HK*Propel* for web links.

Bèlè's Revitalization, Cultural Activism, and Pedagogy

In the early 1980s, a group of young activist-intellectuals returned to their island home following years of university study in Paris. Disillusioned by their experiences with racism, cultural alienation, and second-class treatment in the metropole, and newly radicalized by leftist political ideology, these activists went back to Martinique with a mission to merge cultural activities with anti-colonial political engagement. In collaboration with other local youth organizations, they cultivated relationships with elders and tradition-bearers who passed on their knowledge of the bèlè culture that had nearly vanished over the course of the mid-20th century. Setting themselves apart from professional folkloric performance troupes, the revivalists used a grassroots-oriented approach to promote bèlè through the formation of various community-based cultural associations.

Since the 1980s' launch of the bèlè revival movement, cultural activists have worked to reverse negative stereotypes and promote more affirming images of the bèlè tradition. They have created several bèlè schools and developed a rigorously codified dance pedagogy based on the repertoire of bèlè movements and gestures. They maintain the public performance of these traditions through the swaré bèlè performance

Dancers performing at a swaré bèlè gathering in Martinique, 2019.

Photo courtesy of Benny René-Charles

network. Unlike professional folkloric troupes that perform Martinique's traditional culture in staged, choreographed renditions, the swaré bèlè functions through an unscripted rotation of initiated practitioners. For the most part, these practitioners span three generations, categorized as *la jeunesse* (the youth), *les djoubaté* (the revivalists), and *les anciens* (the elders). Most of the elders come from modest rural backgrounds, having worked as agricultural laborers in the past. The revivalists and youth who were initiated into bèlè through participation in contemporary bèlè school settings, however, come from all social strata and educational backgrounds.

Though the swaré bèlè space is not explicitly connected to religious practice, it is ceremonially organized to uphold a distinct set of values and ethics instilled in bèlè schools, fostering a unique sense of community belonging and cultural citizenship. These events are typically organized and hosted by bèlè cultural associations spanning the island's urban and rural towns. Leaders of these associations have implemented the **larèl swaré bèlè**, a protocol of best practices to ensure the success of bèlè events, centering moral and ethical commitments to mutual aid, collective work, and solidarity, as well as humility and respect for elders. Devoted practitioners are expected to adhere to this honor code, particularly when it involves the age hierarchy and skill level in the rotation of performers. The swaré bèlè space is enlivened by an energy that pays reverence to the ancestors and ignites a spirit of embodied resistance to oppression and suffering.

The **moman bèlè** operates similarly to swaré bèlè but requires less planning and does not formally impose the strict protocol used in the organization of a traditional swaré bèlè. Participation is open to different skill levels, including beginners who wish to apply what they have learned in bèlè schools to live performance gatherings. Most practitioners would agree that moman bèlè is more relaxed and convivial because there is less pressure to follow protocol, adhere to strict moral codes, and compete with other dancers for a spot in the rotation.

Although each association maintains its own identity, many of them tend to promote some form of nationalism to their members, and there is some variation in their perspectives around how bèlè should be transmitted to wider publics and future generations. Overall, the associations are united in their mission of empowering the people of Martinique. Many associations have bèlè schools where they teach dance and drum classes one to two days a week to groups of enrolled students who pay membership fees to sign up for classes. They have developed their own unique approaches to pedagogy and transmission, and some have contributed to a codified repertoire of movements for the various bèlè styles that they teach.

Some of the larger associations perform choreographed concerts (*les spectacles*) inspired by the movement repertoires, music, and characteristic spirit of bèlè. The associations that produce in this genre of performance aim to draw a distinction between their performative work and the work of folkloric troupes. The goal of the grassroots cultural associations is to develop the local arts scene and promote a sense of cultural nationalism, with performance themes that draw attention to social, political, and economic issues and reflect everyday realities on the island, while folkloric troupes primarily target and cater to tourist markets in ways that are perceived to reproduce stereotypes of Antillean culture.

 **See resource 6.7 in HK*Propel* for web links.**

Annual Holidays and Observances

There are specific holidays throughout the year that involve high participation in bèlè activities. *Samedi Gloria* (Holy Saturday), as the first Saturday following the 40-day observance of Lent in this predominantly Catholic society, is one such holiday. During Lent, all dance parties (including bèlè) are suspended; therefore, practitioners look forward to this day to resume their dance gatherings. Religious holidays, such as *Fêtes Patronales* (patron saint feasts), Samedi Gloria, and *Lundi Paques* (Easter Monday), hold special importance for ladja/danmyé combatants, especially those who spend the period of Lent recharging their

strength and physically, spiritually, and mentally preparing themselves for a day of fighting in connection with the holiday.

Martinique's annual observance of Emancipation Day on 22 Mé (May 22) is another festive occasion for bèlè community members, particularly to honor the legendary act of **Romain**, an enslaved man whose public defiance of the prohibition against drumming and subsequent arrest ignited the 1848 rebellion that marked the end of slavery. Much like Samedi Gloria, 22 Mé activities are organized morning, noon, and night in different island communes, and the drum is revered as a heroic emblem of liberation.

 See resource 6.8 in HK*Propel* for web links.

Bèlè: A Celebration of the Life Cycle

Bèlè is acclaimed as a dance of the earth. Many followers use bèlè to memorialize deceased loved ones, particularly those who contributed to the bèlè movement, as well as to welcome new life, to rejoice in love and nuptial rites, and to animate birthday parties. Some pregnant women dance bèlè to prepare their bodies for labor, because the movements help those muscles that are used in giving birth. In most Afro-Caribbean funeral traditions, drum, dance, and storytelling are characteristic of the traditional wake ceremony, and bèlè is said to have historically played such a role in Martinique.

Crosscurrents

While members of the bèlè community share the common objective of diffusing the tradition and advancing knowledge of the island's drum-dance heritage, the contemporary bèlè revival movement has generated a set of debates that persist around how the bèlè tradition should be transmitted and what social functions bèlè should serve in Martinican society. Given the sociopolitical realities of Martinique's ongoing relationship with France, cultural activists often question whether bèlè is truly an expression of resistance and liberation that should operate within, or entirely subvert, the French system of institutions and values that have taken root on the island. These debates appear most prominently in the discourse around (a) political activism, (b) local economic development, (c) conceptions of spirituality and religion, (d) expressions of gender and sexuality, and (e) approaches to pedagogy and educational curriculum. These debates suggest that the contemporary bèlè revival movement contributes to the formation of a distinctive Martinican cultural citizenship and plays an important role in coping with the feelings of cultural alienation experienced by many Martinicans.

Leaders of the bèlè revival have focused on bèlè's potential for refashioning political and economic sensibilities. This was evident in 2009 when a 38-day general strike was mobilized in Martinique, paralyzing the island's economy for more than a month. The strikes led to riots, curfews, and protests against economic exploitation. During the strike, cultural activists and artists became engaged in ways that electrified the public with the performance of local drum-dance expressions and protest songs. Protest repertoires were ignited by the sound of the bèlè drum, with dances and danmyé fights in the streets filling the air with a rebellious energy. The mobilization of bèlè as an expression of protest continues to appear in Martinique to confront local issues of racial injustice and global systems of anti-Blackness, aligning with the current international movement in solidarity with Black lives.

As mentioned above, many bèlè cultural associations ideologically subscribe to some form of cultural nationalism. However, the degrees to which they desire political sovereignty vary. While some wish to see Martinique pursue independence from France, others are more invested in seeing Martinique achieve a greater degree of autonomy within, rather than apart from, the French state. And still others have leftist political orientations in the struggle for greater class equality and fair labor practices, denouncing capitalist exploitation and imploring community members to support local economic production. Bèlè activists are known to gather with their drums and dances in front of large corporate retailers to protest high costs of products, low salaries, and poor treatment of workers who occupy lower-ranking positions in the racialized division of labor.

With regard to religion and spirituality, there is an increasing visibility of bèlè performance in the Catholic church (Maddox-Wingfield 2021). This fusion genre, called **bèlè légliz** (church bèlè) is an attempt to refashion the liturgy with Afro-Martinican cultural references that were once prohibited by the dominant religious order. Debates question whether bèlè proponents should seek recognition by a religious institution that historically repressed the tradition, and if bèlè légliz is compatible with the movement's larger quest for **marronage** (resistance).

Juxtaposed with bèlè légliz, one finds a philosophical orientation and worldview that honors African and Black diaspora religion and spirituality. A subset of bèlè activists engages this perspective by observing the rituals, practices, and symbols of ancestor reverence, **Haitian Vodou**, **Cuban Santería**, **Brazilian Candomblé**, and Martinique's conjure tradition **quimbois**. The cosmologies of African and Afro-Caribbean religious practices are important emblems of Black spiritual authenticity for many individuals who denounce the dogmatic nature of the Catholic church and the church's connection to Martinique's colonial history. Finally, there is the assertion that bèlè is a spirituality in and of itself—a point of view held by an increasing number of practitioners who consider bèlè to be an integral form of social healing from colonial and racial subjugation (Maddox-Wingfield 2021).

Given the courtship style of communication exchanged by dancing pairs, bèlè is a fascinating space to observe the dynamics of gender and expressions of sexuality, as described in the opening scenario of this chapter. In some bèlè circles, this theme has been a subject of debate. Bèlè performance can be interpreted as a space for women's transgression of "respectable" sexuality and gender norms and the associated morality debates around appropriate dance conduct. In a society where Black women are negatively perceived as dependents of the welfare system and stereotyped as hypersexual, bèlè becomes a transformative space where their performance of a provocative sensuality is applauded and celebrated without shame. In the playful, flirtatious game of certain bèlè choreographies in which the woman is the object of her male partner's pursuit, she ultimately decides if she will submit or retreat (Maddox-Wingfield 2018). This aspect of bèlè performance, whereby women are admired and praised for their sensual dance prowess, brings a remarkable sense of affirmation for les dames bèlè (danm bèlè in Kréyòl). Some forms of sensual expressivity among bèlè women, however, provoke discussions about decency and morality in dance behavior, which becomes a reflection of wider societal values and tensions around gender and sexuality. Some question whether these tensions, produced by a respectability politics that regulate women's behaviors, are the product of Eurocentric norms and Catholic religious values, and if they should have a place in the bèlè tradition.

The integration of bèlè into the national education system is another source of debate about tradition, modernity, and the politics of French national allegiance in the transmission of bèlè. Some leaders of the bèlè movement find that teaching bèlè in formal school settings based on a rigorously codified dance pedagogy is an appropriate strategy for putting young Martinicans in touch with their roots. Others criticize this approach, arguing that the improvisational spirit that is intrinsic to Black dance culture—the spirit inherited from the ancestors—is weakened through French-influenced manners of pedagogy and standardization. With the implementation of French educational guidelines, bèlè teachers and tradition-bearers have modified their modes of transmission at the expense of the affective (emotional) elements to satisfy bureaucratic expectations and appease the concerned parents of school-aged children, particularly those who have internalized negative images associated with the tradition. Advocates of the bèlè pedagogical approach and the bèlè baccalaureate program in schools see their work as the most effective means of exposing Martinican children to ancestral traditions, instilling pride in Martinican cultural specificity, and enculturating them with the values associated with bèlè's heritage.

Summary

As this chapter demonstrates, Martinique's bèlè culture was historically influenced by the colonial histories of the Caribbean, the transatlantic slave trade, and the institutions that developed in everyday plantation life among those enslaved and free. The spread of different bèlè variations across different Caribbean societies was the result of the interisland circulation of people, products, expressions, and ideas. Power dynamics of the past and present have determined the trajectory of bèlè's future. The drum-dance traditions of Afro-descended Martinicans have survived systematic repression from the colonial era through the mid-20th century period of political transition as the island became fully integrated with the French state.

Despite modernization and assimilationist practices, bèlè survived on the peripheries of Martinican society among familial networks of the rural poor and was later revived and diffused by committed grassroots activists. Systems of codification and standardization of movements, gestures, and drum techniques have made the transmission of bèlè more accessible to eager students of all ages and social strata. The practice is no longer shamed by the middle and upper class to the extent that it was in recent history. Standardization and codification do not have to mean the tradition becomes static, hardened, or frozen in time. In swaré bèlè performance contexts and in manifestations of protest, Martinique's bèlè heritage continues to be a dynamic, ever-evolving culture where the spirit of improvisation, creativity, and spontaneity in movement styles lives on.

Discussion Questions

1. What is the role of flirtatious or competitive play in bèlè between dance partners?
2. How do the movement styles, postures, and choreographic configurations of bèlè represent the cultures of Martinique's colonial history and plantation life?
3. How did bèlè survive its near erasure from Martinican public life? What was the role of rural performers in professional folkloric troupes?
4. How might we analyze bèlè as a form of cultural politics and its reflection of power dynamics?
5. How does bèlè help us deconstruct the sacred/secular binary as it relates to dance and expressive culture?
6. What might be some pros and cons of standardization and codification of bèlè movements and gestures?

 Visit HK*Propel* for access to this chapter's Application Activity.

Selected Glossary

Antilles—The group of islands comprising the West Indies. *Antillean* is a term commonly used to refer to islanders, or people who identify their home as one of the island societies of the Antilles. French Antilleans are people who identify with Martinique or Guadeloupe (or both).

bamboulas—Drum-dance events from the slavery era that were held on weekends and holidays when enslaved Africans were permitted to rest from work and socialize.

carré—French for square; can refer to (a) square fabric tied around the waist of a female bèlè dancer, or (b) the dance square in the bèlè and quadrille choreographies made up of four dancers (two female–male pairs).

Code Noir—Set of rules established in 1685 by King Louis XIV that enforced the conversion and baptism of enslaved Africans in French colonies; the code prohibited slaves from assembling and participating in nocturnal music and dance gatherings.

danm bèlè—A female dance participant in bèlè, partnered with the kavalyé.

kavalyé—Male dance participant in bèlè, partnered with the danm bèlè.

marronage—The enactment of resistance to oppression, particularly colonial or racist oppression, small-scale (*petit marronage*) and large-scale (*grand marronage*).

monté o tanbou—A sequence in the bèlè linò choreography whereby dancers are displayed in the center of the circle to playfully interact with their dance partners, and give a danced salutation to the drummer.

quadrille—A European court dance that uses the square configuration.

quimbois—Martinique's local practice of conjure and magico-religious ritual.

swaré bèlè—Nocturnal, participatory performance gatherings whereby "initiated" (experienced) dancers, drummers, and singers come together to play bèlè until the early hours of the morning.

tanbou bèlè—A goat-skinned conical drum that rests horizontally on its side and is played in the transversal style, whereby the drummer sits straddled across the body of the drum and uses their heel to alter the pitch of the drum.

tibwa—Wooden sticks used by a secondary percussionist who beats a steady tempo on the back of the drum.

wondi-dewondi—The demicircular procession (counterclockwise then clockwise) danced by the ensemble of eight bèlè dancers during the opening sequence of bèlè linò sets.

Selected References and Resources

Agard-Jones, Vanessa. 2009. "Le Jeu de Qui? Sexual Politics at Play in the French Caribbean." *Caribbean Review of Gender Studies*, Issue 3.

Beriss, David. 2004. *Black Skins, French Voices: Caribbean Ethnicity and Activism in Urban France*. Cambridge: Westview Press.

Cyrille, Dominique. 2002. "Sa Ki Ta Nou (This Belongs to Us): Creole Dances of the French Caribbean." In *Caribbean Dance From Abakuá to Zouk: How Movement Shapes Identity*, edited by Susanna Sloat, 221-244. Gainesville: University Press of Florida.

Cyrille, Dominique. 2009. "Creole Quadrilles of Guadeloupe, Dominica, Martinique, and St. Lucia." In *Creolizing Contradance in the Caribbean*, edited by Peter Manuel, 188-208. Philadelphia: Temple University Press.

Daniel, Yvonne. 2011. *Caribbean and Atlantic Diaspora Dance: Igniting Citizenship*. Champaign: University of Illinois Press.

Franco, Hazel. 1999. Belaire: Aesthetics, Dance and Pan-Caribbean Identity. Paper presented at the 24th annual conference of the Caribbean Studies Association, Panama City, Panama.

Gerstin, Julian. 1996. "Traditional Music in a New Social Movement: The Renewal of Bèlè in Martinique (French West Indies)." Ph.D. Dissertation. Ann Arbor: UMI Dissertation Services.

Gerstin, Julian. 2010. "Tangled Roots: Kalenda and Other Neo-African Dances in the Circum-Caribbean." In *Making Caribbean Dance: Continuity and Creativity in Island Cultures*, edited by Susanna Sloat, 11-34. Gainesville: University of Florida Press.

Gikandi, Simon. 2011. *Slavery and the Culture of Taste*. Princeton: Princeton University Press.

Johnson, Sara E. 2012. *The Fear of French Negroes: Transcolonial Collaboration in the Revolutionary Americas*. Berkeley: University of California Press.

Maddox-Wingfield, Camee. 2018. "The Dance Chose Me: Womanist Reflections on Bèlè Performance in Contemporary Martinique." *Meridians: feminism, race, transnationalism* 16(2): 295-307.

Maddox-Wingfield, Camee. (Forthcoming September 2021) "The Quest for Spiritual Purpose in a Secular Dance Community: Bèlè's Rebirth in Contemporary Martinique." In *Embodying Black Religions in Africa and Its Diasporas*, edited by Yolanda Covington-Ward and Jeanette S. Jouili, xx-xx. Durham: Duke University Press.

Price, Richard. 1998. *The Convict and the Colonel: A Story of Colonialism and Resistance*. Durham: Duke University Press.

Wason, Janet. 2010. "Bèlè and Quadrille: African and European Dimensions in the Traditional Dances of Dominica, West Indies." In *Making Caribbean Dance: Continuity and Creativity in Island Cultures*, edited by Susanna Sloat, 227-246. Gainesville: University of Florida Press.

Dance in Trinidad and Tobago

"Where Everybody Dance"

Elizabeth Fernández O'Brien

Learning Objectives

After reading this chapter students will be able to do the following:

- Describe the setting of a Trinbagonian folk dance, including musical instrumentation, participants' apparel, and motivation for the event.
- Explain the historical significance of the 20th century move to staged performance developments in Trinidad and Tobago dance.
- Compare different backgrounds and initiations of winin' in two cultural environments in Trinidad and Tobago.
- Apply understanding of the historical development of a Trinbagonian dance to a dance form in the United States.

Key Terms

Canboulay—Precursor to today's Trinidad Carnival.

chantuelle—Lead singer in West African–style call-and-response who, at times, dances.

East Indian/Indian/Indo-Trinidadian—Ethnic description of people and things with roots in India. Caribbean people, in general, are known as West Indian.

play mas—From "Masquerade." Costumed participation in Trinidad Carnival.

Trinis/Trinbagonians—People of Trinidad and Tobago (T&T).

win' (wine/winin')—From the English word "winding." Full range of motion in hips, buttocks, and torso, inspired by the music, a partner, or onlookers. Social implications are many.

"Bus' ah Sweet Wine"

"Trinidad, they love dance. It doesn't matter what kind of dance, once you do it properly. Trinidad has space for everyone in culture."

Susan "Baby" Mohip

"Nani wine down so, nani wine down so, nani wine down low. . . ." These lyrics are played at home parties, **limin'** outside of a **creole** restaurant, and at all-night weekend parties leading up and into **Carnival** celebrations. To "**wine**" or "**bus' ah sweet wine**" in the days of Carnival can be a joyous jumble as locals and tourists alike pour into the capital of Trinidad, Port of Spain. **Steel pan** (drums), brass bands, and recorded music playing **calypso**, **soca**, **Indo-Trinidadian chutney soca**, and **off-island** songs all fuel the desire to dance, dance, dance. In more intimate settings, such as a family party, a small child breaks out into winin'. Good intentions pour forth as the surrounding adults clap and sing approval of the child's ability to swing, shake, and circle hips while attempting to sink and rise. The roots of Trini winin' begin with the stunning, exuberant flash that is Carnival.

Here are some key concepts you will encounter throughout this chapter:

- Migration from Africa, Asia, the Caribbean, and Europe to Trinidad and Tobago is central to the preservation and growth of dance.

- The **Prime Minister's Best Village Trophy Competition** for folk dance, drama, and music, with over 30 dance categories, is a government-sponsored national series of events including competitive multi-arts performances. It was initiated in 1963.

- Demonstration of dance skills is a method of gaining social capital within one's community, as well as national and international recognition.

History and Carnival as a Trini Identifier

The many distinct traditions and the merged modern forms of dance and music have long represented the diversity in the Republic of Trinidad and Tobago. The two islands at the southeastern tip of the West Indies were united in 1889. Today, the population of **East Indian** and African descendants and mixed or other heritages (including **First Peoples** [indigenous], Europeans, and descendants of Chinese, Syrian, and Lebanese immigrants), comprise approximately one third each. "Nani Wine Down," a 1986 chutney soca lyric, is a fusion of East Indian and earlier African legacy and is reflective today of being **Trinidadian**, or the more inclusive, **Trinbagonian**. Many residents and those of the **diaspora** call themselves the demonym "**Trini**."

The islands were inhabited for many thousands of years before Columbus arrived in 1498. After the near extinction of indigenous peoples, European colonizers imported enslaved Africans to toil on plantations.

Indigenous "Amerindians": First Peoples of Trinidad and Tobago

Though their populations now are much reduced and mixed with other cultures, Arawaks (Taino), Caribs (Kalinago), and other First Peoples numbered around 40,000 when Columbus named Trinidad for the Catholic Trinity (the concept of God as three persons). Trinidad's Amerindians were part of an interisland and island-to-mainland trade network. Trinidad was the first point of entry to the Caribbean, from what is now Venezuela and Guyana.

From 1783 on, although the nearly empty islands were nominally owned by the Spanish Crown, French Caribbean planters comprised 95 percent of Trinidad's enslaver population (Niranjana, 32). After constant English, Dutch, and French raids on the Spanish colony, the British took control in 1802. Following the official emancipation of enslaved Africans in 1834, and continuing until 1917, planters brought in South Asian indentured immigrants to fulfill labor needs. However, the economy shifted away from agriculture during the 20th century as Trinidad's oil industry boomed in the 1970s. After gaining independence from Britain in 1962, **T&T** (Trinidad-Tobago) has continued to develop as an industrial nation with complex cultural heritages.

Carnival and Catholicism

Despite British control, French presence continues in certain **neo-African dances** of T&T and in the use of French terms such as *artiste* and ***palais***, as well as in the influence of Catholic practices, most vividly recognized through Carnival.

Originating in European religious street performances on Three Kings Day (January 6th), and leading up to Easter, Carnival is celebrated in over 50 countries, and each culture has developed its own unique characteristics born of history and demographics.

Carnival's Trinidadian precursor, **Canboulay**, from the French *cannes bruleé* (burnt cane), was created in the 1800s by the enslaved and freed people categorized as "coloreds." In public, they danced, played **Kongo rhythms** on drums, and sang and chanted, especially on public holidays. After the Canboulay riots of 1881, drumming and masquerading were outlawed. Though required to play European-based music when enslaved, emancipated Africans continued to be banned from French Shrovetide's Carnival season of masked balls and celebrations.

Carnival Today

For lovers of Carnival, what is "wine down low" or winin'? The term *wine* (and *win'*, *winin*, or *winin' down*), derived from "winding" in English, refer to curvilinear movements of the hips and torso. A matter of national Trini pride, the context of winin' shifts by generation, gender preference, and social situation. The female, not the male reveler, is the one who decides whether, how much, and what type of bodily contact occurs

Carnival in Trinidad.

Sean Drakes/LatinContent via Getty Images

(personal communication with A.K. Jones). The female and her cohorts disapprove of "tiefin," thievery by snatching moments of contact. The phrases "**free-up**," "**get-on**," and "**jump-up**" can be used to describe the revelry of winin', dancing, and arm waving, in Carnival parading.

Preparation for Carnival is a monthslong process, culminating just before Ash Wednesday (in February or early March), when Catholics begin observing 40 days of **Lent** prior to Easter. The rollout of calypso tunes begins during the Christmas season, inspiring competition shows for dancers, singers, masqueraders, Panorama steel pan (drums) and, Carnival kings and queens. Impromptu dancing breaks out in music rehearsal yards, while costume orders (both local and from abroad) are filled. After the Friday's Canboulay reenactment, weekend dance parties (*fetes*) through Sunday, and processions out to the streets at dawn, *j'ouvert*, on Monday, Carnival goes nonstop for two days. The last celebration ends Tuesday at midnight with the Catholic Ash Wednesday.

Play mas, or masquerading, begins at dawn on j'ouvert. In a group—often a family legacy—traditional folkloric characters, such as **Jab Molassi (Devil Molasses)**, **Jab Jab**, and **Devil Mas**, covered in sticky black, brown, or blue, may suddenly surprise revelers around a corner or on a parade route. Bystanders scatter or "pay de devil," giving money to avoid a hug, a kiss, or "rub up" from the sticky characters.

Moko jumbie stilt walkers appear. With roots in West African spirit figures, Trini-style stilt sizes range from tailored-for-children to beyond the traditional eight-foot length. Historically, moko jumbies collect offerings from second floor balconies as they execute complex one- and two-legged steps.

Thousands participate on Carnival Tuesday, the people's day, many representing traditional characters, such as sailors, firemen, Indians, and *Jametres/Jamettes* dressed as baby dolls. Band trucks blast and popularize calypso and soca tunes in an effort to be the one to win **road march** tune of the season.

Band themes include history, nature, folklore characters, and reminders of the indigenous peoples. The inclusive nature of Carnival prevails throughout the culture with extensive support from the government. Trini Carnival has become socially acceptable across ethnic identities, and it is a standard copied by nearby Caribbean islands, cities in the United States, and in Toronto and London.

"**Jam-cram**" (throngs) of revelers are **chippin'**, which means taking a break from high energy dancing, drawing feet along in "a kind of shuffling . . . flatfooted" walk (Daniels, 112), as hips swing in opposition. A common goal for many is to be "makin' a **bacchanal** in di road" with other "winers" (personal communication with A.K. Jones).

Band managers marshal parade onlookers onto the sidelines but all, nevertheless, feel like participants. Even an "outta timin" foreigner, met with laughter, is given a helpful on-the-spot dance lesson. Carnival peaks with a choreographed sweep across the Queen's Park Savannah stage in the Parade of the Bands, where members enjoy being seen flaunting their fantastical costumes.

Jametres/Jamettes/Diametres

The name derives from a slanderous 1800s' colonialist term meaning "below a diameter" of respectability. African women, transitioning from enslavement to less than full citizenship, reclaimed the term, similar to baby-doll street masking troops of New Orleans. From the 1890s, many setups for costumes and body paint for devils, characters of yore, and legend came from the hand of female Jametres/Diametres. Jametres were the original costume makers and singers for **kalinda** stick fighting. Nowadays, Jametres signify women who hold the power to control their own bodies in social situations, specifically used when winin'.

Calypso

Calypso, the underlying beat of Carnival whose name and lyrics derive from Kongolese *kaiso* ("go more!") is now manifested in soca, chutney soca, and **rapso** music. In keeping with this musical heritage, traditional calypso dance motifs continue to draw from West and Central African sources that evolved during Canboulay dancing in the streets, as well as from **bèlè**, **piquè**, **bongo**, and **limbo** dances. Calypso is marked by a constant weight shift with hip swings and rolls. Soca developed from 1970s North American soul dance combined with calypso. However, soca dance now features the traditional handkerchief as well as winin' and chutney movements, even as it also integrates hip-hop motifs.

See resource 7.1 in HK*Propel* for web links.

Neo-African Dance in Trinidad and Tobago

Unlike the maintenance of separate African ethnic "nations" in Brazil and Cuba, the forced confluence of **Igbo**, **Kongo**, **Malinke**, and other African ethnic groups evolved into neo-African dances in the Trinbagonian context. Many of these neo-African dances, such as bélé, survived by using a process that anthropologists term **transculturation**, whereby enslaved people would co-opt elements of slave owners' dress and mannerisms to disguise underlying Africanist dance practices.

Bèlè and Piquè: Development in the French Colonies

The bèlè is often considered the Trini national dance. Studied now in middle school curriculum, it originated mainly in French-speaking cocoa plantations that stretched across the north of Trinidad. However, Caribbean "back door" migrants also brought bèlè from "small islands," such as French Martinique, and migration was but 25 miles between Trinidad and French-occupied Tobago.

Today's performance style reflects the tradition of the chantuelle using a handkerchief to extend an invitation to each dancer and maintain "proper" distance while introducing them into the dance. Traditionally, dancers and participants cram into the tented *palais* (meeting space), singing and shouting the chorus and encouragement, much as you might see in a 21st century hip-hop cypher (circle). In the conversation between the dancer and the lead "**cutter**" drummer, the dancer challenges with sudden and sustained skirt gestures. Beating highly syncopated accents, the cutter responds with the bass and **fula** drums' steady, repeated rhythms.

The female dancer's attire features as much as eight yards of fabric over a petticoat. The front opening split allows for many variations of opening, closing, and extending. The undivided torso of bèlè reflects the European ideal of proper, upright posture. However, from West African dance, the torso is angled downward and lengthened to honor the earth. The queen, usually the eldest, or the host signals a break in the action by touching the cutter drum with skirt ends or handkerchief. She later tosses a bouquet over her shoulder to identify the next host.

The bèlè feast (*fete*) often progresses to the livelier piquè, where a precursor to the **breakaway**, a side tilting step of calypso, is seen. With the torso shifting in multiple directions driven by the interlocking drum rhythms, the synchronizing hip movement of one female wrapping her skirt around another can be considered an origin of winin', as well.

Kalinda: Martial Art Dance

Playing the Kongo polyrhythms on drums was regulated, relegated, and prohibited at various times. Instead, percussionists tuned bamboo sticks, and this musical form became known as **tamboo bamboo**. From this, the martial art of fighting with sharpened bamboo sticks, called kalinda, developed. It was banned in 1934 in Trinidad, when authorities blamed it for streets overtaken by "rowdiness." Eventually, however, the kalinda performing group at **Bois Academy of Trinidad and Tobago** developed it into a choreographed reproduction of a challenging duo in the Best Village competitions.

As with the bèlè, a chantuelle (originally a Jametre) accompanies performances of kalinda, encouraging one or both of the stick fighting pair, sometimes "trash talking" one, in the West African tradition of satirical singing about life themes, including local officials' behavior.

Tobago Music and Dance

Tobago, with earlier emancipation and fewer immigrants, remains predominantly of African descendancy, as reflected in its dances and music. The **tambrin**, the banned drum replacement fashioned from a cheesebox, is the higher cutter (lead drum) that directs the dancer's movement, recalling African traditions. European influences do exist, however, including men in top hats, as well as fiddle and triangle used in the lively Tobago Jig (Franco, 315). The dance imitates the rocking motion of the ships, camouflaging African heritages in the European sailors' dances, and helping enslaved people to survive colonial oppression. Dances also closely mirrored the way of life. The **Tobago reel**, for example, is danced to mark boat launchings and for many life events. Libations of white rum and water poured at the beginning of the dance invite the ancestors into the yard, similar to ceremonies invoking **Elegba** (or Eshu), the West African **Yoruba** deity (*orisha*) known to open the door to pathways.

Afro-Devotional Dance

Africanist spiritual practices persist in Trinidad and in the African diaspora, with a common belief in transformation involving a spirit. Just as West African Malinke people adapted the teachings of Islam over centuries into their ancient beliefs, Trinidadians syncretized a Catholic saint with a physically hidden Yoruba orisha behind it (personal conversation with Dr. Pearl Primus).

Shango Ritual

Antecedents of winin' are found within the sacred and secular dances of West Africans enslaved in Trinidad, such as the Yoruba people, who arrived between 1838 and 1870. After an 1884 ban on African-type drumming, "on March 30, 1891, constables moved in to confiscate drums from **Shango** devotees" in Arouca, Trinidad (Campbell, 8). Shango is one of many orishas (deities) in the Yoruba religion (*Ifʊ*), each with unique motifs, colors, gender identities, and artifacts. He is the king of the drums who "comes down" to communicate directly through the body of the priestess/priest or initiate (communicant). In Trinidad, Shango is the name of the entire spirit possession ceremony in the constellation of spiritual dance practice of the African diaspora in the Caribbean and the Americas (personal communication Wándé Abímbọ́lá). Shango practitioners can be found throughout Trinidad and Tobago on all levels of society. The late **Astor Johnson**, founder of the Repertory Dance Theater of Trinidad and Tobago, was an initiate of Shango.

Spiritual (Shango) Baptists

From North American rituals of the "**Merikins**"—African American enslaved soldiers who fought for the British and were freed to Trinidad after the U.S. War of 1812—**Spiritual (Shango) Baptists/**Shouters emerged. All wear Christian hierarchy garb with elaborate head ties for females. They move in procession, often outdoors, and sing seated in meetings. As they "shake (ring) the bell" that starts the mass, drumming and singing inten-

sify. In this faith, a person who is possessed by the Holy Spirit retains his or her own identity, as compared to Yoruba orisha practice, where those who are possessed actually become the spirits.

 See resource 7.2 in HK*Propel* for web links.

From Ritual to Performance

Rituals connect believers with the sacred realm to bring overall wellness to their lives, to make merit, to enter the spirit world, and to bring balance between the physical and sacred realms. While such spiritual practices continue to have deep meaning in Trinidad, aspects of these rituals are also performed onstage to entertain as well as to compete for "Best Village" titles.

Funerary Dances: Bongo and Limbo

Bongo, a neo-African dance, is traditionally danced in a "dead house" to keep the deceased and family company as the spirit is safely guided into the next world (Alladin 1974). The wake night ceremony, preceded by nine nights of ritual, is still observed high in the western mountains of Trinidad and in Tobago.

Bongo is a dance of strength displayed inside a circle, employing many vigorous "crossing over" motifs to demonstrate life–death transition. Originally danced by men, Bongo is now mostly performed by female dancers in university, competition, and government performance settings.

Limbo is danced in the nine nights up to the wake night. Two participants hold a horizontal barrier that might be a pole, two limbs in contact, or a dancer's whole body. Lifted incrementally each night, the barrier signifies how the spirit is urged to rise. A dancer passes under the pole at its lowest point on the first night. With knees fully flexed allowing the upper body to extend out behind the hips, passing becomes easier each night of the ceremony as the dance encourages the soul to rise into life after death. This dance requires one to be limber in both strength and flexibility. To pass under successfully has been interpreted as a metaphor for the freeing of

Cultural Highlight

DOCUMENTING "BÈLÈ/BELAIR"

As part of my documentary project in 1985, I attended and recorded a bèlè feast just outside of Port of Spain in the village of Barataria—a town with dirt floors and roads that is nonetheless more urban than the mountain villages where bèlè began as the essential small community event.

When the fete began, Donald MacCauley, the **chantuelle**, sang the call, and dancers and the circled participants sang the response in vivid African tradition. The gestures of the female's voluminous skirt over petticoats and both genders' use of the distancing kerchief maintained historical propriety and formality at the evening's outset for both male and female soloists. In a low voice, the host, Baptist Bishop Mother Vero, briefly mentioned dancers' familial connections to other islands such as Martinique.

The Queen, in her nineties, was not dressed in a full skirt, but when she was assisted out of her chair, she dance-walked toward the drums using small hand gestures and laid her hands on the drums. They stopped! As the rhythm changed, dancers overlapped each other's entry in the tight circle and responded with livelier, playful piquè steps. The challenges continued as an elderly dancer came into the circle, her head tied high in Congolese style, her torso inclined further forward, her steps and skirt action sharply percussive. Later, Mother Vero whispered "Dat be Igbo she dancin'," referencing the West African origins. The saucy piquè resumed until, in the hours before dawn, the drummers stopped and rearranged their drums.

When they began a new rhythm, I made the decision to turn off our cameras because we had not asked permission to film what was evidently a spiritual invitation to the orishas, deities of the Shango practice. The dancer's control seemed to come from only the drum. He exuded the signature virility of Shango, the deity of lightning and thunder. His body shook as his exaggerated steps filled the circle. We clutched the camera to get out of his way.

The feast then began to wind down at dawn with cups of coffee and quiet conversation. We went home to sleep, then on to the studio to edit. Upon returning to the shrine and setting up to show the video, we discovered other researchers had come, photographed, and never returned to show the congregants and dancers themselves in a bèlè feast. Shy smiles, acknowledging murmurs, and occasional laughter accompanied the showing. We left a copy of bèlè/belair with Mother Vero.

slaves from their captivity, just as the stick itself is spoken of as a threat and coercive exercise on slave ships. Limbo today is a popular secular form of dance. The "First Lady of Limbo," **Julia Edwards**, innovated with fire and with changing the direction of the pole's progression so that it now travels downward incrementally. During the 1940s and 1950s, Edwards' spectacular performances, starting with the **Boscoe and Geoffrey Holder** dance company, cemented limbo's fame around the world.

Folk Performance

Even though stage performance has been part of the larger theater event on sacred "**grong**" (ground) in East Indian communities from the mid-17th century, staging did not start among African-heritage artists until 1940. While presentational elements always existed in the cypher-like circles of bèlè and other folk dances, true choreography for an audience only began with the "Mother of Modern Caribbean Dance," **Beryl McBurnie**. In forming her **Little Carib Theater** with dancers **Molly Ahye**, Geoffrey and Boscoe Holder, **Percival Borde**, and **Cyril St. Lewis**, McBurnie's narrative choreography reproduced local, Brazilian, and Haitian African diaspora dances. She tirelessly promoted folkloric dance as a viable dance form, teaching students of all ages, in Trinidad and abroad. McBurnie had privately taught Shango, Bongo, and Kalinda to the famous **Katherine Dunham** in 1938 in New York. Boscoe and Geoffrey Holder went on to teach their Trini dance style for Dunham's St. Louis school, influencing her internationally recognized technique (Ahye, 28).

As a folk dance activist, McBurnie not only initiated the circum-Caribbean Festival of the Arts (**CARIFESTA**) in 1948, but also invited a classical ballet school's company and steel pan (drum) group, the Invaders, to perform on the same bill with her company. In so doing she initiated some controversy: "[T]here is this leaning toward the American and European dances. Ballet is attractive, Bèlè . . . means going into the hills and valleys, doing research, meeting people, going into the rain and hot sun" (Ahye, 105). Yet McBurnie's determination to maintain connections between different dance genres while promoting folklore would eventually pay off.

Trinidad and Tobago's 1962 independence accelerated the growth of folkloric dance in the streets for Carnival parades and for audience presentations. The Prime Minister's Best Village Trophy Competition for folk dance, drama, and music, launched in 1963, became a hallmark of preserving folk dance and community arts while opening to modern styles.

Best Village Trophy Competition

Originally, towns and neighborhoods throughout Trinidad and Tobago received funding, thanks to oil production taxes, to build community centers. In their new centers, dancers performed on dirt floors just like they had done in ritual events. Judges were sent to determine which villages qualified for the televised Queens Park Savannah stage shows in the capital, Port of Spain.

Today, dances presented through Best Village events cover many categories, reflecting the widely varied cultures and functions of dance woven through the nation's history. Traditional African devotional dance, East Indian–influenced dance, Amerindian dance, and many more are seen when over 180 villages and neighborhoods compete to display their retention of folk art and preservation of national heritage in accordance with the Best Village rules and regulations. The choreographies and dramas draw on the many festivals and religious practices rooted in various cultures on the islands.

 **See resource 7.3 in HK*Propel* for web links.**

Indo-Trinidadian Dance Traditions and Development

The end of slavery in 1838 precipitated a labor shortage on the sugar plantations, and workers from India were brought to Trinidad under the **British Colonial Indenture** system. Over the next century, multiple cultural practices, mainly of northern India, were performed in the ethnic enclaves geographically located in less desirable southern regions of the island, where Indo-Trinidadians were first able to settle independently. The rigid Indian caste system under which the immigrants had previously lived dissolved soon after their arrival in Trinidad. Life was celebrated in Hindu and Muslim practices of story dramas, processions, and folk dances. The community was educated through poetic language and made to feel the emotion through the expressions of the dancers. To the accompaniment of **tassa** stick drums, men danced female roles in weddings, **Hosays**, and **Ramdillas** and later, in Carnival. Despite impoverished and oppressed circumstances, dance proved to be a cultural through line for Indo-Trinidadian immigrants, just as it had been for the Afro-Trinidadians who preceded them.

Repression and Recovery

In 1884, to forestall any Afro-Indian working-class unity, officials extended the ban on Negro drumming to include observances by immigrants from India. When the latter still celebrated their traditions with a passion play, they were assaulted by soldiers and police. Many were killed and wounded in the attack. (Campbell, 16) Nonetheless, by 1917, when the indenture system ended, many Indo-Trinidadians had chosen to remain in Trinidad after their terms of servitude ended, and they were able to expand their cultural capital as settlers on the island. Their wealth grew further through communal land purchase and eventually the 1974 oil boom. Over time, Indo-Trinidadians and their dance events (ranging from private, single-gender events to public weddings, repeatedly presented passion plays, and parades) have gradually received acceptance and participation across all ethnic communities. Prominent Indo-Trinidadian dance events include a Muslim funerary-origin procession, wedding rituals, and a Hindi passion play.

Hosay—A Muslim Festival Procession

The procession of Hosay honors the martyrdom of the **Prophet Mohammed**'s two grandsons, represented by a rotating crew of two dancers holding up half-moon structures that meet and part along the parade route, accompanied by tassa drums. For nearly 140 years, Hosay has been a celebration by Shiite Muslims but also open to any Trinidadian who chooses to participate. Nowadays, contraindicating Hosay's funerary origins, a joyous festival of choreographed **Indo-Trinidadian folk dance** performances is included in the celebrations.

Ramdilla—A Passion Play About the Lord of Dance

Though "**passion play**" performance had waned as Trinbagonian culture became more secular, in the 1990s it surged again with performance groups. The performance illuminates how the divine origin of dance lies with **Shiva Nataraja** as the "lord of dance." Celestial beings such as **Rama**, symbolically on the Earth and in the beyond, perform *deva gatri* (divine steps). With the *yatra gatri* (pilgrim's steps), the audience follows the action (Maharaj 2010). Other Indian dance styles have been incorporated more recently.

Shiva Nataraja—The God as Lord of the Dance

Dance lies at the core of much religious symbolism in India, fully exemplified by the image of the supreme god as Shiva Nataraja, Lord of the Dance. The well-known image combines "Shiva's roles as creator, preserver, and destroyer of the universe and conveys the Indian . . . conception of the never-ending cycle of time" through the god's dancing body and **mudras** (hand gestures) (metmuseum.org).

Filmi—Indian Film Industry

The fantasy of Hindi film, introduced to Trinidad from India in the 1930s, gave descendants of indentured workers a transculturally amplified view of classical and folk dances such as **bhangra**. Accompanied by old folk songs, the choreographies were "influenced by Arabic, western, and ballroom technique" (Maharaj, 322). Dance, music, and elaborate wedding clothes became signifiers of being Indian, not of India itself, with the introduction of films. **Filmi** helped to ratify Indian heritage and maintain the influence of dance within the Indo-Trinidadian culture.

Classical Indian Dance

Classical Indian dances were not brought to Trinidad by East Indian ancestors of present-day Indo-Trinidadians. Rather, as a 20th century cultural insertion directly from India, these dances expressed the Republic of Trinidad and Tobago's new independence in 1962, as well as the divesting of the Euro-colonial perspective. Classical dance directly from India may be seen as counterpoint to the dance that had only been encountered through highly popular filmi. In the 1970s, sponsored by the **National Council of Indian Culture of Trinidad and Tobago**, this dance currency was brought to T&T by cultural ambassadors **Priya and Pratap Pawar**.

Indo-Trinidadian communities, who had been performing folk dance dramas in public Indo-Trinidadian performance spaces and dance schools not only in southern Trinidad but also in Port of Spain, anchored dance traditions of classical **kathak**, **bharata natyam**, and **odissi** styles. Greater study spurred villages to showcase their classical dances for Best Village judges. The goal became to get onstage in the finale at the Queen's Park Savannah stage and to be on Trinidad and Tobago television.

Bollywood's Footprint in Trinidad and Tobago

The Indian musical films most often associated with the term ***Bollywood*** have gained worldwide followings since their emergence in the 1970s. Inspired by folk, classical, filmi dance, and ***matikor*** (female fertility rite) ceremonial songs, with more recent infusions of western pop dance,

Bollywood films typically follow romantic plots with star-crossed lovers and nefarious villains. Since 1970, Trinidad and Tobago's **Mastana Bahar** televised talent competition has featured multiple thousands of dancers who espouse Bollywood style. Schools of dance regularly hire winners to teach Bollywood classes (Manuel, 130). Dancers have charmed their way into Carnival and calypso, creating a fused cultural identity. While it was "uncommon to see Indo-Trinis participating in Carnival during the '60s, '70s, and much of the '80s" (Campbell, 8), Indian dance, characters, and song have integrated slowly from the mid-1980s into the centerpiece of African descendants' culture—the bounteous, overflowing, gorgeous Carnival.

Chutney Soca: "Where Everybody Dance"

Along with classical Indian dance and the tradition of matikor, the pop dance form of chutney soca would have to include the calypso, Indian dances (such as dance dramas and solos inspired by Hindi cinema), Carnival, Hosay, and the television show *Mastana Bahar*. (Niranjana, 104). In its fusion of popular forms, chutney has become the pathway to the heights of Trinbagonian participatory dance. **"Raviji" Maharaj**, an early chutney pop choreographer, has performed the

Matikor—Women's Fertility Dance

"Though . . . reticence is culturally appropriate, women stimulated by the drums (and sometimes alcohol) depict the sex act in dance" with a bride-to-be (Niranjana, 98). With an eggplant or a pillow at the belly, in the sexually explicit (even humorous) *chatti* dance, hips, buttocks, and waist swing, circle, and shake, ostensibly sharing knowledge of wedded life (Alladin 1974). In a night prior to the wedding, a man chips forward using his scarf to emphasize the forward and backward jerk of his hips in Nagara dance (Alladin 1974). These historic acts contributed to the popularity of winin' in today's chutney soca dance.

gamut of Indian, even African dance. Originally, dance was private, segregated, or in a performance. Chutney turned dancing into public participation for all genders. Frequently held on Saturdays in southern and central Trinidad, one fete featured a winin' competition. While controversy still abounds about bringing previously private, gendered, explicit moves to the public eye, chutney soca and Bollywood can be seen as today's cultural nexus of Indo-Trinidadian dance.

 See resource 7.4 in HKPropel for web links.

Other Cultural Infusions

Chinese, Syrian, and Lebanese Dance

Today, **Chinese dances**, such as dragon, lion, ribbon, and tai chi fan, are performed at public events, the legacy of Chinese immigrants who arrived in Trinidad as laborers in the mid-1800s. Despite many returnees to China at the end of indenture contracts and the 1949 revolution in China, Chinese Trinbagonians have a significant presence in the islands. In 2011 they established the Dai Ailian Foundation, granting scholarships for Trinbagonian youths to attend the premier dance university in China—Beijing Dance Academy. The scholarship honors **Madam Dai Ailian**, the famous Trinidadian-born dancer and premier proponent of folk dance and ballet in China in the 20th century.

The early 1900s saw the "last" immigrants, Syrians and Lebanese, who left the Middle East in the tumult leading up to World War I and the dissolution of the Ottoman Empire. They brought with them their cultural dances, such as the men's **dabke** dance and women's belly dance. The shaking, swiveling focus of Trinidadian **Syro-Lebanese–style belly dance** is congruent with what has become the cross-cultural genre of winin'.

 See resource 7.5 in HKPropel for web links.

Crosscurrents

The societal value of leaving to study and perform abroad is exemplified by members of all ethnic communities. Former minister, dancer, and studio director **Eugene Joseph** exhorted dancers to "go, but always carry your Trini culture with you" (personal observation). From local and outside sources throughout the centuries, Trinidad and Tobago's dance has been marked by constant and active avocation, devotion, and reinvention.

Cross-cultural exchanges in dance and music are a hallmark of Trini experience, from the early interweavings of Caribbean, African, European, Asian, and Middle Eastern traditions and peoples to the vibrant collaborations and inspirations of today. For example, the exportation of limbo to the international dance scene and the incorporation of the DJ **Afrika Bambaataa**'s principles of "peace, love, unity, and having fun" into the Trini hip-hop scene are but two of many such exchanges that shaped Trinbagonian performance culture in the 20th century and solidified pathways for such flows to accelerate into the 21st century.

Recently, dancer **Makeda Thomas** described living and working in both Trinidad and New York as critical to her work that is "situated at the intersection of performance practice, diaspora theory, dance studies, ethnography and black feminisms." As the granddaughter of a mas' woman, a dance artist, filmmaker, scholar, writer, educator, curator, and (Jametres) band leader, Thomas dances in multiple geographic and cultural spaces (Thomas 2022).

 See resource 7.6 in HK*Propel* for web links.

Summary

In the vibrant multiplicity of dance within Trinidad and Tobago itself, from winin' down in Carnival and chutney soca concerts to the drummer following the dancer's skirt gestures in bèlè and piquè to breaking's power moves, the body initiates the dancer's message. The body dissolves into multiple actions, as in the facial expressions, hand mudras, and foot stamping play of the ankle bells of kathak dancers. Yet the pauses of the classical Indian pose, the upright torso of bèlè, and breaking's freezes express the wide variety of Trinbagonian dance today. These are reflections of the African and Indo-Trinidadian cultures supplanting European histories. "Change is inevitable, and these dances will certainly continue to change" (Alladin 1974, 3). "We live in such a culturally rich and diverse land and we as a people just love and appreciate any art form, and to merge different cultures through dance is definitely a channel to show unity and harmony in diversity. It reaches beyond the political, ethnic, and religious divides" (Davis 2017).
Aché!

Discussion Questions

1. Reference the geographic influences using dance terminology and demonstration for a neo-African or Indo-Trinidadian dance. Demonstrate how a dance motif communicates aesthetic and cultural values.

2. Define your own personal artistic preferences to critique another Trini dance form. Consider societal and personal values, and a range of artistic expression. How has the analysis expanded your own dance literacy?

3. Explain dance participation beyond a dance performance career, for example, "I have always loved dancing, but cannot claim to be a trained dancer. Yet I have performed as a dancer in Indian and African dance, on television, at formal occasions, at Best Village, and at cooking nights in communities across Trinidad" (Ravindra Nath "Raviji" Maharaj; Sloat, 321).

 Visit HK*Propel* for access to this chapter's Application Activity.

Selected Glossary

calypso—Afro-Caribbean music and dance originating in Trinidad and Tobago in the 1800s. Roots lie in the Canboulay festivals of the French Caribbean islands and in the rhythms and social commentary of West African kaiso music.

Canboulay—From the French *cannes brulées* (burnt cane), this festival of the sugarcane harvest is a precursor to today's Trinidad Carnival.

Carnival—A yearly celebration building for many weeks prior to Easter that incorporates dance, costuming, spoken word, and music into competitions and parades.

chantuelle—Lead singer in West African style call-and-response who, at times, dances.

chippin'—Trini term for the hip-swinging walk that permits parading for hours, adjusting to the packed Carnival crowds.

diaspora (Trinbagonian)—People who live outside of the country and identify with that country, in this case, the Republic of Trinidad and Tobago.

East Indian/Indian/Indo-Trinidadian—Ethnic description of people and things with roots in India. Caribbean people, in general, are known as West Indian.

kaiso—A West African music with social commentary; in Trinidad it now represents a friendly encouragement to dance more intensely, as in winin'. It is an origin of the word *calypso* and of the role that musical commentary plays in the Trinbagonian culture.

neo-African dance—A tradition, newly created, from dances of African origins with changes in event, timing, type of presentation (e.g., stage or participatory), and type of participants.

play mas—From the word *masquerade*, costumed participation in Trinidad Carnival.

transculturation—Cultural transformation, not assimilation, as elements of a new culture equally merge with existing ones.

Trinis/Trinbagonians—People of Trinidad and Tobago (T&T).

win' (wine/winin')—From the English word *winding*, a full range of motion in hips, buttocks, and torso, inspired by the music, a partner, or onlookers. Social implications are many.

Selected References and Resources

Ahye, Molly. 1983. *Cradle of Caribbean Dance*. Petit Valley: Republic of Trinidad and Tobago: Heritage Cultures.

Alladin, M.P. 1974. *Folk Dances of Trinidad and Tobago*. Self-published: Maraval, Trinidad.

Balkaransingh, Satnarine. 2016. *The Shaping of a Culture*. London: Hansib.

Bergman, Sara. 2008. *Matikor, Chutney, Odissi and Bollywood: Gender Negotiations in Indo-Trinidadian Dance*. Centre for Gender and Development Studies Issue 2, University of the West Indies.

Campbell, Susan. "Carnival, Calypso, and Class Struggle in Nineteenth Century Trinidad." *History Workshop Journal*, Volume 26, Issue 1, Autumn 1988, pp. 1-27.

Daniel, Yvonne. 2011. *Caribbean and Atlantic Diaspora Dance: Igniting Citizenship*. Champaign, IL: University of Illinois.

Devi, Ragini. 1972. *Dance Dialects of India*. New Delhi, India: Shri Jainendra Press.

Franco, Hazel. 2010. "Tradition Reaffirming Itself in New Forms, An Overview of Trinidad and Tobago Folk Dances." In *Making Caribbean Dance, Continuity and Creativity in Island Cultures*, edited by Susanna Sloat, 298-320. University Press of Florida.

Jones, Adanna K. 2016. *Take a Wine and Roll "IT"!: Breaking Through the Circumscriptive Politics of the Trini/Caribbean Dancing Body*. UC Riverside eScholarship: https://escholarship.org/uc/item/33d3r5fz.

Hutchinson, Sydney. 2020. *Focus: Music of the Caribbean*. New York: Routledge.

Maharaj, Ravindra Nath "Raviji." 2010. "A Narrative on the Framework of the Presence, Change, and Continuity of Indian Dance in Trinidad." In *Making Caribbean Dance, Continuity and Creativity in Island Cultures*, ed. Susanna Sloat. University Press of Florida.

National Coalition for Core Arts Standards. 2014. National Core Arts Standards. Rights Administered by the State Education Agency Directors of Arts Education. Dover, DE. www.nationalcoreartsstandards.org

Niranjana, Tejaswini. 2006. *Mobilizing India: Women, Music, and Migration Between India and Trinidad*. Durham, NC: Duke University Press.

O'Brien, Elizabeth Fernandez. Laird, Christopher. *Bèlè/Belair*. Directed by Bruce Paddington, Port of Spain, Trinidad: Banyan Production, 1980.

Sloat, Susanna. 2010. *Making Caribbean Dance, Continuity and Creativity in Island Cultures*, xxx-xxi. University Press of Florida.

PART IV

Africa

Africa, the birthplace of the human race, is the second largest continent on earth. Its rich and multifaceted dance cultures reflect Africa's centrality in the story of humanity from ancient times to the present. However, centuries of colonial exploitation and distortion of African realities mean that African dance is often erroneously perceived as a single entity. While there are philosophies and cultural concepts that connect dance practices across different communities, ethnicities, and nations in Africa, the dances themselves and their purposes vary widely. At the same time, the African diaspora—wrought by the enslavement and exile of more than 11 million people over several centuries—cemented the worldwide influence of African dance cultures. At the heart of these Afro-descendant expressions is *dance-musicking*—the reality of dance and music as an inextricable and potent cultural force. However, while the fact of the music–dance relationship may be constant in Africanist traditions, the specific ways in which it is used depend on a given culture's history, yielding a wide range of dance–music practices across the African continent. The following chapters from Ghana, Uganda, and Zimbabwe illuminate dance cultures and histories from the west, central, and south areas of the continent, respectively. Each country has a unique history and thus unique dances that nonetheless serve a similar, critical role of creating, teaching, and supporting communal identity.

 HK*Propel* includes web links to additional resources for this section.

8

Dance in Ghana

Jennies Deide Darko

Learning Objectives

After reading this chapter you will be able to do the following:

- Use dance and its development to recognize essential qualities of Ghanaian history and culture.
- Identify the functions of Ghanaian dance and why these functions are important.
- Identify cultural and religious connections with the dances.
- Compare some regional variations in Ghanaian dance development.
- Analyze the social dynamics of Ghanaian dance culture.

Key Terms

durbar—A public gathering; also the space where the gathering happens.

fontomfrom—Traditional dance among the Ashantis and Akwapims. Also a name of a drum.

Ga people—Part of the larger Ga-Adangme tribal group of Ghana.

Gold Coast—Previous name of the region whose major land area became Ghana.

Homowo—Name of festival among the Ga traditional area in Accra, Ghana.

kpa—Homowo festival dance.

woyei—Fetish priestesses.

Dance in the Ghanaian Worldview

Dance to us is not outside of daily life, not an escape, nor a spectacle. Dance lies at the center of our world, each and every moment of existence.

In an interview, Kofi Owusu, a royal and a son of a linguist from the chief's palace at Adukrom Akwapim in the eastern region of Ghana, said that **fontomfrom** dance features prominently at royal funerals. All citizens of the royal lineages (the ones who have not converted to Christianity) have the fontomfrom played during their burials and funerals. These events provide a platform for the departed to be eulogized for the valiant and virtuous feats they accomplished while alive. The drum also interprets moves of various accomplished dancers as they express shock, sorrow, and a sense of loss at the departure of the deceased. These dancers usually include the deceased's family members, spouses, and children. Through the dance performances, the society assures the bereaved members of support in the absence of their departed relations (K. Owusu, personal communication, Nov. 16, 2019).

"To us life, with its rhythms and cycles is Dance. The Dance is life expressed in dramatic terms. The most important events in the community have special dances to enhance their meaning and significance. To us the Dance is a language, a mode of expression, which addresses itself to the mind, through the heart, using related, relevant and significant movements, which have their basic counterparts in our everyday activities, to express special and real-life experiences in rhythmic sequences to musical and poetic stimuli. For a deeper insight into our way of life, our labours, material culture, aspirations, history, social and economic conditions, religious beliefs and disbeliefs, moments of festivity and sadness—in short, our life and soul, and the realities perceived, conceived, or felt, that make us the people that we have been and are at present, are revealed to the serious seeker, in our dance" (Opoku 1965).

In the statement in the opening vignette, dance artist and scholar Mawere Opoku (1965) captured the essence of dance in the Ghanaian worldview. It is a general perception that people in various Ghanaian cultures enjoy speaking without their voices and use dance as a medium of communication. In most African societies, dancing plays pivotal roles in all the major stages of life from birth through to death. Dance is regarded as one of the leading performing arts forms, manifesting in religious, social, occupational, and ceremonial events. It serves, among other things, as a facilitator of unity, a demonstrator of the complexities of cultures, a communicator, an entertainer, a correction agent, a mode of exercise, and an occupation. Dance is, on the one extreme, spectacular and vigorous, but it is also solemn and graceful on other occasions.

Although dance anthropologist Pearl Primus' (1996) assertion that the African was the first to dance has been variously contested by many scholars, there is certainly no doubt that dancing is important in the Ghanaian worldview. Indeed, in practical terms, you can find dance in most places—most celebrations and most significant events of our life cycle. There are dances during the naming of newborn babies, puberty rites, marriages, festivals, and funerals. Wives dance to spite their rivals in polygamous unions; sports fans dance to celebrate victories. Hedonism seems to be on the ascendency in Ghana, and there is dancing in bars, in nightclubs, on beaches, and on the streets. Dance has even crept into the commercial domain, where it is used for advertising consumer goods (Darko 2016). All these factors probably validate Opoku's claim that to Ghanaians, *dance is life*. Movement and dance have been powerful instruments for keeping community events alive in most Ghanaian societies.

There are four broad categories of dance in the African context: social, religious, occupational, and ceremonial.

- Social dances are used to entertain, to make merry, and to socialize. An example is the **kpanlogo** dance among the **Ga people**, who predominantly live in the south of Ghana. It is performed by the youth of both sexes.

- Religious dances are dances associated with religion. An example is the **yeve** dance performed by the **Anlos** of the Volta Region of Ghana. They are dances associated with the cult and by initiates of a secret society.

The dance helps the citizens to communicate with their ancestors.

- Occupational dances depict the kind of work of a people or actions that characterize a person's occupation. An example is the *adevu*—hunters' dance—from the Volta Region.
- Ceremonial dances, like the fontomfrom dance among the **Akan** people, are performed to commemorate funerals of political leaders and other important events.

This chapter examines, in detail, one social dance and one ceremonial dance from two of the dominant ethnic groups in Ghana to illustrate how dance in Ghana fulfills its central role in the culture.

 See resource 8.1 in HK*Propel* for web links.

Brief History

The area now known as Ghana has been occupied since at least 4000 BCE by various groups. Migration of peoples within the area and from neighboring regions has long defined the shape of Ghanaian society. Colonization by Islamic and European powers also put its stamp on the nation, formerly known as the **Gold Coast**. This name encapsulates ancient Ghana's renown for its wealth of gold mines and mastery of the gold trade, placing the African rulers at the core of a vibrant economy. When Europeans arrived, they colonized Ghana's coastal areas first, starting in 1482 with the Portuguese. In subsequent centuries, Dutch, Swedish, Danish, German, and British colonizers jockeyed for power over the wealthy region. "With the opening of European plantations in the New World during the 1500s, which suddenly expanded the demand for slaves in the Americas, trade in slaves soon overshadowed gold as the principal export of the area" and Ghana became central to the slave trade (GhanaWeb-Gold Coast/Slavery).

Starting in the late 1800s, the British colonized Ghana, and though the African population was largely excluded in the political procedures of the colony, in 1957 Ghana became the first African nation to declare independence from European colonialism. The turning point was the return to the Gold Coast in 1947 of **Kwame Nkrumah** (1909-1972) to become General Secretary of the

The Slave Trade in Africa

Ghana was a major conduit for slaves taken to the New World. "During the heyday of early European competition, slavery was an accepted social institution, and the slave trade overshadowed all other commercial activities on the West African coast. To be sure, slavery and slave trading were already firmly entrenched in many African societies before their contact with Europe. In most situations, men, as well as women, captured in local warfare became slaves. In general, however, slaves in African communities were often treated as junior members of the society with specific rights, and many were ultimately absorbed into their masters' families as full members. Given traditional methods of agricultural production in Africa, slavery in Africa was quite different from that which existed in the commercial plantation environments of the New World" (GhanaWeb-Gold Coast/Slavery).

United Gold Coast Convention, the main political movement agitating for self-government. Following many vicissitudes, Nkrumah became prime minister in 1952 and served again after independence in 1957. The current republic, now led by **Nana Addo Danquah Akuffo Addo**, has endured since 1992.

 See resource 8.2 in HK*Propel* for web links.

Crosscurrents

Most contemporary historians tend to interpret the history of the emergence of Ghana as the creation of an artificially designated nation-state, discounting the natural kinships that exist between the different ethnic groups and their cultures. Sociologists Smock and Smock (1975) opine that several historians and commentators have simply presumed that Ghana's evolution into a nation-state occurred with the onset of colonialism. The effect of such presumptions on Ghana's emergence as a sociopolitical unit is that it comes to be regarded as a conglomeration of disparate tribal units, with no natural connections with one another, either historically or culturally. This perception underestimates the historical role of migration within Africa and cross-cultural exchange in shaping Ghanaian identity, and similarly undervalues the implications for dance in cross-cultural cohesion.

Cultural Bonds Versus Colonial Structures—Migration and Identity

It is noteworthy that, apart from external borders and state structures that were artificially created, cultural bonds between the various ethnic groups are largely natural. While the colonial experience was significant in connecting the peoples of Ghana as a geopolitical entity, it is only one of the several important stages in a natural process of evolution. Colonialism bestowed its structures of modern nationhood to the independent Gold Coast. However, the sense of belonging together as one people started to evolve long before the first Europeans arrived. In fact, colonial rule interfered with what was a fairly natural process of evolution and distorted what would have been the physical borders and naturally evolved political systems of the nation-states that eventually emerged. Historian Ivor Wilks posits that Ghanaian culture grew from various stages of a historical process during which a sense of bonding as a people who belong together emerged progressively, despite the bitter interethnic state rivalries marked by wars, burdensome payments of tributes by the vanquished, and slave raids.

Historians have discussed the extensive cultural interaction among the peoples of West Africa that must have occurred as early as the period between 500 CE and 1000 CE. These interactions involved migrations of peoples from one part of the subcontinent to another. The ancestors of many of the ethnic groups in contemporary Ghana were part of this development. According to scholars, the inhabiting of the land was marked by continuous movements of groups in different directions. Scholars cannot agree on the nature of these migrations, and their exact trails are difficult to reach. But there is almost complete unanimity that such movements did take place (Wilks 1961). Studies of oral traditions that explained origins have enabled scholars to build reasonably plausible theories of migrations and resettlements. Major ethnic groups such as the Akan, **Ga-Adangme**, **Dagomba**, **Ewe**, and others all became established in Ghana over the centuries through settlement, absorbing other groups, and creating independent states within the region (Salm and Falola 2002, 4-8). The migrants did not all move in one sweep but in batches, and by the end of the year 1200 CE, major movements had ended. Though some further migrants did arrive later, they were small groups of invaders that were absorbed by the existing communities (Boahen 1977).

The beginning of the evolution of a common Ghanaian culture must be located in this period. It has been suggested that the fusion of indigenous societies that were mostly stateless with immigrant peoples who already had centralized political systems led to some important changes in that period. Borrowing of cultural ideas and practices between the various peoples who encountered each other in the movements and resettlements that occurred must have been accompanied by a gradual integration of the various groups. Agriculture became an important occupation of the settled communities, and chieftaincy, with its sacral associations, probably began to take shape and spread during the stage of migration. Along with migration, trade and other forms of contact led to cultural fusions among the peoples of Ghana and between them and their neighbors. Such free movements of peoples and contacts no doubt led to the diffusion of cultural ideas and practices.

A Multiplicity of Customs

Ghana is a land replete with numerous tribes and a profusion of languages and customs. Ghana also has many idiosyncrasies that make it inimitable and different. Because the dance is so closely attuned to the daily life of the people, these customs, in turn, can be reflected in the subject matter, settings, participants, and intentions of the dances themselves—for instance, the Ga love the communal life. The families usually live together even after the adults are married, and dances are informal, dealing with community life. Among the Ga and other peoples, Ghanaian customs surrounding gossip, adultery, witchcraft, and the like are engaged through dances such as *gome*, *sikyi*, and *akom*.

Konkonsa—Gossip

Ghanaians love gossiping, especially the women, a trend quite prevalent in the churches and the hair salons. People who chatter a lot are called *konkonsa*, which literally means busybodies. In the typically tight-knit Ghanaian communities, everyone knows everyone else's business. As you will see later, some dances specifically use this penchant for gossip to impart social lessons and manage community relations. An example is the gome dance from the Greater Accra Region.

Jolley—Adulterer

Jolley is a word whose origin is not widely remembered. It refers to a lover, or an intimate acquaintance, that is not one's spouse. Jolleys are very popular in the urban areas of Ghana because they are fun loving, quite a big contrast to the ring-clad wives who are more interested in attending weddings and funerals, where they can show off the ornaments on the finger. Some Ghanaian dances, such as sikyi, feature amorous gestures where the dancers seem to be too familiar with one another.

Anyen—Witch

Ghanaians believe in the supernatural and that there are good, kind spirits who facilitate the progress and well-being of people who have pleased them. On the other hand, they also believe in evil spirits that delight in destruction and bloodshed. There is more talk of witches (female) rather than wizards (men). It is believed that witches live on human blood and can be any age. In Ghana, a witch is called *anyen*, and some dances are used to exorcise such evil spirits. An example is the akom dance among the Akans.

Traditional Dances From Ghana

Customs among the many different ethnic groups in Ghana have led to a wide range of traditional dances, a few of which are named here.

- Social: kpashimo, **gota**, sikyi, **asedua**
- Ceremonial: fontomfrom, **damba**, **kundum**, **adowa**
- Occupational: adevu, gome, kpanlogo
- Religious: **kple**, akom, **tigari**

The breadth of dances in Ghana is truly expansive in each category, and while a few were discussed briefly in connection with the customs that inspire them (such as sikyi, gome, and akom as commentary on adultery, gossiping, and witchcraft, respectively) it is impossible to illustrate them all fully in this chapter. However, by focusing on one social dance (*kpa*), and one ceremonial dance (fontomfrom), the close connections between dance and life in Ghana can be made visible.

 See resource 8.3 in HK*Propel* for web links.

Social Dance

Kpa in the Homowo Festival of the Ga People

The Ga people are an ethnic group in Ghana that belong to the larger Ga-Adangme tribal group. They live primarily in the greater Accra region of Ghana. Their language is also called *Ga*. Gas are generally patrilineal, and family inheritance is through the paternal line. The Ga tribe is divided into towns, and each of them is headed by a *mantse* (chief). The traditional annual festival of the Gas is the **Homowo** festival (Abbey 2010). *Homowo* means "hooting at hunger." During the Homowo festival, there is drumming and dancing at the shrines, on the *durbar* (public reception area) grounds, and in every nook and cranny in the town (homes, drinking bars, streets). "In the afternoon there is a public dance with possessed *"woyei"* (priestesses). There is also a dance competition organized for the youth to enliven the celebrations" (Field 1961, 73).

Homowo is an example of a migration festival, and it commemorates the origin of the Ga people, as well as their migration to Ghana, which was fraught with many challenges, including a famine. They sought to grow millet (a grain), and upon achieving a great harvest they had cause to "hoot at hunger" (Abbey 2010, 5).

Teshie Homowo and Kpa Dance

The Teshie Homowo takes place in August of each year, following the celebrations of the event in the city of Accra (also known as Ga Mashie, home of the original Ga settlers). To commemorate the escape from famine, citizens prepare sumptuous dishes of **kpoikpoi** (the traditional Homowo dish), accompanied by palm nut soup laden with large fishes called **tsile** and **odaa** for their loved ones, friends, and well-wishers. The other aspect is the kpa performances. Abbey (2010) states that "the Homowo festival is preceded by some traditional religious rites, including the **shibaa** (the planting of millet and the ban on noisemaking for thirty (30) days); the **odada** (the lifting of the ban on noisemaking); and the **nsho bulemo** (the purification of the sea, done by the **wulomei**, the fetish priests) between April and July."

Teshie Homowo Festival

Teshie is an important town on the southern coast of Ghana and part of the Greater Accra Region. Its people initially migrated from the town of La, and their main occupations are fishing and fish selling; thus the Teshie festival is a prime example of the Homowo's origins and function. Because the town is situated on the way to the Tema port (Ghana's principal port of entry), Teshie has become an important economic hub, and many artisans and traders have thriving businesses there. Every year the Teshie Homowo is a major event.

The Ga people are deeply religious and ascribe all blessings and good fortune to the Supreme Being and the gods. Similarly, they believe that the deities, the state, and the general public punish people who do not do what is right (Opaku

1978). Each society has its own ideal of what is considered acceptable and unacceptable behavior. Moral decadence is considered a disgrace in the view of the Teshie people, and they continually strive to find ways of dealing with it. Naturally, they expect punishment meted out to offenders to serve as a deterrent to other potential offenders. The Teshie people go to great lengths to remind members that it pays to be morally upright. Nuertey Nortey, a traditional elder of Teshie, says that during Homowo the people of Teshie use song and dance to praise members of good moral standing and expose the nefarious deeds of miscreants (personal communication, July 28, 2019). These methods are very effective because the songs and dances are performed on the streets of Teshie in the full glare of all and sundry. In some instances, national and political leaders are not spared. The society perceives moral decadence as a disgrace, and the punishment meted out to offending individuals is meant to send the message that moral uprightness is a virtue, and therefore no one should in any way attempt to disregard it. There is no doubt in any indigene's mind that one is bound to receive reward or retribution, depending on their behavior in the society.

The main means of addressing the behavior of members of the Teshie society is singing songs and dancing. These mediums are so powerful that anyone who uses them derives the pleasure of telling the society or the whole world about the misdeeds, or the good deeds of a society member on the streets of Teshie. During the Homowo festival, the people air their views on any topic freely, and the bad behaviors of the people are fully sanctioned by the people, with the support of the deity. Anyone airing their views or sanctioning any member of the society during this period works within the confines of the law, as far as the deity (who is responsible for this sanction) is concerned. During the kpa performances, the people are free to openly express their views without fear of retribution, since they believe the gods themselves have granted them permission.

Kpa Music

According to D. Obeng-Bene, a royal of Teshie, kpa music is a vocally oriented musical genre, with performances by individuals or by groups (personal communication, March 7, 2019). During the kpa, the dancers make social commentaries on issues confronting the society while running through the streets of Teshie, singing and stamping the feet in the dance known as *kpashimo* (also *kpaashimo*). There are two types of kpa music, namely, the **Amlakui-akpa** (kpa music for the royals; that is, the chief and members of the chief's family) and **kpashikpa** (music for the nonroyals). During the former, the songs used belong to the royal lineage known as **amlakui** and comprise historical themes.

Royalty of Ghana

In Ghana "the institution of chieftaincy is guaranteed by the constitution. Although chiefs are not permitted to participate in politics, they play an important role in Ghanaian society. The National House of Chiefs has authority over traditional laws and customs, and chiefs have a great deal of influence in the community and government" (The World of Royalty).

There are two types of Amlakui-akpa: the ordinary and the "heavy" songs. The latter songs are used to invoke the deity. This is the type of kpa used by the carriers of the **sese**. The sese is a large dish reputed to contain all the bad things that the Teshie people reject. The contents of this container will eventually be emptied into the Sango Lagoon, signifying the end of the Homowo festivities. The Teshie people believe this act of cleansing paves the way for blessings from the gods, including bountiful harvests and plenty of fish. Hence this lamentation.

> Original: Sese yaabu dzan neke afi
>
> Meeloo abaaye?
>
> Translation: Sese shall not overturn till next year
>
> What fish shall we eat? (D. Obeng-Bene, personal communication, March 7, 2019)

Nonroyal citizens use the kpashikpa to comment on current events in the society and on trending national issues. It serves three major social functions. The first is to punish and to reform misbehaving members of the society. Second, it is used to praise and encourage upright citizens. Third, it is used to caution and counsel everyone. According to dance artist Nii Kwei Sowah, who hails from Teshie, the performance of kpashikpa is organized in four main ways, namely, (1) the solo performance, (2) the all-male performance, (3) the all-female performance,

and (4) the mixed-gender performance (personal communication, March 9, 2019).

In his unpublished thesis, Amakye-Boateng (2006) describes the kpa dance as a rhythmic stamping of the feet on the ground, danced in solos or in pairs that face both away and toward each other. The dancer moves side to side and is free to choose the number of steps to take in any one direction. A key feature of all these variations is that the knees, upper body, and arms are slightly bent. As a venerable elder might say, "One does not perform the *kpashimo* in an upright position."

The right steps often coincide with every strong beat of the song. The dance may begin with the right foot, followed by the left, then there is a pause with the arms in half bent position. Pauses are found in most traditional or folk dances. They are either preparing the dancer for a different movement or bringing the dancer to a different level of dynamics. This stamping compensates for the absence of instrumental support. Lyrics in the songs are used to invoke blessings from the Supreme Being, the lesser gods, and the ancestral spirits.

Social Control Through Kpa

During the Homowo festival in 2016 the youth of Teshie lambasted the man who was then president of Ghana. As indicated earlier, one of the main functions of the kpa dance is to address social and political issues through the medium of dancing and singing. The youth had been unhappy about the high level of unemployment among the youth and corruption among public office holders. They were assuring him they would vote against him. Colloquially put, they will "carry his boxes." They are seen in the video carrying his imaginary belongings and running toward the outskirts of the town. They sing and dance, stomping their feet and chanting.

> Here is the key line of the song, which is repeated many times:
>
> John Mahama eei wo ba tele odeka.
>
> Translation:
>
> John Mahama eei we will carry your boxes.

People of the general public may dress as clowns or in other costumes that both conceal the identities of resisters and incite humor (Kwakye-Opong 2014). For instance, some men wear wigs and heavy makeup and carry handbags, while others put on oversized spectacles and face paint. Members of the groups, however, do not necessarily dress uniformly when they set out to parade in the streets and before houses of celebrities. Also, unlike the Amlakui (royal performance), the groups that engage in this version of kpashimo are not required to be barefooted. Usually, no musical instruments are used for the street parades. The tempo of the song is often guided by the foot stamping of the kpa dance.

Color Symbolism in Kpa Performance

According to semantic scholar Kwakye-Opong, clothing and color symbolisms inform the dress code in the kpa dance performances, driving home their messages. There are seven kpa bands—teams of kpa dancers—representing the seven quarters of Teshie, each with its own emblem and colors. For example, the **pot** band represents the society's diversity and is identified by a mixture of colors. Another carries a black *ananse* (trickster) spider emblem representing greed and cunning, while the fifth band carries the American flag to discourage the "America at all cost" mentality that has bedeviled many of the youth in Teshie. The seventh group, *tsese*, is the leading group, believed to hold the soul of the town. It bears the Ghana national flag's colors, red, gold, and green.

 See resource 8.4 in HK*Propel* for web links.

Ceremonial Dance

Fontomfrom

The Akans are one of the dominant ethnic groups in Ghana. They are homogeneous culturally and linguistically, and these attributes enable them to easily assimilate their immediate neighbors, by virtue of their superior political systems. Music is a prominent feature of Akan culture and is used during most traditional events. The main instruments are the drum, the horn, the rattle, and the bell. Music is used for both entertainment and communication. As a communication tool, music is used in the traditional Akan society for both tangible and esoteric reasons, delivering messages through invocations, proverbs, salutations, eulogies, announcements, and warnings.

Among the Akan people from **Adukrom** in the eastern region of Ghana, the fontomfrom dance promotes unity and social cohesion. Fontom-from is widely referred to as the dance of royals, during which talking drums are extensively used to communicate royal messages. These messages are used to honor chiefs as they ride in their palanquins in public, splendidly attired in royal regalia. The drums also praise the royal processions through the recitation of proverbs. Another function of the fontomfrom rhythm is to replicate the patterns of speech at royal gatherings. It sometimes also supports chiefs in their "state-of-the-union" presentations—in full battle dress, reenacting notable achievements of their states and those of their predecessors.

However, the fontomfrom, while prominent, is not practiced throughout Adukrom. The people of Adukrom are **Guans**, whose main vocations are farming and, to a lesser extent, hunting. Among farming families that require adequate labor for their agriculture, the practice of polygamy, for example, is still in vogue in Adukrom. But both this practice and the use of the fontomfrom are not universal. Instead, their presence depends on whether people adhere to traditional religions or practice Christianity. A key reason for this disparity is that Adukrom was home to one of the Salem settlements set up by the **Basel Mission** to separate converted Christians from those that the colonizers perceived to be fetish worshippers (Agyemang 1997). Thus, one can find a clear demarcation of places where Christians live and places where the other citizens reside who vigorously practice fontomfrom.

Fontomfrom in Funerals

At funerals, the fontomfrom drums are set close to where the chief and his entourage are seated. The drums are played continuously throughout the event, and since it is a funeral, clothes worn have dark shades (red, dark brown, or black). In the past people were only allowed to wear traditional clothes—men with the cloth wrapped over their shoulders over shorts, and women in *kaba* (a local blouse) and cover cloth with no makeup. Now, however, people are allowed to wear urban clothes, as well as some makeup. When fontom-from is played on the funeral grounds, those who are confident of their proficiency in the dance get closer to the performers, and at any given opportunity exhibit their skills. The dances are normally solo, and the dancers interpret the rhythm that is played.

Dancers and drummers communicate through gestures. The raised index finger of the right

Cultural Highlight

I have been privileged to learn about the Adukrom version of fontomfrom through my frequent visits there for different events in the company of my husband, who hails from there. In the olden days, the fontomfrom drum was used to raise alarm in the community to warn citizens of impending danger. Those were times when technology was not so advanced, and populations were smaller and less dense. The most effective means of communication was the call for the people to gather at the durbar grounds. The Akwapim Ridge (where Adukrom is situated) was also a favorite hunting ground for slave raiders. Even today, there is still a big house at the border of the town in which one can find the remains of a dungeon, where captured slaves were kept before onward transportation to the coast. The people of Adukrom had a lookout on a mountaintop, always warning the townspeople when they were going to be attacked by invaders. Because they were on top of the mountain, they could see those who were coming from the valley early enough, and the fontomfrom was used to rally the people to prepare to defend themselves against the invaders. Now in the current peaceful times, the drum is played for the people to remember their good old days of valor and unity of purpose (Y. Okyere, personal communication, November 6, 2019). When the fontomfrom is being played, the talking drum initiates the rhythm while the dancer interprets it. The drum performance occurs wherever royals are gathered and during functions where the whole town meets, such as durbars, funerals, and festivals. All these events serve to unify the citizens.

The drums are kept in the palace, and the performance of rituals (libation and the slaughtering of a ram) must happen before the drums can be played. The typical fontomfrom ensemble includes the **bommaa**, **atumpan**, **apentema**, **agyegyewa**, **adukrogya**, and **dawuro** drums.

The bommaa (which is the master drum) includes one "male" drum and one "female" drum—so named because their functions in the ensemble mirror societal roles for men and women. So too do the atumpan drums that are used to send the messages. Other supporting drums are the apentema, the agyegyewa, and the adukrogya, all of which are one drum each. There are also two dawuro or bells. The master drummer is called the **okyerema**, and he is the leader of the group and their conductor. It must be noted that fontomfrom is essentially a communicative dance; therefore before one could do the dance proficiently, one needs to understand the drum's language and be capable of interpreting the nuances being churned out by the drum.

hand toward the okyerema means the dancer is asking the drummers to play for him to dance. With two palms together, the chief is asking for togetherness. With the dancer's upper arm facing up, putting the right elbow into the left palm is a sign promising the drummers a bottle of drink when they play for the dancer on the floor. A dancer with eyes wide open as if looking for someone among the people and being unable to find them, followed by a sudden clap of hands and open palms, as if asking "why?," means the dancer cannot comprehend why the deceased had departed at that time.

A drumstick can also be taken from the drummers and given to someone among the people. This is an open invitation to good dancers to come to the dancing floor and share their skills. As they dance, there is a point when the drumming stops. Sometimes when this happens, the dancers embrace themselves or sit on people's laps. The chiefs also dance to express their emotions. Normally when they come onto the floor to dance, many people join in and surround them, two fingers up in a victory sign, appreciating the dance. This promotes socialization among members—the bereaved and those who came to mourn with them. At times, people find their life partners during these occasions.

Fontomfrom During Durbars

Unlike funerals, the movements performed in fontomfrom during durbars (public receptions) are normally open and joyous. Clothes for this event are in brighter colors. Royals, including the chief, also dance during durbars, and it is an opportunity for the citizens to judge the chief's

Fontomfrom drum ensemble.

PIUS UTOMI EKPEI/AFP via Getty Images

dancing prowess. Chiefs who are not confident of their dancing skills take private lessons so they are not embarrassed in public. The chiefs do not typically perform forceful movements like jumping. Instead, they communicate with the drumming by raising both arms up when the drumming is cut. Sometimes, the chief is held at the waist to give him stability while he is dancing and also to hold firm the cloth he is wearing. Sometimes someone from the chief's entourage dances the fontomfrom in front of the chief.

 See resource 8.5 in HK*Propel* for web links.

Summary

As noted throughout this chapter, dance in the Ghanaian worldview is a way of life, enabling people to work, learn, and grow together as a community. Social, ceremonial, occupational, and religious dances all have their roles to play in strengthening societal bonds. The kpa social dance unites people of Teshie during the Homowo, especially the youth, as it is a period where young members also choose their suitors. At the end of each Homowo, family members who were at loggerheads are reconciled, bringing peace and growth for all. The kpashimo also serves as an agent of social control for the Ga people. The Homowo festival provides a suitable platform for the performance to negotiate conflicts and correct social wrongs, all in a friendly and carnival-like atmosphere. Apart from its social and cultural importance, the kpashimo promotes tourism and commercial activity. There is good business, especially for the couturiers who create the colorful costumes.

The ceremonial fontomfrom dance is a medium through which the people of Adukrom negotiate their connections to each other. The dance that used to be a male-only performance is now done by both sexes, furthering community cohesion and better socialization in the town. As with the kpashimo, some people find their life partners through dancing the fontomfrom. Those who have problems in their families manage to resolve them. In keeping with the role of dance in African cultures, the complexities of life among people in Ghana are embraced, engaged, and expressed through motion when voices are raised in song and the drums call forth their rhythms.

Thus, kpashimo and fontomfrom illustrate how the vital threads of community, family, and worldview are woven together in the ever-vibrant steps and sounds of Ghanaian dance.

Discussion Questions

1. Why is dance so important in the Ghanaian worldview?
2. What is your evaluation of Mawere Opoku's claim that "Our life and soul, and the realities perceived, conceived, or felt, that make us the people that we have been and are at present, are revealed to the serious seeker, in our dance"?
3. How well are the concepts of social control, unity, and cohesion revealed in the two dances addressed in the chapter?
4. What are the comparative roles of costume in the kpa and fontomfrom dances?
5. Does the fontomfrom drum really communicate? How is its language interpreted?
6. To what extent is dance involved in Ghanaian life and culture?

 Visit HK*Propel* for access to this chapter's Application Activity.

Selected Glossary

Adukrom—Akan town in the eastern region of Ghana.

Amlakui-akpa—Kpa dance music for the royals.

anyen—A witch.

bommaa—Fontomfrom master drum.

durbar—A public gathering; also the space where the gathering happens.

Ga people—Part of the larger Ga-Adangme tribal group.

Gold Coast—Previous name of the region whose major land area became Ghana.

gome—An occupational dance of the Ga people, reflecting the lives and work of people in a fishing community.

Homowo—A Ga word for "hooting at hunger" or "hunger sleeps," this name is used for a festival among the Ga people.

jolley—Ghanaian slang meaning "lover."

konkonsa—Ghanaian slang meaning "gossip."

kpashikpa—Kpa dance music for non-royals.

kpa—Homowo festival dance.

kpashimo/kpaashimo—Art of doing the kpa dance.

kpanlogo—A social dance among the Ga people.

mantse—chief.

Nkrumah, Kwame (1909-1972)—Ghananian nationalist leader who led the push for independence and served as Ghana's president from independence in 1957 to 1966. https://www.britannica.com/biography/Kwame-Nkrumah.

odada—The lifting of the ban on noisemaking before the Homowo festival begins.

okyerema—Master drummer.

sikyi—Flirtatious dance for Asante youths.

Teshie— An important town on the southern coast of Ghana. The Teshie festival celebrating the migrants to the region who overcame famine is a prime example of the Homowo's origins and function.

woyei—Fetish priestesses.

wulomei—Fetish priests.

Selected References and Resources

Abbey, N.H. 2010. *Homowo in Ghana*. Accra: Studio Brian Communications.

Boahen, A.A. 1977. "Ghana Before the Coming of Europeans." In *Ghana Social Science Journal*.

Darko, J.D. 2016. Dance Performance. An Endorsement for Advertised Products on Television in Ghana. *Journal of Performing Arts* 5 (4).

Dickson, K.B. 1969. *Historical Geography of Ghana*. Cambridge: Cambridge University Press.

Field, M J. 1961. *Religion and Medicine of the Ga People*. London: Oxford University Press.

Gyekye, K. 2003. *African Cultural Values. An Introduction*. Accra: Sankofa Publishing Company.

Kwakye-Opong, R. 2014. "Clothing and Colour Symbolisms in the Homowo Festival: A Cultural Means to Socio Cultural Development." *Research on Humanities and Social Science* 4 (13): 118-119.

Nelson-Adjakpey, T. 1982. "Penance and Expiatory Sacrifice Among the Ghanaian-Ewe and Their Relevance to the Christian Religion." Doctoral diss., Rome.

Opoku, M.A. 1965. *African Dances. A Ghanaian Profile. Pictorial Excerpts From Concerts of Ghanaian Dances*. Ghana: Institute of African Studies. Accra: University of Ghana, Legon.

Primus, P. 1996. "African Dance." In *African Dance: An Artistic, Historical and Philosophical Inquiry*, edited by K.W. Asante. New Jersey: African World Press.

Smock, D.R., and A.C. Smock. 1975. *The Politics of Pluralism: A Comparative Study of Lebanon and Ghana*. New York /Oxford/Amsterdam: Elsevier Scientific.

Wilks, I. 1961. "Ashanti and the Muslims: The Northern Factor in Ashanti History." *The Journal of African History* 3 (3), 518-519. https://doi.org/10.1017/S0021853700003492.

Wilks, I. 1996. "The Blackman's Burden." In *One Nation Many Histories: Ghana Past and Present*, 60-73. Accra: Ghana Universities Press.

9

Dance in Uganda

Inherent Community-Based Agendas in Dancing and Dance-Musicking Traditions

Ronald Kibirige

Learning Objectives

After reading this chapter you will be able to do the following:

- Understand and identify key communal objectives inherent in the dance and dance-music traditions of Uganda.
- Understand and view dance and the process and action of dancing and dance-musicking as cultural-specific forms of community-based interaction through which (past, present, and future) community challenges can be declared and mitigated.
- Understand dance and the action of dancing and dance-musicking from a larger and deeper communal perspective, rather than from only a performative one.
- Understand community traditional dancing and dance-musicking as an important aspect of local community life in Uganda.
- Identify major political and social-political events in the history of Uganda that have shaped the understanding and development of dance traditions.

Key Terms

boko lok—Social interactions at a dance event of the Acholi people.

communitarian approach—An approach that views community as a web of interconnections for individuals' and communities' social-cultural being, growth, and development.

community-based agendas—Implicit and explicit communally understood aims/objectives inherent in the action of dancing and dance-musicking.

dance-musicking—Free and nonprescriptive engagement with music for dancing before and during the dancing; a process of making music through the enaction of dance movements.

knowledge-body or knowledge-bodies—A conglomeration/collection of different aspects and elements of the dance tradition that are seen and known as communally rooted knowledge and situated knowing by way of enacting the dance as a complete entity.

social capital (community-based)—Developed social relations of extended families and community members.

A Lamokowang Dance Event in an Acholi Community

On a Saturday afternoon, a community member arrives at the home of Ladit Oringa, an elder in the village of Alel in Kitgum district. The guest brings *awal* (calabash, a half-gourd instrument), and as part of the usual casual greeting, Ladit Oringa asks his son to bring other drums into the sun. Soon, two more community members arrive, each from a different direction. When the drums are in the sun, the boy plays a random rhythm on the two small *lutinobul* (small high-pitched traditional drums), but very proudly and loudly. A few minutes later, a man from a neighboring family walks in slowly while sounding the *bila* (an **Acholi** wind instrument made from a buffalo's, antelope's, or gazelle's horn). Continuing from the sound of the bila, a woman in the family repeatedly sings out *ojili* (a high-pitched trill) three consecutive times in phrases of about 8 to 10 seconds each. Ladit Oringa picks the sticks from his son and plays the lutinobul for a few seconds and then returns to greeting new arrivals. In the mixture of conversational exchanges, Ladit Oringa's wife brings some cups around, and people continue to flock to Ladit Oringa's homestead. Then several children arrive but stay a distance further away from the center to play and run after each other. Conversation topics flow from cattle to children and more. Two men start trying out their awal. As more people arrive, the compound is filled with chanting in the mixture of sounds of bila, sporadic ojili, invocations, and lots of laughter. From the talking, subtle musicking develops with humming, while some women continue to tie their *gara* (ankle bells), trying out some stamping movements with them; the sounds intensify as more men play the awal at random moments. A woman sings the ojili, but now for a longer period of time (about 15 seconds), and she does so repetitively. She is joined by two women from another corner of the homestead as the singing continues to build. Ladit Oringa shifts the drums to the center of the compound. As it all intensifies, people come closer to each other, some just walking, but some subtly singing, dancing. Robust singing and playing of the awal ensues, with the strength of stamping building. People are still coming, and children are playfully engaged in singing, too. An elder starts to play *rigirigi* (a one-string tube fiddle). Some people watch from the roadside for a few minutes before joining. More elders continue coming in slowly with verbal invocations and sounding the bila at random moments. The lutinobul sounds the main repetitive and quite fast rhythmic sounds. Dance movements develop into linear formations, then evolve into a circle. The *minbul* (an Acholi main mother drum) finally sounds, but for only a short time (about five seconds). Its sounding is welcomed by the whole circle through ululations from within the formulated circle and from those dancing subtly outside it. The minbul steadily joins amid further ululations, ojili, and bila sounds, as the lutinobul continues to adapt its play to the minbul. Full-scale dancing develops and goes on for over an hour before a break. In the breaks, practitioners interact even further, elders gracing the occasion to talk to each other and to other people who come to them. Dancing and **dance-musicking** break out again and again as the joyful event flows on through the day.

 See resource 9.1 in HK*Propel* for web links.

Dance events similar to the one in the opening vignette happen in many rural communities in many regions of Uganda. They occur as local events throughout human life, such as twin births, initiation ceremonies, traditional weddings, and funerals, among many other events and rituals of community life. In areas in and close to townships, these events are mostly planned, while those in more rural communities are both planned and spontaneous. Dancing and dance-musicking are almost always at the center of these events.

It may be challenging to imagine a community thriving on a traditional "communal life," where one respectfully looks upon an elder in the family, the clan, and the community for emotional, spiritual, cultural, and educational, as well as social-political, guidance. In local communities, dancing and dance-musicking are pivotal for learning about and understanding oneself and one's place in the environment. Dance-musicking is the free and nonprescriptive engagement with the music for dancing before and during the dancing. It may also refer to the process of making

A communal dance event in Alel Village in Kitgum District of Northern Uganda.

Photo by the author (Alel Village, Ladit Oringa's Homestead, May 2018)

music through the enaction of dance movements (Kibirige 2020a; Small 1998). This perception of local knowing will help us to understand some of the often taken-for-granted aspects of community dance and music of the different ethnicities of Uganda. The term ***community-based agendas*** is used here to indicate the individual and community intentions, sometimes explicit, but mostly implicit, embedded in dancing and dance-musicking. Being mostly implicit, such agendas unfold beyond what is visible and audible in the performative contexts and dance-musicking events. They manifest in the individual's or community's understanding of the tradition and its functions.

Dance in Ugandan communities, as elsewhere in sub-Saharan Africa, is more complex than what people have written about it. Its core community conception is linked to the notion of cultural self-regeneration through an oral tradition. This tradition is mostly understood as one for passing cultural knowledge from one generation to the next, but little is known about it as a way to safeguard this knowledge, even in the most extreme conditions, such as those experienced in northern Uganda—and Uganda in general—during the 20th century. Although implicit and tacit, community-based agendas continue to thrive in the seemingly simple traditional processes, such as those of dancing and dance-musicking. For many local communities, these processes present a system of knowing that includes both the form and content of knowledge. Multiethnicity in Uganda—often considered only in terms of difference and social-political boundaries—can

be a point of cohesion and positive diversity when viewed through the lens of community-based agendas in traditional dancing and dance-musicking. A brief overview of Uganda's major historical events will give us a backdrop for understanding Uganda's dance and music cultures, and their communal functions today.

Brief History

Uganda is composed of 65 different tribes, each with its dance and dance-music traditions embedded in its core cultural fabric, spread over four regions: the south-central region that is mainly bordered by lake Nalubaale (also known as *Lake Victoria*), the biggest lake in Africa; the western region, bordered by the Democratic Republic of Congo; the eastern region, bordered by Kenya; and the northern region, bordered by South Sudan.

Ethnic groups in Uganda were deeply rooted in the administrative structure of monarchies from as far back as the early 14th century. They are organized in two major linguistic groups— the **Bantu** and the **Nilotics**, each of which came from different directions to the land now known as Uganda. The Bantu group entered from the south and southwest around 1000 to 1300 CE and mostly occupied the western, southwestern, central, eastern, and southeastern parts of this land. They include all the Bantu-speaking ethnic groups in these regions: **Baganda**, **Banyoro**, **Batooro**, **Basoga**, and **Banyankole**, among many other groups. The Nilotics are divided into the highland and the plain Nilotes, spread both in Uganda and Kenya. In Uganda, this group is divided into two subgroups, the **Nilo-Hamites**, who include the **Karimojong**, **Iteso**, **Kumam**, and **Langi**; and the **River-Lake Nilotes**, who include the Acholi, **Alur**, and the **Jopadhola** (or the Luo) (Nzita, Mbaga-Niwampa, and Mukholi 2011).

This ethnic diversity ultimately provided a foothold for the British, who had arrived in the region during the 1860s. Using the dominant Baganda people as an administrative springboard, British colonialism capitalized on the differences between ethnic groups—such as language—to administrate Uganda when it became a British protectorate in 1894.

In the early 1900s, along with the missionary agenda of spreading the English language, there was an unimaginable shift in the traditional dance and music scene as different ethnic groups started using English to communicate with each other. After Uganda's independence in 1962, the traditional dance and music further experienced a revolutionary, patriotic, and nationalistic shift through the formation of a national ensemble dance troupe in 1963 known as the **Heart Beat of Africa** (Hanna 1968). However, the unfolding of democratic dispensations led to the abolishment of monarchies in 1966. The king of Buganda, Sir Edward Muteesa II, who had become the first president of Uganda in 1963, was exiled in 1967, and the Heart Beat of Africa was closed in the same year.

Because kingdoms and chiefdoms were the anchors for communal music, dance, and other cultural expressions, political instabilities led not only to the abolishment of the monarchies, but also to suppression of many cultural activities. Civil unrest followed, particularly with the northern Uganda Lord's Resistance Army (LRA) insurgence that caused an unimaginable disruption in the cultural life of children and youth, many of whom were abducted by LRA rebels and others confined in **internally displaced people's camps**.

However, dance and music traditions are adaptive. Having been at the very core of communal activities and communal life, music and dance expressions continued, though less robustly. Some of them adapted to the situations and were used as modes of protests, as well as expression of communal distrust and dissatisfaction. Upon return of the kingdoms by the current leadership of Uganda in 1993 (Africa Report 1993), there was another shift in the modes of performance as a cultural revival ensued. Drawing on ideas from the defunct national ensemble, dancing, music, and dance-musicking quickly started to cross borders from the rural communities to townships and further on to people of the **Ugandan diaspora**. We see the dance troupes springing up, school music and dance festivals becoming rampant, and music bands and individual artists adapting some Western artistic concepts, genres, and aesthetics into the local dance and music traditions. While this chapter cannot examine all the dance and music traditions of the 65 existing ethnic groups in Uganda, a focus on those in northern Uganda, especially among the Acholi people, and references to several cultures from the other three regions should help illuminate traditional dance and dance-musicking in the nation.

Acholi People of Northern Uganda

The Acholi are one of the **Luo-speaking people**—a subgroup of the Nilotic people in South Sudan, northwestern Kenya, and northern Uganda. The Acholi people are said to have originated from Rumbek Shilluk in South Sudan, led by Rwot Kideli, the grandson of Rwot Luo, who was their first king in about 1650 CE. The Acholi were pastoralists (livestock raisers) and hunters and practice agriculture, occupations to which many traditional music and dance activities are attached. Being pastoralists, they never stayed in one place for a long time, because they moved to find greener pastures for their flock. The dancing embedded in most of their activities can be traced to the time of their migration (1400 CE) through legends of famous ancestors whose lives and sometimes magical activities are still represented in dance and music today. *Otole*—an Acholi local combat/war dance, and *lamokowang*—an Acholi social, reconciliatory, and integratory dance tradition, are just two examples of dances originating in the ancient legends.

In the monarchy of the precolonial era, the *rwot moo* was the supreme ruler and anointed chief who marked his authority through a council of elders. The administrative structure of the Acholi extended from the head of the family through the clan system to the rwot moo before the arrival of the colonialists in the late 1860s. Although weakened, such administrative structures still exist in the regions of Buganda, Busoga, Bunyoro, and Ankole. (Note that Buganda is the place where the Baganda people live, Busoga where the Basoga people live, and so forth.) Chiefs and kings are still influential among their people (subjects) and are responsible for upholding traditions, as well as for using these traditions to solve communal conflicts.

Although the continued spread of British colonial influence weakened many monarchies, it strengthened those that they used in war to suppress other monarchies and extend British rule. For example, social anthropologist Lloyd Fallers (1961) says that "the Buganda monarchy located in the south central region was used as the stepping-stone for the British colonizers to invade and weaken Bunyoro and Busoga monarchs" (678). Buganda kingdom therefore grew stronger than many other monarchies with the support and empowerment of the British.

Northern Uganda Civil War: 1986-2006

While community-based agendas embedded in dancing and dance-musicking processes can be identified and seen to unfold in many situations in the Ugandan society even today, the postwar situation in northern Uganda presents particular highlights of these agendas' entrenchment in the core cultural fabric of the Ugandan populace.

Internal strife for political power, fueled by religious (mainly Catholic, Protestant, and Islam) and tribal differences (which, in part, developed due to British occupation before independence) divided the country so much that the British handover of the instruments of power in 1962 sparked a national state of successive political insurgences from 1962 to 1986. A culmination of these instabilities was the northern Uganda two-decade civil war of the LRA, led by Joseph Kony.

The Acholi people experienced a horrendous time during this war, where children and youths were abducted. Many were killed, many were indoctrinated, and many were forced to commit grave atrocities onto their own communities, including, but not limited to human slaughter and destruction of property and homesteads.

A report from **Resolve Uganda Inc.** (2009)—a research and funding program for communities affected by the LRA—estimates that 30,000 children and youths were abducted, and over 1.7 million people were forced into internally displaced people's camps between 1987 and 2006, which accounted for about 98 percent of the Acholi population.

However, even in the face of such atrocities, and upon genuine analysis of the community norms and values in local practices of dancing and dance-musicking, community-based agendas embedded in such practices are unescapable.

 See resource 9.2 in HK*Propel* for web links.

Dancing and Dance-Musicking

Embedment and Activation of Community-Based Agendas

Many communities in Uganda commonly understand dancing and dance-musicking practices as communal **knowledge-bodies**—a conglomeration/collection of material and nonmaterial elements of the dance tradition that are seen and known as communally rooted knowledge. From a communal perspective, dancing is an established system of knowing. Knowledge in the tradition is activated, safeguarded, and transmitted through enacting it, and the knowledge-body is the knowledge itself, rather than a "container" of the knowledge. Both material and nonmaterial elements that practitioners associate with the tradition form this knowledge-body.

In Uganda and other countries of East Africa, the sense of affiliation to a specific group of people with common cultural traits and history is one of the fundamental pillars onto which most communities are built. Having experienced the wrath of colonialism, religious invasion, protracted wars, and weakening of the traditional forms of administration (monarchies and chiefdoms), Ugandans' ethnic identity does seem to be a cohesive force that brings such communities together. Nevertheless, struggles with ethnic ambivalence for those living in major townships arise, springing from current cosmopolitan lifestyles in such cities. The notion of multiethnicity has mainly been looked at from a point of difference and social-political boundary, rather than from a point of cohesion, positive diversity, and **social capital**—an understanding of multiethnicity that is, to a large extent, politically motivated. With in-depth analysis and understanding of ethnicity, important threads of positive community-based agendas emerge in traditional processes of dancing and dance-musicking.

Each of the 65 ethnic groups in Uganda has its own music and dance traditions. Local practitioners identify values and norms from the name of the tradition to its category; from its occasion of enactment to its season of enaction; from its gender constructions to the ages of its enactors; from its "choreography" to its structural form; and from its executed movement phrases down to the smallest meaningful step patterns. It is clear that Acholi communities depend on such traditions not only for individual and communal expression, but also for their interpretation of life itself. Particular ethnic groups and their dance cultures are windows to broader perspectives of the traditions through three community agendas: community coexistences, social capital and protection, and communal knowledge safeguarding and transmission, as illustrated in figure 9.1.

A Communitarian Approach to Coexistence

Myel Bwola and Other Dance Traditions Across Uganda

Community is the fulcrum upon which dance and dance-musicking traditions rest. While local or rural communities are defined as natural and informal groupings of families and clans in regular interactions, those in urban cosmopolitan settings might be formulated somewhat differently. Nonetheless, within a given community, the process of dancing and dance-musicking is still one of activating shared communal agendas. Dance and music traditions being functional, these agendas can be traced from the general communal understanding of a dance tradition, the concept of dance, and the choreographic and nonchoreographic structures down to the individual and communal motivations of the dance in question. For instance, similar to the lamokowang event described in the opening vignette, *inemba* dance is enacted as part of the *imbalu/impalu* circumcision ritual event of the **Bamasaaba** people of eastern Uganda (Makwa 2012; Were 1977). In this tradition, participants share a moment of common action, space, and time—a moment when all individual and communal differences are suspended and mitigated, or even where they begin a process of dissolution. In this **communitarian approach**, society is understood as a web of interconnections for individuals' and communities' social-cultural being, growth, and development. Within this interconnectivity and interhumanism in the imbalu ritual, each individual "is" because others "are"—the core understanding that is at the center of the African philosophy of **Obuntu/Ubuntu**.

In the Acholi communities of Patongo, at different stages in life—for example, birth, childhood, adolescence, marriage, death and burial—specific rituals that involve traditional dancing and dance-musicking are enacted. As journalist Peter Holslin rightly argued, "Anything to do with life in Acholi, whether life, or death, or pleasure, is always accompanied by dancing" (Holslin 2008, 1).

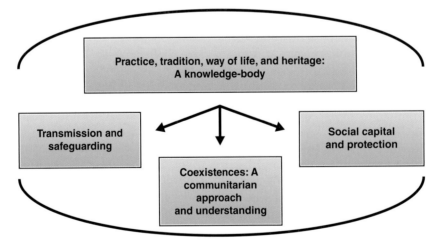

Figure 9.1 Community-based agendas in dancing and dance-musicking.

Dance and music dialogical moment by practitioners George Lukoya and Michael Ocaya.

Community elders in Patongo village have described that the ***myel bwola*** dance was and continues to be performed in the processions, coronation, or even death of the rwot (chief). In addition to being performed in the chiefs' palaces, it is enacted in processions leading the chiefs and the royals to and from a communal event. According to Lajul Ventorino, an elder from the subcounty of Kitgum Matidi, the dance started being performed in the palaces of the *rwodi* (chiefs) in the 1920s. As the powers of chiefs in the Acholi subregion waned due to the colonial administrative influence, and later on due to the abolishment of cultural institutions, myel bwola crossed tribal and ethnic boundaries to the more urban areas, such as Kampala.

Myel bwola is considered a deep-rooted form of expression of pride and admiration of the rwodi that does not necessarily need any formal audience apart from the "royals." Myel bwola dancers of old immersed themselves into the dance without preconditions. With passion, they stood guard

for the chief and paraded their achieved seniority in the repetitive movement patterns of the dance. Today, it is performed at social-communal occasions, at the coronation of chiefs in the Acholi subregion, and at many occasions in the urban areas, especially at social occasions for or socialization by individuals from northern Uganda. The dance is an outstanding marker of Acholi identity. The myel bwola tradition embeds in its people a thick context of traditions, changes, tensions, and unquestioned assumptions and practices (Bell 1997; Turner 1977; Kertzer 1988). It is one of the traditional royal dances of the Acholi people, in which a number of inherent community-based agendas can be investigated and understood from both a micro and a macro perspective.

Organized within a chiefdom structure, the Acholi politics, religion(s), and traditions function in strict conformity with the Acholi social-cultural strata (Atkinson 1989, 1994; Girling 1960; Gray 1952; Bere 1947). This stratum adheres to a communitarian approach to cultural socialization and access to knowledge (Avineri and de-Shalit 1992; Etzioni 2014). In the communitarian approach, the community is seen as an incubator, a continuation, and a maintenance chamber of morals, cultural norms, and values. Although these are both an individual and a communal responsibility, the sense of "the we" is more pronounced than "the I," especially insofar as community culture is concerned. At the same time, however, individual practitioners' skills have a lot of relevance because their individual participation in communal events ratifies the tradition as a whole.

Dance and Music in Dialogue

Myel bwola dancing and dance-musicking are pluralistic in nature. As evident in the dance event described earlier, members of the community talk through dancing and dance-musicking. As such, the communitarian spirit is developed and maintained through individuals who are part of the community, embodying norms and values inherent in the tradition. Learning to dance and the actual dancing are both individual and shared experiences, skills of which are developed over time to benefit both the individual practitioner and the community at large. The process of obtaining and transmitting such skills depends on the individual's interactions within a community of able practitioners. Interdependence and coexistence are paramount. The bodily, sonic, and verbal dynamics inherent in the dancing and dance-musicking ensure an event of interaction—an event that mitigates conflicts through coexistent sharing of moments, space, and time in meaningful dance and dance-music patterns. It becomes a time of building and maintaining good relations, as well as dissolving bitter ones, all of which are part of the notion of coexistence.

The coexistent transfer of community knowledge inscribed in the myel bwola dance event and dance-musicking itself is described by social learning theorist Etienne Wenger as locating "learning not in the head or outside it, but in the relationship between the person and the world, which for human beings is a social person in a social world. In this relation of participation, the social and the individual constitute each other" (1998, 1). Wenger is presenting learning, here, as a product of social structure, where community socialization is key. It is unusual for a dance practitioner in the local communities of Uganda to dance alone, not only in the myel bwola tradition, but also in many other dance traditions, such as

in the circular dance formations and verbal invocations of the lamokowang tradition described at the beginning of this chapter. Further, in the *baakisimba* tradition of the Baganda people of central Uganda, coexistent dialogue is evident in the layering of the dancing and its dance-music (Nannyonga-Tamusuza 2005). The patterns of the main drum (*embuutu*) exist in constant dialogue with the two high-pitched drums (*namunjoloba*), and the long drum (*engalabi*), as well as with the major female dancers' foot and hip movements. Sound and movement patterns coexist even in the smallest meaningful phrases and patterns, structurally enhancing the overarching communal functions of the tradition. In and beyond the sound and movements, dancers and dance-musicians—by doing these and many other dance traditions across the four regions—are always in constant explicit and implicit connection. The communitarian understanding and practice reinforces a communal development of the common core values of coexistence, because one's wellness, growth, and development depend on that of another.

Local Community Safeguarding and Transmission of Knowledge: Bwola Dance Tradition

The communitarian approach to coexistence suggests communal activities of myel bwola, lamokowang, baakisimba, inemba, and other dance and dance-music traditions as methods of safeguarding and transmitting knowledge—an inherent community agenda among Ugandan local communities that was undermined during the colonial period (1894-1962), in the period of abolition of kingdoms (1967-1993), and (for the northern Uganda region in particular) during the northern Uganda civil war (1986-2006). During the war, families were forced into internally displaced people's camps, which constricted the spaces for cultural practices such as dancing and dance-musicking, whose growth and effect in absence of other transmission and safeguarding methods sorely depends on continued enactions. Confining people in camps went against most of their communal modes of life, because it was difficult to convene for communal interactive events of practices such as dancing and dance-musicking, or for the *wangoo*, where families gathered around a fireplace outside to learn through sto-

Lira Palwo dancers performing myel bwola.

ries and other verbal forms of transmitting and learning from traditions (Erling and Bakka 2017).

The introduction of internationally recognized (formal) education during the British occupation caused a positive shift in the transfer of formal and informal knowledge and presented an opportunity to elevate the perception of local communities to the wider world (Pier 2011; Muyanda-Mutebi 1996). Ethnic groups were able to communicate better through a common language, English. However, it is clear that formal education is insufficient to the task of maintaining and transmitting local traditions that rely upon the communal approach to thrive, because the formal system has not yet adopted local ways of knowing. Fortunately, there are scholars now engaged in archiving, repatriating old records of these traditions, advocating for and adapting indigenous pedagogy, and formalizing their access within communities and in formal education institutions to enhance their transmission. This is an effort to bridge the gap between the formal and informal knowledge bases (Mabingo, Ssembatya, Ssemaganda, and Kibirige 2020; Nannyonga-Tamusuza and Weintraub 2012).

The communitarian approach being based on person-to-person relationships and practical experiences propagates an open oral self-regeneration in its transfer from one generation to another. If it had been kept only in a written form, given the unfolding and development of the northern Uganda insurgence, much of it would have been lost during the civil war, when villages were destroyed and people fled into the bush.

Traditional forms of communal expressions in Uganda have existed before the emergence of the formal education as valid systems of knowing, intangible cultural heritage, and pedagogical tools in local communities (Kibirige 2020b; Mabingo 2015, 2019, 2020). Communal and ritual events are seen as the place and time not only where one can access their inherent knowledge, but deeply understand it and its practical functions in the community. Some dance practitioners have described how this knowledge is transferred –or not—when traditional communal settings and practices are disrupted.

Through the communal understanding of dance and music traditions as knowledge-bodies, in which traditional aspects of belonging are engaged, and through the creation and maintenance of individual and communal relations and bonds, dance and music traditions become focal points and events where the young returnees and the older generation interface for the local community agenda of transmission and safeguarding to unfold.

Despite some efforts to document and archive dance and music traditions in Uganda and in East Africa, present practical dancing and dance-musicking processes in many communities are mainly practiced and seen as informal ways

Cultural Highlight

Constantine Odida Ojegele, a myel bwola and lamokowang practitioner from Oguda village, spoke of this learning process. While pointing to a communal form of accessing the knowledge, he articulates the difficulties during the war that hindered local forms of transmission.

Whether in the war time or before, no one would come to you and ask you to go and learn dancing. When you have family gatherings, lamokowang events, when there are rituals, or when for children—when they are playing on their own. This is when we learn. For me I learnt to play the *adungu* (arched harp) and dancing by looking at the elders, for example my father. And also listening. At school, at primary, we only danced during break time as children, not in class. I remember, when we had to hide ourselves from the teachers to try out how people were dancing in the evening so that we can also join the **Orak dance circle**. But in the bush, we did not have time, even a thought to dancing—in the IDPs there was time but not enough space sometimes. It is all different—we [were] always scared everywhere. (personal communication, September 28, 2007)

of knowing. Effective, understood, cherished, and relevant in the communities as they may be, they are neither yet directly incorporated in the formal academic system, nor appropriately documented and systematized as forms of reference in the formal education system. While this fact still limits their transmission to the young generation, especially today, this community agenda of transmission and safeguarding is continued and maintained in the communities through the continuous processes of enaction/reenaction and performance among the bearers of the tradition and beyond.

 See resource 9.3 in HK*Propel* for web links.

Activation of Individual and Community Human Social Capital

Communal moments of dancing and dance-musicking are more than just performance. They embed implicit aspects of cultural and social-cultural life that run deep in family life. Many communities in sub-Saharan Africa are built on a family structure, with many extended family members living in close proximity, where they can reach out and care for each other.

In their communal interactive and inclusive nature, dancing and dance-musicking activate communal healing, inclusion, community coexistence, reconciliation, and reintegration. They also activate social relations that are a form of capital that family and community members—especially the elderly—enjoy, but also depend on, such as in situations of financial difficulty. This activation is achieved particularly through a common denominator of social interaction known as **boko lok** in the Acholi communities.

This activation through boko lok exists not only in the music and dance encounters of the event, but also in the formations, sound and bodily nuances, music phrases, and individual and communal attitudes toward each other developed in the processes of doing. These elements are usually taken for granted. Scholars who have studied the often taken-for-granted societal rules of stigmatized populations (such as those in northern Uganda who endured civil strife) share a view that displaced people strive to compartmentalize their identity in the places they find themselves (Stokes 1994; Turino 1999). "They always strive to erect boundaries between themselves and the people they encounter in the new homes, creating identities of 'them' versus 'us' and 'ours' as opposed to 'theirs'" (Stokes 1994, 317), with a clear, but sometimes unconscious, goal of building social bonds and coexistence, deciding on which relations to embrace, and coping with their new environment—all of which are elemental to understanding of the notion of social capital.

Individuals' social capital is at play during social interaction. People may increase it, risk that it decreases, or depend on it to understand how to interact with each other.

This can be why the Acholi communities explicitly set up procedures where social interaction is used as a tool for integration. Dance movements and healing rituals are at the very core of such tools and have been used as social therapy since time immemorial. Although not yet well studied, especially on artistic micro levels, in communal contexts, the community agenda of social capital is not only evident in the socially interactive dancing and dance-musicking, but also at the core of many dance rituals among traditions across the nation. For example, in highly interactive dance traditions, such as lamokowang, the activation of human social capital is embedded not only in the processes of dancing, but also in the metaphorical *la-moko-wang* existence in the communities. In this *la-moko-wang* existential metaphor, *la* ("I/they/we/it") indicates an individual practitioner or community's intrinsic coexistences and relations with its context—both visible and invisible. The *moko* relates to interaction or negotiation, and the *wang* implies "eyeing/looking/seeing" deeply and understanding the essences of a community challenge or situation that is a function of the lamokowang tradition (Kibirige 2020a). In the lamokowang dance and dance-musicking interactions, a knowledge-based dialogue ensues between the sound, movement, invocations, facial expressions, and material aspects of the traditions, such as the instruments, attire, and props used by the different practitioners, families, clans, and sometimes tribes.

For lamokowang practitioners, to dance is not only to learn, to teach, to inform, and to continuously transform, maintain, and preserve traditional knowledge, but also to initiate, develop, and maintain human relations that turn into social capital for individual practitioners and the community at large. Social capital is activated particularly through the moko section/concept of this tradition. In the lamokowang process, there is a moment that is known as *moko*, where an opposite sex pair intending to begin a marital relationship break off from the normal circular formations and go into seclusion but remain visible within the dancing space.

In tantalizing ululations, they mark the beginning of their possible relationship in the presence of the elders. Knowledge of specific forms of expressions in moko makes this moment possible, but if the couple's negotiation is not successful the community is still aware of their trial. Similarly,

the process also provides for developing and maintaining existing relations—a notion that is very perceptible because individual practitioners' dance knowledge and skill define their individual realizations in the moko moment.

Activation of social capital is also explicit in other dance traditions in other regions, such as the **orunyege-ntogoro** courtship dance of the Batooro of southwestern Uganda, the **ekizino** social dance of the Bakiga of western Uganda, and the baakisimba dance of the Baganda of central Uganda. The Batooro use orunyege-ntogoro dance to navigate individual and communal relationships by engaging positive internal attitudes toward another practitioner, as well as toward members of the community. However, similar to lamokowang, the ultimate moment in orunyege-ntogoro is when two participants interact to initiate, develop, or maintain an established relationship. In all these traditions, there is a very thin layer between practitioner and audience. Rather, there is a high level of interaction and interdependence, all of which translates into individual or community social capital, on which the core concept of community thrives. It is this form of interaction as concrete human action that socioloigist Erving Goffman (1963), in his studies of individuals in mental asylums and other stigmatized social groups to highlight the rules of social-cultural interaction, referred to as "encounters" in daily life. In undesirable conditions, such as civil strife and natural or protracted human disasters, Ugandan communities have always persevered, not only because of the so-called political and religious interventions, but also because of these inherent, core, but often taken-for-granted values in local communities that activate the very essence of life itself.

Crosscurrents

The currents that flow between cultures and eras are made visible through dancing and dance-musicking traditions in Ugandan communities. In a multiethnic African society that continues to endure European colonization, and the long-term consequences thereof, these traditions have allowed Ugandans to navigate remarkable challenges on the individual, community, national, and international levels. Two factors—the Ubuntu philosophy and the unifying effects of the common English language within a colonial education system—amplify the notion of coexistence that is important for harmonious living between the numerous ethnicities. Dancing and dance-musicking in Ugandan communities have, for generations, supported communal systems of knowing. They form an immediate and embodied route for Ubuntu to thrive, aided by a common verbal language, particularly in the more cosmopolitan communities of Uganda. Technology—including online resources and communication that proved critical during the COVID-19 pandemic—continues to spread dance traditions beyond their traditional settings. Thus the simultaneous recognition of Ubuntu in rural, multiethnic, and cosmopolitan communities of Uganda, and in "African dance" forms in the diaspora today, such as in the U.S., is ample evidence of crosscurrents flowing worldwide.

Summary

Although little scholarly attention has so far been paid to micro aspects of Ugandan and East African community dancing and dance-musicking traditions, these traditions have always been understood as the key to safeguarding and transmitting communal agendas. Thus dance and dance-musicking are among the most important cultural resources the communities possess. As a knowledge-body, these traditions provide critical communal content. In the context of civil ethnic strife—for example in the communities of northern Uganda, like many others in Africa—it is through the multilayered processes of dance and dance-musicking that essential community agendas are sustained, enacted, and transmitted, bridging the cultural vacuum between generations. This reality underscores the need to give formal support for the traditions as intangible cultural heritage through academic observations, filming and archiving, and continued enactment. Thus, from the rhythms of the awal, the sound of the bila, voices raised in song, and bodies flowing in shared movement, dancing and dance-musicking in Uganda endure as the very heartbeat of community life.

Discussion Questions

1. How is the community-based agenda of coexistence experienced and developed on a lamokowang dance event and in the actual lamokowang dancing?

2. Can dancing be separated from musicking in the communal traditional dance event? Why or why not?

3. What really makes dance and dance-music traditions of Uganda "knowledge-bodies," and how is "dance-musicking" defined in this so-called knowledge body?

 Visit HK*Propel* for access to this chapter's Application Activity.

Selected Glossary

awal—Calabash, or half-gourd instrument.

bila—An Acholi wind instrument made from a buffalo, antelope, or gazelle's horn.

boko lok—Social interactions at a dance event of the Acholi people.

communitarian approach—An approach that views community as a web of interconnections for individuals' and communities' social-cultural being, growth, and development.

community-based agendas—Implicit and explicit communally understood aims/objectives inherent in the action of dancing and dance-musicking.

dance-musicking—Free and nonprescriptive engagement with music for dancing before and during the dancing; a process of making music through the enaction of dance movements.

Heart Beat of Africa—The first national dance troupe ensemble of Uganda after independence in the 1960s.

internally displaced people's camps—Camps that were used to accommodate and protect

1.7 million displaced people and their property during the civil war in northern Uganda.

knowledge-body, knowledge-bodies—A conglomeration/collection of different aspects and elements of the dance tradition that are seen and known as communally rooted knowledge and situated knowing by way of enacting the dance as a complete entity.

lamokowang—Traditional dance of the Acholi people of northern Uganda.

lutinobul, minbul—Drums in the lamokowang traditional dance-musicking among the Acholi people of northern Uganda.

myel bwola—A traditional dance of the Acholi people of northern Uganda.

Obuntu/Ubuntu—An African ethic of community's unity, humanity, and humility as well as harmony among the Bantu peoples of Africa.

ojili—A high-pitched trill enacted by the Acholi people in the process of dancing.

social capital (community-based)—Developed social relations of extended families and community members.

wangoo—Gathering (family or otherwise) around an outside fireplace for learning through stories and other verbal forms of transmitting and learning from traditions.

Selected References and Resources

Atkinson, R.R. 1989. "The Evolution of Ethnicity Among the Acholi of Uganda: The Pre-Colonial Phase." *Ethnohistory* 36 (1), 19-43.

Avineri, S., and A. de-Shalit. 1992. *Communitarianism and Individualism*. Oxford: Oxford University Press.

Erling, T., and E. Bakka. 2017. "Museums, Dance, and the Safeguarding of Intangible Cultural Heritage: 'Events of Practice'—A New Strategy for Museums?" *Santander Art and Culture Law Review* 2 (3): 135-156.

Etzioni, A. 2014. "Communitarianism Revisited." *Journal of Political Ideologies* 19 (3): 241-260. Routledge.

Girling, F.K. 1960. *The Acholi of Uganda*. London: Her Majesty's Stationery Office.

Goffman, E. 1963. "Behaviour in Public Spaces." Free Press.

Gray, J. 1952. "Acholi History 1860-1901." [Part II.] *Uganda Journal* (1952):36-37.

Hanna, J.L., and W.J. Hanna. 1968. "Heart Beat of Uganda." *African Arts* 1 (3): 42-45.

Kibirige, R. 2020a. "Dancing Reconciliation and Re/integration: *Lamokowang* and Dance-Musicking in the *Oguda-Alel* Post-War Communities of Northern Uganda." Doctoral thesis, Norwegian University of Science and Technology, Trondheim, Norway.

Mabingo, A. 2019. "'African Dances Are Valid Knowledge': Dance Teachers' De/Construction of Meanings From Cultural Heritage Dances in Uganda." *Research in Dance Education* 20 (3): 311-330. https://doi.org/10.1080/14647893.2019.1631271.

Mabingo, A. E. Ssembatya, and G. Ssemaganda, R. Kibirige. 2020. "Decolonising Dance Teacher Education: Reflections of Four Teachers of Indigenous Dances in African Postcolonial Environments." *Journal of Dance Education* 20:148-156. https://doi.org/10.1080/15290824.2020.1781866.

Nziza, R., Mbaga-N., and D. Mukholi. 2011. *Peoples and Culture of Uganda*. Fountain Publishers.

Wenger, E. 1998. *Communities of Practice and Social Learning Systems: The Career of a Concept*. New York: Cambridge University Press. https://wenger-trayner.com/wp-content/uploads/2012/01/09-10-27-CoPs-and-systems-v2.01.pdf.

10

Dance Cultures of Zimbabwe

Solomon Gwerevende

Learning Objectives

After reading this chapter you will be able to do the following:

- Develop an appreciation of the diversity and uses of dance cultures in Zimbabwe.
- Identify and describe key features that characterize Zimbabwean dance heritage.
- Establish the role of dance as an enactment of ethnic cultures, norms, values, and memories from the past.
- Compare and contrast indigenous and contemporary Zimbabwean dance traditions.
- Analyze the influence of modernity, urbanization, and globalization on indigenous dance heritage and the development of contemporary dances in Zimbabwe.

Key Terms

chimurenga—Revolution; armed struggle.

kusvikirwa—Spirit possession or trance.

mukwerera—Rainmaking ceremony of the Shona people.

polyrhythm—A musical term characterized by several frequencies of beats or sounds and sometimes referred to as cross-rhythm.

township dances—Contemporary dance genre performed with popular music genres that flourished in the townships, mining towns, and growth points (government-sponsored settlements).

unhu/ubuntu—Compassion, reciprocity, dignity, harmony, and humanity in the interests of building and maintaining community.

Kongonya Performance at a Political Rally

In 2008, I attended a political rally organized by the **Zimbabwe African National Union–Patriotic Front** (ZANU–PF) in my rural village, known as Mushongwi, in Buhera South District in the Manicaland province of Zimbabwe. My parents did not want me to attend political rallies, but late one night I outsmarted them by simply waiting behind a big rock in the dark as they proceeded to the *bhesi* (secretive political meeting place). I followed a group behind them and went to the *pungwe* (all-night event) to watch and enjoy the *kongonya* dance and music performance. After giving a political speech, the ZANU–PF district leader punctuated his presentation with a rousing chorus of "Muri Musoja" ("You Are a Soldier"), followed by energetic drumming. The music rises on a crescendo and compels everyone—parents, villagers, and youths—to dance kongonya. Stamping the ground, they circle the fireplace, each dancer holding the waist of the one in front of them as they do hops, leaps, jogging steps, waist swirling, and retreating to the center. The performance became so contagious that small boys and girls eagerly joined the dance. Watching, dancing, and experiencing the kongonya music, I learned that kongonya requires a flexible body, energy, and physical stamina. The routines and patterns of the performance went through a few basic moves, starting from a leaping position, then sprang up with stamping of feet through space to the rhythm of the revolutionary music. Their convex posture, controlled in an arch, allowed the dancers' pelvises to drive the body as the dance movements progressed. In that pungwe, I realized how kongonya dance and music were crucial for mobilizing political support, teaching people about political agendas, and fostering values of freedom, patriotism, and nationalism.

Indigenous dances occupy a central place in the political, social, religious, and cultural life of different ethnic communities in Zimbabwe. Dance in Zimbabwe is a significant means of expressing life experiences, honoring kings, celebrating good harvests, and performing ceremonies, such as rites of passages. Today, indigenous dances are also performed for recreation and entertainment, but originally this was not their purpose. Factors such as colonization, modernity, migration, and Christianity have brought changes to indigenous ways of life in Zimbabwe. As a result, the dances have also adapted and survived, albeit with modifications. Indigenous dances are connected to Zimbabwe's rich musical traditions, and performed and expressed in different contexts, as well. To understand this connection, it is crucial to look deeper into the elements that are common to these dances from different ethnic communities in Zimbabwe.

Brief History and Geography

Zimbabwe is a landlocked country in southern Africa. From 1880 to the early 20th century, a combination of colonialism, mercantilism, Christianity, and capitalism gradually transformed the precolonial social and economic landscapes, leading to new commodities, identities, languages, cultures, politics, and religions. The **First Chimurenga** (armed struggle) of 1896/97 against the British colonial forces, in which the Africans of Zimbabwe were defeated, resulted in creating the settler colony **Rhodesia**. Named after British colonial administrator Cecil Rhodes, the colony was administered by the British South Africa Company in the 19th century and heavily exploited for its gold, copper, and coal deposits. Mining became a key industry. The colony lasted until 1965, when the white minority declared independence from Britain to avoid majority rule but ultimately lost the ensuing 15-year struggle to maintain political dominance over the majority Blacks. Another war, known as the **Second Chimurenga** (1964-1979), was carried out by the armed wings of the Patriotic Front, also known as **ZANU–PF**, and the **Zimbabwe African People's Union PF**. This war won the independence of the indigenous people from the British colonizers. **Robert Mugabe** (1924-2019), the late ZANU leader, won the first democratic election in 1985 and maintained his leadership until 2017. Land ownership had been the first cause of all the chimurenga, and *jambanja*—the forced taking of white-owned farms—intensified through the **Third Chimurenga** that began in 2000. Indigenous dances, such as kongonya and *toyi-toyi*, were performed at *chimurenga pungwes* (all-night political gatherings held in the bush) organized as a platform to teach the people about the necessity and justice of the struggle against the Rhodesian government. Chimurenga dance performances facilitated political mobilization, morale-boosting, psychological anchoring, and above all, a comforting sense of the ordinary in an otherwise traumatic context.

Ethnic Communities in Zimbabwe

From the precolonial era to date, Zimbabwe was and still is a multiethnic country, inhabited by the Shangani (or Tsonga), Venda, and **Karanga** in the southern parts, the **Ndebele** and **Kalanga** in the southwest, the Tonga in the north, Korekore and Zezuru in the central and northern parts, and the Ndau and Manyika in the east. However, many scholars have ignored these ethnic-specific names in favor of colonial and broad ethnic blocs, namely **Shona** and Ndebele. These terms are colonial inventions referring to related ethnic communities in Zimbabwe sharing common historical experiences and speaking related dialects (Chitando 2002). However, there are also other ethnic communities not culturally linked to any of the majority groups, representing diverse cultural backgrounds of rich and varied ancestry. Zimbabwe has over twenty ethnic groups, each with its own dance culture. Dance has been and still is an indispensable aspect of life in Zimbabwe, bringing and binding together different communities and helping the people to understand their roles in relation to the community. In sacred contexts, such as *mukwerera* (rainmaking), *kurova guva* (funerary, "beating the grave"), and *bira* (ancestral invocation) ceremonies, dance helps people to understand and remember their role in relation to their ancestors, who are believed to live in the spiritual world (*vari kumhepo*). In secular contexts, indigenous dances strengthen community life, contributing to a sense of safety, continuity, and *unhu/ubuntu* (togetherness, caring, harmony).

As the nature of different communities has changed because of external forces, such as modernity, and with the application of economic aspects in cultural performances, some specific functions of dances have also changed and adapted. Neverthelesss, most indigenous dances, especially in rural areas, remain an imperative aspect in the social well-being and spiritual and emotional life of Zimbabwean communities.

Indigenous dances provide a crucial expression of the nation's unhu/ubuntu philosophy and the living histories, beliefs, and values, as well as the communities' evolution over the centuries and their cultural identity. Dance scholar **Kariamu Welsh Asante** (2004, 45) suggests that Zimbabwean dance is an "artistic way of expression well made, beautiful, pleasing to senses, virtuous, useful, correct, appropriate, and confirming to the customs and expectations in a given cultural context." Indigenous Zimbabwean dances are as diverse and changing as the ethnic communities that create them.

Historical Periods in the Development of Dance in Zimbabwe

The four main historical periods in the development of dance in Zimbabwe are precolonial era (1000-1887), colonial era (1888-1980), early postcolonial era (1980-1999), and late postcolonial era (1999-present).

Precolonial Era (1000-1887)

Precolonial dance performance activities were part and parcel of the community social events that ranged from birth through life to death and were incorporated into social, economic, religious, and political events. Music and dance were found in specific contexts, such as rites of passage, rituals, marriage and weddings, coronation, hunting, harvesting, children's games, and livestock herding.

There are no official written records about dance in this era—only general reports from missionaries, travelers, and colonial representatives who described Zimbabweans and their cultures, dance included (Gwerevende 2019). Dances took place regularly as part of social activities, as well as hunting and ethnic wars mainly between ancient states like Ndebele, **Great Zimbabwe**, and **Mutapa/Munhumutapa** states. For example, *mhande* dance relates to the Great Zimbabwe state, where it was used for kurova guva and mukwerera ceremonies. The structure of dance (motifs, movements, and rhythms) remains the same despite diversity of the contexts in which the dance is performed. Only the song repertoire differs. Historical sources on dance in this period include rock paintings, oral tradition, and written sources by early missionaries.

Ancient rock paintings believed to connect dance and hunting activities during the precolonial era.

Paul Almasy/Corbis/VCG via Getty Images

Colonial Era (1888-1980)

After British rule began in Zimbabwe, the colonial administration established policies and systems that effectively transformed the context and production of dance. Most significantly, local people were barred from practicing their culture, creating a cultural production vacuum in the lives of Zimbabweans, especially in urban areas. European dance and music production filled some of the gaps. The colonialists banned indigenous dances, such as *mbende* (fertility dance) and mhande, and introduced to the local people dances like ballet, **cha-cha**, and ballroom in schools. However, despite the changes and pressure from the white missionaries to abandon their dance and music cultures, local people continued to practice their own cultural activities. During the late colonial era, due to urbanization and establishment of mining towns, people migrated from rural areas to urban areas looking for jobs. Western dances prevailed in these new settlements. Though migrants retained their dance and music cultures in a decontextualized form, they were not allowed to practice such indigenous traditions, nor did they have time for doing so.

Despite exclusionary colonial policies that restricted women to the rural areas, some women found their way into towns (Barnes 1991). These women—usually wives of workers and the unemployed dwellers—were responsible for keeping traditional indigenous dance and music alive in towns.

Early Postcolonial Era (1980-1999)

After independence was attained in 1980 through the Second Chimurenga war of liberation (1964-1979), political change promoted massive participation by local dance and music artists. The government used these arts as a political tool and a means of reviving Zimbabwean cultural values, heritage, and traditions, as well as a source of revenues for the government through foreign currency and taxes. During this era, urbanization resulted in massive movement of people from rural to urban areas. More modern dance and music styles were introduced, the most famous of which were **township dances**, influenced by popular music such as *sungura* and jazz. As more towns were established around the country, these dance and music performances spread nationwide. Dance sparked gatherings for recreation and entertainment, especially at beer drinking and tea parties in small towns around the country.

Late Postcolonial Era (1999-Present)

Several factors have influenced the entertainment industry since the start of the 20th century, most notably migration and cultural diffusion, along with globalization and technology advancement. Performances were broadcast via television and the Internet, and the growth of social media and Internet-based communication sparked the production and distribution of dances for online consumption. More contemporary/modern dance and music pairings arose. For example, **Borrowdale dance** is performed with sungura music, and **Clarks dance**, by various dancehall artist groups like the Expendables Clarks Crew Dance Troupe, is associated with **dancehall music**. According to literature scholar Jairos Gonye (2013, 45), Borrowdale dances have been the most fascinating dance features in Zimbabwe since independence in 1980. Originally emulating **ghetto culture**, its popular moves imitate those of a horse and rider competing at the well-known and affluent Borrowdale Racecourse in **Harare**, Zimbabwe's capital city.

Recontextualization of indigenous dances is also common during this period, whereby indigenous dances are taken from their original contexts and performed for entertainment in different settings. Dance performance continues to change and develop with technological advancements and has continued to be influenced by commercialization, social change, sponsorship, media, education, and government policies like the **75% local content policy**, introduced in 2016 to support Zimbabwean arts.

 See resource 10.1 in HK*Propel* for web links.

Indigenous Zimbabwean Dances

Zimbabwean indigenous dances can be classified into two major groups—sacred and secular. For all indigenous dances, drumming is an indispensable symbol of life—the heartbeat of the community. In both sacred and secular activities, people dance to the beat of the drum accompanied by other musical instruments like *hosho* (shakers), **hwamanda** (horn), and **magagada** (leg rattles).

Sacred Dances

In Zimbabwe, and in Africa in general, religion is not something reserved for a certain time or place, a last resort only in times of crisis: *all* aspects of life are connected to religion, be they political, cultural, social, or economical. Certain dances are performed for similar religious purposes among many different ethnic groups, for example, the mhande dance of the Karanga people, **jichi** of the **Shangwe** people, and **hosana/ wosana** of the Kalanga ethnic group are part of rainmaking ceremonies among their respective people.

Sacred dances represent the broadest and most ancient of Zimbabwean cultures, affirming and enforcing the indigenous belief systems of different ethnic groups. In specific religious events, the dances expedite and facilitate the most powerful modes of communication and expression—community members united in their dance and music. Ritual or sacred dances are usually officiated by the informed and elder members of the community, who are popularly known as **vanasorojena**—meaning elderly people who are knowledgeable about the cultural and religious beliefs, norms, and values. They lead the events in which the dances are performed, as well as

the dance itself. Most of the sacred dances are officiated by the older people only because young people are believed to indulge in sinful activities. Women or girls who still menstruate cannot officiate because this would stop the spirits from manifesting through *masvikiro* (spirit mediums).

Secular Dances

Although secular dances are commemorative and transient (unlike most ritual dances), as well as mainly for entertainment at different social events, such as weddings, political gatherings, and beer drinking parties, they are still important. While the same dance might appear in different settings, the basic movements and rhythms mostly remain the same. However, formations, customs, props, tempo, and songs usually change to fit the secular context. It is important to note that both sacred and secular dances could be recontextualized. In secular contexts, dance performance appears as a component of broader cultural and communal activities. Dances of harvest celebration are performed in **chirimo** (dry, or winter, season), soon after the rain season, because there will be fewer or no agricultural activities in the field. For example, **mbakumba** dance and music of the Karanga people in Masvingo province and **dinhe** dance of the Korekore people in **Mashonaland** West province are performed when fields lie fallow and people have time to celebrate the fruits of their labor. Dances of family, fertility, sexuality, and couples are also of a secular nature. Dance scholars Gwerevende and Chamboko (2019, 94) identify mbende as a fertility, sexuality, and family dance of the Zezuru people in Mashonaland province. The dance is performed by women and men in events related to marriage, such as weddings and bride welcoming ceremonies.

As a result of modernity, urbanization, and acculturation, dances such as **muchongoyo**—originally performed in war and other events by the Ndau people—have been taken out of their authentic contexts, staged, and presented in new contexts, such as competitions and cultural festivals. Muchongoyo dance is now performed to welcome visitors at the Harare International Airport, as well as to show respect and pleasure to the diplomats from foreign countries visiting Zimbabwe. In the case of recontextualization, the dance is misappropriated and performed by members of different ethnic groups, particularly those living in urban areas like Harare, **Bulawayo**,

Mutare, and Masvingo. Secular dance performance expresses the life and culture of the community more than individual traits or sentiments shared by couples. Unlike contemporary dances, indigenous dances are community intellectual property and not individually owned. Social events in which dance is an indispensable component provide the community members a sense of belonging, cohesion, and solidarity realized in the concept of *ubuntu/unhu*. In most cases, the structure of the dance is a replica of the structure and organization of the communities in which they are performed. For example, women are responsible for the production of hosana dance in both secular and sacred settings, reflecting how gender roles within a community are organized. Ethnicity, age, status, and kinship are similarly represented through different dances and their contexts.

 See resource 10.2 in HK*Propel* for web links.

Characteristic Features of Indigenous Dances

Some basic contextual and structural features are characteristic of most indigenous dances in Zimbabwe. These include a spiritual dimension, the centrality of community, and a deep, finely wrought relationship to rhythm.

Spiritual Representation

Indigenous dances in Zimbabwe within the religious and cultural contexts are used as a way of elevating oneself from the human realm to that of the spiritual universe. For example, dances such as mhande and hosana/wosana are performed in rainmaking ceremonies to ask for rain from **Mwari** (God) through the medium of the ancestors. Although mhande of the Karanga people, a subgroup of the Shona-speaking people, and hosana/wosana of the Kalanga people are from different cultures, they are both a mixture of music and dance performed in the rainmaking ceremony. From that functional perspective indigenous Zimbabwean dance makes excellent use of dance's ability to engage mind, body, and spirit to release the conscious into a transcendent, spiritual realm.

Importance of the Community

Indigenous dances in Zimbabwe are performed with and for the benefit of the community. They are owned by the community. The dancers are supported and praised by other members of the community through singing, ululating, hand clapping, and shouted encouragements. The circle formation is a common structure in indigenous dance performances, representing unity and completeness, summed up in the concept of ubuntu (figure 10.1).

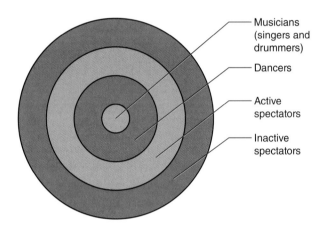

Musicians (singers and drummers)

Dancers

Active spectators

Inactive spectators

Figure 10.1 Formation of tshigombela dance and its participants.

Relationship to Rhythm

Rhythm is fundamental to the existence of Zimbabwean cultural expressions, in general, and dance in particular. It acts as a thread, binding the very fabric of indigenous cultures together through their diverse forms of expression. Dance and music in Zimbabwe are identical twins, almost inseparable. Most indigenous dancers wear leg rattles that produce a guiding beat and dialogue, with instruments such as **mbira** (misrepresented in music literature as "thumb piano"), drums, whistle, and other percussive instruments for tempo. Adjudicators for dance competitions, such as the **Jikinya Dance Festival**, judge the skills of individuals and the whole ensemble by their ability to follow musical rhythm elements.

For example, the Karanga people perform mbakumba (harvest) dance in a way in which their bodily movements are synchronized with an accelerating rhythm beat from the drum-

Jikinya Dance Festival

Founded by The National Arts Council of Zimbabwe (NACZ) in 2002, the Jikinya Dance Festival encourages children in primary schools around the country to appreciate the diversity of traditional dances. Several rounds of competition bring students together to vie for the crown at zone, district, and provincial levels. The signature jikinya dance is a joyous, unifying feature that all participants learn, while each year one traditional dance is designated as the basis for adjudication. For example, the 2019 festival competition was won by students showcasing the mbende jerusalema dance. The event also spurs the production of costumes and musical instruments needed by the schools, ensuring that the children experience the richness of Zimbabwe's cultural heritage.

ming by a master drummer. In the celebratory *jaka* and *ngororombe* dances, the percussive *majaka* (shells or bottlecaps that make a buzzing sound) worn on legs and magagada (leg rattles) in mhande dance create a rhythmic beat that drives the dance and maintains the rhythm. Zimbabwean communities judge the mastery of dancers by their skills in visualizing the rhythm. **Polyrhythm**, the simultaneous sounding of two or more independent rhythms, is an important characteristic of Zimbabwean music. More skillful dancers might express several different rhythms at the same time, often by maintaining a separate rhythmic movement with each of several different body parts.

Zimbabwean dances typically employ repeated motifs. The dances are not arranged into refrains but are an emphasis of one musical motif or thought, one sequence, one movement, or the whole dance. Repetition of major and minor choreographic sections is a common feature in Zimbabwean dances. For example, in the foot-stamping in the muchongoyo dance of the Ndau people, the movements are in stages, patterned and sequenced, but the dancers can improvise within the basic pattern of the dance.

Indefinite Duration of Performance

In both sacred and secular dances, chronological time is not an important factor. Instead, it is a feeling, realization, or state of being that determines when a dance performance is ended. Performances intensify by repetition from one level to another until trance, possession, and satisfaction have been reached. In sacred dances, such as mhande and hosana, the climax of the performance is characterized by a trance known as **kusvikirwa** in Shona language.

Expressive and Mimetic Movements

One of the most crucial characteristics of Zimbabwean indigenous dances is the performance of movements from daily life and imitation of different animals. For example, in jaka dance, there is a choreographic section in which male performers imitate the movements of a male baboon. In mbende dance, the male dancers' movements imitate a mole—representing fertility, familyhood, and sexuality (Gwerevende and Rwaendepi 2019). In most cases, indigenous dances involve the movement of the whole body in sync with the music. Scuffing, stamping, and hopping steps; angular bending of legs, arms, and torso; asymmetrical use of the body; shoulder and hip movements; and fluid motions all characterize Zimbabwean dances. In different ethnic groups in Zimbabwe, dance is a medium of communication that embodies values, norms, enjoyment, sensuality, the experiences of life, and pleasure. Indigenous dance forms are direct expressions of culture through the medium of dance and music. Culture is the impetus for bodily movements and artistic expression.

 See resource 10.3 in HK*Propel* for web links.

Crosscurrents

The nature, characteristics, and purposes of modern/contemporary Zimbabwean dances differ from indigenous dances and from contemporary dances elsewhere. "Contemporary," used interchangeably with "modern," represents

Zimbabwean dances that originated and are mainly found in urban areas, growth points, townships, and other town-like settlements. Cross-cultural interactions—including colonialism, migration among African nations, and foreign artistic influences brought through tours or technology—are at the core of these contemporary dances.

Influences of Colonization

From a historical point of view, modernity finds its way into most African countries through colonization. The origins of contemporary dances can be traced to such dances as ballet, cha-cha, and ballroom, brought to Zimbabwe during the colonial era by the British white settlers around the early 1800s. The colonialists were discovering the economic benefits of imposing Western cultures and tradition on various non-Western communities whom they regarded as "others" in African countries, and Zimbabwe was no exception. Contemporary dances in Zimbabwe are characterized by unfixed and shifting aesthetics, and they draw from different physical techniques often created by individual dancers, thereby making them complex and sophisticated. The historical development of dance in Europe and America has had implications for the origins and development of modern dance in many African countries, and in Zimbabwe specifically, since the 1970s.

Due to the need to gain power not only in the political and economic sectors but also in cultural production, the colonial government banned Zimbabwean indigenous dances to pave the way for the introduction of Western and American dance traditions. As a result, Zimbabwean dance production and performance were censored—Black bodies were monitored and controlled in every sense. Zimbabwean indigenous dances and Black dancing bodies were not allowed in urban areas and were even excluded from government and institutional support, let alone artistic production and consumption.

Yet dance is a formidable source of power and energy. The embodied resistance and reactionary politics in the founding philosophies of contemporary dance and its creators allowed the origin of modern dances as a province of resistance and protest in Zimbabwe. For example, dances such as toyi-toyi, kongonya, and *jiti* were used during the Second Chimurenga war of liberation as a potent mechanism to defy the accepted institution

of Western dance traditions. The idea of modern, or contemporary, dance took form not only through the resistance and rejection of Western dances, but also through the incorporation and recognition of an incredibly rich Zimbabwean dance heritage mixed with foreign cultures from other African countries like **Malawi**, **Democratic Republic of Congo**, and **South Africa**. The foreign cultures that characterize Zimbabwean contemporary dances were brought to Zimbabwe by immigrants from countries such as Malawi and **Zambia** who came to work in farms, mines, and towns across the country.

Kariamu Welsh Asante's Zimbabwe National Dance Company of Zimbabwe

In the Zimbabwean capital city of Harare in the 1970s, Kariamu Welsh Asante started a contemporary modern dance company that specialized in the performance of contemporary dances, primarily from Europe and America. The company performed ballet and other Western dance styles. It started to train "professional dancers"—a foreign concept in the Zimbabwean indigenous dance fraternity, where dance knowledge and skills are transmitted orally through participation and observation rather than through formal training. The company was characterized by an ethos of nonracialism, community development, and social-political commentary. The now defunct **National Dance Company of Zimbabwe** was also responsible for the staging of indigenous dances in urban areas. All forms of contemporary and modern dance techniques were assimilated, accepted, and experimented with. Somatic techniques, such as **release** and **Alexander Technique**, were incorporated, developed, and mixed with African dance styles, such as *pantsula* and *kwasa-kwasa*. As a result, an African dance hybrid known as **Afro-fusion** arose and gained widespread popularity in African countries like South Africa, Zambia, and **Namibia**.

Most of the contemporary dances incorporated concepts, movement styles, and narratives inspired by ritual, trance, and repetition relating to Zimbabwean indigenous dance cultures. Today, contemporary dances are regarded as highly sexualized performances, but during the Second Chimurenga war of liberation they were seen as revolutionary in the racially discriminated against and closed-minded community.

The processes of urbanization, migration, acculturation, and globalization directly influenced the creative and performing arts industry in Zimbabwe. In the mid-1990s and early 2000s cross-cultural, multicultural, and multiracial modern dances were created and upheld as the pinnacle of the new and postcolonial Zimbabwean society. Dance and music productions showcased cultural aspects of Zimbabwean ethnic traditions, such as traditional attire, in performances like those related to kwasa-kwasa and *ndombolo* music. This was an important and exciting era for performing arts in Zimbabwe, but it became apparent that these forms of cultural productions and performances had their own bundle of sophisticated and complex issues.

International Influence on the Development of Contemporary Zimbabwean Dances

The demand for international products and the influence of the mass media have affected the nature, product, and marketing of contemporary dance and music in Zimbabwe. Workers from Zambia, Malawi, and **Mozambique** who worked in mines, farms, and factories in Zimbabwe brought their music cultures from their countries, influencing certain types of dances related to those music traditions. For example, sungura music is linked to the Borrowdale and *chibhasikoro* dances. Other influences from abroad—Europe, America, and the Caribbean—came through blues, jazz, soul, rock 'n' roll, disco, funk, country music, and reggae, particularly during the 1960s to 1970s.

 See resource 10.4 in HKPropel for web links.

Implications of Modernity and Globalization

The evolution of dance and music production in Zimbabwe was shaped by colonization, urbanization, and changes in the political economy of Zimbabwean communities. Many of these forces

were activated by colonialism and implemented through schools, the army, churches, private companies, mass media, and municipalities. According to ethnomusicologist Caleb Dube (1996, 100) commercial cultural workers in Zimbabwe were mainly a product of African adaptations to the colonial political economy that transformed the economic and social systems of existence and occupations in many ways. Industrialization and urbanization, because of colonization, gave birth to new urban lifestyles, gender relations, and social networks, which were in many ways different from those in rural areas. According to sociologists Gilbert and Gugler (1992, 62) these changes, notably in colonial societies, were the result of a historical process of incorporating Africans into the world of capitalism.

Contemporary dances in Zimbabwe are mainly connected with urban areas, townships, and other town-like settlements. Most of these towns are cross-cultural and multiethnic, allowing cultural syncretism and blending to undermine the tight-knit communities so basic to indigenous dance heritage. Although indigenous dances are still being practiced in rural areas in connection with religious, social, political, and cultural ceremonies (*biras*), the urban lifestyle has become a threat to these dances and is giving birth to the new and modern dances mentioned previously. These include chibhasikoro and Borrowdale dances, associated with sungura music, and Clarks Crew dances related to *dendera*, or dancehall music.

Many aspects and features of Zimbabwean indigenous dance traditions change when they are recontextualized—taken from their original contexts in the villages and communal life to contexts such as tourist and entertainment centers in urban and town-like settlements. The recontextualization of indigenous dances is fueled by the need to sustain livelihoods through dance heritage, leading to the monetization of dance. For instance, in sacred and secular indigenous dances, the performers, rather than acting in isolation, interact directly with the onlookers, who participate in the ceremonies and other social events by playing, singing, and exchanging with the performers (musicians and dancers). However, when these indigenous dances are taken out of their cultural contexts and performed onstage for other than social, religious, and political purposes, they often incorporate new features and modify the dance structure to suit the new context. By creating and accelerating the growth of these new settings, the potent forces of globalization, acculturation, urbanization, and colonization have directly led to changes in the structure and features of indigenous dances.

Specific aspects of colonialism, such as Christianity and Western education, have contributed immensely to the transformation of Zimbabwean people and their communities, resulting in new Zimbabwean dance styles for contemporary sociocultural settings. These new dance styles have gained widespread popularity across the whole country, especially among the youths, and are threatening to submerge the indigenous dance traditions, particularly in rural areas that border urban ones. During the colonial era, the colonial authority in Zimbabwe shifted regional boundaries and introduced a cash economy that, in turn, influenced labor migrations. As a result of migration, people from a specific ethnic culture found themselves neighboring a different ethnic culture with very different cultural values, beliefs, norms, and dance styles. As people from rural areas migrated to and gathered in towns, like Harare, the capital city, or Bulawayo, the second largest city, contemporary dance forms gained new significance as markers of ethnic cultural identity. For example, since the 1970s, in different mining towns around the country, such as Hwange coal mine, "**mine dancers**" have vied in competitions organized around ethnic origins.

Hybrid Dance Cultures

During the colonial and early part of the post-colonial eras, hybrid dance cultures that were performed in towns resemble a mixture of Zimbabwean dance style and American and European dance cultural features. **Highlife** was the most famous of these forms of hybrid dance cultures, mixing features of European dances such as ballroom, cha-cha, and waltz with techniques learned by performers in towns with indigenous dance styles and rhythms. Contemporary dances rose to popularity in cities in Zimbabwe mainly after the Second Chimurenga war of liberation. During the war, local African Zimbabweans united across ethnic and cultural borders to oppose the White European settlers, expressing a common national and cultural identity derived from the experience of urbanization and colonialization throughout cities and towns dotted around the country. During the 1990s, this unity was abundantly reflected in hybrid dance styles. People danced to sounds of sungura, kwasa-kwasa, and *kwela* (South African music), mostly borrowed from central and eastern Africa. These music genres gained widespread popularity across the whole country and in other southern African countries, such as South Africa, Namibia, Zambia, and Botswana.

The modern dance styles were modified and indigenized to suit the local contexts and cultural production goals, precipitating remarkable creativity and diversity of dance styles in the postcolonial era. Dance remains an important element of different social events and recreational activities in places such as **Mai Musodzi Hall** (entertainment venue) in Mbare, a high-density residential area in Harare. Entertainment halls built by city councils around the country were

Gumboot Dance—Crosscurrents in Mine Dancing

Mining is a major industry in countries of southern Africa, and migrant workers from different ethnic groups have been the source of much cross-cultural exchange throughout the region. Mine dancing in Zimbabwe was influenced by forms such as South Africa's **gumboot dance** that originated in the late 19th century. Under colonial oppression, workers in the gold mines were shackled to their workstations in dark, flooded tunnels and forbidden to speak to one another. The dance arose as a form of communication, using body percussion and rhythmic stomping of their "gumboots" (rubber boots). As the dance spread beyond the mines into the communities, the mine owners saw it as good publicity and encouraged dance troupes to perform and compete. In their ignorance of traditional culture, the employers did not recognize the anti-colonialist expressions couched in the spirited dances, nor that some parts of the dance mocked how the mine operators themselves moved. By the 1930s gumboot dance had become a more formal practice of shared cultural identity. Now, many decades later, the tradition of gumboots and other mine dancing continues as a vibrant part of the region's performance culture.

used as venues for the night discos. Dance performance remains a strong and changing part of Zimbabwean life. The transformation and modernization of Zimbabwean dance has promoted both innovation and continuity.

Contemporary Dance Venues

The government, through city councils or municipalities during the early days of colonial Zimbabwe, instituted laws as part of the colonial and racial effort to control Black people or Africans in towns through skills training, accommodation, health, and recreational facilities. However, during the colonial and postcolonial eras, the municipalities established municipal halls in residential areas for recreational purposes. The municipality halls are still used as venues that feature dance performances (for example, ethnic dances), ballroom dancing, and other artistic activities, such as films, talent nights, music, drama, and martial arts.

Besides the halls, the council gardens become the loci of cultural activity and an important source of innovation in dance, music, and other forms of performance among urban Africans (Wolcott 1974, 83). Beer gardens, such as those in Bulawayo city, provided space for indigenous singing and dancing. To the colonial state, beer consumption and ethnic dances in municipal beer halls created effective diversions for workers who were potentially hostile to the state (Jackson 1987). Each township had its own halls where, among many activities, ballroom dancing was held. A guild in Bulawayo was formed in Makokomba township to cater to ballroom dancing and other activities like indoor games and table tennis (Masiye 1966). In many mining towns in Zimbabwe, open space dance floors and amphitheater performances were developed. For example, the Mangura Mine Management hired musicians who would entertain mining workers using instruments owned by the mining company (Zindi 1985, 31). These music performances influenced dances. In Bulawayo, Wankie and Shabani mines organized indigenous dancing competitions and artistic activities that were attended by dancing clubs from the two mining companies.

 See resource 10.5 in HK*Propel* for web links.

Summary

The long history of Zimbabwean traditions, cross-cultural dynamics, ethnic identity, and religious and social contexts influenced the development and continuity of indigenous dances in Zimbabwe. These dances are performed in sacred and secular contexts, as an enactment of people's memories, beliefs, histories, spiritualities, and epistemologies. Indigenous dances occupy a central place in the social, religious, and cultural life of different ethnic communities in Zimbabwe. Colonization influenced the transformation of the context of dance and music production by introducing the capitalist economic system and the notion of market and money. Furthermore, colonization also influenced the development of contemporary/modern dance, which is mainly associated with an urban lifestyle. Contemporary Zimbabwean dance thus reflects both the complex history of the nation and its dynamic push toward the future.

Discussion Questions

1. What are the functions of dance cultures in Zimbabwe?
2. Identify and describe key features that characterize Zimbabwean dance heritage.
3. Compare and contrast indigenous and contemporary dances in Zimbabwe.
4. Discuss the role of dance as an enactment of ethnic cultures, norms, values, histories, and memories from the past, with specific reference to indigenous dances in Zimbabwe.
5. How do modernity, urbanization, and globalization influence the modification of indigenous and the development of contemporary dances in Zimbabwe?

 Visit HK*Propel* for access to this chapter's Application Activity.

Selected Glossary

bira—An all-night ceremony performed by the Shona-speaking people in which members of an extended family call on ancestral spirits for guidance and intercession.

Borrowdale dance—A dance characterized by fancy footwork and galloping body movements as if on racing horses. It is named after a horse racing track in the Borrowdale suburb of Zimbabwe's capital city, Harare.

chimurenga—Revolution; armed struggle.

Clarks dance—A modern dance and youth culture performed with Zimbabwean dancehall music, popularly known as "Zim dancehall." It was influenced by Jamaican dancehall culture.

dancehall music—A music genre that emerged in Jamaica after a political disturbance in the 1970s and became popularly known as *raga* in both Jamaica and the international community; the music uses a heavy four-beat rhythm driven by a combination of drums, bass guitar, electric guitar, and a corrugated scraper that is rubbed by another plain stick.

Great Zimbabwe—An ancient settlement in the southeastern region of Zimbabwe. Its stone houses are thought to have been built by ancestors of the Shona-speaking people.

hosana/wosana—An indigenous Zimbabwean dance of the Kalanga people performed in the rainmaking ceremony.

kongonya—A contemporary dance characterized by movements and sounds of resistance performed during Zimbabwe's liberation struggle by freedom fighters as they danced at political gatherings addressing the people.

kurova guva (*beating the grave*)—A funeral ceremony performed after one year of burial to welcome home the spirit of a deceased member of the family. Dance and music are components of the ceremony.

kusvikirwa—Shona word that means *spirit possession* or *trance*. It happens when the ancestral spirits arrive in the bodies of the mediums and communicate the ancestral message to the people.

mukwerera—Rainmaking ceremony of the Shona people.

polyrhythm—A musical term characterized by several frequencies of beats or sounds and sometimes referred to as cross-rhythm.

township dances—Contemporary dance genre performed with popular music genres that flourished in the townships, mining towns, and growth points.

unhu/ubuntu—Compassion, reciprocity, dignity, harmony, and humanity in the interests of building and maintaining community.

Welsh Asante, Kariamu (1949-2021)—An influential and pioneering scholar of African diaspora dance and a professor emerita of dance at Temple University. She published many books, including *Zimbabwe Dance: Rhythmic Forces, Ancestral Voices—An Aesthetic Analysis* and *Umfundalai: An African Dance Technique*.

Selected References and Resources

Barnes, T. 1991. *Different Class Experiences Amongst African Women in Colonial Harare, Zimbabwe, 1935-1970.* Harare: University of Zimbabwe.

Chitando, E. 2002. "Singing Culture: A Study of Gospel Music in Zimbabwe." Uppsala: Nordiska Afrikainstitutet. http://urn.kb.se/resolve?urn=urn:nbn:se:nai:diva-192</div.

Dube, C. 1996. "The Changing Context of African Music Performance in Zimbabwe." African e-Journals Project.

Gilbert, A., and J. Gugler. 1992. *Cities, Poverty and Development: Urbanization in the Third World.* New York: Oxford University Press.

Gwerevende, S. 2019. "Zimbabwean Indigenous Dance Research: A Reflection on the Past and Present Approaches." *International Journal of Music and Performing Arts* 7 (2): 15-24.

Gwerevende, S., and F. Rwaendepi. 2019. "Operations to Restore Cultural Legacy: Past and Present Voices on the Revival of Mbende Dance in Zimbabwe." *Journal of Humanities and Social Sciences Studies* 1 (5): 92-102.

Jackson, L.A. 1987. "Uncontrollable Women in a Colonial African Town, Bulawayo Location 1893-1958." Columbia University, Unpublished.

Masiye, P. 1966. "The City Housing and Amenities Department." Bulawayo: Bulawayo City Council, No. 18.

Mbiti, J.S. 1969. *African Religions and Philosophy.* London: Heinemann.

Mudenge, S.I.G. 1988. *A Political History of Munhumutapa, c. 1400-1902.* Harare: Zimbabwe Publishing House.

Welsh Asante, K. 2004. *African Dance (World of Dance).* Philadelphia: Chelsea House Publishers.

Wolcott, H.F. 1974. "The African Beer Gardens of Bulawayo: Integrated Drinking in a Segregated Society." New Brunswick: Rutgers Centre of Alcohol Studies.

Zindi, F. 1985. *Roots Rocking in Zimbabwe.* Gweru: Mambo Press.

PART V

Europe and Russia

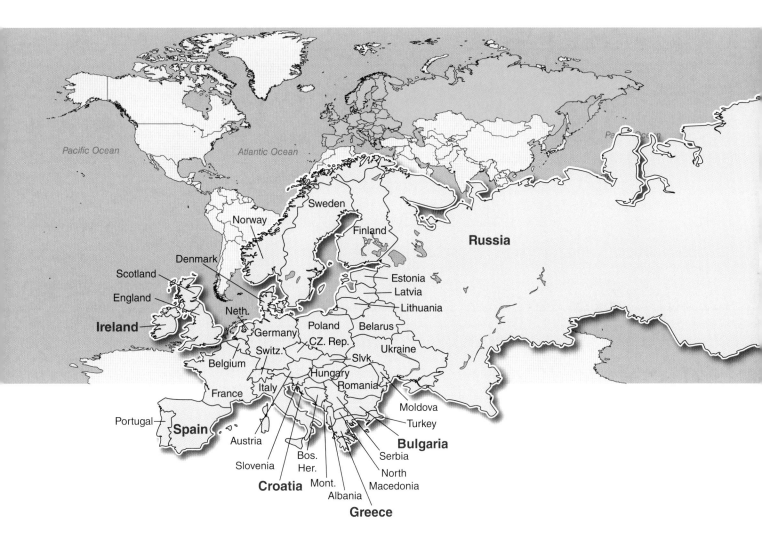

The six chapters in part V range from western Europe through several countries along the Mediterranean Sea, into Eastern Europe, and finally Russia. While there are no northwestern European countries included here, due to contributor availability, the major elements of history, geography, politics, and religion that shaped dances in the region can be seen through the different chapters. Of these elements, the reign of the Ottoman Empire, World Wars I and II, and the Cold War between Russia (former Soviet Union) and the West had great influence on the continent and thus on the implications for dance. Similarly, colonial exploits and migration of people between different countries both within the continent and abroad have affected the types of dance found in the region and the dispersion of these dances around the world. At times, the presumed superiority of Western European culture dominated the choices and expressions of dance throughout the continent, most noticeably in the prevalence of ballet. Throughout the ages, religion has shifted the cultural relationship with dance in Europe and Russia, as the major monotheistic forms wrestled for dominance on the continent. The dynamics between Christianity, Islam, Judaism, and more localized practices loom large in this process, shaping perceptions of dance traditions even into the present day.

 HK*Propel* includes web links to additional resources for this section.

11

Dance in Irish Culture

Sharon Anne Phelan

Learning Objectives

After reading this chapter you will be able to do the following:

- Place different Irish dance types into sociohistorical contexts.
- Explain stages in the Irish dance master tradition.
- Identify connections between nationalism and Irish dance.
- Describe developments in Irish dance during the 20th century.
- Justify the placement of Irish dance into competitive and theatrical contexts.

Key Terms

céilí (singular), **céilithe** (plural)—The Irish céilí is a social and recreational event featuring live music for group dances to traditional Irish dance tunes.

feiseanna—Originally the term *feis* or *feiseanna* (plural) referred to native arts and culture festivals in Ireland. Since the turn of the 20th century, the term is usually associated with Irish dance competitions.

figure dance—A group dance that also exists in Scotland. There are several similarities between the Irish and Scottish figure dances.

set dances—Irish group dances with fast rhythms and intricate floor patterns that originated from quadrilles and cotillions during the 19th century.

Siamsa Tíre—The National Folk Theatre of Ireland, founded by Fr. Pat Ahern in 1968.

step dance—A solo Irish dance type.

The World Irish Dance Feis

The **World Irish Dance Feis** (festival) is thronged with people. Irish dancers from around the world wait nervously to be called to the stage. Between the sound of tapping shoes, Irish dance music, and loud voices, the noise is deafening. Some dancers twitch nervously, daunted by the atmosphere. They have trained and competed all year to win a place at the World Irish Dance Championship.

Now, as they practice their step dances for the last time in soft black pumps (**ghillies**) or shiny black hard-soled **batter shoes**, they know the time has come to realize their dream—to win the world championship. Garbed in colorful costumes, the female dancers adjust their wigs and dresses, while the male dancers fix their waistcoats. The hall becomes silent as the first three Irish dancers appear on stage. They each take position and point their right foot in front in anticipation. Their arms are held rigidly by the sides of their bodies. Suddenly, the music starts and the dancers shine as they jump, hop, and batter their feet in front of adjudicators. The latter apply strict criteria as they note the dancers' techniques and skills. The music stops and the dancers bow and smile as the audience applauds. They have done their best. They can do no more. As they leave the stage to rejoin their teachers, they fantasize walking onto the winner's platform, later in the day, to accept the World Cup.

This account of an international Irish dance feis reflects the competitive context within which most Irish dancers operate today. Many people commend the feis; it encourages self-discipline and perfection in skill and technique. Others believe that the dance repertoire has become standardized, the dancers' goals are external, and their mindsets are exclusive. They believe that the dancers are dancing to win, not dancing to dance.

 See resource 11.1 in HK*Propel* **for web links.**

This chapter focuses on key points in the Irish dance tradition to provide a framework within which the evolution of Irish dance can be addressed from traditional and contemporary perspectives.

Keep the following points in mind as we explore the development of Irish dance over the past centuries:

- The impact of colonization on the Irish dance tradition.
- The political undertones that shaped Irish dance during the Gaelic Revival at the turn of the 20th century.
- The impact of popular culture on Irish dance during the 20th century.
- The movement of Irish dance into competitive and theatrical contexts in the latter half of the 20th century.
- The Irish dance diaspora.

Brief History

The island of Ireland is situated in the north Atlantic, west of mainland Europe. The earliest inhabitants were hunters and fishers who entered Ireland approximately 10,000 years ago, during the **Mesolithic period**. Subsequently, the first farmers arrived in Ireland around 4000 BCE. This marked the start of the **Neolithic period**, when the Irish cultivated land, raised cattle, formed communities, and built stone buildings. Around 300 BCE, Iron Age warriors called **Celts** invaded Ireland, eventually becoming the dominant influence on Irish culture. The first official language of Ireland, *Gaeilge* or **Gaelic** originated in their Celtic language, and today early Irish literature is steeped in Celtic mythology.

During the fifth century, **Saint Patrick** and fellow missionaries brought Christianity to Ireland. This led to the creation of large monasteries, where scholarly monks documented Latin, Greek, and Christian theology in such works as the **Book of Kells**. Art forms that emerged included manuscript illumination, elaborate jewelry, and the engravement of stone crosses that incorporated **Celtic designs**.

The missionaries were followed by Norwegian invaders, **Vikings**, in the eighth century. Like their predecessors, many settled into Irish society, and they built Ireland's capital city, Dublin, in 998 CE. The Viking influence diminished from the early

11th century, when they were defeated by **Brian Boru**, the high king of Ireland.

The **Anglo-Normans** invaded Ireland in 1159 CE. These warriors were descendants of invaders from Normandy, France, who conquered **Anglo-Saxon Britain** in 1066 CE. Over time, the Anglo-Normans became part of Irish society and today, the Irish landscape features many Anglo-Norman castles, walled towns, and churches (just like the British mainland). In the 17th century, Ireland became completely colonized by Britain and remained under British rule until the early 20th century. Between 1845 and 1852 the **Great Irish Famine** swept the nation. Almost a quarter of the native population disappeared due to death and emigration. Those who emigrated largely traveled to Britain, British colonies, and America.

There was renewed effort to gain freedom from Britain in the late 19th century, and Ireland achieved independence in 1922. However, six counties in the north of Ireland remained under British rule, causing much anger and violence in Ireland. The discord continued until the 1990s, when a united peace process was enacted between the British and Irish governments.

 See resource 11.2 in HK*Propel* for web links.

Irish Dance Culture From the 13th Century CE

Our exploration of Irish dance culture begins in 1265 CE, during the Anglo-Norman era, when the first written reference to dance in Ireland was recorded in a poem entitled *Rithmus Facture Ville de Ross* ("The Entrenchment of New Ross").

Then the youths advanced in turn,

And the town they made it ring.

With their merry caroling.

Singing loud and full of mirth.

During this era, Irish natives danced *caroles* that had been brought to Ireland by the European invaders. Caroles were usually danced in a circle. The chief performer stood in the middle of the circle, and he sang a love song. The other participants responded as they danced in a circular pathway around him, holding the hands of their suitors.

Because this poem was the first written reference to dance in Ireland, some historians have assumed that dance did not exist prior to the Anglo-Norman era. This is unlikely, given that the early Irish inhabitants, the Neoliths and the Celts, often illustrated dancers in rock paintings, and international Celtic stories referred to spiritual and prebattle dances. Both these groups held music in high esteem; the Neoliths had bells, horns, and trumpets, and the Celts had harps, pipes, and stringed and wind instruments. Because dance preceded music in other cultures, it is probable it evolved in the same way in Ireland. The relationship between music and dance has always been strong in Ireland.

After "The Entrenchment of New Ross," the next known reference to Irish dance appeared in the 14th century in a short Middle English lyric poem titled *Ich am of Irlaunde* ("I Am of Ireland"). The exact date of the reference is unknown and, like most Middle English lyric poems, its authorship is anonymous or unknown. It is uncertain whether the dancer in *Ich am of Irlaunde* existed. She seems overly dramatic as she "begs" the poet to visit her "holy londe." The term *holy* has mythical connotations.

Icham of Irlaunde ("I Am of Ireland")

Icham of Irlaunde	(I am from Ireland,
Ant of the holy londe	And from the holy land
Of Irlande.	Of Ireland.
Gode sire, pray ich the,	Good sir, I beg of you,
For of saynte charite,	For holy charity,
Come ant daunce wyt me	Come and dance with me
In Irlaunde.	In Ireland.) (Anon.)

In 1933 the famed Anglo-Irish poet William Butler Yeats wrote a longer poem based on the older poem's first line. He titled it "I am of Ireland."

 See resource 11.3 in HK*Propel* for web links.

Dance During the Colonial Era

Between 1536 and 1691, Ireland was colonized by Britain, and this had a significant impact on Irish dance. British travelers who visited Ireland provided valuable written records of Irish dance. The British also introduced differing dance types, country dances and French court dances. Finally, the Irish **dance master system** evolved from the British dance master system, which entered Ireland in the early 18th century.

British Travelers and Irish Dance

Beginning in the 18th century, British travelers toured Ireland while gathering information about Irish folk culture in logs and journals. In the main, their writings indicated a genuine respect for Irish folk culture and folk dance. (This comports with cultural theorist Albert Memmi's view that the cultural dominion is low in most colonizers' priorities [1991].) British Lieutenant Sir Henry Sidney described Irish female dancers as "magnificently dressed, very beautiful and first-class" (Whelan 2000, 10). Distinguished Scottish physician and humanitarian Sir John Forbes concurred. As he watched a woman dance, he remarked: "If she had not been long and strictly drilled in her vocation, she must have been born with all the aptitudes of original genius in this harmonious art" (1853, 7). Rev. Dr. Thomas Campbell, a Protestant clergyman, took this further when he compared British dancers unfavorably with Irish dancers: "We frog-blooded English dance as if the practice was not congenial to us, but here they move as if dance had been the business of their lives" (Forbes, 189).

British travelers also compared dance events in Ireland and Britain. In Britain, as in Ireland, the dances were "enjoyed upon the slightest excuse . . . at weddings, fireside gatherings, on "May Day" (first of May), New Year, or simply on dry moonlight nights at some favorite part of the road or green" (Emmerson 1971, 71). In Ireland, "every village (had) a bagpiper, who every fine evening, after working hours, collect(ed) all the young men and young maids in the village about him, where they dance(d) most cheerfully" (Grattan Flood 1911, 152).

Irish Dance Types and Styles

Several dance types were introduced into Ireland during the **colonial era**, including **round dances**, **quadrilles** and **cotillions**, **figure dances**, and **pantomimic dances**. The native **step dancing** tradition also evolved during this era. All these dance types remain today in different shapes and styles.

Round Dances

The British travelers documented circle dances when they visited Ireland. There, unlimited numbers of and male and female dancers occupied alternate positions. The round **hey dances** received specific reference, because they had existed in Britain as well. However, Irish hey dancers had a faster dynamic; English dramatist Thomas Dekker considered the dancers "mad" and "wilde" (Bowers 1961, 361).

Quadrilles and Cotillions

British traveler Arthur Young referred to the arrival of cotillions in Ireland in his notes, which were dated between 1776 and 1779 (Harrington 1991, 183). Cotillions existed in Europe throughout the 1700s, and they arrived in Ireland via British dance masters. Cotillions were succeeded by quadrilles in the 1800s. Cotillions were improvised, but quadrilles had set sequences. During cotillions, dancers moved continuously, whereas in quadrilles, the dancers paused to allow other dancers to move. Techniques in these dances included les **ronds**, les **grande chaines**, and les **moulinets**.

In time, cotillions and quadrilles entered Irish society, where they were adopted, adapted, and renamed **set dances**. In the set dances, the positioning and pathways (the imaginary trail a dancer leaves while doing the dance moves) remained similar to the cotillions and quadrilles. Irish females also turned under their male partners' arms and moved to the right and left while facing them. However, unlike their European counterparts, who walked, paused, and bowed to each other, Irish set dancers moved to a faster dynamic tempo, and their leg actions involved hopping, skipping, and jumping. During the 19th and 20th centuries, set dancers often congregated at crossroads in the countryside in the evenings, where they danced for many hours.

Figure Dances

During the colonial era, figure dances resembling those in Scotland were popular in Ireland. It is likely that the Irish dancers who left Ireland to work on farms in Scotland during harvest time adopted the dances while residing in Scotland. British dance masters would also have carried figure dances into Ireland when they came to work for the landed gentry. There were two-hand, three-hand, four-hand, six-hand, eight-hand, and sixteen-hand figure dances in Ireland and Scotland. In these dances, women and men adopted alternate positions; they held hands as they advanced and retreated from each other. They swapped positions, and women danced under the arms of their male partners. The leg actions in both countries involved hopping, skipping, and jumping, and lines of dancers advanced and retreated at the beginning and at the end of the dance. Figure dances are still performed today in both Ireland and Scotland, though with slight differences; unlike the Scottish figure dancers, the Irish never employed hand gestures. (It is possible the men considered them effeminate.)

Pantomimic Dances

There are accounts of pantomimic dance in Ireland since the 1600s. Theater scholar Farley Richmond defined pantomimic dance as the acting out of a story through costume, makeup, and body language. The focus is on the final performance (Richmond, Swann, and Zarrilli 1993, 41). *The Dancing Cobbler*, a dance for men, was the first pantomimic dance documented in Ireland. The dancers would first squat on their haunches, then fling out their feet while moving round the floor. The repetitive sound of the toes and heels on the ground recreated the sound of the cobbler hammering, while the arm movements signified the cobbler sewing his shoes. Usually, due to exhaustion, the dancers stopped and assumed their starting position once more. The performance always provoked much jollity among the spectators. *Bata na bPlandaidhe* (planting stick) was a pantomimic dance during which dancers mimicked the use of long pointed sticks to cultivate potatoes and cabbages. The accompanying tune was in double **jig** time with two sections of eight bars each. As the musician moved into the second section of the tune, the dancers moved into the second section of the dance.

Other pantomimic dances centered on the theme of war. During *Rince an Chlaidhimh* (sword dance), the dancers placed their swords on the ground and danced around them. British traveler Fynes Moryson referred to the "**Bulrudery**" and the "**Whip of Dunboyne**." There, dancers used *withies* (flexible rods or branches), to entice each other toward flames (O'Rafferty 1953, 9). Having observed one such martial dance performed by potentially rebellious Irish soldiers in front of officials aligned with the British occupiers, Moryson commented that "it seemed . . . a dangerous sport to see so many naked swords" (O'Rafferty, 9).

One of the most famous pantomimic dances, called "**The Burying of the Wren**," is still practiced today on the 26th of December, **St. Stephen's Day**. A wren is a small bird found in Ireland. On Wren Day, the participants parade from house to house telling the story of a dying wren, using song, dance, mime, and music:

The Wren Boys' Song

The wren, the wren the king of all birds,

St. Stephen's Day he got caught in the furze,

Although he is small his family is grey

Cheer up old woman and give us a cake.

Up with the kettle and down with the pan

And give us some money to bury the wren.

(Anon.)

The lead wren boy often wears a white horse's head and carries a decorated pole with a fake wren placed at the top. As the wren boys dance, they sing the "Wren Boys' Song." The costumes and the song remain today. After the performance, the wren boys request payment from the onlookers. Today, this is usually given to charities.

Solo Step Dance Tradition

From the late 18th century, Irish dance masters started to choreograph solo step dances. There were five solo dance types: light and heavy **reels**, jigs, **hornpipes**, and slip jigs. These solo dance types were largely distinguished by different time signatures in their musical accompaniment. The heavy jigs and hornpipes had downward battering actions and were danced only by men wearing hard-soled shoes. Their movement style was earthy, or grounded. Women performed light dances, with an upward focus to the body and

143

a fast, flowing dynamic. Sometimes they wore pumps—soft shoes in cloth and leather. Today, women also dance the heavy dances, but they continue to use pumps.

Dance masters cultivated novel footwork techniques that still exist today. These include **drums** and **double drums** and **batters** and **double batters**. These techniques create a rhythm by tipping toes and heels on the ground. "**Rocks**" were also common. There, the dancer places one foot closely behind the other and sways from side to side using the ankles.

The dance master system moved from east to west across Europe and entered Britain during the 1600s. In 1651, renowned British dance master **John Playford** published his most famous book, *The English Dancing Master*.

Playford's book contained music and instructions for English **country dances** of the era. Many of the dances in his manual are echoed in Irish dances, with similar rhythms, pathways, and positioning of the dancers.

British dance masters entered Ireland in the early 18th century because the British landed gentry needed them to teach their children court dances while in Ireland. The first dance master, **Charles Stanton**, arrived on the 21st of October 1718, contracted to work for a British landlord.

As the century progressed, an Irish dance master tradition emerged. There were three types of masters. The first taught the children of landed gentry. They adopted the European dance master image, carrying silver canes and wearing tall hats, white stockings, and turn-pumps (soft shoes with upward-turned toes). The second type of Irish dance master was weak, technically, and taught simple group dances to Irish natives. The last type of dance master was the most capable; he adopted and adapted European group dances and was also responsible for the creation of the Irish solo step dance tradition. These dance masters had a unique movement style and, accompanied by musicians, they traveled from place to place teaching dance for up to six weeks at each stop. At the end of their stay, these dance masters held "benefit nights." During these social events, the parents observed their children dance a new repertoire of group and solo pieces. At the end of the night, a hat was circulated to collect money for the dance master, who would leave the following day.

 See resource 11.4 in HK*Propel* for web links.

Dance at the Turn of the 20th Century

At the turn of the 20th century, Ireland was seeking independence from Britain. Consequently, Irish **Nationalists** created formal structures to promote native art forms. For dance, they established conventional dance schools and competitive dance events called **feiseanna**. They also started social events called *céilithe*, where people danced traditional Irish group dances, devoid of British influences. Throughout this Gaelic Revival, Irish Nationalists strove to preserve and promote traditional Irish culture.

Dance Schools

New dance schools established during the Gaelic Revival had little in common with the original traveling dance masters. The schools hired **dance teachers**, and these new teachers rarely traveled. They had a standardized dance canon and movement style, and their opportunity to choreograph original dances was restricted. Still, their approach to teaching echoed that of their predecessors. They were perfectionists and equally dictatorial.

Nevertheless, outside this new system, many dance masters continued to teach as they always had. They still moved from one place to another, taught all the original dance types and techniques, and refused to dance in a standardized mode. Instead, they retained their own unique dance repertoires and movement styles.

As mentioned previously, dancers from these conventional schools competed at feiseanna (festivals). There, the goals became external, because the dancers fought to win trophies and medals. Some students of lesser ability often felt ill at ease. (It is an emotion that feis dancers can still experience today.) These students wore standardized costumes, usually made from traditional Irish materials (wool, lace, and tweed) and embroidered with Celtic designs.

Céilithe

Nationalists established social dance events called *céilithe*, which they considered to be purely Irish. In reality, the repressive atmosphere surrounding them had little in common with traditional

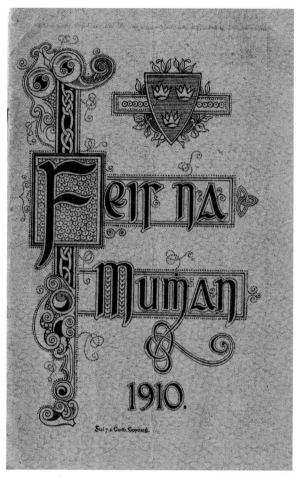

Feis na Mumhan (Feis of Munster), held in Cork City, in the south of Ireland, on September 9-11, 1910. Irish dancers from the province of Munster competed.

Courtesy of the Irish Traditional Music Archive.

Irish cailíní (girls) during the Gaelic Revival: Mazie McCarthy, dancer, piper, and drummer; Alice Dunne, dancer; May McCarthy, Union Piper.

Courtesy of the Irish Traditional Music Archive.

dance gatherings. At céilithe, the dancers danced standardized routines, and clergymen patrolled the dance. Alcohol was rarely served, and the gatherings finished early. Dancers had to sing the national anthem before they went home.

These events were intended to be devoid of British influences, and as a result, several dance types of British origin, such as figure and set dances, were banned. However, there were inconsistencies. For instance, similar events in Scotland, which is part of Britain, were also called *céilithe*. Ironically, the first Irish *céilí* (singular form of *céilithe*) took place in Bloomsbury Hall, in London, where the attendees were Irish emigrants.

 See resource 11.5 in HK*Propel* for web links.

Dance During the Postcolonial Era

From the 1920s onward, the popularity of Irish dance grew in urban areas. The international dance scene also flourished as Irish natives attended popular dance events in Americanized dance halls.

In 1927, Ireland's first formal dance organization, ***An Coimisiún Le Rincí Gaelacha*** (the Irish Dancing Commission), was established, and its members strove to revive dances that had disappeared during the Gaelic Revival. Feiseanna increased in popularity, retaining the nationalistic undertones. Before a feis, the Irish dancers often marched behind a piper in military style to the location of the event. Like their predecessors, the dancers sang the national anthem before they competed, and their costumes had Celtic designs.

As the century progressed, An Coimisiún Le Rincí Gaelacha increased in importance, and branches were established across the world. The World Irish Dance Championship was created, and dancers competed annually. A grading system was instituted, where dancers trained to become teachers and adjudicators. More recent Irish dance organizations have also evolved. These include **Comhdháil Muinteoirí Rincí Gaelacha** (the Congress of Irish Dance Teachers) in 1970 and **WIDA** (World Irish Dance Association) in 2004. Like An Coimisiún Le Rincí Gaelacha, these organizations operate nationally and internationally, promoting Irish dance around the world. They also have fixed repertoires and grading systems, and their students compete in feiseanna to maintain the prestige and integrity of Irish dance.

International Dance Scene

The international dance scene grew during the early and mid-20th century as the Irish took up **jazz dance**—a generic term for imported ballroom dances, such as the Charleston, black bottom, tango, quickstep, or foxtrot. The Irish had started to listen to American jazz music on radios and gramophones and see jazz dance at the cinemas, and returning emigrants brought jazz tunes and footwork back with them. The Irish danced jazz in Americanized halls that had names such as the Crystal, the Silver Slipper, and Ricardo's Ballroom.

Unsupervised jazz dance events were all-night affairs, during which alcohol was served and the dancers reveled as they swung and clasped each other. These events aggravated Nationalists, who believed they were undermining traditional dance. In addition, the sensuality of the movement patterns annoyed the clergy. As a result, the **Public Dance Halls Act** was established in 1935. Now, dance hall licenses were issued in district courts, and the court hearings were witnessed by the clergy. Dances that occurred in local parish halls were overseen by guards and the clergy, and the proceeds from these dances were donated to the government and sometimes the church.

A poster advertised a ballroom dance held in a town hall in Killarney, County Kerry (southwest

Ireland), in 1949. Unlike posters advertising feiseanna and céilithe, the colors of the Irish flag (green and gold) and common Irish motifs (e.g., Celtic designs, shamrocks, and harps) are absent.

The Irish Dance Scene

Céilithe started to decline in the 1930s, and by the late 1940s, they were rare in urban areas. As a result, district judges started to grant restricted dance hall licenses (i.e., only those approved by the clergy, police, and judiciary), on the premise that céilithe would occur in them. The events bore little resemblance to the traditional dance scene, with people dancing standardized dances under well-lit bulbs in impersonal Americanized halls. The professional music bands played standardized tunes on nontraditional instruments (pianos, banjos, saxophones, and drums). They focused on volume versus technique.

 See resource 11.6 in HK*Propel* for web links.

Theatricalization of Irish Dance in Ireland

By the mid-20th century, the traditional social scene had faded in importance, and most Irish people attended musical theater productions, light operas, and Anglicized plays. It was during this era that traditional Irish dance became theatricalized, mainly to preserve and promote Irish dance as an art form. It was also used as a tool through which traditional Irish folklore could be communicated, in shows at **Siamsa Tíre** (National Folk Theatre of Ireland) and in more recent productions such as ***Riverdance***, ***Lord of the Dance***, and ***Celtic Tiger***.

Siamsa Tíre: The National Folk Theatre of Ireland

Fr. Pat Ahern founded Siamsa Tíre, the National Folk Theatre of Ireland, in the early 1970s and used traditional Irish dance as a tool of expression. (*Siamsa Tíre* translates to "merriment of the country.") In his first show, ***Fadó Fadó*** ("long, long ago"), he portrayed his youth on a rural farm in North Kerry. It was a way of life that had dis-

Cultural Highlight

THE NORTH KERRY STEP DANCE

Today, people usually see Irish dance at feiseanna and at performances like *Riverdance*. The style of dance tends to be fast and furious; the upper body is rigid and there is an emphasis on jumping high from the floor. My own Irish dance experience was different. I learned in the *Teach Siamsa* ("house of Siamsa"), which was the training school for performers in Siamsa Tíre. There, I adopted the traditional North Kerry step dance style. It was also called the Molyneaux style of dance, because it was handed down to the founder of Siamsa Tíre, Pat Ahern, by traveling North Kerry dance master Jeremiah Molyneaux. The style involves dancing close to the ground, and the arms flow in a relaxed manner in conjunction with the feet. As I danced the Molyneaux style of dance with Siamsa Tíre, I became part of a dance tradition that is ever-changing and responds to Ireland's heartbeat.

appeared and could only be visited in a theatrical context. Ahern used unique **occupational dances** to portray farm chores: milking cows, thrashing corn, feeding chickens, and beating butter in churns. He choreographed the dances with a local dance teacher, **Patricia Hannifin**. The show also contained solo step dances performed to jig, reel, slip jig, and hornpipe rhythms. Although some of the step dances were choreographed more recently, the dances retained traditional characteristics. The dancers had relaxed upper shoulders and their arms moved with their feet. They also danced close to the floor, using their feet to weave patterns on the floor.

Ahern told the life story of famous North Kerry dance master **Jeremiah Molyneaux** (1881-1967) (or "Munnix" as he was more affectionately known) in his final full-length production, *Ding Dong Dederó*. Molyneaux taught dance during the early 20th century. While the show focused on Molyneaux, it also drew the essentials of the dance master tradition together. These included the common dance types taught by the masters, the specific styles of movement they employed, their commitment to dance, and their method of "handing on" their repertoires and styles as they grew older.

Today, Irish dance remains core at Siamsa Tíre. Ahern's successor, **Oliver Hurley**, used dance to reflect the traditional life of the people on the Blasket Islands, off West Kerry, in his show *Oileán*. The island became uninhabited when the natives left for the mainland in the 1950s.

More recently, *Anam* ("soul"), premiered. Codirected by **Jonathan Kelliher** and Australian choreographer Sue-Ellen Chester, the show provided a cross-analysis of four differing Irish step dance styles: the Appalachian "flatfoot" style, the traditional North Kerry style, the Ottawa Valley (Canada) style, and the modern Irish dance style common to feiseanna and shows like *Riverdance*.

Riverdance

On the 30th of April 1994, a group of singers and dancers performed the interval act for the **Eurovision Song Contest** in Dublin, Ireland. The title of the performance piece was "Riverdance." It was choreographed by lead step dancers **Michael Flatley** and **Jean Butler**.

During the act, lead female dancer Jean Butler emerged from an Irish green cloak to dance in soft pumps. Then Michael Flatley burst onto the stage in hard shoes to the sound of loud beating drums. The act culminated with a large chorus of Irish dancers streaming onto the stage. Specific factors were worth noting: the young chorus adopted linear pathways; they danced the same steps; their movement style was standardized; and the women wore short, black, figure-flattering dresses. These consistencies complemented Flatley. Unlike the chorus, his pathways were unique, his dynamic varied, and he used differing accompaniments (silence, percussion, and music). His costume, like Jean Butler's, was also distinctive. This act evolved into a full-length production, *Riverdance*, in 1995, exploring chief themes like Irish mythology, the Irish famine (during which many Irish people emigrated), and the Irish diaspora in America. The final scene, "The Homecoming," focused on the notion of the Irish emigrant returning home. After *Riverdance*, Michael Flatley directed *Lord of the Dance*, *Feet of Flames*, and *Celtic Tiger* using this modernized approach.

The Dance Diaspora

It was interesting that the two lead dancers in *Riverdance*, Jean Butler and Michael Flatley, were from America and of Irish descent. Inadvertently, this symbolized a cross-relationship between Irish dancers in Ireland and America that has existed since the turn of the 20th century. Then, Irish people emigrated to America in search of a better life. In America, the Irish dance tradition remained an integral part of their lives, for they could imagine they were on Irish soil while they played music and danced together.

 See resource 11.7 in HK*Propel* for web links.

Crosscurrents

When later *Riverdance* productions intertwined Irish dance with other folk dances, including Spanish flamenco, Russian folk, and American tap, many people assumed that this was a ground-breaking feature. However, as we discussed, Irish dance masters adapted French and British folk dances during the colonial era. Furthermore, the founder of **Cork Ballet Company**, **Joan Denise Moriarty**, combined Irish dance and ballet in 1978 to convey an Anglo-Irish play. Clearly, cross-fertilization has long been part of Irish dance.

There was also a connection between Siamsa Tíre and *Riverdance*. In 1992, Spanish flamenco dancer **Maria Pages** performed "Salute to Seville" with Siamsa dancer **Michael Murphy** at the World Expo in Seville. The music was by *Riverdance* composer **Bill Whelan**, and the performance was a unique blend of Spanish and Irish folk dance. Subsequently, in 1995, Pages performed "Firedance" with Michael Flatley in *Riverdance*. Again, the music was by Bill Whelan and, like "Salute to Seville," the male and female dancers answered each other using flamenco and Irish dance steps. The male and female dancers finished their performances dancing together. However, the underlying tones of these performances differed. In "Salute to Seville," the tone was friendly as Pages and Murphy swapped folk dance styles, whereas in "Firedance," with Flatley, the tone had become more sensual.

 See resource 11.8 in HK*Propel* for web links.

Summary

The evolution of dance in Ireland, from historical and social perspectives, is filled with the travails and triumphs of an ancient people. Through religious shifts, colonialism, famine, political upheavals, and more, Irish dance has emerged as a complex dance form, fully reflective of Ireland's storied history. With the spread of dancing traditions through the Irish diaspora and the stunning popularity of performances such as *Riverdance*, Irish dance is now a worldwide phenomenon.

Discussion Questions

1. What influences did the French and British dance traditions have on the Irish dance tradition?

2. How was Irish dance nationalized at the turn of the 20th century?

3. Compare the methods of teaching employed by traditional Irish dance masters and current Irish dance teachers.

4. How did Pat Ahern, founder of *Siamsa Tíre*, develop Irish dance?

 Visit HK*Propel* for access to this chapter's Application Activity.

Selected Glossary

caroles—Medieval European ring, chain, or linked circle dances with accompaniment sung by the dancers. Originating in the seventh century, the carole peaked across Europe during the 13th century, then started to decline from the 14th century onward.

céilí (singular), **céilithe** (plural)—The Irish céilí is a social event attended by women and men who dance various céilí dances to live traditional Irish music.

colonial era—During the period 1536 to 1691, Ireland was colonized by Britain. The full island remained under British control until the early 20th century, when Ireland gained freedom. However, the six counties of Ulster province in Northern Ireland remained under British rule as a compromise.

cotillions—French formation dances performed in places across Europe and America during the 18th century. The term translates to "petticoat," probably referring to the long dresses of the French female dancers. Cotillions entered Britain in the mid-18th century and were introduced into Ireland by British dance masters. Usually, there were four couples in a square formation. Cotillions were the precursor of the quadrille and the square dances of the USA.

country dances—The term *country dance* is usually associated with social dances in the British Isles. The first printed source for "country dance" in Britain was a publication by British dance master John Playford in 1651. Traveling dance masters brought English country dances to Ireland in the 18th century, and the Irish adopted and adapted them. These dances are danced in circular and longways formations to provide the opportunity for many participants. Other geometric formations used in country dancing, such as squares and triangles, are more restrictive in the numbers of participants. Country dances are danced to a set piece of music. The dances are social, and the dancers honor each other as they dance. Also called "English country dances" or "British country dances."

dance master system—During the 15th century, the dance master tradition traveled across Europe and became popular in Britain in the 17th century. In the early 18th century, British landlords settled in Ireland and employed British dance masters to teach their children court and country dances of the time. Soon, Irish dancers adopted the material of the British dance masters, and they became dance masters in the houses of the British landlords. When the Irish dance masters returned to their communities, they adapted British and French dances while also creating their own unique individualized step dance tradition. These dance masters traveled from one place to the next teaching their own repertoire and movement style. They were held in high regard, and their contribution to the spreading and popularization of Irish dance remains recognized today.

dance teachers—At the turn of the 20th century, Irish Nationalists created a dance teacher system. These teachers largely taught a standardized repertoire in urban areas, and they ceased teaching dance during the summer holidays. Their students wore costumes when competing for medals and trophies at feiseanna. At the same time the traditional dance masters continued to teach in rural areas. Unlike the dance teachers, their repertoires remained individualized, and their movement styles remained unique to themselves.

feiseanna—Originally the term *feis* (singular) or *feiseanna* (plural) referred to native arts and culture festivals in Ireland. Since the turn of the 20th century, the term is usually associated with Irish dance competitions.

figure dance—A group dance. It also exists in Scotland. There are several similarities between the Irish and Scottish figure dances.

hornpipe—The hornpipe resembles the reel. Both are in simple 2/4 or 4/4 time. The chief difference between both is the emphasis on the rhythm. The hornpipe largely emphasizes the first and third beats, whereas the reel has less emphasis and is usually played faster.

jig—The term *jig* can refer to a tune or a dance in Ireland. From a music perspective, it is in compound meter. There are three types of jig: single jig, double jig, and slip jig. Single and double jigs are usually in 6/8 time, whereas slip jigs are in 9/8 time. A jig dance accompanies a jig tune.

quadrilles—These French dances were fashionable during the late 18th and 19th centuries in Europe, entering Ireland via British dance masters and French soldiers. During quadrilles four couples dance in a square formation. There were at least five sections to the dance, which was performed largely among the upper classes in their courtyards.

reel—A dance or a tune, it is in simple 2/4 or 4/4 time. Dances performed to reel music are faster than jigs or hornpipes.

set dances—These group dances evolved from quadrilles during the 19th century. Today, many set dances still carry the term *quadrille* in their title (e.g., "Fermanagh Quadrille"). The dance formations, male–female relationships, and pathways resemble quadrilles, but the rhythm is faster. Originally, these dances were danced at crossroads in Ireland. Today, set dances can be performed in many different social contexts, including feiseanna.

Siamsa Tíre—The National Folk Theatre of Ireland. Founded by Fr. Pat Ahern in 1968.

step dance—A solo Irish dance type.

Selected References and Resources

Bowers, F., ed. 1961. *The Dramatic Works of Thomas Dekker*. Cambridge: Cambridge University Press.

Brenann, H. 2021. *The Story of Irish Dance*. Niwot, CO, USA: Roberts Rinehart Publishers.

Emmerson, G. 1971. *Rantin' Pipe and Tremblin" String: A History of Scottish Dance Music*. London: J.M. Dent and Sons.

Foley, C.E. 2016. *Step Dancing in Ireland*. London: Routledge.

Forbes, John. 1853. *Memorandums Made in Ireland in the Autumn of 1852*. London: Smith, Elder and Co.

Grattan Flood, W.H. 1911. *The Story of the Bagpipe*. Newcastle Upon Tyne: Walter Scott Publishing.

Harrington, John P. 1991. *The English Traveller in Ireland*. Dublin: Wolfhound Press.

Kenrick, W., ed. 1767. *The London Review of English and Foreign Literature*. London: T. Evans and Paternoster Row.

Memmi, A. 1991. *The Coloniser and the Colonised*. Boston: Beacon Press.

O'Rafferty, P., and G. O'Rafferty. 1953. *Dances of Ireland*. London: Max Parish and Company.

Phelan, S. 2014. *Dance in Ireland: Steps, Stages and Stories*. Newcastle Upon Tyne: Cambridge Scholars Publishing.

Playford, J. 1651. *The English Dancing Master or Plaine and Easie Rules for the Dancing of Country Dances, With the Tune to Each Dance*. London: Harper.

Richmond, Farley P., D.L. Swann, and P. Zarilli, eds. 1993. *Indian Theatre: Traditions of Performance*. Delhi, India: Motilal Banarsidass Publications.

Whelan, Frank. 2000. *The Complete Guide to Irish Dance*. Belfast: Appletree Press.

12

Dance in Spain

Bridgit Luján

After reading this chapter you will be able to do the following:

- Define flamenco.
- Synthesize the historical influences that developed the art and culture of flamenco.
- Understand where flamenco fits in the pantheon of dances in Spain.

Key Terms

Andalucía—Southern region in Spain where flamenco originated.

cante—Flamenco song.

floreo—Hand movement and circles that embellish the dance and illustrate the rhythm.

jaleo—Rhythmic calls and shouts (e.g., "olé!") from the musicians and audience that encourage the dancer and enliven the performance.

palmas—Rhythmic hand clapping used as percussive accompaniment in flamenco.

palos—Different song forms in flamenco, each with a distinctive emotion, musical beat, lyrical style, and musical melody.

Flamenco of Spain

It was a cool humid morning. The sun barely peeked through the clouds, and there was an energy that seemed to rumble the city—an unexplained feeling in the air that made the heart race with excitement and anticipation. I made my way around the front of the Villamarta Theater along to the street, where I spotted the force that had descended on the city. It was **Farruquito** and his company disembarking from their bus. The entire day was filled with an energy of excitement that seemed to touch every visitor and resident of the small southern Andalucían Spanish town of Jerez de la Frontera. Everyone could feel the "rock star" had arrived, bringing the mythical **duende** with him. Finally, when the energy level was nearing frenzy, nine o'clock came, and the curtain lifted on the theater stage. A burst of exuberant hand clapping, guitar, song, and cheers exploded from the stage as the lights exposed a seated line of the most powerful singers and musicians in flamenco, with the presence of a cavalry ready to attack. Hearts beat in the throats of the audience as flamenco dance icons Farruquito and **Karime Amaya** charged into a center-stage duel of footwork and turns that defied the imagination, revealing the ancestral forces that continue to thrive within the dance of descendants of the flamenco creators' dynasties (Festival Jerez 2010, Jerez de la Frontera Spain).

"'All that has dark sounds has *duende*.' And there's no deeper truth than that. Those dark sounds are the mystery, the roots that cling to the mire that we all know, that we all ignore, but from which comes the very substance of art. . . . So, then, the *duende* is a force not a labour, a struggle not a thought. I heard an old *maestro* of the guitar say: 'The *duende* is not in the throat: the *duende* surges up, inside, from the soles of the feet.' Meaning, it's not a question of skill, but of a style that's truly alive: meaning, it's in the veins: meaning, it's of the most ancient culture of immediate creation" (García Lorca, Trans. Kline 2007).

The area known as Spain today is said to have been inhabited since 800,000 BCE. The famed cave paintings of **Magdalenian** in northern Spain date back to 15,000 BCE. Cádiz, an important city of **Andalucía** (the southern province where flamenco developed) was founded by the **Phoenicians** in 800 BCE. In 237 BCE the foundation of the **Carthaginian Empire** was established, followed by Roman rule. Today there are still many well-preserved Roman structures throughout Spain. Later, the **Visigoths** would occupy Spain until the Muslim forces between 711 to 720 CE would overrun the Visigoth kingdom. The Muslim kingdom occupied Spain until 1492, when the final Muslim stronghold in Granada fell to the newly united Christian kingdoms under the Catholic monarchy of **King Ferdinand II and Queen Isabella**. The **Inquisition**—a judicial body designed to combat heresy in Spain—had already been persecuting non-Catholics since 1478, and Muslim and Jewish people were faced with the choice of converting to Catholicism or leaving Spain. These groups had lived in harmony in Spain for centuries, and it was their home, but they were threatened nonetheless. After years of such persecution, 1492 had brought not only the defeat of the Muslims, but also the official expulsion of **Sephardic Jews** from Spain, along with Queen Isabella's financing of Christopher Columbus to sail to Asia. The latter resulted in the "discovery" of the New World and the extensive Spanish colonization that followed. Many Jews and Muslims left Spain for the New World or other countries, while some remained as **conversos** (people forced to convert to Catholicism) in a persecuted shadow existence, marginalized from society, oppressed by racist and religious intolerance.

It is believed that the influences of the numerous cultures that occupied Spain, the persecution of groups like the Muslims, Jews, and Roma people (originating from the Indian subcontinent), and the influence of the American colonies set a unique stage for flamenco to develop and appear in the public sector during the mid-19th century. Political conflict riddled the 19th and early 20th centuries, eventually leading to the **Spanish Civil War** in 1936, which ended in 1939 with the victory of Nationalist forces led by fascist dictator **Francisco Franco** (1892-1975). Franco would remain in power until his death in 1975 when **Juan Carlos I** was crowned king. Juan Carlos led the transition into democracy, elections being held in 1977. Today Spain is a member of the **European Union** and **NATO** and is a contemporary cultural leader.

Mercedes de Cordoba
Photo: Farruk

Roma, Gitano, Gypsy

It is important to clarify that for this chapter the term **Gitano**, which is the Spanish word for *gypsy*, is used to reference the **Roma** people living in Spain who practice the art form of flamenco. While the term *Roma* is the preferred term for the people also known as *gypsies* in Europe, the Roma people of Spain who specifically do flamenco take great pride in being *Gitanos*. It is important to call a group by the term they prefer and self-identify with and, in the case of the Roma people of flamenco, they call themselves *Gitanos*. There are references of pride sung in flamenco music about Gitanos, and it is a bloodline coveted by non-Roma and foreign flamenco artists and aficionados. Dancing or singing like a "Gitano" is a great compliment in flamenco for those not of Gitano descent. The Roma people outside of flamenco do not like the term *gypsy*, or its Spanish equivalent, *Gitanos*, and self-identify as *Roma*. Hence, *Roma* is the accepted term in academic research and should be used outside of flamenco.

Flamenco

Flamenco is associated with Spain's national identity in popular culture throughout the world. The dance form is a fusion of local and global influences that formed a new and unique tradition rooted in the geography of southern Spain that continues to evolve today. Political, religious, and economic oppression of Spain's unwanted groups forged a rebellious, resistant, and fierce art form practiced by artists of numerous nationalities and enjoyed by audiences globally. The people who created flamenco and contributed to its early development would be surprised by this global understanding of the dance form and the meaning attached to it.

A Brief History of Flamenco's Development

Centuries of political, religious, racial, and economic oppression in the form of expulsion, imprisonment, forced assimilation, and extermination are the driving forces behind the development of flamenco. Marginalization of unwanted

Is Flamenco Spanish Dance?

Outside of Spain, Eurocentric ideals result in flamenco being incorrectly categorized as traditional or heritage dance. Flamenco is not dedicated to preserving traditions or celebrating past historical events; it is actually a vibrant living art form. Flamenco is sometimes believed to be a folk dance from Spain, and while it has influences from folk dance that have been fused into the music and dance, that alone does not make it a folk dance. If such criteria did apply, ballet could be considered folk dance as well. Flamenco also is not "Spanish dance"; it is a fusion of the various groups of ethnic minorities in Spain that makes it an ethnic dance of Spain, rather than a national dance style. There is confusion and debate about including it in the canon of Spanish dance. While Flamenco is native geographically to Spain, it did not arise from the people in power; it is born from the ethnic minorities, foreign newcomers, and nomadic Roma, precluding it from the canon of Spanish dance.

groups in Spain, such as Jews, **Moors** (Muslims), Gitanos (Roma people), and Africans, pushed them into the lowest social classes, intermixing with thieves, sex workers, and other powerless groups. A melting pot of music, dance, and traditions in Andalucía created the foundation for what would eventually evolve into the art form of flamenco as we recognize it today. Flamenco is not considered a protest art but was born of protest against oppression and as a therapeutic release from the pain and suffering of marginalization. Today, flamenco is a highly sophisticated set of complex dances to particular song forms (*palos*) that each display a unique movement technique and style, coupled with rapid footwork and emotive expression.

Flamenco is said to have begun taking shape in the 15th century with the arrival of the Roma from India. After centuries of nomadic existence and persecution in every area they passed through, they arrived in Spain with a collection of various folk dances encountered along their journey. Once in Spain, the Roma were further influenced by the folk dance traditions of rural Christian Spain, as well as the traditions of the Jews and Moors.

At the same time these unwanted fringe people came together, other influences were also circulating into the ports of Andalucía from the New World (North and South America and the Caribbean). Folk music of the Americas was blended into this new style. The slave trade brought the music and dance of the Black Africans to Spain. As all these influences became blended among a mixed group of oppressed people, the early form of flamenco began to take shape. The release of pain that lived in the historic memory of the various peoples first appeared as song that, with time, was set to the rhythm of handclaps. Dark songs, called **cante jondo**, would generate intricate rhythmic meters, accompanied by barefoot dancing that fused the movement of the Moors, Jews, Gitanos, Africans, and southern Christian Spaniards. This barefoot dancing would evolve into one of the most intricate and sophisticated forms of percussive dance in the world today. The art was first generated within the family and later become part of pop culture. Today, such blending continues as flamenco absorbs influences from all over the world. American music, such as rock, jazz, blues, and reggaetón, have played a role in the evolution of today's flamenco sound. Modern dance of northern Europe and the United States has also influenced the movement aesthetic.

Flamenco in the 19th to 21st Centuries

The 19th century marked over 300 years of oppression by the Christian monarchy in Spain; however, that century was a turning point for when flamenco began to be recognized and appreciated by the mainstream public. The Romantic era of Europe set into motion a time of prominent status for the arts, driven by interest in bohemian cultures and all things exotic or foreign. This was the time period when flamenco as we know it today emerged. In the late 19th century, flamenco was seen publicly in the **café cantantes**, or song cafes (1847-1920), which led to a period known as the Golden Age of Flamenco (1869-1910), when growth and invention transformed and defined flamenco as we recognize it today.

Shortly after the Golden Age of flamenco, Spain endured a time of intense political upheaval. The monarchy lost power and Spain

Iván Vargas.
Photo: Farruk

flamenco to the entire world from the late 1940s to the early 1970s. His touring schedule was described by his daughters Lola and Carmela as 364 days a year; they said they only saw him one day a year, on Christmas. Greco is said to have performed in every country in the world.

After Franco died in 1975, King Juan Carlos I transformed Spain away from autocratic rule into a parliamentary constitutional monarchy. This transformation opened Spain to the international economy, and flamenco artists could easily tour and teach all over the world. Roma children were integrated into the public schools during the mid-1980s, while Spain joined the European Union (1986) and was one of the first countries to adopt the euro currency (1999). In 2010, the United Nations Educational, Scientific and Cultural Organization (**UNESCO**) recognized flamenco as an **Intangible Cultural Heritage of Humanity**. The descendants of exiled Sephardic Jews were given the opportunity to apply for a Spanish passport from 2015 to 2019 in a government gesture to atone for the Jews' expulsion, the Inquisition, and religious intolerance.

The Spanish Language and Flamenco

Today the Andalucían form of Spanish, which is peppered with local Andalucían dialect and **Caló** words, is viewed as the only authentic language of expression in flamenco. Spanish being flamenco's primary language, however, is not a reflection of flamenco being Spain's national art form but, instead, evidence of political oppression. Many regional Indo-European languages spoken throughout Spain, such as **Galician** (related to Portuguese), were overtaken by the language of central Spain, called ***Castellaño*** (Castilian)—the language of Queen Isabella's province of Castile. Other languages spoken in Spain, such as the remaining Arabic languages of the Moors, **Ladino** (Judeo-Spanish) of the Sephardic Jews, and Caló of the Gitanos, were also nearly wiped out. Castellaño became what the rest of the world refers to as Spanish, or *Español*, the language of Spain, and was brought to the conquered lands of the Americas. Today, very few Gitanos speak Caló. In many cases its remaining usage has evolved into a dialect of Spanish. So while flamenco is expressed in Spanish, that does not connect it to being a Spanish art form. Rather, Spanish connects flamenco to its geographic area of development

entered into a bloody civil war (1936-1939). In 1939, fascist dictator Francisco Franco took power and ruled Spain until his death in 1975. Under Franco's rule, Spain suffered a time of intense oppression, with many people subjected to exile, held as political prisoners, and in some cases assassinated. In Franco's efforts to draw tourists into Spain and improve the image of his oppressive regime in the eyes of the international community, flamenco—the dance style from the despised people of Spain—was co-opted as propaganda. Performed alongside Spanish dance, its true identity was suppressed because Franco, a Nationalist, banned all regional music, dance, and languages. The contribution of the Gitanos and the melting pot of cultures that developed flamenco became blurred and misrepresented.

Meanwhile, outside of Spain, **Carmen Amaya** (1913-1963), revered in flamenco as the "Queen of the Gypsies," had left Spain and was performing in North and South America (1936-1947), bringing a pure and fiery interpretation of flamenco to the global stage. Then, Italian-born American dancer **José Greco** (1918-2000), one of the most well-recognized flamenco dancers on Earth, was touring and bringing live performances of during a time when its developers' languages were being extinguished.

In 1981, the film version of **Antonio Gades'** (1936-2004) dance drama *Blood Wedding* was released, bringing flamenco dance through media to the international community. The dance drama, directed by Carlos Saura, interpreted the play written by famed poet **Federico García Lorca** (1898-1936) who was assassinated by the Nationalist militia in 1936. People throughout the world who had never seen flamenco now had their appetites whetted for this resonant, intriguing art form. More recently, social media, YouTube, and the Internet have further popularized flamenco around the globe.

Flamenco is not a stand-alone dance form; it is danced as a direct response to the *cante* (song), which is considered the root of the entire art form. During the singing, the dancers perform *marcaje*, which are steps that mark the basic music accents in the feet while drawing visual images characterized by dynamic shapes and swirls in the upper body. These are the "dance," or artful, sections of flamenco that highlight the basic rhythm of the song through full-body lyric expression. The breaks in the song are where sections of footwork are done by the dancer and contrast the lyrical movement with intense percussion. Footwork, or percussiveness created by striking with the feet, is when the dancer transforms into an additional musician and uses the floor and their feet to create intricate rapid rhythms with various types of strikes from different parts of the foot. These sections of complicated, intricate, and forceful striking of the foot add another layer of percussion to the music. The dancer is supported by music, in most instances guitar, and hand clapping known as *palmas*. This hand clapping gives the percussive support to the music and dance. Hand clapping to create percussion and voice as the melody were the first elements of flamenco. These elements were born of extreme poverty where marginalized groups often had not much more than the tattered clothing they were wearing. Without the luxury of instruments other than what their own bodies provided, they found creative ways to make music with body movement, voice, clapping, snapping, and stomping. The rhythms, thought to have originated from repetitive work, evolved into extremely complicated unique rhythmic meters and accents and a complex system of song styles, which generated a difficult and highly sophisticated instrumental and dance technique.

Flamenco Footwork

Flamenco footwork is called *zapateado* (shoe work) or *taconeo* (heel work). Individual steps do not have names but are described using the parts of the foot—*planta* (striking just the ball of the foot), *golpe* (striking the entire foot), *tacón* (striking the heel in a jab motion or pushing a lifted heel downward), and *punta* (dropping the front, or point, of the shoe). A section of footwork is called an *escobilla*, and footwork sections that speed up are called *subidas* (to speed up) or *redobles* (four or five percussive steps, with the loudest accent on the final sound).

Flamenco Music

Flamenco dance as we recognize it today evolved from barefoot dancing into what is called a percussive dance. Similar to the American style of tap dance, the dancer creates with the feet not only visual movement, but also rhythmic sounds. A flamenco dancer wears specially designed shoes that have many small nails in the front and heel to create a louder sound when the shoe is struck against the floor. The dancer contributes to the music as an instrumentalist, providing a percussive layer to the music while also visually describing the rhythm and emotion evoked by the music. A flamenco performer must be skillful in both dance and body percussion, enhancing the music through clapping, finger snaps, slapping the body, and footwork. In 2020, flamenco dancer **Nino de los Reyes** became the first dancer to win a Grammy Award for dancing. The percussion from his dance was part of the album *Antidote* by Chick Corea that won the 2020 Best Latin Jazz Album Grammy. Thus, the flamenco dancer's talent as a musician is as vivid and important as the dance to which it is intricately bound.

Polyrhythms, Lyrics, and Emotional Aesthetics of Flamenco

The flamenco dance technique includes movement of the arms that is called *brazeo* and circling of the hands, called *floreo*. The circling of the hands is an aesthetic embellishment as well as a visual description of the meter being pulsed in the music. The hand movements do

Nino de los Reyes.
Photo: Farruk

not directly describe the narrative the way they do in Hawai'ian **hula** or **kathak** of India, where the hand movements often actively narrate the story. Polyrhythms (many rhythms) are used; the feet, arms, and hands are often all moving at different speeds, making flamenco difficult to master. Performers support one another with various shouted cheers, called *jaleo*, such as "olé!" These shouts of encouragement and approval can also come from the audience but should occur at the culturally appropriate times. An exquisite flamenco performer is said to conjure a force known as *duende*, which is an intangible form of inspiration and passion that adds a unique magical quality to a flamenco performance.

Because a flamenco song has lyrics, people often believe that the lyrics are the narrative

that is being interpreted by a dancer's movement. However, flamenco dance is not normally a direct narrative of the poetic lyrics. Instead it is an emotional reaction to the pain evoked by the sound of the voice; the dance interprets its own emotional abstract narrative. Emotion and rhythm are primary in flamenco, with aesthetics being secondary. The aesthetic is driven by emotion presenting a challenge when supporting varied contemporary narratives and subjects. So today's **neo-flamenco** choreographers, such as **Belén Maya**, Rocío Molina, and Israel Galván, are seeking to widen the vocabulary of flamenco movement by blending it with contemporary dance and performance theater to address social issues and wider gender explorations beyond the cliché often expected of flamenco.

Instrumentation

In the 19th century, the guitar joined flamenco as the primary musical instrument. Instrumentation remained somewhat static, without percussion beyond hand clapping, until the mid-20th century, when the *cajón*, a percussive instrument of Peru, made its way into flamenco music to become the current quintessential percussion instrument. The introduction of the cajón into flamenco was made by form-changing guitarist **Paco de Lucía** (1947-2014), the most well-known flamenco guitarist in the world. Today, flamenco instrumentalists, such as violinist **Paco Montalvo** and pianist **Laura de los Ángeles**, among others, use these classical instruments to express flamenco's emotive qualities. **Ana Crismán** recently became the first person in the world to use the harp to interpret flamenco.

Costumes

Costuming in flamenco is a real-life rags-to-riches story and generally reflects the popular trends of clothing outside of flamenco and high fashion. As a tradition from indigent people, flamenco costumes started out as the clothing that you might be lucky enough to have, but they have evolved into an entire design industry. As flamenco developed during the late 19th century, the elaborate dress of the aristocrats infiltrated the dance. Female dancers today still perform in long-trained dresses (**bata de cola**), which recently have become a dance accessory for men, as well. Women most often dance in ankle-length skirts with wide panels. These panels have become narrower and skirts lighter as the speed of the dance has increased. In the 1950s, when petticoats were popular, skirts were a few inches shorter, with many ruffled layers. Stretch fabric, once taboo in flamenco costuming, is now common, because it suits the fluid torso-bending in today's dance. Women's shoes have also changed; at one time a high narrow heel was worn, but today a thicker, shorter heel is ideal for the type of footwork women perform. It is not unusual for dancers to be wearing $2,000 worth of costuming for just one dance: handmade shoes, fine combs and earrings, silk hand-embroidered shawls, and, of course, all those ruffles on the dresses that rival wedding gowns.

Men wear low-heeled ankle boots and dress in fashionable suits, sometimes designer clothes, such as Armani. At one time, high-waisted pants with a short vest was the fashion of flamenco (*traje corto*). Today, the traje corto is still worn alongside the most current fashions, such as skinny jeans.

Flamenco fashion is so popular in Spain that there are specialist designers and many shops and factories that manufacture the dresses and shawls, such as Molina Moda Flamenco and Artesania Textil, respectively. Specialists, such as Luna Flamenca, Artefyl, and Don Flamenco, make the shoes by hand. There is an annual high-fashion flamenco event called **SIMOF**, the Salón Internacional de Moda Flamenca. In 2020, the event presented 1,500 dresses, with 42 professional presentations on the catwalk, featuring 80 designers. The cutting-edge fashion of flamenco is worn to festivals and events, and sometimes weddings, similar to designer evening wear in the United States.

Technique and Improvisation

Flamenco's use of bound energy creates tension within the body and is a constant visual and physical reminder of its blended past. The lower body, from the waist down, is heavy and weighted into the ground, similar to African dance. The upper body is regal and proud, reminiscent of the posture of aristocrats in corsets. The arms sometimes use clean positions, influenced by early ballet and folk dance, but they also twist and curve as dancers rapidly whirl around in numerous turns, similar to Arab styles of dance. The leg is lifted and strikes the floor from behind, as is done in traditional dance in India. There is stillness and wildness, a constant shifting of restraint.

Improvisation in flamenco is not free in the way the word might lead one to believe. In other dance styles, such as modern dance improvisation or hip-hop freestyle, dancers can move as they please. By contrast, there is a considerable amount of ritual that must be learned and understood to correctly improvise in flamenco, and those skills require time and practice. Improvising is one of the most difficult things in flamenco, since there is an extremely complicated structure and method of communication between the dancer and musician. Not being able to stay within the prescribed structures during improvisation is viewed as not being ready to improvise and honor the art. Those who master this complicated system of the supposed "free dance" are highly revered. Mastery requires an instantaneous understanding and ability to respond to the music while positioning oneself in the space with a command of gestural and rhythmic cues.

Flamenco training today is considerably different than it was in the past. Flamenco used to be a tradition passed down in the family. Children learned flamenco, which served as profession, entertainment, celebration, and emotional release. Many Gitanos practice flamenco as part of a familial tradition, even if they never do it for a profession or in public. Although most professional flamenco dancers today train in academies, the familial history remains an important part of the tradition and philosophy. It creates a mode of multigenerational and multiability community inclusivity when it is practiced outside of the profession as a celebratory social form of dance.

 See resource 12.1 in HK*Propel* for web links.

Spanish Dance and Flamenco

Today, flamenco as "Spanish dance" is in dispute. There are respected written publications that include flamenco in Spanish dance and others that do not. Some artists, aficionados, and researchers of flamenco do not categorize flamenco into Spanish dance solely because it was developed in Spain, but some do. Flamenco may best be described as "made in Spain of foreign and domestic ingredients." The Gitanos view categorizing flamenco as Spanish dance as a racially motivated mechanism to erase their contribution. Because of the debate and broad confusion, it is important to understand what Spanish dance is.

Cultural Highlight

FLAMENCO, AN INCLUSIVE DANCE

In early flamenco, the family setting once provided an inclusive experimental platform for everyone: disabled and abled, children and elderly, large and small, short and tall. The desire for economic success gave way to myths and stereotypes during the past 200 years of flamenco's public evolution, for the most part shelving flamenco's endemically inclusive core ideal. However, over the past 20 years flamenco has made strides in developing and offering diverse inclusive programming and classes. The primary trailblazer and foremost expert of inclusive flamenco dance is choreographer **José Galán**, who presents theater performances that include disabled and abled dancers on the professional stage, demonstrating appreciation for these dancers as expressive artists. The inclusion in flamenco met a milestone in 2018 when the **Bienal of Sevilla**, the most important professional flamenco dance festival in Spain, was dedicated to diversity. The opening flash mob honored the inclusive nature of this universal art.

No existen barreras para el flamenco.	There are no barriers for flamenco.
El Flamenco no tiene edad.	Flamenco has no age.
El Flamenco no tiene género.	Flamenco has no gender.
El Flamenco no tiene de razas.	Flamenco does not know race.
El Flamenco no entiendo de fronteras.	Flamenco does not know borders.
El Flamenco no tiene límites.	Flamenco has no limits.
El Flamenco es un arte universal.	Flamenco is a universal art.

From *Cierra los ojos y Mírame*
Written by José Galán
For the 2018 Bienal Sevilla Flash Mob

Spanish dance is often a misused term for any dance style from a Spanish-speaking country, such as Argentine tango, salsa, or Mexican folk dance. As a broad term, *Spanish dance* really should be reserved for styles of Spain and, more specifically, dances that represent the Spanish people's culture and traditions. Flamenco is a blending of foreign influences and the artistry of ethnic minorities that were located in Spain. Even though it has uniquely developed in Spain, it developed alongside—not within—the mainstream Spanish culture and does not truly represent this larger culture.

Spanish dance remains important and vibrant in conservatory studies and is required for a dance diploma (equivalent to a BFA) in Spain. However, it is not often seen on the global stage because there are few professional Spanish dance companies remaining in Spain, and even fewer outside of Spain. The government-supported **Ballet Nacional de España** is the largest and most prestigious Spanish dance company in Spain.

Spanish dance is generally subdivided with several distinct and unique forms of dance indigenous to Spain; the **bolero school** (*escuela bolera*), **classical Spanish dance** (*clasico Española*), **stylized dance** (*danza estilizada*), and **regional folk dance** (*folklórico*). Following are brief descriptions of each subtype of Spanish dance.

Bolero School

Bolero school (escuela bolera) is an 18th-century academic dance style. It is a balletic dance performed in soft slippers and influenced by the Italian and French dance masters of the time. Based on the principles of classical ballet, it is adorned with the playing of castanets and influence from Iberian folk dance. This is a unique form of early ballet that is still performed in Spanish dance repertory.

Classical Spanish Dance

Classical Spanish dance (clasico Española) is performed in heeled shoes with castanets, using much of the upper-body technique and arm positions of escuela bolera. It often resembles flamenco because there is footwork; however, an important key difference between this style of dance and flamenco is that classical Spanish dance is performed to classical music, while flamenco is performed in response to live flamenco song.

Stylized Dance

Stylized dance (danza estilizada) is a complicated term that loosely refers to a style that incorporates folk dance, classical Spanish dance, and flamenco dance. Today you will see elements and concepts from modern dance, as well. This style of dance is generally performed to classical or other contemporary arrangements while maintaining the unique aesthetic character of Spanish dance.

Regional Folk Dance

Regional folk dance (folklórico) encompasses all the traditional and regional dances of Spain, including hundreds of folk dances. Many of these dances stem from Greek, Phoenician, Celtic, Jewish, and Moorish origins.

Traditional folk dances unique to each region of Spain are part of celebrations in nearly every city in Spain and are clearly representative of the term *Spanish dance*. These traditional folk dances, in most cases, do not resemble flamenco at all. The folk dance of Spain has qualities that we normally attribute to northern European folk dance. The music may sound Celtic, with bagpipes, and in some regions costumes may resemble traditional Dutch dresses. One of the most well-known styles of folk dance in Spain is from the northern province of Aragon, called *jota aragonesa*. This partner dance includes high kicks and is performed in sandals in traditional costumes with castanets held in a uniquely different way than in classical Spanish dance and flamenco.

Sevillanas

The four short dances of the **sevillanas** make up the most recognized Spanish folk dance in the world, taught globally. As a whole, sevillanas is a festive partner dance commonly performed at outdoor celebrations in Andalucía. It is often confused with flamenco dance, because it has been adopted and stylized by flamenco and is performed within flamenco performances. Sevillanas are also taught in flamenco classes all over the world and are often, ironically, students' first introduction to flamenco. The sevillanas as a folk dance is a Spanish dance separate from flamenco, even though it enjoys a nearly interchangeable association within flamenco and is popular worldwide solely based on its association with flamenco.

Tamara Lopez.

Photo: Farruk

 See resource 12.2 in HK*Propel* for web links.

Crosscurrents

Flamenco is growing in popularity throughout the world and is an important part of Spain's creative economy, both domestically and as an export. In June 2021, **Macarena Ramírez** won the Spanish TV dance competition *The Dancer*, which was not only a triumph for her as a dancer but for flamenco overall. This competition relies heavily on popular votes, and flamenco has rarely captured this level of support above other more well-known dance styles, such as modern, ballet, and other popular mainstream forms of dance.

Ruben Olmo, the artistic director of the Ballet Nacional de España, describes flamenco's current popularity as eclipsing Spanish dance. And while this is true, flamenco's international popularity has eclipsed more than Spanish dance;

internationally, Spain's entire dance community is eclipsed by flamenco. Spain has vibrant companies and performances in modern dance and ballet—and there are many more highly skilled dancers in these genres than there are companies for them to work in. American styles, such as musical theater and hip-hop, are growing in presence because interest in their associated musical styles has increased. Dance in Spain is much more than flamenco and Spanish dance. Of course, proximity to these other styles influences flamenco's evolution, including how flamenco is taught, dancers' cross-training, and fusion of technique.

Ballet is rarely the image people conjure when thinking of dance in Spain; however, many Spanish-trained ballet dancers have had stunning international careers. A great example is **José Carlos Martínez**, who directed the **Compañía Nacional de Danza** (National Dance Company of Spain) from 2011 to 2019. He returned to Spain with several international ballet prizes after two decades with the Paris Opera Ballet. Modern dance is also flourishing, particularly in Spain's two largest cities, Barcelona and Madrid. **Ramon Oller** is an example of many of the fine contemporary choreographers. Oller directed his own, now defunct, Limón technique–based company, *metros*, and today works as a choreographer internationally, recently (2019) creating a work for **Ballet Hispánico in NYC**.

Spain is also growing in dance styles from the United States. In 2019, Spanish-born Hollywood star **Antonio Banderas**' Spanish-language revival of the musical *Chorus Line* opened in Malaga, Spain, selling 40,000 advanced tickets. Hip-hop dance is also becoming more popular as **reggaetón** music, a style originating in Puerto Rico, takes hold in the pop music scene of Spain. These are just a few examples of the internationally recognized dance talent of Spain beyond flamenco.

 See resource 12.3 in HK*Propel* **for web links.**

Summary

Flamenco is a unique mode of dance from Spain's southern region of Andalucía that has a presence in nearly every country in the world. It is an art form of contradictions, mystery, tradition, and evolution. It is a dance form based on the sacred tradition of the song. Filled with history only beginning to be uncovered, the physical body and music continue to evolve, developing fresh frontiers. As a global phenomenon, flamenco's technique and form are readily acclaimed, but its deepest resonance comes through the fusion of many cultures centered in suffering. Efforts to define or lay claim to flamenco are complicated by the relationship between flamenco and Spanish dance—a wide-ranging field of European heritages and Greek, Phoenician, Celtic, Jewish, and Moorish influences. As a dance "made in Spain of foreign and domestic ingredients," flamenco has a paradoxical interaction with the past, present, and future that fuels constant evolution, embodying the dynamic heritage of dance in Spanish culture.

Discussion Questions

1. Discuss why flamenco is not "Spanish dance."
2. Briefly list some of the historical events discussed in the chapter that influenced flamenco's development.
3. What are the two root musical elements of flamenco before instrumentation? What is the most-recognized instrument of flamenco music? What are some other instruments used in flamenco? What is the name of the percussive instrument commonly used in flamenco today?
4. Discuss some of the types of oppression that the developers of this art form experienced.

 Visit HK*Propel* **for access to this chapter's Application Activity.**

Selected Glossary

Andalucía—Southern region in Spain where flamenco originated.

bata de cola—Long-trained dress reminiscent of styles from the aristocracy that dancers manipulate to embellish the dance.

brazeo—Movements of the arms.

café cantantes—Performance venues of early flamenco.

cajón—Drum box adopted from South America and used for percussion in flamenco.

cante—Flamenco song.

floreo—Hand movement and circles that embellish the dance and illustrate the rhythm.

jaleo—Rhythmic calls and shouts (e.g., "olé!") from the musicians and audience that encourage the dancer and enliven the performance.

marcaje—Patterns of dance steps with accents and passive sounds that mark the beat.

palmas—Rhythmic hand clapping used as percussive accompaniment in flamenco.

palos—Different song forms in flamenco, each with a distinctive emotion, musical beat, lyrical style, and musical melody.

Roma/Gitano/Gypsy—Romani people are an Indo-Aryan group of nomadic people that live in Europe and the Americas. Those dancing flamenco prefer the term *Gitano*. The term *gypsy* is considered derogatory.

traje corto—Costume worn by men that includes well-fitted high-waisted pants with a short vest.

Selected References and Resources

Barton, S. 2004. *A History of Spain*. London: Palgrave MacMillan.

Hayes, M.H. 2009. *Flamenco Conflicting Histories of the Dance*. Jefferson, NC: McFarland & Company.

Holguín, S. 2019. *Flamenco Nation: The Construction of Spanish National Identity*. Madison, WI: University of Wisconsin Press.

Leblon, B. 1994. *Gypsies and Flamenco*. Hertfordshire, UK: University of Hertfordshire Press.

Liégeos. J. 1986. *Gypsies: An Illustrated History*. Trowbridge: Dotesios.

Marcellus Vittucci, M. 2003. *The Language of Spanish Dance*. Hightstown, NJ: Princeton Book Company.

Pohren, D. 1990. *The Art of Flamenco*. Madrid: Society of Spanish Studies.

Thiel-Cramer, B. 1991. *Flamenco*. Lidingo, Sweden: Remark AB.

Totton, R. 2003. *Song of the Outcasts*. Cambridge: Amadeus Press.

Washabaugh, W. 1996. *Flamenco Passion, Politics and Popular Cultural*. Oxford: Berg.

13

Dance in Croatia

A Small Country With Rich Dance Diversity

Tvrtko Zebec, Ivana Katarinčić, and Iva Niemčić

Learning Objectives

After reading this chapter you will be able do the following:

- Describe Croatian traditional folk dance culture.
- Identify the main regional dance differences in Croatia.
- Explain an array of folk music instruments and the interrelationship between musicians and dancers.
- Compare and contrast Croatian dance culture in connection with other dance cultures and influences.
- Describe how Croatians learn dance through formal and informal education.
- Define UNESCO intangible cultural heritage designation.

Key terms

Catholic calendar rituals—Dance events performed by organized groups in processions at Christmas and New Year, and during Carnival, Easter, and similar significant days of the Catholic calendar.

drmeš—The best-known and most popular dance in northwestern Croatian villages.

ethnochoreology—Study of dance through disciplines such as anthropology, musicology, ethnomusicology, and ethnography.

kolo—Circle dance, the most common form of traditional folk dance in Croatia.

round dances—Pairs dance in a circle in a counterclockwise direction.

tamburitza—A long-necked, pear-shaped plucked lute, a typical south Slavic instrument; within orchestras became a symbol of national identity during the 19th century.

The Sung Kolo

In a mix of joy and reverence after the midnight mass on Christmas Eve, churchgoers grasp their neighbors' hands and set the **kolo** in motion—an ancient tradition of circle dancing still woven into the fabric of some areas of 21st century Croatia. Though the area outside the church is too narrow for a true circle, the townspeople are joined in a single loop that weaves around the plaza, hands tightly linked, arms crossed, and a steady rhythm of small steps keeping time as their voices rise in song. At other times and other places, the kolo is more formalized, with folk dancers performing in traditional costumes for an audience. The kolo as a dance and as a social gathering was originally the main way young women and men could get to know each other, express mutual liking, make pledges of unity, and also indulge in mockery and social criticism. Because of its simple form, in which the dancers follow each other around in the circle, the kolo is unusually widespread and can even be called a general human phenomenon. Within a circle, everyone can be seen, and each individual must be aware of the circle as a whole if the group is to move effectively. No wonder, then, that the circle dance is regarded as the oldest form of dance, manifesting a marked need for expression of community (Torp 1990, 27-68).

 See resource 13.1 in HK*Propel* for web links.

Croatia is a small European country situated between central and southeastern Europe on the Adriatic Sea, at the crossroads of multiple political and cultural centers that have shaped its development from ancient times to the present. Three geographic areas partly align with ethnographic distinctions in Croatia: the plain (Pannonian valley), mountains (Dinarides area), and coast (Adriatic region). Croatia is a country with thousands of islands, islets, and reefs, 67 of which are inhabited. Both the physical terrain and the influence of bordering cultures and history have affected the development of dance in Croatia.

Croatia is rather new as an independent country, but with a long and rich history. In the remote past it developed under the influence of many European cultures, such as Greek, Illyrian, Roman, Ottoman, and Slavic. Croatia was a part of the **Austro-Hungarian monarchy** until the end of the First World War in 1918. After the fall of the monarchy, Croatia, together with Slovenia, Serbia, and Bosnia and Herzegovina, declared itself the *State of Slovenes, Croats and Serbs*, then entered into the *Kingdom of Serbs, Croats, and Slovenians*, which was renamed the **Kingdom of Yugoslavia** in 1929. After the Second World War, Croatia under president Josip Broz Tito (1892-1980) became one of Yugoslavia's six federal socialistic republics and, since the 1960s, one of the leading partners of the Third World organization (nations not involved in the Cold War between Western capitalists and Soviet socialists). In the early 1990s, with the war and collapse of Yugoslavia—occurring almost simultaneously with the breakdown of the Eastern Bloc at the end of the 1980s—Croatia became an independent state.

Most (79%) of Croatia's 3.87 million people are Roman Catholics. Almost the same number of Croats have been living in emigration for several generations in Europe, the Americas, Australia, and New Zealand, and in neighboring Bosnia and Herzegovina, where Croats are one of three constituent peoples. Croatian Catholicism developed on one of Europe's most sensitive frontiers with the Eastern Orthodoxy. The Catholic base in Croatia, no less than in Ireland and Poland, helped to define Croats as an ethnic group in modern times. (For more on the historical complexities of Croatian national identity, see Banac 2011.)

Social Context

From Ritual to Social Dances, Stage Performances, and Cultural Tourism

Dance events and music-making are intrinsic parts of **Catholic calendar rituals**, performed by organized groups in processions at Christmas and New Year, during Carnival and Easter, and on St. George's Day, Midsummer Day (aka St. John the Baptist Day), and so on. These groups make door-to-door rounds through villages, and their songs express good wishes to the members of the households at which they stop to sing. The tunes and their sometimes strictly set performing styles were believed to have magical powers.

Kolo Circle Dance

In the northwestern part of the country, leading the kolo circle dances at Easter and during the customs of the spring cycle, around bonfires, and around the tables at weddings to the singing of ballad verses was a familiar feature in the older dance traditions until the end of the 19th century. The kolo had ritual function, usually connected with the cult of fertility. With the introduction of couple dances from central Europe, the circle dances were almost completely neglected and forgotten. However, the sung circle dances, such as the sung kolo described at the beginning of this chapter, remain dominant in lowland Croatia among the dances of the Pannonian Valley.

The circle dance that does remain—the kolo—is one of the basic forms of Croatian traditional folk dance. Throughout a large part of Croatia, right up until World War II, and in some places as late as the 1950s, the kolo was the center of village social life. The peasantry was the largest social group in Croatian society until the middle of the 20th century.

Interrelationship Between Musicians and Dancers

Musicians often play their instruments while standing or sitting in the center of the kolo circle dance. Their position already indicates their importance, especially where the closed circle dance has been changed to a **round dance**—couples dancing in the circle, around one or more musicians. The place in front of the musician is particularly significant for all the participants. Dancers perform primarily for the musician, but also for other dancers and observers—the latter sometimes joining in the dance, as well. All participants want to show themselves and compete with each other before and around the musician.

A clear example of the music-dance relationship can be seen in the traditional wheel dance known as *kolo, poskočica–lindo*, where the dance leader calls out verses while dancing. All the couples swirl in front of the musician (or *lijeričar*) who plays a *lijera*—a three-stringed solo instrument used to accompany dance, and, less frequently, singing. It was imported from the southeast—from Greece—and reflects the long history of Mediterranean influences.

Lindo dance in front of the musician with lijerica.

Courtesy of the Archive of the International Folklore Festival.

Kolo dance.
Courtesy of the Institute of Ethnology and Folklore Research in Croatia.

Diversity of Dance Practices in Croatia

There are many dance forms and diverse dance practices in Croatia. Traditional, or folk, dances are shaped by the uneven cultural heritage of the regions, with significant variation resulting from historical development and context, as well as contemporary practices. Their diversity shows how they cannot be reduced to just one traditional dance form. As with many elements of traditional culture in Croatia, folk dance repertoire is heterogeneous, reflecting varied cultural heritages

Diverse Influences on Croatian Folk Culture

"When we speak of traditional (folk) music, we are usually referring to the music of the peasant communities. . . . [Researchers focused on peasant culture] during the time of the intensive development of ethnology, and similar disciplines such as ethnomusicology, during the 20th century" (Marošević 2000, 409). The various cultures that met in the Croatian regions brought with them dance, music, and other elements of their heritage: Mediterranean (Italian, Greek, and Arab), Slavic (brought by the Slavs migrating from more eastern parts of Eurasia), Middle Eastern (the heritage of centuries of Ottoman imperial influence), and central European influences.

throughout the country. The musical instruments and their geographic lineage are particularly important in traditional Croatian dance. The dance centers on the music, and "the main characteristics of traditional musical instruments in Croatia are their number and diversity over what is a relatively small territory" (Ćaleta 2000, 421). Thus the richness and color of the dance styles, and the songs, music, and musical instruments that accompany them continue to reflect Croatia's multifaceted heritage.

 See resource 13.2 in HK*Propel* for web links.

Central and Southeastern European Influences

Round Dances (Couple Dances)

Central European influences are most obvious in the couple dances (**mazurka**, **waltz**, **polka**, **schottische**, *siebenschritt*, *rašpa*, *štajeriš*, *furlana*, *palaisglais*) in northwestern, northern, and central Croatia, and in Istria and the Gulf of Quarnero region. The round dances were mostly neglected by ethnographic research on dance during the 20th century. These kinds of couple dances were not readily accepted at the festivals organized by the **Peasant Harmony Association** (*Seljačka sloga*) during the late 1930s, since they showed the influence of urban and non-Croatian centers.

Peasant Harmony—the cultural, educational, and charitable association driven by the populist ideology of the Peasant Party—has since the 1920s attempted to inspire self-confidence in the peasants, to gradually enlighten them, and to introduce them to national political life. As a result, folklore festivals today continue to mirror cultural policy and are places for public presentations of recognized national practice.

Social Dances

Round dances are danced in pairs, mostly man and woman. The pair can be a part of circle, square, or **contra dances**; these are all social dances. The appearance of social dance in Europe was linked with the growth of the larger European cities and conditioned by the development of trade and crafts. Despite the fact that they were not readily acceptable to the older generation, round dances became part of the Croatian dance repertoire in the second half of the 19th century and the first decades of the 20th, and sometimes arose in opposition to the influence of outside dances such as the waltz. For example, the ***salonsko kolo***—a domestic urban couple dance—was very popular in the 19th century. At the time, Croatia was part of the Hapsburg empire, and the dance sprang up as a patriotic reply to the foreign "waltz" by proclaiming and promoting national colors, national fashion, and patriotic verses. The Croatian or Slavonic kolo dance was born in this environment (Katarinčić and Niemčić 2020). *Narodno kolo*, which later became known as *salonsko kolo*, emphasized the national identity of the Croatians in opposition to the other popular European social dances of the 19th century like the waltz and polka (Dunin 1988, 110).

Round dancing was almost always a form of entertainment, although sometimes these dances, too, could have ritual characteristics; for example, the waltz was often, and still is, the first dance of the newly married couple at weddings. The bride is also expected to dance a lot and with verve to show her capability and stamina (the idea being that she is seen as hale and capable). Dancing with the guests also brings her material gain, since everyone who dances with the bride has to pay for the privilege.

The polka and the waltz—highly popular throughout Europe—were danced often, because everyone knew them. Indeed, the highly controversial waltz changed the history of dancing in many ways (Knowles 2009). Round dances before the waltz were less continuous, and face-to-face contact changed with the appearance of the waltz.

Energetic Dances

In performance of dances with obvious central European influences, there is a noticeable tendency for the dancers to rotate quickly. The couples spin intensively, for example, in the ***drmeš***—a couple dance often done in smaller or larger circles. This is the best-known and most popular dance in northwestern Croatian villages. People of all ages dance drmeš in social settings (Carnival, wedding, or other social dance events), as well as on stage. It features small steps with relatively little traveling through the dance area, but with marked vertical shaking of the entire body (*drmati* in Croatian means "to shake"). In the second section of the dance, the dancers rotate at unusual speed. This is definitely one of the most dynamic Croatian dances.

The ***dučec***, ***kozatuš***, and the ***staro sito***, also from northwestern Croatia, are dances that utilize energetic jumps and are performed during Carnival. In some places they have survived until the present day and are danced when a "magical" consequence is sought. It used to be believed that by forcefully striking the foot on the floor and leaping high in the air, the performer could increase the yield of the turnip, flax, hemp, and other harvests. From the 1930s onward, these dances were passed on as stage performances. Gradually losing their ritual significance, the dances became symbols of cultural identity in their life on the stage or as part of festival performances.

Ethnochoreology— Understanding Humanity Through Dance

In Croatia, **ethnochoreology** has been part of educational processes since 1998 and has become even more intensive recently (Zebec 2009). Croatia now has a dance academy (since 2015), but there is still no dance or ethnochoreology among formal academic disciplines. Ethnochoreology, with ethnomusicology, is studied within the Institute of Ethnology and Folklore Research in Zagreb, which has been the main center for studies of these disciplines since 1948.

 See resource 13.3 in HK*Propel* for web links.

Regional Styles of Dance and Music

Ethnochoreologists note how the profusion and variety of styles existing in traditional music and dance in Croatia result from the overlapping of different cultures—central European (Pannonian and subalpine), Balkan, and Mediterranean. It is therefore possible to see the totality of Croatian traditional music and dance through summarizing the specific musical characteristics of its broader regions.

Plains and Pannonian Region (Central European)

In Slavonia, in the northeastern Pannonian region, the kolo was danced to song but also to the music of a ***gajde*** (bagpipe)—a wind instrument known among many European and non-European peoples. In Bilogora, a hilly region in central Croatia, dance was accompanied by a similar instrument called the ***dude***.

Since the beginning of the 20th century, ***tamburitza*** bands have provided most of the kolo dance music and are seen as highly popular icons of Croatian culture. Amateur tamburitza orchestras were formed in the mid-19th century by Croatian intellectuals who recognized the tamburitza as a typical south Slavic instrument. The tamburitza (also called ***tamburica***) "is a long-necked, pear-shaped plucked lute. It is regarded as part of the heritage among Croats and other neighboring ethnic groups and was probably introduced by the Turks during their 14th- and 15th-century Ottoman invasions of the territory of the Balkans. The term for this instrument is a diminutive of ***tambura***—an ancient Persian instrument" (Ćaleta 2000, 427). Its use became a symbol in the struggle for Croatian independence and identity under the rule of the Austro-Hungarian Empire, and it created a refined, national music suited to elite aesthetics but based on the folk, rural music (Bezić 2001).

The enclosed circle dance that is performed around the tamburitza players who stand playing and singing in the middle of the circle is characteristic of the entire Pannonian region, particularly Slavonia. There are varying step structures in kolo dancing that often take their name from the accompanying song. Still, the circle dance performed is usually simply called the kolo. It is the best-known and most popular dance among all ages and is performed in a specific pattern in each particular village, but with minimal difference in step structure. With its liveliness, song, and shouting dancers, it became the trademark of Slavonia—a symbol of regional identity. The kolo commences with energetic dancing and slight shaking of the body, with rhythm and style of performance similar to the *drmeš* dance performed further to the west. The music and dance are interrupted by the dancers, who sing verse couplets that they improvise on the spot. At such intervals, the dance calms and transforms into a light walk, and then takes up the fast tempo again after the verse—until the following interjection in song. During the faster part of the dance, *poskočica*, witty verses with double meanings are shouted out by the individual dancers, mirroring social relations in a community where everyone knows each other's business and social status.

Mountains and Dinarides Region (Balkan)

The old **silent circle dance** (***nijemo kolo***), without musical accompaniment, is typical of the dance repertoire in the mountainous region. The nijemo kolo has a **six-part dance pattern**. In step structure, this dance is almost identical to the kolo from the Faroe Islands (of Denmark) performed to the singing of ballads throughout the Balkans (Torp 1990) and to the Arab dance called the *dabke*. In this mountainous region with its largely stock-raising culture of sheep and goats, the kolo is performed in large steps and leaps. People are generally tall and strong because terrain is rough and full of stone. The main accompaniment is the clanging of the women's jewelry and the deep breathing of the dancers. The circle dance can be open or enclosed, and couples can separate from the kolo group. The circle form has been almost completely lost in some areas, so that dancing by couples has retained only the kolo name. The dance is not compact the way it is in the northern lowland, because the young men and women hold each other by their belts in keeping with the old tradition, and their movements use all of the floor space available. In performing the various figures in the dance according to the directions of the dance caller, dancers mutually test each other's physical capabilities.

Coast/Adriatic Region (Mediterranean)

The island ***hrvatski tanac*** (a dance accompanied by another bagpipe-like instrument called the ***mijeh,*** or by two ***sopela*** instruments) is similar to the ***balun*** dance in Istria, the peninsula in the northern part of coastal Croatia. The historical

links of Istria and the Gulf of Quarnero region exposed them to direct influences from the medieval Frankish state, and later to influences from Bavaria, Carinthia, and Carniola.

The dance repertoire and style of performance in this coastal region show somewhat stronger central European rather than Adriatic influences, and these are most marked in the very popular and widely accepted polkas and mazurkas. The specific aspect of their performances in Istria, which is around the Gulf of Quarnero and in the northern Littoral area, is the musical accompaniment provided by the *sopela*, or ***roženica***, aerophonic musical instruments with a double reed of the oboe type, which makes a piercing sound.

Reed Instruments of the Adriatic Region

"The *sopele* are built in two sizes—the *vela* (or large) *sopela* and the *mala* (or small) *sopela*—and they are usually played together or in two-part renditions. This musical instrument produces a penetrating sound which is largely dependent on the quality of the reed" (Ćaleta 2000, 434).

On the islands and in the cities, these elements are mixed with dances under obvious central European influence, with names indicating their origins. The *šotić* (the *Schottische* or *Scotish*), *kvatropaše* (from Italian *quattro passi*), *Siebenschritt* (German for "seven step"), *furlana*, *valcer* (waltz), *manfrina*, *kvadrilja* (quadrille), and *polka šaltina* are accompanied by mandolin ensembles, which are very popular in the Dalmatian cities, similar to the tambura bands in the lowland.

 See resource 13.4 in HK*Propel* for web links.

Legacies of Cross-Cultural Trade and Travel

New fashions spread quickly in the Adriatic area, emanating out from Venice, Italy, and the ancient coastal city of Dubrovnik. As a trading center and travel junction, Dubrovnik was an intermediary throughout history in disseminating various influences through ceremonies at the Dubrovnik court (of Spanish and Neapolitan origins). These influences then spread largely through the crafting guilds. For example, in the 15th century, there were written records of dances with arches, staves, and kerchiefs being performed by shoemakers and other craftspeople. These were derivatives of the chain sword dances fashionable throughout Europe during the 16th and 17th centuries, and they were performed in several of the Dalmatian towns. They have survived up to the present day on the Pelješac peninsula and on the islands of Lastovo and Korčula.

The chain sword dances in the villages of the island of Korčula are performed by the **kumpanije**, male societies from which the dances take their name, *kumpanije*. These dances are organized at Carnival time. The dancers are accompanied by a *mijeh* (bagpipe) and drum as they perform various figures. After the chain sword dance is completed, the dancers are joined by the young women, and together they perform the *tanac* dance.

The **Moreška** is a famous sword dance performed in the town of Korčula. Two groups perform a dance drama, in which two sides, variously identified as Whites and Blacks, Christians and Moors, or Turks and Moors, clash swords over the fate of a veiled young woman. This mock combat dance with two swords is believed to have spread from Spain throughout almost all of Europe.

"Hidden Transcript" of Moreška

"The dramatic narrative of the *moreška* clearly locates the dance in the widespread tradition of mock battles among Muslims and Christians (Harris and Čale Feldman 2003-04, 297). . . . We suggest, therefore, that the Korčula *moreška* was not imported to the island intact but was developed as an original creation by the citizens of Korčula (309). . . . Land is almost everywhere imagined in female terms. . . . We believe that the abducted young woman of the hidden transcript represented the island of Korčula itself, repeatedly captured by external forces (312)."

International Folklore Festival: From Village to Stage

The modern age brings numerous changes that have significantly influenced rural life. Many peasants have become laborers, and many rural communities have become suburban or even urban ones. In today's local communities, musical and dance traditions are preserved and fostered in performing groups that bring together members of all generations. What distinguishes them from urban amateur ensembles is that their repertoire includes only music and dance forms of their own local community, while urban ensembles perform folk dance choreographies from all parts of Croatia. Urban ensembles predominantly consist of young dancers, mostly high school and university students, while village performing groups have a more varied membership in terms of age. They include more elderly members, in whose youth those traditions were still part of everyday life. They are typically formed as non-governmental organizations or as cultural clubs within their own communities following traditions developed in the years between the two world wars.

Dance and Politics

In Croatia, the representation of traditional culture and folklore on stage began as early as the 1930s. The intention was to promote national, rural, ancient, local, and traditional heritage of the Croatian village that was gradually being supplanted by urban culture. After only about 20 years (in the 1950s), under the pressures of the new socialist ideology, the representation of folklore on stage was suppressed due to a bias in favor of the proletariat and the working classes. In the socialist regime, "[d]ance was an essential element in the project of creating a new citizen and a new, united, unified socialist and Yugoslavian culture. The building of a national culture, which operated as the dominant social framework in the late nineteenth and the early twentieth centuries, shifted to a socialist concept of unified, non-national or supranational ideology in the second part of the twentieth century. The aesthetics have shifted according to social and political changes, but also as a result of expert influences that have directly affected cultural politics" (Zebec 2018).

Following further social and political changes, and owing to great efforts from the experts in the field, the first international folklore festival was held in 1966 and welcomed with enthusiasm by large audiences and numerous performers. It signaled a "reaffirmation of the values of rural peasant culture, from which most of the population of Croatia and Yugoslavia at the time originated," as well as appealing to those who moved to Zagreb, the nation's capital, and other cities looking for work (Vitez 2016, 11). The festival has been held in Zagreb every July since then, with the exception of 1991 due to threat of war.

The festival is conceived as an event mostly representing rural performing groups, ensembles of national minorities living in Croatia, and foreign ensembles as guests. When selecting the performers, the aim is to ensure equal representation of all Croatian regions, and priority is given to older forms of dance, music, and heritage repertoire of the local native area. Direction of the festival has always been delegated to experts, mostly ethnologists who specialize in the study of dance and are working at the **Institute of Ethnology and Folklore Research** in Zagreb, or in the professional ensemble **LADO** (National Folk Dance Ensemble of Croatia).

The preconceived path to the festival stage is clear: There is a local community with a living tradition practiced in their everyday life or weekly at their cultural clubs. Then a smaller group forms and chooses the most representative parts of their musical, dance, and customary heritage and arranges them for a stage performance lasting up to 10 minutes that is presented at the festival.

 See resource 13.5 in HK*Propel* for web links.

Institutionalized Dance Education

The status of different dance forms in Croatia varies and so, too, does their funding. Many dance communities are organized as courses or associations and are not included in official programs funded by the state. Most of them operate on their own, primarily funded by membership fees. For example, there are communities of acrobatic rock and roll, hip-hop, step dance, and others, as well as the community of competitive sport dances (e.g., ballroom dancing). Most of these are imported dance forms. It is interesting that the imported competitive dances, such as

ballroom, are not recognized by the broader public as different from urban social dances and are constantly mixed, interlaced, and related to the social dances, using the aesthetics of one in order to advertise the other (Katarinčić 2012).

Dance Education

The schooling of dancers for classical ballet, contemporary and modern dance, and folk dances is provided in official specialized art schools financed by the state. Because modern and contemporary dance programs have few requirements for enrollment, there are several schools for these genres. However, classical ballet and folk dance are taught at only one arts high school in Croatia.

Informal Education

Apart from being taught through formal education in school, folk dances are taught at many local folk dance associations called *kulturno-umjetnička društva* (**KUD**)—cultural art associations. These are usually members of the county network of associations and clubs, and their umbrella organization at the national level is the **Croatian Cultural Association** (*Hrvatski sabor kulture*). It organizes county and national dance meetings and festivals, as well as folklore seminars and courses for dance leaders and members of dance clubs.

In the **Zagreb School for Classical Ballet**, there are two departments, one for classical ballet and another for folk dance. Students receive a high school degree as a classical ballet dancer or a dancer (or singer) of folk dances. The school in Zagreb was established in 1949. Passing the audition is the only way to get admitted into the school program. Students receive standardized ballet education and ballet technique. The final exam at the school is usually also an audition for the ballet ensemble in the **Croatian National Theater** in Zagreb. Before Croatia gained its independence in the 1990s, ballet students living in what was then Yugoslavia would have continued their education in Russia. In the 1990s, after the fall of the Soviet Union, that practice ended, so after formal high school education, classical ballet dancers audition for several national theaters in Croatia or abroad. Apart from Zagreb, there are national theaters

Cultural Highlight

GANGA SONGS FROM THE EIFFEL TOWER

In 2012, a year before Croatia was accepted into the European Union, during a cultural exchange project with France known as *Croatie la Voici*, several small groups of singers were invited to perform in Paris, in the **Maison des Cultures du Monde**. A woman who was singing with the group was surprised when they were invited to Paris. She commented, "I am a simple woman from the village, a shepherd and worker in the field. I have never ever been in the theatre, and now, when UNESCO recognised *ojkanje*, I flew for the first time in my life! To Paris, and I performed in the theatre. That was quite an experience." During their time in Paris, some of the singers climbed up to the Eiffel Tower and sang their *ganga* songs. "To come to Paris and not to sing *ganga* from the top of the Eiffel, that would be like you have never been in Paris. We blessed Paris with *ganga*!" (*Ganga* is a type of *ojkanje* singing and sung by people in the mountains of Dalmatia.)

with drama, opera, and ballet ensembles in the cities of Split and Rijeka.

For the first time in Croatia, a higher education for dance artists and specialists was made possible recently by the founding in 2013 of the three-year undergraduate programs in dance: bachelor of arts in contemporary dance (performance and teaching strands) and bachelor of arts in ballet pedagogy at the dance department of the **Academy of Dramatic Art at the University of Zagreb**. These programs provided a path to higher education for classical ballet dancers and contemporary dancers, but not for folk dancers. One of the reasons for this difference lies in the traditionally informal and noninstitutionalized way of passing folk dances down from one generation to the next.

Classical ballet dancers usually begin their higher education at the University of Zagreb after or near the end of their performing career, to prepare them for a future career in choreography or teaching.

Unlike dancers of classical ballet and folk dancers, who can audition for LADO, dancers of contemporary forms do not have as many opportunities for employment, even with a college degree. Most of them become freelance artists, with irregular and uncertain sources of income.

Department for Folk Dance and LADO

The aforementioned high-school-level Department for Folk Dance at the School for Classical Ballet was founded in 1983. The department has worked ever since on the education and preparation of young dancers for performances in LADO. At the school, a minimum of four students must enroll for a grade to be created, with a maximum of about 10 students. The department's curriculum is based on the LADO ensemble's curriculum and is organized according to traditional folk dance expression. Such school and education policy for a dancer or singer satisfies the needs for educated artistic leaders in professional and amateur folk ensembles and schools. Since there has not been any academic higher education for a dancer or singer of folk dances, a high school degree is the only such degree in that kind of dance.

Despite this fact, there are still more active dancers in LADO who pass auditions, and who come from amateur companies, than from the dance school. Young dancers with a very good dance education and a degree as a dancer and singer of folk dances often have no advantage over those candidates who have gained their dance education only in amateur ensembles. There has not been any long-term need analysis for the employment of dancers and singers in LADO, and therefore there are no criteria for determining the real need for young dancers' education and their targeted selection for enrollment in the school.

From its beginning in 1949 until today, LADO has developed a recognizable performance style characterized by the high level of professionalism established by its founder, **Zvonimir Ljevaković** (1908-1981). Ljevaković was a long-standing leader and choreographer of many works that are still widely performed. However, apart from his exceptional talent and authority in folklore, Ljevaković did not have any formal education in that kind of dance and performing art. The LADO professional ensemble stemmed from gathering the best amateur dancers and singers in Zagreb, who became professionals by the very fact that LADO was founded.

 See resource 13.6 in HK*Propel* for web links.

Crosscurrents

Croatia is one of the most-recognized countries for intangible cultural heritage designations at UNESCO, with 17 inscribed elements. One of them is *nijemo kolo*—the silent circle dance of the Dalmatian hinterland. Another element, *ojkanje* singing, is part of the living heritage from the same region and broader vicinity, and is desig-

nated by UNESCO as part of intangible cultural heritage that is in urgent need of safeguarding.

 See resource 13.7 in HK*Propel* for web links.

Summary

Croatia is a rather newly independent country but with a long and rich history. In the remote past it developed under the influence of many European cultures. Croatia's unique heritage and geography yield many dance forms and diverse dance practices across the different regions of the country. Continuing these historical patterns, today's political, religious, and societal forces are interwoven with Croatian dance. Just as the kolo pulls ancient traditions and contemporary lives into its circle, the dance of Croatia carries us toward the future.

Discussion Questions

1. How can you interpret folk dances and the context of their performance according to politics?
2. Which folk dance is connected with calendar rituals and bonfires in Croatia and why?
3. Why can we say that the kolo was the center of village social life?
4. Why is the relationship between music player and dancer important?
5. Which cultures met in the Croatian tradition and which ones influenced its tradition with dances and instruments?
6. Why do we consider folk dance and music in Croatia as mostly peasant?
7. When was the National Folk Dance Ensemble (LADO) founded, and why?

 Visit HK*Propel* for access to this chapter's Application Activity.

Selected Glossary

Catholic calendar rituals—Dance events performed by organized groups in processions at Christmas and New Year, and during Carnival, Easter, and similar significant days of the Catholic calendar.

drmeš—The best-known and most popular dance in northwestern Croatian villages.

ethnochoreology—The study of dance through the application of a number of disciplines such as anthropology, musicology, ethnomusicology, and ethnography; a discipline within the Institute of Ethnology and Folklore Research

in Zagreb following southeast European dance research traditions.

gajde—A bagpipe-like wind instrument.

kolo—Circle dance, the most common form of traditional folk dance in Croatia.

Kingdom of Yugoslavia (1929-1941)—Centralistic monarchy headed by the Karađorđević dynasty.

LADO—The professional National Folk Dance Ensemble of Croatia.

lijera—A three-stringed solo instrument used to accompany dance, and, less frequently, singing.

mazurka, waltz, polka, schottische, siebenschritt, rašpa, štajeriš, furlana, palaisglais— These are all couple dances of central European provenance.

mijeh—Bagpipe-like instrument.

round dances—Pairs dance in a circle in a counterclockwise direction.

tamburitza—A long-necked, pear-shaped plucked lute, a typical south Slavic instrument; within orchestras became a symbol of national identity during the 19th century

Selected References and Resources

Banac, Ivo. 2011. "Independent Croatia: History, Issues, and Policy." *Délkelet-Európa—South-East Europe. International Relations Quarterly* 2 (1): 1-7. www.southeast-europe.org.

Bezić, Nada. 2001. Tamburica—hrvatski izvozni proizvod na prijelazu 19. u 20. stoljeće ("Tamburitza—Croatian export product on the turn of the 19th into the 20th century"). *Narodna umjetnost—Croatian Journal of Ethnology and Folklore Research* 38 (2): 97-15.

Ćaleta, Joško. 2000. "Traditional Musical Instruments." In *Croatian Folk Culture at the Crossroads of Worlds and Eras*, edited by Zorica Vitez and Aleksandra Muraj. Zagreb: Gallery Klovićevi dvori, Exhibition Catalogue, 420-437.

Dunin, Elsie Ivancich. 1988. "'Salonsko kolo' as *Cultural Identity* in a Chilean Yugoslav Community (1917-1986)." *Narodna umjetnost Special Issue* 2:109-122.

Harris, Max, and Lada Čale Feldman. 2003-04. "Blackened Faces and a Veiled Woman: The Early Korčula Moreška." *Comparative Drama* 37 (3-4): 297-320.

Katarinčić, Ivana. 2012. "Paradoksi sportskoga plesa." *Etnološka tribina* 42 (35): 207-223. https://hrcak.srce.hr/94124.

Katarinčić, Ivana, and Iva Niemčić. 2020. "Dancing and Politics in Croatia: The *Salonsko kolo* as a Patriotic Response to the Waltz." *Waltzing Through Europe: Attitudes Towards Couple Dances in the Long Nineteenth Century*, edited by E. Bakka, T.J. Buckland, H. Saarikoski, and A. von Bibra Wharton, 257-282. Cambridge, UK: Open Book Publishers. https://doi.org/10.11647/OBP.0174.

Knowles, Mark. 2009. *The Wicked Waltz and Other Scandalous Dances. Outrage at Couple Dancing in the 19th and Early 20th Centuries*. Jefferson, NC, and London: McFarland & Company.

Marošević, Grozdana. 2000. "Traditional Music." In *Croatian Folk Culture at the Crossroads of Worlds and Eras*, edited by Zorica Vitez and Aleksandra Muraj.

Zagreb: Gallery Klovićevi dvori, Exhibition Catalogue, 408-419.

Torp, Lisbet. 1990. *Chain and Round Dance Patterns—A Method for Structural Analysis and Its Application to European Material*. Copenhagen: University of Copenhagen; Museum Tusculanum Press.

Vitez, Zorica. 2016. "Half a Century of the Zagreb International Folklore Festival." *Smotre folklora i simboli identiteta. U povodu 50. Međunarodne smotre folklora [Folklore Festivals and Symbols of Identity. On the Occasion of the 50th International Folklore Festival]*, edited by Z. Vitez, K. Bušić, and J. Forjan, 11-24. Zagreb: Etnografski muzej.

Zebec, Tvrtko. 2009. "Development and Application of Ethnochoreology in Croatia." Edited by S. Kazić and J. Talam, 136-150. 6th International Symposium "Music in Society," October 29-31, 2008. Sarajevo: Muzikološko društvo FBiH.

Zebec, Tvrtko. 2015. "Intangible Culture as Heritage: The Linđo – Kolo Dance, from the Dubrovnik Littoral." *Translingual Discourse in Ethnomusicology* 1:44-56. https://doi.org/10.17440/tde004.

Zebec, Tvrtko. 2018. "Folklore, Stage and Politics in the Croatian Context." In *Folklore Revival Movements in Europe Post 1950. Shifting Contexts and Perspectives. Prague, Institute of Ethnology of the Czeck Academy of Sciences*, edited by Daniela Stavělová and Theresa Jill Buckland, 183-196. Prague: Institute of Ethnology of the Czech Academy of Sciences.

Zebec, Tvrtko. 2020. "A Twenty-First Century Resurrection: The Potresujka, the Croatian Polka Tremblante." In *Waltzing Through Europe: Attitudes Towards Couple Dances in the Long Nineteenth Century*, edited by E. Bakka, T.J. Buckland, H. Saarikoski, and A. von Bibra Wharton, 417-432. Cambridge, UK: Open Book Publishers. https://doi.org/10.11647/OBP.0174.

14

Dance in Greek Culture

Christos Papakostas and Nick Poulakis

Learning Objectives

After reading this chapter you will be able to do the following:

- Understand the evolution of Greek dance through the centuries.
- Appreciate the structural, stylistic, and aesthetic variety of Greek music and dance genres.
- Identify the specific cultural and performative context of Greek dances.
- Understand the fundamentals of ancient, traditional, popular, and contemporary dance heritage of Greece.

Key Terms

bouzouki—A type of long-necked plucked lute of popular Greek music.

Hellenic—Of or pertaining to Greece and Greek people.

logos-melos-kinesis—In Greek, the indivisible triptych of text, music, and dance.

syrtos—Major genre of Greek folk dance, characterized by "dragging."

Iconic Greek Dances

In 1964, the film *Zorba the Greek* brought notice to a neo-folk dance, **syrtaki**, or "**Zorba's Dance**," choreographed from steps of the earlier Greek folk dances **hasapiko** and **hasaposerviko**. On a windswept Cretan beach in the last scene of the film, Zorba dances to teach his European-educated boss how to be truly Greek. He moves spontaneously to the music of the lute-like **bouzouki**. His measured steps and leg lifts glide slowly across the sand, then gradually gain speed and power as the two men dance in the fading light. Thus, Zorba reveals and shares his inner world. He is authentically Greek, "in tune with himself. The metaphor is one that would have appealed to Plato, for it is through the means of music and dance . . . that Zorba, in contrast to the 'boss' . . . achieves a secure sense of his place in the universe" (Holst-Warhaft 1997, 233).

In 1804, the village of Souli on the mountains of Epirus was in imminent danger of falling into the hands of the Turks. The women, in order to avoid slavery and shame, formed a circle hand in hand with their children and began dancing around the precipice, singing a sad farewell song. When the leader of the circle reached the brink of the precipice, she separated herself from the rest and fell to her death; then followed, after each verse, the second, the third until all had perished. A few words of their song illuminate the character of this dance: "Farewell! poor world of sorrow, farewell! sweet life. Farewell! little fountains, hills and mountains, and to you my unfortunate Country farewell forever. . . . Souliot women know not only how to live; they also know how to die rather than submit to slavery" (Michaelides 1956, 39).

This "Dance of Zalongo" continues to be reenacted on Greek national holidays in schools or cultural associations "and endures inasmuch as it is so inextricably tied to the notion of a glorious, coherent, and continuous past" (Loutzaki 2011, 220). "Zorba's Dance" had a great impact abroad, and "together with the bouzouki, became common national musical symbols of Greece from the mid-1960s onward" (Loutzaki and Poulakis 2019, 1035). These two dances remain relevant in Greece of the 21st century, revealing both the internal and external perceptions of Greek dance, as well as its rich functionality on an individual and cultural level.

 See resource 14.1 in HK*Propel* for web links.

Though distant from one another in time and purpose, "Zorba's Dance" and the "Dance of Zalongo" illustrate how Greek dance is tightly woven into the individual, community, and national psyche. Always accompanied by music and song, Greek dances have generally been performed as parts of a folk tradition of popular entertainment and festivity, rather than cultural forms of a pure and sophisticated art. Despite any historical or local peculiarities, they are characterized by their social, egalitarian, inclusive, and "democratic" nature. In Greece, playing music, dancing, and singing together constitute a threefold concept symbolizing Greekness—or other regional cultural identity—as well as an experiential, expressive, and communicative process through an interconnection of instrumental, vocal, and body-movement performance. Passing from one generation to the next, traditional dances have been characterized as representative customs and rituals of Greek folklore. That being the case, in Greece nowadays, folk dances are still a substantive dynamic tradition interrelated with the daily lives of local communities and individuals.

Brief History and Geography

Located on the Balkan Peninsula of southern Europe, Greece has the largest coastline on the whole continent, due to its numerous islands. Inland Greece is a mountainous region with a continental climate, while its seaside regions are influenced by the Mediterranean Sea. The current population of Greece is about 10 million, its official language is Greek, and its constitutionally recognized religion is Eastern (Greek) Orthodox Christianity. The country covers nine geographic areas: Macedonia, Central Greece, Peloponnesus, Thessaly, Epirus, Thrace, and more than 200 inhabited islands in the remaining zones of the Aegean Islands, Ionian Islands, and Crete. Athens is one of the world's oldest cities and is the capital and largest cosmopolitan metropolis of the country. The **Greek diaspora (*homogenea*)** is also one of the oldest and largest in the world, with an extensive and powerful presence in the United States, Germany, Australia, Canada, and the United Kingdom.

Over the centuries, Greek culture has been formulated and expressed as a continuous blend of variable extrinsic cultural flows and its own deep-rooted traditions. Greek language has played an important role in cementing the influence of ancient Greek culture, because it is the language in which primary scientific and philosophical texts were originally inscribed and its basics have remained quite unchanged over the centuries. Nestled between three continents (Europe, Asia, and Africa), Greece has always been considered a melting pot of peoples, cultures, economies, and customs at the crossroads of East and West. In addition to being the birthplace of democracy, Greece is widely referred to as "the cradle of Western civilization" since the rediscovery of ancient Greek ideas on art, architecture, literature, philosophy, science, and language during the Western Renaissance period. This period followed the ignorance and restrictions of the medieval era and led to the idolization of ancient Greek culture as an essential part of the Enlightenment and intellectualism. The ancient writers **Socrates** (470-399

BCE), **Plato** (427-347 BCE), and **Aristotle** (384-322 BCE), along with the gods **Zeus**, **Dionysus**, and **Apollo** are just a few of the most renowned figures in Greek mythology and philosophy that set the stage for modern-day Western aesthetics. Table 14.1 presents a chronology of Greek history.

 See resource 14.2 in HK*Propel* for web links.

Ancient Greek Dance (800-146 BCE)

Dance in ancient Greece was a component of the tripartite concept *logos-melos-kinesis*, meaning "text-music-dance." Ancient Greek dance had these three basic characteristics: (1) the combination of verbal and nonverbal attributes, (2) the recurrent mimetic dimension (that is, the repeating of specific basic patterns), and (3) the balance between its playful nature and its serious form of ritual communication. Two key words that designate the umbrella of dance practices in ancient

Table 14.1   Chronology of the History of Greece

Prehistoric [Cycladic, Minoan, and Mycenaean] Greece (3000-800 BCE)
Painted and sculpted figures of ancient Greek women dancing suggest a fundamental relationship between dance and religion.

Ancient Greece (800-146 BCE)

Dance is a virtue, and anyone who could not dance is considered uneducated and unrefined, while an accomplished dancer is cultured and appreciated.

Archaic Greece (800-500 BCE)

Classical Greece (500-323 BCE)

Hellenistic Greece (323-146 BCE)

Medieval Greece (146 BCE-1453 CE)
Greek dance aesthetics deteriorate, and the trimodal entity of "text, music, and dance" breaks down into three distinct units.

Roman Greece (146 BCE-324 CE)

Byzantine Greece (324-1453 CE)

Early Modern Greece (1453-1821 CE)
Dancing is suppressed by the Orthodox Church, although people in the villages continue to dance as a daytime entertainment and a means to maintain their identity and tradition.

Venetian Greece (1204-1797 CE)

Ottoman Greece (1453-1821 CE)

Modern Greece (1821 CE-today)
Various forms of dances (local, traditional, formal, popular, art, etc.) exist and are performed, making Greece one of the richest dance regions in the world.

Greek culture were *orchesis* (improvised individual kinetic performance) and *choros* (group music, singing, and dance in various formations). Ancient philosophers Plato and Aristotle believed that dancing was inherently necessary to illustrate words by body gestures, revealing actions, characters, and passions by means of postures and rhythmic movements.

According to Greek mythology, performing arts were of divine origin, and the gods themselves taught music and dance to people. **Hesiod**, one of the greatest poets of ancient Greece, in the opening lines of his epic oeuvre *Theogony* (700 BCE) vividly describes the creation of the world and deities while the **Muses**—the goddesses of literature, science, and the arts—danced on Mount **Helicon** (a mountain in southern Greece).

> *From the Heliconian Muses let us begin to sing,*
>
> *Who hold the great and holy mount of Helicon,*
>
> *And dance on soft feet about the deep-blue spring*
>
> *And the altar of the almighty son of Cronos, and,*
>
> *When they have washed their tender bodies in Permessus*
>
> *Or in the Horse's Spring or Olmeius,*
>
> *Make their fair, lovely dances upon highest Helicon*
>
> *And move with vigorous feet.*

> *[English translation by Hugh G. Evelyn-White]*

Although our knowledge of ancient Greek dance is limited to some visual references in vase paintings, statues, and other artifacts, as well as to literary sources that cannot capture the vibrancy of the real performance, it would be no exaggeration to say that dance was the symbol of conscious presence of life through bodily motion. "When we consider that the ancient world was an essentially oral culture, where performance, including nonverbal components, was as important as any contents, we might begin to understand exactly how indispensable dance was within the whole of the cultural repertory" (Naerebout 2004, 140). Dance was a participatory process—and not a grandiose spectacle—closely tied to all facets of life in ancient Greece (education, religion, celebration, work, theater, athletics, peace, war, love,

and death). It is quite evident that "the ancient Greek concept of the dance differs considerably from our own" (Lawler 1947, 345). Ancient Greeks believed that the stars and the planets perform a cosmic dance, manifesting a perpetual harmonic motion to create, maintain, and evolve the whole world. They did not perceive dance as a separate entity, but one closely associated with other kinds of human experience and a powerful tool for self-knowledge and development. At that time, everyone learned to dance from a young age, since this was considered to be a means for physical conformation, mental integration, and internal balance.

Ancient Greek dances could be categorized according to five different attributes: their place of origin (e.g., Laconic, Troezen, Cretan, Ionic, Mantinean), their choreography (processional, mimetic, kinetic, and acrobatic), their style and expression (following either the Apollonian **ethos**—based on the character/reputation of the performer, or the Dionysian **pathos**—based on emotional appeal), their place of performance (public or private), and their character and purpose (martial, religious, and secular).

In the latter category, martial dances prepared men for struggle. The most important war dance was the *pyrrhic*, accompanied by a flute or lyre, which, according to Plato, was an imitation of a battle representing its phases. Pyrrhic was danced in full armor. In the beginning, there was a kind of parade with side turns, backsteps, high jumps, and bending. This was followed by a series of paces symbolizing the postures of attack and defense, and generally all the movements of the warrior, such as the moment when he throws his spear or raises his sword. These actions were rhythmically adapted to the sound caused by the clashing of the arms. The dance was mainly performed by the Spartans—an ancient Greek warlike people—who considered it light military training. Furthermore, the ancient writers **Homer** and **Xenophon**—who also documented this dance—refer to the pyrrhic as a festive or competition dance. At present, the pyrrhic dance is being revived through *serra* folk dance—a kind of accelerating dance from the Black Sea area.

Religious dances were dedicated to specific deities. *Geranos*, a ritual winding dance with mythological origins, is believed to have been devoted to Apollo and invokes the mythological Labyrinth where Theseus slew the Minotaur. Geranos continued to be performed during the Hellenistic and Roman times. It was danced at night under the light of torches by women and men holding branches, ropes, and cords in a chorus line, with a leader at each side.

Among secular dances, **hormos** was common in ancient Greece and, according to the ancient satirical writer Lucian, was a chain dance performed by young men and women. A young man would lead by showing off his talents, followed, in contrast, by a young woman, who represented the solemnity and modesty of the female dancers.

 See resource 14.3 in HK*Propel* for web links.

Theatrical Dances of the Classical Period

During the classical period of ancient Greece (500-323 BCE), some dances were closely related to theatrical drama. In particular,

- **emmeleia** was the serious and majestic dance of tragedy and included a code of symbolic gestures, enhancing the events enacted on the stage;

- **kordax** was a provocative and often obscene mask dance of comedy using lascivious body spins; and

- **sikkinis** was danced by **satyrs**—mythical male spirits—in satirical drama, imitating animal movements and aerial tricks.

By the fourth century BCE, several centuries of Roman rule had led to a devaluation of ancient Greek dances. Their initial harmonious nature was disrupted by the public mass entertainment shows of low aesthetics, abruptness, and vulgarity found throughout the far-flung and multicultural Roman empire. The idea of dance competency and exclusiveness was promoted; the prominence of the theater had already established a deep distinction between dance amateurs and professionals. Dance was no longer a regular part of daily life. "It became an ungentlemanly thing, suitable only for the social inferior, or . . . for drunkards" (Fitton 1973, 260). Gestural and postural arts prevailed, dance lost its religious and

An engraving depicting the Pyrrhic dance.

Stefano Bianchetti/Corbis via Getty Images

educational character, and pantomime developed into the emblem of the Greco-Roman period.

Greek Dance in the Middle Ages (146 BCE-1453 CE)

The Middle Ages in Greece constituted a transitional era from the ancient to the 1400s and the early period of modern Greek history. It was the time when Greece became a major crossroads of maritime trade and the Greek language and culture spread across the Western world. Nevertheless, this was also an ambivalent phase for almost all the performing arts. Information concerning Greek dance during this epoch dates back to the last years of the cosmopolitan—but decadent—Roman Empire, when stagecraft and other dramatic arts revealed a historical decline by becoming popular vulgar spectacles. The satirical phrase **panem et circenses ("bread and circuses")** implied that two things (food and entertainment) were provided by the state to keep the poor people from rioting. As a consequence, dance, along with other forms of folk performance, gradually lost its original texture and aesthetics. Its trilateral substance—logos-melos-kinesis—was dismantled. Artistic movement became independent from music and text and eventually turned into a commercial show and an occasion for sensual licentiousness. Dance was connected with horrendous public events in the **amphitheaters** and the arenas and was strongly condemned by the later moralists.

When the Christian religion became an official state institution of the **Byzantine Empire (324-1453 CE)**, the Greek Church proclaimed war against all performing arts that mirrored the cultural decay of that era. Dance was dismissed by the official clergy as the devil's conception. Its correlation to the worship of nature divinities and sexual license led to the frequent conflation of women performers with prostitutes, since the ecstatic and sensual moves went against the feminine ideals of modesty and sexual purity. "Male participation in dance was condemned by Christians and pagans alike as 'unbecoming' (*aprepes*) and 'unmanly' (*anandros*)" (Webb 1997, 126). John Chrysostom, a significant Church Father and archbishop of Constantinople, "is

well known for his condemnations rather than praise on any type of dancing, private or public. His basic position was that the sight of a performer, mostly female, had a devastating effect on the audience, especially the male and his soul" (Kalavrezou 2004, 281). This reflected the clergy's dualistic approach to psyche and **soma**—mind versus body, morality versus corrupted sensuality.

Despite all aphorisms, denunciations, and prohibitions, folk tradition was so powerful that major social events were always accompanied by secular dances. People danced for celebration—either in public or in private—during wedding ceremonies, birthday fests, holy day events, and **symposia** (postprandial drinking parties), and also to celebrate great war victories in the **hippodrome** (arena) and the imperial court. At the time, it was possible to notice a gradual transmutation from rural to urban staged dance. The Byzantines distinguished between **orchesis** (simple, calm, and nonviolent dance) and *ballism* (outrageous, noisy, and frantic dance). Several ancient Greek dances survived during the Middle Ages through their popularity. Circular or spiral dances (similar to the medieval carole form) were performed by sets of women or men who, at the same time, were singing group **call-and-response** chants. These dances were often accompanied either by clapping the rhythm or by such musical instruments as guitar, flute, tambourine, finger cymbals, and drum.

 See resource 14.4 in HK*Propel* for web links.

Early Modern Dance (1453-1821)

From the fall of the Byzantine Empire in 1453 to the Greek War of Independence in 1821, Greece was primarily ruled by the **Ottoman Turks**, while a small number of Greek areas were under **Venetian rule**. During this period of about 400 years, formal types of dances were banned in public events through prohibitions imposed by the Orthodox Church, since dance was considered unethical and was not part of official religious ceremonies. However, because both the Church and the Ottomans were not interested in popular culture of the countryside, Greeks in the villages continued to dance as a daytime entertainment and as a means to maintain their identity and traditions. Dances of Ottoman-ruled Greece were described in Western travelers' narratives, often enhanced with a sense of exoticism and antiquarianism. Since Ottoman Greece was a multiethnic society, several cultures influenced popular Greek music and dance practices, especially Eastern cultures, creating a colorful mosaic of multiple local music and dance idioms that eventually spread throughout the country.

Hellenic Terms

Both the ancient and the modern term for *Greece*—as asserted by its natives—is *Hellas*, which at present can be mostly found in archaic, literary, and official frameworks. Its adjectival form (**Hellenic**) operates either in formal cases or when Greek nationals refer to their own language and civilization, emphasizing their connection with Greek antiquity. According to the fourth-century BCE historian Herodotus, Hellenic identity consists of mutual characteristics, such as shared descent, shared language, shared sacrifices, and shared customs. The word **Neohellenic** is used to denote modern Greek culture and dialect, and the term **Panhellenic** signifies something relating to all of Greece or representing all people of Greek origin or ancestry.

 See resource 14.5 in HK*Propel* for web links.

Traditional Dance in Modern Greece (1821-Present)

The "Dance of Zalongo" (reenacting the 1804 self-sacrifice of the Soulian women) is one of the long-lasting myths of modern Greek history. Whether derived from a legend or from an actual incident, the dance signifies the performative—while, at the same time, tragic—reaction of Greek women to the ruthlessness of the Ottoman enemy

and their dedication to homeland. Through various theatrical depictions, romantic paintings, and musical representations, this dance has become an emblematic symbol of national self-sacrifice and courage.

The symbolism and relevance of "Zalongo" exemplifies how a tradition can be invented and preserved for historical, ideological, and aesthetic reasons. However, Neohellenic folk dance reflects the plentiful performative culture of modern Greece. There are diverse forms, styles, and expressive idioms from both the mainland and islands of Greece. Traditional dances are generally identified with the place of their origin (Cretan, Thracian, Epirotic, etc.). One could enumerate thousands of traditional dance types spread over the entire country. Greek folk dances are manifestations of oral practice and physical communication that evolved according to the choices of people who share a mutual system of ideas, symbols, behaviors, and beliefs. Despite the fact that ancient Greek dances, in and of themselves, have not survived, the inextricable relation between text, music, and movement in ancient performative rituals never abated and continues today as a living tradition.

During the 19th and 20th centuries, Greek dance—in full conjunction with the corresponding music and songs—held clearly functional and habitual connotations, primarily in rural and island areas, given that it "has long been at the literal center of communal social life as a central activity within ritual and secular celebrations" (Cowan 1990, 20). There are two major genres of Greek folk dance, **syrtos** ("dragging dance") and **pidichtos** ("leap dance"). The main characteristic of dragging dances is that the performers are moving with a light shuffle, using minimal or no jumping steps at all. These dances vary significantly in terms of their moves, names, tunes, and rhythms, and they are reputed to be the oldest ones. Leap dances are characterized by the performers' dynamic bouncing motions—especially the leader, who reveals technical and expressive skills through a series of striking hops, twirls, and other patterns. Certain types of those dances—such as **kalamatianos** and **tsamikos**—have been recognized as the most predominant dances in the country and in Greek diasporic communities. These are better known as "Panhellenic dances," because they have been taught and performed nationwide.

Regional and Other Variants of Traditional Dance

The genre of **dimotika** includes the inland music and dance performed in the prefectures of Epirus, Thessaly, Central Greece, Peloponnesus, Macedonia, and Thrace. The island music and dance, called **nisiotika**, derive from isles of the Greek archipelago (Sporades, Cyclades, Northeast Aegean Islands, and Dodecanese). Music and dance of Crete, Ionian Islands, Asia Minor (the coastline of present-day Turkish Anatolia), and Pontus (the area of current eastern Black Sea Region of Turkey) are typically explored as independent areas because of their highly differentiated cultural dialects. Apart from the *kalamatianos* and *tsamikos*, Greek folk dances—along with their local versions differentiated by place, music and kinetic style, and functionality—number over 4,000. The most common of them are *antikristos, baidouska, ballos, berati, chaniotikos, gaitanaki, hasapiko, ikariotikos, kangeli, kerkyraikos, koftos, mandilatos, omal, pentozali, serra, sousta, sta dyo,* *sta tria, trata, tsakonikos, zeibekiko, zervos,* and *zonaradikos.*

Traditional Greek dances are performed to the tunes sung by the dancers or other participating singers and to the music played by folk ensembles, generally referred to as **zygia** (duo) or **kompania** (band). Zygia originated in mainland Greece and kompania in the Greek islands. The correlation between traditional Greek dances and musical rhythm is readily perceived. Greek dance rhythms show great variety, as do those in other Balkan and Western Mediterranean countries. "Many of those rhythms are familiar to the western ear: 2/4, 3/4, 4/4. These are common in both the islands and the mainland. In addition, there are many rhythms not often used in western music: 7/8, 9/8, 5/4, 12/8, 5/8, 3/8, 11/8, 7/16. Those rhythms are frequently referred to as 'asymmetric'" (Hunt 2004, 141). Although danced in irregular meters, Greek dances comprise varying patterns of quick and slow steps, always keeping an appropriate balance between constancy and improvisation in movement.

Greek folk dance group.
LOUISA GOULIAMAKI/AFP via Getty Images

Cultural Highlight

DORA STRATOU

Dora Stratou (1903-1988) was an actress, choreographer, and stage producer who founded the **Greek Dances Theatre**. She was born in Athens in 1903 and grew up in an urban bourgeois lifestyle, studying piano, dance, singing, and theater. After her father's political execution, she left the country to pursue further studies abroad. Returning to Greece in 1932, Stratou was initially involved in theater and, later on in folk art performances, by establishing a school of traditional Greek dances in Athens. Motivated by the romantic idea of saving and disseminating Greek folklore, she organized regular theatrical performances of Greek dances and songs at a professional level in the open-air theater of Philopappou. Dora Stratou pioneered a unique system of presenting folk dances, where there was "no choreographer and no artistic director per se" but principal dancers who led "each regional section represented in the program" (Shay 2002, 181).

During her outstanding career, Stratou received several distinctions, such as the World Theatre Award of the International Theatre Institute, the Academy of Athens Award, and a research grant from the Ford Foundation. She worked together with prominent ethnomusicologists and folklorists to produce an archive of recorded music and interviews and films of dancers, costumes, jewelry, and more. In 1979, she wrote a book entitled *Traditional Greek Dances* that likened Greek folk dance to a living bond with antiquity. It was translated into numerous languages around the globe. She died in 1988, leaving behind an extremely rich legacy. Today, there are hundreds of local and diasporic folklore groups consisting predominantly of young adults that present Greek dances from almost every region of the country in various festivals, concerts, and competitions, all motivated by Stratou's work on traditional Greek dance.

Dance and Community

The majority of traditional Greek dances are group formations in open circle, semicircle, line, or face-to-face pairs. In almost every round dance, the first person acts as the leader while the others are the followers, moving in a counterclockwise direction. They hold their hands at a 90-degree angle—at their shoulders, with outstretched arms. The leader performs elaborate steps, leaps, and squats, usually linked with the second dancer by a handkerchief. The dancers move together by simply stepping to the side (right or left) or back and forth with one foot following the other, and sometimes by swinging the position of their legs, their movement direction, or their speed.

It was only recently that mixed-sex dances were widely accepted by most Greek communities; in earlier times there was a clearer distinction between the dances performed by men and those performed by women. The most common occasion for performing these dances is the *panigyri*, "an annual religious feast that takes place out-doors, usually in large open-air plazas at the side of the church. These festivities . . . bring together local inhabitants and operate like symbolic venues that reinforce social and cultural coherence" in the context of the community (Poulakis 2020, 601). In Greek provinces, folk dance skills have been learned and transferred from one generation to the next through personal participation in the communities' rituals. On the other hand, in modern Greek cities, these dances are taught through institutional and typical music/dance education, mainly in dance schools and formal dance groups. In the present day—although transferred away from its rural background and positioned inside urban settings, following more systematic training and performance processes—traditional Greek dancing is starting to find its way back to the lives of the younger generations (local as well as diasporic) as a way to rediscover and reinterpret their folk culture.

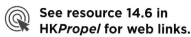 **See resource 14.6 in HK*Propel* for web links.**

Anastenaria—Firewalking Ritual

A vestige from the past Dionysian worship that persists to this day is the **Anastenaria** dance ritual, celebrated during the Greek Orthodox holiday of Saints Constantine and Helen in some villages of northern Greece and in southern Bulgaria. Dancers carry the saints' holy icons to help induce them into a wild trance so that they can dance ecstatically for hours before entering a fire and walking barefoot over the glowing-red coals as the saints direct and protect them. The ceremony concludes with the sacrifice of animals, from which a special meal is prepared for all to partake. In 2009, the ritual was inscribed in the UNESCO Intangible Cultural Heritage lists.

Popular Dance

During the first half of the 20th century, due to the fundamental changes that took place in the country as a result of two world wars and associated political upheavals, some traditional rural dances—for example *aptalikos*, *hasapiko*, *hasaposerviko*, *kamilierikos*, *karsilamas*, *tsifteteli*, and *zeibekiko*—were transformed into popular urban dance forms within metropolitan settings. The emergence of the *rebetika*—the popular song and dance blend that was initially spread among the Greek urban lower and working-class populations in the early 20th century—and the subsequent introduction of the bouzouki as the main instrument of popular music inside and outside the country—led to the advance of a song and dance counterculture of the Greek underworld, followed by a period of massive acceptance and artistic upgrading.

By the middle of the 20th century, the alteration of music and dance practices and tastes, the influence of Western popular dances (such as waltz, tango, foxtrot, polka, and rumba), the disengagement from closely local contexts, and the invention of modern sound technology and commercialized staged representation transformed the earlier rebetika to the newer *laika* genre. Since then, "people have been able to witness a gradual ever-increasing 'transference' or . . . 'deterritorialization' of dancing" (Papa-

kostas 2007, 374). Popular Greek dances are considered simplified versions of old traditions that have incorporated folk, rebetika, Anatolian, and European dance formulas, aiming at becoming easier to perform—by means of free movement and extended improvisation—as well as appropriate for mass entertainment. Nightclubs, tavernas, and live stages offering popular Greek music became fashionable dance locations patronized by the wealthy working class and the bourgeoisie. Within these places, known as *bouzoukia* or *skyladika*, you can find hundreds of people drinking, smoking, singing, and dancing while throwing flowers and smashing plates, a common practice showing Greek excitement that is considered a part of a *glendi* (celebration) with *kefi*—the Greek word for "high spirits, amusement, and joy"—and a way of showing one's social status or emotional situation.

 See resource 14.7 in HK*Propel* for web links.

Contemporary Art Dance

The sociopolitical and economic conditions of the 1980s and 1990s facilitated the reformation and promotion of contemporary art dance in Greece. A substantial number of young dancers and choreographers—including notable dance professionals **Dimitris Papaioannou**, **Konstantinos Rigos**, **Konstantinos Mihos**, **Sofia Spyratou**, and **Apostolia Papadamaki**—adopted some of the most influential techniques, theories, and ideas of the Western dance scene. They have trod new paths within the globalized dance milieu by diverging from previous attempts of earlier pioneers such as **Koula Pratsika**, **Rallou Manou**, and **Zouzou Nikoloudi**.

Characterized by a fusion of personal experiences, Western aesthetics, and national cultural heritage, this new wave of Greek art dance of the last 30 years has stressed a more experimental, internationalized, postmodern, and panhuman attitude. "This era suggested a turning point for the local dance affairs, introducing a direction away from national concerns and towards a post-national, anthropocentric focus on the individual" and was interpreted by many "as a revolutionary rejuvenation . . . away from parochial prototypes towards inspiration, independency, and open-mindedness" (Tzartzani 2007, 279). Nowadays, contemporary Greek dance is particularly presented in major art festivals in Greece, for instance **Greek festivals** (which also take place around the world in diasporic Greek communities) and the **Kalamata International Dance Festival** in southern Greece.

 See resource 14.8 in HK*Propel* for web links.

Crosscurrents

"The Greeks of the 21st century have continued to identify themselves with the rhythms of the rural folk dances and the national values they encase" (Kalogeropoulou 2013, 62). The opening and closing ceremonies of the **2004 Olympic Games in Athens** could be seen as concrete examples of this tendency to focus "once more on 'Greekness,' folk tradition, and urban contemporary embodiments, [through the] artistic choices of **Dimitris Papaioannou** that unified the past with the present in modern Greek history" (Savrami 2019, 45-46). One year later, **Helena Paparizou**—a Greek-Swedish pop singer—won the Eurovision Song Contest by representing Greece and singing the song "My Number One." In order to entertain a global audience and represent current trends, the show incorporated a fusion of music and dance styles, including "a Euro-pop music melody and dance rhythm, naïve English lyrics, bouzouki accompaniment and passages, a Cretan lyra solo, as well as a 'traditional' Pontian dance performance imitation" (Loutzaki and Poulakis 2019, 1036).

Folk dance is a crucial element in the life and culture of the Greek diaspora. Through dance, traditional values and attitudes—generated through customs and enhanced through practice—gradually become embodied by diasporic Greeks and contribute to the formation of mutual memories, as well as personal and collective identities. Moreover, Greek folk dances are closely bound to other aspects of diasporic Greek culture, such as annual and life cycle rituals and customs. It is in the context of Greek folk dance teaching, practice, and competition, formal or informal, that diasporic Greeks become introduced to age, gender, and ethnoregional values. Two major events that serve as excellent examples of the role of traditional dance for the Greek diasporic communities are the **Folk Dance and Choral Festival (FDF)** and the **Hellenic Dance Festival (HDF)** in the United States, both organized by the Greek Orthodox Church of America. They both include a "folk dance competition that exclusively involves the dance groups of Greek communities of the United States" (Papakostas 2016, 293).

 See resource 14.9 in HK*Propel* for web links.

Summary

Greek dance is a component of a threefold performative phenomenon engaging text, music, and movement—logos-melos-kinesis—as a means of personal and social experience, expression, and communication through the ages. Its roots can be traced back to Greek antiquity, where ethos and pathos characterized dance as a path for mind and body wellness. Overcoming a period of degradation and disapproval during the Byzantine era, Greek dance was revitalized through the collective traditions of rural folklore in later years. Regional practices in every part of the country revealed a variety of local dances but gradually led to the establishment of a Panhellenic dance repertoire that now continues the ancient heritage of Greek dance both at home and abroad.

Discussion Questions

1. What is meant by *logos-melos-kinesis* in Greek culture?
2. Which dances are considered as traditional Panhellenic forms?
3. What are the differences between the *dimotika* and the *nisiotika* dances?
4. What were the reasons that led to the transformation of the *rebetika* to the *laika* dance genres?
5. What are the main influences of the contemporary Greek art dance scene?

 Visit HK*Propel* for access to this chapter's Application Activity.

Selected Glossary

bouzouki—A type of long-necked plucked lute used in popular Greek music, with three or four pairs of strings, a round body, and a fretted fingerboard.

call-and-response—A musical form consisting of a succession of two phrases in which the second one is heard as a commentary in response to the first.

choros—Group dance in ancient Greece.

dimotika—Traditional inland music and dance from the Greek prefectures of Epirus, Thessaly, Central Greece, Peloponnesus, Macedonia, and Thrace.

ethos—The Apollonian spirit of ancient Greek music and dance that called attention to concepts such as reason, self-restraint, morality, and form over function.

Hellenic—Of or pertaining to Greece and Greek people. From the ancient Greek word "Hellas," meaning "Greece."

kompania—Traditional music ensemble of the Greek islands consisting of either the lyre and a small davul or the violin and the lute.

logos-melos-kinesis—In Greek, the indivisible triptych of text, music, and dance.

nisiotika—Traditional island music and dance of the Greek archipelago.

orchesis—Improvised individual dance in ancient Greece.

pathos—The Dionysian spirit of ancient Greek music and dance that emphasized emotions, sensuality, desire, and function over form.

pidichtos—A major genre of Greek folk "leap" dance.

syrtos—Major genre of Greek folk "dragging" dance.

zygia—Traditional music ensemble of the Greek mainland consisting of either the shawm (woodwind instrument) or the clarinet and the davul (Turkish drum).

Selected References

Cowan, J.K. 1990. *Dance and the Body Politic in Northern Greece*. Princeton: Princeton University Press.Fitton, J.W. 1973. "Greek Dance." *The Classical Quarterly* 23 (2): 254-274.

Holst-Warhaft, G. 1997. "Song, Self-Identity, and the Neohellenic." *Journal of Modern Greek Studies* 15 (2): 232-238.

Hunt, Y. "Traditional Dance in Greece." 2004. *The Anthropology of East Europe Review* 22 (1): 139-143.

Kalavrezou, I. 2004. "Dance as Ritual, Dance as Performance." In *Greek Ritual Poetics*, edited by D. Yatromanolakis and P. Roilos, 279-296. Cambridge and London: Harvard University Press.

Kalogeropoulou, S. 2013. "Greek Dance and Everyday Nationalism in Contemporary Greece." *Dance Research Aotearoa* 1:55-74.

Lawler, L.B. 1947. "The Dance in Ancient Greece." *The Classical Journal* 42 (6): 343-349.

Loutzaki, I. 2011. "The Dance of Zalongos: An Invented Tradition on Canvas." In *Imaging Dance: Visual Representations of Dancers and Dancing*, edited by B. Sparti and J. Van Zile with E.I. Dunin, N.G. Heller, and A.L. Kaeppler, 195-224. Hildesheim and New York: Georg Olms Verlag.

Loutzaki, I., and N. Poulakis. 2019. "Greece: History, Culture, and Geography of Music." In *The SAGE International Encyclopedia of Music and Culture*, vol. 3, edited by J. Sturman, 1029-1036. Thousand Oaks, London, New Delhi, and Singapore: Sage Publications.

Michaelides, S. 1956. "Greek Song-Dance." *Journal of the International Folk Music Council* 8:37-39.

Naerebout, F.G. 2004. "Dance in Ancient Greece: Anything New?" In *Orchesis: Texts on Ancient Greek Dance*, edited by Anna Lazou, Alkis Raftis, and Malgorzata Borowska, 139-162. Athens: Way of Life.

Papakostas, C. 2007. "Repertoire: Practice vs. Theory. The Greek Paradigm." In *Re-Thinking Practice and Theory International Symposium on Dance Research: Conference Proceedings*, 374-378. Paris: Society of Dance History Scholars.

Papakostas, C. 2016. "(Re)Searching in the (You)Tube: Digital Archives and Dance Practices." In *Congress on Research in Dance: Conference Proceedings*, 292-298. Cambridge: Cambridge University Press.

Poulakis, N. 2020. "Nisiotika." In *Music Around the World: A Global Encyclopedia*, edited by Matthew Mihalka and Andrew R. Martin, 601-603. Santa Barbara, CA: ABC-CLIO.

Savrami, K. 2019. *Tracing the Landscape of Dance in Greece*. Newcastle Upon Tyne: Cambridge Scholars Publishing.

Shay, A. 2002. *Choreographic Politics: State Folk Dance Companies, Representation and Power*. Middletown, CT: Wesleyan University Press.

Tzartzani, I. 2007. *Interplays of Ethnicity, Nationalism and Globalisation Within the Greek Contemporary Dance Scene: Choreographic Choices and Constructions of National Identity*. Doctoral thesis. Guildford: Department of Dance Studies, University of Surrey. Webb, R. 1997. "Salome's Sisters: The Rhetoric and Realities of Dance in Late Antiquity and Byzantium." In *Women, Men and Eunuchs: Gender in Byzantium*, edited by Liz James, 119-148. London and New York: Routledge.

Avgoulas, M.I. and R. Fanany. 2019. "The Symbolic Meaning of Greek Dancing in Diaspora." *Athens Journal of Social Sciences* 6(2): 99-112.

Blagojević, G. 2012. "Research on Dance in the Byzantine Period: An Anthropological Perspective." *Pax Sonoris* 6: 87-95.

Dorf, S.N. 2019. *Performing Antiquity: Ancient Greek Music and Dance from Paris to Delphi, 1890-1930*. New York: Oxford University Press.

Niora, N., M.I. Koutsouba, V. Lalioti, and V. Tyrovola. 2019. "The Phenomenon of Greek Traditional Dance Workshops in Greece: The case of the Cultural Association 'En Choro'." *Journal of Education and Social Policy* 6(2): 95-105.

Petrides, T. 1980. *Greek Dances*. Athens: Lycabettus Press.

Poulakis, N. 2018. "Music and Dance." In *Modern Greece*, edited by E. Thomopoulos, 273-295. Santa Barbara: ABC-CLIO.

Raftis, A. 1998. "Greece: Dance in Modern Greece." In *International Encyclopedia of Dance*, edited by S.J. Cohen, 296-301. New York: Oxford University Press.

Vesterinen, M. 1997. "Communicative Aspects of Ancient Greek Dance." *Arctos: Acta Philologica Fennica* 31: 175-187.

Torp, L. 1992. "'It's All Greek to Me": The Invention of Pan-Hellenic Dances—and Other National Stories." In *Telling Reality: Folklore Studies in Memory of Bengt Holbek*, edited by M. Chesnutt, 273-294. Copenhagen: Nordic Institute of Folklore Publications.

Zografou, M., and M. Pateraki. 2007. "The 'Invisible' Dimension of Zorba's Dance." *Yearbook for Traditional Music* 39: 117-131.

15

Dance in Bulgarian Culture

Iliana Petrova Salazar

Learning Objectives

After reading this chapter you will be able to do the following:

- Identify the main characteristics of Bulgarian dance culture and their sociocultural impact within the region.
- Find and contrast the historical path of Bulgarian dance forms among other Balkan and European examples, following their identification codes and their development.
- Recognize and observe Bulgarian geographic areas and how they influenced the Bulgarian folk dance styles.
- Relate key dance structures to the sociocultural orientation and evolution of the Bulgarians.
- Understand practical applications of the main principles rooted in Bulgarian dance.

Key Terms

Bogomils—The followers of "Bogomilism," a spiritual-practical esoteric teaching that arose in the middle of the 10th century in Bulgaria.

horo—The most popular national folk ensemble dance in Bulgaria.

rachenik—In the Rhodope area, a headscarf a bride wears during the rachenitsa dance.

rachenitsa—The distinctive dance and musical signature of Bulgaria.

kukerski dance plays—An ancient form of masquerade group dance plays in Bulgaria, still performed at certain times of the year.

Liberty, Equality, Brotherhood—A moving motto of the Bulgarian cultural and spiritual enlighteners.

Panevritmia—An ensemble choreographic and musical practical method developed by the spiritual master Beinsá Dounó in the first half of the 20th century.

rusaliiski/kalusharski dance—A pre-Christian ritual dance to ensure fertility, well-being, or healing among the Bulgarians.

Horo and Panevritmia

The sun rises in the morning and brings life, joy, and energy to Earth and its inhabitants. People gather in Nature, hand in hand or side by side, circled around musicians to participate in this revival process. United in common philosophy, rhythm, songs, and movements, in couples or in ensembles, the performers exchange electromagnetic energies holding their hands—right on top of the left, clapping or waving them up and down. Their movements are always in conjunction with the musical beats, while tracing symbols or cosmic cycles with their feet—often bare—to complete the Earthly connection with Nature. This ensemble round dance has been performed on Bulgarian land from pre-Christian times and is a constant thread in Bulgarian cultural memory. "From the beginning of the times is the healing Bulgarian dance *horo*" (Majarov 2012, 58). It is believed that the **horo** prepared the physical base and cultural memory of the 20th century spiritual and renewal Sun dance **Panevritmia**. These two ensemble dance compositions are key representatives of the Bulgarian dance culture today.

In the beginning of the song that accompanies the Panevritmia dance in part 2, the following lines pay homage to the Sun:

> Miraculous dawn arises,
>
> she manifests new life,
>
> A Sun dance in the mountain
>
> we start playing,
>
> and jointly we start singing
>
> the songs of the Sun.

Beinsá Dounó, 1942

Translation by Iliana Petrova Salazar.

 See resource 15.1 in HK*Propel* for web links.

Bulgaria, throughout history, lay at ethnical, historical, physical, and spiritual crossroads. From pre-Christian times, its territory was home to Bulgarians and Thracians. The Odrysian Kingdom of Thrace was established between the fifth century BCE and the first century CE. Later on, the royal dynasties of the First Bulgarian Empire flourished from 681 to 1018 CE. During this time Christianity was adopted (around 864 CE) and the pre-Christian ritual dances mixed with the church holy days. Through the church practices, disciples of Slavic-speaking clergy developed the second Old Bulgarian alphabet, the Cyrillic alphabet, which has spread among the Slavs. (Note that when the Cyrillic alphabet is rendered in Latin form it can yield several different versions of the same word, such as the horo and *khoro* or *kolo* you will find later in this chapter.) Bulgaria entered into the so-called Bulgarian Golden Age, the best cultural and economic period in Bulgarian history, under the rule of Tsar Simeon the Great (893-927 CE). A century after his death, Bulgaria fell under Byzantium rule (the eastern part of the Roman Empire) for almost 200 years.

Following this Second Bulgarian Empire (1185-1396 CE) Bulgaria was trapped in Ottoman rule for about 500 years, until the early 20th century. Yet even after independence in 1908, the nation was buffeted by turmoil in Europe, including the Russian Revolution, two world wars, and communism. But Bulgaria has been fortunate to host some of the greatest European enlighteners and healers of the society—**Orpheus, Boyan Magesnik, Beinsá Dounó,** who shared their methods of spiritual and societal renewal. Along this historical path, natural, political, and spiritual forces continue to shape Bulgarian dance culture.

Bulgarian Dance Culture

Ensemble dances such as horo and Panevritmia illustrate the importance of unity and cultural identity in Bulgaria, as well as how the geography and landscapes that define the country as a part of the Balkan peninsula play a key role in the dance culture. Borders with the Black Sea, the Danube River, and the Balkan Mountains define six ethnographic areas in Bulgaria: (1) Thracian area/Thrace, (2) Dobrujanska area/Dobruja, (3) Northern area/Severnyashka, (4) Shopska area/Shopluk, (5) Pirin area/Pirinska, and (6) Rodopi area/Rhodope. The characteristics of these six areas differentiate and reflect the form and content of Bulgarian folk dances. These dances also spring from pre-Christian spiritual beliefs of proto-Bulgarian cults that revered the life-giving properties of the Sun. Concepts of the Sun God, whose powers resided in the sun's rays and its circular shape, are deeply rooted in the ancient history of Bulgarian culture. Images of sun-worshipping dance figures can be observed on the wall paintings in the **Magura Cave** dating back beyond 8000 BCE, along with figures moving in circles, lines, and serpentine paths on the walls of pre-Christian Thracian tombs. The Thracians were ancient Indo-European tribes inhabiting a vast area of east and southeastern Europe. They were one of the first who populated the region now known as Bulgaria, and they strongly influenced the ancient Greek and Roman cultures. The circular and linear patterns of sun worship and horo can be observed in pre-Christian dance rites, Thracian Orphic mysteries that kept the ritualistic practices alive for centuries, and many more dances, extending even to the present day in Panevritmia. The importance and potency of ensemble dance remains central to Bulgarian dance culture.

Magura Cave

The Magura Cave is situated in the Danube River region in Bulgaria. Its complex cave paintings depict animals, astral bodies, symbols, and dancing or hunting human figures dating back to 8000-4000 BCE. The first Sun calendar in Europe is found in the Magura Cave, as well as one of the first "dancing woman" figures depicted in Europe. Other frequent images show dancers with hands in circle shapes above their heads, evidently in a sun-worshipping enlightenment ritual.

The three nymphs dancing on a Thracian sanctuary stone near Burdapa (Ognyanovo, Pazardjik).

Pre-Christian Dance Rituals

Since time immemorial, dance and spiritual teachings have had the same function: to connect the earthly and the ineffable, synchronizing their eternal cosmic and natural cycles. Bulgarian dances have roots in such pre-Christian practices and continue their mysterious dance codes in choreography, eurhythmic rites, dance plays, and health-based renewal practices. For example, the Thracians—like the Egyptians and Buddhists—believed in life after death, but also in reincarnation, and they bade farewell to the dead with music and dancing. Rites such as these were developed in antiquity and encoded during medieval times, but after the conversion of Bulgarians to Christianity (864-866 CE) the culture took a very different course. The daily life of the people and the views about dance art were dictated through the official Christian church, where the concept of reincarnation was denied. The church successfully banned many dance rituals, and for centuries almost no sources acknowledged the ancient dances. Nonetheless, some pre-Christian dance practices were absorbed into the church calendar and still appear in traditional dance performances and festivals today. Three of the most prominent are the **nestinarski dance**, **kukerski dance plays**, and **rusaliiski/kalusharski dance**.

Fire Dancing Rites

Dancing or walking on hot coals is a ritual practice performed all around the globe—Africa, India, China, North America, and elsewhere. In Europe there are the nestinarski dance in Bulgaria, Anastenaria in Greece (Greek Αναστενάρια), and the paso del fuego in Spain. Fire dances are performed for special occasions: initiation, worship, transformation, divination, healing. To this day, many cultures celebrate one or more of these occasions through such practices.

Nestinarski Dance—A Fire-Dancing Rite

The nestinarski dance is performed on hot coals as the culmination of an ancient ritual complex called "nestinarstvo." It is danced during one of the two main celebrations in the Bulgarian culture, summer equinox, now equated with celebrating the Orthodox Christian saints Constantine and Elena. Its performers are called *nestinari*—women and men specially initiated in the fire dance steps. The peculiar mental state that allows dancers to cross the hot embers is characterized by little steps and a glimpse into an icon held by the performers that depicts one or both of the saints. The main purpose of nestinarski dance is to make a sacred connection that will secure good health and fertility for the people.

The Kukerski Dance Plays—Masquerade

The kukerski dance plays in Bulgaria are commonly held in the days between winter equinox (around December 21st) and Epiphany (January 6th). In the Bulgarian folk tradition this period is considered as the "**dirty days**," when malicious spirits and unclean powers walk freely outside and can harm the people. That is why at this time of year male performers called **kukeri** don masks and scary animal leather costumes hung with bells and then dance to protect and bless people's homes, villages, and cities. The dance-ritual symbolism encoded in their masquerade is performed mainly to banish the winter and evil forces, but also to provide a good harvest, health, and happiness in the upcoming year.

Rusaliiski/Kalusharski Dance

The rusaliiski/kalusharski dance is a complex ritual connected with the most important periods in the year—winter and summer equinox. In Bulgaria this dance has traditionally had double calendar location: In winter, the rusaliiski/kalusharski dance takes place between Christmas and Epiphany. Similar to the kukeri, male dancers—rusalii/kalushari—parade through the villages with sticks or swords wearing masks and costumes and bells to drive away the evil forces and the winter. They dance to call forth protection, health, and fertility (Arnaoudov 1969, 545).

In summer, the rusaliiski/kalusharski dance culminates in a healing dance rite performed during the Pentecostal Orthodox Feast (the 50th day after Easter), also known as the Mermaid Week or the *Rusalijska Nedelya*. Unlike the kukerski dance plays, the rusaliiski/kalusharski dance in Bulgaria is an occult dance rite of pre-Christian origins (Arnaoudov 1969; Shapkarev 1884; Venedikov 1995) and has its accompanying healing dance ritual. Connected to biblical rituals in the Old Testament, the dance invokes fertility, herblore, worship, balanced life, and protection from "**folklore diseases**" caused by mistreated supernatural beings. It can be performed as a healing rite for a specific individual whose illness is seen as the result of harmful actions by these beings.

Medieval Dance Rituals: From Boyan Magesnik to the Kolo Dance

Scholars of pre-Christian rituals note that many elements—such as dance poses and symbols by members of secret societies or brotherhoods—were carried forward into the Middle Ages through Christian mysteries and their practitioners. One of these practitioners, the **Bogomils** society, founded by Boyan Magesnik (910-970) (also known as Veniamin-Boyan, Bayan, and Boyan the Magician), left lasting influences on folk customs and dances that are still performed today.

Bogomils

The Bogomils—literally "endeared to God"—were people brought together by Boyan Magesnik in his esoteric teachings that rejected the trappings of Orthodox Christianity. They followed the early Christianity and its divine principles of **Liberty, Equality, Brotherhood** through love (origin of the *Liberté, égalité, fraternité* motto used in the French Revolution 800 years later [Pophristov 2015, 176-178]), along with the belief in reincarnation. For such Christian heresy, the Bogomils were brutally persecuted by the church and chased out of Bulgaria. Their perception of the body as a tool of the soul led to the use of dance in their mysterious rites.

Boyan Magesnik

Boyan Magesnik, son of the Bulgarian tsar Simeon the Great, was one of the strongest and most famous shamans and enlighteners from medieval times in all of Europe. He renounced his royal life and went to live with, protect, and heal the Bulgarian people. The magical shaman practices were bound with his abilities to transform into a wolf and other animals. In Bulgarian folklore and mythology, the wolf is considered one of the smartest and most powerful animals, and it is a liaison between the material and the spiritual worlds—a function also held by dance in medieval Europe. Similar to North American shamanic practices for calling "power animals," this son of a Bulgarian king practiced what were known as the "wolf mysteries" and brought his followers, the Bogomils, into his teachings.

As esoteric practitioners, the Bogomils were banned from the church and chased out of Bulgarian land. They spread in small societies around Europe as missionaries of Bogomilism and predecessors of main European esoteric societies. Unfortunately, the Bogomils left few traces of their dance rites and practices, though we do know that the main one among them was the kolo dance.

Kolo Dance in Europe and Bulgaria

Kolo, as a term, can be found in all Slavic languages in variants in both meaning and form, connected with "circle" and circle shape (wheel). It is also found in the ancient Bulgarian word *kolobur*, a title meaning enlightener/shaman/priest, and in the dance *kalabrismos*. The kolo existed long before Christianity but was officially adopted through the Orthodox church and is associated with South Slavic traditional dances in several countries. The Serbs preserved the kolo dance as their national heritage, listed in UNESCO's **Intangible Cultural Heritage of Humanity** in 2017.

The kolo dance is connected with the cultural and archeological heritage left by the Bulgarian Bogomils, who escaped to live outside of Bulgaria. They left gravestones called **stechki**, on whose surfaces, along with cosmological references about Sun and Earth worship and calendar cycles, the Bogomils engraved a complex system of female, male, and mixed-sex dances that follow circular, row, serpentine, or concentric curving line patterns. Proof of their ancient history can be seen in similar images found in the Magura Cave of dancers moving with hands above their heads. Though for now the dance culture and symbolic elements of kolo remain a mystery, historians confirm the resemblance between the Bulgarian horo and the kolo of the Bogomils, its choreographic shapes, and Sun–Earth cyclicity connections. For centuries, this connection has been preserved in the folk forms and character of Bulgarian dances, especially in the many variations of the horo that define Bulgaria's national dance.

Table 15.1 gives a brief view on the people and historical periods of cultural development of Bulgarian dance, particularly ensemble dances.

 **See resource 15.2 in HKP*ropel* for web links.**

Table 15.1 Historical Periods of Bulgarian Dance

People/Culture	Period	Dance
Proto-Bulgarians	Pre-Christian times	Horo, in the Sun–Earth cults
Thracian Orpheus	6-1 BCE to 4 CE	Thracian and Orphic mysteries
Christianity	Bulgarian Empire I	Cult and religious dance mix
Boyan Magesnik	10th century CE	Christian and wolf mysteries
Bogomils	Medieval Europe	Kolo, dance of the Bogomils
Reforms of scholars	19th-20th century	Horo, in the six folk areas
Beinsá Dounó	20th-21st century	Panevritmia

The Horo

Bulgaria's National Dance Form

In addition to the nestinarski, kukerski, rusaliiski/kalusharski, and kolo, many other dances with ancient origins still exist in Bulgaria today. The horo (plural *horá*) is the most popular of these folk forms. Vocal or instrumental music accompanies this hand-holding ensemble dance. Both amateurs and professionals perform the dance, and groups can be divided by sex or mixed. This dance form is characteristic of the pre-Christian ritual dance culture in Eastern and southeastern Europe and is associated with medieval European *carole* dances. In the horo the dancers continuously repeat patterns or vary them according to the music, voice modulations, instructions from the leader of the horo, or the performance purpose. People learned to communicate and celebrate many things through the horo—from rituals and customs to expressions of love or other emotions to national celebrations. As a key part of large fairs and festivals in the beginning of the 20th century, the horo became a way to mediate economic, religious, and political issues in Bulgarian society, taking its place as a national dance and a hallmark of Bulgarian culture around the world. This important role grew out of the horo's communicational and social orientation carried over from its pre-Christian origins. As such, it is well-suited for the regional adaptations that characterize its performance in Bulgaria.

Caroles

Caroles were "medieval European dances in a ring, chain, or linked circle, performed to the singing of the dancers. An indefinite number of persons participated, linking arms and following the step of the leader. The origins of the carole are in ancient ring dances of May and midsummer festivals and, more remotely, in the ancient Greek *choros*, or circular, sung dance. Mentioned as early as the 7th century, the carole spread throughout Europe by the 12th century [CE] and declined during the 14th century" (Encyclopedia Britannica 2016).

Regional Variants of the Horo

After the liberation of Bulgaria from Ottoman rule in 1878, the country formed into six ethnographic areas (discussed at the beginning of this chapter). Shortly thereafter, Bulgarian folk dance became an important academic topic. Up through the 1950s, prominent Bulgarian scientists and researchers (Dzhudzhev 1945; Tzonev 1950) and their associates in choreography (K. Haralampiev,

Shopsko horo dancers at the 21st Vitosha International Folkore Festival in Sofia (2017).

Photos: Stefi Rumenova.

K. Dzhenev, T. Kyuchukov, and P. Zahariev 1952) systematized Bulgarian folk music and dance elements. This led to the typology of six folk dance styles. Further variations within the six styles are related to specific events (religious festivals, folk customs) and the creativity of individual choreographers.

The main Bulgarian folk dance elements include the following:

Dance Elements for the Legs

Leg movements in Bulgarian folk dance are quite varied, thanks to the dominance of the horo group dance and its intricate footwork. The many element combinations include steps, foot dabs, hammering (on foot, toe, or heel), hops, vaults, knee bends, bounce, trigger, leaps, springs, scissor steps, high or low *hlopki* (feet clapping, low or high, with jump), kicks, squats, and *pleti* (foot cross).

Dance Elements for the Hands

Hand elements are much less varied in Bulgarian folk dance and generally relate to regional differences in dance styles. The movements by solo dancers represent common actions (clapping, swaying) or manipulating different props from everyday life such as spoons, sieves, and handkerchiefs. However, in Bulgarian group dances there are several distinguishing handholds: down-facing-palm handhold, up-facing-palm handhold (elbows pointing down), shoulder hold (hands holding at shoulder level side by side), **za poyas** ("by belt" hold—each partner in the horo holds their two neighboring dancers' belts), and arm-in-arm hold. A typical hand hold in Bulgaria is **na lesa**, a kind of belt hold when the dancer holds the belts of the partner on their right side (with left hand over the right hand of the partner) and left side (right hand under the left hand of the partner). There are also "front *lesa*" and "back *lesa*." In the past, to avoid direct contact, people joined together by holding the opposite ends of a handkerchief.

Different handholds and choreographic patterns help to define the regional variants and correspond with Bulgarian folk music and songs. As with many other folk dances, every city, small village, or dance group can have its own dance variations and horo style with specific musical rhythms and melody. Costuming also reveals local characteristics in the traditional **shevici** (embroi-

dery), of symbolic images used everywhere on dance costumes and props—like handkerchiefs or bridal clothing—often connected with the name of the performed dance. Many kinds of hora are named after calendar holy days or folk customs, after their performers, or after the ethnographic area where they were created. The **pravo horo** ("straight" horo)—a basic form of **vito horo** (winding horo)—is the most common, because its basic steps can be performed by people from any gender, religion, or social status, and almost every age.

Thracian Folk Dances

Folk dances of the Thracian region—the largest of the six—have solo or group forms with rich dance ornamentation both in the legs and hands. Movements reach toward Mother Earth, showing gratitude for her fertility, or up to the sky, greeting the Sun, reflecting beliefs derived from proto-Bulgarian and Thracian religious cults and expressed in the region's nestinarski and rusaliiski dances.

Dobruja Folk Dances

Dobruja is known as the "wheat garden of Bulgaria." Its dances are mainly associated with agriculture, grain and wheat, and they are typically very mild and focused on the earth. Movements reflect those associated with sowing, harvesting, and utilizing crops, especially in the hands, steps, and props for these actions, and music often uses a 2/4 beat.

Northern (Severnyashki) Folk Dances

Dances in the northern lands of Bulgaria (the Danube Valley) are among the most lively of all. The open air of the valley inspires uplifted dance movements, and the music also connects with air through instruments like the *kaval* (flute) and the pipe. Typical musical measures are 9/8, 11/16, and 2/4.

Shopski (Shope) Folk Dances

The landscape is as open and wide as the free soul of the dances here. Fast and vivid, the Shopski folk dance has dynamic rhythms, typical shoulder shaking—*natrisane*—and skillful dance combinations, especially in the legs. The most used hand hold is za poyas, while the music beats are commonly 2/4, 11/16, 5/8, 13/16, and 7/16.

Pirin Folk Dances

The area named after the Pirin Mountains in southwest Bulgaria shows cultural similarities with bordering Greece and North Macedonia. The dances are slow and temperate, female or male but not often mixed. The movements in the hora, specifically for men, often evolve from slow, light, and wide ones to very skillful spins and pirouettes. Music is mainly in meters of 2/4, 3/8, 7/8, 8/8, 12/8, and 11/8.

Rhodopes Folk Dances

Unlike the Pirin Mountains, the namesake Rhodope Mountains have a lower altitude and cover a wider area. Dancers in this different mountain climate wear heavy folk costumes that limit lively or high movements and slower rhythm with minimal variation of elements. The most characteristic folk dance is the hora, accompanied either by profoundly lyrical songs sung by both women and men or by the famous **kaba gaida**, or kaba pipe, a bagpipe-type instrument. Rhythms are often in 2/4 or 4/4 meter.

Signature of Bulgarian Dance and Musical Form—Rachenitsa

The **rachenitsa** dance form unites the hora variants of the six regions within one dance and musical structure. It is defined by three basic steps that can be performed with a leap, foot tapping, spring, and turn. The rachenitsa is a very vivid dance with ancient roots and is considered the signature form of Bulgarian national folk dance. Some researchers connect the name with the Thracian words *runk* or *rink*, meaning fast, movable, or lively, which corresponds to its vivid character. Others refer to the word **rachenik**—which in the Rhodope area is a headscarf a bride wears during the dance. Rachenitsa can be a solo, duo, or ensemble dance (male, female, or mixed). The most distinctive Bulgarian dance form, the rachenitsa is defined by a special musical rhythm and measure—7/8 or 7/16—where the most used variant of the 7 beats is "quick, quick, slow" (2+2+3, with accents on 1).

Bulgarian Uneven Rhythms

Bulgarian uneven rhythms are asymmetrical music structures of the musical meter, built up around complex harmonic scales. Used in classical and jazz music, they are also typical for Balkan folk music and deeply rooted in Bulgarian folk culture. In the first half of the 20th century, professor Stoyan Dzhudzhev systematized the uneven rhythms and their metrical structure common for Bulgarian folklore music: 5/8, 7/8 (rachenitsa), 9/8, and so on, plus their complex combinations: 11/16, 15/8, 25/8, and the like.

 See resource 15.3 in HK*Propel* for web links.

Folk Dance Education and Bulgarian Music

The syncretic connection between music and dance in all Bulgarian folk forms combined with a need to reestablish Bulgarian national identity to create a key role for folk dance in the country's education systems after Bulgaria left the Ottoman Empire in the late 19th century. Bulgarian folk dances hora and rachenitsa entered the physical education system not as a sport, but as an effort to rebuild national consciousness, traditions, and culture while improving general physical and mental health. By the mid-20th century, the intricate, uneven rhythms of folk music and associated dances had become part of the educational system at all levels. Bulgarian folk dances and hora were taught along with elementary theory of music, and in 1951 a national folk music and dance ensemble was founded by composer **Filip Kutev** (1903-1982).

 See resource 15.4 in HK*Propel* for web links.

Crosscurrents

Major historical events, such as long periods of Orthodoxy and socialism in Bulgaria, two world wars, and the Russian Revolution helped to shape the development of Bulgarian ballet and contemporary dance forms throughout the 20th century. Key threads of influence were Soviet ballet, Bulgarian folk dance, and German expressionist dance—the latter promoted by "New Dance" artists who toured throughout Europe in the first decades of the century (Yaneva 2002, 50). Ballroom dances also left their mark as "city" dancing, attuned to new European ballroom styles, contrasted with "village" dancing that adhered to Balkan folk dance. Under these varied influences, the Bulgarian national ballet was established in the 1920s and '30s. Concurrent with the influences from other European cultures, Bulgarian folklore dance became a major creative resource for many Bulgarian dance artists after the country gained independence in 1908, and it continues as such to this day.

Choreographer **Margarita Arnaoudova** (1941-1994) and the experimental ballet company that she directed best exemplify this synthesis. The company, "Arabesque," was founded in 1967 and continues to be the primary symbol of Bulgarian contemporary ballet culture both at home and abroad (Yaneva 2015).

After the fall of Communist rule in 1989, contemporary dance works in ballet and modern dance idioms joined forces with other artistic and performative forms including theater, music, and even gymnastics. The early 20th-century push for integrating the dance and music arts through physical education at all academic levels paved the way for the national recognition achieved by rhythmic gymnast and trainer **Neshka Robeva** (b. 1946) who weaves Bulgarian folklore with folk dance elements, gymnastic combinations, and props. The syncretic approach that shaped Bulgarian ballet and contemporary works underlies another vibrant development in Bulgarian dance—the Panevritmia.

 See resource 15.5 in HK*Propel* for web links.

A New Choreographic Culture

Panevritmia

After the devastations of Ottoman rule, Bulgarians sought to revive and transform the dance culture in different dimensions—physical, aesthetic, mental, and spiritual. In the first decades of the 20th century, a new syncretic composition arose to meet the challenge—the Panevritmia (discussed in the opening vignette). This new choreography emphasized a connection with Nature along with ancient unitive practices that had long been at the core of Bulgarian dance, such as the pre-Christian and Thracian sun-worship rituals. According to **Beinsá Dounó** (1864-1944), the creator of Panevritmia, this circle dance composition weaves cosmic rhythms and laws, ideas, music, and natural movements, and it is *an eminent universal harmony of the movement* (Beinsá Dounó 1938, 62). The Panevritmia is a physical implementation of Beinsá Dounó's philosophical principles and teaching.

Etymology of Panevritmia

"**pan**" means *everything, supreme,* or *cosmic*

"**ev**" or "**eu**" in its Latin original form means *veridical* (truthful) or *supreme*

"**ritmia**" means *regularity in the movements*

Thus, *Panevritmia* means *supreme cosmic rhythm* (Beinsá Dounó 1938, 62).

Translated by Iliana Petrova Salazar

Structure of Panevritmia

Panevritmia, a tripart circle dance, is performed primarily by a balanced number of male and female couples moving counterclockwise around a group of musicians. Unlike the horo, where the dance movements are concentrated in the legs,

Master Beinsá Dounó (in white in the center) and his followers performing Panevritmia at 7 Rila Lakes.

the hands and upper part of the body initiate movement in Panevritmia. While the dance elements and rhythms are easy to perform, dancers—wearing clean, light-colored clothing—do not improvise and must know precisely all the steps, lyrics, and underlying philosophy.

Underlying Philosophy of Panevritmia

Based on ancient concepts of human unity with Nature and the universe, two key tenets of Panevritmia are the principle of rhythm and the principle of correspondence. Rhythm organizes the elements of the Panevritmia, and the principle of correspondence fixes the exact relationships between musical and choreographic text. Evidently, Beinsá Dounó worked for decades on the traditional 7/8 and 7/16 musical measures of rachenitsa and Bulgarian music to remove the tones and vibrations that held sadness within melodies and rhythms layered negatively in the history of Bulgaria. By partnering his music with specific movements, lyrics, and ideas, Beinsá Duonó structured each part of Panevritmia to

Female couple practicing the Sun Is Rising exercise from part 1 of Panevritmia, "Awakening."
Photo: Stefi Rumenova.

awaken and have precise meaning and impact on the body, psyche, soul, and spirit.

Cultural Highlight

A PERSONAL EXPLORATION OF PANEVRITMIA

Panevritmia is not new religion but new practical teaching. By personal experience I can say that going from dancing under stage lights to dancing in a circle under the first rays of the Sun is a profound and healthy experience. That's why Panevritmia represents the beginning of dance therapy in Bulgaria. It is a triad of physical, mental, and soul therapy. Along with years of investigating its theories, I personally practiced the method. Years after I learned to follow its holistic psychophysiological applications, spending six months barefoot every day, I realized that I healed my painful flatfoot and curved posture, which hurt my whole being and dance career. As an interdisciplinary dancer I had to rehearse and dance on heels in different settings—arena sand, floating ship—and to wear heavy costumes. Eventually I was in such pain that doctors forbade me to dance. The Panevritmia lifted me with its positive lyrics about human values, together with the recommended body posture and direct body and soul contact with Nature and the performers. Not only as an academic researcher, but also as a Panevritmia performer for more than seven years, I can surely say that its main purpose is to put natural and universal principles into practice in order to prepare the way toward a new united culture rising with the circle of life that is the Sun—the choreographic signature of the Panevritmia.

Beinsá Dounó's approach ensured that Panevritmia was aligned with the needs of a Bulgarian population still reeling from the tumult of the Ottoman occupation, and on the precipice of another world war. It also incorporated concepts similar to expressive art therapies and psychotherapies that were emerging in early 20th-century Europe—one of the most valuable renewals of the connection between *telos* and *psyche* (body and soul) at that revolutionary time. While the societal value of Panevritmia kept it relevant during the early years, its holistic therapeutic effects on individual mental and physical health helped it to survive during decades of repression under communism (1945-1990). With the fall of the Soviet Union and the end of Communist rule in Bulgaria, Panevritmia reemerged in 1991 to grow throughout the 20th century and into the present day.

 See resource 15.6 in HK*Propel* for web links.

Summary

From ancient times until today, Bulgarian dance culture has been shaped by universal principles and laws, rooted in dance practices and rites known from pre-Christian times. The dances are encoded or artistic messages following mainly natural forms—circles, lines, and serpentine patterns that invoke the Sun–Earth connection with their social, unitive, and health impact for humans. These metaphorical and physical connections are preserved in the Bulgarian dance culture through the rusaliiski/kalusharski and nestinarski dances, horo, kolo, and Panevritmia. Bulgarian dance history—built on the synthesis of sociocultural, spiritual, traditional, and contemporary diversity within the motto of Liberty, Equality, Brotherhood—now continues its trajectory with the Panevritmia to create a dance culture fully embracing the physical, moral, and spiritual potentials of our human existence.

Discussion Questions

1. Why and how did the motto Liberty, Equality, Brotherhood become the moving power in the Bulgarian dance culture?
2. What is the main dance form repeated in the history of Bulgarian dance culture, and why did it have such a strong impact?
3. What is the national folk dance signature of Bulgaria and what are its distinctive features?
4. Which principles shape the choreographic structure of the Panevritmia, and how does this lead the performers to the idea of new cultural horizons and their practical application?

 Visit HK*Propel* for access to this chapter's Application Activity.

Selected Glossary

Bogomils—The followers of the spiritual practical movement "Bogomilism," established by Boyan Magesnik in the 10th and 11th centuries CE in Bulgaria.

Bulgarian uneven rhythms—The asymmetrical tendencies of the Bulgarian folk music art.

horo—The most popular national folk ensemble dance in Bulgaria.

kukerski dance plays—An ancient form of masquerade dance ritual plays, performed around Christmas and preserved in folk festivals today.

Liberty, Equality, Brotherhood—A moving motto of the Bulgarian cultural and spiritual enlighteners.

nestinarski dance—Ancient fire dance in southeastern Bulgaria.

Panevritmia—An ensemble choreographic and musical practice developed by the spiritual master Beinsá Dounó in the first half of 20th century.

rachenitsa—The distinctive folk dance and musical signature of Bulgaria.

rusaliiski/kalusharski dance—A pre-Christian ritual dance to provide fertility, well-being, or healing among the Bulgarians.

Selected References and Resources

The official Bulgarian transliteration is used from the following link: Transliteration of proper names in Bulgaria

https://web.archive.org/web/20071014000612/http:/transliteration.mdaar.government.bg/trans.php [Wayback Machine]

Arnaoudov, M. 1969. *Essays on the Bulgarian Folklore*. Vol. 2. Sofia: Academic Edition Prof. Marin Drinov.

Biks, R., A. Yaneva, R. Karakostova, M. Tzenova-Nusheva, and E. Zhunich. 2015. Bulgarian Musical Theatre. Opera. Ballet. Operetta. Musical. 1890-2010. Recensions, Reviews and Comments. Vol. IV, Institute of Art Studies, BAS, Sofia: Geya Lybris, 767:162-461.

Chervenkova, L. 2013. *Paneurhythmy, Health and Wellness: A Bulgarian Model of Physical Activity*. Sofia: Snt. Kliment Ohridski.

Eliade, M. 1973. "Notes on the Căluşari in the Gaster Festschrift." *The Journal of the Ancient Near Eastern Society of Columbia University* 5:115-122.

Encyclopedia Britannica. 2016. "carole." *Encyclopedia Britannica*, September 14, 2016. www.britannica.com/art/carole.

Encyclopedia Britannica. 2019. "kolo." *Encyclopedia Britannica*, August 28, 2019. www.britannica.com/art/kolo.

Georgieva, I. 1993. *Bulgarian National Mythology*. 2nd revised and expanded ed. Sofia: Academic Edit. Prof. Marin Drinov.

Leach, M. 1950. *The Dictionary of Folklore, Mythology and Legend*. Vol. 1. New York: Funk & Wagnalls.

Majarov, H. 2012. *Forerunners of Panevritmia*. Varna: Alfiola.

Petrova Salazar, I. 2021. *European Choreographers Orientated in Dance Therapy and Its Application in the XX and XXI Century*. Sofia: Institute of Art Studies, BAS.

Pophristov, D. 2015. *About the Bogomils from "Mouth to Year."* Sofia: VBB.

Venedikov, I. 1983. *The Copper Threshing-Floor of the Proto-Bulgars*. Sofia: Science and Art.

Venedikov, I. 1995. *Myths on Bulgarian Land. Mednoto gumno (The Copper Threshing-Floor)*. Book I. Stara Zagora: Idea.

16

Traditional Dance in Russia

Anthony Shay

Learning Objectives

After reading this chapter you will be able to do the following:

- Articulate Russian aesthetics as reflected in traditional dances.
- Recognize how idealized gender roles are enacted through the dance.
- Consider how staged ethno identity dances, like those of the Igor Moiseyev Dance Company, have been used for purposes of diplomacy, especially during the cultural Cold War.
- Identify authentic folk dances and how they differ from ethno identity dances.
- Understand dance as a political tool in Russian culture, not simply an art form or social activity.

Key Terms

cultural Cold War—The Cold War rivalry (1947-1991) between the Soviet Union and the West extended into all areas of society, including cultural products, such as dance.

ethno identity dances—Staged dances, based on folk forms, that are coordinated, rehearsed, and choreographed.

folk dance in the field—Authentic folk dance performed as an organic part of people's lives, especially, but not limited to, the rural populations.

khorovod—A round dance containing many figures and regional styles. It is the oldest of the Russian folk dances and is generally accompanied by singing.

Moiseyev Dance Company—The first state-supported, official representative of the former Soviet Union, and later the Russian Federation. Founded by Igor Moiseyev in 1937.

socialist realism—The concept upon which all Russian music, dance, literature, and visual art were based during Joseph Stalin's authoritarian rule (c. 1924-1953).

Traditional Russian Dance

It is a feast day, and after church, a number of men have gathered in front of the village tavern. Vodka flows freely among them with much laughing and shouting. The accordion player begins to play a lively dance tune, and the men, seeing Ivan emerging from the small wooden church, call him over. Here is some fun. Ivan dreads the moment, for he sees that Vladimir, his chief rival and the current winner in competitive dancing, has begun to warm up. Vladimir begins a series of *kolentsa* (knee movements) and, giving Ivan a wink as a challenge, he squats close to the well-packed earth where village dances take place. In his loose pants and well-worn boots, Vladimir throws out first his right leg, reaching as high as possible with his right foot, and then his left. He repeats the movements, and the men surrounding the dance space begin to call out the numbers of kicks (*prisiadki*). But Ivan has not been idle over the past month since he last lost the competitive *pereplias*, yet again, to Vladimir. Behind his wooden log house, he has been practicing to exhaustion and building his leg muscles. At last, Vladimir falls to the ground with a comical thump, his knees giving out to the strain of the dance. Ivan takes his place. He begins by warming up to the music with a series of traveling squatting figures circling the dance space and then commences the same series of squat kicks that Vladimir performed before him as the men count. Luck is with him. The men count out numbers, their voices rising louder when the number of steps are higher than Vladimir accomplished. Finally, Ivan gives one last glorious kick before his leg muscles turn to mush. One of the men rushes over and pulls him up, raises his arm in victory, and proffers him a drink of vodka in a wooden cup to celebrate. Ivan turns red with pride as a cheer goes up for him among the reveling viewers.

The most important issue for those interested in traditional Russian dance is the division between actual Russian **folk dance in the field** (Buckland 1999), that is, authentic folk dance performed as an organic part of people's lives (especially the rural populations like the one described in the imaginary scene in the opening vignette), and **ethno identity dances**—staged dances that are coordinated, rehearsed, and choreographed. Most viewers see Russian dance only in its ethno identity iteration. For centuries, Russian folk dances in their most authentic form have been part of both ritual and social life, typical of weddings, harvests, and informal, often spontaneous, social events like *sedelki*. Ethno identity dances, by contrast, are prepared for audiences and frequently performed by non-natives, such as Russian urban dwellers who did not grow up performing these dances. The dancers, both professional and amateur, learn them from a choreographer in a studio—not as part of their social lives. While ethno identity dances are frequently called "folk dance," they may land anywhere along a spectrum from stylized interpretations of original folk dances to physically spectacularized and theatricalized choreographies. The latter constitute an entirely separate dance genre with little remaining of the original folk dancing. This chapter addresses both dance genres, because Russian ethno identity dances have been popular for over a century, and many, if not most Russians believe them to be authentic Russian folk dance. These dances first appeared in **Imperial Russia** (1721-1917) in musical comedies and in character dances during **Russian Imperial Ballet** performances. They were elaborated and professionalized in the former **Soviet Union** with the founding of numerous professional state folk dance ensembles. Thus, it is important to carefully distinguish folk dance in the field from Russian ethno identity dance because they are both often called "folk" dance.

Brief History

The Russians belong to a large linguistic population known as **Slavs**, who are predominant throughout Eastern Europe. The Slavic people are not a hereditary genetic race or ethnic group, but they share a common language origin.

The first Russian state, **Kievan Rus**, centered in Kiev, located in today's **Ukraine**, was founded in the ninth century CE. Its Russian line of kings, the **Riurikid dynasty**, embraced the Orthodox branch of Christianity, although it took centuries before the majority of the population accepted Christianity. Today, the **Russian Orthodox Church** plays an important role in Russian life. Russia has always been a difficult nation to govern because of its size; it is geographically the largest nation-state in the world. The early Russians lived in northern forests and fields in scattered villages over a vast region, mostly living on a subsistence economy, farming, hunting, and fishing.

In the 13th century the **Mongols**, led by **Genghis Khan**, invaded and conquered much of the Eurasian continent, from central Asia to Eastern Europe. After massive destruction of the burgeoning Russian economy, they dominated the Russian lands for more than a century. During this period, the power center of Russia shifted to **Moscow**, the present-day capital. After the end of Mongol rule came the **Grand Duchy of Muscovy**, led by a branch of the Riurikid dynasty. They established an empire whose ruler was called a **tsar**. When the Riurikid dynasty died out because it had no more heirs, the **Romanovs** were selected to succeed them. Throughout this period, the Russian state expanded.

The greatest ruler of the Romanov dynasty was the towering figure of **Peter the Great** (1672-1725). (He literally towered—he was 6′7″ at a time when people in Europe were much shorter.) Throughout the 17th century, the greatest struggle in elite Russian society was whether to embrace the modernity of Western European culture or remain traditional. Peter the Great came down on the side of modernity. While waging constant war and expanding the nation, Peter also forced the Russian elite to adopt European fashions. In the beginning of the 18th century, he founded and built the city of **St. Petersburg**, with grand palaces in the style of a Western European city. Built on a series of canals, it is called the "Venice of the North." Hundreds of thousands of **serfs** perished in the extreme cold and mud while building the future capital of the Romanovs on a marshy site. Peter the Great is still a revered figure in Russian history.

One of the major events of the 19th century was **Napoleon Bonaparte's** 1812 invasion of Russia. Though Napoleon burned Moscow to the ground, his invasion ultimately failed and greatly weakened his rule in Europe. As a result, the Russian elite, in a burst of national pride, began to embrace Russian culture, especially folklore and the Russian language.

Russian Serfs

Well into the 19th century, the vast majority of Russians were serfs who, like slaves, were owned by their landlords. This medieval system meant that Russia remained economically backward throughout its history. Standards of education and literacy remained low until the Communist period (1917-1991). Like slavery in the United States, the question of freeing the serfs dominated Russian political life until their emancipation in the 1860s.

Slavs

Slavs are a European people who originally spoke the same language (known today as Church Slavonic or proto-Slavic), and one of the branches of the Indo-European language group. As these people spread out from the space in which the original language was spoken (this space is unknown, but highly speculated about), the Slavic language slowly evolved into three groups: Western (Polish, Czech, and Slovak), Eastern (Russian, Ukrainian, Belorussian), and Southern (Serbian, Bulgarian, Croatian, Macedonian, Slovenian). Many people adopted Slavic speech as this language developed and differentiated. Therefore, the term *Slavic* does not refer to a genetically related group, but a linguistic group.

The Romanov dynasty fell in the bloody **Communist Revolution of 1917**. Throughout the subsequent Communist period, especially after World War II, Russia constituted half of the population and territory that became the **Union of Soviet Socialist Republics** (U.S.S.R.). During the Communist period, the Soviet Union expanded its political control over most of Eastern Europe, becoming a rival to Western Europe and the United States. This **Cold War** of the 20th century was largely a struggle between two very different political and economic systems that played out in many venues—science, technology, armaments, and even the arts. Ultimately, however, the Soviet Union's turbulent past and neglect of its citizens' well-being led to political and economic collapse in 1991. Out of this dissolution and the resulting scramble, a number of territories together emerged as the **Russian Federation**. Today, the Russian Federation under **Vladimir Putin**, a former secret police operative, is again becoming an increasingly authoritarian state and a political rival to the United States and Europe. Table 16.1 presents a time line of major periods in Russian history.

 See resource 16.1 in HK*Propel* for web links.

Ethno Identity Dance and Socialist Realism

Most people outside Russia have only experienced Russian traditional dance in its idealized ethno identity form in concert settings—a manifestation of **socialist realism** (Shay 2002, 2019a). *Socialist realism* is the term and never-clearly-stated concept upon which all Russian music, dance, literature and visual art were based during **Joseph Stalin's** authoritarian rule (1924-1953). The artist, writer, or composer was to depict Soviet life, in spite of all of the flaws, as if it were perfect and everyone was eternally happy.

Through a number of political and economic events, especially collectivization of agriculture and the rapid development of heavy industry in the 1930s, a vast majority of the rural population settled in cities, often leaving only very old women behind. This rural population was further drastically reduced by the 1941 to 1944 German invasion that burned and destroyed every village the German army and their allies encountered. In addition, the Soviet Union's **Red Army** practiced a scorched-earth policy destroying all food sources that would potentially fall into the hands of the German enemy, including the villages that produced them. This destruction wreaked havoc on traditional village life and its customs. Over 27 million Soviet citizens, most in the Russian area, lost their lives as a result of the fighting and destruction in World War II (Gaddis 2007).

Such widespread destruction severely disrupts the continuity of folkloric practices like singing and dancing (see Ichikawa 1989, JVC World Music, volume 23). Finding old traditional music and dance in its original setting is difficult today. Furthermore, the former Soviet Union rarely permitted non-Soviet individuals into areas in which folk dance could be observed. What is left of the original folk genres is largely reconstructions of former practices by amateur urban

Table 16.1 Time Line of Major Periods in Russian History

Period	Dates	Event
Kievan Rus	882-1240 CE	First Russian kings embrace Orthodox Christianity
Mongol rule	1240-1340	Rule by Ghengis Khan and his heirs
Grand Duchy of Muscovy	1340-1584	Expansion and rise of the tsars
Time of Troubles	1584-1613	Extensive political chaos
Romanov dynasty	1613-1917	Influence of Western European aesthetics
Revolution of 1917	1917 CE	Massive political change and new concepts of Russian identity
Communist period (U.S.S.R.)	1917-1991	Socialist realism in the arts
World War II	1941-1945	Catastrophic destruction and loss of life during and after the war
Cold War	1947-1991	Dance diplomacy in cultural Cold War between U.S.S.R. and the U.S.
Collapse of the U.S.S.R.	1991	Economic and political turmoil with cultural impacts
The Russian Federation	1991-present	An increasingly authoritarian state and a political rival to the United States and Europe

Dancers of the Igor Moiseyev Russian ballet.

FRANCOIS GUILLOT/AFP via Getty Images.

enthusiasts. It is more common to encounter the ethno identity dances and music performed by government-supported professional music and dance groups, such as the world-renowned Igor **Moiseyev Dance Company** or the **Pyatnitsky Choir** and its dance ensemble. The Soviet state considered original, authentic folk dances to be backward, so instead it promoted the idealized performances of the professional state ensembles.

One of the major results of the creation of ethno identity dance for professional and amateur performing ensembles is that regional differences in the field dances, like the traditional singing-circle/chain dances called *khorovod*, are lost and blurred. Only one model of "Russian" folk dance remains. In this case, the Moiseyev style of Russian dance becomes the iconic example with which most people today are familiar, featuring spectacular performances of women's gliding steps and men's athletic prowess. These endless displays of *prisiadkis* (high kicks) symbolically represent Russia as a young, powerful, athletic, and resilient nation.

A second issue in looking at Russian folk dance is to recognize that the land mass that constitutes today's Russian Federation stretches from the Baltic Sea to the Pacific Ocean and contains more than purely Russian culture. It has always, to this day, had relatively small, but important, non-Russian populations who speak other languages. All have their own dance and music traditions (Zhornitskaya 1998, 447-449; Zemtsovsky 2000).

 See resource 16.2 in HK*Propel* for web links.

Russian Folk Dances in the Field

One of the most typical and important aspects of most Russian traditional dancing is improvisation. Many individuals think that folk dance is handed down unchanged and unchanging through time, like an heirloom piece of jewelry. However, improvisation in most folk dances is a vital means of maintaining the dances as dynamic living parts of cultural expression (Shay 2019b).

Unlike dances found in the Balkans, which have a number of specific foot patterns that define its genre, much of Russian folk dance is almost wholly improvised, within specific stylistic parameters. In fact, entire genres, like spontaneous solo improvised *pliaska*, the pereplias competition dances (which dance historian Valeria Uralskaya characterizes as "outdo in dance" [1998, 444]), and ***chechyotka***, a type of rhythmic tap dancing, performed by male dancers that form part of *pliasky* (plural of "pliaska") emphasize this improvisational pattern. Improvisation is also found in many of the khorovod dances (round and circle dances). These are most often accompanied by singing, and sometimes instrumental music, while a dance leader improvises choreographic changes. Thus, spontaneity is an overarching aspect of traditional Russian folk dancing.

Dances of Peasants and Elites

As part of village life, peasants dance and make music as ritual, as well as for informal social gatherings. For example, as is true for most Slavic ethnic groups, weddings often feature a series of dances and songs performed in a particular order to ensure the happiness and fruitfulness of the ritual and the marriage. Social settings for dance include working bees, evening gatherings, and informal gatherings of young people.

The distance between the elite and the peasantry in Russia was much more blurred than in France or England where, for centuries, the elite performed different dances and listened to different music than the peasantry. In Russia, cultural differences between elites and peasants were much smaller and only changed to some degree in the 18th century when Peter the Great's westernizing project introduced Western music and dance for the elite but not the peasantry.

After this change, "The autochthonous [indigenous] music of Russia, the tonal products of the soil and its peasant denizens, were not admired and not discussed" (Taruskin 1997, xvi). However, the building of St. Petersburg threw together peasant and elite in the same milieu again, which had consequences for later Russian classical music, since the classical musicians were always surrounded by folk music whose themes sometimes appeared in their compositions. "The most immediate musical consequence of the Petrine reforms was the sudden mass transplantation of folk song, together with its singers, into Peter's newly created metropolis on the Neva" (a river) (Taruskin 1997, 19). This transplantation had important implications for the dances that people perform, as well. As historian Orlando Figes notes in his analysis of a scene in Tolstoy's ***War and Peace***, the heroine—Countess Natasha Rostov—joins in a peasant dance, in which she executes an improvisational pliaska like a native peasant maiden (2002, xxv-xxvi). The fictional countess was not the only noblewoman to dance rustic dances. After the French invasion in the **War of 1812**, when Russian nationalism was on the rise following Napoleon's ignominious retreat, "Recreations were going Russian, too. At balls in Petersburg, where European dances had always reigned supreme, it became the fashion to perform the *pliaska* and other Russian dances after 1812" (Figes 2002, 105). The Russian elite and urban dwellers retained a deep and abiding love for the countryside, its music, and its dance as part of their growing Russian identity.

 See resource 16.3 in HK*Propel* for web links.

Three Russian Folk Dances

There are three basic genres of Russian folk dances: khorovod (circle/chain dance), improvised solo dancing (pliasky; pliaska), and patterned dances, of which the most popular are many variants of the European **quadrille** (*kadril*) (Tkachenko 1954, 15). Russian ethnomusicologist Izaly Zemtsovsky recognizes several dance traditions: individual dancing, "*pliasky*, accompanied by instrumental *ostinato* [continuous rhythm] dance tunes (***naigryt*** 'dance until you drop' which I refer to as *pereplias*); and collective circle and figure dances (sing. *khorovod*, ***tanok***, pl. ***krugi*** 'circles') accompanied by the dancers' singing and/or, in the late twentieth century, instrumental music" (2000, 769). It is likely that Zemtsovsky ignores the patterned dances (like the widespread quadrille) as foreign in origin and therefore not indigenous forms.

Khorovod (Circle/Chain Dance)

As with many forms of folklore, Russian dances demonstrate layers of different historical periods, the oldest level of which is the khorovod. This dance—like the **medieval carole**—is generally performed with simple steps (often a gliding walk), and the performers sing as they dance. Singing by the participants is one of the most important elements of the khorovod, often aligned with seasonal and calendric rites. "It is widely believed that *khorovod* songs and, linked to them, dance songs, emerged from **calendar ritual songs**" (Prokhorov 2002, 8). Yet in several khorovod choreographed by **Igor Moiseyev**, the dancers never sing, and the dance is performed solely to instrumental music. In 1948, **Nadezhda Nadezhina** founded and became choreographer for the female dance ensemble **Beryozka**, which specialized in staged versions of khorovod without singing.

Medieval Carole Dance

The khorovod is an example of the old medieval carole dancing, a kind of walking dance with singing, in which the singing and folk poetry are as important as the movements of the dance. The form exists throughout Eastern Europe. Though seemingly out of fashion in Western Europe by the 1400s, its legacy persisted throughout the continent and in the use of the term *carol* for songs of the Christmas season.

Complexities of Khorovod

There are also complex khorovods with many figures, such as passing under the arms of two of the dancers, or the ***zmeyka*** (snake), in which the leader of the dance creates a serpentine figure, especially in a large space such as a field or through the central road of a village. "However, whereas in content the [khorovods] are richer than the couple and solo dances, their technique is poorer inasmuch as every dancer is willy-nilly compelled to coordinate his movements with those of his partners. Hence complicated movements requiring individual skill are hardly ever used" (Iving 1947, 140). There is generally a dance leader who creates the degree of complexity of the dance. Some khorovods are performed only by female dancers, and others are mixed sex. We know that this is one of the oldest layers of dance because it is widespread among other Slavic and East European peoples, as well. Another sign of

its historical depth is that "Most often, the entire *khorovod* forms a circle in which the participants hold hands, or the ends of cloths they carry, or sometimes their hands are left free" (Tkachenko 1954, 16). This links the Russian khorovod to a number of European dances, from the **Faroe Islands** (Denmark) to Greece, in which dancers use simple steps and sing—hallmarks of their common ancestry in the ancient medieval carole.

Khorovod Variations

The khorovod, especially given its historic depth, can be considered a complex of dances with many variations and different local styles. Sometimes, the khorovod takes the form of a pantomime party game where some or all of the participants mime the themes of the accompanying song, which often feature agricultural movements. Other themes that abound are about the meeting of a bride and groom, quarreling and making up, and the treatment of a husband by his wife. Some khorovod songs and accompanying movements are about animals or birds. "Utyona," for example, is about how a duck swims, floats, and makes a nest (Tkachenko 1954).

Zemtsovsky notes of the khorovod that "in some places, a *khorovod* is performed exclusively by girls, and elsewhere girls are the main performers, sometimes paired with bachelors" (769). The characterization of the khorovod as a female-dominated choreographic genre fits with the way in which singing circle dances are performed in much of Eastern Europe, often with miming movements, either by soloists or the whole group. One signature characteristic of Russian khorovods is that "sometimes the dance rhythms and the song rhythms create polyrhythmic effects" (Zemtsovsky 769). Khorovods were performed both inside and outside, depending on the weather. "In addition to its entertainment value, *khorovods* were believed to influence magically the harvest of flax and hemp" (Zemtsovsky 769). Thus, the khorovod serves in both secular and sacred events, creating one of the most basic and varied of Russian folk dance traditions.

Solo Improvised Dances

Solo improvised dances could take the form of competition, known as pereplias or *naigryt*, as described in the opening vignette. In the competitive *pereplias* (meaning "to outdo in dance"), "two men, surrounded by their male companions,

A performance of the Igor Moiseyev Russian ballet ensemble.

MLADEN ANTONOV/AFP via Getty Images.

alternated in performing increasingly difficult step combinations (*kolentsa*, literally 'knee joints,' meaning 'tricks') until one of the dancers emerged victorious. Then someone else challenged the winner with new combinations, and the competition continued" (Uralskaya, 444). Young women also did solo improvised dances, sometimes dancing within the khorovod and executing the mimetic movements of the song. In addition to the steps, "Movements of the arms are important, especially in dances for women. All gestures should be soft and flowing. The play of the arms, neck, and shoulders is a key to the mood of the dance" (Uralskaya 1998, 445).

Among the movements in khorovods and solo improvised dances, dance scholar Uralskaya (1998, 445) describes three common steps:

1. Simple, slow, measured, rhythmic steps with alternating right and left feet.
2. A small stamping step. Before stepping forward, the heel brushes the floor from back to front.

3. Changing step. Three steps are performed on the first three eighth notes of 2/4 music. The fourth eighth note is a pause that prepares for the next combination of three steps. The basic three-step has a multitude of versions, such as putting the legs together before moving out, stepping on demi-pointe, adding a small jump, or stamping on the floor.

Patterned Dances and Quadrille

The most recent layer of dances is patterned dances, such as the widespread quadrille. "Of the social forms of folk dance, quadrilles were common in Russia at the end of the seventeenth and the beginning of the eighteenth century" (Uralskaya 1998, 445). Instead of having four couples, a format with which many people in the West are familiar, Russian quadrilles featured as many as 8 or 16 couples. Typically, quadrilles have four, five, or six figures. Each figure has its own musical motif and can be musically accompanied either by accordion or singing (Tkachenko 1954, 16). Some of the quadrilles took on regional characteristics. For example, the Ural region quadrille ended each figure with a stamp or a clap, which makes it distinctive from other regions among the quadrille genre.

Quadrilles, like khorovods and the lyrical dance tradition, have a local and regional character (Tkachenko 1954, 17). Among the quadrilles, Russians perform "The **Lancers**," which was popular in Europe and North America in the 19th century. Quadrilles come from the dancing masters of the elite classes of that period; however, so popular is the quadrille that "scores have been created by the people themselves," generating new forms and content vastly different from that of old quadrilles (Tkachenko). The quadrille is the main figure dance of certain minorities, as among the **Sami**, a reindeer-herding group found in Finland and **Karelia** in northwest Russia.

 See resource 16.4 in HK*Propel* for web links.

Russian Ethno Identity Dance

In 1937, the Moiseyev Dance Company (now Moiseyev Ballet) was officially established as the **State Academic Folk Dance Ensemble of the Peoples of the U.S.S.R.** Its founder, Igor Moiseyev (1906-2007), was trained as a ballet dancer in the **Bolshoi Ballet**, where he performed as a soloist and choreographer in his younger years. The world-famous dance company that bears his name still flourishes. One of the main goals of this company was to participate in the 1930s-era artistic endeavors to valorize and promote Russian national and ethnic identity through language and folklore. To achieve this, he created a new theatricalized dance style and genre that was more aligned with ballet character dance than it was with authentic folklore. His genre combined elements of ballet technique, character dance, dance in the field, and heavy dollops of athletic and gymnastic feats. Moiseyev "believed that a professional group's rendering of a folk dance ought to be quite different from its performance by the people. To deliberately stress this difference became one of his aesthetic principles" (Chudnovsky 1959, 29). Thus, although

both were called "folk dance," "Moiseyev is against *literal* transplantation of the folk dance to the stage" (Chudnovsky 1959, 28, emphasis in the original). Igor Moiseyev intended to create a new dance genre. The traditional solo improvised dance, which may be performed individually by several soloists or couples, can be highly competitive. "The movements of young men demonstrate strength, adroitness and passion; he dances intricate stamping, clapping, and jumping (***prisyadkas***) showing his mastery" (Tkachenko 1954, 16). Moiseyev made his trademark of the Moiseyev Dance Company with the spectacular, virtuosic *prisyadkas* (squat-kicks), coffee grinders, and barrel rolls included in most of his dances, which have awed audiences for nearly a century. It is this athletic component that left the most long-lasting impressions on the viewers. "His dancers, especially the men, could without exaggeration be described as sensational, capable of executing an exhausting number of split jumps, turns on the head or forearm, and, of course, the signature step in which legs are kicked out from a squatting position—the *prisyadka*" (Reynolds and McCormick 2003, 254). Moiseyev utilized every possible athletic step in Russian folk dance to create and spectacularize his new invented tradition (Hobsbawm and Ranger 1983).

The most important link between character dance and Moiseyev's new invented tradition of Russian folk dance was the belief in "informed character," sometimes referred to as "national" dance, and that the choreographer (called at that time the "ballet master") had the ability to distill the essence of a "national character" into two or three characteristics that would be recognizable to the audience as the essential "Russian," "Polish," or "Hungarian" character. Typical of the characterizations of his Russian dances, it was said that the ***Russian Suite*** "reflects all that is best in the Russian character—its fervour and reserve, modesty and recklessness, pride and a sense of humour. Take any part of the *Russian Suite* and you will see a new facet of the national character" (Ilupina and Luskaya 1966, 11).

Russian ethno identity dance is widespread. It is found in professional and amateur ensembles that one sees in Russia as a tourist. In concert stages around the world, companies such as the Moiseyev Dance Company, the Siberian-Omsk Folk Chorus Beryozka, and Pyatnitsky Choir and dance ensembles perform them. They're also found in online videos and in adaptations in Hollywood films and Broadway musicals. While the steps that Valeria Uralskaya describes in her article in the *International Encyclopedia of Dance* are a feature of traditional in-the-field dance, they can also be seen in Moiseyev performances, but their performance in the ethno identity form is spectacularized and smoothed over with professionalism. These steps are useful to move large numbers of dancers during staged presentations. The viewer of Moiseyev's work will note that stylized Russian arm movements provide the "Russian" feeling in his choreographies, and while they are related to ballet *port de bras* (arm movements), they are distinctly different.

In the former Soviet Union, art was only useful if it could be harnessed to support the state, and the government authorities were not interested in the backward folklore of the old women still left in the villages—they wanted "improved" folk dances. Igor Moiseyev and all others involved in the creation of "improved" folk dances fulfilled this goal, and the state rewarded them for their creations (Shay 2019a).

Cultural Cold War

The Cold War rivalry between the Soviet Union and the West extended to every aspect of the society, including cultural products. As the first state-supported folk dance company in the world, the Moiseyev Dance Company launched the **cultural Cold War** in the 1950s with performances in London, in Paris, and throughout the United States. It became the model for other national folk dance ensembles, such as Ballet Folklorico de Mexico, Bayanihan of the Philippines, and Mazowsze of Poland, among dozens of others.

Popularity of Russian Folklore

The appeal of the new government-controlled folk dance in the former Soviet Union "can best be explained by the popularity of folklore throughout Russian society, which has traditionally accorded special status to professional folk performers" (Miller 1990, 4). Folk singers and dancers were popular as performers among the Red Army during World War II, and the Moiseyev Dance Company traveled throughout that period to entertain the troops in a way that would be incomprehensible to many people in the West (Stites 1995). That popularity continues today because Russian folklore is linked to Russian national identity. But since the 1930s, Russian folk dance had to be state-sanctioned.

"The revival of folk music [and dance] that was viciously assaulted during the [Russian] Cultural Revolution [of the 1920s] therefore became a natural part of the 1930s normalisation in culture. Its peasant content, though stylized, reinforced love of the land and thus of the nation or **narod** [its people]. . . . Folklorism—i.e., political folk adaptation—became a major industry in the Stalin era. Folk music and dance came back into favour on the wave of the Stalin's '**Great Retreat**,' a campaign to preserve or revive certain elements of Russian history and culture" (Stites 2004, 25). At the same time, non-Russian forms like ballet were privileged over Russian folklore, so it is understandable why Stalin loved what Moiseyev did with Russian folk dance.

Dance Promotion and Education

Like much folklore, in general, Russian dances are not frozen, museum-like artifacts, but living phenomena that change with contemporary needs. Part of that change came about through the intervention and support of the government, the support of amateur groups, and the establishment of professional folk song and dance ensembles. Tens of thousands of groups were established throughout the country. "As a result of the emphasis given to national cultures in the mid-1930s, folk dance groups sprouted in hundreds of towns and cities, with even the NKVD [Soviet national law enforcement agency] having its own Song and dance Ensemble. . . . In 1956, 3,000,000 people were reported to have taken part in the preliminary contests in the U.S.S.R." (Swift 1968, 241).

Another feature of folk dance in the former Soviet Union, not only in Russia, was that many new dances were "created." This became a feature of each of the Soviet Republics. Igor Moiseyev, for example, to represent the state of **Belarus**, created the choreography **bulba** (potato), which depicted the planting, growth, and harvesting, "and the happiness of the people over a plentiful harvest" (*Moiseyev Dance Company* np.). The region subsequently adopted Moiseyev's choreography as the official representation of Belarus. Agricultural dances like bulba became a feature of all the state-supported folk dance ensembles of the Soviet Union, further ratifying the connection between national identity and folklore.

 See resource 16.5 in HK*Propel* for web links.

Cultural Highlight

INSPIRED BY MOISEYEV

Seeing the Moiseyev Dance Company on their visit to the United States in 1958 moved me very deeply, and it planted the seed for founding my own dance company two years later, the UCLA Village Dancers. The Moiseyev event was the first performance in the newly minted cultural exchange program established between the United States and the Soviet Union. Inspired by the scope and professionalism of Moiseyev and other Eastern European touring ensembles I had seen, I envisioned creating a large company with one hundred dancers, singers and musicians. I began my first attempts at choreography with dances from Iran and Turkey, and the choreographic models from the professional companies like the Moiseyev Dance Company would not work for dances from the Middle East. I had to develop unique works, but I wanted to have the professional level of performance and the authoritative look of those professional companies. The company I founded eventually became AVAZ International Dance Theatre.

Crosscurrents

Throughout the former Soviet Union and continuing into the post-U.S.S.R. period, special schools for dance (and other art forms), grades 1-12, were designed to train children to dance both ballet and staged traditional folk dance. The ballet course was eight years, and the folk dance course was five years. After graduation, the various dance companies would select the best students for professional careers. The Moiseyev Dance Company had its own school, and 95 percent of their performers came from the company school. Through this education system and other venues, many young people today are involved in performing and learning Russian folk songs and dances. Some of them emulate the Moiseyev Dance Company, while others perform a more authentic type of folklore. The government provides funding and rehearsal spaces for many of these groups. As with the education and professional systems, much of this amateur activity began during the Soviet period and continued into the post-Soviet period. Because the historical impact of Russian dance has long extended beyond Russia, it is not surprising that folk dance—so well-supported and promoted by the state—should have a significant effect on folkloric dance around the world.

Largely due to the national and international successes of the Moiseyev Dance Company, and, in the case of Eastern Europe, partly falling in line with the organizational structures of the powerful Soviet Union, large state folk dance ensembles based on the model of the Moiseyev Dance Company rose to prominence in many countries around the world, including the United States of America.

Post-Soviet Union Russian Village Folk Festival

Young enthusiasts reacted to the state-supported Russian packaging of ethno identity dances by going to villages to seek the "real" Russian dances and music (Olson 2004). After the fall of the Soviet Union, a program featuring the authentic music and dance of seven Russian villages toured the United States. In 1997 this Russian Village Folk Festival was hosted at UCLA.

 See resource 16.6 in HK*Propel* for web links.

Summary

Authentic Russian folk dances, especially the khorovod, are ancient. Though their origins are lost in time, they are still danced, largely in rural areas and small towns. The khorovod is probably the most ancient dance form and was among the dances performed all over Europe in the Middle Ages, and perhaps earlier. It is a successor to the carole (as in Christmas carol), in which the dancers use simple walking steps to move in a circle while singing ballads with many verses. The various Russian folk dances can be divided into two types: group dances like the khorovod

213

and quadrille, and solo improvised dancing like pliaski and pereplias. Under the former Soviet Union, the government sponsored several dance and music ensembles to perform staged folk dances (ethno identity dances) for entertaining local audiences and as diplomatic representatives of the nation. After the collapse of the Soviet Union, the Moiseyev Dance Company continues to represent the Russian Federation around the world.

Discussion Questions

1. What is ethno identity dance, and why did the Soviet Union prefer this style of dance over authentic folk dance?
2. What is improvisation in traditional dance and why is it important?
3. What part did dance play in the cultural Cold War from the Russian perspective, and why?

 Visit HK*Propel* for access to this chapter's Application Activity.

Selected Glossary

Belarus—Belarus, meaning *White Russia*, is the region, now an independent state, between Russia and Poland. The Belarus people (Belarusians) are Eastern Slavs; they speak a language so close to Russian that it is almost a dialect rather than a separate language. The capital city is Minsk.

beryozka/Beryozka Dance Company—Literally "birch tree"; the name of a professional folk dance company whose choreographer is Nadezhda Nadezhdina; "Beryozka" is the title of the company's signature khorovod, in which the female dancers carry birch branches.

Bolshoi Ballet—The Bolshoi Ballet, named for the "great" (*bolshoi*) Bolshoi Theatre in Moscow in which they perform, is one of the most famous ballet companies in the world. The other famous Russian ballet company is the Kirov Ballet (Mariinsky Ballet), located in St. Petersburg.

calendar ritual songs—Folk songs that are attached to a specific ritual holiday, just as "Jingle Bells" is sung only at Christmas.

cultural Cold War—The Cold War rivalry (1947-1991) between the Soviet Union and the West extended into all areas of society, including cultural products such as dance.

ethno identity dances—A term created by dance scholar Anthony Shay in 2014 to distinguish folk dances in the field from staged dances that are prepared for performance. Authentic folk dances refer to specific ethnic groups and are based on or inspired by dances in the field.

folk dances in the field—The term coined by dance scholar Theresa J. Buckland to indicate authentic folk dances that people, especially peasants and tribal peoples, perform as part of their lives. These are in contrast to ethno identity dances prepared for the stage.

Igor Moiseyev (1906-2007)—Moiseyev was trained and performed in the Bolshoi Ballet, and in 1937 he founded and directed the State Academic Ensemble of Folk Dances of the Peoples of the Union of Soviet Socialist Republics, which is more commonly known in the West as the Moiseyev Dance Company.

khorovod—A round dance containing many figures and regional styles. It is the oldest of the Russian folk dances and is generally accompanied by singing.

Moiseyev Dance Company—Founded by **Igor Moiseyev** in 1937; the first state-supported, official representative of the former Soviet Union, and later the Russian Federation.

Pyatnitsky Choir/Pyatnitsky Russian Folk Chorus—Founded in 1910 by Mitrofan Pyatnitsky, who presented a group of peasants singing authentic Russian folk songs; the vocal version of the Moiseyev Dance Company. Also spelled *Piatnitski* or *Pyatnitskii*.

sedelki—An informal village gathering to relax, eat, drink, sing, and dance; from the Russian verb "to sit."

socialist realism—The concept upon which all Russian music, dance, literature, and visual art were based during Joseph Stalin's authoritarian rule (1924-1953).

Selected References and Resources

Buckland, T.J. 1999. "Introduction." In *Dance in the Field: Theory, Methods, and Issues in Dance Ethnography*, edited by T.J. Buckland, 1-10. New York: St. Martin's Press.

Chudnovsky, M.A. 1959. *Folk Dance Company of the U.S.S.R.: Igor Moiseyev, Art Director*. Moscow: Foreign Languages Publishing House.

Figes, O. 2002. *Natasha's Dance: A Cultural History of Russia*. New York: Picador.

Ichikawa, K. 1989. *The JVC Video Anthology of World Music and Dance: Russia*. Multicultural Media. https://clarkuniversity.on.worldcat.org/oclc/1048450106.

Prokhorov, V. 2002. *Russian Folk Songs: Musical Genres and History*. New York: Scarecrow Press.

Shay, A. 2002. *Choreographic Politics: State Folk Dance Companies, Representation and Power*. Middletown, CT: Wesleyan University Press.

Shay, A. 2019a. *The Igor Moiseyev Dance Company: Dancing Diplomats*. Bristol, UK: Intellect Books.

Shay, A. 2019b. "In the Moment: Improvisation in Traditional Dance." In *The Oxford Handbook of Improvisation in Dance*, edited by V.L. Midgelow, 705-718. New York: Oxford University Press.

Shay, A. 2021. *Dance and Authoritarianism: These Boots Are Made for Dancing*. Bristol, UK: Intellect Books.

Stites, R. 1995. "Frontline Entertainment." *Culture and Entertainment in Wartime Russia*, edited by R. Stites. Bloomington: Indiana University Press.

Stites, R. 2004. "The Ways of Russian Popular Music to 1953." In *Soviet Music and Society Under Lenin and Stalin: The Baton and Sickle*, 19-32. London and New York: Routledge.

Taruskin, R. 1997. *Defining Russia Musically: Historical and Hermeneutical Essays*. Princeton: Princeton University Press.

Uralskaya, V.I. 1998. "Russia: Traditional Dance." *International Encyclopedia of Dance, Vol. 5*, 443-445. New York: Oxford University Press.

Zemtsovsky, I. 2000. "Russia." *The Garland Encyclopedia of World Music, Vol. 8: Europe*, edited by T. Rice, J. Porter, and C. Goetzen, 754-789. New York: Garland Publishing.

Zhornitskaya, M.I. 1979. "The Study of Folk Dancing in the Soviet Union: Its State and Tasks." In *The Performing Arts: Music and Dance*, edited by J. Blacking and J.W. Kealiinohomoku, 79-96. The Hague: Mouton Publishers.

PART VI

Middle East

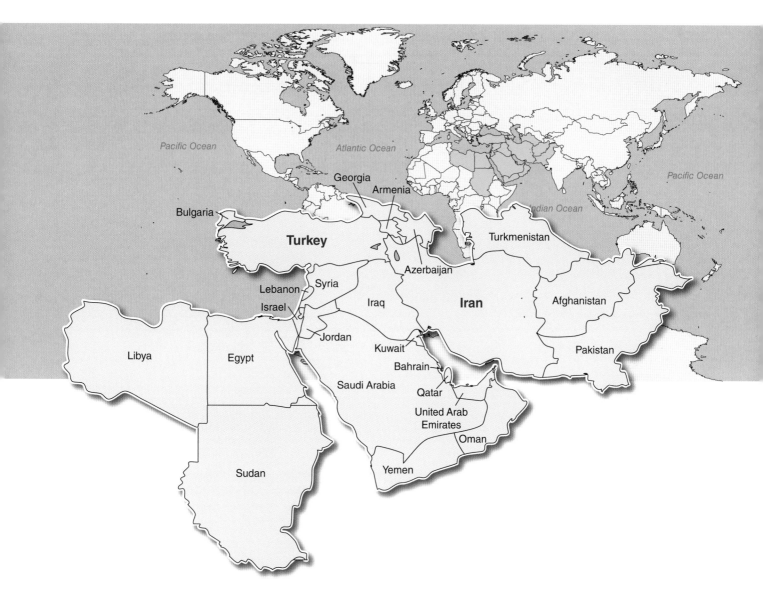

The Middle East is largely characterized by the presence and influences of Abrahamic religions—Islam, Judaism, and Christianity, with varying degrees of secular culture along with other localized religious traditions. The two countries discussed in part VI, though they share a border and responded to similar historical forces, present very different cultures of dance. Religious and political dynamics have operated differently in each country to yield this result. As with Europe and Russia, the major forces at play included the spread of the Ottoman Empire and World Wars I and II, along with Western European influences as empires shifted and the secular, Western cultures became more prominent, exemplifying modernity. Additional complexities have been brought about by theocratic governments throughout history and into the present. Technology has proven to be a significant player in the dance cultures, altering the dynamics of cultural relevance by enhancing cross-cultural and diasporic effects. Despite religious constraints on viewing and participating in dance, especially for women, the proliferation of video technology in the mid-to-late 20th century and the development of the Internet thereafter provided unprecedented opportunities for dance to be seen and shared. As a result, the active participation in a given dance culture is no longer bound to the land of its origin, sometimes becoming a larger presence in exile than within the country.

 HK*Propel* includes web links to additional resources for this section.

17

Dance Cultures of Turkey

Zeynep Gonca Girgin

Learning Objectives

After reading this chapter you will be able to do the following:

- Understand relationships between dance and the history and culture of Turkey.
- Identify and label key factors in the history of dance cultures in Turkey, noting why these factors operate as they do.
- Compare and contrast social and artistic stage formations in dance cultures of Turkey.
- Analyze the historical, religious, political, and geographical dynamics as they affect the dance culture.
- Take general understanding from the specifics of dance cultures in Turkey and apply this understanding to other dance cultures.

Key Terms

alafranga and alaturka—Terms indicating the two major parts of cultural repertory in modern Turkey, "westernized" (*alafranga*) and "like Turk" (*alaturka*).

artistic stage—Staged performances. The term *folk dance* refers to social dance, but "Turkish folk dance" means staged artistic performances.

folklor oynamak—"To dance folklore," the overall folk dance activity in the 1960s and 1970s of Turkey.

hybrid aesthetic or **hybrid dance aesthetics**—Multisourced hybrid choreographies and performances throughout the 2000s in Turkey.

Turkish folk dance—An official performance of folk dances, framed by Turkish republican politics.

Debates on Turkish Ballet Over the Years

In 1965, the ballet *Çeşmebaşı* (*At the Fountain*) was choreographed by Dame **Ninette de Valois**, founder of the British Royal Ballet, who had come to Turkey in 1947 to establish the nation's first state-run ballet institutions. De Valois's choreography highlighted a Western European view of Turkish culture, rather than an **Anatolian** (Ancient Turkish) one. However, *Çeşmebaşı* was set to the music of Turkish composer Ferit Tüzün's *Anatolian Suite*, used folk dance steps, and even incorporated **Turkish shadow theater** (Karagöz-Hacivat) to create a recognizably Turkish atmosphere for the otherwise European classical ballet (Başar 2018). Turkish critics responded favorably, saying that the dance "looks pretty much like us on the stage, you cannot watch it without gushing" (Sağdıç 1965, 24). At its core, however, the ballet remained a European construct.

By 1991, political shifts created a push for more genuinely Turkish creations and the Minister of Cultural Affairs deemed that ballet dancers should learn "our national rhythms." On the heels of this decree, ballerinas of the State Ballet Ensemble of Turkey found a traditional *davul* (hanging drum) player in their rehearsals for a new, truly Turkish ballet. "The following day's newspapers gave broad coverage to the event, displaying on their front-page ballerinas crying in shock, despair, and humiliation" (Öztürkmen 2001, 139). By 1998, however, the shock had worn off and the State Ballet Ensemble of Ankara's performance of *The Harem*, a ballet with a fully Turkish theme and set to classical Turkish Art Music, was playing to full houses. *Harem* was seen as "the first Turkish ballet example that narrates its history by its own instruments" (Kalyoncuoğlu 2019).

 See resource 17.1 in HK*Propel* for web links.

Introducing the dance cultures in Turkey through ballet is fairly ironic. However, these examples, though couched in ballet, accurately reflect political and ideological modulations in traditional folk dance, religious movement systems, and popular dances, as well as ballet history in Turkey. To be specific, "traditional" concepts are usually associated with Turkish political power, while "modern" ones are usually associated with Western European standards. In this way, the history of ballet in Turkey is not only crucial in terms of early politics of modernity and westernization in the Republic of Turkey, but it is also crucial for exposing the new national view of neoliberalism that developed during the 1980s.

Brief History

The **Republic of Turkey** derives its name from the states of Turks (Turkish people) and has described the nation since the end of the **Ottoman Empire** in 1923. Turks as a distinct people lived in Central Asia from 2000 BCE and settled on the Anatolian plateau (in modern Turkey), later establishing states and empires independent from each other within a vast area of Asia and Europe. "Anatolian Turkey possesses a rich and splendid vocabulary of gestures and movements

of dances . . . created by the separate traditions and ultimate blending of five great cultural trends over a period of 900 years" (And 1976, 6). Ancient Anatolian culture was shaped by neighboring civilizations, including Greek and Byzantine. Asian culture is the second influence. The third influence is Islamic culture, with the 11th-century arrival of the Turks. Fourth, the highly influential Ottoman Empire period covered the 15th through 19th centuries. The current modern republican period began with Turkish independence in 1923 and has continued to the present with many shifts along the spectrum between conservatism and liberalism, religious fundamentalism and secularization.

Historically, dance is an inseparable part of social and ritualistic life in Turkish culture, illuminating concepts and metaphorical meanings that have carried through from the Ottoman Empire to the present. Table 17.1 presents a time line of dance in modern Turkey.

Ottoman Period

Raks (Arabic, meaning "motion") was the term used for dance during Ottoman times. These movement systems can be classified as religious practice performances, professional dances in urban life, and local dances in rural life. The main

Table 17.1   Time Line of Dances in Modern Turkey

Era	Folk dance categories	Classical dances	Religious movement systems	Popular dances
Late Ottoman period				
Westernization (end of 19th century	First milli raks, Tarcan Zeybeği, 1909	Non-religious urban practices (Çengi-Köçek)	Whirling dervishes (Sema)	(Raks)
Republicacan period				
Nationalism, westernization, modernity 1920s	First collections, Halkevleri and national bayram performances	Classical ballet performance and training in Istanbul, Institutionaliza-tion of ballet in Ankara (1948)	First sema public performance of republican period (1943), semah in ritual occasions	Jazz, waltz, tango, foxtrot, Charleston
Liberal economy, heritage tourism 1950s	Creation of "Turkish folk dance," to dance folklore; folklore market	National ballet choreographies, Keloğlan (1950), Çeşmebaşı (1965), Hürrem Sultan (1976)	Sema and semah performances in heritage tourism	Western steps, rock 'n' roll, twist, çiftetelli, belly dance, Greek sirtaki
Neoliberal economy, new conservative nationalism, globalization 1980s	Identities in Turkish folk dance repertory, like Romani/Gypsy case	Institutionalization of modern dance (1992).	Expanded public visibility of semah and sema, especially in touristic and cultural represen-tations	Cultural jungle; disco dance, pop dance, lambada, breaking, belly dance, Gypsy/Romani dance
Globalization 2000s	Hybrid aesthetic; Sultans of the Dance		UNESCO	Hybrid aesthetic; Sultans of the Dance, fetishism on Romani dance, belly dance. New regional choreographies, kolbastı, "Erik Dalı"

historical references to professional urban and religious movement systems are their portrayals in miniature paintings (Öztürkmen 2016). A look at two different dancing traditions for the nonreligious urban practice is illustrative: *çengi* and *köçek*.

Court Dancers: Çengi and Köçek

Since the 17th century, nonreligious urban performances in the court and in coffee houses refer to the çengi and köçek dancing traditions,

in which soloists entertained dignitaries at the court with dancing, singing, and instrument playing. While köçek performers are generally male, çengis are females and young boys. Documentation of entertainment life during Ottoman rule and in the capital city of Istanbul in the early republican period describe çengi and köçek dances as exotic "belly dancing, toe hits, shaking and backward-bending body, swaying of breasts, walking on the balls of the feet, swinging heads and waist" (Koçu 2002; Baykurt 1995; And 1976). However, the status of women in Islam certainly influenced köçek's development in male settings. "Whereas ancient Turkic communities had a very rich entertaintment culture and both sexes coexisted in entertainment settings as in other spheres of life, after the adoption of Islam and the new culture that came with it, sexes were spatially segregated, and coexistence was lost. Especially in all-male entertaintment settings, this loss was first compensated through the mimicry of female dancers by the male köçek performers; later the performances acquired functions that evoked sexuality" (Beşiroğlu and Girgin 2018, 47).

 See resource 17.2 in HK*Propel* for web links.

Traditional Folk Dance

In Turkey, "**Turkish folk dances**" are official performances of folk dances under the auspices of republican politics. Consequently, there is a perceived difference between traditional "folk dances" and "Turkish folk dances"; the former are social events and the latter are performed on the **artistic stage**. As folk dances were regularized and set in geometric patterns for the stage, regional and other distinctions between various folk dance traditions became blurred. (Öztürkmen 2001). However, such distinctions are more easily maintained in the social realm. While artistic stage performances create a push for formal learning to ensure consistency and build technique, traditional folk dances in social settings are different. These dances are performed on ritualistic occasions, such as birthdays, weddings, circumcision feasts, military celebrations, and festivals, and as general entertainment. The communal joy of these events allows people to absorb dances and dance steps without any official learning process.

Traditional Turkish Folk Dance Categories

Although folk dances in Turkey share several general characteristics, such as mimetic or representational versions, accompanying music and materials, and common religious or social orientations, they differ in terms of structure and form, setting, geography, and cross-generational aspects. Of particular significance, Islamic religious doctrines require separate dances for women and men, keeping women associated with the domestic and interior space while men are free to engage with the outside world, both literally and symbolically. Table 17.2 illustrates the range of dances you might encounter throughout Turkey.

The Concept of Turkish Folk Dance: First Choreographies (1923-1950)

During the republican times, **Selim Sırrı Tarcan** (1874-1956), founder of Turkey's National Olympic Committee, used the term ***milli raks*** (national dance). Milli raks is exemplified by the dance ***Tarcan Zeybeği***, which reestablished traditional ***zeybek*** dance motifs in a national context, further shaped by Tarcan's personal experiences studying physical education in Sweden in 1909. The national context here engages central Asian and Anatolian folklore through a modernized concept of the body.

The formalization of folk dance in Turkey began under the ***Halkevleri*** (local cultural centers or "people's houses"). In the 1930s, the Halkevleri identified local dances for sponsorship by the **Cumhuriyet Halk Partisi** (Republican People's Party). In the early republican period, dances were collected and classified by geographic regions, not by ethnic origins. These dances in villages and towns were performed by local people at domestic celebrations, such as national holidays (e.g., Republic Day on October 29, Youth and Sports Day on May 19) and local festivals, including those hosted by the Halkevleri. The regional and local characteristics of these dances were faithfully maintained by using their original music and instrumentation, ensuring a diversity of representation even as the dances were elevated to national prominence. Local dances were performed not only by local practitioners, but also by nonlocal students who learned these dances at their educational institutions. As a result, the 1930s and 1940s were the years when the tradition of performing folk dances took on the additional role of promoting national identity.

The role of women was also shifting during this early republican era; the linkage of traditional dances with national identity joined with the focus on secularization and westernization to reshape perspectives on women's dances. In addition to staging women's dances that reflected

Table 17.2   Select Traditional Turkish Folk Dances

Dance	Description
Bar ("shamanic drum")	An open-area group dancing in a common public space. Music uses irregular rhythms.
Halay ("gathering")	Another open-area group dance similar to bar, but the music uses regular 2/4 or 4/4 meter.
Horon	Group dance in lines and circles. Music uses irregular and regular rhythms for different dances.
Hora	Group dance in lines and circles accompanied by instrumental music with irregular rhythmic structure.
Zeybek	Group circle dance without contact between dancers. Music is instrumental, with irregular rhythmic structure, commonly in 9/8.
Karşılama ("face-to-face")	A couple or group dance. Music uses irregular rhythms.
Çiftetelli ("two strings")	A solo or couple dance common all over Turkey. Music uses regular rhythms in vocal and instrumental accompaniment.
Kaşıklı oyunlar ("dancing with spoon")	Male, female, or mixed couple dance in a circle or a line without contact between dancers. Dancers use spoons as percussion instruments. Music uses regular rhythms.
Kılıç-Kalkan Oyunu ("sword and shield dances") and Bıçak Horonu ("knife dances")	Masculine, martial dances with props, representing prescriptive war scenes.

social life, the practice of women and men dancing together gained emphasis. Women's identity was highlighted not only in dance performances, but also in other arts, such as music and theater, in direct opposition to "the segregation norms (*haremlik-selamlık*) and gender practices that [were] dominant in small cities and towns" (Lamprou 2014, 8).

To Dance Folklore: Transition to Liberal Economy (1950s-1970s)

In 1951 the Halkevleri were closed, and the local dances of the towns shifted to big cities (such as Istanbul, Ankara, or Izmir) to be performed by students at newly private folk dance clubs. By popularizing folk dance practices as "cultural capital," folk dance competitions between schools proliferated, and the performance of folk dance spread throughout the country.

After the 1950s, different local dances from around the country were centralized and designated as "Turkish folk dances." In this period,

watching folk dance performance became popular entertainment, and folk dance activity was referred to as *folklor oynamak*—to dance folklore (Öztürkmen 2001).

During the 1950s and 1960s, folklor oynamak spurred a growth in tourism, and the grand folk dance market was developed by increasing stage performances, competitions, folk dance clubs, and educational programs in cities, reaching a peak by the 1970s. From 1977 onward, through government-sponsored competitions, new dances were added to the traditional repertory and the folklore market became bigger than ever.

The second major shift in the state-sponsored approach to dance occurred after 1970, when the Soviet Union's (Igor) Moiseyev Dance Company performed in Istanbul. Moiseyev was heralded for having revolutionized folk dance and for embodying the "New Soviet Man . . . the acrobatic, muscular builders of socialism" in the Soviet Union (Morrison 2015). A corresponding concept of the **"Turkish Man"** arose. Another point of influence was Moiseyev's appropriation of traditional folk dance repertory that represents a rich national culture. The Turkish **State Folk Dance Ensemble** (Devlet Halk Dansları Topluluğu) was founded in 1975, building a remarkable dance repertory "through the network of folk dance festivals and competitions [that had arisen since] the inception of the republic" (Shay 2002, 219). *Halays*, *bars*, zeybeks, and other dances were shaped into the new folk dance repertoire.

New Identities, Hybrid Aesthetic: New Nationalistic Perception (1980s-Present)

After the 1980 coup d'état, the cultural policies of the new liberal neoconservatisim approach appeared in the choreography of the Turkish State Folk Dance Ensemble. In 1983, the ensemble performed one of the most debated genres of dance history in Turkey, *çiftetelli* (belly dance), which was criticized for vulgarity, reference to Ottoman tradition, and links with the **Gypsy/Romani** culture (see Girgin 2015). Despite the belly movements and shoulder shimmying, çiftetelli is quite gentrified from the original belly dance, and the dancer's costume is completely concealing, creating an "amenable and professional version of *Çiftetelli*" (Shay 2002, 195). In that context, it is not a coincidence that çiftetelli choreographies were added to the State Folk Dance Ensemble repertoire. Çiftetelli carries the meaning of Turkish-Islamic woman's palace tradition to the stage, from both conservative and global perspectives.

In the 1990s, "Turkish identity" in folk dances became more flexible regarding identity politics and in conservative liberalization that emphasized the Ottoman past. For example, Gypsy/Romani dance motifs in çiftetelli and the **Thracian karşılama** (Thracian "face-to-face" dance) choreographies of the State Folk Dance Ensemble (and many other independent folk dance groups) echo the identity politics from the second half of the 1990s.

Concurrently, given the laissez-faire economy, the productions of a global-cultural industry gained extensive audiences in the 1990s through newly founded private radio and television studios. The first broadcast of the Irish *Riverdance* performance, choreographed by **Michael Flatley**, was at a **Eurovision Song Contest** in 1994. It kindled memories of the Moiseyev Dance Company's impact in the 1970s and predisposed Turkish dancers to the influence of Flatley's *Lord of the*

Dance later in the 1990s, spurring new performance models.

In 1999, the Turkish performance *Sultans of the Dance* initiated the trend of **hybrid dance aesthetics** (Dehmen 2001) that took hold in the 2000s. The new aesthetic view overlapped with a new multicultural identity and explained the current dance repertories' embrace of previously stigmatized dance genres such as belly dance and Gypsy/Romani dance.

 See resource 17.3 in HK*Propel* for web links.

Classical Dance

Classical dance is used to imply classical ballet and modern dance in Turkey. The adjective "classical" refers to Western European geography and culture, engaging the realities of westernization, Europeanization, and secularization. In Turkey, ballet education is an institution based on the aesthetics of European classical ballet, but it is framed by the endeavor to create a Turkish national ballet. On the other hand, since classical ballet is performative, not social, it emerges from educational institutions and a field of professional dancers equipped with technical knowledge, rather than cultural traditions. Thus, the meaning of Turkey's classical ballet history carries the meanings of classical ballet training history.

Classical Ballet

The famous national art historian and researcher **Metin And** (1927-2008) described ballet as a "newcomer" (And 1976). Indeed, it was only in 1948 that the ballet was institutionalized. Ninette de Valois, the founder of the British Royal Ballet, was invited to establish a ballet school in Turkey. In 1950, it was moved to the capital, to the **Ankara State Conservatory**, and soon grew to a capacity of a hundred students (And 1976, 167). Although ballet had been performed in the region as far back as the 16th century, ballet during the republican period was first introduced to Turkey by Russian dancer **Krassa Arzumanova**, who established a private ballet school in Istanbul in 1921. The 1931 and 1933 performances by her students are touchstones in Turkish ballet history.

In the republican period, synthesizing Eastern or Western with traditional or modern dominated the ballet repertory. In 1950, Ankara State Conservatory students performed their first ballet performance, ***Keloğlan*** ("Bald Boy"), which is based on a character from Turkish folklore and echoes this East-West traditional and modern dichotomy. The first graduates of the school established the core team of dancers, instructors, and choreographers at the State Theater and the Conservatory's Ballet Department (founded 1960) (Deleon 1992). Their first performance, the 1965 ballet mentioned in the opening vignette, *Çeşmebaşı* ("Top of Fountain"), was designed using national images: stylized costumes, ballet-like Turkish folk dance motifs, and characters of traditional **Turkish shadow theater** ("Karagöz-Hacivat") (Öztürkmen 2016).

The ballet prototypes of this period represented a European **Orientalist** view, and the "exotic" quality of choreographies continued in subsequent years if choreographers were Turkish—as an obvious example of **self-Orientalism**. In 1968, however, the Turkish State Ballet first performed an abstract work, ***Çark*** ("The Wheel"), by native choreographer Sait Sökmen, who was a soloist in the company (And 1976). In contrast with earlier works, this short "pure dance" ballet interprets musical dynamics within Ravel's String Quartet.

"It is possible to find different images of nationality" (Öztürkmen 2016, 46) in the choreographies of the State Ballet, which also staged many original ballets from the world classics repertoire: The culturally resonant elements—clues of the village, Anatolian culture, **meddah** (storyteller), folk dance motifs, and Ottoman Empire culture—comprise these national images. For example, the *Hürrem Sultan* ballet, which was staged in 1976, is about the palace intrigue of Haseki Sultan, wife of 16th-century Ottoman Sultan Süleyman I.

The emphasis on Ottoman history in the 1970s is evident in many areas, from national language policies to culture and art politics. Staged by the State Opera and Ballet since 1998, *The Harem* echoes the final state of the changing nationality content in the national ballet debate. It is conceived as "the first Turkish ballet that narrates its history by its own instruments" (Kalyoncuoğlu 2019). These instruments evoke Ottoman court and Middle Eastern music cultures, and were seen as the most effective way to anchor the ballet in Turkish culture.

Modern Dance

Institutionalization of modern dance is newer than the ballet in Turkey. It was initially added in 1992 to the **Mimar Sinan University State Conservatory** master's programs—opera, ballet, theater—as a section, and a modern dance ensemble was founded within the body of the **Ankara State Opera and Ballet** in the same period. Rather than focusing on a single artist's work, the ensemble's repertory consisted of pieces by different Turkish modern dance choreographers (Evci 2002). Earlier, in the 1920s, Selim Sırrı Tarcan's daughter **Selma Selim Sırrı** had introduced modern dance to Turkey as ***bedii raks*** (aesthetic dance). "Selma was interested in liberating her movement system as a young woman of the republic and she wanted to promote 'modern dance' as well as to give dance a respectable place in the nation-state" (Öztürkmen 2003).

Istanbul State Ballet performed a modern dance, *Seyahatname* ("Travel Log"), in 1992, based on the famous writings of a 17th-century Ottoman Turkish traveler. The dance contains images intrinsic to Turkey, such as the **slender teacup** and the *ney* instrument that is identified with music of the Islamic **Sufi** religion and motifs of **sema** (Sufi whirling dance) (Öztürkmen 2016). The emphasis on national themes occurred in private modern dance companies, too. **Turkuaz Dance Company** (1990-1993) is one of the early examples. It used belly dance rhythms (*Bir Rüya Gördüm*, "I dreamed a dream"), traditional Turkish woman narratives (*Son Bakış*, "Final Look"), and folk song rhythms (*Dejavu*).

 See resource 17.4 in HK*Propel* for web links.

Religious Movement Systems

Sufi Whirling Dervish Dance

Music and dance are the unapproved parts in Islamic thought, but when conceived as a religious movement system—that is, in the Sufi (Islamic philosophy) tradition—both gain acceptance as part of the ***ayin*** (ritual). Among the different sects of Sufism, the rituals of those associated with **Sunni** Islamic thought, or with **Alevilik** (Alevism) play a central role. Ideological conflicts between **Alevi** and Sunni adherents over the centuries of Ottoman rule and into the present day have shifted their dances (***semah*** and ***sema***) from a ritualistic context to public visibility. As a result, both the religious dances and the touristic performances create an environment of conflict that is at once a cause and a consequence of political history.

Semah

Semah ("listening") is a ritual dance of the Alevi community, crucial to their Islamic worship. However, among most Sunni groups, the Alevi communities were not deemed "proper Muslims," and their villages and neighborhoods were marked as "the other" (Öztürkmen 2005, 250). While Alevis do consider themselves Muslim, "the influences of Christianity, Shamanism, Buddhism, Manicheanism and prehistorical Anatolian religions" (Ocak 1996) have made their practices and views far more diverse than those of the Orthodox Sunnis.

Since the 16th century, women and men in Alevi communities have performed together in an important cultural ritual known as *cem* ("meeting"), an "Islamized form of religious rituals among Turkish nomads, especially Shamanist ones in Anatolia during pre-Islam" (Ocak 1996, 253). Cem rites reinforce unity and solidarity through the doctrines of Alevism, and are conducted by a *dede* (holy man) who belongs to a hereditary priestly caste. In Alevi terminology, the movement system is called *semah dönmek* ("to turn semah"), referring to the whirling individuals in the circular form of the group (Öztürkmen 2005, 252). As a structured movement system in both Sunni and Alevi traditions, the whirling emphasizes *devir* ("rotation") to express the reunion with God and symbolize a mortal journey in which nothing stands still but changes ceaselessly. The way of devir is *zikr* ("remembrance"), and music and dance are the central parts of the zikr. The cem ritual has regional variations that include references to local ways of subsistence—*tahtacı semahı* (dance of forestry workers)—or traces of shamanism: *turnalar semahı* (dance of the cranes) evokes the transformation of shamans into birds who take flight.

Sema

Sema is also a ritual dance like semah but related to the **Mevlevi** order, a different sect associated with Sufism that is aligned with teachings of the 13th-century mystic **Mevlana Celaleddin Rumi**. The ritual of the sect, Mevlevi Ayini (Mevlevi

ritual) consists of trances and ecstatic statements based on devir and zikr.

The ritual is commonly performed in the **Mevlevihane** (Mevlevi lodge) and starts with a poem known as *naat*, a style that praises the prophet Muhammad, sung a capella and composed by **Itri** (1640-1712, composer of Ottoman-Turkish music). **Taksim** (improvisation) is introduced by the ney (flute), and then a prelude is performed by all ritual musicians who play Ottoman court music instruments, such as **kanun**, **ud**, and **tambur** (stringed instruments), ney, and **kudüm** (small double drum). Sequentially, "the *sema* (whirling dance) is performed to music in four sections. . . . During the third [section] there is an increase in tempo and a slowing down during the fourth where an air of restraint is once again maintained by the **dervishes** as they end the dance" (Markoff 1995, 158). The whole ritual takes approximately two hours and is performed by male participants called **semazen**.

Public Performances and Politics of Sema and Semah

Whereas sema dances during the cem ritual are traditionally performed in the Mevlevihane and *tekke* (religious lodges, places of worship), over time audiences started to be admitted to these venues. By the late Ottoman period, the sema began turning into a public performance. When the tekkes were closed during the republican era, public viewings of sema dwindled until the ritual performances were revived in the Halkevleri starting in 1943 (Tarhan 2007). Over the next several decades, the Sufi whirling dervish dance rose in prominence as a representation of Ottoman and Turkish-Islamic legacy, both at home and abroad. After 1980, with the changing neoliberal policies, sema even joined the folk dance repertoire and fully entered the global market. Female performers were added to this men's dance during the 1990s, when it became a touristic form in all media and event venues, especially during religious holidays, such as **Ramadan**. In the 2000s, UNESCO added the whirling dervish ceremony to its Intangible Cultural Heritage list (Uyar 2009), while sema also developed further to unite fundamentalism and modernism as a wedding and celebration dance of Islamic families.

The semah of the Alevi communities followed a similar path to public visibility. The Alevis' inclusion of women in the public sphere and their use of Turkish language (rather than Sunni Islam) in their prayers aligned with the modernization efforts of the early republic. In the years following the 1980 coup, urban Alevi intellectuals began to write openly about their religious identity, and through the 1990s Alevi organizations rapidly emerged and expanded, providing sites of communal ritual expression in cities (Şahin 2005; Tambar 2010). Despite being sidelined as a "minority" group, their visibility grew as radio, television, and the Internet gave public voice to the Alevi communal expression, and the Turkish state's ongoing failure to adequately recognize Alevi ritual is cited as a blot on Turkey's efforts to join the European Union. In 2010, UNESCO added the **Alevi-Bektaşi** cem ceremony to its Intangible Cultural Heritage list, as semah continues its uneasy dance between the pressures of Islamic fundamentalism and the boom in the cultural industry.

 See resource 17.5 in HK*Propel* for web links.

Crosscurrents

There is no specific categorization of "popular urban dance" in Turkey's dance history, although such dances take place in the cities and have become widespread throughout the country. Popular dance is difficult to define, because it is not anchored to a geographic region, it contains little common sociological meaning to the dancers, and it is practiced in any medium where dance can exist. The content and visibility of some dances depend on the political and cultural climate. Prior to the rise of mass media—especially television—popular dance was identified with big cities like Istanbul but quickly spread more widely after 1975.

Until 1950s: Dancing Disease, Jazz Appreciation

In the 19th-century Ottoman Empire, couple dances such as *vals* (waltz) and polka were very popular in ballrooms of the European bourgeoisie. The visibility of these dances coincides with the early republican period, and they are indispensable demonstrations of modern social life. The official balls organized in Istanbul became the popular entertainment of the new "high soci-

ety" class. Ballroom dance presented "hyperfeminized women" and "overdetermined men" (Picart 2006, 250) and depicted the ideal new woman as *alafranga* (westernized), as opposed to *alaturka* (like Turk).

Ballroom dancing became widespread during the 1920s and 1930s in different venues, such as balls organized between families, solidarity balls, and masquerade balls. As the essential dances of these balls, waltz and tango reflect the cultural capital of Western society life. Like the waltz, tango reflects interest in the European lifestyle and became popular during the "**tangomania**" period that spread to many countries. Tango was included in the training program of the Halkevleri—a symbol of "civilization" in Turkey during these years.

From the early republican period and into the 1950s, *fokstrot* (foxtrot) and *Çarliston* (Charleston) dances were the dominant genres within *dansings* (dance halls), along with the Western *cazbant* (jazz orchestras) that accompanied them. In contrast with the civilized appearance of waltz and tango, foxtrot and Charleston were considered unbuttoned, dangerous forms of the Western lifestyle, especially for women. Many popular culture journals published in the 1920s described dance as the addiction of the 20th century, an epidemic of *dar'ü raks* or "dance disease" (Toprak 2017). However, in the *Çarliston olayı* (Charleston debate) of that time, while you could find persuasive articles to stave off potential moral dangers for youths, you could also find published guides for teaching the Charleston.

1950s to 1970s: Western/Latin Steps, Middle Eastern Bellies

In addition to student groups, folk dance associations, and culture houses that opened beginning in the 1950s in city centers such as Istanbul, Izmir, and Ankara, private dance courses teaching popular urban dances have also proliferated. A book titled ***Tangodan Mamboya Bütün Danslar* (All Dances from Tango to Mambo)**, published in 1955, illustrates the steps of the foxtrot, waltz, rumba, swing, mambo, samba, and tango. During this period, all these dances were called "modern dance" and emphasized the ongoing relationship with the West.

Rock 'n' roll dance, which was popular in Europe and America in the same period, joined this repertoire at the end of the 1950s, and in a short time it became the most popular urban youth dance, creating a resistance that recalled the previous Charleston debate: "When the Charleston was just released, there was a lot of confusion. When the tango was just released, the Pope condemned it (the Tango) in the Vatican. But rock 'n' roll cannot be compared with the Charleston, the tango, or any of the later more modern dances because in none of those dances was the man's hand on the hips of the woman or below" (Bengi 2020, 250).

The twist, which was added to the repertoire of rock 'n' roll in the 1960s, had the same luck as its predecessors. Popular culture magazines and newspaper headlines of the period describe the dance's movements on the one hand and its drawbacks on the other. Unlike its predecessors, the twist was perceived as "the hip curling of western modern dances." Music and films of the period that variously criticized or appreciated youth gained traction through the twist.

The favorites of the alaturka (Turkish) style repertoire—çiftetelli and *Oryantal* (Middle Eastern) belly dances—were outside the repertoire of traditional folk dances and also excluded from the alafranga (Western) style. However, in the urban entertainment of this period, these dances were popular in places such as pubs, dance halls/clubs, and ballrooms, where Western forms were also seen, as well as as in the ***gazino*** (music halls), ***meyhane*** (taverns), and ***müzikli kahvehane*** (musical coffee houses) where alaturka dance forms predominated. Gazinos, in particular, catered to Turkish-style entertainment, such as drinking programs with a nightlong lineup of singers and other performers, with Turkish classical music playing and belly dance shows. The "other entertainment" of the city, which includes both European and Turkish styles, became hybridized in these gazinos because the tourist market was growing and a new rural-urban culture arose among those who migrated to urban areas. During this period, the booming tourism industry and a push for "national cultural representations" often juxtaposed conflicting aspects of alafranga, alaturka, *resmi* (official), and *piyasa* (commercial) dance genres.

Because the traditional çengi, köçek, and çiftetelli had been associated with belly dance in urban areas since the 1950s, these urban practices were classified as belly dance, though Anatolia's traditional çiftetelli dance practices also were maintained. Throughout the 1950s and 1960s, belly dance of the alaturka entertainment was associated with nudity in striptease and revue shows. In the 1970s, this perception changed somewhat, but the dangerous femme fatale image of the female body persisted. During this period, ***dansöz oynatmak*** (to make a belly dancer dance), and ***oryantal yapmak*** (to dance in a Middle Eastern manner), a settled form of entertainment, continued to be "the other" of the official discourse until 1981.

At the same time, while the concept of Western culture in this period was rapidly shifting from European to American lifestyles, imported forms were also settling in the content of Turkish culture—alaturka Turkish culture. Indian movies that were shown in cinemas in the 1950s and the ***sirtaki*** dance, which became popular with the movie *Zorba the Greek* in the 1960s, updated the content of the alaturka with the Far East and the Balkans.

1980 Onward: Toward a Cultural Jungle and Identities in Dance

Social life, which halted after the military coup of 1980, soon resumed through the entertainment media. Consumption of melodrama films and a booming cassette industry fueled the neoliberal transition, largely through the spread of ***oyun havası*** (dance tune) albums released throughout the 1980s. The pop and ***arabesk*** (Arabic) sounds in these albums cover all popular genres and local dance music accumulated up to that time and are a collective archive of musical styles.

During this period, the dansings were supplanted by ***diskoteks*** (discos), the first of which were seen in the 1970s. By the 1980s, the global pop music repertoire also attracted intense attention in Turkey. In diskoteks, the hit pop songs of the period sparked "swinging, spinning, jumping movements," amid pop-techno-electronic sounds at a volume that prohibited conversation. The disco scene hopped with globally popular songs (e.g., **"Comanchero" by Raggio di Luna**), as well as local dance music and disco covers of folk songs.

The random movement of dance practices in disco dance changed with the **moonwalk** figure introduced in the 1990s through Michael Jackson's concert in Istanbul. Through tours and music videos, Jackson and other pop music artists were a profound influence on popular music and dance in Turkey throughout the 1990s. Visuality and dance became indispensable for sound and music, thanks to the broadcast of video music channels (MTV in 1981, Kral TV in 1994) that existed throughout the 1990s. Video music by dance-trained or professional dancer-singers was particularly influential in popularizing "disco-pop dance" throughout the 1990s. The music video of "**Lambada**," by the band Kaoma, pioneered the Latin-pop genre in discos of the 1990s. **Breaking**—the bodily manifestation of **hip-hop** culture—became more visible in the 1990s, spreading from dance clubs to the streets with dances such as the "**Electric Boogie**."

The alaturka side of the 1980s' popular dances begins with the special demonstration of belly dance (previously banned), on TRT (Turkish Radio and Television) screens in the 1981 New Year's celebration. Thus, belly dance was officially recognized in the dance category; the ongoing presence of belly dance in social practices was reconstructed through this official recognition. TRT's belly dance performances in 1983 poured oil on troubled waters as heritage tourism continued and the dancer's body was framed with costumes that did not threaten the conservative image of Turkish women.

In the 1990s, despite TRT's "restricted" performances, private channels increased the exotic, erotic, and Middle Eastern content of belly dance as much as possible, making it a part of musical entertainment programs, in particular. Though belly dance did increase its presence in competition, and squeezed in state ideology, it was never fully supported by the government. However it has been embedded as a genre of the national cultural heritage in the brochures of the ministry of tourism, or in "Turkish Night" programs (events with Turkish themes), and in the Turkey promotional films of the 2000s. This contradictory relationship continued after 2010 with the bans imposed by the state media regulator RTÜK, even on private television channels, despite prior normalization of belly dance in staged folk dance and general social practices.

On the other hand, especially after the second half of the 1990s, the expansion of centralized identity politics added Romani dance to Turkey's dance culture as an autonomous genre. The dance soon became an icon of Romani/Gypsy identity. While it was previously an improvisation moment of the Thracian karşılama dances or çiftetelli choreographies in the traditional folk dance repertoire, it was repositioned as a discreet and ultimate genre in the 1990s. By the 2000s it was one of the most popular forms of entertainment;

Romani dance competitions on TV channels, choreographies of Romani dance in shows, and Romani dance added to dance courses indicated a wide market.

Throughout the 2000s, global markets spurred the addition of regional repertoire and private, local dance titles to the repertoire of dance culture in Turkey—a feedback mechanism that neatly sidestepped ethnicity and religious identity. The pop sound of *horon*, one of the traditional folk dances that entered the market in the early 2000s, brings the Black Sea region to the stage. Along with the basic patterns of horon dance and a local instrument (*kemençe*, a pear-shaped lute), lyrics in a dialect of the Black Sea region were added to a substructure with pop-disco sound. Examples in this context refer to a popularity resulting from regionalism unlike Romani dance, which works with the exoticism of the global world music market.

Kolbastı/hoptek, one of the most popular dances of the 2000s, is an improvised dance known since 1920, identified with the eastern Black Sea region and performed by two or more people. *Kolbastı*, which means "law enforcement raided us" (in back translation) according to local sources, is a narrative dance. Imitations of fishing and rowing, youthful fights, and drunken behavior are included in these demonstrations. Between 2007 and 2010, it reached a prevalence beyond regions and cultures, with YouTube videos on how to dance kolbastı, choreographies announced as "kolbastı shows," birthday celebrations, and wedding entertainment (Şahin 2020). Another regional dance popularization of the 2000s came through dance tunes of Ankara (capital of Turkey), especially the song "**Erik Dalı**" (*Branch of Plum*) that spread throughout the nation. Ankara dance tune productions and video clips in the popular music market reveal the popular-cultural-local flow, which provided must-have music for weddings at the time.

In order to understand any dance culture in Turkey, it is necessary to know the national ideologies, as well as the ideological or technological interactions outside the country. For example, the staging experiences of the early republican period, in the process of creating the national dance repertoire, take the European as a modern and Western model. European ballet and its successor, modern dance, have survived to the present day as the only classical dance categories for Turkey. In urban popular dance repertoires, we see the popular dances of Europe and Amer-

Cultural Highlight

DISCOVERING MY ROMANI HERITAGE

I was born in Istanbul, Turkey. I completed my undergraduate education by studying music at the conservatory. While I was studying for a master's degree in ethnomusicology, I learned by chance that I was of Gypsy/Romani origin. During the process of writing my doctoral thesis, I started to get to know myself, to get to know the Roma neighborhoods that I have been kept away from since my childhood. I learned Romani dance from a professional folk dance teacher (who is not Rom) by participating in a Romani dance course opened by another university in Istanbul. While making participant observations during my field research on Romani dances, I learned about true Romani dance when informants objected, saying things like "this is not the real Romani!" While trying to understand the past and present form of Romani dance in Turkey by associating it with its popularity in those days, I met the magical worlds of other dance forms and cultures. Being able to read Turkey's social history through dance cultures is an indispensable focus of motivation for me, and producing knowledge in this field is essential for the hope for a more equal and just world struggle.

ica, too. Cultural forms that opened to the world market with globalization are associated with dominant markets and changes in the repertoire of folk dances, classical ballet, and popular urban dances. The transformation of the closed traditional structures of religious movement systems, their stage representation, and their increasing presence in popular markets can also be explained by the same global relations.

 See resource 17.6 in HK*Propel* for web links.

Summary

Turkey's dance culture can be divided into four main categories: traditional folk dance, classical dances, religious movement systems, and popular urban dances. Although this classification includes different repertoires, each of them is closely related to social change and disruptions that can be explained in terms of modernity, westernization, nationalism, and globalization. The articulation of folk dances in the commercial market and the developments in ballet reflect transitions from the Ottoman era to different phases of the republican period during the 20th century and into the 21st century. The dances of ethnic or religious minorities—such as the Alevi whirling dance—have become significant to the European Union membership process and the global market, while the close relationship with worldwide popular dance ensures that imported dances find a ready home in Turkey. Recently these varied dance forms have intertwined through **hybrid aesthetic** approaches and new media tools, further blurring the line between alaturka (Turkish) and alafranga (Western) conceptions. A 21st-century example is the dance company **Anadolu Ateşi** (Fire of Anatolia)—a melting pot of concepts partially conservative, encompassing the "other," radically mystical and nostalgic, extremely contemporary, absolutely global, and inevitably Turkish.

 See resource 17.7 in HK*Propel* for web links.

Discussion Questions

1. Why and how is the concept of "to dance folklore" crucial for traditional folk dance culture in Turkey?
2. What is the "hybrid aesthetic approach" of the folk dancing market?
3. What is the concept of national ballet in Turkey after the 1950s?
4. How did the different nationalistic approaches influence folk and classical ballet dance repertory in Turkey?

 Visit HK*Propel* for access to this chapter's Application Activity.

Selected Glossary

alafranga and alaturka—The two major parts of cultural repertory in modern Turkey; the words mean "westernized" (alafranga) and "like Turk" (alaturka).

arabesk—A genre particularly popular in Turkey in the decades from the 1960s through the 1990s; dominant popular music style of the 1980s in the music industry of Turkey. Means "in Arabic style."

artistic stage—The term *folk dance* refers to social dance, but "Turkish folk dance" means staged artistic performances.

bedii raks—Translated as "aesthetic dance," defines bodily expressions of sensations in terms of narratives, and the first choreographies contained Western modern dance themes.

cazbant—Jazz orchestra; though the term originated with jazz orchestras in dance halls accompanying popular Western dances like the foxtrot and Charleston, it was also used for all music-making forms in which European art music instruments were used, during the early republican period.

dansöz oynatmak (to make a belly dancer dance)—In rural and urban culture, the hiring of professional belly dancers for entertainment venues.

diskoteks—Places in which verbal communication is minimized while dancing to pop-techno-electronic sounds during the 1970s-1990s in urban places. Also called *disco*.

folklor oynamak—Phrase meaning "to dance folklore," the overall folk dance activity in the 1960s and 1970s in Turkey.

gazino (music hall)—A type of nightclub primarily located in Istanbul, Turkey, that features most types of Turkish-style entertainment.

hybrid aesthetic or **hybrid dance aesthetics**—Multisourced hybrid choreographies and performances throughout the 2000s in Turkey.

oryantal yapmak (to dance in Middle Eastern manner)—The popular expression of the most preferred belly dance performance of the Turkish repertory in the urban dance market of the 1970s.

Turkish folk dance—An official performance of folk dances, framed by Turkish republican politics.

Selected References and Resources

And, M. 1976. *A Pictorial History of Turkish Dancing*. Ankara: Dost Yayınları.

Baykurt, Ş. 1995. *Anadolu Kültürleri ve Türk Halk Dansları*. Ankara: Yenidoğuş Matbaası.

Bengi, D. 2020. *50'li Yıllarda Türkiye: Sazlı Cazlı Sözlük*. İstanbul: Yapı Kredi Yayınları.

Beşiroğlu, Ş., and G. Girgin. 2018. "Entertainment Spaces, Genres, and Repertories, Ottoman Musical Life." In *Made in Turkey*, edited by A.C. Gedik. New York, London: Routledge.

Dehmen, B. 2001. "Yeni Paradigma: Melez Danslar." *Art-izan*. August 27, 2001. www.art-izan.org/artizan-arsivi/yeni-paradigma-melez-danslar.

Ocak, A.Y. 1996. *Türk Sufiliğine Bakışlar*. İstanbul: İletişim Yayınları.

Öztürkmen, A. 2003. "Modern Dance Alla Turca: Transforming Ottoman Dance in Early Republican Turkey." *Dance Research Journal* 35:38-60.

Öztürkmen, A. 2005. "Staging a Ritual Dance Out of Its Context: The Role of an Individual Artist in Transforming the Alevi Semah." *Asian Folklore Studies* 64:247-260.

Shay, A. 2002. *Choreographing Politics: State Folk Dance Companies, Representation and Power*. Middletown: Wesleyan University Press.

Toprak, Z. 2017. "Rakstan Dansa: Erken Cumhuriyet ve Çarliston Gençliği." *Toplumsal Tarih* 283:64-79.

Woodall, C. 2008. "Sensing the City: Sound, Movement, and the Night in 1920s Istanbul." PhD diss., New York University.

Dance in Iran

Raqs-i-Irani: The Persian Dance

Nathalie M. Choubineh

Learning Objectives

After reading this chapter you will be able do the following:

- Understand formal and creative differences between Persian dance and belly dance.
- Appreciate the fundamental importance of inner feelings and attitudes and a high sensitivity to Persian music in performing Persian dance.
- Identify and compare classical, popular, folk/regional, and contemporary/pop/fusion genres of Persian dance.
- Understand Iranian cultural, political, and musical history.
- Understand the concept of choreophobia and its explicit and implicit impacts on social, religious, and political constraints imposed on Persian dance, and follow its applicability to other Islamic cultures.
- Identify various forms of Persian dance practiced around the world today and their ease of access through dance institutions, online courses, and, most crucially, Persian music videos.

Key Terms

choreophobia—Fear of dance, particularly a fear injected into social, cognitive, and behavioral traditions through ideologic propaganda.

kereshmeh—Essential attitude in Persian dance shown in flirtatious body movements, such as twists and turns; the word can denote either a dance or dance moves.

Persian classical dance—Foundational and formal dance to Persian music.

Persian pop dance—Persian popular dancing to contemporary pop songs and music.

Persian popular dance—Spontaneous, informal party/cabaret Persian dance.

qir—Persian hip/waist work; the most characteristic dance movement in Persian popular dance.

raqs-i-Irani—General term for Persian dance in Farsi (Persian language).

The Magic of Persian Dance

It is a late autumn day in 2019. Evening has just fallen over the Masonic Hall, in Bath, England, where an international conference on biochemistry has been going on the whole day. Exhausted participants prepare to doze through the predinner entertainment. But then the 1001 Nights dance group takes the stage. The dancers glide up the front steps to their positions around the gilded pillars, waiting for the music to start, glittering in their beautiful outfits of white, blue, pink, and red. Pearl drops of mild staccatos sound through the evening air. The first steps are soft and fairy light, with a trembling of tambourines. In solemnity, each dancer lays her tambourine down and then glides and swings with waving arms to express wonder and mystery. Wiping phantom tears from their eyes, the dancers raise their arms and heads to heaven.

Then the music changes. Grief is over. Joy is granted. Dancing ladies leap, run and turn, bend and bounce, twist and sweep their limbs. As **kereshmeh** dancing reveals their utmost beauty in sheer joy, they share their profound happiness with their audience, inviting them to rejoice in the loveliness flowing on the stage. Ecstatic moments culminate with tambourines swept off the floor to fill the air with happy jingles. The conference attendants are mesmerized, tiredness long forgotten. The world around shines with beauty, love, music, and jubilation. That's the magic of Persian dance.

> *Thou whose ways are kereshmeh and coyness*
> *How long would they last to be your ways?*
>
> Attar Neyshabouri (c. 1145-c. 1220), Book of Poems, ghazal 410

 See resource 18.1 in HK*Propel* **for web links.**

Persian cultural practices, including dance, can be understood through five evolutionary turning points in the history of Iran:

1. Foundation of the Persian Empire by Cyrus II of Persia around 550 BCE.

2. The Arab conquest of Iran in 651 CE and the substantial infusion of Islamic elements into Persian culture.

3. Conversion of Iran to Shi'a Islam in the 16th century and popularization of strict religious views, resulting in **choreophobia**.

4. Modernization and westernization of Iran, initiated/supervised by the ruling dynasties from the mid-19th century onward.

5. The Islamic Revolution of 1979, imposing an overarching ban on dance in Iran.

The cultural changes prompted by each of these upheavals drags Persian dance practice forward or backward along the spectrum between full existence and complete elimination. Therefore, in Persian dance discourse, to dance or not to dance counts as far more crucial than professionalism or competence of performance.

Myths and Assumptions of Persian Dance

What is the difference between Iran and Persia? Do Iranians speak Arabic? Can we identify all Iranians as Muslims by definition? These questions often come to mind respecting the Iranians and Persian culture. The answer to many such questions is a simple "no." However, further explanation is needed to unfold the mystery of Persian culture, although the available information about this culture may vary depending on your sources. For example, many Iranians may identify themselves as Persians, while others may insist on being Iranians. The picture of Iran promoted in media reflects the ruling political climate of the day. Similarly, accounts from non-Iranian visitors and observers about Iranian customs and beliefs are not always reliable.

Myths and assumptions arise when talking about the underrepresented aspects of Iranian/

Persian culture, such as ***raqs-i-Irani*** (Persian dance). The mystery of raqs-i-Irani is twofold, one pertaining to its appearance, the other to its origins, development, and survival in a society marked by "choreophobia" (Shay 1995, 62). In its appearance, Persian dance represents an interesting cross-cultural confusion: It appears, to many, as a version of the Arabic-origin **belly dance**. And not without reason. There is no doubt that Iranians use the Arabic alphabet for writing (of Farsi, the Persian language that is essentially different from Arabic). Many Iranians, if not all of them, are Muslims. Iran is a country in the Middle East, a region that immediately reminds most non-Iranians of the Arabian culture, of a land of deserts, sands, and camels: Certainly, this must be the dance performed by the beautiful slave-girls in the sultans' harems from *The Arabian Nights*. Or, is Persian dance something else entirely? A comparison between Persian dance and the more familiar belly dance will help dispel the prevailing myths about Iranian and Arabian cultures.

Persian Dance and Belly Dance

Persian dance and belly dance are different, dwelling on the two sides of the same gap that separates Farsi from Arabic, Iran from Iraq and other Arab countries, and **Persian music**, art, costumes, and customs from their Arabic counterparts. The difference between Persian dance and belly dance is in the philosophy of a dance—the cultural pretext and attitude that shapes our dance moves and gives them their meaning and purpose. In this sense, belly dancing has an extroverted nature. Its main purpose is to evoke sensuality and sensation. In contrast, Persian dance is a relatively introverted practice, engaging inner perceptions, worldviews, dreams, and desires. The moves and routines of belly dancing display a commanding control of each and every muscle with an emphasis on sensually attractive body parts, namely the breasts and the hips; Persian dance movements are performed to create meaningful compositions. In terms of technique, belly dancing consists of sharp, quick, and short moves, staccato momentums and muscle shivers, all in contrast to the soft and fluid swings and sways of Persian dance. That said, it is also true that, thanks to their parallel development under the umbrella of the Persian-Arabic-Turkish musical tradition, the two dances share technicalities, such as the soft hip undulation, the vertical waving of the body, and the sophisticated hand and wrist twists.

Notwithstanding those, belly dancing accommodates relatively large-scale stretches and swings compared to the delicate sways of kereshmeh in Persian dance.

Kereshmeh

The Farsi word *kereshmeh* is a complex one in translation and onstage. Grammatically, it is a noun, but it tends to be rendered as an adjective in English because kereshmeh pertains to an image, rather than a literal concept. When it crops up in a text or conversation, it evokes a coquettish/flirtatious behavior through which ladies, mainly, conceal their true feelings. In effect, a kereshmeh might connote being anything from coy or cold to shrewd or mischievous. Covering all these amorous strategies has secured a special position for kereshmeh in the ancient arts of poetry and **Persian miniature painting**, the latter artform having reached its pinnacle in the 14th and 15th centuries. Kereshmeh is recognizable through dancing figures in these paintings because the depiction of human figures in Persian art was not completely forbidden despite Islamic rule. The literary and illustrative images of coquettish women tie kereshmeh to many figurative moves depicted in Persian murals and miniature paintings. Recent scholarship of Persian dance, therefore, positively identifies kereshmeh as a kind of dance. However, other scholarship indicates that it is more of a quality of movement and an aesthetic concept than a specific dance form.

Main Categories of Persian Dance

Raqs-i-Irani, as it is known today, may appear in two forms. The one more widely promoted is an elegant performance of Middle Eastern professional or semiprofessional dancers on stage, graceful in multilayered drapes and ethereal silk headpieces. Dances of this form may be defined as "classical," "traditional," or "ritual" and are associated with a variety of historical or mystic elements.

In contrast with classical dance, a more intimate form of Persian dance is performed spontaneously and individually at a disco or party dance. This popular dance is widespread among Iranians, even seen in Persian dance competitions, all held necessarily outside of Iran, such as the **Mohammad Khordadian Dance Competition** series in Turkey and Germany. This dance form is

Shah Abbas I receives Vali Muhammad Khan of Turkistan at the Chehel Sotoun Palace, Isfahan, 17th century.

often considered the original—or national—raqs-i-Irani, since it features the most characteristic movement of Persian dance, **qir**, the smooth and rhythmic side-sliding or rotating of the hips. Persian popular dance has been termed *urban*, *pop*, or *Tehrani* (after the capital city, Tehran) in scholarly writings. Here, I will use the terms "classical" and "popular," respectively, for the first and second dance forms, because these terms are prevalent and comfortably approved in both theoretical and practical fronts. Therefore, the two main categories of raqs-i-Irani discussed here are **Persian classical dance** and **Persian popular dance**, with a subcategory of **Persian pop dance**.

A third category of **Persian regional/folk dances** attracts dance ethnographers and those who seek further variations of Persian dance, such as dance ethnologist Robyn Friend who directs the Institute of Persian Performing Arts. Space limits here do not allow a review of this vast category. It must be noted, however, that some regional dances, such as the Azeri-Turkish *lezgi* of the northwest and the **bandari** dance of southern Iran are to be found, in moderated forms, in the repertoire of Persian popular dances.

The two categories of Persian classical and Persian popular dance share a broad set of characteristic moves, particularly the head-and-neck and the hand-and-arm movements fundamental to creating a typically Persian kereshmeh. The frequency of characteristic moves in both categories may bring about confusion in their identification. To avoid this, it is helpful to concentrate on "the philosophy" of each type of dance. Persian classical dance embodies ideas, historical events, folk legends, or personal stories. Persian popular dance tends to share an inner joy and delight. In practical terms, Persian classical dance feels gentle yet somehow exotic or remote, whereas the popular raqs-i-Irani looks and feels intimate, exciting, and contagious. Accordingly, movements and gestures characteristic of Persian dance may be enlarged to fit large-scale choreographies of the classical genres or, contrastingly, encapsulated in the finely detailed routines of the popular format. Taking footwork as an example, you may stretch your strides to dance a Persian classical work or keep your steps tight and tiny in a Persian popular dance.

 See resource 18.2 in HK*Propel* for web links.

Historical Highlights

How did these two distinct categories of dance develop from the same cultural tradition that accommodates only one specific set of figurative moves? History and geography suggest an answer. Archaeological evidence about the existence of dance in the Iranian plateau, including painted pictures of dancing figures on pieces of pottery, date back to 8,000 years ago (Taheri 2011, 43). Written indications of dance, however, begin to appear in the ancient manuscripts only from the mid-fifth century BCE, a hundred years after Cyrus II of Persia (c. 601-530 BCE) conquered a vast portion of central Asia and the Middle East and founded the first empire (in the modern sense of the word), the Persian Empire. Xenophon of Athens (c. 431-354 BCE), in his historical novel about Cyrus, *Cyropaedia*, indicates "the Persian national dance" as the cultural heritage left from the ancient Achaemenid kings (book 8, chapter 7). Around the same time, Ktesias of Knidos, in his *Persika*, mentions a favorite dancing girl of

Farzaneh Kaboli performing a Persian regional dance under the title of *hararkat-i-mawzun*.
Courtesy of Farzaneh Kaboli.

the Persian king, Artaxerxes II (404-358 BCE). Writings of this kind suggest that dancing in ancient Persia was a luxurious entertainment, presumably exclusive to the royal court. This is somewhat at odds with the overall picture of dances in the ancient cultures of the region that were chiefly performed for sacred purposes and in public festivals. However, it may also be that because many of these written works were revived in the Middle Ages, their transmission might have been affected by the biases of their transcribers of Persia. Ktesias' writings, for example, had been lost for centuries, only to come to light in fragments in the ninth century CE. The Persian practice of keeping harems and enslaved performers was widely known and acknowledged by then.

From Court Dance to Choreophobia

Historical records of a Persian national dance and the dancing girls of the royal court are ubiquitous in the form of Persian miniature paintings and murals, as well as in the accounts of European travelers to Persia. The dance form illustrated in these records is what we consider Persian classical dance. Dancers appearing in the paintings are entertaining the courtiers, and the non-Iranian visitors who mention dancing were mostly guests of rulers and nobles.

The popular form of raqs-i-Irani, in contrast, is a modern phenomenon whose development can only be traced back to the early 20th century. Because the establishment of the Islamic tradition of choreophobia (fear of dance) affects any dance that might have existed outside of the high-class sphere, it is not easy to decide whether the popular dance of Iranian casual gatherings today actually derives from classical dance or whether it has some roots in an older tradition of dancing in private spaces and occasions (Shay 2006).

The perception that music and dance could only exist as an elite pastime arose because historical sources mainly focused on the political, social, and religious activities of the upper classes. Assumptions about the presence and functioning of music and dance in people's daily life find little or no evidence in pre- or even post-Islamic Persia. Still, it is generally safe to say that no cultural group in the world could go without some sort of musical activity; music and dance were evidently widespread in the eastern Mediterranean and central Asia. Music and dance must have been part of ritual and theatrical traditions all over the Iranian plateau.

Following the conquest of the Persian Empire by the newly converted Muslim Arabs in the seventh century CE, Persian music and dance had to survive and develop in the intolerant climate of religious/traditional choreophobia. The Islamization of political power imposed ethical restrictions on musical activities in both public and private spheres. While the development of Persian music and dance continued throughout medieval times and beyond, their very existence remained largely dependent on sponsorship by elites who had enough power to relax religious grips. Breaking through choreophobic restraints became possible only at the beginning of the 20th century (see, for example, Mozafari 2013; Meftahi 2016). Within eight decades, three historical events took place that brought about liberation, systematization, and popularization of Persian dance:

1. Iranian **modernization**
2. The development and commercialization of **Persian pop music** and the *filmfarsi* industry
3. The **Islamic Revolution of 1979**

 See resource 18.3 in HK*Propel* for web links.

Modernization of Iran

The modernization of Iran that began in the early 20th century had its roots in Europe. From the 1500s onward, commercial trade, military assistance, and cultural exchanges between Europe and Persia fueled the Persian affinity for the Western world. Persia, in return, became known as a welcoming destination in the exotic East for travelers from the West. Political exchanges, archaeological expeditions, discovery of oil fields in Persia, and evolutions in the education system through new schools built and run by European missionaries were among the most remarkable highlights of Persian contact with "foreigners" between the 17th and 19th centuries. Persia was among the first Asian countries to import the latest innovations of the day, thanks to the last three kings of the **Qajar dynasty** (1789-1925) who traveled through Europe.

The idea of westernization, of reconstructing the country according to world—that is, Euro-

pean—standards, became thus consolidated. The rapid course of modernization was amplified by Reza Shah Pahlavi, who overthrew and succeeded the Qajars in 1925. He sought to empower Iran, renamed as such to his command in 1935, with the most up-to-date infrastructures in technology, industry, public services, and sociocultural practices. His progressive projects turned the face of old Tehran into a 20th-century capital city with a vibrant nightlife featuring mostly well-educated men and women dressed up in the latest European fashions.

Reforms and developments continued to a greater scale under Reza Shah's son and successor, Mohammad Reza Shah Pahlavi (1919-1980). Integration into the mainstream world culture was now broadly encouraged by the government, the media, and the growing class of highly educated "intellectuals." Persian dance was part of this modernization process, although the idea and the initiatives came, ultimately, from abroad.

"French Ballet" in Iran

In the waves of migration subsequent to the 1917 revolution in Russia and the 1909 massacre of the Armenians in Turkey, several ballet dancers landed in the north and northwest cities of Iran. These artists set up the first dance classes in Tabriz, Qazvin, and Tehran. They taught **"French ballet"** (so called because ballet terms

Achaemenid takuk or rhyton. 5th century BCE.
The Metropolitan Museum of Art, New York, Fletcher Fund, 1954.

are French) into which they also recast popular Persian folk songs and dances, attempting both self-adaptation to their host culture and marketing promotion.

Ballet in 20th-Century Iran

Attracting and training young dancers from Persian families was challenging. Nesta Ramazani (b. 1932), one of the prominent dancers trained in these classes, tells us about this in her richly informative autobiography, *The Dance of the Rose and the Nightingale*:

> The prospects of my being able to pursue any sort of dance career in the 1940s in Iran were dim, in spite of its rapid modernization. But, thanks to the Russian Revolution, there was a ballet studio in Tehran. I was also lucky that my mother was English . . . and that my father's family were Zoroastrian, not Muslim, and somewhat open to new and modern ideas. (2002, 6)

By the mid-20th century, ballet-based teachings and Persian hybrid choreographies by the Russian- and Armenian-origin dance masters had already become popular. Given this situation, Nilla Cram Cook (1908-1982)—an American dance ethnologist assigned to the American Embassy in Tehran—convinced the Iranian Ministry of the Interior to help her establish the Iranian National Opera and Ballet Organization in 1946. Nesta Ramazani, a founding member of the Iranian National Ballet Company (established in the 1950s), expounds on Nilla Cram Cook's fostering of professional dance culture in Iran:

> And so Mrs. Cook's dream of an Iranian performing dance company, so at odds with ancient traditions, became a reality. Conceiving of the company as a blending of the East and the West, the traditional and the modern, the ancient and the contemporary, this singular woman . . . managed to overcome the objections of traditionalists by imaginatively showcasing Persian poetry, legend, and folk dance, even as she grafted these elements onto a foundation of Western concepts of dance as an art form buttressed by ballet training. (2002, 10)

Other dance teachers soon joined the flow, setting up popular dance studios, particularly in Tehran. The most significant of these were Madam Yelena Dance Group, founded by Yelena Avedisian (1910-2000), and Tehran Ballet School, founded by Sarkis Djanbazian (1913-1963).

Nilla Cram Cook's success in gaining official sponsorship for her national dance projects owed immensely to the performances of her dance group for the royal family and their high-class Iranian and non-Iranian guests between 1943 and 1945. Between the 1920s and 1950s, Persian classical dance and its subgenres were widely practiced in Iranian private dance schools. At the same time, the dance enjoyed royal sponsorship and was presented in different countries by Iranian state-sponsored dance groups. Enthusiasm for fostering a world-class Iranian national dance was upheld strongly by the government, right up to the 1979 revolution. The Iranian collective perception of professional dance practice became equated with learning, absorbing, and nationalizing Western contemporary forms. This approach has remained unchanged up to the present.

Emergence of Iranian Popular Music and Dance

The development of Persian popular dance took a somewhat different path from that of Persian classical dance. Never regarded as worthy of being taught in a class or deserving official attention, Persian popular dance was dismissed as suitable only for women's private gatherings and notoriously vulgar ***ruhawzi*** ("on the pond" plays, so-called because their stage was typically a large wooden cover on the pond or pool in the yards of private houses). These functions tied Persian popular dance closely to Persian popular music, a light and untechnical variation of Persian music. Since the historical accounts of Persian popular dance before the 20th century are meager, we can surmise its background through a brief look at the history of its close relative, Persian music.

While dance in historical Persia had to cope with the double standard of explicit condemnation with implicit protection under the political supremacy of Islam for more than 12 centuries, music fared slightly better. Early in the Islamic era, the Persian-Arabic-Turkish musical tradition allegedly flourished under the Persian-named musician **Ziryab** (789-857), the inventor of the standard *oud* (lute).

Ziryab's Legacy: Persian-Arabic-Turkish Music in the Ninth Century

Ziryab lived and served under the Muslim rulers of Andalusia, Spain, in the early ninth century, and it was thanks to their enthusiastic sponsorship that the Persian-Islamic musical system Ziryab developed could continue its growth and dissemination all around the Abbasid Empire from South Spain to North Africa, Arabian territories, Turkey, and Iran. The characteristic sets of tunes, rhythmic patterns, modal structures, instruments, and vocal and instrumental forms that comprise the Persian-Islamic musical system was an ever-flourishing stream nourishing hundreds of musicians, vocalists, poets, and scientists, who eventually left a huge number of treatises about theoretical, instrumental, and vocal aspects of this music for us today.

Dance, however, remained broadly underrepresented in this treasury of musical accounts (Mozafari 2011, 226). Records about dancing in ritual and seasonal celebrations, daily occasions, local festivals, theatrical displays, and even puppet shows cover only up to the last 350 years of Persian history. Nevertheless, the majority of such records imply that dancing was rarely acknowledged as an independent or professional occupation and despite its obvious prevalence, it had little social esteem. Right up to the late 19th century, both music and dance were considered indecent professions, suitable only for "merry-making servants" or *motrebs*, leading to the genre of *motrebi* **music**.

The Iranian modernization and the increasing social value of high education and emancipation dramatically changed this picture. In March 1924, **Ali-Naqi Vaziri** (1887-1979), a high-ranking officer but a musical virtuoso with outstanding knowledge, founded the Superior School of Music in Tehran. There, Western classical music and Persian classical music were taught side by side. This cross-pollination carried over into popular music and dance. However, hybrid genres of Persian popular dance appeared much later than the music.

Early in the 20th century, the popular format of Persian dance was part of the comic ruhawzi plays, performed by professional or semiprofessional troupes hired for such ceremonies as weddings and circumcision parties. All-female parties and gatherings were another traditional, and secluded venue for practicing this dance form (Shay 1995; Mahdavi 2007, 493). Moreover, Persian popular dance underlines the basic structure of a group of men's dances associated with, and named after, some typical Iranian jobs or characters. **Shateri** (the baker dance), **jaheli** (the hypermasculine dance of "the fearless"), and **baba karam** (inspired by the fictional love story of a *jahel*, or macho man, chasing his beloved), are examples of dances based on iconic male characters (Shay 2017, 16).

By the mid-1950s, the early hotels and restaurants that provided musical entertainment for the elite and the youth were replaced by music halls, nightclubs, theater houses, and cabarets (locally called *cafés*). Each of these places sponsored specific categories of Persian dance in resonance with the social status of their typical customers. Music halls, often part of a school or college, held concerts for Persian classical singers, featured Western-style dramas, and put on Persian classical or regional dance shows for middle-class families and people of higher education. Theaters hired Persian popular dancers and musicians to accompany their ruhawzi plays and entertain their lower-class audiences with Persian popular dance and belly dance during the intervals. The same sort of program was available in cafés, called the *cabaret* if located in places to be frequented by the middle-class, wealthy families, or bachelors. Later, in the 1960s, nightclubs and discos opened their doors to young generations to party and practice modern pop dances in Tehran and other major cities (Nettl 1972, 220). Persian pop dance thus developed from frequent exposure of Persian popular dance to Western pop music and new contemporary dances of the day.

Filmfarsi

All these trends coalesce in filmfarsi, the Iranian filmmaking industry. Between the initiation of Iranian national cinema in 1906 and the Islamic Revolution of 1979, most filmfarsi productions contained one or more dance scenes to guarantee their success in the box office. Many movies were categorized as melodrama or musical, with heroes and heroines singing and dancing in parts of the story. The main dance genres used in filmfarsi were Persian popular (particularly baba karam and jaheli) and belly dancing. However, a good number of contemporary genres, such as twist, cha-cha, rock 'n' roll, swing, and tango can also be found in these films. Regional/folk dances, mixed with some fundamental movements of Persian popular dance and rearranged to meet the standards of the Iranian folklore national organization (founded in 1967), were used by the filmmakers who tended to advocate national art forms (Meftahi 2017, 113).

The Iranian modernization can be compared to the European Renaissance in terms of relaxing class stratification, on the one hand, and expanding urbanization, on the other, which allowed a prosperous, well-educated, and economically and politically empowered middle class to grow. Dramatic cultural changes were soon to follow. Modern big cities attracted masses to their thriving pool of business and industry, Western goods, and fascinating modes of entertainment. In contrast with such progressive thoughts, however, a reductive and deeply critical view denigrated popular culture. Accordingly, French ballet (Western) and Persian classical dance (national emblem) were hailed as embodiments

of high culture, but Persian popular dance forms were confined to nonartistic domestic purposes: informal parties, downtown cafés, theater houses, and filmfarsi productions. Persian popular dance was absent from sponsored stage performances and considered inappropriate for teaching or systematization. The same segregation was applied, more or less, to Persian music, with praises for Western and Persian classical music as belonging to "high culture" (Meftahi 2016, 8). By the end of the 1970s, the serious, artistic, Persian classical dance had its distinctive position in the Olympus of the National Iranian Radio and Television (launched in 1958) and the Roudaki Hall for opera and concerts (opened in 1967), whereas Persian popular dance was still struggling to justify its artistic worth through its connections with authentic Iranian traditional celebrations unearthed by Iran's national folklore organization (Meftahi 2016, 212).

 See resource 18.4 in HK*Propel* for web links.

Islamic Revolution of 1979

Interestingly, the social and conceptual stratification of Persian dance was bound to collapse through a dance-destructive upheaval. The theocratic republic that eventually took power from the centuries-long monarchy in 1979 put Islamic religious laws in force. The government reading of Islamic teachings rejected all sorts of musical activities, particularly dance, which was, and is, equated with eroticism. For several months after the establishment of the Islamic regime, the sole *mojaz* (authorized) formats of music were revolutionary hymns and songs, which were sung a capella or to the beats of a snare drum by all-male groups. This almost complete ban on music, however, abated before long. Persian classical music gained a hazy and hesitant license as a source of national pride that was justified in the Islamic regime propaganda. Apart from that and the world classics, all sorts of Western and Persian pop music remained in the forbidden zone of *qeyr-i-mojaz* (unauthorized). The forbidden zone also included women solo singing, showing musical instruments on television, and dance in every form and in any public

Apulian bell-krater.
Digital image courtesy of Getty's Open Content Program.

Cultural Highlight

FARZANEH KABOLI: CIRCUMVENTING CHOREOPHOBIC CONSTRAINTS

When the resident dancers of the Ministry of Culture and Art were told they could hold on to their positions in the new Ministry of Culture and Islamic Guidance, but they were no longer allowed to dance, Farzaneh Kaboli was the one who decided to preserve what she had learned and worked on. She started her own "aerobic" classes at home and began to teach women the basic steps of ballet, Persian popular dance, and routines of various regional dances. With the help of her husband, Hadi Marzban, she took videos of her choreographies to be watched and learned from. In four decades, she trained hundreds of dancers, who then performed on private and official stages, in theatrical projects and in dance displays for all-female audiences.

place. Iran, by then a pioneer in performing and creating the most recent forms of music, dance, and theatrical shows, stepped into the 1980s with severe restrictions imposed on music, along with musical instruments, movies, sports, clothes, food and drink, and many other things, dividing everything into the two categories of the tolerable mojaz and the punishable qeyr-i-mojaz (Gholami 2016, 85; Meftahi 2016, 10).

Still, any political change, no matter how revolutionary in nature, cannot resist the overwhelming waves of cultural trends in the long term. Modernization, westernization, and progressive ideas had already been rooted deeply in Iranian collective thought. Persian pop music and dance, despite their disappearance from public life, were and are indispensable parts of Iranian culture. Consequently, any division between mojaz and qeyr-i-mojaz blurred before long. In addition, the music and dance artists who had left the country began to produce new repertoires and new styles. The postrevolution Persian music and dance, therefore, can be investigated in two separate categories of "home" and "abroad," with subcategories of "overground" and "underground" at home (Nooshin 2005).

Dance in Postrevolution Iran

In Iran, government censorship made the substantial reconfiguration of music and dance inevitable. To merit an overground presence, Persian dance had to be cleared of those choreographic elements that could be deemed erotic and corruptive. One crucial change was to disguise the prohibited dance as *harakat-i-mawzun* ("rhythmical movements"). This title could justify dance as physical exercise that was deemed necessary for a "soldier of Islam." Harakat-i-mawzun, in their original form, are limited to a few coordinated movements. The similarities between rhythmical movements and some traditional Islamic rites helped harakat-i-mawzun to get integrated into the big, state-sponsored theatrical productions in the 1980s, focusing on Islamic history or on the various revolutionary movements around the world. The next decade, with the relative opening of the political climate after the end of the Iran-Iraq war (1980-1988), witnessed the first choreographed group dances by men in historical and political dramas onstage and on television (Nazmjoo 2017). Women's dance in theater for mixed audiences had to wait longer—and still faces challenges to this day. Nevertheless, it is not unusual for theatrical plays to have one or more dance scenes of a sort—from French ballet to flamenco to hip-hop—performed by actor-dancers that included women. This happens, nevertheless, on the condition of observing the red lines: fully clothed bodies with head coverings for women, zero contact between genders, and no eroticism.

The underground dance groups in Iran are difficult to trace for obvious reasons. These are generally founded by dance teachers. Following the relaxation of governmental restrictions on popular music in 1998, several postrevolution pop music bands tried to bring their music overground (Nooshin 2005, 463). Similarly, dance classes ventured from private houses to some elementary schools, teaching harakat-i-mawzun to children under age 9 as part of their after-school activities. The 21st century saw yet another step toward the unearthing of dance classes in ladies-only gyms and leisure centers, disguised as aerobics, Zumba, ballet for kids, and the like. Persian and non-Persian dances, including belly dancing, are thus taught in a semisecret mode. Persian pop dancing—solo, improvisatory, and structurally a fusion of Persian-style movements with Western disco dancing—is widespread in private venues

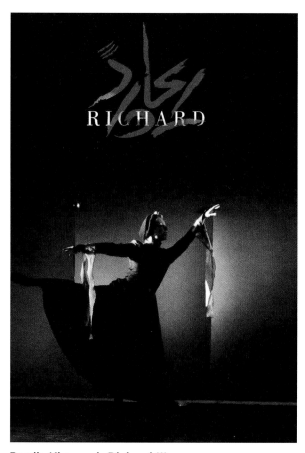

Pardis Khosravi, *Richard III*.

inside and out of Iran. Pop, rock, street dance, and hip-hop are very popular among the younger generations, who are now more than 50 percent of the Iranian population. None of these dances, however, are allowed on public stages, and there is no professional or competitive structure to bring dancers, teachers, choreographers, and celebrities together. That said, it is also the case that videos of private dance classes, dancing groups, or dancing individuals are posted and circulated in social media in great numbers.

 See resource 18.5 in HK*Propel* for web links.

Crosscurrents

After the revolution, most Iranian dancers, pop musicians, and singers left the country. Many of them found new opportunities in California, which soon turned into a home away from home for a great population of Iranians. Since the first

Iranian restaurants and nightclubs were located in or around the Los Angeles area, almost all prominent musicians, singers, composers, and dancers settled there. ***Losangelesi*** music became the new cultural brand. It carries all the connotations assigned to it by the so-called high culture, deeming the popular and mass culture unfit for serious attention (Shay 2000, 61). The losangelesi performing arts, likewise, were considered of low quality and dependent on public taste. Nevertheless, losangelesi music was valued as nostalgic. Although weakened by the exile from Iran, Persian pop music found an ever-growing and enthusiastic audience that yearned to resume the prerevolution procedure of modernization. Only a few years after the revolution, new albums by famous Iranian pop singers who had (mostly) settled in Los Angeles swept Iranian music markets. Dancing to such music became a symbol of protest against the limitation of social freedoms by the Islamic regime and a means for expressing a non-Islamic Persian identity.

In the 1980s, a great majority of Iranians found themselves dancing feverishly. Shoulder to shoulder with Persian pop music, Persian popular dance began to be taken seriously and seen as fit for systematized choreography and instruction. The pioneering figure in this field is **Mohammad Khordadian** (b. 1957). His work is significant for being grounded fully in Persian dance movements and totally independent, for the first time, from French ballet.

For more than a decade, Mohammad Khordadian, his dancers, and his dance style were fixed elements of every Iranian music video that contained dancing. Many Iranian dancers and dance teachers followed his choreographic patterns and routines or developed their own on this basis. In recent decades, however, Persian classical dance is widely promoted as an Iranian cultural agent. Consequently, raqs-i-Irani as instructed and choreographed for stage lies somewhere between the purely Persian-based Khordadian light moves and the stylish classical dance inspired by centuries-old miniature paintings. Some Persian dance academies active today are **Niosha Dance Academy** in California, USA (www.niosha.com); **Helia Dance Academy** in Enschede, the Netherlands (www.helia.nl); **Fereshteh Nasr** in Paris, France; and **Anahita Dance Class** in Toronto, Canada (www.anahitadanceclass.com).

 See resource 18.6 in HK*Propel* for web links.

Summary

Persian dance today is taught in dance schools and appears on stages worldwide. Persian classical dance develops fusion formats through importation of intricate figures and pantomimic gestures from folk/regional dances. Persian popular dance borrows extensively from contemporary dance styles, such as street dance, hip-hop, and Latin American-style dances, to keep up with medleys of Persian pop songs. Young generations' mastery of these dances to Persian pop songs and their pure execution of them (i.e., unmixed with Persian dance moves) elevates Persian pop dance to the high levels of kinetic challenge. Although the governmental ban on dance in Iran cannot be lifted, the strength of Persian dance outside of the country has caused the concept of choreophobia to lose its relevance in the collective consciousness of Iranians. Leaving behind centuries of hiding in choreophobic shadows, Persian dance can now breathe in the atmosphere of freedom and well-deserved attention beyond Iranian borders and in social media.

 See resource 18.7 in HK*Propel* for web links.

Discussion Questions

1. What are the main differences between Persian dance and belly dance, and what do these differences tell us about Persian dance?
2. What is choreophobia and how did it change the historical development of Persian dance?
3. What is kereshmeh, and how does it appear in different genres of Persian dance?
4. What is qir, and how does it characterize Persian dance specifically?
5. What are the main genres of Persian dance, and what is the fundamental factor that defines their difference?
6. When and why were harakate-i-mawzun introduced into the Persian dance repertoire?
7. How can we compare losangelesi music/dance to its underground counterpart?

 Visit HK*Propel* for access to this chapter's Application Activity.

Selected Glossary

belly dance—The generic name for Arabic-style dance.

choreophobia—Fear of dance, particularly a fear injected into social, cognitive, and behavioral traditions through ideologic propaganda.

"French ballet"—Principal system used as a foundation for dance teaching and choreography in Iran. Because of ballet's French terminology and despite major developments of the form in other countries such as Russia, Iranians call it "French ballet."

harakat-i-mawzun—A set of sporty, rhythmic movements that replaced dance in public venues in postrevolution Iran under the guise of physical exercise.

Islamic Revolution of 1979—The political change of ruling regime from monarchy to an Islamic leadership in Iran.

jaheli dance—The main category of supermasculine Persian popular dancing that includes baba karam dance.

kereshmeh—Essential attitude in Persian dance shown in flirtatious body movements, such as twists and turns; the word can denote either a dance or dance moves.

modernization—Adoption of Western lifestyle in Iran.

Mohammad Khordadian—Persian popular dancer, champion of teaching and systematization of Persian popular dance. After the 1979 revolution forced him to flee Iran, Khordadian performed Persian dances in exile and taught dance to the post-revolutionary generation through secret videotapes.

Persian classical dance—Foundational and formal dance to Persian classical music, using movements inspired by dancing figures in Persian miniature paintings.

Persian miniature paintings—Miniature paintings to depict religious or mythological themes flourished from the 13th through the 16th centuries. Dancing figures in the paintings confirm the existence and general aesthetics of Persian dance from centuries ago.

Persian pop dance—Dancing to Persian pop or other sorts of pop music, using Western-style dance moves.

Persian popular dance—Dancing to Persian light classical, popular, or pop music, using Persian dance moves, particularly qir.

qir—Persian hip/waist work; the most characteristic dance movement in Persian popular dance.

raqs-i-Irani—General term for Persian dance in Farsi (Persian language) often understood as Persian popular dance.

Selected References and Resources

Ameri, A. 2006. "Iranian Urban Popular Social Dance and So-Called Classical Dance: A Comparative Investigation in the District of Tehran." *Dance Research Journal* 38(1-2): 163-179. www.jstor.org/stable/20444669.

Beaini, J., and K. Newman. 2014. *For the Love of Mohammad, A Memoir: With Mohammad Khordadian.* Createspace Independent Pub.

Cram Cook, N. 1949. "The Theatre and Ballet Arts of Iran." *Middle East Journal* 3(4): 406-420.

Gholami, S. 2016. *Dance in Iran: Past and Present.* Wiesbaden: Reichert Verlag.

Kiann, N. 2016. "The History of Ballet in Iran." In *Dance in Iran: Past and Present*, edited by S. Gholami, 91-175. Wiesbaden: Reichert Verlag.

Mahdavi, S. 2007. "Amusements in Qajar Iran." *Iranian Studies* 40(4): 483-499. www.jstor.org/stable/4311920.

Meftahi, I. 2016. *Gender and Dance in Modern Iran: Biopolitics on Stage.* London and New York: Routledge.

Meftahi, I. 2016. "The Sounds and Moves of Ibtizāl in 20th-Century Iran." *International Journal of Middle East Studies* 48(1): 151-155. https://doi.org/10.1017/S0020743815001579.

Meftahi, I. 2017. "Intimate Embraces With Ajnabi (Strangers): A Political History of Partner Dancing in Tehran, 1920-1950." *Clio. Femmes, Genre, Histoire* 46(2).

Mozafari, P. 2011. "Negotiating a Position: Women Musicians and Dancers in Post-Revolution Iran." Doctoral thesis, University of Leeds. www.semanticscholar.org/paper/Negotiating-a-position-%3A-women-musicians-and-in-Mozafari/e44e28b2d047495eb783690f065702df119a0e8d.

Nazmjoo, T. 2017. "From Veshtan to Harakat-i-Mawzun: Dance in Iranian Theatre." *Tableau*, September 2017. https://www.taylorfrancis.com/chapters/mono/10.4324/9781315753294-14/harikat-mawzun-post-revolutionary-iranian-theatrical-dance-ida-meftahi

Nettl, B. 1972. "Persian Popular Music in 1969." *Ethnomusicology* 16(2): 218-239. www.jstor.org/stable/849722.

Nooshin, L. 2005. "Underground, Overground: Rock Music and Youth Discourses in Iran." *Iranian Studies* 38(3): 463-494. www.jstor.org/stable/4311744.

Ramazani, N. 2002. *The Dance of the Rose and the Nightingale: Gender, Culture, and Politics in the Middle East.* New York: Syracuse University Press.

Shay, A. 1995. "Bazi-ha-ye Namayeshi: Iranian Women's Theatrical Plays." *Dance Research Journal* 27(2): 16-24.

Shay, A. 1995. "Dance and Non-Dance: Patterned Movement in Iran and Islam." *Iranian Studies* 28(1-2): 61-78. www.jstor.org/stable/4310918.

Shay, A. 2000. "Six-Eight Beat Goes On: Persian Popular Music From 'Bazm-e Qajjariyyeh' to 'Beverly Hills Garden Party'." In *Mass Mediations: New Approaches to Popular Culture in a Transregional World*, edited by Walter Armbrust, 61-87. Berkeley: University of California Press.

Shay, A. 2017. "A Rainbow of Iranian Masculinities: *Raqqas*, a Type of Iranian Male Image." *Iran-Namag.* https://pdfs.semanticscholar.org/10f7/c3dc39dd4b1d-8117b6ae4f13f50c161b2652.pdf.

Taheri, S. 2011. "Dance, Play, Drama: An Investigation on Dramatic Activities in the Iranian Pre-Islamic Works." *Honarha-yi-Ziba* 43(Spring-Summer): 41-49. https://jfadram.ut.ac.ir/article_24776.html?lang=en

PART VII

South and Southeast Asia

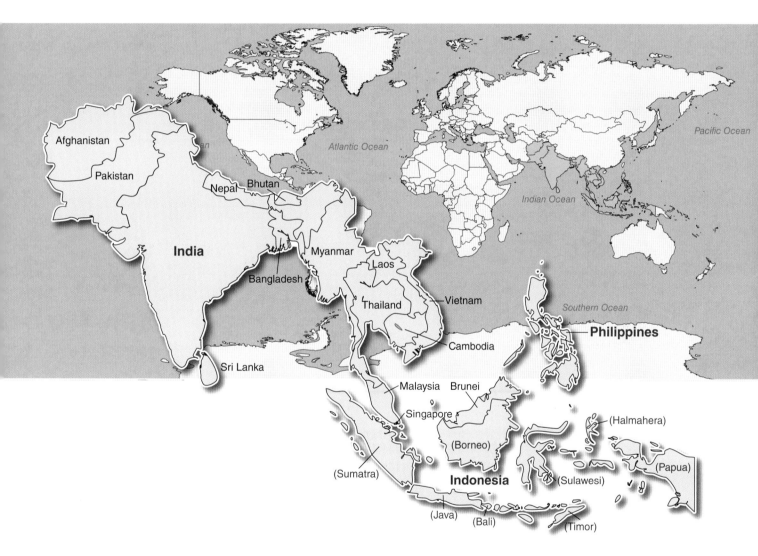

As in the Americas and Africa, colonialism has affected the forms, purposes, and perceptions of dance in this region, though the deep historical roots of traditional forms allowed them to endure. The primary colonial powers involved here were the Dutch in Indonesia, British in India, Spanish in the Philippines, and lastly the United States. While the latter had a relatively short (but nonetheless impactful) presence in 20th century Philippine culture, the European powers had a much longer reign. It is important to note that many of these colonial efforts were instigated by corporations seeking to monopolize trade routes and resources, with both direct and indirect influences on dance cultures. While direct effects such as marginalization and outright bans on dance were common under colonial rule, other more subtle effects and consequences can be seen. For example, pop-up markets are an integral part of some traditional folk dances in Indonesia—a possible connection between the dance and the country's position along ancient trade routes that attracted commercial exploitation. In India, though the forms of many dances were able to maintain their ancient characteristics, the perceptions of the dances (and of dancers) were greatly affected by British laws and sensibilities as corporate colonialism became full-scale governmental control. In the Philippines, Spanish dance forms themselves have been extensively integrated into Philippine dance culture. Thus the impacts of colonialism have played out in varying manners through the dance cultures of this region.

 HK*Propel* includes web links to additional resources for this section.

19

Indian Dance

Justine Lemos

Learning Objectives

After reading this chapter you will be able to do the following:

- Understand how embodied research as a fundamental technique of dance ethnography can be applied to dance of India.
- Understand the relationship between Indian nation-building and the reformation of classical Indian dance.
- Understand the relationship between dance and religion in Indian contexts.
- Identify and label key concepts in classical Indian dance performance.
- Compare and contrast regional variations in classical Indian dance.

Key Terms

abhinaya—The art of expression used in classical Indian dance. *Abhinaya* leads the audience toward an experience (*bhava*) of a sentiment (*rasa*).

bharatanatyam—Neoclassical Indian dance with origins in South India in the state of Tamil Nadu.

devadasi—Women historically dedicated to temple service. Some were trained in music and dance.

kathakali—A style of dance-drama from Kerala known for its elaborate costume and makeup.

kuchipudi—A style of neoclassical dance from the Indian state of Andhra Pradadesh.

Mohiniyattam—A style of neoclassical Indian dance with its origins in the southern Indian state of Kerala.

mudras—Single and double hand gestures used in dance, ritual, and yoga.

A Journey Into Classical Indian Dance

I arrive at the dance *kalari* (studio) after a long, hot, and bumpy bus ride. But once I enter the kalari I relax a bit. I *get* it here. I understand the protocol and what will go on. I know how to act, how to behave, how to fit in (mostly). I change into my dance **sari** and prepare to begin my practice of *Mohiniyattam* classical dance. I perform the *namaskaram* prayer, indicating that I am ready to start my lesson. As a dance ethnographer conducting research via embodiment, I am investigating my relationship to the movement technique, to my teacher, to the lineage of dance that she carries in her lived memory of movement and to a community of dance and dancers within the larger landscapes of Ernakulam city, **Kerala** state, and the Indian nation-state. Each correction given by my **guru** requires me to re-think and re-move through the sequence, refine my attention, and recalculate my attempt to investigate and integrate on a bodily level. As a foreigner in Kerala, India, it is so refreshing to be able to do something relatively correctly; from long-term practice the pathways of the dance technique are cut deeply into my body-mind. I just have to set my body in motion through the already-formed conduit of the technique. This is not a mindless operation; it is fully mindful and body-ful. I am completely engaged in allowing and creating the technique through my body. Teacher says to the students who are watching "Oh yes, she has studied **Odissi**, and also some Mohiniyattam, so these *adavus* (series of steps) come easily." I feel triumphant.

 See resource 19.1 in HK*Propel* for web links.

India is a complex nation-state. According to the *Indian Express*, "more than 19,500 languages or dialects are spoken in India as mother tongues" (India Express 2018). The democratic country with over one billion citizens is divided into 29 states and seven union territories. Perhaps the most accurate thing to say about India is that one cannot generalize about the people or culture. India is one of the most diverse places on Earth, with a history of civilization in the Indus Valley dating to at least 2500 BCE. Following the **Indus Valley civilization** (or more precisely known as **Harappan civilization**) was the **Vedic period** (c. 1500-c. 500 BCE) sparked by the arrival of **Aryan** people from central Asia. It was during this time that the **Vedas**, liturgical texts that formed the basis of the influential **Brahmanical (Hindu)** ideology, were written in the **Sanskrit** language. Important for our study of dance, it was during this period that the famous *Natyashastra* (Sanskrit: नाट्य शास्त्र), a Sanskrit treatise on the performing arts, was written. The text is attributed to sage **Bharata Muni**, and its first complete compilation is dated between 200 BCE and 200 CE, though estimates vary between 500 BCE and 500 CE. *Natyashastra* deems itself the fifth of the major Vedic texts: "Let Natya (drama and dance) be the fifth Vedic scripture. Combined with an epic story, tending to virtue, wealth, joy and spiritual freedom, it must contain the sig-

nificance of every scripture, and forward every art" (*Natyashastra* 1.14-15). Importantly, the *Natyashastra* connects the arts to spiritual and religious realization and is a resource text used by many dancers of India's classical and neoclassical styles of dance. Flowing from the *Natyashastra*, these dances embody religious tenets and iconic images of key deities, such as **Shiva Nataraja**.

Shiva Nataraja

Shiva, the destroyer, one of the most important gods in the Hindu pantheon, has been portrayed as a divine dancer from early times. In his form as Nataraja, king of the dancers, Shiva dances in a pose depicted in the *Natyashastra*. The image of Shiva Nataraja can be seen in many Hindu temples, in rock reliefs dating to the sixth century CE, and in contemporary classical Indian dance performances.

Brief History

Throughout the history of India, the continent and its peoples have experienced waves of foreign invaders, traders, colonizers, and looters. Of relevance to our study of dance in India is the first wave of Aryan invaders from central Asia into India around 1500 BCE. While we do not know how this early invasion affected dance of the earlier Harappan civilization in India, we do know that the invading Aryans brought with them the Sanskrit language. Most of what we know about the Aryans comes to us via the Vedas, their religious texts. Among these texts, the *Natyashastra* demonstrates that the Aryans had a very sophisticated system of dance, music, and other performing arts. The Aryans also brought with them a system of dividing society into **castes** and subcastes to determine a person's occupation and social class.

Castes

There were five major categories of caste, or *varna*, defined in documents from the Aryan civilization: **Brahmin**, **Kshatriya**, **Vaisya**, **Sudra**, and **Dalit**. Brahmins were the priestly caste who oversaw religious rituals. Kshatriya were the warrior caste who defended the kingdom. Vaisya were farmers and merchants. Sudra were non-Aryan manual laborers. The Dalit caste lived separated from others and did jobs deemed unclean, such as butchering or garbage collection. However, contemporary scholars suggest that people could—and did—move between castes with relative ease prior to the 18th century. The current rigid system is seen as a product of British colonial efforts to simplify governance and solidify control over the populace.

Buddhism: From 563 BCE

Of significance to the history of dance throughout Asia is the origin of **Buddhism** in India. The historical Buddha, **Siddharta Gautama**, was born in India in 563 BCE, but it wasn't until 260 BCE, when Indian **Emperor Ashoka** converted to Buddhism, that the religion began to have a significant impact in India. As Buddhism moved throughout Asia, northward into Tibet and Mongolia and China and southward to Sri Lanka and Indonesia (and through much of southeast Asia), the influence of Indian culture and arts is felt throughout the entire region. We can see stylistic similarities between the classical dances of India, Bali, Java, Cambodia, Thailand, and elsewhere. While the earlier Vedic religion that later became Hinduism focused on ritual, sacrifice, and chanting hymns, Buddhism focuses on the **noble Eightfold Path**, and the attainment of Enlightenment, which is said to be a state of being completely free of lust (*raga*), hatred (*dosa*), and delusion (*moha*).

Following the Buddhist empire of Ashoka, the **Gupta Empire** was established throughout much of India in 320 CE. This empire is considered to be the golden age of Indian history and relevant to our study of dance, for it was during the Gupta period that the two great Indian epics, **Mahabharata** and **Ramayana** were written. The *Mahabharata* tells the story of the five Pandava brothers and their attempts to hold their kingdom against their evil cousins, the Kauravas. The *Ramayana* tells the story of King Rama and his fight against the evil King Ravana, who has kidnapped Rama's wife, Sita. These epic poems contain characters, stories, and concepts frequently used in Indian dance and drama.

Mughal Empire: 13th-18th Centuries CE

In 1200 CE, Muslim armies began to conquer northern India. This wave of invaders brought with it massive cultural and religious changes and ushered in the **Mughal Empire** in the 16th century. Some Mughal emperors sought to convert the populace to Islam, while others were relatively religiously tolerant. For the Mughal rulers, dance and music became an important part of court entertainment. In the north of India, Mughal rulers brought dancers from Persia to entertain at court. Their dance mixed with Indian dance, creating **kathak**, one of the major styles of classical Indian dance. Ultimately, the Mughal Empire dissolved under the British colonial push in the 19th century that built upon the initial corporate occupation by the **British East India Company** in the 18th century.

British Occupation

To varying degrees each wave of invaders influenced India's regional cultures and the histories of its people and its arts. India also has been and continues to be a major influence on other cultures. For example, influences on Chinese dance traveled along the **Silk Road**, and the **Indian indenture system** under the British meant that Indian culture—and dance—can be found in places that were part of the British Empire as far away as Trinidad and Tobago in the Caribbean. As the last wave of invaders, the British occupied India for two centuries, from the mid-1700s to 1947. The British colonizers enacted levies on peasants throughout India, actively impeded local craft manufacturing, and placed emphasis on cash crops, undermining local food production and causing famine. The emphatically racist, colonizing, and extractive policies of the British had a massive impact on local cultural, religious, and artistic practices throughout India, including dance and dance cultures.

Most, though not all, dance in historical India had a relationship to the rich mythic landscape of the country, its epic stories, gods, goddesses, saints, and heroes. To this day, much of India's dance culture is still a part of religious traditions and cultures. Dances are performed as part of ritual, for festivals, to celebrate common history, for calendrical events, and as part of worship. It is also performed for entertainment and theater, to convey teachings and tell stories, and to celebrate and have fun. In particular, stories of Hindu gods and those of the heroes of the *Mahabharata* and *Ramayana* epics feature prominently in staged dance performances. Temple festivals often include dance performed to and sometimes *with* the energies of the deity. Important in the danced cultures of India are the major figures of the Hindu pantheon, which is rich with multiple gods and goddess. Dance, drama, and ritual frequently feature these gods and goddesses, including, for example, **Krishna**, the flute-playing lover of **Radha**; **Durga**, a fierce form of the goddess; **Ganesha**, the elephant-headed remover of obstacles; **Shiva**, the god of pure consciousness; and **Parvati**, or **Shakti**, the feminine principle, to name just a few.

Indian Nation-State: 1947 to Present

There are eight nationally recognized forms of **classical/neoclassical** dance in India. These classical forms have linkages with Sanskrit texts, connections to Hindu religious rituals, or connections to the Mughal courts of the 16th and 17th centuries. Classical dance forms are representers of state and national identities. India is divided into many states, each with unique language, heritage, cuisine, and culture. The resurgence of classical Indian dance forms in the 1950s and beyond was linked to the creation of the Indian nation-state and to regional identities within that larger nation-state. The maintenance and construction of tradition in Indian dance is important to the participants in these dance forms; however, Indian dance is dynamic and changes throughout time without losing its identity as "traditional." Regional and folk dances of India are too numerous to count. Dance events are common in India and are found in nearly every context—street theater, community parties, religious rituals, parades, celebrations, and just for fun. **Bhangra**, for example, is a lively and energetic folk dance from the state of Punjab in Northern India that has been popularized in other countries by college students from India who are studying abroad. **Garba**, on the other hand, is one of the chief folk dances of west India, performed on religious occasions like Navaratri (the nine nights in celebration of the goddess). Garba is danced in a circle, with participants singing and clapping musically to the rhythm of a drummer.

 See resource 19.2 in HK*Propel* for web links.

Classical Dances

There are at least eight distinct regional styles of classical dance in India. These styles share common core features, including the use of rhythmic footwork to accent musical accompaniment. Classical Indian dance is performed barefoot, and dancers use their feet to strike the stage in precise rhythmic patterns that match the pattern of the drum. Ranging from strong percusive striking to light rhythmic tapping, footwork using the ball, heel, whole foot, and sometimes even the sides of the feet is an almost universal characteristic of classical Indian dance. The footwork is usually accentuated by the dancer's rhythmically tinkling ankle bells. In classical dance there is a synergistic and harmonious relationship between music and movement, especially in terms of the rhythmical aspects. Both classical dance and classical music are ruled by a complex system of *tala* (rhythmic cycles) that are counted in *bols* (nonsense syllables that relate to the rhythm). This might sound like "tha ita na kita thay thay." These syllables have no direct meaning; they simply mark time in four beats. Dancers and drummers use these bols—spoken rhythms—to indicate rhythmic patterns throughout a dance piece. Drums for classical dance might be the *tabla*, *pakhavaj*, or *mridangam*. These are wooden drums with a leather head, played with the hands. Music for classical dance almost always derives from classical styles of Indian music and can include **sitar**, flute, **vena**, and other instruments. It may be avant-garde to perform classical dance to nonclassical music, and purists might deem such fusions experimental.

All classical styles of dance have elements of facial expressivity, or *abhinaya*, including complex eye, eyebrow, and cheek movements used to indicate mood (*bhava*). Most classical dance styles have some element of storytelling through dance (**natya**) that may explore the *navarasa*—the nine main emotional states conveyed by the dancer to invoke a mood in the audience. Classical dance also features the use of **mudras** (hand gestures) in two ways: as decorative motifs without explicit meaning, and as iconic meaning-making vehicles for storytelling. Intricate and complex mudras are a cardinal feature of classical Indian dance. In fact, the use of mudras in dance may be more highly developed in classical Indian dance than in any other dance form in the world. In "pure dance," or **nritta**, there is no story, but the dancer re-creates the mood of the music through graceful movements of the body, punctuating the rhythm of the music with their feet. The movement of classical dance is sculptural and harmonically balanced; there is a sense of equipoise in movement throughout all forms of classical Indian dance. Nothing should be discordant or jarring to the viewer, who is wrapped into an aesthetic experience of the dance and music.

Navarasa—The Nine Emotional Tastes

In classical Indian dance aesthetics there are nine (*nava*) emotional "tastes" (*rasa*) that form the cardinal emotional states transmitted by a dancer to the audience. These *rasa* are love (*shringara*), laughter (*hasya*), anger (*raudra*), compassion (*karuṇa*), disgust (*bibhatsam*), fear (*bhayanaka*), heroism (*veeram*), wonder (*adbhutha*), and peace (*shanta*).

All classical dance features elaborate costuming, jewelry, and makeup that may reference traditional regional styles of dress and regional textile design. While each style of classical dance has its own specific costume protocol, the ornamentation is always elaborate and may include bracelets, anklets, and hip belts. Each of the eight major classical dances is emblematic of a particular region or state within India and, along with distinctive costuming, has a unique vocabulary, syntax, and style. While all forms of classical Indian dance have similarities, such as rhythmic footwork and the use of mudras, an informed viewer can recognize characteristic elements of each form. For example, Odissi dance has a distinct triple-bend position, known as *tribhanghi*, and kathak dance is notable for virtuosic turns.

Bharatanatyam

Bharatanatyam has its origins in **Tamil Nadu**, a state in southern India. The dancer's knees usually remain bent in *aramandalam* position while the upper body is used in directionally precise constellations of movement. The footwork of bharatanatyam is complex, fast, and

Nritta, Nritya, and Natya Dance Movements

Sanskrit texts on dance distinguish between three categories of danced movement. Because "dance" is a Western term, we should be careful not to conflate our definitions of "dance" with these three terms, which are both inclusive and exclusive of Western ideas of danced movement. The three categories are nritta, nritya, and natya. Nritta is "pure dance" or "abstract dance," through which rhythmic footwork and bodily movements reflect the mood of the musical composition. In nritya, mudras and facial expression (abhinaya) relate to the lyrics of accompanying songs. Natya is dramatic acting within a piece of danced movement to elaborate on poetry or story using mudras and facial expression. Thus, natya contains elements of nritya.

spectacular. The dancer either interprets myths from Hindu texts and traditions in expressive, storytelling dance (natya), or performs nonnarrative (**nritya**) dance expressing or responding to song lyrics. There are several distinct schools, or styles, of bharatanatyam, distinguishable by signature movement characteristics that are apparent to informed viewers. The precursor to bharatanatyam was known as **sadir nac**, a style of dance performed by temple dancers before the renaissance of bharatanatyam in the 1960s. Both men and women perform classical bharatanatyam dance.

Kathak

Kathak hails from North India. Like bharatanatyam, there are several subschools or lineages of the dance form. Kathak emphasizes rhythmic foot movements and virtuosic turns. The kathak repertoire emphasizes verticality, and in the movement and costume one can observe the influence of Persian culture and the Mughal courts of northern India. Because of these origins, kathak is unique in having both Hindu and Muslim cultural influences. Kathak is performed to instruments that were brought to Muslim courts in India during the Mughal period. Kathak dancers in ancient India were traveling bards, men known as *kathakars*. Today both women and men perform kathak as entertainment on stages throughout the world. Improvisation and lively call and response challenges between drummers and dancers can be another feature of kathak.

Mohiniyattam (Mohiniattam)

Mohiniyattam classical dance, easily distinguishable by its white costume and gold border, is known as a **lasya**, or "feminine," style of dance. Uniform effort, continuity of movement, and the use of the torso and arms in curvilinear patterns are the hallmarks of a good dancer. Unlike bharatanatyam and Odissi, which have direct links to temple dancers and their dance practices, the history of Mohiniyattam dance is linked to dances of the historically polyandrous and matrilineal **Nayar caste** women of Kerala in South India. Mohiniyattam's roots as a temple dance practice are debated by scholars. It is rare to find a male performer or teacher of Mohiniyattam dance. The tradition is held almost exclusively by women.

Lasya, Tandava—Feminine, Masculine

Lasya is a term used to mean "feminine" and is related through myth to the dance of the goddess Parvati. The term *lasya* is often contrasted with **tandava**, the dance of the god Shiva, which is considered more "masculine." Whereas lasya is "slow and gentle," tandava is faster and more intense. These two terms, *lasya* and *tandava*, are relative qualitative generalized terms. For example, one might describe bharatanatyam as more tandava and Mohiniyattam as more lasya, as a generalization. That said, Mohiniyattam is known as "the lasya dance."

Odissi

Odissi is a classical style of dance with its origins in the eastern Indian state of **Odisha** (formerly Orissa). Odissi classical dancers use a distinctive body position known as *tribhangi*, a triple bend of the body that is seen in many statues and sculptures throughout India. The tribhangi is unique to Odissi dance, a hallmark of its style. The classical style of Odissi dance was re-created

Odissi.

STR/NurPhoto via Getty Images

from the dances of female temple performers known as *mahari* in Odisha and from the dances of **goti puas**, young boys who dress as women and perform more vigorous and acrobatic dances. Like bharatanatyam and Mohiniyattam, today Odissi is performed as a classical art on stages throughout the world. Also like bharatanatyam and Mohiniyattam, Odissi emphasizes use of abhinaya (facial expression) and mudra (gesture).

Sattriya

Sattriya has its origins in the eastern Indian state of **Assam**. A dance-drama performance form, it originated in the Krishna-centered monasteries of Assam. Traditionally, sattriya was performed by **bhokots** (male monks) in monasteries as a part of their daily rituals and as part of religious festivals. Today, in addition to this practice, sattriya is also performed onstage by secular women and men.

Kathakali

Kathakali is a dance-drama form from Kerala, India, with complex costuming that includes face paint, masks, and elaborate clothing. The face makeup can take many hours to complete. The traditional plays of kathakali are performed all night long, with some being performed over several nights. Some of these longer plays have been shortened to be performed over the course of a few hours. The traditional themes of the kathakali are folk stories, Hindu epic myths, and stories of heroes. Kathakali is performed for festivals, as entertainment, and to mark religious holidays. Historically, kathakali was performed only by men, with men taking both the male and female roles in a drama. Today there are a few women kathakali performers.

Kathakali.
Anshuman Poyrekar/Hindustan Times via Getty Images)

Kuchipudi

Kuchipudi comes from the southern India state of **Andhra Pradesh**. Unlike the other styles of classical dance, kuchipudi dancers also sing. Historically kuchipudi was performed by troupes of male dancers. "It is said that Siddhendra Yogi, the founder of Kuchipudi art form, once dreamt of Krishna dancing with his consorts Rukmini and Satyabhama and he ever since went upon a mission in search of dancers and in Kuchipudi village, every Brahmin family had to train one of their sons to learn dance-drama that included both male and female roles. It is noteworthy that women of elite castes of the days were not allowed to be part of the dances per the social norm of those days, hence men playing female roles" (Chavali 2018). Today the style is also performed by women. While kuchipudi resembles bharatanatyam, its movements are more subtle and playful.

Kuchipudi.

Jack Vartoogian/Getty Images

Manipuri

Manipuri dance, from the region of Manipur, is also known as **Jagoi**. A dance-drama form, Manipuri is famous for the depiction of the *raslila*, the dance of the god Krishna with the milkmaids, or *gopis*.

Devadasi—Temple Dancers

Devadasi dancers, having a variety of duties, customs, traditions, and statuses, were a sociocultural entity throughout much of the Indian subcontinent for centuries. Ethnographic records show that these women were "ever-auspicious" (*nitya-sumanagli*) and were ritually married to regional Hindu gods. In many cases, devadasis had obligatory ritual practices that included dancing, singing, offering lamps, and waving fans for the gods. Though not concubines or prostitutes, devadasis engaged in highly codified sexual relations with upper-caste men. Far from being morally repudiated, devadasis were historically treated with considerable respect by their communities. Many devadasis had ritual sanction to dance inside the *nata mandapa* (temple dance space) and were prohibited from dancing outside the temple, though enforcement of this prohibition was uneven (see Kersenboom-Story 1987; Marglin 1985, 1990; Vijaisri 2004; Coorlawala 1992; Meduri 1996, 2001; Kothari 2010).

Devadasis Under British Colonialism

Nearly all classical dance styles have a relationship to temple dance practices of the devadasis. The notable exceptions to this rule are possibly kathak in the north (though this is debated) and kathakali dance-drama in the south. Important to the history of classical Indian dance, devadasi dedication in South India waned in the mid-1850s due to crises in the subcontinental colonial political economy and cultural pressures of British colonialism (Meduri 1996; Parker 1998; Kersenboom-Story 1996; Vijairsri 1998). Throughout

Cultural Highlight

DANCING THE DIVINE

"I enter the stage, dressed in golden yellow with a necklace on my bare chest, a peacock feather in my hair knot, and I hold a flute in my left hand. I am 7 years old. The audience roars with applause and women cry out 'Govind (Krishna) has appeared.' That is the first clear memory I have of performing on stage as the divine Lord Krishna. From that time on and well into my twenties, I danced as Krishna in multiple dance-dramas that were centered on Krishna Radha themes, and each time I was lifted off the stage and carried by the audience members. Flower garlands were placed around my neck, and audience devotees of Lord Krishna bent down to touch my feet. Such is the power of seeing/imaging the Divine for people, especially those devoted to the ritual of prayer in dance.

"Seeing a divine spirit appear through a visualized human body in dance is not a unique phenomenon in ritual and prayer. The mind and imagination play a powerful role in cultural belief. As in most ancient cultures, religious rituals in India were the earliest inspiration of visualized body movements that later became known as classical dance and developed into a highly codified style with vocabulary and aesthetics for dramatic interpretations. While training in technique and skill are of paramount importance for a dancer, yet the 'rasa and bhava' (emotion and flavor) of a character role exhibited by the dancer may surpass the technique, bringing into being a genuine divine image for the devotees/audience. The clarity of such a vision is resonant for both, leaving the dancer somewhat bewildered and overcome with a sense of inner joy, while the audience blessed by this vision bows with folded hands. I recall hearing my mother and Gurus speak about these backstage.

"Dance has been my life in all these years of living—from active hard movements to lyrical, and now I reflect on my breath as it dances in my body each moment." (Written by Ranjanaa Devi, 2021)

this time, a series of legal cases classified devadasis as prostitutes; their dance practices were rendered degenerate. The result of these legal and cultural changes was, in economic terms, quite simple: thousands of women found themselves unemployed. Their dance and music no longer had financial patronage from the temples and courts. After a period of decline, contemporary forms of classical Indian dance were reformed and codified from a variety of sources. This project of codification and regeneration happened in tandem with the cultural renaissance that began in 1947 with Indian independence. These sources included the dance traditions of the devadasi and their teachers (though at times the actual dancers were marginalized in this process), Sanskrit texts, and sculptures in temples and cultural sites.

Today, classical dance is not performed inside the nata mandapa, and the tradition of dedicating dancers to perform in temples is no longer practiced. Nonetheless, classical dance retains many hints of religious traditions and rituals—the stage as akin to a ritual space and bowing to the earth

prior to practice and performance, for example. The content of most contemporary classical dance choreography is religious in nature and often uses the myths of Hinduism as a subject (Dandekar 1998; Mahesvara et al. 2001; Royo 2006; Srinivasan 2012). As an expression of devotion, dancers perform the namaskaram, or **bhumi pranam**, prayer prior to beginning dance practice. Dances pay special reverence to our teachers, gurus, and their knowledge. In the tradition, or **parampara**, of classical dance it is not typical to study with many teachers. The lineage of teachings that are brought through a single teacher to a student is a process that is cherished and respected. A relationship with one's teacher will often last a lifetime. My guru of Odissi dance, Ranjanaa Devi, began dancing the role of the god Krishna from a young age. She tells the story in her own words in the Cultural Highlight sidebar.

 See resource 19.3 in HK*Propel* for web links.

Tradition and Reconstruction

From the 1920s onward, reconstructions, or re-creations, of traditional dances gave rise to many forms of classical Indian dance. In the case of bharatanayam, Mohiniyattam, and Odissi, the renaissance of these "traditions" was tied to aestheticizing the female body. The re-creations were also tied to bringing dance into the sphere of the nuclear family, thereby involving dance with the projects of state consolidation and nationalism that defined India's independence from British colonialism. What was previously a panoply of styles and traditions became standardized into classical styles with a variety of substyles of dance.

In the case of Mohiniyattam, for example, a practice that was reconstructed (and radically refashioned), now represents India and traditions of the south Indian state of Kerala wherever it is performed and practiced. This process was not a simple "invention of tradition" (Hobsbawm and Ranger 1983). Rather, it was a complex exchange of repertoire, informed by arts maestros. An archive of Sanskrit texts, along with the raga (melodic mode) and tala (rhythmic cycles) systems of classical Indian music, enabled these creations of classical Indian dance forms. These exchanges of repertoire do not, however, diminish the importance that dancers and choreographers place on these styles as "traditional" and "spiritual" practices. Dance can be radically refashioned and still be completely traditional, retaining its value as "tradition" even without the absolute replication of repertoire from one generation to the next (Lemos 2015).

Many (though, by all means, not all) South Asian dance scholars trace contemporary classical dance traditions to Sanskrit textual origins, especially to the *Natyashastra*. While there are strong correlations between Sanskrit textual evidence of historical dance practices and contemporary classical dance, there were also many international exchanges that shaped the styles of classical Indian dance.

Throughout the formation of classical Indian dance, Indian dancers traveled west while western dancers traveled east (Shelton 1981; Srinivasan 2012). As dancers traveled, so did their repertoires. Western dancers, most notably ballerina **Anna Pavlova** (1881-1931) and modern dancer **Ruth St. Denis** (1879-1968), directly influenced the re-creation of classical dance throughout India (Coorlawala 1992; Desmond 1991; Srinivasan 2012). The performances of ***nautch*** dancers ("dancing women") and devadasis in Europe and America inspired ballet choreographers and modern dancers (Meduri 2004; Mehta 2002; Srinivasan 2012). Classical Indian dance practices that were reconstructed in the past 60 years have come to represent "ancient" Indian tradition. A complex transfer (and invention) of repertoire bolstered by an archive of truly ancient Sanskrit texts enabled the creation of classical Indian dance, arguably giving the dance a justified grounding in ancient traditions. In the contemporary sphere, classical Indian dance is a signifier of ancient tradition, of Indian culture, and of Indian nationality.

 See resource 19.4 in HK*Propel* for web links.

Crosscurrents

Dance in India has long been a confluence of global cultures. Dance scholarship has attended to sociocultural analysis, conceptualizing dance as a commodity positioned for exchange on the global market (Savigliano 2004). In the case of Indian dance, bharatanatyam has, from its inception, been a "global" form of dance developed through a complex transnational exchange. Because of the myths of "cultural purity" and unbroken "tradition" pervading the dance practice, it is important to position our discussion of classical Indian dance with research that has examined the transnational roots of contemporary/classical dance forms. The cross-influences of and on Western dance icons such as Pavlova and St. Denis were key examples of such interactions in the late 19th and early 20th centuries.

Today, many contemporary choreographers who are trained in classical dance styles continue to explore and expand genres of Indian dance in and out of India. For instance, Padma Menon's choreography is an artful synthesis of embodied knowledge, including modern dance, kuchipudi, and **kalaripayyatu** (Indian martial arts). Finally, no survey of dance in India would be complete without mention of bhangra and **Bollywood**. Dances in Indian films, often termed "Bollywood dance," have a significant presence in popular culture within India, throughout much of Asia and Africa, and through the Indian diaspora. Early Bollywood dance had influences from the Indian classical dance traditions, and many Bollywood dancers are classically trained. Bollywood dance now includes influences from hip-hop, salsa, ballroom dance, and modern dance. Contemporary dance in India includes experimental fusions of classical, folk, modern dance, hip-hop, ballet, Bollywood dance, and uncategorized styles of experimental dance. Bhangra was originally an exuberant style of folk dance from the Punjab region of India but is now a global style that has been influenced by hip-hop dance and music.

 See resource 19.5 in HK*Propel* for web links.

Summary

Like India, the world's largest democracy with an ethnically and religiously diverse population, "Indian" dance is a vast and multifocal subject. India is a cornucopia of dance styles and traditions. Dance events happen in nearly every context, from the most secular to religious ritual and festivals, and they can be found in villages and cities throughout the continent. Because there is such a diversity of dance in India, it is nearly impossible to make any blanket statements about Indian dance. Even so, the classical dance styles of India are rich repositories of aesthetic, religious, cultural, and historical knowledge. To master a classical Indian dance form takes a lifetime. A consummate performer of classical Indian dance has mastery over rhythm, melody, music, poetry, mythology, costuming, makeup, aesthetics, movement, and expression. These elements coalesce to express and invigorate the rich cultural heritage of India that is now seen around the world.

Discussion Questions

1. What is "tradition"? Do you consider classical Indian dance to be "traditional"? Why or why not? Would a dance ethnographer consider classical Indian dance to be "traditional"? Why or why not?

2. What does it mean for a dance form to be classical? Compare and contrast Indian classical dance to other forms of classical dance. What features do they share?

3. What similarities do you see between classical Indian styles of dance? Watch examples and explain.

 Visit HK*Propel* for access to this chapter's Application Activity.

Selected Glossary

abhinaya—The art of expression used in classical Indian dance. Abhinaya leads the audience toward an experience (bhava) of a sentiment (rasa).

aramandalam—A primary position used in bharatanatyam, with the legs turned out and knees bent deeply.

bharatanatyam—Neoclassical Indian dance with origins in South India in the state of Tamil Nadu.

devadasi—Women historically dedicated to temple service. Some were trained in music and dance.

guru—Teacher.

kalari—Dance classroom or dance studio; traditionally open-air on the sides with a roof.

kathak—A style of neoclassical Indian dance with origins in the Mughal courts of North India.

kathakali—A style of dance-drama from Kerala that is known for its elaborate costumes and makeup.

kuchipudi—A style of neoclassical dance from the Indian state of Andhra Pradesh.

Mohiniyattam—A style of neoclassical Indian dance with its origins in the southern Indian state of Kerala.

Manipuri—Anything from or related to the modern-day Indian state of Manipur. Specifically, this term can relate to the classical dance from Manipur, known as "Manipuri" or Ras Leela, which is inspired by the god Krishna and his dances with the gopis, or milkmaids.

mudras—Single and double hand gestures used in dance, ritual, and yoga. Mudras range from very complex to simple gestures. Some mudras are abstract and have no direct meaning; they are used decoratively. Other mudras have direct meaning and represent ideas, things, people, and places.

namaskaram—Namaskar (or namaste) is a traditional greeting performed with hands placed together. Dancers perform "namaskaram" at the beginning of dance practice (also termed *bhumi pranaam*, literally "bowing to the earth"). In the context of dance this is a short sequence of movements performed prior to practicing dance. Bowing to the earth, to the teacher, and to the teachings. The namaskaram creates a sacred space for the dance practice that follows.

Odissi—A style of new classical Indian dance with its origins in the western Indian state of Odisha.

Selected References and Resources

Chakravorty, P. 2000. "From Interculturalism to Historicism: Reflections on Classical Indian Dance." *Dance Research Journal* 32(2): 108-119. https://doi.org/10.2307/1477983.

Keshaviah, A. 2008. "Decoding the Modern Practice of Bharatanatyam." *Congress on Research in Dance Conference Proceedings* 40(S1): 140-150.

Kothari, S. 2010. *New Directions in Indian Dance*. Mumbai: Marg Publications.

Meduri, A. 2004. "Bharatanatyam as a Global Dance: Some Issues in Research, Teaching, and Practice." *Dance Research Journal* 36(2): 11-29. https://doi.org/10.2307/20444589.

Pillai, S. 2002. "Rethinking Global Indian Dance Through Local Eyes: The Contemporary Bharatanatyam Scene in Chennai." *Dance Research Journal* 34(2): 14-29. https://doi.org/10.2307/1478457.

Samson, L., and Pasricha, A. 1987. *Rhythm in Joy: Classical Indian Dance Traditions*. New Delhi: Lustre Press.

Singha, R., and R. Massey. 1967. *Indian Dances: Their History and Growth*. London: Faber.

Soneji, D. 2004. "Living History, Performing Memory: Devadasi Women in Telugu-Speaking South India." *Dance Research Journal* 36(2), 30.

Srinivasan, A. 1984. "Temple 'Prostitution' and Community Reform: An Examination of the Ethnographic, Historical and Textual Context of the *Devadasi* of Tamil Nadu, South India." PhD thesis, Cambridge University.

Srinivasan, P. 2012. *Sweating Saris: Indian Dance as Transnational Labor*. Philadelphia: Temple University.

20

Dance in Indonesia

Jathilan Trance Dance

Abdul Haque Chang

Learning Objectives

After reading this chapter you will be able to do the following:

- Identify the differences and similarities between the court dances and folk dances of Indonesia.
- Consider the role of religion in Indonesian dance.
- Discuss the greater economic and social benefits of traditions like jathilan.
- Trace the influences of outside cultures and beliefs on the arts and traditions of Indonesia.

Key Terms

gamelan—Traditional Javanese musical ensemble consisting of metal percussive instruments.

jathilan—Javanese dance involving spirit possession (trance) and horse figures.

Javanese Ramayana Theater—Performance derived from the Indian Hindu epic tale of the legendary prince Rama.

Kejawen—Traditional Javanese beliefs with different regional variants incorporating local or indigenous spiritual practices.

Kyai Samandiman—Sacred whip used in Javanese rituals such as jathilan. Also called *pecut*, *cemethi*, or *cambuk*.

pawang—Trance master.

sajen—Specialist who manages the offerings during religious rituals.

Jathilan Dance—The Moment of Spectacle

January 5, 2020, was a cloudy and rainy Sunday. I was attending a morning *jathilan* performance at the community ground in my family's village in Central **Java**, Indonesia. The organizer of the event was the *kepala desa*—the village headman—and an old friend. It was his son's circumcision celebration. Musicians were playing **gamelan**, the traditional **Javanese** ensemble of musical instruments on a wooden stage full of singers and children. The *sajen* (offering ritual specialist) stood near an array of flowers, boiled chicken, rice crackers, perfume, and much more.

The stage and dance ring were fenced off with bamboo. In the center, eight jathilan dancers were performing in pairs on either side of their woven bamboo horses. Both male and female dancers wore makeup and colorful costumes resembling those of the **Javanese Ramayana Theater**. Dancers mounted the "horses" and moved forward in pairs, changing their rhythmic movements with the varying musical tones. The tempo altered dramatically from very slow moments to frenetic climaxes. Suddenly the *pawang* (trance master) grabbed the flower offerings and moved to the center of the ring. Dancers gathered in a tight circle holding their horses. The pawang closed his eyes and raised one hand in the air, holding the flowers in the other, and recited something. Junior pawangs stood next to the performers, holding whips in their hands.

The audience went utterly silent. The master flung the floral offering onto the dancers, and at that moment, the three junior pawangs waved their whips in the air and cracked them, making the sound of a thousand thunderstorms. The musicians played a haunting beat that built to a frenzy, sending the dancers into a trance (*surup*). They moved wildly in all directions, slamming into each other, the pawangs, helpers, and volunteers. The dancers lost all control as they were possessed (*kesurupan*) by different supernatural or ancestral entities and guardian spirits in fulfillment of the jathilan ritual.

 See resource 20.1 in HK*Propel* for web links.

Jathilan follows Javanese **Kejawen**, a syncretic tradition that interweaves old Javanese religions, local faiths and beliefs (*Aliran Kepercayaan*), animism, **Hinduism**, **Buddhism**, and **Islam**. Kejawen is also referred to as *agama Jawa*, or the Javanese religion. *Jathilan* means "dancing like riding a horse" and is also called *jaranan*, *kuda lumping*, *jaran ebleg*, *kuda kepang*, *jaran kepang*, or the "horse dance." This ritual offers a glimpse of traditional culture in the setting of a village festival, which provides an opportunity for local vendors to sell their products in a **pasar**, or pop-up market.

Jathilan dance occurs regularly all around Java and follows no specific calendar. It can occur during any social, cultural, or religious ceremony—Muslim, Christian, Hindu, or other—but has no affiliation to any specific religion. The performance can take place anywhere in the open. Most often it happens on the side of a road where there is enough space for the performance and an audience. Anyone can invite a jathilan group, provided they can pay for the performance. Some communities have their own groups who perform for the community during the Islamic annual

Jathilan Woven Bamboo Horse

The jathilan bamboo horse (kuda lumping or jaran kepang) is decorated with designs unique to the village or region and represents a mythical character in traditional Javanese culture. One myth concerns Dewi Songgolangit, a princess whose father offered her in marriage to anyone who could make an art form that had never been seen before. To prevent bloodshed among the many princes who came to fight for her hand, Dewi Songgolangit decided to end her own life. People from East Java invented jathilan and another trance dance, **Reog Ponorogo**, to commemorate her story and her sacrifice. Stereotypically, the white horse is considered good, and the black one represents evil forces. Offerings of food are presented to jathilan horses at a pawang's (master's) home for guardian spirits that protect jathilan dancers and the pawang during the event.

events of **Idul Fitri** and **Idul Adha** (in Arabic, Eid al-Fitr and Eid al Adha), when many people return to their village for the holidays. These characteristics of jathilan illustrate key elements of Indonesian dance culture, illuminating the unique confluences of places, times, and peoples in Indonesian history.

Crosscurrents

Indonesia is a culturally diverse country in Southeast Asia at the crossroads of the world, stretching from the Indian border near the tip of **Sumatra** to the Pacific Ocean near Australia. Located along the **Pacific Ring of Fire**—an arc of volcanoes and seismic activity—Indonesia has long been subjected to frequent natural disasters. The official language is **Bahasa Indonesia**; however, there are more than 700 dialects and languages. The country consists of 17,508 islands containing 1,340 recognized tribes and cultural, religious, ethnic, and linguistic groups. Most significant are Javanese, Sundanese, Malay, Batak, Madurese, Batawi, Minangkabau, Buginese, Bantenese, Banjarese, Balinese, Achenese, Dayak, Sasak, Chinese Indonesian, Makassarese, Minahasan, and Nias. The country has 34 provinces, each headed by a governor.

Indonesia is on an ancient global trade route that has significantly shaped the region's development. Though indigenous populations in the archipelago can be traced back at least 40,000 years, Indonesia has always influenced and been influenced by people from other parts of the world in its languages, cultures, religions, and population. Buddhism, Hinduism, Islam, and Christianity spread to Indonesia through trade and missionaries from China, India, the Middle East, Europe, and more. On the island of Java, **Jakarta** city has been the capital of Indonesia since the Dutch colonial era and is the center of economic, cultural, and political life.

The main islands are Sumatra, Java, **Borneo**, **Timor**, **Bali**, **Sulawesi**, and **West Papua**. The population of Indonesia is 270.6 million. According to 2018 statistics, 86.70 percent are Muslim, 10.72 percent Christian, 1.74 percent Hindu, and 0.84 percent are categorized as Aliran Kepercayaan—those who have different faiths or belief systems. Until 1945, when Indonesia achieved independence, the region was called **Dutch East Indies** or **Hindia Belanda**. The term *Indonesia*

was first used by the English ethnologist George Windsor Earl in 1850 when referring to the culture of the region as "Indonesian." Indonesian people preferred it after 1913 instead of "Dutch East Indies" to remove the Dutch colonial influence from the name of the country.

Early Kingdoms: 2nd to 12th Centuries CE

The early kingdoms were a time when many currents in culture, language, philosophy, and history arose, heavily influenced by Indian Hinduism and Buddhism (table 20.1). Most people followed one of those religions in some form or another, especially in Sumatra, Java, Bali, and Kalimantan (on Borneo). During this period, Indian culture began to blend with local traditions, and many Hindu and Buddhist states in different parts of the nation rose in power.

Borobudur—Buddhist Temple in Java

Borobudur was constructed on the island of Java between the eighth and ninth centuries and is the largest Buddhist temple in the world. A unique and remarkable manifestation of Indonesian art, architecture, and local motifs, this Mahayana Buddhist temple was designated a UNESCO World Heritage site in 1991.

During the **Sailendra** (750-850 CE), Javanese Buddhist styles of architecture and traditional elements of ancestor worship influenced temple design. From the ninth century onward, the old Javanese language flourished; in the 16th century, it began to change and is now referred to as new Javanese. When Islam arrived, Javanese, Malay, and other inscriptions began to be written in *Jawi*, which was derived from Arabic writing, especially Islamic religious texts, poetic works, and local literature. In the 17th century, Javanese was the predominant language. This was the time of the royal court culture of Java. Declining kingdoms were succeeded by more powerful kings, and royal dances, poetry, art, and elevated language (*halus*, or aspects of "high" culture) developed.

Table 20.1 Time Line of Indonesian Kingdoms

Kingdom	Time period	Events
Srivijaya kingdom	c. 683-1286 CE	First kingdom to consolidate much of the region in Sumatra, West and Central Java, Malaysia, Vietnam, and Cambodia as a Buddhist empire. It was a maritime kingdom with trade and business links in other coastal areas of the region, as well as China, India, and the Malay Archipelago.
Majapahit kingdom	c. 1293-1527	Rose into power from West Java and controlled a vast part of Southeast Asia, paving the way for a modern empire with a strong military and trade presence in the region. Around 1365, most of current Indonesia was conquered by the Majapahit kingdom at its peak, after which it started to decline.
Aceh sultanate	c. 1496-1903	Located on the northwestern tip of Sumatra, it was a strong maritime kingdom prior to Dutch control. The Dutch government, after occupying Java in the 1800s, took another 100 years to overtake Aceh.
Mataram kingdom	c. 1586-1755	Introduced Islam to Indonesia through Indian and Arab traders and religious scholars, establishing Islamic kingdoms in Java and Sumatra. Most of the ruling Hindu dynasty from Java retreated to Bali. Also during this time, Christianity was first introduced.

Sultanate of Yogyakarta and Surakarta Sultanate

Due to internal conflict in the royal court, the Mataram sultanate was divided between two empires in 1755, the **Sultanate of Yogyakarta** (1755-present) and **Surakarta Sultanate** (1745-1946). The Sultanate of Yogyakarta continues to prevail as a ceremonial kingdom under the shadow of the Indonesian government. During the 1945-1949 war against the Dutch colonial empire, Yogyakarta was the center of the independence movement, providing military, financial, and political support. In appreciation, the territory was given Special Region status in the newly independent nation.

Surakarta Sultanate's legacy continues today with Sri Susuhunan Pakubuwono XIII, who has been sultan since 2004. However, unlike in Yogyakarta, the Surakarta sultan's role is symbolic. He has palaces and property but no role in administration of the city. However, these two royal courts are considered the modern center of Javanese culture, art, and dance and a continuation of the historical legacy. Many traditions in art, dance, language, and culture have close connections with them. Classical dance (including the royal court dances mentioned in this chapter), dramatic arts, **Javanese shadow puppets (wayang kulit)**, traditional fabric printing (**batik**), music, handicrafts, and poetic traditions originated in these courts and survive today through their patronage. The families of the sultans maintain the royal palaces in Yogyakarta and Surakarta, shrines of saints, royal tombs, and cultural artifacts. Numerous annual festivals, rituals, and processions are organized by the courts in Yogyakarta, Surakarta, and parts of Central Java. They are a source of Javanese culture, and their promotion has been a priority of Yogyakarta's government. The royal courts have become an essential part of the cultural heritage of Indonesia. Many art schools, universities, and institutes have received their patronage in the past; currently, the national government is supporting them to continue the legacy of art, education, culture, and performing arts.

Kingdom of Bali

The Kingdom of Bali (914-1908 CE) became the last refuge for Hindu-Buddhism when Java was overtaken by Islam in the 16th century and Javanese and other followers of Hinduism fled to Bali. In 1908, the Dutch conquest of Bali ended its thousand-year legacy. Over a millennium of existence, the kingdom's Hindu religion interwove with Buddhism and indigenous beliefs to take center stage in Balinese life. As a result, the culture encompasses vibrant architecture, arts, and crafts, all of which contribute to Bali's highly renowned culture.

Dutch Colonial Empire

The Dutch colonial empire (1610-1945) is one of the longest eras of Indonesian history. It started with the **Dutch East India Company** in 1610; by 1800 a Dutch government was established, and the region was called the Dutch East Indies. From 1610 to 1945, including a brief period of British rule from 1811 to 1816, the inhabitants endured colonization and rule by force until the brutal war of independence from 1945 to 1949, after which Indonesia was recognized as a sovereign nation-state.

Japanese Occupation (1942-1945)

The Japanese occupation (1942-1945) occurred during the Second World War. Following this period, Indonesian youth began to struggle against reoccupation by the Dutch and the British, ultimately gaining Indonesian independence (1945-1949). On August 17, 1945, resistance leaders **Sukarno** and **Mohammad Hatta** proclaimed the independence of Indonesia from the Dutch, who had lost the moral ground and political power in the region. Before surrendering to the British army, which came to take charge until the Dutch returned, the Japanese army gave all its weapons and resources to the Indonesian resistance, giving them a chance to fight first the British and then the Dutch to prevent the reestablishment of colonial rule.

During the **New Order** (1965-1998), **General Suharto**, the self-proclaimed second president of Indonesia, ruled an authoritarian government until 1998, when a student-led movement and the Asian financial crisis forced him to resign. Under Suharto in 1965 and 1966, between one million and two million people were massacred on the pretext of an anticommunist purge. The Communist Party of Indonesia was banned. Its members, sympathizers, and leaders were arrested and executed. Thousands were imprisoned until the late 1980s without any charge or proper judicial process. Civil liberties and human rights were violated. It was a harsh time in Indonesian history, where the state had control over lives, the media, and the flow of information.

Indonesia today is a growing country with excellent prospects for development. Tourism is a major attraction, particularly in Central Java and Bali. The economy is growing fast. The majority of the population is young. Social media is enormously popular among the younger generations. Arts and culture are popular, and the government is strongly motivated to grow these sectors further.

 See resource 20.2 in HK*Propel* for web links.

Diversity of Indonesian Dance

The geographic and cultural diversity of Indonesia is evident in its regional dance culture. While dance throughout Indonesia has sacred, folk, and cultural origins, Java and Bali are most significant, because these regions exhibit distinct characteristics in their dances. Furthermore, according to the Ministry of Education and Culture, there are around 3,000 different styles of dance in the Indonesian archipelago. Of these, the ***saman*** dance from the Gayo region of **Aceh** province, **Javanese court dance** from the Yogyakarta region, and **Balinese temple dance** have been designated **UNESCO Intangible Cultural Heritage** dances. The unique styles of dance and their music and costumes have become representative of Indonesian culture nationally and internationally. Balinese temple dance is considered sacred, and Javanese court dances are a refined classical art form. Saman is a type of folk or traditional dance with captivating rhythms and quick, synchronized movements.

These dances are regularly performed in public accompanied by the gamelan orchestras that are an essential part of most Indonesian dance events. The two prominent Javanese court dances of Yogyakarta, ***bedhaya*** and ***serimpi***, are formal, ritualized, and performed by women. They are considered sacred and classical and referred to as high (halus) culture, in comparison to jathilan or ***dangdut***, which are considered lowbrow public dances. Dangdut is a popular dance music throughout Southeast Asia, considered vulgar by cultural elites due to its erotic dance steps and gestures. However, it is wildly popular and performed all around Indonesia. Just hearing the dangdut rhythms can make people start to dance.

Gamelan—Traditional Indonesian Music for Dance

"Across Indonesia, but particularly on the islands of Java and Bali, gamelan is the most popular form of traditional music. A gamelan ensemble consists of a variety of metal percussion instruments, usually made of bronze or brass, including xylophones, drums, and gongs. It may also feature bamboo flutes, wooden stringed instruments, and vocalists, but the focus is on the percussion" (Szczepanski 2019).

Regional Dances of Indonesia

Each island in Indonesia has many traditional, religious, and folk dances that invoke the diverse local practices, traditions, and history. Table 20.2 presents a small sample of those found all over Indonesia. This topic would require a separate book-length volume, but a brief look at the remarkable range of dances will help to illuminate the forces working to shape Indonesian

Javanese Ramayan Theater—Indian Hindu Epic in Indonesia

The *Ramayana*—an ancient Indian Hindu epic from a sacred text written in Sanskrit—is a story of patience, commitment, wisdom, and the fight between good and evil. The protagonist, Rama, follows the dharma—an aspect of truth or reality—and succeeds at the end. Based on this epic, the Javanese Ramayana performance is adapted to the vernacular to become an essential part of local culture. Regular performances take place in cities, towns, and villages throughout Indonesia as a Javanese or Balinese shadow puppet show. The Ramayana dance performance is also popular in Thailand, Cambodia, and other areas of Southeast Asia influenced by Indian Hinduism. The costumes and style of feminine makeup used in the Ramayana also appear in jathilan and Javanese and Balinese sacred and folk dance and performing arts.

dance through the ages. In each region a few of the many dances have been described to give a sense of the variety and characteristics within the regional dance culture.

While the sheer number of Indonesian dances can seem overwhelming, we can begin to understand their nature more deeply by looking at a specific form. Some dances are considered formal classical art by and for the cultural elite and others are popular entertainment for the general public, yet all are firmly woven into Indonesian culture and can be examined to reveal some specific dynamics at work. The widespread occurrence of trance dance is particularly significant. From ancient times to the present, trance rituals have been an integral part of Indonesian culture in every social realm, from rural villages to the royal palaces.

 See resource 20.3 in HK*Propel* for web links.

Ancestor Worship, Trance, and Religion

Trance, in one form or another, is an ancient tradition in Indonesia with its origins in ancestor worship. These practices are part of Kejawen religion in Java, **Aluk To Dolo** in **Toraja**, and **Sang Hyang Widhi Wasa** in Balinese Hinduism. In Indonesia many beliefs that are not part of such mainstream religions as Islam, Protestantism, Catholicism, Hinduism, Buddhism, or Confucianism are considered *Aliran Kepercayaan*. These local religions

Kejawen—The Javanese Religion

Kejawen is an ancient Javanese belief system that transcends religious boundaries and is followed by many Muslims, Christians, and Hindus. Its central principles are based on harmony in society, between humans and nature, and between humans and God. It can be observed in jathilan dance, ancestor worship days (*sadranan* or *nyadran*), offering rituals, everyday prayers, and shrine and grave pilgrimage rituals.

Table 20.2   Select Dances Found in Indonesia

Balinese dances	
Baris	A warrior's dance that shows off a dancer's martial skills.
Barong	Dramatic performance about a mythical being who protects a village from an evil witch.
Cendrawasih	Reenacts the mating ritual of the bird of paradise.
Condong	Accompanied by *pangulingan*, a style of gamelan. It involves a stock character, a maidservant, who appears in many other dances.
Gambuh	An ancient dance drama accompanied by a gamelan *gambuh* ensemble.
Topeng	Another dramatic dance accompanied by a gamelan orchestra and involving performers in masks and ornate costumes interpreting traditional stories of kings and heroes.
Javanese dances	
Gambyong	A blend of folk and court dance.
Gandrung	A dance drama throughout Indonesia; the most popular variation is from the well-known region of Java, giving the city the nickname of Kota Gandrung, or "city of gandrung."
Golek wayang wong	Also known as *wayang orang* ("human wayang"). A classical, stylized performance of stories from the *Ramayana* or *Mahabharata*. The epitome of Javanese aesthetic unity, it involves dance, drama, music, visual arts, language, and literature.
Reog Ponorogo	A traditional folk dance performed in an open space that involves magic and dancers dressed in animal masks or costumes
Dances of the Sudanese culture in West Java	
Bajidor Kahot	Typically performed by eight young women and involves specific movements, costumes, and sometimes props; it is accompanied by gamelan and a distinctive regional drumming style.
Jaipongan	A popular dance created by Sudanese composer Gugum Gumbira and based on traditional music and movements. Also known as *jaipong*.
Sisingaan	A traditional dance in which dancers carry an ark or palanquin that resembles a lion; children ride inside it, and the dance often celebrates a child's ritual circumcision.
Dances of the Betawi culture of Jakarta	
Cokek	Performed by a woman and a man; the name is taken from the *kebaya* (traditional shirt) worn by the dancers.
Langgang Betawi	A traditional dance derived from a folk tale that invokes the theme of women's freedom.
Ondel-ondel	A dance involving a large, iconic puppet figure.
Ronggeng	A dance in which couples exchange verses of poetry accompanied by a *rebab* (two-stringed lute) or violin and a gong.
Topeng Betawi	A traditional masked dance with songs, comedy, and drama, often performed at weddings, circumcisions, and other celebrations.

and beliefs embrace syncretic spirituality, ancestor worship, shamanism, **dynamism**, totemism, and animism. Trance tradition is found in most cultures in Indonesia. In Java and Bali, it originated in ancient religious practices and persists as part of the culture in modern times.

While in trance, the dancers become mediums through which a divine presence communicates with the mortal world. From a cultural perspective, trance is a way to ask ancestors for blessings, help, protection from disaster, safeguarding of crops from diseases and drought, and avoidance of evil spirits. Many trance dance traditions in Bali are part of the agricultural cycle and engage local cosmological beliefs. These trance dances are believed to provide protection for the local economy, people, and environment. They create balance between the mortal and immortal world through intervention by the ancestors. Halting these trance dances creates imbalance in the social and economic life of these communities and can cause disasters, earthquakes, ruined crops, death, and misery.

In Java and Bali, ancestors are worshiped through trance dance, as well as other means. For example, the Toraja people's treatment of corpses as if they were still alive (see sidebar) highlights the importance of ancestor worship in Indonesia. In a similar vein, it is believed that deceased ancestors who observe rituals and performances, such as trance dances, will help protect the community. These events are regularly held in the rural areas of Java and Bali. Every year before the Islamic fasting period of **Ramadan**, ancestors are commemorated during the "month to remember ancestral spirits" (**Ruwah**). Pilgrimage to graveyards is a special rite of this tradition. Graves are cleaned and maintained and decorated with flowers. Food is shared, and the living ask their deceased family members for protection.

Ancestor Worship in Indonesia—Toraja People

The many faces of ancestor worship and traditions surrounding death undergird the uniquely extensive presence of Indonesian trance rituals, such as dance. In the Toraja culture of South Sulawesi, the sixth most populous province in Indonesia, the dead are not buried immediately but instead are kept in their homes and treated as living people until they are buried— which may happen years after death. Every few years after they are buried, their bodies are taken from their graves for a cleaning ritual. In Toraja culture, a person never really dies.

Ancestor worship, as manifested through trance rituals such as jathilan in Java and **kris dance** in Bali, is a key element of Indonesian dance culture. Many of these rituals have been explored by researchers over the years, most notably in anthropologist **Margaret Mead**'s 1937 film ***Trance and Dance in Bali***. Research such as Mead's film documents the cultural centrality of trance rituals to illuminate the unique elements that define Balinese dance culture. A focus on jathilan dance will provide a deeper understanding of Indonesian culture as a whole.

 See resource 20.4 in HK*Propel* for web links.

Jathilan Trance Dance

The Horse Dance

Historically, jathilan was considered vulgar and common by the Javanese cultural elite, and the trance aspects were even banned for several decades. However, after 1998, with the increasing demand for traditional arts, jathilan became an essential social and cultural event. Its flexibility allows village groups to develop their own creative variants of the performance without departing from its rich traditions. Thanks to its increasing popularity, jathilan has become an emerging cultural industry in Central Java.

Banning Trance Dance

During the dictatorship of General Suharto from 1965 to 1998, trance dance was prohibited. The jathilan dance was allowed, but trance, or anything esoteric or supernatural, was banned because it was considered a threat to the New Order. In urban areas, jathilan happened under the watchful eye of the state to prevent any expression of dissidence. In the post-1998 era, jathilan has reemerged as a trance dance and is now a very popular tradition on Java.

Jathilan is a traditional trance dance; accordingly, there are great variations not just between Central and East Java but within each village and region. The pawangs (trance masters) have different ways to conduct the performance. This

Cultural Highlight

PAWANG—TRANCE MASTER

The pawang is the leader and master of ceremonies; he is also called the trance master or the handler. In East Java the pawang is called a *gambuh*. Most pawangs have a family history of traditional dance, music, or puppetry. Many claim to have received orders from a spirit in a dream or a **wangsit**—divine inspiration—urging them to be jathilan dancers or masters. The pawang manages the musical instruments, woven bamboo horses, sacred whips, and other paraphernalia. His house is often used for rehearsals and group gatherings. It is the pawang's job to lead and support his jathilan group. This requires capital, time, and networking to obtain invitations to perform. A pawang is usually heavily involved in local cultural tradition. Every group has one master and a few junior pawangs. A pawang may also perform occasionally and become possessed.

A junior leader receives permission (called **izjin**) through a guru or spiritual teacher to become a pawang. This indicates that he has the spiritual powers to handle the rituals, training, and performance. A pawang acts as an intermediary between this world and the **dunia alus**, or supernatural realm—it is a sacred responsibility. The pawang is believed to have esoteric knowledge: **mata tiga**, or the third eye, and **ilmul al-ghaib**, divine knowledge about the unseen, secret world. This spiritual position gives a pawang authority, legitimacy, and the power to conduct spells and initiate and then end possession of the jathilan dancers. Dancers and members of the public believe a pawang is a spiritual master and have full confidence in his knowledge and powers.

variation offers the dancers some level of creativity. Unlike highbrow Javanese performing arts, which have less flexibility, jathilan is based on improvisation; many acts are created without preparation, which also makes it a more adaptive and inclusive folk tradition for the common people.

Pawang (trance master) doing ritual prayers before the start of the jathilan dance.

Standard Jathilan Ritual

The day before the event, the pawang, dancers, and assistant pawangs pay homage to the sacred water source in their area by performing the cleaning ritual called **siraman**. During this ritual, incense is burned and the pawang offers prayers to the spirits for safety and success in the trance dance. Jathilan horses and other props are cleansed at the pawang's home with this sacred water. The pawang and dancers take a ritual shower. Sacred water is also taken to the pawang's home for the next day's event.

On the day of the ritual, the jathilan horses, sacred whips (**Kyai Samandiman**), and masks are put in the middle of the ring, where the *sajen* (offering ritual specialist) sprinkles them with sacred water, uncooked white rice, flowers, and aromatic oil. The pawang spreads coconuts around the arena to protect the performers from evil spirits. He chants prayers as smoke from burning incense billows around the ring. Then the dancers form pairs, a minimum of two and maximum of eight. They begin without the horses, moving slowly to the beat of the gamelan orchestra. As the pace of the music quickens, they mount the horses and dance faster. One dance session can last an hour or two. Dancers move from one side of the ring to the other, bend down, and then turn back. This sequence continues until the session is over or the dancers fall into a trance—the major attraction in jathilan dance. When the pawang throws flowers onto the dancers, the junior pawangs crack their sacred whips and the music intensifies. The dancers are thrown into trance, their bodies possessed by supernatural entities.

Kyai Samandiman—The Sacred Whip

The sacred whip used in jathilan dance has many names: *Kyai Samandiman*, *pecut*, *cemethi*, or *cambuk*, which simply means "whip." The term *kyai* refers both to someone who teaches religious subjects and to cultural objects or entities having supernatural abilities. In traditional Javanese beliefs, the Kyai Samandiman harnesses the unfathomable power of a thousand thunderstorms to cast a spell on the dancers.

The state of possession creates fear, shock, and a sense of being transported to a world of the unseen, and the dancers' bodies are controlled by nonhuman forces. Only the master has the knowledge, education, and power to release this force from a human body and let it return to the spirit world. This trance state is desirable and culturally approved throughout Indonesia.

At the end of the performance, the pawang sits cross-legged near the stage and gestures for the dancers to move toward him. When a dancer comes near, volunteers, junior pawangs, and the sajen hold the dancer's body, and the pawang touches it, rubbing the body from head to toe to take the spirit out. When the spirit is out, the dancer lies still on the ground until volunteers and junior pawangs carry them to the dressing room. Some of the spirits are powerful, however, and refuse to leave, controlling the dancer's body until the following day, in some cases. When this happens, the entranced person might convey messages to the public, utter strange words, and make prophecies.

Traditional Jathilan Masks

The word for mask is **topeng** in Bahasa Indonesia, Javanese, and Balinese. The most important function of the mask is to cover the dancer's face during performances. A topeng is a ritual object in traditional ceremonies, court theater dances, religious customs, and other performing arts of the different cultures of Indonesia. A topeng allows the dancer to embody a character. There are two kinds of masks: the face mask and the **barong**, which covers the entire head of the performer. A topeng can represent historical, mythical, or religious characters, animals, ogres, demons, evil forces, or heroes. In Central and West Java and Bali, most of these topengs are ritual objects. In Bali they exist in both the religious domain and the performing arts. jathilan performances use multiple masks: knights (**Toh Bagus** and **Pujangga Anom**), clown (**penthul**), tiger (**macan**), monkey (**kethek**), and mythological animals or ogres (tiger masks of **Singakumbang** and **Singa Barong** and the boar **celeng**).

In Jathilan, the celeng mask is carried in one hand by a dancer who behaves like a wild forest boar. Barong dancers wear a mask with long pieces of fabric attached. The dancers are hidden by the masks and fabric as they make the creature walk and dance. The ogre dancers wear face masks and **gongseng** (ankle bells) that ring with each step. Ogres dance in groups of four, and when they reach a peak of intensity, they take off their masks and dance in circles. These and other masked dancers who roam around the dance ring and frighten people are an essential part of the jathilan tradition.

The Pasar—Markets at Public Performances

Any festival or cultural ceremony in Central Java, including jathilan dance, is accompanied by a pasar, or pop-up market, for local vendors. Items such as Javanese face masks, jathilan whips, traditional foods, toys, and more are sold outside any public event. These markets at public performances are significant because they generate income for the vendors, and for the local government through various fees paid by the vendors and spectators. Thus, pasars are a culturally and economically essential part of jathilan and other performances in Java.

Jathilan Practitioners/Performers

Dance groups may contain children, adults, and seniors and are mixed gender. Most of the

Ogre dancers ready for performance.

performers earn nothing directly, but they expect food, gifts, and sometimes cash from the spectators. The girl groups often receive offerings of money during the performance; some of the dancers walk around with a basket inside the ring and outside in the market to collect donations. Dancers have been known to grab things from vendors without paying, but because these performers are considered to be in a state of possession, this behavior is tolerated. In a way, these holdups are part of the performance—spectators follow the dancers outside the ring to watch. Many dancers go outside the ring in the state of possession and let the public have another show.

Performers may be students, artisans, traders, part-time workers, carpenters, daily wage earners, seasonal laborers, construction workers, agricultural laborers, unemployed people, young boys and girls, government servants, and teachers—all kinds of people from different backgrounds. Each group also features girls who perform before the trance begins. Sometimes children perform separately in opening sessions before the main event. The practice varies according to the master's vision. Most of the young boys and girls are from local villages and surrounding areas. They meet regularly at the master's house to rehearse, plan events, or help someone through the mutual aid system locally called **karja bhakti**, or mutual community service. These groups provide aspiring dancers a chance to learn and perform. The growing popularity of jathilan, via social media and cultural capital, has drawn an increasing number of youngsters to pursue this tradition.

 See resource 20.5 in HK*Propel* for web links.

Revival of Traditional Dance Arts

Locally, jathilan dance is called *kesenian tradisional*, which means "local traditional art form."

Temporary shop in pop-up market during the Jathilan performance.

The word *seni* is used to refer to traditional arts, such as batik, which is part of the national costume of Indonesia. There has been a demand recently for reviving this traditional dance in the rural and semi-urban areas of Central Java, along with handicrafts, textiles, music, and other tangible and intangible aspects of Javanese cultural heritage.

In small villages and towns and on the side of the road, one often sees these shows taking place along with other traditional Javanese music and dance performances. They appear in village festivals, independence day celebrations, before and after the Muslim religious festivals of Eid, annual days of remembrance for ancestors and saints, at weddings, circumcisions, birthday gatherings, and other social events.

The revival and cultural reemergence of traditional performing arts are also due to strong support from the local government, the national Ministry of Education and Culture, cultural enthusiasts, and the general community. More and more of the local people in Central Java are patronizing jathilan, wayang kulit (Javanese shadow puppet show), **laras madyo** (sung poetry), Reog Ponorogo (lion-masked trance dance), and other traditional performing arts. Arts initiatives are also developing an infrastructure of festivals

and pop-up markets, boosting the local economy and supporting artists and artisans.

Many pawangs have started new groups while still belonging to another group somewhere else. Every group is an offshoot of an older one. Most regular performers dream of one day being the master of their own jathilan group. Many children are actively involved as performers and audience members, and the younger generations are always well represented in the audience.

 See resource 20.6 in HK*Propel* for web links.

Summary

Indonesian dance emerges from an extraordinarily complex history, interweaving ancient practices, cross-cultural influences, and a volatile natural environment. Jathilan is an example of this rich folk culture in Java, providing a glimpse of tradition, religion, history, and Kejawen. Because it hasn't been strictly controlled like other, more highbrow Javanese arts, jathilan dance has adopted the expressions of its locale and provided new ways to think about folk dance in rural areas. It also incorporates village-level cultural sensibilities, allowing local artists and artisans to take part, in comparison to classical or courtly art traditions that remain the province of the upper classes. Perhaps this cultural inclusivity and flexibility is the reason jathilan dance is wildly popular in Java, becoming the impetus for social gatherings in rural areas, nurturing the local economies and helping artists, artisans, and communities grow. The dance also acts as a medium between the human and non-human world, bringing the mythical past into a living animated act of dance and performance.

In this way, jathilan both reflects and extends the deep relevance of Indonesian culture and dance. From the catharsis and communal vitality of trance dances to the precise movements of court rituals and dance dramas—all interwoven with traditional arts and aesthetics—Indonesian dance continues its dynamic representation of the past, present, and future.

Discussion Questions

1. What is trance, and how it is embedded in different cultures in Indonesia?
2. How is the concept of Kejawen historically rooted in the wider sacred cosmology of Java?
3. What important role does a pawang play in jathilan?
4. Give three examples of why Hindu-Buddhist traditions and beliefs are an important part of many Indonesian cultures.
5. How have the religions of India, the Middle East, and Europe affected the sphere of religious life in Indonesia from a historical perspective?

 Visit HK*Propel* for access to this chapter's Application Activity.

Selected Glossary

Aliran Kepercayaan—Local faiths and beliefs that fall outside the majority religions of Indonesia—Islam, Protestantism, Catholicism, Hinduism, Buddhism, and Confucianism.

Balinese temple dance—Sacred dance performed for rituals and ceremonies, including Rejang, Sanghyang Dedari, and Baris Upacara.

dangdut—A genre of dance and folk music from Java with Indian and Arabic influences.

gamelan—Traditional Javanese musical ensemble consisting of metal percussive instruments.

gongseng—Ankle bells worn by jathilan and other performers.

halus—High language or cultural forms used for certain expressions of arts, language, poetry, and dance in Central Java.

jathilan—Javanese dance involving spirit possession (trance) and horse figures.

Javanese Ramayana Theater—Performance derived from the Indian epic tale of the legendary prince Rama.

Kejawen—Traditional Javanese beliefs with different regional variants incorporating local or indigenous spiritual practices.

Kyai Samandiman (also called *pecut*, *cemethi*, or *cambuk*)—Sacred whip used in Javanese rituals such as jathilan.

pasar—A traditional market.

pawang—A trance master.

Reog Ponorogo—A traditional dance from Ponorogo Regency, East Java in which dancers wear huge lion masks to enact a tale of war while in an intense trance.

sajen—A ritual offering expert.

topeng—A dance with masks performed in different styles and with different narratives in various parts of Indonesia.

Selected References and Resources

Acri, A., H. Creese, and A. Griffiths, eds. 2011. *From Lanka Eastwards: The Ramayana in the Literature and Visual Arts of Indonesia*. Verhandelingen van het Koninklijk Instituut voor Taal-, Land en Volkenkunde, vol. 247. Leiden, Netherlands: KITLV Press.

Bagus Laksana, A. 2016. *Muslim and Catholic Pilgrimage Practices: Explorations Through Java*. Routledge: London.

Harnish, D.D. 2006. *Bridges to the Ancestors: Music, Myth, and Cultural Politics at an Indonesian Festival*. University of Hawai'i Press: Honolulu.

Hughes-Freeland, F. 2010. *Embodied Communities: Dance Traditions and Change in Java*. Berghahn Books: New York

Lemelson, R. 2011. *Jathilan: Trance and Possession in Java*. DVD. Elemental Productions.

Mauricio, D.E. 2002. *Jaranan of East Java: An Ancient Tradition in Modern Times*. University of Hawai'i at Manoa: Honolulu.

Mead, M., and G. Bateson. 1951. *Trance and Dance in Bali*. Video. Library of Congress. www.loc.gov/item/mbrs02425201.

Van Groenendael, V.M.C. 2008. *Jaranan: The Horse Dance and Trance in East Java*. Brill Academic: Leiden.

21

Dance in the Philippines

Desiree A. Quintero and Wayland Quintero

Learning Objectives

After reading this chapter you will be able to do the following:

- Understand that dance in the Philippines is premised on cultural ideas of mutual cooperation, is place-centered, is entered into with others as a communal practice, and that music is intrinsic to movement.
- Understand how colonization and the resistance to colonization in certain regions in the Philippines affected dance practices.
- Comprehend "indigenous" within the Philippine dance context.
- Recognize the development of dance, the plurality of practices in the Philippines, and national efforts in the perpetuation of forms.
- Analyze how dance has become an important identity marker among the Philippine global diaspora, with the United States as an example.
- Make connections between the Philippines and neighboring countries, and situate the country within Southeast Asia.

Key Terms

bayan—"Nation" or "motherland" in the national language of Filipino.

folk dance—A classification of Philippine dances and music within particular ethnolinguistic or regional communities that have been codified and nationalized to represent Filipino identity both nationally and internationally.

gangsa—Handheld flat gongs found primarily in the mountainous Cordillera Administrative Region on the island of Luzon.

kapwa—A Filipino term for "being with others" that refers to a Philippine shared identity.

kulintangan or **kulintang ensemble**—A musical ensemble comprising an assortment of gongs and drums.

pangalay—"Dancing with the hands" among the Tausug people, an Islamized ethnolinguistic group from the island of Jolo in the Sulu Archipelago.

rondalla—An ensemble of stringed instruments including bandurria, octavina, laud, bajo, and guitarra.

Confusion About Dances and Music in the Philippines

International conference delegates, scholars of the performing arts of Southeast Asia, sat quietly in the small auditorium at the Philippine Women's University in the capital of Manila, awaiting what would be a cultural experience of Philippine dance and music. It was 2012, and the evening performance was part of the opening ceremony for the weeklong conference. As the lights dimmed, the sound of the *rondalla* string ensemble filled the air, evoking historical times. Female performers dressed in long **Maria Clara** or **Filipiniana** gowns walk casually beside male performers dressed in embroidered sheer **Barong Tagalog** shirts onto the stage. Both attires are considered traditional Philippine formal fashion. The atmosphere created an imagined Spanish-esque time and place, of couples strolling down cobblestoned streets or riding *kalesa*—horse-drawn carriages. The six couples walk into formation and begin moving in a side-to-side waltz step, women holding their gowns as men swing their arms in a lateral position. They break into a fundamental Philippine folk dance step, the sway balance, with arms crossing from second position into fourth position as the feet end with a waltz. The dance opens the **Maria Clara Suite**, an assemblage of dances that are at times lively or slow, using props such as castanets, lace umbrellas, or handkerchiefs. Four dances later, a short intermission break began. As the lights came up, one ethnomusicologist loudly voiced a sincere confusion, "Why are all the dances and music European? I thought we were supposed to be watching Philippine dance, not this European stuff?" Another scholar from Southeast Asia replied with exasperation and annoyance, "Don't you know about the history of Spanish colonization of the Philippines for almost 350 years?"

 See resource 21.1 in HK*Propel* for web links.

This vignette prompts a discussion about Philippine Indigenous Peoples and their dance practices, the diversity of Philippine cultures, and—despite colonialism—local processes of indigenization that have come to dominate dance in the Philippines. Table 21.1 presents a time line of significant Philippine dates.

The diversity of Philippine cultures is represented in the diverse terrain that covers over 7,100 islands, spans approximately 300,000 square kilometers (115,831 miles), and features over 35,000 kilometers of coastline, many mountain ranges, and river systems. The archipelago is divided into three major island groupings: the **Luzon group**, which includes the islands of **Luzon**, **Palawan**, and **Mindoro**; the **Visayan Islands (Visayas)**; and the **southern Philippines**, inclusive of **Mindanao** and the **Sulu Archipelago**. The island nation is bound by the Philippine Sea and Pacific Ocean on the east, the South China and Western Philippine Sea on the west, the South China Sea to the north, and the Sulu Sea and Celebes Sea in the south. The archipelago is located within the Pacific typhoon belt and the Pacific Rim of Fire, and it is therefore prone to typhoons, volcanic eruptions, earthquakes, and their subsequent disasters both natural and caused by humans.

As a result of its natural environment, a diversity of communities and histories that both connect and separate ethnolinguistic groups throughout the archipelago have come to make up the people and their cultural practices.

Key historical points in the history of the Philippines are as follows:

- Trade with China throughout the region beginning in the seventh century
- Arrival of Islam in the 13th century
- Spanish colonization from 1565-1898
- Philippine Revolution 1896-1898
- Philippine–American War 1899-1902
- American colonization 1898-1946
- Philippine independence in 1946

The "Philippines" as a unified nation-state did not exist prior to the 16th century, when it received its name from Spanish colonizers. Given the region's history, current political boundaries should be viewed in terms of historical circumstances, such as trade, commerce, and the competition for colonies between European powers, set within a complex physical geography. Many local histories undergird the estimated 175 ethnolinguistic groups in the archipelago.

Table 21.1   Time Line of Significant Philippine Historical Dates

Dates	Events
618-907 CE	Contact is established between the islands that would later be named "Philippines" and China's Tang dynasty. Tang porcelain wares are brought by Muslim traders to the Philippine Islands.
13th century	Islam is brought to the Philippine Islands via Arab and Chinese traders.
c. 1450	Sayyid Abu Bakr establishes the Sulu sultanate.
1521	Explorer Ferdinand Magellan, under the Spanish flag, lands on Limasawa, and the first mass Catholic conversion (of native rulers Rajah Humabon and Hara Humamay and their people) is recorded.
c. 1525	Sharif Kabungsuwan from Johore in present-day Malaysia arrives in Mindanao and establishes the first sultanate in Maguindanao.
1542	The naming of Las Islas Filipinas or Philippine Islands is bestowed to the archipelago in honor of King Philip II of Spain.
1565-1815	250 years of economic and cultural exchange through the Manila-Acapulco Galleon Trade. Trade between Mexico and China is conducted, with Manila as the transshipment hub. European performing troupes arrive in the islands, instigating the indigenization of foreign cultural art forms.
16th-19th centuries	Moro wars or conflicts fought between Muslim groups and the Spanish colonizers in six stages. *Moro moro* plays, as a form of propaganda, help facilitate the proselytization of Catholicism.
1565-1898	Spanish colonization of the Philippine archipelago brings the minuet (locally *minueto*), fandango (*pandango*), jota, mazurka, polka, and the waltz (*balse*). The dance forms are adapted to local contexts and communities.
1896-1898	Philippine Revolution, where Filipino revolutionaries succeeded in ending Spanish rule.
1898	Spanish–American War is initially fought over Cuba, but ends with Spanish surrender to the Americans in a mock battle in Manila Bay and a secret agreement between Spanish and American authorities. The Treaty of Paris is signed, with no Filipino representation present, where the United States purchases the Philippines from Spain for $20 million.
1899-1902 (north and central Philippines) 1899-1913 (southern Philippines)	Philippine–American War between the U.S. Army and the Philippine Army and other native freedom fighters that ultimately resulted in American takeover and colonization of the archipelago.
1898-1946	American colonization of the Philippines brings vaudeville (localized as *bodabil*); social dances, such as foxtrot; Charleston; ballet; and modern dance.
1942-1945	Japanese occupation of the Philippines during WWII.
1946	U.S. grants independence to the Philippines.
1969	Cultural Center of the Philippines is built and becomes an important venue for staging ballets and other dance performances.

Oral traditions among different communities in the Philippines are important historical and cultural resources that are ways of sharing generational knowledge through performance, recording, and transmission. Oral traditions are laden with sociocultural values, genealogies, lessons, knowledge of the environment, and religious beliefs—cultural traits found throughout Southeast Asia.

Southeast Asia encompasses the countries of the Philippines, Malaysia, Indonesia, Thailand, Vietnam, Myanmar, Cambodia, Laos, Brunei,

East Timor, and Singapore. The neighbors share countless commonalities—words, ritual practices, bilateral kinship (wherein families trace descent from both parents' lines), and the prominence of bamboo, coconut, rice, fishing, and weaving. Gong music and associated movement traditions are found throughout Southeast Asia, comprising a "**gong belt**" that indicates the social and cultural significance of gongs. The overwhelming influence of trade between the Philippines and its neighbors reverberates over centuries and into the present day, underscoring the interconnectedness of histories and cultures in Southeast Asia.

Place-Based Dance Practices

Dance in the Philippines is intrinsically related to the environment, where mountains offer natural obstacles to outside intrusions and are home to *anitos* (ancestral or nature spirits), where waterways and oceans connect different ethnolinguistic groups, where fertile grounds and irrigation networks provide rice and other sustenance for communities, and where an array of animals and flora coinhabit the diverse landscape. These surroundings permeate the aesthetics of a community, influencing movement. Examples include the extension of arms displaying a bird's wingspan, curving hands like curling foliage, and the scratching or mincing of bare feet on a dirt ground. The connectedness to and dependence on the natural landscapes yield practices that concern movement, sound, and shared identity. For example, *kawayan* (or bamboo) growing in the forest provides material for *tallelet* (bamboo clappers), indigenized musical instruments for marching *musikong bumbong* (bamboo music) and parade dancing, and long bamboo poles that are rhythmically clapped on the floor as dancers weave in and out of the clacking poles.

Tinikling and Kasingkil: Dances With Bamboo Poles

The two most iconic dances that foreground displays of Filipino national identity are also two dances with long bamboo poles found in the archipelago: **tinikling** from the Visayas and *kas-*

ingkil of the **Maranao** people in Mindanao. Tinikling gets its name from long-legged tikling birds who forage the rice fields while avoiding bamboo traps set by farmers. Dancers jump between a set of bamboo poles in rhythmic coordination with the rondalla string ensemble. *Kasingkil*, meaning "to tangle or trip," is a small part of a larger performance by the *onor*, a professional female artist who incorporates *kambuyok*/chant-singing and playing the *kulintang* (also spelled *kolintang*). In 1957, Manila-based artist **Lucrecia Reyes-Urtula** choreographed the dance **Singkil** that has come to be identified as Philippine folk dance.

Dance in Muslim Communities

The Philippines was part of a foreign trade network from as early as 971 CE. Around the 14th century (before Roman Catholicism arrived with the Spaniards), **Islam** became the first **Abrahamic religion**—religions that trace their origin to prophet Abraham—to take root in the Philippines. It has been theorized that Muslim communities existed in the archipelago prior to this (Majul 1973) due to trade within the maritime Southeast Asian region, South Asia, and China. Islam took root in the Sulu Archipelago, western Mindanao, along the coasts of Mindoro and Batangas, and all the way to *Maynila*, Filipino word for the Manila Bay area (Aguilar 1987, 151). Islamization in the archipelago was already underway when Portuguese explorer **Ferdinand Magellan**, sailing under the Spanish flag, arrived in 1521 on Limasawa Island in the Visayas, but

Maranao dance in Marawi, southern Philippines.

its spread was attenuated by Spanish colonization. The term **Moro**, coming from the Christian European term *Moor*, referring to Muslims, is attributed to the Muslim population in the Philippines. It originated when the Spaniards encountered Muslims in the archipelago.

Defining dance in the Islamic world has its permissibility challenges that are tied to the history of Islam and its relationship to pre-Islamic religions (al-Faruqi 1978), and is distinct from European-American conceptualizations of "dance." The misnomer "Muslim dance" has dominated dance classifications and performance descriptions in the Philippines and should be differentiated from Islamic aesthetics that permeate the performing arts in Muslim ethnolinguistic communities. Exploring dance as an *expression* of Islamic culture, with wording such as "dance in Muslim communities," concerns Islamic notions of beauty and truth (al-Faruqi 1978). Endowed with a holistic worldview, Islam and its ideals pervade political, social, economic, and family structures, including the visual arts, movement, and music.

See resource 21.2 in HK*Propel* for web links.

Music and Dance

Most of the early written documentation of music and dance in parts of the archipelago is found in the chronicles of Europeans about their encounters with native peoples. Italian explorer Antonio Pigafetta (1521) wrote of being invited into the house of a native prince:

> Four young girls were playing [instruments]—one, on a drum like ours, but resting on the ground; the second was striking two suspended gongs alternately with a stick wrapped somewhat thickly at the end with palm cloth; the third, one large gong in the same manner; and the last, two small gongs held in her hand, by striking one against the other, which gave forth a sweet sound. . . . [The prince had three girls dance for us]. . . . Those gongs . . . are made of brass and are manufactured in the regions [of] China." (Blair and Robertson, xxxiii)

Gong cultures pervade parts of Southeast Asia. Within the Philippines, different types of gong ensembles are found from the mountainous

regions of northern Luzon all the way to coastal areas in the southern reaches of the Sulu Archipelago. Although early written documentation is attributed to European contact with native peoples in the archipelago, oral traditions account for a continuity of local aesthetics and music and dance practices among different ethnolinguistic groups. A good example of this is the **Darangen**, the Maranao epic poem that existed prior to the 14th century Islamization of Mindanao. The dance kasingkil that is based on this epic is said to depict **Paramata (Princess) Gandingan**, who, despite mischievous forest spirits that cause an earthquake with falling trees and earth cracking beneath her feet, gracefully maneuvers as if gliding over the land. The dangers she navigates are represented by bamboo poles, clacking together with increasing speed.

Onor—Female Performing Artists of the Maranao People

"An *onor* is a professional female performing artist who has to master an entire repertoire of kulintang compositions, sing excerpts of the Darangen epic, and then gracefully execute gestures in this holistic performance known as Kaganat Sa Darangen. These gestures consist of kapagapir, the act of gracefully manipulating the jeweled fan. Kasadoratan, manipulating both a scarf and a fan, while attracting attention with sideward glances. Then executing a graceful kakini-kini walk. . . [she attracts attention from young suitors while] showing off her expertise to entertain her audiences and . . . acknowledging dignitaries and sponsors of that festive occasion or wedding" (Ellorin, 2021, 19).

The **kulintangan ensemble** is found among different ethnolinguistic groups in the southern Philippines, but under different names. For example, it is known as *kulintang* among the **Maguindanao** people, *kulintangan* among the **Tausug**, and *taggungu'* among the **Sama** groups. The origins of the word *kulintang* are unknown, although the playing of an ensemble called *culintangan* during a trance ceremony was recorded by Francisco Combes in 1667, suggesting its existence in the region for centuries. Kulintang may have arrived in the Philippines from Borneo to Sulu and from Celebes to Mindanao (Cadar 1971), becoming incorporated into local communities and conforming to existing indigenous musical cultures. Although kulintang exists in various communities in the southern Philippines, ethnomusicologist José Maceda notes that kulintang is played in places where Islam has historically had a strong presence (1963, 216-217 in Jimenez 2008). Kulintang is part of a larger gong-chime culture that spans Southeast Asia, with ensembles existing among different ethnolinguistic groups in Borneo, such as the Dusun, and in Maluku and Sulawesi in Indonesia.

The function of kulintangan varies for each ethnolinguistic group and depends upon the particular occasion. The ensemble may be part of a welcome celebration among the Maranao; as *agung* (gong instrument) competition among the Maguindanao (Kalanduyan 1996, 12-13), for ritual purposes with the Sama; or as part of wedding celebrations among the Tausug. Certain kulintangan pieces are played for listening and others for dancing.

Kulintangan music for dancing invokes an exchange between dancers and musicians and is exemplified in *pangalay* dancing. Pangalay is a dance form found among the Tausug peoples in the Sulu Archipelago in the southern Philippines (who are referred to as *Suluk* in Sabah, Malaysia). *Pangalay ha kulintangan* means "pangalay with kulintangan." Dancers respond enthusiastically to a kulintangan ensemble that plays well together, with interlocking rhythms creating a drone-like soundscape as dancers adjust micro and gross movements and become inspired by the music.

Pangalay is understood within a larger context of Tausug/Suluk **ethnoaesthetics**—aesthetics that are shaped within culture (Royce 1977). One such aspect is curvilinearity: the qualities of curving and curling in space (Quintero 2016; Quintero and Nor 2016). Curvilinearity is seen in the visual arts, such as *ukkil*—referring to carved flora, fauna, and scroll motifs—and in music as the rising and falling of sounds of the kulintangan ensemble (Nor 2003). Curvilinear ethnoaesthetics also translates into pangalay dancing through the curving and curling of movement, the *malantik* (curve) of flexed hands or "broken" double-jointed elbows, and the asymmetry of the body-position (Quintero 2016).

Aesthetics rooted within culture are experienced, rather than just seen. In pangalay, it is what is heard, what is felt; it's the process of dancing that is appreciated by Tausug/Suluk. There are particular ways of listening to what is played by the ensemble, focusing one's attention on the interlocking rhythms struck on large gongs (agung), or perhaps the *tambur* played by a musician who starts to quicken the speed. These rhythms and beats become manifested in each dancer's distinct ways of executing movement

Lang-ay Festival in Bontoc, Philippines.

motifs as slow, sustained motions, enhancing the curvilinear effect.

 See resource 21.3 in HK*Propel* for web links.

Acapulco-Manila Galleons and the Melding of Forms

The first Spanish settlement in the Philippines was established in 1565 by **Miguel Lopez de Legazpi**, a Spanish colonial official sent from New Spain (Mexico), and over the centuries this settlement became modern day Cebu City. Legazpi's expedition from New Spain coursed through the **Mariana Islands** and **Guam**, which were "claimed" for Spain and eventually became part of the trade route to and from the Philippine Islands—a major global trading route connecting Asia with the Americas. Spain ruled the Philippine Islands from Mexico from 1565 to 1815, then later through direct rule in the archipelago from 1815 to 1898. The establishment of the **Manila Galleon Trade Route** (or the Acapulco-Manila galleon trade) not only transported silver and gold to the east via Manila in exchange for porcelain, Chinese silk, spices, and other goods that were in demand in European countries, but also transported people, and thus cultures, whereby "Foreign dance influences were witnessed by Filipinos with the arrival of European troupes. These travelling groups greatly popularized European dances and plays" (Reyes-Urtula et al. 2017, 29). With the arrival of foreigners to the Philippines came different cultural influences that are evidenced in the country's languages, foods, customs, and dances and music.

Dance of the Moros and Christians

Moros y Cristianos ("Moros and Christians") in Spain and Mexico, known also as the *moro moro komedya* in the Philippines, are playlets with music and dance that were brought to the Philippines to facilitate the process of Catholic evangelization. The plays focus on the conflict between the Moors, who are Muslims, and Christians during the Middle Ages. Through prose and verse, music, dance, and a mock battle as the finale, the Christians usually win while the Moors

are defeated and sometimes baptized. There was a process of indigenization with the incorporation of native languages in the playlets and in some variations situating the conflict between different ethnic groups in the Philippines, such as the Moros of the southern Philippines in conflict with people of the Visayan Islands in central Philippines.

The *moro moro* dance or **baile de cristianos y moros** (the movement aspect of the moro moro komedya) depicts the mock battle between Christians and Moros with shouting, jumping, and large movements. One of the most popular dances, called **maglalatik** or **magbabao** (*bao* meaning *coconut shell*), originating in Biñan, Laguna, on the island of Luzon, portrays Christians and Moros who fight over *latik*, condensed coconut milk. The dancers are typically all men who wear coconut shells split in half attached to the body and who beat particular rhythms with handheld coconut shells while dancing. Maglalatik is performed as part of the religious procession held during the feast of San Isidro Labrador, the patron saint of Biñan (CCP 2017, 178) and also for entertainment purposes.

From Spanish Dances to Philippine Folk Dance

Spanish dances, such as **jota**, **fandango**, and **paso doble**, with their basic steps and music, were introduced by missionaries, soldiers, traders, and families of bureaucrats. Over time, these dances became integrated with native aesthetics to eventually become folk dance (Rivera and Villaruz 2017, 209). Through Spanish colonization, the combination of foreign elements with native aesthetics has come to characterize some Philippine cultures, including dance and music.

A good example of the localization of foreign forms is the jota, a couple dance originating in Aragon in northern Spain. Filipino jotas differ from the Aragonese dance in several ways: Smooth movements lack the characteristic hop and kick of Aragonese jota; two bamboo slabs are freely held in the hands (unlike Spanish castanets that are fastened to the hands); and the rhythm of the rondalla string ensemble predominates, along with the waltz step, throughout the dance. There are said to be hundreds of jotas found throughout the archipelago, usually taking on the name of their locality: *jota manileña* (Manila), *jota cagayana* (Cagayan), *jota pangasinan* (Pangasinan), and the like. Jotas are performed for weddings, baptisms, fiestas, and other special occasions, but they take on different religious meanings when performed during **guling guling**, the celebration day before the Catholic Ash Wednesday, and *tambora* on Christmas Eve. The dance **jota moncadeña**, originating in Moncada, Tarlac, on the island of Luzon, and also known as *jota florana*, is a unique jota performed during funerals and wakes, with a section in the dance called *patay* (dead) or *desmayo* (fainting), where dancers act as though they comfort each other in their grief. Movements are said to be a mixture of Spanish-influenced and indigenous motifs, with the patay section characteristic of the Ilokano (also spelled *Ilocano*), a northern Luzon people.

Influences From New Spain (Colonial Mexico)—La Cucaracha

Kuratsa, a dance found primarily in the Visayan islands and popular among the Waray people, is said to have been introduced by Mexican soldiers and traders when Spain controlled the Philippines through its viceroy in Mexico. Localized from "**La Cucaracha**," a Mexican dance and folk song, kuratsa in the Visayas is believed to have been derived from **kigal** (**quigal**), a courtship dance involving flirtation and teasing between dance partners (Kwan et al. 2017, 170-171). The dance itself depends upon the local styles and the skill of the dancers, who improvise with basic movements such as waltzes, turns, brushes, and chasing steps.

 See resource 21.4 in HK*Propel* for web links.

Dance as Part of Festivity

Throughout different parts of the Philippines, whether commemorating a religious holiday or tied to indigenous agricultural practices, dance as festivity unites a community. Many Roman Catholic festivals within the Philippines have indigenous origins, and over time native peoples integrated Catholic beliefs, incorporating celebrations and holidays with existing indigenous practices. The Catholic conversion of much of the population was successful simply because evangelization did not completely eradicate native practices. Instead, native people associated their practices with Catholic ones and melded the two. As an example of this process, the **Sinulog Festival** in Cebu City, **Ati-Atihan** of Aklan, and Dinagyang Festival of Iloilo City, although held in three different geographic locations in the Philippine archipelago, all celebrate the **Santo Niño**. The festivals center on the child Jesus (Santo Niño) statue that was given by Ferdinand Magellan to **Hara Humamay**, who was later baptized as Queen Juana, the wife of the prominent ruler of Sugbo (Samar) island Rajah Humabon. According to 16th-century explorer Antonio Pigafetta, the queen was so overwhelmed by the baptism and so taken with the statue that she asked to keep it. It is said that the origins of the adoration of the Santo Niño statue come from a pre-Spanish animistic children's healing ritual that was adapted in the 16th century (Ness 1995, 1), whereby the Santo Niño was accepted by native people who believed that particular objects hold spiritual significance.

The *sinulog* (or *sinug* in Visayan language), meaning "flowing or moving water," are ritual dances found throughout the central Philippines (Ness 1995, 1). Sinug dance movements are said to be related to the movement of water, although it is theorized that sinug steps were a part of a precolonial war ritual. Praying to the Santo Niño happens intermittently in Latin when the dancing stops (Ortiz 2017). The Sinulog Festival in Cebu involves street dancing competitions between people from many other cities and provinces. Due to the popularity and success of the Sinulog Festival and Ati-Atihan Festival in the Philippines, different kinds of festivals emerged throughout the archipelago to promote tourism.

 See resource 21.5 in HK*Propel* for web links.

The "Mother" of Philippine Folk Dance

Folk dance refers to dance as practiced within particular ethnolinguistic or regional communities. Folk dances have been codified and nationalized to represent Filipino identity both domestically and internationally. The transition of folk dances as practiced by communities to folkloric events intended for audiences into nationalized "Philippine folk dances," representative of Filipino-ness, is partly attributed to the dance pioneer known as the "mother" of Philippine folk dance (Castro 2011). In 1927, **Francisca Reyes Tolentino** (1899-1984;later known as Francisca Reyes Aquino) and Petrona Ramos (1899-1983) published ***Philippine Folk Dances and Games***, based on fieldwork conducted by Reyes Tolentino as part of her master's thesis. This work created an elaborate system of movement terminologies as "fundamental" dance steps used in what would become national folk dances of the Philippines. As a result of the research and work of Reyes Aquino, who eventually became the superintendent of physical education for the bureau of public schools in 1947, Philippine folk dances became a part of the physical education curriculum in public schools. Reyes Aquino established the **Philippine Folk Dance Society** in 1949, an institution that conducts research and workshops to support folk dance and teachers in the education system. The dances gathered by Reyes Aquino, as well as their eventual stagings by dance companies, have become standardized and performed within the Philippines and in the Filipino diaspora around the world.

 See resource 21.6 in HK*Propel* for web links.

Indigenous Peoples

The Philippines has an estimated 14 to 17 million **Indigenous Peoples** (IPs) belonging to 110 ethnolinguistic groups. They are mainly concentrated in northern Luzon (Cordillera Administrative Region, 33%) and Mindanao (61%), with some groups in the Visayas area. In Luzon, the term ***Igorot*** is used to refer to a large grouping of many different northern highland ethnolinguistic groups, compared to place-derived group identities that local people ascribe to themselves. In Mindanao, IPs are collectively referred to as **Lumad**, with 18 ethnolinguistic groups recognized by the government. The 13 Muslim ethnolinguistic groups are also classified as IPs.

There is a connection between IPs, their traditions that come out of the ancestral lands where they have lived since time immemorial,

Pangalay danced by Norhaimah binti Halid in Semporna, Malaysia.

and the change in those traditions when IPs are displaced, leave their homelands, or are no longer able to continue their indigenous practices. For example, the **Aetas of Nabuclod, Pampanga**, were resettled in the area after the eruption of **Mt. Pinatubo** in 1991 destroyed their ancestral homeland. Their cultural practices suffered as a result. With Christianization and the loss of their hunter-gatherer way of life, storytelling and healing traditions (including the practice of ***talipe***, a ritual dance with tapping and clapping performed for healing purposes) are on the decline due to the limited number of *mang-aanito* (ritualists), and other factors (Martinez 2019). The change in values of indigenous beliefs and practices are related to the changes of the lifestyles and tenuous status of IPs.

 See resource 21.7 in HK*Propel* for web links.

Kapwa

A Filipino Value

In the 1970s, Filipino psychologist Virgilio Enriquez introduced what was called ***sikolohiyang Pilipino***, or Filipino psychology, to reveal

Cultural Highlight

THREE GENERATIONS OF DANCE LINEAGE FROM SIASI, PHILIPPINES, TO SABAH, MALAYSIA

In Spring 2014 I was already a year into my research on pangalay as practiced among the Suluk (known as Tausug) in Sabah, Malaysia. One consistent theme was evident: Most Suluk performers learn the aesthetics of pangalay dancing from a young age through observing other dancers at celebrations, not through formal instruction. Then I met sixteen-year old **Innamorata Lidz**. Although young, she already exhibited nuanced dancing described by other Suluk as "old" and not seen in the younger generation. As I got to know Innamorata, I learned that pangalay was something she had always wanted to do since a very young age. She would go to gatherings where the majority of dancing would be to electronic music, but she then would go home and try to recreate it in front of a mirror. One day her mother saw her and asked if she really wanted to learn pangalay, and when she voiced an enthusiastic "yes," a more formal training with her mother started. When younger, Innamorata's mother was a well-known dancer, and I came to learn that Innamorata also studied with her grandmother. Her family lineage traces back to the island of Siasi in the southern Philippines. While Innamorata, her mother, and her grandmother have distinct ways of arranging movements, stylistically, all three are connected in their sustained movement to the fast tempo of the kulintangan and the general reserved way of dancing without exaggerated hip movements, backbends, or overuse of the shoulders. The "oldness" noted by others is attributed to Innamorata's family's style of dancing and conventions that were common to the island of Siasi. In this way, Innamorata's family is the living, thriving bodily link connecting the Sulu Archipelago in the Philippines and Sabah, Malaysia—the perpetuation of dance traditions through people who fully embody their cultural lineage.

 See resource 21.8 in HK*Propel* for web links.

what he believed to be native knowledge systems that were culturally and intrinsically "Filipino," found in all societies in the Philippine archipelago. The best-known concept by Enriquez is **kapwa**, which means "other" or "other person" but is interpreted to be "a recognition of shared identity, an inner self shared with others" (Enriquez 2004, 5). *Kapwa* refers to one's unity, connection, or oneness with other people—regardless of "blood" connection, social status, wealth, level of education, place of origin, or other factors typically used to separate or distinguish people (David, Sharma, and Petalio, 48).

Kapwa and the related ideas of cooperation and communality can be seen in the music and dance practices collectively called **gangsa**. The playing of handheld flat gongs while dancing gangsa requires coordination between producing sounds and the movement of bodies in circum-ambulatory formations. Striking an individual gangsa instrument generates a singular sound. And although you can play a particular rhythm on the gong, no clear melody can be heard from one gong. It is only when you have all the gongs

playing together that playing gangsa becomes comprehensible as gangsa music, a collaborative effort to make a melody suitable for dancing. All participants must cooperate with each other for a successful music-making event, interconnected in a true manifestation of kapwa.

Gangsa is common to many groups in the northern Philippines' highlands and traditionally was performed for ritual and celebratory purposes. Today, in addition to its use in specific community rituals, gangsa also unites people from different ethnolinguistic groups from the northern Philippine highlands as an expression of their collective highland identity. An example of this is **BIBAK**, an organization started during the 1950s by students from various universities in Baguio in northern Luzon to combat prejudices and discriminations faced by highland indigenous groups of the Cordillera Administrative Region. This was addressed through cultural dance performances that educated and empowered BIBAK members and created solidarity among highland IPs (Indigenous Peoples).

BIBAK

BIBAK is an acronym for the five original provinces—Benguet, Ifugao, Bontoc, Apayao, Kalinga—in the Cordillera Administrative Region of the northern Luzon highlands. The region's indigenous people are collectively known as "Igorot," a term initially seen as derogatory but then reclaimed by its members as a source of solidarity and empowerment. Members of different highland ethnolinguistic groups come together through BIBAK to perform gong dancing (W. Quintero, 2016), educating its own members about each other's cultures while developing a collective Cordillera identity. Since its advent, BIBAK satellites have popped up internationally.

 See resource 21.9 in HK*Propel* **for web links.**

Crosscurrents

Although pegged as a Catholic nation in Southeast Asia, the Philippines geographically, historically, economically, and linguistically—and thus culturally—has been connected to its Southeast Asian neighbors. The trading of gongs as significant heirloom objects endowed with spirit and power is found in many communities in maritime Southeast Asia, a "gong belt." Whether the gangsa being used during a ritual period called *begnas* in Sagada, Mountain Province, or the kulintangan in a *pag-igal jin* ritual among the Sama Dilaut in Tawi-Tawi, Philippines, and Sabah, Malaysia, the sounds produced from gongs can have spiritual significance. Gong ensembles for entertainment and ritual purposes are found throughout the region and extend to the diaspora, such as gamelan ensembles from Indonesia that are found throughout the United States and Europe. Kulintang ensembles and gangsa playing among the Filipino diaspora, and especially among Fil-ipino Americans as part of the "kulintang zone," garner different expressions related to kapwa, belongingness, and identity (W. Quintero 2011).

Philippine Culture Nights

Filipino, Pilipino, or **Philippine Culture Nights** (PCNs) showcasing music and dance began in the 1980s at U.S. universities and high schools, primarily on the West Coast. Driven by young adults, PCNs deal with various themes, including identity (Gonsalves 2010). A central and creative theme anchors a variety of folk dances performed to recorded music (with the occasional live accompaniment), interspersed with DJs and singing (Talusan 2020, xxxvi). Borrowing primarily from the widely documented **Bayanihan Folk Dance Company** repertoire ("*Bayan*" means "nation") that is based largely on the work of Francisca Reyes Aquino, PCNs express "Filipino-ness" through the repetition of what have become nationalized folk dances.

 See resource 21.10 in HK*Propel* **for web links.**

Summary

The diversity of dances within the island nation of the Philippines is due to the various histories, geographies, and languages found in the archipelago. For these reasons, "Philippine dance" is difficult to define as a monocultural idea. Instead, the term *dances in the Philippines* is more suitable to understand the complexity of the people and their histories. Simultaneously, common ideas that link dance cultures in the Philippines are related to expressions of belongingness, of collaboration, embracing the philosophy of kapwa as Filipino communities at home and abroad gather to express their rich, vibrant heritage through dance and music making.

Discussion Questions

1. What is kapwa and how can this concept relate to dances in the Philippines?
2. In what ways did colonization of the Philippines affect dance practices? Name one example.
3. What can "indigeneity" mean within the Philippines' dance context?
4. Define "folk dance" within the Philippines' context. Describe the process of nationalizing folk dances in the Philippines.
5. How has dance become an important identity marker among Philippine diaspora in the United States?
6. Discuss how the Philippines is connected to the rest of Southeast Asia.

 Visit HK*Propel* for access to this chapter's Application Activity.

Selected Glossary

agung—Suspended knobbed metal gong. Also called *agong*.

bayan—Means "nation" or "motherland" in the Tagalog language. Used as part of the name of the Bayanihan Folk Dance Company.

BIBAK—An acronym for the five original official provinces—Benguet, Ifugao, Bontoc, Apayao, Kalinga—in the northern Luzon highlands. Students from various universities in Baguio City in northern Luzon started the organization during the 1950s to empower and create solidarity among highland peoples through cultural dance performances and education.

folk dance—Dance as practiced within particular ethnolinguistic and regional communities. Within the Philippines, folk dances have been codified and nationalized to represent Filipino identity both nationally and internationally.

ethnoaesthetics—Aesthetics that are shaped within culture.

gangsa—Handheld flat gongs found primarily in the mountainous Cordillera Administrative Region on the island of Luzon.

Igorot—A collective term to refer to many different ethnolinguistic groups including Kankanaey, Ifugao, Apayao, Tingguian, Ibaloy, and Kalinga.

kapwa—A Tagalog term that refers to "being with others" and refers to a Philippine shared identity.

kulintangan or **kulintang ensemble**—Musicians playing a set of instruments that include the kulintangan, a set of gongs laid horizontally in a row, with the highest pitched gong referred to as *tung tung*; *agong*, large gongs (two or three), and *tambur*, an indigenized snare drum. The term has several other spellings, including *kulintang*.

onor—A Maranao female professional artist who incorporates kambuyok (chant-singing), playing the kulintang, and dancing.

pangalay—Popularly referred to as "dancing with the hands," it is dancing specific to the Tausug people, an Islamized ethnolinguistic group whose ancestral home is the island of Jolo in the Sulu Archipelago.

rondalla—An ensemble of stringed instruments comprising the bandurria, octavina, laud, bajo, and guitarra.

Sinulog Festival—An annual cultural and religious festival that involves street dancing competitions and is held in Cebu to venerate the Santo Niño (child Jesus statue).

Selected References and Resources

Cadar, Usopay H. 1996. "The Role of Kolintang Music in Maranao Society." *Asian Music* 27(2): 81-103. https://doi.org/10.2307/834489.

CCP. 2017. *CCP Encyclopedia of Philippine Art, Vol. 8, Dance*, 2nd ed. Manila: Cultural Center of the Philippines.

Donoso Jiménez, I. 2008. "Historiography of the Moro Kulintang." *Trans: Transcultural Music Review 12*. www.sibetrans.com/trans/article/102/historiography-of-the-moro-kulintang.

Faruqi, L.I. al-. 1978. "Dance as an Expression of Islamic Culture." *Dance Research Journal* 10(2): 6-13. https://doi.org/10.2307/1477998.

Lipat-Chesler, E., and M. Talusan, eds. 2020. *Our Culture Resounds, Our Future Reveals: A Legacy of Filipino American Performing Arts in California*. University of California, Los Angeles, Ethnomusicology Archive. https://californiarevealed.org/islandora/object/cavpp%3A209355.

Maceda, J. 1998. *Gongs & Bamboo: A Panorama of Philippine Music Instruments*. Quezon City: University of the Philippines.

Ness, S.A. 1992. *Body, Movement, and Culture: Kinesthetic and Visual Symbolism in a Philippine Community*. Philadelphia: University of Pennsylvania Press.

Nor, M.A.M. 2003. "Arabesques and Curvilinear Perimeters in the Aesthetics of Maritime-Malay Dances." *Yearbook for Traditional Music* 35 (2003): 179-181. https://doi.org/10.2307/4149328.

Nor, M.A.M., and K. Stepputat. 2016. "Sounding the Dance, Moving the Music." *Choreomusicological Perspectives on Maritime Southeast Asian Performing Arts*. Abingdon, Oxon; New York: Routledge.

Quintero, D.A. 2016. "Inhabiting Pangalay Ha Kulintangan as Suluk in Sabah, Malaysia." PhD diss., Pusat Kebudayaan, Universiti Malaya.

Quintero, D.A., and M.A.M. Nor. 2016. "The Curvilinear Ethnoaesthetic in Pangalay Dancing Among the Suluk in Sabah, Malaysia." *Wacana Seni Journal of Arts Discourse* 15.

Quintero, W. 2011. "Kulintang Zone: Gong Chime Playing, Dancing, and Costumed Filipino Americans." *Tirai Panggung* 11:96-117.

Quintero, W. 2016. "Mengangsa: Sounding Men in Motion in Sagada, Mountain Province, Northern Philippines." PhD diss., Pusat Kebudayaan, Universiti Malaya.

Santaella, M. 2016. Sounding Movement Extrinsically and Intrinsically: An Ethno-choreomusicological Analysis of Tarirai Among the Bajau Laut in Semporna, Sabah. *Musika Journal* 12:70-90. Manila: UP Center for Ethnomusicology.

Tolentino, F.R., and P. Ramos. 1927. *Philippine Folk Dances and Games*. United States: Silver, Burdett and Company.

PART VIII

East Asia

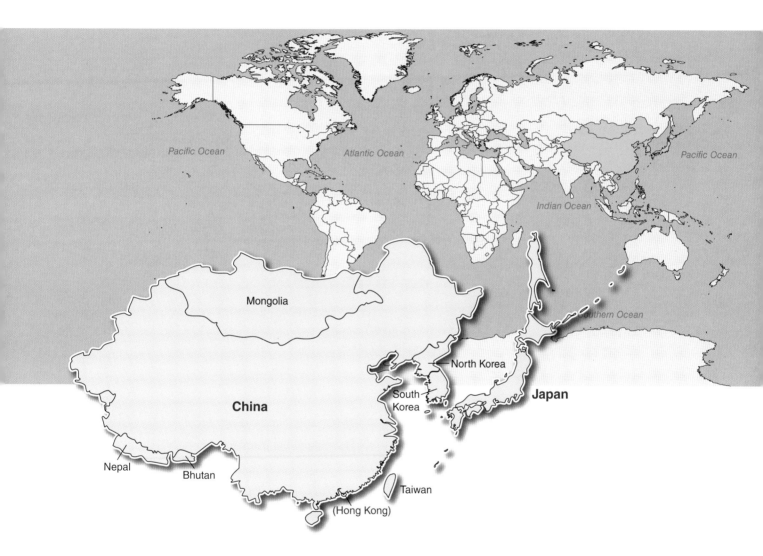

The three major countries in this region are China, Japan, and Korea. While we were only able to provide chapters on the first two of these, they illustrate how geography, religion, and politics—both national and international—can be significant forces shaping East Asian dances. The vast area of China contains a dramatic range of climate and topography with a population of almost 1.5 billion people, many of whom belong to different ethnic groups with unique dance traditions. Japan, by contrast, is an archipelago of several thousand islands, only five of which are large enough to support the population of 124 million people. Both countries have classical and other dances as well as traditional folk forms. The largest presence of folk dance in Japan is through year-round festivals connected to different religious and cultural practices involving the entire nation. In China and the diaspora, Chinese New Year is the most prominent nationally observed folk dance festival, and there are many regional and local events as well. However, from imperial times through to the present, the Chinese government has been directly involved with the development of dance, whereas in Japan (despite its imperial history), government involvement is more indirect. Throughout this history, relations between East Asian nations and with the West—both amicable and otherwise—also affected dance. The 20th century brought massive changes to the region through the second Sino-Japanese war, the Chinese Civil War, World War II, and more, with both immediate and long-term effects on dance development.

 HK*Propel* includes web links to additional resources for this section.

22

Dance in Chinese Culture

Shih-Ming Li Chang and Lynn E. Frederiksen

Learning Objectives

After reading this chapter you will be able to do the following:

- Use dance and its development to recognize significant aspects of Chinese history and culture.
- Identify and label key factors in the development of Chinese dance, noting why these factors operate as they do.
- Compare and contrast regional variations in Chinese dance development.
- Understand the concept of spectator orientation in Chinese history, dance technique, and the societal functions of Chinese dance.

Key Terms

"bigger the better, more the merrier"—Translation of "yijuweimei, yizongweiguan," a common saying about how the status of the viewer is raised when more spectacles and many participants are involved.

Chinese opera—Theatrical form developed during the Song dynasty incorporating singing, poetry, storytelling, acrobatics, dance, and more.

Han dynasty, Tang dynasty, Song dynasty—Historical eras important to Chinese dance; China has had 15 major dynasties.

military dance—Dance troupes are formed within the military to entertain the troops and to represent the country at regional, national, and international events.

spectator orientation—The value of an artistic work is determined by the status of the viewer or owner.

Zhongguogudianwu—A dance training system and aesthetic developed in the mid-20th century.

Lantern Festival at Anfu Gate, 713 CE—Dancing Ta Ge 踏歌

The evening air tingles with anticipation at the Daming Palace, royal residence of the **Tang dynasty** emperors. More than a thousand court ladies—their sumptuous clothing glistening with jade, pearl, and intricate brocade—gather along the balcony high above the Anfu gate. They murmur to one another and gaze down at the courtyard outside the palace walls where the square blazes in the glow of 50,000 lanterns. To entertain the royalty, the court has selected over a thousand girls and women from neighboring towns and adorned them to complement the clothing of the royal ladies. The dancers' garments, headpieces, and facial decorations glitter as long sleeves swirl, shoulders tilt this way and that, feet prance, and voices rise in song under the towering lights. They dance **Ta Ge** 踏歌, a folk dance, as it has been done for at least nine centuries. They dance for hours, over three days and three nights, and all the while the royal ladies watch and learn. Later, as the poets will write, the ladies make Ta Ge their own, bringing it into the court where it takes on new life as a classical palace dance of the Tang dynasty (Qiang 2004, 124-125).

The story of Ta Ge does not end here. In the 20th century, 1,200 years after the Lantern Festival at Anfu gate, professor **Sun Ying** 孙颖(1929-2009) at **Beijing Dance Academy** reconstructed Ta Ge by researching ancient poetry and artworks that referenced this lively stepping dance (Chang and Frederiksen, 158). Thus, Ta Ge's transformation from a folk dance to a dance of the elites, many centuries ago, allowed it to be documented and brought into the present as a staple of Chinese cultural events.

 See resource 22.1 in HK*Propel* for web links.

Ta Ge is just one example of the complexity of Chinese culture, where 5,000 years of documentation provide a unique window on the relationships between dance and imperial history. In a land spanning more than 3,000 miles of Asia through a dramatic range of climate and topography, the region's cultural history is expansive. Over the course of several millennia, shamanistic communities gave rise to theocratic governments and then to a series of 15 major **dynasties** that finally ended with the upheavals of the 20th century. Many different ethnic groups have long existed in the region, and today the Chinese population consists of the **Han** 漢族 majority plus 55 different ethnic minority groups spread through mainland China and **Taiwan** 台灣. When the Han dynasty opened the **Silk Road** 絲路 trading routes in 130 BCE, China's network of cultural influence expanded to reach the Middle East and Europe. The Silk Road routes remained a major source of intercultural exchange until they were closed by the **Ottoman Empire** in 1453 CE.

Trade and other interactions with foreign cultures had wide-ranging effects throughout Chinese history. The Netherlands, Russia, Britain, Japan, and other nations engaged with China through methods both peaceful and belligerent. Many effects of these cross-cultural interactions converged during the 20th century when the **Chinese Communist Party (CCP)** 中国共产党 prevailed in the civil war that followed the end of the empire. Until this time, however, significant eras in Chinese history were largely characterized by dynasties, reflecting the overwhelming importance of imperial rule.

Dynasties

Prior to the **Qin** 秦 (221-206 BCE), dynasties consisted of small kingdoms whose rulers were often in competition. The kingdoms were united in 221 BCE under the first emperor, **Qin Shi Huang** 秦始皇. Although Qin's rule was quite brief, most subsequent dynasties lasted several hundred years and were ruled by single family lines. As a result of this dynastic legacy, Chinese family names are considered most important and are listed first in a name. Over the millennia, most of these family dynasties—except the **Yuan** 元(Mongolian) and **Qing** 清 (Manchurian) dynasties—were ruled by the Han people, who constitute the majority of the Chinese population.

Dance in Chinese Culture Over 5,000 Years of History

Each dynasty developed its own aesthetic, and the many styles of dance that arose over the millennia illuminate different functions of the art in Chinese culture, confirming the continued importance of dance in today's world. Table 22.1 presents a time line of Chinese history related to dance. The following are some key points to note:

- Imperial history is critical for understanding the cultural perspectives that shape Chinese dance, specifically **spectator orientation** (where the status of the viewer determines the nature and status of a per-

Table 22.1   Significant Eras in Chinese History Related to Dance

Time frame	Dynasty/era/events	Notes
1750-1040 BCE	Shang dynasty	Shaman rulers dancing Oracle bone inscriptions Beginning of Chinese writing
1100-256 BCE	Zhou dynasty	Confucius 551-479
221-206 BCE	Qin dynasty	First emperor Terracotta warriors Beginnings of Great Wall
206 BCE-220 CE	Han dynasty	Golden age of Chinese culture Silk Road trade with the West established
618-907 CE	Tang dynasty	Golden age of dance Foreign dances incorporated into palace
960-1279 CE	Song dynasty	Rise of Chinese opera Foot-binding starts Documentation of Han folk dance (yangge) noted
1279-1368 CE	Yuan dynasty (Mongolian rule)	Grandson of Ghengis Khan establishes Monglian rule
1644-1911 CE	Qing dynasty (Manchurian rule)	Heyday of Chinese opera Manchurian rulers promote opera Opium Wars (1840-1894) British take Hong Kong
1912-1949	Republic period	End of dynasties in 1911
1937-1945	Second Sino-Japanese War	Madame Dai arrives in China Japanese defeated 1945 Taiwan returned to China after 50 years of Japanese occupation.
1931-1949	Chinese Civil War	Communists win over the Nationalists in 1949 Nationalists relocate to Taiwan
1949-present	People's Republic of China	Beijing Dance Academy established Wuju (dance dramas) popularized Zhongguogudianwu developed
1966-1976	Cultural Revolution	Only yangbanxi performances allowed Artists persecuted
1978	Open Door policy	Increased artistic exchange with Taiwan and the West

formance), and a **"bigger the better, more the merrier"** (*yijuweimei, yizhongweiguan*) approach.

- There is a strong impulse to bring elements of the past forward into the present.
- With the strengthening of empire came a willingness to incorporate things foreign and make them Chinese—a strategy that still persists today.
- The connections between imperial history and dance mean that even after the end of the dynasties, dance is still intertwined with politics and government.

As the dynasties rose and fell, classical and folk dance forms developed among the varied populations in the region. These dances include those of the majority Han population, as well as those of the 55 ethnic minority groups. They range from ceremonial dances, palace dances, and folk dances to contemporary forms that engage varied techniques from Chinese culture, as well as those from foreign nations.

 See resource 22.2 in HK*Propel* **for web links.**

Ta Ge in Poetry

Here is a rough translation of a verse from the poem "Ta Ge" by Liu Yuxi (772-842), renowned poet of the Tang dynasty. The original verse had far fewer words than this translation, because each character/word in Chinese can hold a great deal of information.

Ta Ge—Stepping Song

The spring river moon rises shining on the dam,

Where young women walk side by side a sinuous path,

Heads tilt and shift, gazes connect, release,

Shoulders touch as they turn,

Long sleeves entwine and flow,

Hair cascades forward as they lean down.

Translation by Shih-Ming Li Chang and Lynn E. Frederiksen

Classical Dance

The Chinese term for classical dance, **gudianwu** 古典舞, translates as "ancient standards dance" (Su 2004). Unlike Western classicism, the aesthetics of Chinese classical dance change with the aesthetics of each dynasty and emanate from the world of the palace. For example, **foot-binding** for women that started in the court during the **Song dynasty** (960-1279 CE) would lead to a technique of small, mincing steps in women's dance that persisted for hundreds of years. Although concepts of classical dance were reinterpreted and reconstructed in the 20th century, ancient dances from the dynasties are still part of Chinese culture.

The sheer length of dynastic rule—4,000 years from the Xia dynasty starting in 2100 BCE to the final Qing dynasty, which ended in 1911—ensured that dance and empire were inextricably entwined. Several key elements of Chinese culture, such as the high status of literacy, the relationship between bureaucracy and the arts, and even the architecture of imperial palaces, all play out through the dance.

Shaman Dance and Beginnings of Chinese Writing

In the early dynasties before the many small kingdoms were united into an empire, rulers evidently performed along with shamans, or sometimes *as* shamans themselves, carrying out religious ceremonies through dance. The complex relationship between government, dance, and literacy in Chinese history may have arisen from the religious or shamanistic use of symbols and crafted artifacts in these dances to guide and govern the community.

Over the course of the **Shang dynasty** (1750-1040 BCE), the roles of the shaman and the ruler slowly separated as political power rose above religious power. Though the focus of ritual dances was ultimately on the god, the ruler was the intermediary. Later on, however, the focus of palace dances stopped at the ruler, who was seen to reign by divine right (Wang 1985, 8-9).

Dancing Bureaucracy and the Rise of Empire

By the Zhou dynasty (1100-256 BCE) the rulers were far less likely to dance, and special classes of dancers—sometimes concubines or professional dancers—performed to entertain the royalty. The shift from religious ritual to entertaining royalty is just one part of how dance remained caught up in the dynamics of government. As prominent Chinese dance historian **Kefen Wang** (王克芬, 1927-2018) noted, "To consolidate their [power, the rulers] strengthened the concept of rank as much as possible and worked out a system of ritual music and dance" (Wang 1985, 13-14). The renowned teacher and philosopher **Confucius** (551-479 BCE) made such rituals a key to his philosophy, and his teachings took hold throughout the culture.

Confucius Dance and *Bayiwu* 八佾舞

Pre-dating Confucius, the ancient *bayiwu* 八佾舞 dance had formal configurations reflecting numerology and cultural status. It became known as "**Confucius dance**" after the philosopher—ever concerned with the form and function of bureaucracy—reinforced a strict association between numbers of dancers and hierarchy in the court (Wang et al. 1994, 638).

Spectator Orientation and the Imperial Palace

For the next two millennia, the most important role for Chinese palace dance was to be seen by the emperor, leading to the spectator orientation in Chinese dance that persists today. In ancient times, the props, costumes, and large numbers of performers helped to make dances visible to a distant emperor whose power and prestige were represented by the amount of space around him and the size of the palace. Emperor Qin set the standard for massive construction projects, not only with the **Great Wall**, but also with his mausoleum/palace complex that eventually covered 22 square miles and contained the famous 6,000 life-size **Terracotta Warrior statues** 兵马俑. Later palaces were designed to show the emperor as the center of the universe, with only the highest-ranked officials and royal concubines allowed anywhere nearby (Steinhardt, 290).

This arrangement fostered an audience-centered perspective on performance that differs from the Western one, where artwork is judged primarily on its form and content, and on the skill and notoriety of the artist(s). While these factors do apply in Chinese culture, the primary value of an artwork lies in the status of the audience or recipient.

Spectator orientation also affected technical aspects of dance. When your main goal is to be visible to a distant emperor, you must use every means at hand to increase your visibility, such as organizing huge numbers of performers in unison movement. From the audience's perspective, a massive unison performance reflects the ruler's importance while also conferring honor on the viewer through the performers' willingness to make such an effort. In this light, the well-known phrase **yijuweimei, yizhongweiguan** (以巨為美, 以眾為觀)—roughly translated as "bigger the better, more the merrier"—aptly describes how spectator orientation and the emperor's power shaped cultural perceptions over the millennia.

To augment the impact of "bigger the better," dancers also employed elaborate costumes with headpieces and twirling sleeves, and props such as ribbons, fans, and swords, showcasing precision and discipline while enhancing the dancers' visibility to others. Of these elements, props have a particularly complex connection to culture and history.

Props

While not all Chinese dances use props, the most popular and recognizable ones do so to demonstrate the technical skill and intense discipline that are highly valued in Chinese culture. Consequently, the meaning and value of technical form itself goes beyond the symbolic use of props that is common in many other cultures, and the sheer skill and discipline of using props becomes a goal in and of itself.

Classical Palace Dances

The two main categories of palace dance were *wenwu* 文舞—civil or "graceful" dance—and *wuwu* 武舞—martial or "energetic" dance. Many dances within each of these forms employ props, though the objectives of their use might differ. They are also somewhat gendered. Civil forms are more strongly associated with women, while both men and women dance the martial ones. However, all palace dances—civil or martial— were centered on the emperor and performed at his pleasure.

Wenwu—Civil/Graceful Dance

Wenwu dances are generally light and elegant, either done bare-handed or with props such as sleeves, ribbons, and feather fans that serve to emphasize these qualities in performance. Some of the most iconic wenwu images in both ancient and contemporary artworks are those of **water-sleeve dance** 水袖, or of **ribbon dance** 彩绸舞. Both dances use varying lengths and widths of fabric, with longer fabrics requiring considerable strength and skill, and shorter fabrics emphasizing posture and gesture.

As with the ribbon and watersleeve dances, choice of materials also identifies styles of another well-known form, the **fan dance** 扇子舞. While wenwu fans can be made of many different materials—paper, fabric, or feathers—the way the fans are manipulated defines the dance. For example, the delicate **feather fan** 羽扇—usually danced indoors—evokes elegant, feminine qualities appropriate to the court setting. By contrast, fans for folk versions of the dance are made of sturdy fabric, rather than feathers, and their movements, danced outdoors, are embellished far beyond utilitarian purposes.

Wuwu—Martial/Energetic Dance

As with wenwu, wuwu can be done bare-handed or with props. But since the dances are related to Chinese martial arts, props serve to emphasize personal strength and dexterity. The **wuwu fan** (made of hard bamboo to evoke the lethal iron fans used in martial arts) is a prime example of how an ordinarily delicate item could be transformed into a deadly weapon. Other props are unmistakably weapons from the beginning: whips, knives, spears, sticks, and more are often used in dance. Swords, in particular, are a popular prop in martial dances around the world, including China. Though Chinese **sword dances** are usually done by professionals now, in ancient times, sword routines were also practiced by scholars and government officials for physical fitness or martial practice, and occasionally they were presented as a form of entertainment for the court.

Imperial Dynamics Reflected in Dance

Besides wenwu and wuwu, the ceremonial dances discussed earlier—such as shaman dances and Confucius dance—also helped to reinforce the protocols and structures of the court. These ancient imperial dynamics have persisted in art forms to this day, their elements preserved thanks to events during the Song dynasty (960-1279 CE). During a time of great political unrest in the early part of the dynasty, the emperor, short on funds, exiled many of the dancers, musicians, and other performers who entertained the court. Left to their own devices, these artists together created one-stop shopping for entertainment through a variety show format, eventually giving rise to **Chinese opera**, where the classical dance forms were preserved (Chang and Frederiksen, 22).

Chinese Opera

Both Chinese and Western opera contain singing, dancing, and acting, but in Chinese opera all the movements are highly stylized, and the lead performers must be able to dance and sing and act simultaneously. Chinese opera includes acrobatics, martial arts, face painting, magic, clowning, mime, poetry, elaborate costumes, and numerous props. The Chinese opera audience also shoulders more responsibility than a Western audience and must have knowledge of symbolic meanings in traditional opera movements. For example, depending on the context, walking in a large circular path could mean that the character has traveled many miles, although in pure dance sections such a movement would be simply locomotive steps without specific meaning. These opera conventions emerge from common cultural touchpoints that developed as Chinese opera grew from the Song dynasty onward.

Chinese opera remained the premier performance art of China even after 1911, when the fall of the Qing dynasty brought an end to thousands of years of Chinese empire. With the opera serving as a touchstone for cultural history and identity, two opera stars in particular—**Mei Lanfang** (梅兰芳, 1894-1961) and **Ouyang Yuqiang** (欧阳予倩, 1889-1962)—played an important role in the development of Chinese dance during the turbulent years of the 20th century. Both men were female impersonators in the opera tradition, and their technique shaped the aesthetics of female movement in the most prominent art form of the time. However, their influence also reached beyond the immediate realm of performance into Chinese culture and politics.

Mei was a cultural ambassador through the early part of the 20th century whose performance introduced and articulated the image of Chinese theater and dance for the West. Though Ouyang did not tour abroad, his diverse work as a theater educator, scholar, playwright, and Chinese opera performer brought Western training methods and perspectives into the ancient Chinese performing arts, including dance. Mei, Ouyang, and other artists would become key players in the politics of modern China, shaping cultural perceptions and realities both within the nation and abroad as tumultuous political strife engulfed the entire world. However, to get to this critical collaboration between dance and politics, we must first address folk dance—a complex wealth of dances woven through the tapestry of Chinese culture.

 See resource 22.3 in HK*Propel* for web links.

Chinese Folk Dance

Chinese folk dance includes both the Han majority dances and those of the 55 minority groups. All have been practiced for thousands of years but were rarely documented for most of that time. While some minority and foreign dances (along with Han folk dances like Ta Ge) were ultimately assimilated into the court, not until the 20th century were folk dances officially included as part of mainstream performances in China and documented as such.

Chinese Minority Folk Dance

The 55 non-Han ethnic groups across China and Taiwan, each with their own history and functions for their dances, represent a wide variety of techniques, costumes, and choreography. The minority groups whose dances are most readily visible in mainland China include **Dai**, **Chaoxian**, **Uyghur**, **Mongolian**, and **Tibetan**, because they are part of the higher education curriculum. In Taiwan, the indigenous **Yuán zhùmín** 原住民 of Austronesian descent have their own dances, recognized as part of Taiwanese cultural heritage.

These prominent minority dances have been brought into the curriculum of many dance schools and universities and are now often seen outside of their original contexts, their traditional functions sometimes altered or fused with other cultural forms. The Dai peacock dance (see sidebar) is a clear example of the journey from village to national stage. Yet despite this recent national

Tibetan minority dance in Wujingsiang Township.

presence, minority folk dances still maintain deep cultural relevance for their people. Both presentational and participatory dances continue in the villages, even as folk dances of the Han majority maintain a proportionally large presence in the nation.

The Dai Peacock Dance: From Traditional Folk Dance to Staged Performance

When **Yang Li Ping** 杨丽萍 first staged her solo version of the Dai people's peacock dance in the 1980s, it was unfamiliar to Chinese audiences—a highly stylized form unique to the Dai culture. Yang's dance was stunning and new, highlighting her singular performance of the peacock dance and bringing it to national renown.

Han Folk Dance—Yangge

The word *yangge* 秧歌 refers to a specific rice-sprout song and dance but is also a general term for the widespread folk dances of the Han people. While minority folk dances were not readily visible outside of their communities until they were brought to national notice in the 20th century, Han folk dances had always been seen throughout the nation in local and national festivals, especially during **Chinese New Year** 春节/新年. In these multitudinous and widely varying dances, presentation seems more prominent than participation—perhaps a manifestation of spectator orientation in Han folk dance. One of the most well-known Han folk dances, seen around the world, is the **dragon dance** 龙舞, an ancient form documented for over 2,000 years. Besides the dragon dance, many other Han folk dances are the highlights of festivals, varying in style across the vast geographic range of the Han Chinese population. The greatest differences are between styles of the colder northern and warmer southern regions. For example, in the **lion dance** 狮舞, the northern costume is much heavier than the southern one. The dance, therefore, stays somewhat earthbound, with more emphasis on mimicking animal movements and on acrobatic tumbling. The southern lion dance costume is lighter, and the performers are not bound together, allowing for remarkable martial arts feats. Southern lion dances have been more influenced by martial arts than were the theatrical northern forms and are intensely competitive at local, regional, national, and international levels.

 See resource 22.4 in HK*Propel* for web links.

Martial Arts, Competition, and Military Dance

Southern lion dance exemplifies how martial arts and competition have been an integral part of Chinese culture for thousands of years and highlights the value of competition throughout the society. Competition reinforces the common saying *chidekuzhongku, fangweirenshangren* 吃得苦中苦 方為人上人, that hard work and sacrifice will make one superior to others; in other words, "**no pain, no gain.**" This perspective is especially applicable to performance, making technique and virtuosity key elements of Chinese performing arts. The physicality of dance as an art form thus leads to the emphasis on ever-more-intense technical prowess, along with a nationwide affinity for dance competitions. Out of this competitive milieu arose the uniquely Chinese form of **military dance**.

The main function of dance in the Chinese military is to entertain the troops and to represent military divisions in regional and national competitions with civilian dance groups. Chinese military dance groups are often invited to perform at national and international events. This system resembles that of military bands in the United States. Although U.S. musicians and Chinese dancers may go through basic training, they do not receive further training for combat and are unlikely to be called to fight. In mainland China, people often join the military for a career in dance, as did **Zhang Jigang** 张继钢 (b. 1958), the graduate of Beijing Dance Academy who choreographed the famous ***Thousand-Hand Guan Yin*** 千手观音 and many of the spectacular works seen in national and international events, such as Olympic ceremonies. Dance competition has been the major influence on the growth and dissemination of dance, raising the level of artistry and technique as different Chinese dance forms

Ansai waist drum dance.

Han Chinese New Year Celebrations, Beijing, China.

emerged from the tumultuous changes of the 20th century.

 See resource 22.5 in HK*Propel* for web links.

20th-Century Political Turmoil

In the crucible of war that defined 20th century China, new concepts of national and international identity crystallized around traditional folk forms—both Han and minority—and later drew on classical traditions, as well. The result was an engine of creativity and virtuosity that presented vividly on the world stage while solidifying political power in China. Factors as immediate as the **Japanese invasion** of China in 1937 and as widespread as World War II influenced the trajectory of dance in the region.

The Japanese invasion brought out a huge patriotic response from artists throughout the country and abroad who devoted their expertise to supporting the national interest. Among them was **Madame Dai Ailian** 戴爱莲 (1916-2006), born in Trinidad to Chinese parents and trained in ballet and modern dance in London.

Though she arrived in China for the first time in 1941, Madame Dai spoke of her journey as "coming back home." Her cross-cultural experiences would inform her life's work and propel her to become the "mother of dance" in modern China (Wilcox, 16). The commitment of Madame Dai and countless others helped the Chinese prevail in the war with Japan, but fractures widened between the two political parties in China—the **Kuomintangzhengfu (KMT; Nationalist Government Party)** and the Chinese Communist Party (CCP). With the Japanese surrender in 1945, the parties were no longer held together in facing a common enemy, and China was riven by civil war.

 See resource 22.6 in HK*Propel* for web links.

Chinese Civil War

1945-1949

The Chinese victory over Japan that marked the start of the civil war further complicated cross-cultural heritages of dance in the region. The island of Taiwan (Formosa) was returned to Chinese rule in 1945 after 50 years of Japanese occupation and cultural influence—influence that included Western dance forms. Then in 1949, after **Mao Zedong** 毛泽东 (1893-1976) led the CCP to establish the **People's Republic of China (PRC)** in the mainland, the KMT government, led by **Chiang Kai-Shek** 蔣中正 (1887-1975), relocated to Taiwan.

From this point onward, Chinese dance followed different trajectories on the two sides of the Taiwan Strait, although both pathways emerged from the same Chinese dance history (Chang and Frederiksen, 40).

The war and its aftermath were not only a manifestation of Chinese politics, but also of cross-cultural interchange and turmoil involving China, Japan, and Korea most immediately, but also England, Germany, Russia, the United States, and more nations. The international elements in the work of Madame Dai and other artists show how the currents of politics, colonialism, and commerce flow through 20th-century Chinese dance. More critically, the outcome of the war and the subsequent political restructuring of China turned, in part, on the Communist party's effective use of the arts—particularly dance—as propaganda.

New Yangge/Struggle Yangge

During the Second Sino-Japanese War, a dance form—**new yangge** or **struggle yangge** 扭秧歌—was developed out of traditional yangge into a highly effective propaganda tool. The comic characters and ribald sections in traditional yangge were replaced with elements extolling the virtues of workers, peasants, and soldiers who supported the revolution, though the dance form and technique retained its folk origins. While new yangge was specifically crafted to meet the needs of the new government, other dance forms would prove equally significant in the early years of the PRC.

Postwar Developments in Chinese Dance

The 1950s proved to be a very productive time for the arts in China. **Wuju** 舞剧, or dance dramas, were created and modeled the process of pulling together many different cultural forms: ballet, modern, folk dance, and more.

Dance academies were developed and supported by the government after 1949 to direct the growth of dance as a national art form, firmly wedded to socialist ideologies. The national curriculum first developed at Beijing Dance School—predecessor to the Beijing Dance Academy—had both Chinese and European dance tracks. The former encompassed Chinese Han and minority folk dances, as well as classical opera dance. The latter covered ballet and other Western forms (Wilcox, 75). Aspects of all these were woven into the new wuju dance dramas.

With government support and training through national academies, such as the **Central Academy of Drama** (led by Ouyang Yuqiang and Madame Dai), performance ensembles around the nation were soon creating dance dramas for both national and international stages (Wilcox, 103).

Films of these performances extended the reach of the dance far beyond the stage itself—a most fortunate process, given that disaster loomed for the newly blossoming Chinese dance field. These films would later aid in the recovery of Chinese dance following systematic destruction of the arts and artists during the **Cultural Revolution**.

 See resource 22.7 in HKPropel for web links.

Yangbanxi

Dance During the Cultural Revolution: 1966-1976

Mao instigated the Cultural Revolution after the disastrous results of **The Great Leap Forward** (1958-1960)—a failed effort to industrialize agriculture that caused massive famine and over 30 million deaths. He sought to recapture the spirit of the Communist victory and reverse what he saw as growing stratification in society. From traditional folk festivals to Chinese opera, all arts and literature that harkened back to feudal systems or times of the dynasties were summarily dismissed, including dance that integrated Chinese folk and classical forms.

Even new yangge was purged from the culture. In place of the exiled performing arts, Mao's wife **Jiang Qing** 江青 (1914-1991) dictated the creation and dissemination of **the Eight Model Works**, or *yangbanxi* 样板戏—the only form of performing

arts permitted anywhere in the nation over the entire decade.

The Eight Model Works included two "modern revolutionary ballets." The formats for these works—contemporary dress and themes, Western staging elements, and Western ballet technique—were the only permitted formats throughout the country. These ballets—*and only these ballets*—were performed as staged full-length works, excerpts for smaller productions, competitions, and films that permeated the entire nation. Yangbanxi served as propaganda tools and to identify dissenters; your loyalty to the party was suspect if you did not fully embrace the performances. The two ballets—**Red Detachment of Women** and **White-Haired Girl**—depicted real-life stories of women in 20th-century China to promote Communism. These works proved how powerful the arts could be when wielded as a method of social control, inserting political propaganda directly into the daily lives and emotions of an entire nation's population.

 See resource 22.8 in HKPropel for web links.

Zhongguogudianwu

Chinese Ancient Standards Dance

After the Cultural Revolution finally ended in 1976, schools and performance ensembles were reassembled by those who had survived the decade of repression. Dances integrating Chinese classical and folk forms returned to the stages, joining the ballet performances that now could diversify far beyond the strict limits of yangbanxi. Using films, written documents, photographs, and memories held in the bodies of dancers and choreographers, innovative works from the 1950s and early 1960s were revived and transformed at the request of the government. New techniques and teaching practices were also being developed during this time.

One such development was *Zhongguogudianwu* 中国古典舞, which incorporates training methods from Chinese opera, martial arts, Western ballet, and modern dance. The direct translation of *Zhongguogudianwu* is "Chinese classical dance," but the term literally means "Chinese ancient standards dance" and was developed as a universal national form to incorporate Western scientific methods with Chinese classical

Professor Kefen Wang, Madame Dai Ailian, and Shih-Ming Li Chang in Madame Dai's apartment.

dance training. Zhongguogudianwu's versatile dancers could meet or exceed the demands of both contemporary and Chinese ancient standards dance. Although it was met with skepticism when first introduced, Zhongguogudianwu's

highly effective training system eventually was widely embraced both in China and abroad.

 See resource 22.9 in HK*Propel* for web links.

Paths to Contemporary Dance

In mainland China, exposure to Western modern dance started as far back as the early 1900s, when such modern dance pioneers as Isadora Duncan and **Denishawn** toured the world. However, because the aesthetics and functionality of dance in China differed from that in the West, modern dance in its Western form was slow to take hold in the region. Political alliances and conflicts helped shape developments in dance. For example, the first professional modern dance company in Hong Kong emerged in the late 1970s, while the city was still under British rule and more receptive to this Western import. In mainland China, modern dance slowly became accepted over time after the government's **Open Door policy** was

Cultural Highlight

A PRECIOUS FRIENDSHIP WITH PROFESSOR KEFEN WANG AND MADAME DAI AILIAN

I was born and raised in Taiwan, so when I first set foot in China in 1998, I knew no one. All I had to guide me was a book written by Professor Kefen Wang, the premier dance historian in China. On arriving in Beijing, I went to Beijing Dance Academy, hoping to find her there, but instead I was given her phone number. When I called introducing myself and my hopes for interviewing her, she immediately invited me to her home for dinner. We ate together in her tiny kitchen as if we were old friends. Through Professor Kefen Wang, I had the privilege of befriending both Madame Dai Ailian and the highly regarded choreographer Zhang Jigang, and later of hosting them in my Ohio home when they visited the United States. Over a decade, I visited them in China frequently and also invited Professor Wang to give lectures in Ohio. When Madame Dai stayed in my home with my family for a week, she shared stories of her life and loves, and also told me how she hoped to host the Laban Notation conference in Beijing one last time before she was too old to do it. And Mr. Zhang made special arrangements for me to videotape minority dances in the high mountains of Yunnan province.

I feel so fortunate to have known these three wonderful people as friends and mentors. Even though Professor Wang and Madam Dai are now both deceased, they remain vibrant in my memory. I will never take for granted the privilege and honor I was given, all through that first meeting with Professor Wang. Thank you, *Wang Laoshi*. You and Madam Dai are forever in my heart. (Written by Shih-Ming Li Chang)

 See resource 22.10 in HK*Propel* for web links.

enacted in 1978. Spurred by cultural exchanges with Western dance companies and schools, Chinese modern dance companies began appearing on the mainland in the 1990s. On Taiwan, dancers explored new vocabularies sparked by early 20th-century forays into Japanese and European modern dance, and by Western dance company performances in Taiwan during the 1950s and 1960s (e.g., Martha Graham, Alvin Ailey, Paul Taylor). Inspired to study abroad in the United States and elsewhere, the dancers then returned home to start their own companies. From the 1970s onward, many modern dance companies emerged in the region and continue to flourish into the 21st century.

 See resource 22.11 in HK*Propel* for web links.

Crosscurrents

While cross-cultural exchange and scholarship has grown tremendously in the 21st century, dance has always activated these interactions and continues to do so, now aided by rapidly changing technologies. Thanks to global travel and the internet, young people everywhere have access to a multitude of dance forms—ballroom, tap, jazz, hip-hop, and many more. (These forms are fully present in mainland China and Taiwan, though their popularity might not always align with government objectives. For example, recent censorship of hip-hop by the mainland China government indicates that enforcement of moral codes still guides government actions regarding artistic expression.) In addition to affecting the dissemination of dance, new technologies, such as virtual reality, are sometimes woven in the dances themselves, generating videos of hybrid choreographies that proliferate on social media. And in another arts–technology interaction, lockdowns during the COVID-19 pandemic sparked innovative uses of the virtual realm to share dance around the world.

 See resource 22.12 in HK*Propel* for web links.

Summary

The long history of Chinese dance, cross-cultural dynamics, vastness of the land, and the intertwining of dance with government all influence dance in Chinese culture. Most significant and unusual in the dance world is that Zhongguogudianwu was created by governmental decree, incorporating foreign techniques to achieve a new Chinese national dance training system. The scale of this effort and its ultimate success in shaping the standards for technical prowess among a large number of the world's dancers is a remarkable achievement and a testament to the complexity of Chinese dance in today's world. As you can see from a the topic of hip-hop in Chinese culture, the many crosscurrents of dance are not easy to navigate but knowing how these currents flow—their origins and their dynamics—will help people reach a safe harbor of understanding and engagement in the world of Chinese dance.

Discussion Questions

1. What is "spectator orientation," and why is it important in Chinese dance?
2. How does the concept "bigger the better, more the merrier" apply to Chinese dance, and why?
3. When was Zhongguogudianwu developed, and why is it important?
4. Watch dance videos, and note whether the Western forms are visible in the dances and how.
5. What was the Cultural Revolution, and how did it affect the development of dance in mainland China?
6. How did the approach to dance in Taiwan differ from that of mainland China, and why?

 Visit HK*Propel* for access to this chapter's Application Activity.

Selected Glossary

"bigger the better, more the merrier"—Translation of 以钜为美，以众为观, a common saying about how the status of the viewer is raised when more spectacles and many participants are involved.

Chinese opera—Theatrical form developed during the Song dynasty that incorporates singing, poetry, storytelling, acrobatics, dance, and more.

Cultural Revolution 文化大革命—A decade-long (1966-1976) attempt to reignite the spirit of the Communist Revolution through ideological cleansing of perceived bourgeois influences and mass mobilization of Chinese youth.

the Eight Model Works or **the 8 Model Works** 样板戏 **yangbanxi**—Performances created to promote Communist policies during the Cultural Revolution.

gudianwu 古典舞—"Ancient standards dance," often translated as "classical" dance.

Han dynasty 汉朝, **Tang dynasty** 唐朝, and **Song dynasty** 宋朝—Historical eras important to Chinese dance.

military dance—Dance troupes are formed within the Chinese military to entertain the troops and to represent the country at regional, national, and international events.

spectator orientation—The value of an artistic work in Chinese culture is determined primarily by the status of the viewer or owner.

wenwu 文舞—Civil or "graceful" dance.

wuwu 武舞—Martial or "energetic" dance.

yangge 秧歌—"Rice-sprout song and dance"; also used as a general term for all Han folk dance.

Zhongguogudianwu 中国古典舞—Dance training system and aesthetic developed in the mid-20th century.

Selected References and Resources

Blake, C. Fred. 1994. "Foot-Binding in Neo-Confucian China and the Appropriation of Female Labor." *Signs* 19, no. 3 (Spring 1994): 676-712. University of Chicago Press.

Chang, Renxia. 1985. 中國舞蹈史 *Chinese Dance History*. Taipei: 蘭亭書店 Orchid Pavilion Books.

Chang, Shih-Ming Li, and Lynn E. Frederiksen. 2016. *Chinese Dance: In the Vast Land and Beyond*. Middletown, Connecticut: Wesleyan University Press.

Graezer, Florence. 1999. "The Yangge in Contemporary China: Popular Daily Activity and Neighborhood Community Life." *Chinese Perspectives* 24 (1999): 31-43.

Kang, Liu. 2004. *Globalization and Cultural Trends in China*. University of Hawai'i Press.

Gunde, Richard. 2002. *Culture and Customs of China*. Westport, CT: Greenwood Press.

McCurley, Dallas. 2005. "Performing Patterns: Numinous Relations in Shang and Zhou China." *TDR: The Drama Review* 49, no. 3 (October 05, 2005): 135-156.

Qiang, Ning. 2004. *Art, Religion, and Politics in Medieval China: The Dunhuang Cave of the Zhai Family*. University of Hawai'i Press.

Steinhardt, Nancy. 2009. "Imperial Palaces." In *Encyclopedia of Modern China*, vol. 1, edited by David Pong, pp. 289-293. Detroit, New York, London: Charles Scribner's Sons.

Su, Ya. 2004. 苏娅. 求索新知-中国古典舞学习笔记 *Seeking Insight: A Study of Zhongguo Gudianwu*. Beijing: 中国戏剧出版社 China Drama Publishing House.

Wang, Kefen. 1985. *The History of Chinese Dance*, translated by Ke Ruibo. Beijing: Foreign Languages Press.

Wang, Kefen, Liu Enbo, Xu Erchong. 1994. 中国舞蹈辞典 *Chinese Dance Dictionary*. Beijing: Cultural Arts Publishing.

Wilcox, Emily. 2019. *Revolutionary Bodies: Chinese Dance and the Socialist Legacy*. University of California Press.

Zhao, Sophia Tingting. 2016. "Reorienting the Gaze in Mei Lanfang's Lyrical Theatre: Performing Female Interiority." *Asian Theater Journal* 33(2):395-419. University of Hawai'i Press.

23

Dance in Japanese Culture

Inoue Atsuki

Learning Objectives

After reading this chapter you will be able to do the following:

- Use dance and its development to recognize essential qualities of Japanese history and culture.
- Understand how regulation of dance by those in authority has affected its development over time.
- Recognize the central role of religion and tradition in Japanese dance.
- Describe how Japanese dance has been subject to influences from overseas cultures.

Key Terms

butoh, yosakoi—20th-century Japanese dance forms.

furyu, wabi-sabi, basara, and **suki**—Aesthetic perspectives and cultural movements that have influenced the development of dance.

geisha—Performer of traditional Japanese arts as entertainment for a private event.

kagura, Noh-mai, Kabuki-mai, Nihon-buyo—Japanese traditional dance, generally performative. Mai means dance, and Noh-mai is the dance in the Noh theater.

mai, odori—Japanese words for "dance."

matsuri—Japanese festivals originating in religious rituals.

Bon Festival—Dancing Bon-Odori 盆踊り

"During the season of Bon [summertime Buddhist-Confucian festivals celebrating the ancestors], a folk dance known as Bon-odori was common in various districts. Bon-odori, which may be seen in many districts even today, affords a delightful pastime for the young folk, who gather at the compounds of local shrines or temples and dance far into the night. The dance consists of simple, monotonous steps and clapping of hands; common folk songs are sung, usually without the accompaniment of any musical instrument. Bon-odori is really the simplest dance ever seen in Japan. Why is it so simple? It is simple because it requires a great number of participants, old and young, men and women. Any and every person can participate but has to dance as he is without wearing a special kind of kimono. Dancing in everyday clothes is the original form of Bon-odori, which is one reason why it is simplicity itself; it naturally will not require any technical skill in dance movement. It is absolutely necessary that every movement of Bon-odori, steps, clapping of hands, and singing, be uniform; that is, the manifestation of the united strength of the masses is required" (Ashikaga 1950, 225).

 Resource 23.1 in HK*Propel* includes a web link to a map of the general geography of Japan.

This notable passage was written 70 years ago, and the situation remains almost the same today. **Bon-Odori** (盆踊り), or *Bon* (盆) dance, is one of the most traditional and popular dances in contemporary Japanese communities at home and abroad. For over 500 years, people of all ages have participated in summertime Bon-Odori, honoring their ancestors in the Buddhist-Confucian festival of Bon. In Japan, it is no exaggeration to say that everyone knows Bon-Odori, and it is widely represented among the numerous festivals that abound in Japanese communities around the world.

Matsuri

Unique Cultural Phenomenon of Japanese Festivals

The term **matsuri** 祭 technically refers to religious festivals. The character 祭 means offering, or worship of gods and ancestors. Every year in

Bon-Odori festival at Tottori prefecture.

Japan, at least 270 festivals are held at various times and places throughout the country. While some matsuri are small, local events, others have national or even international presence, and many are tied to local and regional economic health. Dances are integral to these festivals, their participatory nature supporting rituals that unite people in common worship. Matsuri originated in rites to commemorate ancestors, ensure good harvests, and promote community stability. They continue to fulfill these functions through events that have been held for many centuries, as well as others born in the 20th and 21st centuries. Through gathering together as spectators and participants in dancing, *taiko* 太鼓 (Japanese-style drum), eating and drinking, talking, praying, carrying the altar or propelling a float in a procession, people strengthen their ties to one another but also commemorate their traditions and heritage.

Taiko 太鼓: Japanese-Style drum

Outside of Japan, "taiko drum" is one specific style of ensemble Japanese drum performance, developed in 1951. However, in Japan, the ancient term *taiko* (太鼓) literally means "drum" and represents the full range of percussion instruments, many of which are "indispensable in matsuri. The history of taiko in Japan is said to have started around 500 BCE. . . . According to one theory, the word *taiko*, which means 'drum,' was transmitted from China, and [later became] a general term for drums used in Japan" (Wadaiko History 2020).

 See resource 23.2 in HK*Propel* for web links.

A Confluence of Cultures

Japan has been heavily influenced by cultures on the Asian continent, with its earliest settlers crossing from the easternmost point of Russia many thousands of years ago, giving rise to the **Jomon period** beginning in 14,000 BCE. Much

later, starting around 300 BCE, the **Yayoi people** arrived from China via the Korean peninsula. These two cultures are the primary ancestors of Japanese people. Buddhism and technology were introduced from China throughout the Asuka, Nara, and Heian periods (592-1185 CE). In the process, new aesthetic concepts were cultivated. In the **Edo period** (1603-1868 CE) exchanges with most foreign countries were greatly restricted under *sakoku* (鎖国, 1639-1854), a policy of national isolation. Some body expressions, including **Kabuki** (歌舞伎), were heavily regulated and repressed under the isolationist rule of the Edo **shogunate**. On the other hand, the performing arts of **Noh** (能) and **kagura** (神楽) received patronage from the shogunate as ritual performance rooted in Japanese tradition. Such regulation of physical expression has continued to greater or lesser degrees up to the present. An example is the ban of Bon-Odori in the **Meiji period** (1868-1912) and the regulation of pair dances in the Showa and Heisei periods (1926 to the present). After the **Kanagawa Peace Treaty** between the United States and Japan was signed in 1854, exchanges with the West—which had been restricted until then—increased dramatically. In addition to Western military training and social styles, Russian ballet, German expressionism, American jazz, and more were brought to Japan over time, and the Japanese absorbed many new forms of body expression. During the 20th century, these changes accelerated greatly with the reverberations of World War II, and along with Japan's embrace of technology, helped shape Japanese dance culture into its current form. Here are several key points to note about Japanese dance:

- Some Japanese dances are strongly protected and promoted by the state and powers, while others are not, as can be seen in the contrast between Noh and Kabuki. The relationship with power in the formation and succession of dance is important for understanding dance in Japanese culture.

- In some Japanese dances, there is a large gap between perceptions in Japan and overseas. For example, few Japanese **geisha** (芸者) perform **Nihon-buyo** (日本舞踊), one of the styles of Japanese dance, in **tatami** (畳), or "straw mat" rooms, called *ozashiki* (御座敷). From abroad, however, geisha is often seen as a major component of Japanese culture. This means that the presence of geisha is symbolically large, but is extremely small in a statistical sense.

- Some Japanese dances are strongly participatory while others are performed for spectators. For example, Bon-Odori and **yosakoi** invite participation, while Noh, Kabuki, and **butoh** are strongly presentational.

- Japanese aesthetics are quite important to the dance. Many Japanese people use the word **wabi-sabi** (侘寂) to describe the simplicity of utensils for the tea ceremony and the beauty of a garden surrounded

by silence. From the late Heian period through the Muromachi period (1392-1573 CE), wabi-sabi shaped an image of Japan's unique aesthetic sense, embracing simple, quiet appearance and imperfections. On the other hand, **furyu** (風流) has been one of the dominant aesthetics of Japan since around the Heian period. It refers to an elegant, surprising design that, along with **basara** (婆娑羅) and **suki** (数寄), confronts the wabi-sabi aesthetic.

Table 23.1 presents a time line of Japanese periods.

Table 23.1 Time Line of Japanese Periods

Japanese character	Period name	Duration	Notes
縄文	Jomon	10,000-300 BCE	Hunting-gathering culture arrived in Japan. Early forms of Shinto as animism arose.
弥生	Yayoi	300 BCE-250 CE	Economy based on agriculture centered on rice. Influences from Korea and China.
大和	Yamato	250-710 CE	Emergence of central governing power. Arrival of Buddhism from China.
奈良	Nara	710-794	Exchange with mainland China continues to be popular.
平安	Heian	794-1185	Sarugaku, dengaku, and ennen become popular. Furyu aesthetic movement. Mi-kagura and kagura arise.
鎌倉	Kamakura	1185-1333 CE	Nembutsu odori (one of the roots of Bon-Odori).
南北朝	South and North	1336-1392 CE	Beginning of Noh.
室町	Muromachi	1392-1573 CE	Development of the wabi-sabi aesthetic, especially in tea ceremony. Rise of basara aesthetic.
安土桃山	Azuchi-Momoyama	1573-1603 CE	
江戸	Edo	1603-1868 CE	Period of isolation, or sakoku (1639-1854). Beginning of Kabuki.
明治	Meiji	1868-1912	The start of modernization and encountering Western dances, including ballroom dance. Government situated Shinto as a national religion.
大正	Taisho	1912-1926 CE	European-inspired Romanticism appears in Japanese arts.
昭和	Showa	1926-1989	Beginning of butoh.
平成	Heisei	1989-2019	Yosakoi Soran festival starts in 1992

Note: The Japanese characters for each period/era include dynasty, location of capital, and gengo. The term *gengo* is the era name given to the period of an emperor's reign. In Japan, we use the year in the Western (Gregorian) calendar, but we also give eras names based on the reign of the emperors. Gengo accompany a change of administration, when the monarch takes the throne or during their reign.

The extermination of Yamata no Orochi, the big snake monster.

Prototypes of current dances were created during the Heian and Edo periods. Since the Meiji period, Japanese dance has been heavily influenced by contact with Western dance.

 See resource 23.3 in HK*Propel* for web links.

Japanese Aesthetics

Ancient dance forms are often associated with particular aesthetic principles intertwined with religious, political, and sociocultural dynamics that prevailed when the dances were first enacted. For example, there are various theories on the origin of Bon-Odori, but the most prominent theories concern the *nembutsu odori* (念仏踊り) and the furyu aesthetic movement. Nembutsu odori is a Buddhist invocation with chanting, drumming, and dancing that originated in the middle of the Heian period (794-1185 CE). The furyu aesthetic sense also emerged in this era and developed further during the Edo period (1603-1868), as a cultural movement among the common people. Kagura, Noh, Kabuki, Nihon-buyo, and Bon-Odori all originated in the furyu

aesthetic, embracing ornate design with elaborate taste. Furyu was recognized as a confrontation with the relative clarity and directness of wabi-sabi, and when considered along with basara and suki aesthetics, it is clear that dynamics between different aesthetics continue to inform and shape Japanese cultural expression.

 See resource 23.4 in HK*Propel* for web links.

Kagura

Ritual Dance and Japanese Religion

Kagura dance is aligned with the **Shinto** religion in Japan. It is composed of two types: those that have been performed by the royal family, *mi-kagura* (御神楽), and those that have spread to the people through furyu aesthetics, known as *sato-kagura* (里神楽) or "village" kagura. These rituals greatly influenced the formation of Bon-Odori in connection with shrine-based rituals of the Shinto religion. After the Meiji period (1868-1912), these rituals became a national unification device called *Kokka Shinto*, or state-sponsored Shinto.

See resource 23.5 in HK*Propel* for web links.

Noh and Kabuki Theater

Two Classical Dance Dramas

Noh theater arose during the South and North period (1336-1392) and Kabuki developed a few centuries later during the Edo period (1603-1868). It is said that the mothers of both art forms are *sarugaku* (猿楽) (a variety show), *dengaku* (田楽) (an agricultural ritual), and *ennen* (延年) (part of a Buddhist ceremony). Sarugaku was thought to be created when the art called *sangaku* (散楽) was introduced from China. The art, which was full of variety, such as singing, dancing, pantomime, acrobatics, and magic was performed with governmental protection as *sangaku*, but when it was abolished in the Heian period, the actors continued to perform as *sarugaku* their arts at festivals and within the protection of large temples and shrines.

Dengaku was originally a rice planting ritual with dance and music performed in the paddy fields. With ties to Buddhism and the addition of specific drumming it became a performing art. Eventually, the group of professionals, *dengakuza*, became associated with the landlord and became part of the sacred rituals, along with **sumo wrestling** and kagura dance at Shinto shrines.

Ennen is a performing art presented at Buddhist temples by monks and children after the *Dai-ho-e*, a grand Buddhist memorial service. It is not a single form of entertainment, but a general term for a mix of aristocratic and popular performing arts, such as dance and acrobatics, poetry, a style of dialogue, and songs with a strong local flavor. These three types of performing arts gave rise to the multifaceted theater events now known as Noh and Kabuki.

Noh

Noh dance drama is conducted on a main stage about six square meters large, with a roof, a bridge, and a backstage area for costume changes. A group of qualified professionals wearing traditional Japanese **kimono** costumes follow strictly defined story lines inspired by legend and history. The furyu movement that arose during the Heian period greatly affected the formation of Noh, as did the level of sponsorship and protection given to artists by the **shogun**—the powerful military leader appointed by the emperor. However, the protection was a double-edged sword. While it allowed Noh to develop refined techniques, it also limited its growth beyond the strict codification enforced by the shogunate (government of the shogun) through the *za* (座) system—a set of rules governing merchants and trade guilds. With the fall of the shogunate at the end of the Edo era, Noh actors lost their guardian. During the following Meiji period (1868-1912) of modernization (aka Meiji Restoration) many were forced to go out of business or change jobs. However, due to the recent influence of worldwide art protection policies, such as the **UNESCO Intangible Cultural Heritage** listing, Noh has come alive with the support of the government, the imperial family, and the emerging conglomerates who have realized the necessity of traditional national art. Nonetheless, not many Japanese people will encounter Noh on a daily basis, and the profession's strict adherence to tradition excluded female Noh performers until recently.

Kabuki

Kabuki, the theater of the common people, is said to have been founded by **Izumo no Okuni** (出雲阿国 1572-1613 CE), a *miko*, or shrine maiden, who danced in Shinto rituals. Over the 25 years of Okuni's career, Kabuki dance (also called ***onna-Kabuki*** (女歌舞伎), or women's Kabuki) gained in popularity and in imitators, until it was banned by the shogunate in 1629 for "contributing to the turbulence of morals." ***Waka-shu Kabuki*** (若衆歌舞伎), with men dancing as women, replaced onna-Kabuki, but this form caused similar "moral turbulence," along with political disruption, and was also banned until 1652. Thereafter, despite this history of repression and regulation, Kabuki grew to become one of Japan's leading traditional performing arts. Ironically, Kabuki has survived into the 21st century as a male-only performing art, with men who train as ***onnagata***, or female-role specialists. Actors selected from a closed Kabuki actors' community called ***Rien*** (梨園) are all members of Kabuki families, with roles passed down through generations.

During the Edo period when it arose, Kabuki catered to the tastes of the common people, with plays about historical events and lifestyles of the powerful, tales highlighting the foibles of ordinary people, and nonnarrative dance. These three components still make up the Kabuki program, but the genre has expanded greatly. Now there are collaborations with contemporary playwrights and directors, new performances based on, among other things, **manga** (comic books) and **anime** (animation), attracting a wider audience than ever before. As Kabuki theater evolved from the Edo period to today, Kabuki dance combined with other ancient dances into a separate performance form, Nihon-buyo (日本舞踊).

Geisha Dance and Nihon-Buyo: Legacy From Dance of Kabuki Theater

The term *geisha* is often used to represent Japanese culture from abroad, though the Japanese themselves rarely use the word on a daily basis. In Japan, a geisha is a professional entertainer and sophisticated conversationalist who welcomes guests to a banquet with dances, instrumental music, storytelling, and song. Though foreigners may see geisha as emblematic of Japan, there are only about 500 geishas in the country today.

A performing art closely related to—and often confused with—geisha is Nihon-buyo, an art with a history of nearly 400 years. It includes dance forms of ***Kabuki-mai*** (歌舞伎舞) or Kabuki dance, ***Kamigata mai*** (上方舞), with stiff torso characteristics inspired by the life-sized puppets of **Bunraku** (Malm 1977, 21), and ***Kyo mai*** (京舞), often

associated with traditional banquets. The main elements of Nihon-buyo were greatly influenced by Noh and Kabuki that precede it. First of all, Kabuki dance was created by extracting elements of dance from the early stages of the 17th century, when Kabuki was not yet an independent theatrical form. Therefore, the movement of Kabuki dance in part shows the realistic movement of everyday life in an abstract, theatricalized manner, and in part shows the stylistic beauty that is exaggerated in the theater. Second, techniques from the 15th-century predecessor Noh, such as the turning movement and the style of walking, were absorbed and utilized in Nihon-buyo. The instruments used for Noh music are also indispensable for Nihon-buyo music. The third antecedent is folk performing art, which preceded Noh. The jumping movements in folk dances became part of Noh in its earliest stages and subsequently influenced Nihon-buyo. Fourth, in the 20th century, a group of works were created from the momentum of Western influence, but the technique does not stray far from Kabuki dance. The key point to remember is that Nihon-buyo and Kabuki greatly overlap. From the viewpoint of dance performance, we can recognize Kabuki as a part of Nihon-buyo, but not the other way around. But from a historical point, it can be said Nihon-buyo and Kabuki have a common originator, the shrine maiden Izumo no Okuni.

Geisha

The original geishas were men, known as ***taikomochi*** (太鼓持ち), who acted as jesters and advisors to feudal lords, even accompanying them in battle. During the relative peace of the Edo era, the taikomochi turned more toward hosting and entertainment duties, evolving into the official geisha role. By the late 1700s, female geishas had taken over the roles of host and entertainer, often at banquets that featured ***oiran*** (花魁), high-class Japanese courtesans (Toki 2016). This relationship, coupled with the popularity of female geishas, led to the conflation of geisha with prostitutes. Male geishas still exist today, but the number is small.

 See resource 23.6 in HK*Propel* for web links.

Folk Dance of Indigenous People in Hokkaido and Okinawa

The Japanese island of **Hokkaido** is the southernmost in an archipelago extending from Russia's Kamchatka Peninsula to Japan, and has been a nexus of activities between Russia, Japan, China, and Korea over many centuries. Its indigenous inhabitants, the **Ainu**, have a complex history that has only recently been acknowledged.

Okinawa, the largest of the Okinawa, or **Ryukyu**, Islands, lies in the south of the Japanese archipelago, approximately 450 miles from Taiwan. Current research suggests that indigenous Okinawans migrated from Taiwan over 30,000 years ago. After World War II, Okinawa was occupied by the United States, and extensive military bases on the island today are a source of friction between Okinawans, Japan, and the United States.

The Ainu

The Ainu are an indigenous people who have inhabited Hokkaido, Sakhalin, and Kuril Islands for centuries, perhaps even thousands of years. Their main occupation was fishing, hunting, and gathering. Their animist religion centered on the *iomante* (brown bear sacrificial ceremony), with the bear as the highest god among animal deities.

Records from the 1600s (Edo period) about the Matsumae region of Hokkaido note Ainu dances were performed to mark events of iomante and fishing ground labor and trade ceremonies for Japanese feudal lords and clans of the Edo shogunate. However, it is said that Ainu dance was performed not only in such ceremonies but also in daily life.

In the early modern era, the Edo shogunate placed the Matsumae clan in Hokkaido, and initially clan officials traded with Ainu. Gradually, however, the merchants took over the area and the Ainu became conscripted laborers in their own fishing grounds. Meanwhile, the Ainu were subject to the shogunate's assimilation policies.

In the Meiji era (1868-1912) the government began colonizing Hokkaido, usurping natural resources such as fisheries and forestry. An Ainu protection policy, the Hokkaido Former Aborig-ines Protection Act, enacted in 1898, advocated Ainu assimilation into Japanese culture. In exchange, the Ainu were encouraged to take up agriculture and were given land, medical care, and educational assistance. Through this process, the inheritance of Ainu traditional culture, including dance, was severely restricted.

On the other hand, dance performances were often incorporated into the sightseeing tours for Japanese visiting Hokkaido, and the tourism boom of the Showa era (1926-1989) turned Ainu traditional culture into a tourism resource. Ainu dances are now performed for visiting guests from overseas. The prominence of these music and dance performances is central to the rebirth of Ainu culture (Cobb 2020), and the dance was registered in 2009 on the UNESCO Intangible Cultural Heritage list.

Ainu Dance

Ainu dance emphasizes "coexistence with nature, and represents subjects like brown bears and birds, hunting and play. The variety of dances is truly spectacular. They include large group ring dances, small group dances to offer prayers to the spirits, dances to show gratitude for successful fishing and harvests, dances to drive away evil spirits, and dances which show styles of work. Depending on the area of Hokkaido, the songs and dances may have their own traditional styles and names" (Akanko Ainu Kotan 2020).

Eisa Dance of Okinawa

From its beginnings in 1429, the Ryukyu (Okinawa) Kingdom thrived for 450 years in a delicate balance of trade and sovereignty under the sequential influences of the Chinese Ming dynasty (1368-1644) and Japan's Edo shogunate (1603-1868). But the Meiji government's Ryukyu annexation (琉球処分) of 1879 effectively destroyed the kingdom and made Okinawa a part of the Japanese empire. After World War II, with the deployment of many U.S. military bases on the island, Okinawa came to occupy a significant historical, political, and socioeconomic position in Japan. Today's Okinawan dances, such as *eisa* (エイサー), must be understood in light of this history.

Eisa has its origins in indigenous Okinawan arts and the nembutsu odori, a memorial service for ancestors. In 1603, it is said that a Buddhist monk from mainland Japan translated Buddhist scriptures into songs in the Ryukyu language. The name *eisa* is said to be based on the shout "eisa eisa hieruga-eisa" in the song. In eisa, the drums (taiko) are important tools. In addition to the larger drum dance by the men, there is also a circle dance only for women using a small taiko called *usu-daiko* (臼太鼓). Eisa is popular both inside and outside Okinawa, but connections to the local community remain paramount. There are clear rules for participation connected to the lives and traditions of the Okinawan people.

Zento Eisa Matsuri (All-Island Eisa Festival)

"The Okinawa All-Eisa Festival started as the Whole Island Eisa Contest with the birth of Koza City in 1956, which is held every year on the first weekend of the old *Bon* Festival, and now represents Japan as a summer feature of Okinawa" (Zento Eisa Matsuri Official Site 2020).

 See resource 23.7 in HK*Propel* for web links.

Crosscurrents

A major crosscurrent in Japanese arts is exemplified by sangaku, the "variety show" arts that reached prominence in China's Tang dynasty (618-906 CE) and arrived in Japan during the Nara period (710-794 CE). Sangaku is one of the foundations for many Japanese theatrical arts, including Noh and Kabuki. By contrast, nembutsu odori (based on Buddhism from India that also arrived via China) was a more participatory dance that gave rise to Bon-Odori as an important means of social interaction among Japanese people. Thus, currents that flowed from abroad centuries ago ultimately shaped both presentational and participatory Japanese dances both at home and internationally.

The 20th century saw another rush of influences on Japanese dance, this time from far beyond Asia. European ballroom dance, ballet, modern dance, and other forms arrived as Japan's

isolation ended. National and international events—such as World War II—accelerated the flow of currents in all directions, and new Japanese dance forms, such as butoh (舞踏), found audiences and practitioners around the world.

Butoh, an Avant-Garde Dance Form Born in Japan

Butoh is an avant-garde dance that responded to the profound trauma experienced by the Japanese culture following World War II. The dance also became a medium for connecting to Western cultures through roots in European artistic movements, such as German *Neue Tanz* (new dance), expressionism, and surrealism. Strong connections with postmodern dancers include the rejection of a "pleasing" dance aesthetic while embracing the raw and the grotesque. The first butoh performance was 1959's *Forbidden Color*, directed by butoh's cofounder **Tatsumi Hijikata** (1928-1986) and costarring **Yoshito Ohno** (1938-2020). The dance explored homosexuality—a societal taboo in mid-20th century Japan and many other parts of the world. The founders' explorations of extreme and socially forbidden experiences were a soul-baring response to the destruction caused by the bombing of Hiroshima and Nagasaki and the upending of Japanese culture that followed World War II.

Butoh

"Co-founded by Hijikata and Kazuo Ohno, the genre's iconic tropes—near-naked men in white makeup performing slow, intensely controlled micro-movements—only really took hold from the 1970s. Today, butoh encompasses a range of styles, from the grotesque to the austere, and from the erotic to the comic. It is frequently regarded as surreal and androgynous, and focuses on primal expressions of the human condition rather than physical beauty" (Andrews 2016).

To the Japanese, butoh is "postmodern dance," the antithesis of modern dance that had been learned from Europe and the United States, even though the form was created from a uniquely Japanese experience and culture. On the other hand, overseas, butoh is regarded as "Japanese modern dance." Ironically, while in the eyes of the world butoh is one of the most representative dances of Japan, the scale of its presence at home has always been limited.

 See resource 23.8 in HK*Propel* for web links.

Popular Dance in Contemporary Japan

In contemporary Japan, the dances that ordinary people (mainly nonexperts) are familiar with are street dances, hip-hop, dances spun off from TV shows, folk dances performed at schools and community facilities, festival-derived **Yosakoi Soran**, and ballroom dance, in which many young people in Japan once participated. These dances are popular as part of matsuri (festivals), social gatherings, sports, and extracurricular lessons, and many are also taught in art colleges.

Among these dances, Yosakoi Soran and ballroom dance are notable for their nationwide presence and organization. Although Yosakoi Soran is relatively new, it has spread beyond its origins in Hokkaido and is now a social activity of teams from universities and workplaces around the country throughout the year. On the other hand, ballroom dance—once undertaken by many Japanese youths in social settings—is mainly a competitive sport nationwide.

Ballroom Dance

Ballroom, or couple, dancing was imported from the West in the late Meiji (1868-1912), "as a way to quench a local desire for modernization and westernization" (Godel 2012). However, Japanese society did not generally approve of couple dancing unless the partners were in an established relationship, such as marriage. These social norms led to both legal and social regulation of pair dancing from the 1930s onward. Nonetheless, many dance teachers and fans were determined to popularize the dance in Japan, despite these restrictions. Through their efforts, ballroom dance after World War II became especially popular among young Japanese people during social gatherings, and the form is now widely perceived as a healthy sport or graceful performing art in Japan.

Ballroom Dance in Japan

"[B]allroom dancing has consistently been embodied as a way to express the Japanese self in a Western way. . . . By deviating from the country's norm, specifically in displays of sexuality, the practice of ballroom functioned not as a way to become more Western, but as a form of resistance to a fixed cultural identity and a way to identify not simply as Japanese" (Godel 2012). In effect, ballroom dance was "translated" into Japanese.

Social gathering of couple dancing.

Yosakoi Festival, One of the Most Energetic Matsuri

While ballroom is notable as an imported dance, yosakoi festival dance has become the opposite—a significant Japanese export to the rest of the world. Japanese festivals, or matsuri, serve to unify the people in common effort, celebrate cultural identity, and reinforce religious or social traditions. Unison movements diligently practiced by large groups are the hallmark of these events, and yosakoi festival dance is no exception. However, unlike other traditional festivals, yosakoi matsuri did not emerge over time out of religious and societal trends. It was a competitive event deliberately created in 1954 by the Kochi prefecture's chamber of commerce to counter the post–World War II recession, rejuvenate the citizens, and spur the local economy during the summer lull in shopping. The first festival drew 750 participants from 21 organizations; the 30th event exceeded 10,000 dancers, and the numbers have continued to grow each year for this four-day matsuri in early August. As an entirely new festival, the dances were not greatly constrained in style, music, or content, with only the following requirements:

- Participants must use *naruko* (wooden clappers used to scare birds from the rice fields).
- Music must include something from the original "Yosakoi Naruko Dancing" song.
- Teams are limited to 150 participants.

In 1992, a student from Hokkaido, fascinated by the yosakoi festival, held the Yosakoi Soran Festival in the city of Sapporo, Hokkaido. The success and visibility of this event had a ripple effect, inspiring the spread of yosakoi festivals throughout Japan. As in the original festival, dancers were required to use clappers of some sort, but the musical requirement was adapted to use a phrase from Hokkaido's traditional folk song "Soran Bushi." Other than that, the teams have completely free reign over their choreography, song, and costumes. This is a good example of cultural diffusion.

Today, yosakoi is being shown in more than 200 locations in Japan and 29 countries and regions overseas. Since 2016, the Kochi prefecture has invited representatives of the overseas yosakoi teams to Kochi and certified them as "yosakoi ambassadors" to further disseminate yosakoi to the world. To date, 65 people from 23 teams in 19 countries have been certified as yosakoi ambassadors. Through this accreditation, the world of yosakoi expands and promotes international exchange.

 See resource 23.9 in HK*Propel* for web links.

Summary

In looking at the history of Japanese dance, it is important to know that dances developed under different levels of protection and regulation by those in power and through the ingenuity of the Japanese people. The resultant dances can be divided into performance-oriented (such as Nihon-buyo) and participatory forms, the latter usually happening during the many matsuri (festivals) that take place throughout Japan. From Bon-Odori to yosakoi, the inclusive nature of these dances creates the unifying energy that all Japanese festivals promote. It is also useful to note how Japanese views on the culture's dance might differ considerably from those of foreigners, with butoh being a key example. Thinking from these perspectives as you examine each dance in detail will take you more deeply into the richness of Japanese culture and history.

Discussion Questions

1. What are some of the dances that were protected or repressed by authorities in Japanese culture, and why?
2. What are some of the predecessors of Noh and Kabuki?
3. How has influence from abroad affected the formation of Japanese dance?
4. What is one of the significant Japanese aesthetic movements that affected the development of dance, and how?
5. What are the key features of Japanese festivals, and what is unique about yosakoi matsuri?

 Visit HK*Propel* for access to this chapter's Application Activity.

Selected Glossary

Bon-Odori/Bon dance 盆踊り—A style of dancing performed during Bon festivals that originally welcomed the spirits of the dead.

butoh 舞踏—Avant-garde dance created by Hijikata Tatsumi and his disciples as a response, in part, to the trauma of World War II and influenced by dance movements such as German Neue Tanz (new dance).

furyu 風流—An aesthetic sense and cultural movement from the mid-Heian period to the Edo period (1603-1868). Its focus on elegant design with elaborate taste shaped the development of kagura, Noh, Kabuki, Nihon-buyo, and Bon-Odori, and it was recognized as a confrontation with wabi-sabi, basara, and suki (数寄) aesthetics.

geisha 芸者—Usually (but not always) a woman who performs traditional Japanese arts, such as dance and *shamisen* (three-stringed Japanese guitar) to entertain guests. Geisha entertainment is also known as ozashiki asobi (御座敷遊び). *Ozashiki* is a tatami-floored banquet room where customers can enjoy eating and drinking and geisha performances.

Kabuki 歌舞伎—A performing art originated by shrine maiden Izumo no Okuni (出雲阿国) in the early Edo period.

kagura 神楽—Singing and dancing dedicated to gods in Shinto rituals in Japan. It started with the mi-kagura (御神楽) of the royal family around the Heian period and was inherited as a village kagura or sato-kagura (里神楽) by the common people.

matsuri—Japanese festivals originating in religious rituals.

Nihon-buyo 日本舞踊—Literally "Japanese dance," established through inheriting the techniques of performing arts that existed in advance, such as Noh and Kabuki.

Noh 能—A performing art based on the theatrical aspects of sarugaku in the Heian era that became known as Noh in the Kamakura era. In the Muromachi era, it was further developed by Kanami and his son Zeami under the protection of the shogun Yoshimitsu Ashikaga.

odori, mai—Japanese terms referring to dance. Roughly corresponding to whether the dances are more participatory, such as Bon-Odori and other dances in matsuri (Japanese festivals), or performative, as in Kabuki-mai.

Selected References and Resources

Please note that the way Japanese names are written has recently changed. As of 2019, the system reverted back to writing the family name first, given name second (as is done in Chinese). Since the late 19th century, after the end of the period of isolation, the names were written in the Western fashion with the family name last. Thus the order of names in this text may differ, depending on when the person lived.

Andrews, William. 2016. "'Butoh': The Dance of Death and Disease." *Japan Times* May 28, 2016. www.japantimes.co.jp/culture/2016/05/28/books/book-reviews/butoh-dance-death-disease/.

Ashikaga, Ensho. YEAR. 1950 "The Festival for the Spirits of the Dead in Japan" *Western Folklore* 9, no. 3: 217-228. Western States Folklore Society.

Feldman, Martha, and Bonnie Gordon. 2006. *The Courtesan's Arts: Cross-Cultural Perspectives.* Oxford University Press.

Hahn, Tomie. 2007. *Sensational Knowledge: Embodying Culture Through Japanese Dance.* Wesleyan University Press.

Hokkaido Government Board of Education. 1991 *Investigation Report of Ainu Traditional Dance in 1990.* https://ci.nii.ac.jp/ncid/BN11944999?l=en

Kato, Etsuko. 2004. *The Tea Ceremony and Women's Empowerment in Modern Japan: Bodies Re-Presenting the Past.* Routledge.

Kato James, Hyojiro. 1930. "Ballroom Dancing in Japan." *The Dancing Times.* September:559-561. London: Dancing Times.

Keio University Art Center. 2000. "The First Step." Hijikata Tatsumi Butoh Archives. www.art-c.keio.ac.jp/en/archives/list-of-archives/hijikata-tatsumi/.

Kodera, Yukichi. 1928. *Nihon to Oushuu no Gorakutekibuyou no hikaku* [A comparison of recreation dance of Japan and Europe.] *Minzoku Geijyutsu* [The folk art] 3, no. 8: 51-57. Tokyo: Minzoku Geijutsu no Kai.

Takechi, Tetsuji. 1986. *Kabuki wa donna Engekika* [What kind of drama is Kabuki?] Tokyo: Chikuma Syobo.

PART IX

Oceania

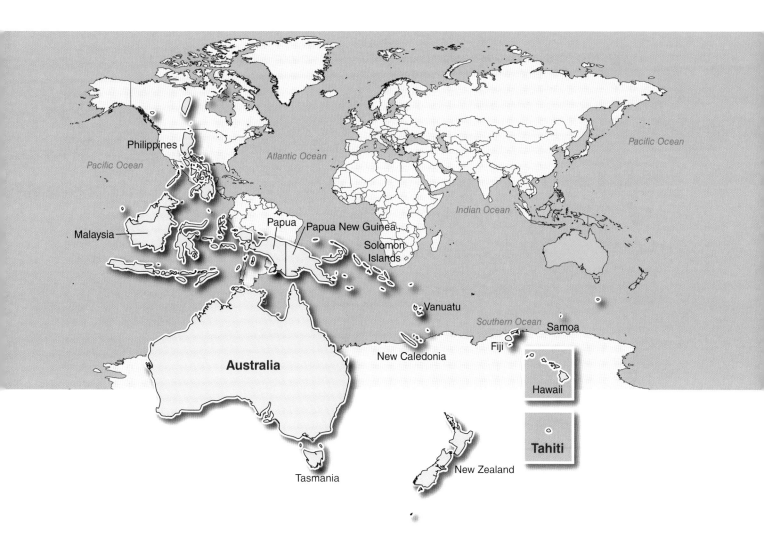

Oceania consists of Australia, New Zealand, and island groups in the Pacific Ocean. The chapters in part IX illuminate the different patterns of dance development in Australia and the French Polynesian island of Tahiti. While Aboriginal dances emerge from 60,000 years of history on the continent of Australia, Tahitian dances, like those of other Pacific islands, developed after seafaring people from Southeast Asia arrived around 1500 BCE. Dances in Australia and Tahiti therefore have different societal and environmental contexts. Colonization in the region—including by the United States in Hawai'i, Britain in Australia, and France in Polynesia—has also affected indigenous dance in recent centuries. In Australia, impacts of colonization were felt more in the south, allowing Aboriginal practices to survive in the central and northern areas. On the island of Tahiti, the effects were more widespread, including complete bans that complicated the use of dance as a form of cultural identity. More recently, issues of institutionalization versus community-based transmission of Tahitian dance have arisen as the dance becomes a potent cultural marker. Since Aboriginal practices are still closely bound to community, the issues of institutionalization might appear more in contemporary practices that integrate Aboriginal traditions. In recent decades, Aboriginal people have been gaining official recognition as original and rightful owners of the land, and their dance rituals have helped to mediate relations with the colonial settlers. Tahitian dance also is increasingly visible both at home and abroad as an enactment of Tahitian identity. Accordingly, the chapters in part IX illustrate how indigenous and colonial histories have intertwined to shape dance cultures in the region.

 HK*Propel* includes web links to additional resources for this section.

24

Dance of Aboriginal Australia

Stephen A. Wild

Learning Objectives

After reading this chapter you will be able to do the following:

- Use dance to differentiate among regional cultures of Aboriginal Australia.
- Understand the stylistic elements of Aboriginal dance, and use this to analyze dance patterns at different times and places.
- Appreciate the strong interconnection among dance, music, and visual design in Aboriginal performance.
- See the results of non-Indigenous settlement on Aboriginal dance performance in Australia.
- Apply what you have learned to analyze Indigenous dance of other colonized countries, such as the United States and Canada, countries in Latin America, and New Zealand.

Key Terms

clan, moiety—Social groups that define inter- and intra-community relations.

spiritual ancestors, the Dreaming, sacred sites—Aboriginal spiritual contexts.

manikay, kuruwarri—Cluster of songs, dances, and visual designs representing a spiritual ancestor of the members of a clan.

mimetic versus generic dances, Island dance (Island-style dance)—Styles of Aboriginal dance.

song man, exclusive/inclusive participation in singing and dancing—Clan elements defining relationships between singing and dancing.

Rom—One of a class of ceremonies performed by Aboriginal Australians to resolve conflicts between individuals or groups of people (Anbarra).

Rom Ceremony in Canberra, Australia

Male Aboriginal dancers from Arnhem Land rounded the east wing of Acton House in Canberra while two singers and two **didgeridu** (a wooden trumpet) players alternately performed verses from the two-song series associated with the dances. Two dancers held two decorated poles, each representing one of the song series being performed. Other dancers held other ritual objects. Aboriginal women danced along the vertical axis of the ceremonial ground formed by the male dancers advancing from the southern end toward a line of gift-bearing officials waiting at the northern end, facing the dancers. Forming a crescent around the officials was an estimated crowd of 1,500 Canberra residents witnessing this auspicious event. When the male dancers reached the line of officials, the decorated poles and other ritual objects carried by the dancers were exchanged for the gifts held by the officials. Thus ended a historic event in the life of the Australian Institute of Aboriginal Studies, now called Australian Institute of Aboriginal and Torres Strait Islander Studies (AIATSIS) and the Commonwealth of Australia. The ceremony was initiated by the Aboriginal performers as an act of reconciliation between the Indigenous people of Australia and the settler community (Wild 1986).

This chapter focuses on dances of Aboriginal Australia, rather than all Australian Indigenous dance. Australian Aborigines originally occupied the entirety of mainland Australia, as well as some off-shore islands, most notably Tasmania, located off the southeast coast, and Melville and Bathurst Islands (also known as the **Tiwi** Islands, named after the Aboriginal people who occupy them), located off the central north coast of the continent. At the time of the first British settlement of Australia in 1788, some 250 languages were spoken. Estimates of the original Aboriginal population are up to one million. In addition to Australian Aborigines (or Aboriginal Australians), a second group of Indigenous Australians—known as **Torres Strait Islanders**—occupies the small islands between the northeastern tip of the continent (Cape York) and Papua New Guinea. Their culture and languages are closely related to those of coastal Papua New Guinea and other nearby islands. This chapter mainly considers Torres Strait Islander dance as it has influenced Aboriginal dance.

From 1788, Aborigines were gradually dispossessed of their land and forced onto missions and reserves. The southern regions of the continent, including Tasmania, were the most intensely dispossessed, leaving much of the central and northern regions of the continent in Aboriginal hands. Thus, we know more about traditional Aboriginal dance in central and northern Australia. We consider Aboriginal dance in northern Australia (**Anbarra Aborigines**) and Central Australia (**Warlpiri Aborigines**) in some detail, with less detailed reference to Tiwi dance and dances of Cape York. We also discuss Aboriginal

Decorated poles are presented by dancers at a Rom ceremony.

responses to increasing pressures on traditional dance and dance contexts. Last, we consider contemporary fusions of Indigenous Australian dance with Western theatrical dance.

"Welcome to Country"

For over 200 years, the aborigines were dispossessed by European colonizers. Only in 1992 did the High Court of Australia recognize that Indigenous people were the original owners of the land. This led to the performance of ceremonies called "**Welcome to Country**."

Aboriginal Culture

Clans, Moieties, and the Dreaming

As you can see from the description of **Rom**, Aboriginal dance incorporates a sense of physical place with ancestral identity that can mediate relationships both within Aboriginal societies and with other cultures. For more than 60,000 years Aborigines lived as seminomadic hunter-gatherers, each community within a well-defined territory. Primary social identity was defined by membership of **patrilineal clans**, that is, determined through the male line. Each community consisted of several intermarrying clans. Each clan owned songs, dances, visual designs, and sacred sites, all related to the activities and characteristics of spiritual ancestors of the clan. Only clan members had the right to perform the dances that represented their ancestors.

Another social feature in Aboriginal Australia is the division of each community into two **moieties**, each consisting of a number of clans. While a clan is partly defined by the requirement for its members to marry someone outside the clan, members must also marry outside one's own moiety. This division of a community into two moieties has particular significance in ceremonial performance, including songs and dances.

Traditionally, Australian Aborigines believe that the members of each clan are descended from ancestors that represented conceptual categories of the world they created and inhabited. Thus, in addition to human characteristics, the ancestors were identified with natural species (e.g., kangaroo, yam) or natural phenomena (e.g., fire, wind, Milky Way), categories that the ancestors created. Members of a clan have a spiritual bond with both human and non-human descendants of their spiritual ancestor. They are, in this belief, contemporary expressions of these ancestors. The ancestors also created the land and its features, such as rocks, watercourses, and hills. Places of special significance during the creative period became **sacred sites**, treated with special reverence. Songs and dances are often performed at these sites or on ceremonial grounds representing them. Song lyrics, dance movements, and graphic designs are believed to depict the activities of the ancestors during the creative period. These beliefs are universal among Australian Aborigines, although finer details vary among different communities. The name of the creative period differs among the many Aboriginal languages but is given the common English name of **the Dreaming** (or "the Dreamtime").

Australian Aboriginal dance must be seen as part of a complex of expressions of the Dreaming, when the ancestors sang, danced, and created visual designs to celebrate their creative activities. They taught these arts to the first generation of human descendants, who then passed them down through the ages. Contemporary Aborigines, in re-creating these expressions of the Dreaming, ensure the continuing existence of the Aboriginal universe and Aboriginal identity.

Reminders of the Deceased

Australian Aborigines do not like to be reminded of recently deceased people, such as in photographic images or by mentioning their names, because their spirits may haunt living people. They are meant to return to their ancestral clan country. On the other hand, these spirits are a potential source of new songs, dances, and visual designs.

 See resource 24.1 in HK*Propel* for web links.

Rom in Northern Australia

The eastern half of the north-central peninsula of Australia is called Arnhem Land. Rom is one of a class of ceremonies performed by Aboriginal

Australians as a means of resolving conflicts between individuals or groups of people. In Arnhem Land, elaborately decorated poles and other ritual objects are presented to the people with whom a reconciliation is desired; the presentation is made after days of singing and dancing by the presenters as a token of respect to the recipients. The people who performed Rom in Canberra are called Anbarra, whose homeland is at the mouth of the Blyth River. Their country is occupied by both freshwater and saltwater species that they sing about in their clan songs, perform in their dances, and paint in clan visual designs. Each named cluster of songs, dances, and visual designs (e.g., **Jambich** and **Goyulan**), called a **manikay**, has a number of "subjects," representing bird, animal, and plant species; human-made objects, such as spears and boomerangs; and spiritual categories, such as "spirit man." Each subject, in turn, represents an ancestral spirit. Jambich has 21 subjects and Goyulan has 30.

Other Contexts of Dance in Arnhem Land

Dances in Arnhem Land are performed in contexts other than Rom, such as ritual initiation, **mortuary ceremonies**, and a cult ceremony called **kunapipi** that centers on birth and rebirth,

but also on purely social occasions after dark in the light of a fire. Mortuary ceremonies—not termed "funerals" because they may occur some time after the disposal of the body following a death—are traditionally focused on the placement of the bones of the deceased into a hollow log. At the end of the ceremony, the **hollow log coffin**, elaborately decorated with clan designs, is placed vertically in the landscape. During the ceremony the disinterred bones of the deceased are crushed, painted with ochre, and placed into the hollow log.

Interspersed with this activity and the painting of the log coffin, clan songs and dances of the manikay of the deceased are performed. A roughly rectangular dance ground is cleared. The musicians sit at one end, female dancers forming a line along one side and male dancers gathering at the opposite end of the singers. The male dancers run from one end to the other, toward and away from the musicians. Women dancers lift their feet alternately, throwing sand on the other foot. A defined item of performance consists of one verse of a subject accompanied by rhythmic beating of **clapsticks** and the playing of a didgeridu (a wooden trumpet). At the last approach of the male dancers they perform a closing pattern of movements, ending precisely with the closing pattern of the musicians. This structuring is considered "formal" or "straight-line" dance. The male dancers also engage a small number of manikay subjects through "elaborate,"

Dancers performing at a Rom ceremony in Arnhem Land.

or circle, dancing. These dances present the characteristic behavior of an ancestor and embody sacred elements, thus expressing the cosmology of the people through imitations. Other dances are standardized movements with no imitation involved (Clunies Ross and Wild 1984; Clunies Ross 1998). We classify the former as **mimetic dances** (imitative) and the latter as **generic dances** (non-imitative). (Clunies Ross and Wild [1984] give a detailed description of the relationships between songs, dances, and the manikay Jambich, including a table of the subjects in Jambich, those that are danced elaborately and those danced generically.)

The Song Series and Its Relationship to Dancing in Arnhem Land

Of the 21 subjects in the Jambich **song series**, only seven are danced, and only two of these dances are in mimetic style. The simpler straight-line dances follow a standard movement pattern for all subjects, whereas in the more complex elaborate dances, each subject has its own unique movement pattern. All of these dances, women's and men's, have somewhat standardized body movements. During the dances, the singer—aka **song man**—chooses the order of subjects to be performed, the number of verses to perform of each subject, and the tempo.

Song Man—Exclusive and Inclusive Participation

The song man learns the repertoires of musical and textual phrases belonging to the song series exclusively owned by his moiety. He accompanies himself with clapsticks and is joined by the didgeridu player, who takes his cue from the singer, as do the dancers. It is the singer, rather than the dancers, who makes the distinctive contribution to, and holds the primary responsibility for, the performance of the ceremony in Arnhem Land. This differentiation of responsibility and specialization between singers and dancers can be summarized as **exclusive participation** (singers) versus **inclusive participation** (dancers).

 See resource 24.2 in HK*Propel* for web links.

Central Australia

Warlpiri People

Among the Warlpiri people of Central Australia, dances are again related to named song series, each representing a particular spirit ancestor. Dances may be either mimetic or generic, depending on whether they are performed by members of the owning clan (mimetic) or by members of managing clans (generic) (Dail-Jones 1998). Members of the owning clan are believed to be spiritual descendants of the ancestor being represented in the dance and thus share the same spiritual identity as the ancestor. In a sense, the mimetic dancers are representing themselves.

A member of an intermarrying clan of the owning clan is responsible, along with their fellow clan members, for "managing" the ceremonial performances of the owning clan. A manager ensures the correct performance of the dance and usually applies the body decorations to the dancer, makes any required ceremonial objects, and generally keeps order. Managers also dance, but in a generic style: feet apart, the dancers move forward by jumping with both legs together, uttering shrill cries in time to the jumps.

Unlike Arnhem Land, women dance separately from men in Central Australia, as well as together in common ceremonies. Women also have their own song series, associated with the same ancestors as the men's song series. Customs aligned with ownership of dances and body designs also vary between men and women.

In Central Australia, the complex of songs, dances, and visual designs representing a spiritual ancestor is called a ***kuruwarri***—equivalent to *manikay* in Arnhem Land. The body designs worn by male owners of the dance (mimetic) are specific to particular ancestors, whereas the body decorations worn by managers are variants of a standard (generic) design. Female dancers may wear designs they own, whether or not they are owners of the dance being performed.

Fire Ceremonies

Warlpiri ceremonies with a similar role to the Rom ceremony in Arnhem Land are generally called ***fire ceremonies***. They are intended to resolve conflicts between intermarrying clans,

Manager instructing mimetic dancer in Warlpiri ceremony.

that is, between owners and managers. There are two named fire ceremonies, **Ngatjakula** and **Jardiwanpa**. The kuruwarri (ancestral spirit representations) in the first ceremony are birds (e.g., owl, budgerigar, emu) and in the second they are marsupials (e.g., rat kangaroo, rock wallaby) or snakes.

In ceremonies involving the whole community, as is usually the case in fire ceremonies, individuals not only belong to a particular clan but also the moiety to which their clan belongs. Ownership of a ceremony is extended from a clan to a moiety, and similarly, the management role is extended from individual clan members to the whole moiety. Moieties are not named in the Warlpiri language, except in relation to each other. The clans of one moiety are owners (*kirda*) of the Ngatjakula ceremonies, and managers (*kurdungurlu*) of Jardiwanpa ceremonies. The roles of each moiety are reversed when the other ceremony is performed. This change of roles between owners and managers according to which fire ceremony is being performed is important because it represents who is punishing whom.

The central theme of fire ceremonies is that managers punish owners for real or imagined derelictions of duty toward members of the intermarrying clans. Male owners, decorated with their clan designs, approach the gathered managers, who shower them with sparks from burning bushes. While burning embers rain on the owners, women managers dancing beside their male counterparts try to mitigate the burning effect by protecting the owners with green boughs of eucalyptus trees. Nevertheless, sparks do penetrate their body decorations and burn their skin. At the climax of the ceremony, the owners sit in a pit holding protective branches above their heads while managers light long poles tied with eucalyptus branches and shake the burning foliage over the owners. This very dramatic conclusion occurs on the final night of the ceremony, which lasts several weeks and is preceded and followed by singing and dancing the kuruwarri being performed.

The Song Series and Its Relationship to Dancing in Central Australia

In Central Australia, singing is a group activity, while dancing is more individualized—the reverse of that in Arnhem Land. There are exceptions to this pattern, but it holds true on most occasions. The differentiation between male singers and dancers in Central Australia can be described as inclusive (singers) versus exclusive (dancers). Each song series in Central Australia is concerned with one or a few related ancestors and consists of 20 or more verses.

The standard musical accompaniment to singing varies between women and men. On some occasions, women cup their hands together and slap the inside of the thighs while sitting cross-legged on the ground—the action produces a dull thud that coincides with the beginning of each word in the song text (**hand-lap percussion**). On other occasions women singers use no percussion accompaniment. Men almost always accompany themselves, usually by tapping together the ends of a pair of boomerangs, one held in each hand (**boomerang clapsticks**). The performers mark the end of each item by rattling the boomerangs end to end.

The Song Series and Women's Dance in Central Australia

Although a song series is owned by a clan or moiety, owners may allow anyone (within gender and age restrictions) to join in the group singing. For women's dances, members of the owning clan are decorated with the appropriate clan design in ochres (clay pigments) applied directly to the body; a headband often holds bird feathers, usually of white cockatoos. Dancers use parallel legs, bent knees, body bent forward from the hips, with very little movement in the hips, changes taking place mostly in the upper body and arms, and a relaxed performance manner (Dail Jones 1984).

Boys' Initiation in Central Australia

Whereas mortuary rituals are a focus of ceremonial life in Arnhem Land, in Central Australia the emphasis is on boys' initiation ceremonies. It is believed that pubescent boys must be separated from the care of women (particularly mothers). In the past, a mock "tug-of-war" was enacted over the initiates between the mothers of the boys and the men responsible for the ceremony. In a large cleared area, women and men gather separately to perform the dances associated with the initiate's clan. Solo male dancers are vigorously instructed on the correct movements by managers, while others sing the appropriate verses of the song series. The boys to be initiated are brought to the

dance area by their **ritual guardians** (described shortly) to witness the dances. Meanwhile, shields are decorated with the designs of the owning clans. At the end of the day, the decorated shields are hidden under a bank of bushes specially constructed for the occasion.

After nightfall, the community gathers to sit behind the barrier of bushes, men in front, with a dancing space between women and men. Women, particularly mothers, and maternal and paternal aunts of the initiates, dance to the men's singing. Fathers and paternal uncles of the initiates are expected to take a prominent role in the singing to demonstrate support for the newest recruits to their clan's ceremonial life. All the participants face east, watching for the sun to rise. One song series, "Travelling Women," is always performed by the men at this stage of the ceremony. It is concerned with a group of ancestral women and children traveling east, followed by a group of men. In the Dreaming story, the men periodically grab a pubescent boy to initiate him, a direct analogy

Shield decorated with clan design at boys' initiation ceremony, Central Australia.

to the ceremony. The male singers accompany themselves by beating shields on the ground. This is the only ceremony when this accompaniment is performed, giving rise to the name of this all-night performance as *Kurdiji* ("shield").

Initiation is also about arrangements for future marriage. Potential brothers-in-law become ritual guardians who supervise the initiates as they witness the dances or wait under a shelter of eucalyptus boughs. These "brothers-in-law" act as guardians to initiates during their long period of ritual learning that begins with their initiation. For several years, the novices do not return to family life but live with other initiates in a kind of bachelors' camp. Eventually, they are "given the boomerangs" by their ritual guardians to enable them to accompany the singers and, in time, join in the singing. It is only after they are permitted to sing that they have ancestral designs applied to their bodies, each design enabling them to become dancers. Thus, dancing is the most privileged activity of a Warlpiri male, because in the act of dancing he is taking on the role of his spiritual ancestor and assuming the responsibility of maintaining the Warlpiri universe.

Warlpiri Women's Generic Dance

The women's public, or generic, dance style, as represented in boys' initiation ceremony, involves a simple rhythm and a small repertoire of repeated movement patterns. They dance en masse in an arc or a line, facing certain directions, using limited ground patterns. The basic footwork is a slight bounce created by lifting the heels (the feet are parallel, apart, and under the hips), and having the knees alternately open out and then return to parallel. The movement accents the pulse. The women finish the dancing prior to the end of each song item, within which each woman has a certain amount of freedom to choose when she will start and stop dancing. The maternal and paternal aunts further have distinguishing roles in the dance, determined by the women's relationship to the initiate (Megan Morais, personal communication).

Other Contexts of Warlpiri Dance

There are various degrees of restrictiveness in the ceremonial contexts of dancing that have been described above or alluded to. These restrictions are based on gender and ritual status. Women's exclusive ceremonies are called *yawulyu*, which have various degrees of constraint. One of the most restricted contexts of male ceremonies is a cult ceremony called *kajirri*, which is the second stage of the boy's initiation ceremony and related to the kunapipi ceremony of Arnhem Land. However, there is one context of dancing that is unrestricted; men, women, and children, Aboriginal and non-Aboriginal people are welcome to attend. These events are called *purlapa*. In some respects, purlapa performances are like other ceremonial performances: They are named after and are concerned about a single ancestor or group of ancestors, the dancers are decorated in a similar manner to other ceremonial performances, and the differentiation between singers and dancers can be characterized as inclusive (singers) versus exclusive (dancers). Unlike other kuruwarri, purlapa are received from spirits by contemporary women or men. The originating spirits are agents of the Dreaming, sometimes the spirits of recently deceased kin. It is believed that purlapa have always existed but have not been previously revealed. Ultimately, all creativity belongs to the Dreaming. The spiritual origin of traditional music and dance is generally held to be true in Aboriginal Australia, except for the Tiwi Aborigines.

 See resource 24.3 in HK*Propel* for web links.

Other Traditions of Aboriginal Dance

The Tiwi Aborigines emphasize individual creativity in dance (Grau 1998). Like elsewhere in Aboriginal Australia, songs and dances are seen as single and indivisible complexes, called *yoi*. However, they are not seen as originating in the Dreaming but in the creative activity of individuals. The dances may be inherited, and only descendants of the originator are eligible to perform them. The yoi repertoire consists of those whose original creators are known and those whose original creators are forgotten. Hence the believed origins and performance eligibility of yoi are not very dissimilar to these characteristics elsewhere in Aboriginal Australia. Yoi is performed in social contexts more than in ceremonies, but sometimes it is performed in the annual yam ceremony (***kulama***) and in elaborate mortuary ceremonies (***pukumani***). (See films *Mourning for Mangatopi*, directed by Curtis Levy [2013] and *Goodbye Old Man*, directed by D. MacDougall [2013].) Women and men often perform together, and children are encouraged to participate. Accompaniment to dancing consists of singing (usually on a single note), hand clapping, and buttock slapping.

In Cape York, in northeastern Australia, Aboriginal culture is diverse, and clan-based performance traditions tend to be very localized. The general belief is that dances, with their associated songs, were created by spiritual ancestors, like elsewhere in Aboriginal Australia, but skilled dancers exploit the opportunity to interpret the received traditions. Skilled dancers are greatly admired and considered sexually attractive. Most dancing is performed in ceremonial contexts. In addition to clan songs and dances, some performance complexes transcend clan borders, binding clans together in common traditions. Women and men have their own repertoires of songs and dances, and the sexes perform complementary roles in combined ceremonies. Like elsewhere in northern Australia, mortuary rites are prominent ceremonial contexts for dancing. As they do in Arnhem Land, these occur some time after the death of the person, to persuade the spirit of the deceased to return to its spiritual origin. There are also public ceremonies akin to the purlapa of the Warlpiri. Finally, a performance genre called

Shake-a-Leg Dance Celebrating Court Win

One of the well-known Aboriginal communities in Cape York is the Wik people. On the occasion of a High Court of Australia's decision in favor of a native title claim, a Wik woman performed a shake-a-leg dance on the forecourt of the building. It was televised nationally and remains in the minds of many Australians who saw the broadcast on that day, a good example of the power of dance to communicate.

shake-a-leg, performed solo by either sex, is believed to have originated outside Cape York. However, the dances consist of movements that are characteristic of other dances in Cape York. It is a non-ancestral dance, usually performed solo, surrounded by onlookers who sing and clap hands and shout encouragement to the dancer. In addition to its main purpose of entertainment, the songs and dances are said to ridicule the behavior of the settler community (Sturmer 1998).

Cape York Aborigines have adopted the so-called **Island dance** of the Torres Strait, a modern adaptation of a Pacific Islands style of dancing. Dancers perform in straight-line formations, gestures and movements are well coordinated, and the dancers are accompanied by singing and percussion. The dances are rehearsed prior to public performance. Island dancing is invariably accompanied by drumming, rather than clapsticks, and the dancers commonly wear seedpod rattles attached to their legs or held in their hands.

 See resource 24.4 in HK*Propel* for web links.

Crosscurrents

New Contexts of Aboriginal Dance

In the 20th century, there have been many attempts by Aboriginal people to communicate with other Australians through music and dance performance. One kind of attempt has been the Welcome to Country events—the practice of acknowledging traditional Aboriginal ownership of places where public events are held. On another front, as pressure on Aboriginal communities to adapt to mainstream Australian society has increased, traditional dances and their contexts have declined. Ceremonies that lasted weeks or even months have been truncated to festivals that last a day or two, and elements of Aboriginal ceremonies have been modified to appeal to invited, non-Aboriginal audiences. They have become spectator events, in which performers and audience are separated. A third current arose in the 1970s with a flowering of urban Aboriginal culture in Australia, including the short-lived but notable National Black Theatre in Sydney; an Aboriginal music school, the Centre for Aboriginal Studies in Music, in Adelaide; several Aboriginal media associations, including the Central Australian Aboriginal Media Association

(CAAMA) in Alice Springs, which has radio and television stations, a recording studio, and a CD label; and finally an Aboriginal and Torres Strait Islander dance college in Sydney. The dance college has had several names and identities, including Aboriginal and Islander Dance Theatre, eventually becoming the **National Aboriginal and Islander Skills Development Association (NAISDA)**. These three currents of change—Welcome to Country events, festivals, and urban organizations—have created different paths of influence for Aboriginal dance.

Welcome to Country and Cultural Center Performances

The Welcome to Country events sometimes consist only of speeches of welcome by a representative of the local Aboriginal community, but they often include singing and dancing. Local performance traditions in the settled regions of southern Australia have suffered substantial loss, and traditions of central and northern Australia (particularly the latter) are often adopted for Welcome to Country practices. Another example of the recontextualizing of Aboriginal music and dance has been their presentation at Aboriginal cultural centers, where performances are simplified and adapted for tourist consumption. In these situations, both Welcome to Country and cultural center performances, the often-simplified dances take on new meanings, especially for the audiences. Stripped of their original meaning, these performances may be open to simplistic interpretation.

Aboriginal Festivals

Modernized Aboriginal performances are often promoted as "festivals" and are used to generate income for the community. Non-commercial purposes are also present. For example, national political leaders are invited to the **Garma Festival**, established in 2000 and held annually in Arnhem Land. The festival addresses issues affecting Aborigines in public forums, lectures, and seminars, and features performance music and dance. Some Aboriginal festivals include both traditional and non-traditional performances, sometimes by communities outside the host community, such as at the annual **Barunga Festival** in northern Australia. The well-known **Djuki**

Mala (formerly Chooky Dancers) got their start at the **Ramingining Festival** in Arnhem Land.

Djuki Mala

From an Aboriginal community in Arnhem Land, this group of young men has choreographed popular music and dance genres using a combination of traditional Aboriginal movements and elements of the borrowed genre. They are particularly popular with non-Aboriginal audiences. Djuki Mala (formerly known as the Chooky Dancers) have toured beyond Arnhem Land, including a season at the Sydney Opera House.

In Central Australia, one of the better-known Aboriginal festivals is called **Milpirri** ("storm cloud"), held every two years in a Warlpiri community called Lajamanu. The community has forged a relationship with the Tracks Dance Company, based in the northern Australian city of Darwin. Each festival embraces the essence of one traditional ceremony, such as the fire ceremony or the boys' initiation ceremony, for an evening's performance lasting a few hours on the community's basketball court. Older women and men perform traditional dances, with traditional singing, while boys and girls perform dances choreographed and taught to them by members of the Tracks Dance Company. The basketball court is transformed into a stage through lighting and large backdrops painted with the designs associated with the ceremony being performed. During the performance, an amplified commentary in English provides information on the ceremony and its traditional meaning.

NAISDA and Bangarra: Development of a National Indigenous Dance Genre

As NAISDA settled into being a college rather than a production company, it became known as **NAISDA Dance College**. Founded by Carole Johnson, the college set about trying to create a national Indigenous dance genre using Aboriginal and Torres Strait Islander elements. Indigenous students are recruited from all over Australia. Indigenous dancers from central and northern

Australia visit the school to teach traditional dances on an annual basis; students visit those same communities to witness and participate in the dances. In addition, ballet, jazz, and modern dance are taught by practitioners of those traditions. Students choreograph their own dances using the many influences they experienced. Each year, an end-of-year program is presented to the public.

In 1989, **Bangarra Dance Theatre** was established by NAISDA graduates, assisted by Carole Johnson. Stephen Page, a NAISDA graduate, was appointed artistic director in 1991. The company has its own Aboriginal composer in residence, and choreographers and dancers are Indigenous. The company adopted NAISDA's practice of involving dancers from Indigenous communities, mainly from Arnhem Land and the Torres Strait. The productions have resembled traditional dances, adopting quasi-ancestral subjects and incorporating traditional dance movements and gestures. However, dances are fully choreographed and rehearsed, the productions are theatrically presented on a stage, and the costumes and body decorations are contemporary in style. Bangarra has enjoyed significant success, has toured nationally and internationally, and is considered one of Australia's major dance companies (Johnson 2000).

 See resource 24.5 in HK*Propel* for web links.

Summary

Aboriginal dance evolved over more than 60,000 years with different regional traditions linked by common religious beliefs and broad cultural values. Dance traditions in the south were lost when European settlement took hold beginning in 1788. It was in Central and Northern Australia, the last regions settled by Europeans, that Aboriginal culture survived and flourished into the 20th century.

Dances were almost always connected to songs and visual designs named after a spiritual ancestor of both humans and other natural phenomena. Each named package of dances, songs, and designs was owned by a clan and, more broadly, a moiety of which the clan was a part. The distribution of song or dance performance rights between clans and moieties varied according to ownership. These Aboriginal dances, as well as songs and visual designs, were believed to have originated in the Dreaming by the ancestors, even if contemporary humans accessed them for the first time from spirit agents of the Dreaming.

In recent years, Aboriginal performance occasions have been truncated and modern forms have been incorporated to attract younger generations of Aborigines and appeal to the general public. Another response has been to modify performances for presentations at tourist destinations. In the southern regions of the continent, local Aborigines have adopted Central and Northern traditions to perform at "Welcome to Country" occasions in which the public are invited to acknowledge prior Aboriginal presence and ownership.

Finally, in an upsurge of urban Aboriginal cultural revival that began several decades ago, an Aboriginal and Torres Strait Islander dance college is creating a national Indigenous dance genre which has enjoyed national and international success. Through these efforts, Aboriginal Australian dance continues, tens of thousands of years beyond the first Dreaming.

Discussion Questions

1. Name three regions of Indigenous Australia, and identify the similarities and differences among them in relation to dance.

2. What are the stylistic elements of Australian Aboriginal dances? Describe their occurrence in one region of Aboriginal Australia.

3. What is meant by inclusive and exclusive participation in Aboriginal performance? Compare Arnhem Land and Central Australian performance traditions to illustrate these concepts.

4. Discuss the local and national Aboriginal dance responses to non-Indigenous settlement of Australia.

 Visit HK*Propel* for access to this chapter's Application Activity.

Selected Glossary

Anbarra Aborigines—Indigenous people whose traditional country is located at the mouth of the Blyth River in north-central Arnhem Land.

exclusive and inclusive participation—Eligibility to perform songs or dances, generally by membership of a clan or by specialist skill.

generic dances—Dances that do not imitate the characteristic behavior of ancestors.

kuruwarri—A cluster of songs, dances, and visual designs representing a spiritual ancestor of the members of a clan in Central Australia (Warlpiri).

manikay—A cluster of songs, dances, and visual designs representing a group of spiritual ancestors owned by the members of a clan in Arnhem Land (Anbarra).

mimetic dances—Dances that imitate the characteristic behavior of ancestors.

moieties, moiety—Two intermarrying halves of a community, each consisting of several clans. This division is more relevant to ceremonial activities, including dancing and singing, than social life.

patrilineal clans—Social groups in which membership is determined by descent through the male line. Traditionally, they are the most common social groups in Aboriginal Australia and are referred to as "clans" in this chapter. Clans are exogamous; that is, marriage is between clans, not within them. Each clan owns dances, songs, visual designs, and sacred sites.

Rom—One of a class of ceremonies performed by Aboriginal Australians as a means of resolving conflicts between individuals or groups of people (Anbarra).

sacred sites—Places of special significance during the Dreaming.

the Dreaming—A general term for Aboriginal religion, it is the creative period when spiritual ancestors created the world that contemporary Aboriginal people occupy.

Tiwi Aborigines—Indigenous people traditionally occupying Melville and Bathurst Islands lying off the middle-north coast of Australia.

Torres Strait Islanders—Indigenous peoples traditionally occupying islands lying between the northeast tip of Australia and Papua New Guinea. They are ethnically different from Australian Aborigines and are usually separately identified.

Warlpiri Aborigines—Indigenous people whose traditional country is located in northern Central Australia.

Selected References and Resources

Clunies Ross, Margaret. 1998. "Aborigines of Arnhem Land." *International Encyclopedia of Dance*, vol. 1, edited by Selma Jeanne Cohen, pp. 223-224. New York: Oxford University Press.

Clunies Ross, Margaret, and Stephen Wild. 1984. "Formal Performance: The Relations of Tune, Text and Dance in Arnhem Land Clan Songs." *Ethnomusicology* 28(2): 209-235.

Dail-Jones, Megan. 1984. *A Culture in Motion: A Study of the Interrelationship of Dancing, Sorrowing, Hunting, and Fighting as Performed by the Warlpiri Women of Central Australia*, pp. 82-84. M.A. thesis, University of Hawai'i Dail-Jones (Morais), Megan. 1998. "Warlpiri Dance." *International Encyclopedia of Dance*, vol. 1, edited by Selma Jeanne Cohen, pp. 227-229. New York: Oxford University Press.

Grau, Andree. 1998. "Tiwi Dance." *International Encyclopedia of Dance*, vol. 1, edited by Selma Jeanne Cohen, pp. 224-25. New York: Oxford University Press.

Johnson, Carole Y. 2000. "NAISDA – Reconciliation in Action." *Oxford Companion to Aboriginal Art and Culture*, edited by Sylvia Kleinert and Margot Neale, pp. 363-366. Melbourne: Oxford University Press.

Levy, Curtis, Dir. 2013. *Mourning for Mangatopi*. Film, Canberra: Ronin Films/Australian Institute of Aboriginal Studies (2013/1974). https://aiatsis.gov.au/publications/products/mourning-mangatopi

MacDougall, David, Dir. 2012. *Goodbye Old Man*. Film, Canberra: Ronin Films/Australian Institute of Aboriginal Studies (2012/1977). https://raifilm.org.uk/films/good-bye-old-man/

Magowan, Fiona. 2000. "Dancing with a Difference: Reconfiguring the Poetic Politics of Aboriginal Ritual as National Spectacle." *The Australian Journal of Anthropology* 11(3): 308-321.

Perkins, Rachel, and Ned Lander. 1993. *Jardiwanpa—A Warlpiri Fire Ceremony*. Film, City Pictures.

Sturmer, John von. 1998. "Aborigines of Cape York." *International Encyclopedia of Dance*, vol. 1, edited by Selma Jeanne Cohen, pp. 225-227. New York: Oxford University Press.

Wild, Stephen, editor. 1986. *Rom: An Aboriginal Ritual of Diplomacy*. Canberra: Australian Institute of Aboriginal Studies.

Wild, Stephen. 1998. "Australian Aboriginal Dance: An Overview." *International Encyclopedia of Dance*, vol. 1, edited by Selma Jeanne Cohen, pp. 219-223. New York: Oxford University Press.

25

Dance in Tahitian Culture

Jane Freeman Moulin

Learning Objectives

After reading this chapter you will be able to do the following:

- Use dance to recognize and understand fundamental Polynesian approaches to performance.
- Identify key factors in traditional Tahitian dance that reflect Polynesian aesthetics in the performative arts.
- Recognize Tahitian approaches to innovation and modernization in dance and understand the problematic issues of the term *tradition*.
- Analyze contemporary social and political dynamics in modern Tahiti and how these affect Tahitian dance culture and its transmission.
- Understand some of the issues surrounding dance in a globalized world.

Key Terms

'aparima—A large group storytelling dance.

'aparima vāvā—A seated large group mute ("vāvā") storytelling dance.

'ori tahiti—Dance that features gender-specific movements.

'ōte'a—A large group dance.

deterritorialization—The process of separating a cultural practice from the homeland.

haka—A posture dance originally from New Zealand.

Heiva—A pastime; an assembly of people who come together to dance.

Heiva i Tahiti

The backstage bustle and excitement are palpable as the dancers of the École de Danse Heiragi make their way to the stage of the Grand Theatre. Thrilled to perform in the annual Heiva i Tahiti as part of a special multinight series dedicated to schools of traditional dance, this group of amateur dancers has been preparing for the last six months under the careful guidance of their teacher, Véro Clément. As with most dance schools on Tahiti, this group is female and ranges in age from 4 to 73 years old. Students come to the studio because of their love for dance and their desire to engage with Tahitian dance culture, but lessons are also a favored way to pass time with others and to stay fit in an increasingly sedentary life. The **Heiva** performance is the highlight of the year, one for which they have learned a series of newly choreographed dances, spent hours creating elaborate fabric and **vegetal costumes**, devoted countless class and weekend hours to rehearsal, and endured pointed critique and repeated correction in their effort to move as one. They have come to the capital city of Pape'ete to share their work with appreciative friends and family in the audience, as well as those who will watch the nationwide television broadcast and, hopefully, take to heart the group's overall theme of respect for Tahitian culture and the knowledge of the ancestors. Given the communal nature of Tahitian dance, this 45-minute performance includes successive same-age groups, but only two duets. The final song, performed as an *'aparima* story-telling dance, brings together all dancers to drive home the following message:

> People of respect, the Mā'ohi people—time passes, and
>
> we have become tied to practices from outside.
>
> Never forget who you are. Never forget where you come from.
>
> Reflect well on the place where we have arrived.

> *(From the song "Mai tahito mai ra" by Rai Kaimuko; translation by J. Moulin)*

The song text addresses a modern world where many Tahitian youth search for a sense of grounding and belonging, one in which adults want them to be part of a continuum that links them to a distant past and flows through them in a continuous line to the future. Some of Tahiti's most prominent artists, however, note changes that accompany modernity and openly express worry that they are seeing a dance far removed from the source. This chapter addresses the questions raised by their concerns, the history behind recent changes, and some issues that underscore and mold dance performance in a contemporary Tahiti.

 See resource 25.1 in HK*Propel* for web links.

In looking at traditional dance in Tahiti, this chapter underscores four important areas of reflection:

1. Polynesian artistic values.
2. The effects of colonization on the performative arts.
3. The contemporary emphasis on creativity and innovation.
4. Issues of ownership and deterritorialization as Tahitian dance traverses the globe.

These four points provide a framework for approaching dance in a modern and global Tahiti and for understanding the critical social context that nurtures dance performance and celebrates it as a communal activity that is widely enjoyed by both participants and audiences in French Polynesia.

Brief History

The settlement of Tahiti and the islands of French Polynesia presents the saga of wayfarers from the area of Taiwan who developed long-distance voyaging skills and traversed the Western Pacific in outrigger canoes to settle the islands of Fiji, Tonga, and Samoa around 950 BCE. Moving outward over the centuries, they eventually populated the far-distant islands of the "Polynesian Triangle," an area roughly outlined by Hawai'i in the north, Rapa Nui (Easter Island) in the southeast, and Aotearoa (New Zealand) in the southwest. Europeans also traversed the Pacific, beginning with Magellan in 1521, as their scientific, religious, and economic goals gradually gave way to the long arm of colonial expansion. Some of the islands of French Polynesia were annexed by France as early as 1842; all were firmly under French control by 1889.

Tahiti is only one island in French Polynesia, which encompasses 118 islands grouped into five archipelagos, each with a distinctive culture, language, and life ways. As French Polynesia's political and economic center, Tahiti has witnessed especially rapid and far-reaching social changes, including the move to a cash economy prompted by the opening of an international airport (1960), an influx of personnel and services associated with French nuclear testing (1966-1996), and the subsequent growth of a tourism industry that attracts around 250,000 visitors a year. Although granted a certain amount of autonomy in 1984, this island state remains a French colony, one molded by strong French governmental, economic, and cultural influences. The term *Tahitian* applies to cultural practices on Tahiti but also to the language and culture shared throughout the archipelago of the Society Islands.

Tahiti's political reality presents an interesting case of cultural survival and the triumph of the human need for cultural expression through the performative arts. In Tahiti, these include dance, music, oratory, and more recently, theater. Modern times offer a view of the insidious and widespread grasp of colonialism and the psychological effects of unheard or muted Islander voices, prompting reflection on ideas of "tradition," how people learn and understand and perpetuate it, and even what this word means in a contemporary island world.

The search for tradition traces back to the period of 18th-century European contact and the arrival of navigators **Samuel Wallis** (1767), **Louis Antoine de Bougainville** (1768), and **James Cook** (1769), who sparked the Western imagination with their published accounts describing Tahiti as a mythical place bathed in ideotypes of plentiful nature and beautiful, welcoming people. Fixated on the South Pacific woman, their portrayals of dance tended to relegate men to the shadows, view female movement as an unrefined and titillating shaking of the hips, and provide only cursory descriptions of the dance itself, such as "the dancers moved their hips in a rotatory fashion" or "the dances employed a measured sideways step." One emerges from the pages with little real idea of what dance may have looked like. In sketching out this vague 18th- and 19th-century history, however, the following is apparent:

- Tahitians performed a wide variety of dance types at the time of contact.
- Dance was presentational with different movements, and often different dances, for men and women.
- Nineteenth-century legal codes, reflecting missionary influence, forbade many traditional practices; by 1835-1836, dance was banned.
- Public dance groups from individual districts of the island began to form once again with the institution in 1895 of yearly dance competitions associated with the French Fête Nationale on July 14th.

In short, when contemporary Tahitians lament not knowing about their cultural history and past practices in dance, they are absolutely justified. Moreover, the absence of a native voice in most of the existing records presents a decidedly one-sided view of history with little reliable documentation to expand our knowledge of Tahitian dance, known as **'ori tahiti** ('*ori* for "dance"; *tahiti* "of Tahiti" or "in Tahitian style"), as Tahitians understood and performed it. It is this 'ori tahiti that is the focus of this chapter.

By the time photography appears around the turn of the 20th century, dance had already been banned for 60 years and rebirthed in a form that drew on basic ideas of Tahitian movement as people remembered them (and practiced them in secret over the years), but presented in a version appropriate for a 20th-century Tahiti. With the arrival of film, a clear image of dance in the 1930s emerges to confirm a presentational dance anchored in group activity and geographic place, with little locomotion but distinctly different movements for women and for men that focus on the legs and lower torso. These early moving images also document—finally!—the details of these movements and the overall choreography at that point in time.

In 1956, schoolteacher Madeleine Moua (1899-1989) formed Tahiti's first professional dance troupe, named Heiva, with the goal of restoring a sense of dignity to the dance so that it could be enjoyed and respected as the national dance of the Mā'ohi (indigenous) people. Since then, this icon of Tahiti has taken its place on the national and international stage, ever-evolving as a changing and creative art, rather than a historical practice fixed in the past. The basic identifying feature that defines this Tahitian style of dance and marks it as unique to this island and neighbor-

A beautiful costume made from dried and plaited pandanus leaves, fibers from the inner white bark of the purau tree, and brown cowry shells.

ing lands centers on the use of **gender-specific movements**—for men, an opening and closing of the bent knees in a scissors-like motion (***pā'oti***), and for women, various lateral and rotational hip movements (e.g., ***tā'iri*** and ***fa'arapu***) performed with a completely still upper torso. Other forms of dance—whether hip-hop, ballet, or Western partner dances—are practiced in Tahiti, but by far the most popular form of dance—among both youth and their elders—is 'ori tahiti. In what might appear to be a contradiction, the world of traditional dance is where things are "happening," where choreographers try new ideas to help in expressing the message of the dance, and where young dancers find a symbol of cultural identity that expresses their generation.

Artistic Values—Text, Dance, and Music

Performative arts in Tahiti blend together in holistic ways that contrast with the Western penchant for putting the arts into separate categories. For example, dancers in Tahiti are also singers, dance programs include oratory, dancers make their own costumes, and musicians sculpt their drums.

Values are different, as well. At an academic meeting in Tahiti organized by a European researcher and dedicated to the use of the body, Tahitians—at every possible turn—guided conversation to what they consider the most important part of music and dance performance—language and song text. For them, the basic premise was "How can you study the body in dance without first considering the language?" This section tackles that question and emphasizes the importance of recognizing a new and sometimes bewildering space when approaching the dance of another culture. It endeavors to guide the reader to an insider view of what Tahitians consider when they present their dances and opens the door to a different way of considering organized movement systems.

There are three main elements in Polynesian dance—poetic text, dance, and music. The text, which Tahitians consider the primary element, is the basis of all performative arts (oratory, music, dance, theater). In dance, hand gestures guide the listener to a deeper understanding of the words. The text is animated by the addition of rhythm and melody (music), which facilitates learning, aids the brain to fix the words in memory, and allows performers to synchronize their movements more easily. Musical instruments further underscore and elaborate the basic rhythm, accompanying danced text with string instruments or replacing text with percussion rhythms (which historically were likely based on speech patterns). The lower torso and feet provide a visualization of this rhythm; hand and arm gestures guide the onlooker to a clearer comprehension of the meaning of the text or, in the case of rhythmic accompaniment, the overall theme of the dance. The dancing body is a visual aid, the perfect integration of movement and text (or narrative theme). While some gestures, or even whole dances, such as the **'aparima vāvā**, are mimetic in nature, the overriding importance of most dance is to amplify word-based performance, whether sung or interpreted through drum rhythms.

The conceptual structure is thus very different from that found in many other cultures. Not surprisingly, when European researchers at that meeting kept wanting to talk about the body as something that can be explored apart from the dance, the Tahitians—both presenters and audience members—kept coming back to the language. For them, this was the logical place to start.

Dance and Community

Another fundamental value of 'ori tahiti anchors the dance in community and geographic place, with performance as a way to create shared experiences and entertain attendees while displaying and reinforcing a sense of community pride. Traditionally, dance is a group activity and the communication of group feelings, not individual emotions. Performance represents the establishment and confirmation of relationships—with the past, with fellow dancers, with the musicians, with the audience. The notion of expressing one's inner and deep feelings through dance, so dominant in the Western arts, is different from the relational experience Tahitians expect from performance. The sentiments the Tahitian dancer feels on moving into the performing area are similar to the following:

> Look at us, the people of this place! We are here as a group, moving in perfect harmony to show you what we can accomplish as an effective, well-rehearsed team. We are the sacred cord that links the past to the present. Admire the vitality of our song, our hours of preparation, the costumes we carefully prepared to delight your eyes and help you to understand our message, the heady perfume of the flowers and fragrant oils we wear to enhance your senses, and the beauty of our coordinated moving bodies. Accept our greetings and our love for all of you.

Not surprisingly, similar sentiments echo through many songs that have long opened dance presentations. Traditionally, this dance was open to the community and transmitted informally; the idea was that anyone could do it by being with people engaged in the activity and eventually learning through doing it together.

This traditional view of dance and its role in community building, however, does not always align with the thinking of many youth today. Brought up learning French at school and speaking it among friends and family, this generation is often more attracted by the rhythms and movements of the dance rather than the nuances and beauty of the Tahitian song poetry. Communal elements have morphed as well. Although some youth may join district dance groups, more frequently they dance for school or church performances, with many perfecting their skills by attending paid classes at private dance

Voted "best costume" at Heiva 2006, with its use of yellow more, white tapa, polished coconut shell, and the long white fibers of the unopened, bleached coconut leaf (nī'au).

studios or the official **Conservatoire Artistique de Polynésie Française** (CAPF). Their goals also differ in focusing on the personal acquisition of technique and repertoire rather than collective action and strong community-based group cohesion. It is constructive to examine this and why elders bemoan this new face of culture and the consequences of both the increasing loss of language and the move to greater institutionalization in the dance.

 See resource 25.2 in HK*Propel* **for web links.**

The Colonial Institution

Increasing reliance on the French language is the result of colonization and the educational policies of the French state, including the implementation of the French national curriculum in island schools and islanders' realization that increased education can enhance employment opportunities in an environment where unemployment was 21.8 percent in 2017. Without a school curriculum

The annual Heiva competitions are the height of the dance year in Tahiti, featuring Tahiti's very best in presentation themes, song texts, choreography, music, and costuming.

that follows local history, language, arts, and epistemologies, however, students express feelings of not knowing who they are and sadness over not understanding more about the lives and cultural practices of their ancestors. Dance is one way for them to connect with their culture and to express pride in being Tahitian.

Institutionalization of the arts is another product of the colonial state. In 1979, CAPF opened its doors in Tahiti, offering lessons on Western instruments and voice. By 1985, instruction came to include "traditional arts," specifically Tahitian dance and drumming, and later expanded to traditional choral singing, ukulele, oratory, and (eventually) theater and visual arts. This recognition of indigenous expression initially appeared as a forward-thinking boon to cultural continuity; Tahitian performance was validated at the Conservatory, where students could enroll in multiyear programs and receive a diploma equivalent to those awarded in France. The move to the classroom, however, encompassed radical changes. First was the method of transmission. Traditionally, a young person who wanted to learn a skill (whether dancing or canoe-building) went to the place where people engaged in that activity—carefully observing, listening, and imitating to gain experience and knowledge or **'ite** (to see, to know) by *doing*. With little verbalization and correction, you became as good a dancer as your eyes and your ears allowed. The number of isolatable "dance steps" was restricted, and repertoire was learned by rehearsing complete dances from beginning to end. Aside from the handful of professional troupes that danced for hotels and government occasions, groups came together in response to a specific upcoming event, rather than rehearsing year-round. The move to formalized classroom learning, however, changed all of that.

Navigating Change

In the classroom, instruction in technique dominates, and CAPF was instrumental in developing and standardizing new movements, some of them imported from Hawai'i. Teaching methodology also shifted to perfecting isolated techniques or segments of a choreographed work, rather than rehearsing complete songs and dances. With some dancers beginning as young as three or four years old, the dance has become more virtuosic. Well-trained youth progress through multiyear programs, thereby increasing creative possibilities for a growing number of young choreographers. Students view the Conservatory as the site of new and exciting movements, their study as an individual acquisition of technique, and the goal as the diploma offered at the end—all of which contrast with traditional approaches to dance transmission.

Dance classes extend what previously was the normative age, adolescence through the mid-20s, to include both very young and mature dancers. As a culture that viewed dancers as the beautiful, well-toned, physically fit, strong, and sexually attractive members of society, Tahitians long regarded the efforts of the two extremes as humorous parodies of the "real" dance. Expanding the age range therefore triggered major change. People questioned the appropriateness of certain movements for very young dancers, considered adaptations in a dance requiring stamina and fitness not always possible for very young or old dancers, and realized the need for

Cultural Highlight

COCO (JEAN) HOTAHOTA (1941-2020)

On March 8, 2020, Tahiti mourned the passing of Jean "Coco" Hotahota, a pillar of Tahitian culture and one of the most significant figures in the history of Tahitian dance. A former dancer in Madeleine Moua's troupe, he branched out in 1962 to form his own dance group, Temaeva. Over his 58 years with Temaeva, he won the prize for best dance group 14 times, touched the lives of generations of young dancers, and molded the cultural climate of Tahiti.

   A staunch advocate for his culture, Coco used music and dance to voice his observations of the world and Tahiti's place in it. He believed strongly in the importance of tradition, but was always open to seeing how the ideas of today might align with this tradition to create something meaningful and powerful. A legendary strict disciplinarian with high standards and a strong vision of what he wanted, he conveyed his love for his homeland and instilled in his dancers the knowledge that they were part of something important and infinitely beautiful. I feel privileged to have started dancing 'ori tahiti under Coco, to have danced with Temaeva at two Heiva competitions, and to have shared many hours over the years talking with him about dance and ideas of culture. Watching him rework or refine a piece was always a wonderful lesson that allowed a peek into how he viewed and understood dance. He was the most creative person I have ever met.

 See resource 25.3 in HK*Propel* for web links.

modified costumes to accommodate the bodies of those outside the teenager and young adult age group. The growth of the widely popular Heiva des Écoles created a new venue that today bears witness to the successful reconfiguration of technique, choreography, repertoire, and performance attire to accommodate a range of dancers.

Invoking Tradition

By the mid-1990s, however, resistance to the Conservatory and its teachings began to surface. Some of Tahiti's older and best-known dancers complained of feeling culturally dispossessed when youth accused them of teaching only the "old stuff." Although many dance directors subsequently came to recognize the serious work done by Conservatory teachers, tension between the Conservatory and tradition erupted once again in 2019 when Heiva officials required all competition troupes to conform to the movements and the terminology employed by the Conservatory. In an explosive rebuttal, dance director **Marguerite Lai** (winner of multiple Heiva awards for best dance group, including the 2019 competition) publicly countered, "We were here long before the Conservatory started. . . . If that is the Heiva, then we stop everything, and I'll return to my island" (Polynésie la 1ère 2019). For her, there

was no question of accepting the new rules and defining the dance by Conservatory standards.

   Some of Tahiti's respected elders in the arts express concern over the continual change that fuels Tahitian dance. **Coco Hotahota** (1941-2020), himself a well-known innovator, lamented in 2017: "Tahitians today no longer speak the language or eat our own food; they give priority to everything that is from the exterior and not ours. What will we do tomorrow? The generation that is coming, what will they do? It's sad" (Polynésie la 1ère 2017). In 2020, **Iriti Hotu**, one of Tahiti's most respected drummers, addressed youth attending a lecture on music saying: "You young Tahitians have a long way to go in knowing about your culture" (Moulin 2020). **Heremoana Maamaatuaiahutapu**, minister of culture and a former best dancer awardee (along with multiple other Heiva awards), bemoaned deeper changes underlying the dance, commenting that 40 years ago the dance troupe was like a clan that embraced a strong sense of belonging (personal communication 2012). He contrasted this with contemporary dancers who, in their pursuit of repertoire and personal experiences, flit between groups and place knowledge acquisition above group identity.

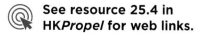 **See resource 25.4 in HK*Propel* for web links.**

Creativity and Innovation

The balance between maintaining tradition and allowing the dance to evolve by opening it to creation and innovation is a hotly debated topic in many Pacific islands. Urbanization, colonial education, and institutionalization of the arts all feed the constant search for the new, but Tahiti also has an established history of reaching out to the exterior, borrowing from neighbors and not hesitating to incorporate new ideas as a part of "tradition." For the annual Heiva, everything must be new—there are no previously recorded songs, no recycled choreography, no replicated costumes—fostering an environment that admires creativity. There are downsides to this, however. As renowned choreographer and dance director Coco Hotahota said in expressing his regret, "We have not kept one single historic dance" (personal communication 2012). Nevertheless, there are important elements that remain, and the person who is open to seeing how Tahitians weave the past into a modern expression will find some of the most creative people and spectacular dancing in the Pacific.

Dance in a Contemporary World

Persistent features of dance include the fundamental movements of ʻori tahiti and a gender distinction that highlights the contrast between male and female dancing and reinforces proper male and female behavior in a heteronormative society—through costume, placement on the dance, choreography, and gender-specific movements. An *ʻōteʻa*, for example, can be choreographed for only women (*ʻōteʻa vahine*) or only men (*ʻōteʻa tāne*) to display the beauty of female or male movements; when choreographed for a mixed group (*ʻōteʻa ʻāmui*), the idea is to contrast and confirm the differences between the two groups. The two main genres of dance are the ʻōteʻa (accompanied by drums) and the ʻaparima (accompanied by string instruments and a drum), both of which place a high value on coordinated large-group dancing in rank and file formation with changes to allow variety in the choreography. Words are important, and dancers are simultaneously singers who are expected to sing and to harmonize with full voices. Costumes draw on the colors, fragrances, and textures of island resources, including the famous "grass skirt" (*more*), made from the bark of the *purau* tree. This skirt forms the base for the **grand costume**, which features a large headdress, an elaborate dance belt, and occasionally hand whisks, with a bra and neckpiece for the women and a shawl, bandolier, or neckpiece for the men. Although the dance schools have expanded the age range for dance, Heiva groups rely on adolescent and young adult participants, and competition rules specify a minimum age of 16.

The Tahitian dancer is also a singer and a skillful costume crafter. Minor differences between the headdresses, for example, confirm the Tahitian practice of valuing communal space and action, but with a tolerance for individuality within the group.

Contemporary performances, however, also reinterpret tradition. The wide variety of lower torso and foot movements introduced in the 1990s supports choreography that is increasingly complex, with formation changes occurring at a much faster pace than 40 years ago; male dancing has become very athletic, with frequent leaps and level changes that can dominate and replace the iconic pa'oti male movement. Heiva troupes have expanded up to 200 members, showing the phenomenal interest in dance today. The accompanying musicians, who formerly sat in a front corner where they could see and communicate easily with the dancers, are now relegated to the rear of the stage and often joined by a small group of female singers, a contemporary aesthetic that foregrounds the dancer and moves some of the primary responsibility for singing and text delivery to a small specialized group of microphoned singers. The inclusion of a vegetal costume in the Heiva regulations brings a stunning variety of materials to the dance stage, offering a veritable stroll through Tahiti's gardens. Costumes in Tahiti expose a lot of skin, but this is different from Western ideas of sexualizing the dancer. Rather, the costume designer aims to celebrate the beauty of the dancers' youthful bodies. Other changes happen on the level of overall presentation; rather than a series of related dances that tell a somewhat vague story, performances now have elaborate "themes" and the dance has assumed an increasingly narrative and dramatic feel. Here, the influences of colonization are clear and mark a major shift that starts to set Tahiti apart from its Polynesian neighbors. This creates an interesting "show," especially for a generation raised on videos and losing fluency in the language, but it represents a major change from traditional aesthetics.

 See resource 25.5 in HK*Propel* for web links.

Crosscurrents

Tahitian Dance as a Globalized Art

In the 21st century, ideas, people, and products all crisscross the globe with astonishing speed. As Tahiti increases its internationalization, its dance culture is also on the move, defying borders in a process of **deterritorialization** that takes it far from its island homeland. 'Ori tahiti dance groups, often directed by non-Tahitians, have been active for many years in the United States and in Mexico. Recent expansion to other areas—including Europe, South America, and China—demonstrates global interest in the art of Tahitian dance, but the biggest development in recent years has occurred in Japan. Given its large population base and its cultural zeal for new fads from the exterior, Japan offers an especially interesting picture of what occurs when dance navigates the waters of geographic displacement, intercultural representation, and cultural interaction.

Cultural Sharing: Friendly Borrowing or Appropriation?

In 2017 there were an estimated 300,000 students of 'ori tahiti in Japan, more than the entire population of French Polynesia! Tahitian dancers, dance directors, and musicians regularly travel to Japan to judge competitions, work with "sister" studios, and give short-term workshops for teachers and students. Accompanying all of this activity, important questions have started to surface. In subtle ways Japanese dance troupes still do not look completely Tahitian, raising the prospect that—if dance is ultimately tied to culture, as scholars argue strongly—perhaps it can be difficult to resituate it completely in a new environment. The sheer numbers involved are staggering and give rise to critical discussions surrounding the commodification of culture and who can or should (or does) benefit from the sale of culture, issues concerning representation in what is presented as Tahitian on far-off shores, and uncertainties about maintaining ownership and control of cultural resources overseas. One overwhelming question concerns how much of the enormous profit generated by dance instruction, competition events, workshops, and the sale of dance paraphernalia (e.g., audio/video recordings, practice attire, costumes) comes back to Tahiti to nourish and support the creative artists who transmit and treasure this dance as a link to their culture and their *tupuna* (ancestors).

Critical focus shifts to the opposite side when Islanders appropriate the culture of their neighbors. An example is the **haka**—a traditional Marquesan term, but now applied to a dance very different from the original haka practiced in the Marquesas Islands of French Polynesia. Inspired by a visiting group of New Zealand **Māori** in the mid-1990s, the new haka incorporates Māori-inspired movements, but with drumming and a Marquesan text. Subsequently traveling to Tahiti as a traditional Marquesan dance, it now appears in dance presentations there, raising questions about whether Marquesans and Tahitians have the right to appropriate the traditions of others and use them to excite tourist audiences or to reframe their own arts.

In the search for costume materials, Tahitians turn to a global marketplace. With today's extremely large competition groups of 100 to 200 dancers, local suppliers simply cannot meet the demand for costume resources. Tahiti now competes with international dancers for access to the same goods—shells from the Philippines, dance skirts from Micronesia, and feathers from wherever they can locate them. Dance culture and dance costumes, like other aspects of modern life, are intimately bound to international circuits of commodification.

Summary

Tahitian dance in the 21st century is an incredibly vibrant, exciting, and spectacular dance form. Based on the fundamental gender-specific movements of 'ori tahiti, it embraces long-held Polynesian ideals related to the importance of text, a preference for storytelling as a primary element of presentational performance, and a view of dance as the embodiment of community, group effort, and relational space. The 1990s witnessed a significant evolution in the dance culture, along with the codification of many new dance movements and the expansion of dance to all age groups. Extremely popular, both at home and in the many countries to which it has traveled, this dance culture does not retain historical repertoire or view dance as fixed in the past. Rather, Tahitians prefer to draw from both traditional and external ideas and to interpret them in ever new and original ways that have high appeal to Tahiti's youth. For Tahitians, dance is a creative activity that reflects a contemporary modernity, yet still draws from the wellspring of tradition. Now Tahitian dance travels far beyond the island's shores, flowing through cultures of dance around the world.

Discussion Questions

1. What are important aesthetics of your own dance culture, and how do these contrast with Tahitian views of dance? What do these priorities tell us about culture?

2. Considering generational views of change, youth tend to seek what is new. In Tahiti, what are the potential dangers and benefits?

3. What are the dominant ways of learning dance in your culture? Does this change from one genre of dance to another? Is there a difference between informal learning and what is transmitted in the dance classroom?

4. Some Polynesians are criticized for "selling" their culture abroad. What happens when a non-Tahitian takes, borrows, or "buys" a tradition? Does it matter if they do not respect it, decide to change it, or feel they can do it better? Does this devalue the source, or is it part of a natural process of borrowing and innovation?

5. How do the issues of copyright, ownership, and cultural appropriation affect the arts? What are the current international laws regarding intellectual property in folk traditions? How do these processes affect (1) the host culture or (2) those places where dance travels? Should Polynesians even be concerned about this?

 Visit HK*Propel* for access to this chapter's Application Activity.

Selected Glossary

'aparima—A large group storytelling dance for an all-male, all-female, or mixed group conveyed through song and movement, accompanied by a string band and bass drum.

'aparima vāvā—A seated large group "mute" (*vāvā*) storytelling dance conveyed through mimetic gestures and accompanied by a drum ensemble.

'ori tahiti—Dance that features the gender-specific movements of Tahitian dance, accompanied by a drum ensemble.

'ōte'a—A large group dance accompanied by a drum ensemble. This dance can be performed as 'ōte'a tāne for all men, 'ōte'a vahine for women, or an "ōte'a 'āmui for a mixed group.

deterritorialization—The process of separating a cultural practice from the homeland, some-times with an accompanying loss of power and control on the part of the original culture.

gender-specific movements—Defined male and female leg and lower torso movements that highlight the gender differentiation in Tahitian dance.

haka—A posture dance originally from New Zealand, this Māori haka arrived in the Marquesas Islands of French Polynesia in the latter 1990s. Adapting it as Marquesan, complete with drumming and a text in their own language, Marquesans later exported it to Tahiti as a Marquesan dance.

Heiva—A pastime or an assembly of people who come together to dance; an annual period of cultural display and competitions in June and July; name of Tahiti's first professional dance group.

Selected References and Resources

Diettrich, Brian, Jane Freeman Moulin, and Michael Webb. 2011. *Music in Pacific Island Cultures. Experiencing Music, Expressing Culture*. New York: Oxford University Press.

Kahn, Miriam. 2011. "Moving onto the Stage: Tourism and the Transformation of Tahitian Dance." In *Changing Contexts, Shifting Meanings: Transformations of Cultural Traditions in Oceania*, edited by Elfriede Hermann, pp. 195-208. Honolulu: University of Hawai'i Press.

Oliver, Douglas. 1974. *Ancient Tahitian Society* [3 vols]. Honolulu: University of Hawai'i Press. www.hawaiiopen.org/?product=ancient-tahitian-society.

O'Reilly, Patrick. 1977. *Dancing Tahiti*. Dossier tahitiens, 22. Paris: Nouvelles éditions latines.

Moulin, Jane Freeman. 1998. *The Dance of Tahiti*. Papeete: Les Éditions du Pacifique/Hachette.

Moulin, Jane Freeman. 1998. "Tahitian Dance." In *International Encyclopedia of Dance*, vol. 6, pp. 77-79. New York: Oxford University Press.

Moulin, Jane Freeman. 1998. "Tahiti—Dance." In *Garland Encyclopedia of World Music*, edited by Adrienne Kaeppler and Jacob Love, pp. 873-879. New York: Garland.

Moulin, Jane Freeman. 2010. "Dance Costumes in French Polynesia." In *Encyclopedia of World Dress and Fashion, vol. 7, Australia, New Zealand and the Pacific Islands*, pp. 419-424. Oxford: Berg Publishers/Oxford International Publishers.

Moulin, Jane Freeman. 2017. "Touristic Encounters: Imag(in)ing Tahiti and Its Performing Arts." In *A Distinctive Voice in the Antipodes*, edited by Brian Diettrich and Don Niles, pp. 269-307. Sydney: Australian National University.

Moulin, Jane Freeman. 2020. Gods and Mortals (Dieux et humains): Le monde de la musique aux îles Marquises. ("The Musical World of the Marquesas Islands"). Lecture given at the Salle Vaiparaoa, Musée de Tahiti et des Îles and sponsored by the Direction de la Culture et du Patrimoine. Puna'auia, 20 February, 2020.

Polynésie la 1ère. 2017. Television emission on L'Hebdo: *Le Journal*, 25 June 2017. www.youtube.com/watch?v=Pls-LIXiuqs.

Polynésie la 1ère. 2019. "Heiva: 'Notre règlement est peut-être devenu un peu obsolète.'" 24 June 2019. https://la1ere.francetvinfo.fr/polynesie/tahiti/heiva-notre-reglement-est-peut-etre-devenu-peu-obsolete-724642.html.

Stevenson, Karen. 1990. "'Heiva': Continuity and Change of a Tahitian Celebration. *The Contemporary Pacific* 2/2 (Oct 1990): 255-278.

Index

Note: The italicized *f* and *t* following page numbers refer to figures and tables, respectively.

About the Editors

Courtesy of Mariah Minigan.

Lynn E. Frederiksen is a hard-of-hearing modern dancer, choreographer, educator, and author from St. Croix, U.S. Virgin Islands. She holds a BA in biology and an MA in environmental affairs from Clark University, and she has an MFA in dance from Smith College. Frederiksen was on the drama and dance faculty at Tufts University and is currently an adjunct professor of theater arts at Clark University, where she teaches African Inspirations: A Dance Collaboration, a course based on the dances *Fanga* and *Buschasche*, which she learned from Dr. Pearl Primus. Over the years, Frederiksen has presented her research on rhythms of bipedalism in the dance of language at various conferences, touting our facility for learning as a legacy of the human body in motion. Having danced a variety of forms beyond modern dance—including Caribbean, odissi, and Korean drum-dance—Frederiksen currently performs in Massachusetts with Lynn & Paul Dance, The 4:30 Collective, and Jen Lin Dance. Her choreography has been presented in New England and the Virgin Islands. In addition to her collaborations with Shih-Ming Li Chang, Frederiksen has also published poetry and prose in *The Caribbean Writer*. She received the 2016 Marvin E. Williams Literary Prize for her poem "The Courage of Egrets" and the 2020 Worcester County Poetry Association award for "Flowers."

Courtesy of Wittenberg University.

Shih-Ming Li Chang is a choreographer, performer, educator, author, and emeritus associate professor of dance at Wittenberg University. She earned her BA in dance at the University of Chinese Culture in Taiwan and her MFA in dance at Smith College. At Wittenberg Ms. Chang taught ballet, modern, jazz, Chinese classical and folk dance, and dance composition and dance ethnology, and she directed Wittenberg's annual dance concert. While serving as chair of the theater and dance department, Chang hosted the 2019 ACDA East-Central conference at Wittenberg, and throughout her career she developed cultural festivals both on and off campus. Over the years Chang has given lectures and demonstrations on Chinese dance and culture in numerous universities, festivals, and conferences in Taiwan, Poland, and the United States. As a performer, Chang danced with Van Pelt Dance and also presented her own solo works in many venues. Chang served on the boards of directors of OhioDance, the Ohio Alliance for Arts Education, and American College Dance Festival Association. She also was executive director for Weaving Pine—a nonprofit organization promoting Chinese Culture and performing arts in Ohio.

———

Chang and Frederiksen coauthored the book *Chinese Dance: In the Vast Land and Beyond* (Wesleyan University Press, 2016) as well as an article on Chinese dance in *Encyclopedia of Modern China* (2009) and "Dance Is the Prism: A Collaborative Journey Through Chinese Dance" in *Taking a Bite of the Big Apple: Exploring Resources to Promote Best Practices* (NDEO 2009 Conference Proceedings).

About the Contributors

Nora Ambrosio is a professor of dance at Slippery Rock University. Her publications include *Learning About Dance*, 8th edition, and *The Excellent Instructor and the Teaching of Dance Technique*, 3rd edition (Kendall Hunt Publishing Company, Iowa, 2018). Nora was a seven-year member of the Commission on Accreditation for the National Association of Schools of Dance and served a three-year term as chairperson of the commission. She is a member of the NASD board of directors. She is on the editorial board for the journal *Dance Education in Practice* and serves as a writing mentor for journal submissions. Nora is an active choreographer, creating work for both student and professional venues.

Inoue Atsuki obtained his PhD in anthropology from Hokkaido University, Japan. His primary research interest is in ballroom dance, a couple dance in east Asia including Japan, with a focus on commoditization of dance, the dance–music relationship, and sexuality. He is a part-time lecturer of body expression at Fuji Women's University and of anthropology at Tokai University. He is also an instructor and performer of ballroom dance for 20 years as a member of Japan Ballroom Dance Federation (JBDF), while conducting his ethnographic research in several dance communities in Japan.

Abdul Haque Chang is an assistant professor of Anthropology in the Social Sciences and Liberal Arts Department at the Institute of Business Administration (IBA), Karachi. His ethnographic research area is Sindh, Pakistan, and Java, Indonesia. He was a Sunan Kalijaga international postdoctoral fellow at Sunan Kalijaga State Islamic University in Yogyakarta, Indonesia. He has been visiting faculty in various universities in Indonesia. His research interests include ethnomusicology, Sufi music and poetry, history, religion, and environmental anthropology in Pakistan. Since 1995, he has been conducting ethnographic research on Shah Jo Rag, a Sufi musical tradition of Sindh, Pakistan. In Indonesia, his research focuses on Javanese Sufism, Islam in Java, and emergent Indian religious movements and networks. In Central Java, one topic is traditional Javanese dance, such as jathilan and reog. These dances provide an interesting ethnographic perspective on the syncretic connections of traditional Javanese religion, spirit possession, and traditional performing arts. Dr. Chang completed his doctoral studies at the University of Texas at Austin in 2015.

Nathalie M. Choubineh is a freelance researcher of ancient dances, rituals, and religions, especially focused on dance images in classical Mediterranean cultures. She holds a PhD in classics and a master's degree in classical Mediterranean civilizations. She is a member of the Classical Association since 2019 and was head of the Greece and Rome Department at the Iranian Institute of Anthropology and Culture, 2014 to 2018. She has worked as a translator and researcher in musicology and ethnomusicology at the Mahoor Institute of Culture and Art, Tehran, since 1998. Her publications include 47 books and 300 essays. She is a member of the 1001 Nights Society since 2013, performing Persian dance, belly dance, and other varieties of West Asian and North African dances.

Amélia Conrado is a former postdoctoral fellow in Visual Arts and Contemporary Art at the University of Paris 8 in France (2010-2011). She is a professor at the School of Dance at the Federal University of Bahia (UFBA) and is a member of the postgraduate programs in dance and professional masters in dance at UFBA. She worked for 19 years as a professor at the faculty of education at UFBA. In 2014, she received the Distinguished Visiting Professor Award from the Five College Consortium's Department of Latin American, Caribbean, and Latino Studies (Massachusetts, USA). She is the editor and author of the international collection entitled *Dancing Bahia: Essays on Afro-Brazilian Dance, Education, Memory, and Race*, which together with professors Lucía M.

Suárez from the State University of Iowa (USA) and Yvonne Daniel, Professor Emerita, Smith College (USA), bring together eight authors from Brazil, the United States, and Cuba, whose field of investigation is Afro-Brazilian dances from different perspectives.

Beatriz Herrera Corado is a researcher, dance artist, and writer based in Guatemala City. She holds a BA in Anthropology and Literature UVG (GUA) and completed her MA in the program Choreomundus: International Master in Dance Knowledge, Practice, and Heritage, awarded with the Erasmus+ scholarship (2016-2018). She has published her research about contact improvisation, multicultural performance practices, and Guatemala's contemporary dance scene. She is the cofounder of the webinar "Multílogos: Danzas, cuerpos y movimientos." In Guatemala, she has curated the contemporary dance exhibition "Respirar/Germinar" (Centro Cultural de España En Guatemala, 2021), and she has engaged with Caja Lúdica to develop participatory action research and digital antiracist pedagogies for approaching traditional games as intangible cultural heritage.

Jennies Deide Darko is a dance lecturer specializing in teaching the dance forms of Ghana and Africa. She is also the examinations officer for the Department of Dance Studies at the University of Ghana. Jennies is a dancer and has performed with the university's resident dance ensemble for 16 years. She holds a PhD in ethnomusicology from University of Cape Coast. She holds a diploma, BFA (first class honors) in dance from the University of Ghana. She has previously published a chapter on creative and mental health intervention in Ghana in *Performative Inter-Actions in African Theatre 2: Innovation, Creativity and Social Change* (pp. 81-90). She is a member of the specialized ministry of the Presbyterian Church of Ghana and of the Witness Tree Institute of Ghana.

Colleen Porter Hearn spent her early childhood in Southern California, where she celebrated the Mexican culture and learned many of the dances, with the tales that inspired them, in school and at social gatherings, including Rancho Santa Margarita. These memories have grown with her, and as an educator and choreographer, she has expanded her knowledge in folk dance. Colleen has performed or studied multicultural dance in Mexico and internationally. She gives presentations and writes articles on this topic, including in

Preparing Educators for Arts Integration (Teachers College Press, 2017) and as the senior editor for Dance Arts Now!, an honors student publication of the National Dance Education Organization. At Skidmore College, she was elected to Phi Beta Kappa, and she received a master's in education, with dance concentration, at George Washington University.

Zeynep Gonca Girgin is an associate professor at Istanbul Technical University, Musicology Department of Turkish Music State Conservatory. She is a musicologist, ethnochoreologist, author of *9/8 Roman Dansı: Kültür, Kimlik, Dönüşüm ve Yeniden İnşa (9/8 Romani Dance: Culture, Identity, Transformation and Reconstruction)*. Her research deals with the subjects of music, dance, cultural identity, and politics. She is a member of International Council for Traditional Music. She teaches music, dance and cultural theory, tradition, music and politics, performance theories, and critical musicology in master's and doctoral programs. She has taught Romani dance at workshops, and has performed as a kanun player and vocalist at home and abroad.

Solomon Gwerevende holds a BA general degree in music and religious studies and BA special honors degree in music, both from Great Zimbabwe University. He also graduated with a post-graduate diploma in education from Zimbabwe Ezekiel Guti University. In 2020, he graduated with an Erasmus Mundus international master's degree in dance knowledge, practice and heritage, jointly offered by the Choreomundus Consortium, which comprises the University of Clermont Auvergne, France; Norwegian University of Science and Technology, Norway; University of Szeged, Hungary; and University of Roehampton, United Kingdom. In 2021 he graduated with a first-class master of arts in ethnochoreology from the University of Limerick, Ireland, which was funded by an Irish organization called the Stepping Stone. He is a PhD candidate in applied ethnomusicology at Dublin City University in Ireland, funded by the Irish Research Council Government of Ireland scholarship. He is a member of the International Council for Traditional Music and has presented papers at peer-reviewed international conferences and published in peer-reviewed journals.

Ivana Katarinčić is a former professional classical ballet dancer at the Maribor's National Theater in Slovenia. She holds a degree in history from the University for Croatian Studies in Zagreb.

Since 2005, she has been working at the Institute of Ethnology and Folklore Research. She participated in Erasmus Intensive Program on Dance Knowledge (IPEDAK), Trondheim, Norway, in 2008. She holds a PhD from the Faculty of Humanities and Social Sciences of the University of Zagreb (urban dance tradition—historical, ethnological, and cultural-anthropological aspects). She predominantly deals with the diverse dance forms, historical (Renaissance and Baroque) dances, ballroom (social and sport dances), classical ballet, dance research methods, the body in dance, and dance techniques. She is a member of the International Council for Traditional Music.

Ronald Kibirige is a lecturer in dance, music, and dance-music, and head of the Dance Section at the Department of Performing Arts and Film of Makerere University, Kampala, Uganda. He is a community music and dance practitioner, instrumentalist, East African instruments craftsman, educationist, and researcher of East African dance and music traditions. He was the first ethnochoreologist in East Africa, having completed his doctoral studies at the Norwegian University of Science and Technology in 2020. He also obtained an international master in dance knowledge, heritage, and practice (Choreomundus) from four universities: the Norwegian University of Science and Technology in Norway; University of Szeged in Hungary; University of Clermont Auvergne in France; and Roehampton University in the UK funded by the European Commission. His research focuses on on community-based traditions, development, and intangible cultural heritage.

Justine Lemos has studied and performed classical Indian odissi dance for over 20 years with her guru, Ranjanaa Devi. In addition to holding a master's degree in dance studies, Justine holds a PhD in cultural anthropology with a focus on the study of embodiment in South Asian cultures. Justine was a Mohiniyattam student at Kerala Kalamandalam Institute for the Arts, as well as Nyrthashetra in Ernakulam. She has published articles on Mohiniyattam dance in *Semiotic Inquiry* and in a collective volume *Liberal Arts Lore*. Justine also co-wrote an article on ancient Maya dance for the *Journal of Mesoamerican Studies*. First and foremost, Justine is a student of transformation embodied techniques, and as such, she is administrative faculty at Western Yoga College, where she offers 200- and 300-hour yoga teacher trainings. Justine is also an Ayurvedic practitioner.

Bridgit Luján is a dance researcher who specializes in dance influenced or developed in Spanish-speaking Iberia. She has an MA in dance history from the University of New Mexico and an MFA in choreography from Wilson College. Bridgit has been recognized with various awards, including the 2017 *Dance Teacher Magazine* Higher Education Award for curriculum development in flamenco dance, a 2018 Paul Bartlett Ré Peace Prize Career Achievement Award for fostering inclusion of students with disabilities in flamenco dance, and a 2020 Distinguished Faculty Award from the Central New Mexico Community College. Bridgit is a journalist for *Dance Magazine* and in 2003 copublished the chapter "Mexican and New Mexican Folk Dance" in *The Living Dance: An Anthology of Essays on Movement and Culture*. She is a 2022-2023 recipient of a Fulbright Research Scholar Award to Spain.

Camee Maddox-Wingfield is an assistant professor of anthropology at the University of Maryland, Baltimore County. Her ethnographic research interests center on cultural activism and identity formation in Caribbean and African diaspora dance communities, with a primary focus on the French Caribbean. As a dance ethnographer, Dr. Maddox-Wingfield analyzes the various ways that dance expression contributes to the emotional health and wellness of communities suffering from colonial and racial oppression. She is working on her book manuscript on the cultural politics of the bèlè drum-dance revival in contemporary Martinique, with a particular focus on the intersections of spirituality, religion, and French secular nationalism. Dr. Maddox-Wingfield is an active member of the Association of Black Anthropologists and the American Anthropological Association.

Jane Freeman Moulin is professor emerita of ethnomusicology at the University of Hawai'i In addition to a PhD in music from UCSB, she holds an MA in ethnomusicology from UCLA and a BA in music from the University of Hawai'i. A singer with the pupu hīmene of Papara district and dancer with Tahiti's top professional dance troupes (Te Maeva, Tahiti Nui, and the touring company the Royal Tahitian Dancers), she has participated in five years of prize-winning performances at the Heiva i Tahiti. Publications include *The Dance of Tahiti, Music of the Southern Marquesas Islands*, and the coauthored book *Music in Pacific Island Cultures: Experiencing Music, Expressing Culture*, as well as numerous journal and encyclopedia articles on the music and dance of French Polynesia.

Iva Niemčić has been a senior research associate, assistant director (2011-2015), and director (since 2019) at the Institute of Ethnology and Folklore Research in Croatia. In 2007, she obtained a doctoral degree in the humanities, the field of ethnology, with the PhD dissertation entitled "Dance and Gender" at the Faculty of Social Sciences and Humanities, University of Zagreb. Fields of interest are research into dance, methodology, and development of ethnochoreology, performance studies, dance events in the past and in the present, dance ethnology, role and function of dance in the context of gender aspects, applied work, and a phenomenon of intangible cultural heritage.

Elizabeth Fernández O'Brien holds an MA in dance ethnology; a BS from Springfield College; and studied the Art and Science of Movement at Chelsea College in Eastbourne, England. Initially on a Fulbright-Hays Group Projects Abroad, she studied dance and worked in Trinidad and Tobago periodically for 10 years and coproduced the Banyan Productions' internationally award-winning documentary "Village to Best Village." While living in Trinidad, she taught dance in schools, studied with Astor Johnson, worked with the Ailey Dance School, and documented many local dances with a focus on bèlè. She has performed with Dr. Pearl Primus, and was producer, dancer, and costumer for the African Brazilian and Caribbean Dance Group and the Iroko Nuevo Afro-Cuban Dance and Music Company, and has been artist-in-residence in many settings including Illinois State University, Normal, Illinois.

Christos Papakostas is assistant professor in the Department of Primary Education in the University of Ioannina. He served as an assistant professor of traditional Greek dances at the Department of Physical Education and Sport Science (National and Kapodistrian University of Athens). Christos Papakostas is a scholar, master folk dance teacher, and percussionist. For the past 20 years, he has served as a folklorist, choreographer, dance tutor, and percussion instructor for multiple performing groups. Dr. Papakostas is well known in the Hellenic circles in Europe (Belgium, France, UK), USA, and Canada for teaching at Greek dance workshops, lecturing at universities, and serving as a judge in dance competitions. He is the author "Saha is varo ni nai." *Romani Dancing & Music Identities in Macedonia* (Pedio Books).

Sharon Anne Phelan lectures on folk dance and contemporary dance at the graduate and post-graduate levels at the Munster Technological University, Ireland. Her doctorate focused on Irish dance history. In 2014, her academic book *Dance in Ireland: Steps, Stages and Stories* was published, and she is completing another book focusing on performing arts as instruments of social change. She presented an online special purpose award in Irish dance history at the MA level. Her interest in Irish dance started at Siamsa Tíre, the National Folk Theatre of Ireland, where she performed for 30 years. She is secretary with the Irish Society for Theatre Research, she was responsible for the first dance syllabus in second-level education in Ireland, and she was national dance facilitator in the Department of Education in Ireland.

Nick Poulakis is an ethnomusicologist who serves as laboratory staff at the Department of Music Studies at the National and Kapodistrian University of Athens and an adjunct instructor of music/dance and cinema in the Modern Greek Culture Program at the Hellenic Open University. He has been teaching a number of courses on Greek music and dance, ethnomusicology, film music, ethnographic films, and musical multimedia. He participated in various research projects concerning Greek music and dance, and he is the author of *Musicology and Cinema: Critical Approaches to the Music of Modern Greek Films*, published in 2015 by the Editions Orpheus.

Robin Prichard is an artist/scholar working between the worlds of concert dance and indigenous dance. She has won two Fulbright Fellowships (2002 and 2022) to research indigenous dance in Australia and New Zealand. She writes on Native American dance and has published on powwows in *Dance Education in Practice* and on Native American dance history for an upcoming Routledge textbook. She was a professor of dance for two decades at universities in the United States and Australia. She has received awards from the Australian Federation of University Women, Ohio Arts Council, the Puffin Foundation, and Puffin West. She was a grant reviewer for the National Endowment for the Arts and the MAPFund, and she serves as a reviewer for *Journal of Dance Education*.

Desiree A. Quintero is a lecturer at Leeward Community College, Hawai'i, in the Philippine Studies program. She earned her PhD in ethnochoreology at the University of Malaya and conducted research as an Asian Cultural Council fellow in 2019. Her research is inclusive of dance forms found in the Philippines and Sabah, Malaysia. She is a member of the International Council on Traditional Music study group Performing Arts of Southeast Asia, is a member of the Philippine Folk Dance Society, and is a community outreach liason for the Asian Pacific Dance Festival. She has edited articles for *Borneo Research Journal*, *Malaysian Journal of Music*, and ICTM PASEA proceedings publications. She is coauthor of "The Curvilinear Ethnoaesthetic in Pangalay Dancing Among the Suluk in Sabah, Malaysia."

Wayland Quintero is the discipline coordinator for the only Philippine Studies program within the community colleges of the University of Hawai'i system. Under his direction the program aims to shift to becoming Filipino/a/x Studies, bringing in content on dance and other performative practices of the Philippines. He earned his MFA in dance from NYU Tisch School of the Arts, his doctoral degree from the University of Malaya Cultural Centre, conducted fieldwork among highland and maritime indigenous people, and served as cochair of the publications committee of the Performing Arts of Southeast Asia Substudy Group, International Council on Traditional Music (ICTM) UNESCO. He brings three decades of dance and theater training and experience. His latest publication is titled "Northern Philippine Highland Dancing as Indigenous Knowledge: Enculturation, Embodiment, and Performativity," in the Cordillera Press.

Kelly Sabini is a Fulbright Fellow in dance anthropology. She conducted research on Brazilian notions of citizenship, community, and social responsibility as informed and influenced by the Orixá dances of Candomblé in Bahia, Brazil. She is a former assistant professor of movement at Boston University's School for Theatre and an English language coordinator in Massachusetts. She holds an MFA in dance, an MEd in TESOL, and extensive and diverse additional studies in movement, theater, and voice. Kelly's understanding of the dance as an expression of culture in Brazil and her command of the Portuguese language is deep, having lived in Brazil for 14 years. She choreographed and performed with Filhas de Oxum (Salvador, Brazil); Companhia de Danças Sagradas (Brasília, Brazil); Behind the Mask Dance Theatre and Patric LaCroix Haitian Dance Co. (Boston, USA); and Pace Dance Company (Cape Town, South Africa). She also served

as assistant choreographer, translator, rehearsal coach, and dancer to Brazilian choreographer Marlene Silva (Black Orpheus, 1959, and others), both in Brazil and the United States. She was a visiting artist in Afro-Brazilian and modern dance at the London Academy of Music and Dramatic Arts. With residences in Bahia, Brasília, and in Boston, she continues her inquiry in defining a Brazilian national identity through dance and therapeutic implications of Candomblé's Orixá Dances.

Iliana Petrova Salazar holds a PhD in Bulgaria, defended in the Institute of Art Studies, Bulgarian Academy of Science (BAS), which stresses the dance and choreographic methods used in dance therapy in Europe and worldwide. Her areas of specialization are choreographer-pedagogue in Bulgarian folk dance (BA), choreographer director (MA), and dance science researcher (PhD). As a member of CID UNESCO and leader of association for art, education, and culture "Al Art Visions," she has authored many research texts in national and international congresses and scientific collections on her areas of research. For the last two years she was two times a recipient of the National Fund Culture in Bulgaria with the author's project "I Dance Bulgaria"—knowledge, creativity, health.

Anthony Shay is professor of dance and cultural studies at Pomona College, Claremont, California. He holds a PhD in dance history and theory from UC Riverside (1997). In his academic career, he is the author of eight monographs, author of over 60 peer-reviewed scholarly articles, and editor or coeditor of four edited volumes. In his dancing career as director and choreographer of the acclaimed Aman Folk Ensemble and the Avaz International Dance Theatre, 1960-2007, he choreographed over 200 works and, in recognition of his outstanding choreographies, was awarded fellowships from the National Endowment for the Arts, the James Irvine Foundation, and the Rockefeller Foundation, among others. His most recent publications include *Dance and Authoritarianism* (2021) and *The Igor Moiseyev Dance Company* (2019). His book *Choreographic Politics* (2002) won the Committee on Research in Dance (CORD) award for best scholarly dance book for 2002.

Stephen A. Wild is an expert on Australian Aboriginal music and dance, with an MA from the University of Western Australia and PhD from Indiana University. He was research fellow and later research director of the Australian Institute of Aboriginal and Torres Strait Islander Studies (1978-2001). He taught at Monash University (Melbourne), Brooklyn College (CUNY), and the Australian National University. He has published widely on Australian Aboriginal music and dance, including in *The International Encyclopedia of Dance* (1998). He was president of the Musicological Society of Australia and executive board member, vice president, and secretary general of the International Council for Traditional Music (ICTM). He was elected a fellow of the Australian Academy of the Humanities and an honorary member of the ICTM. In 2017 Stephen was presented with a Festschrift honoring his achievements by the ICTM Study Group on Music and Dance of Oceania.

Tvrtko Zebec is a senior researcher/scientific advisor; director (2011-2015), assistant director (since 2019) at the Institute of Ethnology and Folklore Research in Croatia; honorary full professor, guest lecturer at universities in Croatia; visiting scholar at Choreomundus International MA, UCA (France); ethnologist; ethnochoreologist; author of the bilingual book *Krčki tanci—plesno-etnološka studija*/Tanac dances on the Island of Krk—Dance Ethnology Study (2005) (awarded for the scientific and educational work by Croatian Ethnology Society); chair of the publication committee and member of the board of the International Council for Traditional Music Study Group on Ethnochoreology. Participates in scholarly and UNESCO's experts' congresses. Artistic director of the Zagreb International Folklore Festival.